RACE IN AMERICAN LITERATURE AND CULTURE

Exploring the unsteady foundations of American literary history, *Race in American Literature and Culture* examines the hardening of racial fault lines throughout the nineteenth century and into the twentieth, while considering aspects of the literary and interrelated traditions that emerged from this fractured cultural landscape. A multicultural study of the influential and complex presence of race in the American imagination, the book pushes debate in exciting new directions. Offering expert explorations of how the history of race has been represented and written about, it shows in what ways those representations and writings have influenced wider American culture. Distinguished scholars from African American, Latinx, Asian American, Native American, and white American studies foreground the conflicts in question across different traditions and different modes of interpretation, and are thus able comprehensively and creatively to address in the volume how and why race has been so central to American literature as a whole.

JOHN ERNEST is the author of over forty-five essays, and author or editor of twelve books, including *Liberation Historiography: African American Writers and the Challenge of History, 1794–1861* (2004), *Chaotic Justice: Rethinking African American Literary History* (2009), and *The Oxford Handbook of the African American Slave Narrative* (2014).

CAMBRIDGE THEMES IN AMERICAN LITERATURE AND CULTURE

Twenty-first-century America puzzles many citizens and observers. A frequently cited phrase to describe current partisan divisions is Lincoln's "A house divided against itself cannot stand," a warning of the perils to the Union from divisions generated by slavery. America seems divided in almost every way, on almost every attitude. Civic dialogue on issues often seems extremely difficult. America is an experiment always in process, a remarkable union of 300 million diverse people covering all races and faiths. As a forum in which ideologies and interpretations abound, Literary Studies has a role to play in explanation and analysis. The series **Cambridge Themes in American Literature and Culture** addresses the key cultural themes that have brought America to its current moment. It offers a summation of critical knowledge on key cultural themes as well as an intervention in the present moment. This series provides a distinctive, authoritative treatment of the key literary and cultural strains in American life while also pointing in new critical directions.

Titles in the Series

RACE IN AMERICAN LITERATURE AND CULTURE

EDITED BY

JOHN ERNEST

University of Delaware

CAMBRIDGE
UNIVERSITY PRESS

CAMBRIDGE
UNIVERSITY PRESS

University Printing House, Cambridge CB2 8BS, United Kingdom

One Liberty Plaza, 20th Floor, New York, NY 10006, USA

477 Williamstown Road, Port Melbourne, VIC 3207, Australia

314–321, 3rd Floor, Plot 3, Splendor Forum, Jasola District Centre, New Delhi – 110025, India

103 Penang Road, #05–06/07, Visioncrest Commercial, Singapore 238467

Cambridge University Press is part of the University of Cambridge.

It furthers the University's mission by disseminating knowledge in the pursuit of education, learning, and research at the highest international levels of excellence.

www.cambridge.org
Information on this title: www.cambridge.org/9781108487399
DOI: 10.1017/9781108766654

First published 2022

Printed in the United Kingdom by TJ Books Limited, Padstow Cornwall

A catalogue record for this publication is available from the British Library.

Library of Congress Cataloging-in-Publication Data
NAMES: Ernest, John, 1955– editor.
TITLE: Race in American literature and culture / edited by John Ernest.
DESCRIPTION: Cambridge, UK; New York : Cambridge University Press, 2022. | Series: Cambridge themes in American literature and culture | Includes bibliographical references and index.
IDENTIFIERS: LCCN 2021060642 (print) | LCCN 2021060643 (ebook) | ISBN 9781108487399 (hardback) | ISBN 9781108720144 (paperback) | ISBN 9781108766654 (epub)
SUBJECTS: LCSH: American literature–History and criticism. | Racism in literature. | Race in literature. | United States–Race relations–History. | BISAC: LITERARY CRITICISM / American / General | LCGFT: Literary criticism. | Essays.
CLASSIFICATION: LCC PS169.R28 R33 2022 (print) | LCC PS169.R28 (ebook) | DDC 810.9/3529–dc23/eng/20220301
LC record available at https://lccn.loc.gov/2021060642
LC ebook record available at https://lccn.loc.gov/2021060643

ISBN 978-1-108-48739-9 Hardback

Contents

Contributors

JOSÉ ANTONIO ARELLANO is Assistant Professor of English and Fine Arts at the United States Air Force Academy. His most recent essays have appeared in *Forma Journal, Teaching American Literature*, and *Quarterly Horse*. His current research studies the history of aesthetics and formalism in twentieth-century Mexican American literature.

MITA BANERJEE is Professor and Chair of American Studies at the University of Mainz, Germany. In her research, she has explored issues of race, citizenship, and naturalization (*Color Me White: Naturalism/ Naturalization in American Literature*, 2013), and the role of health justice for the promise of American democracy (*Medical Humanities in American Studies*, 2018). She is co-speaker of the research training group "Life Sciences, Life Writing: Boundary Experiences of Human Life between Biomedical Explanation and Lived Experience," which is funded by the German Research Foundation.

ANNA BRICKHOUSE is Linden Kent Memorial Professor of English and American Studies at the University of Virginia. Her first book, *Transamerican Literary Relations and the Nineteenth-Century Public Sphere* (2004), received Honorable Mention for the ASA's Lora Romero First Book Prize. Her second book, *The Unsettlement of America* (2014), was winner of the MLA's James Russell Lowell Prize, co-winner of the Early American Literature Book Prize, and Honorable Mention for the ASA's John Hope Franklin Publication Prize.

CARI CARPENTER is Professor of English at West Virginia University and is also a core member of the Native American Studies Program. She is the author or editor of four books: *Seeing Red: Anger, Sentimentality, and American Indians* (2008); *Selected Writings of Victoria Woodhull* (2010); *The Newspaper Warrior: Sarah Winnemucca Hopkins's Campaign for*

American Indian Rights, 1864–1891 (2015); and *What the Curious Want to Know: Collected Writings of Ora Eddleman Reed* (forthcoming).

KATY CHILES is Associate Professor of English at the University of Tennessee and the author of *Transformable Race: Surprising Metamorphoses in the Literature of Early America* (2014). Her work has appeared in journals such as *PMLA*, *American Literature*, and *Early American Literature* and has been supported by the Mellon Foundation and the National Endowment for the Humanities.

JOHN ALBA CUTLER is Associate Professor of English and Latina/o Studies at Northwestern University. He is the author of *Ends of Assimilation: The Formation of Chicano Literature* (2015) and is currently working on a book about Latinx modernism and Spanish-language print culture.

MARTHA J. CUTTER is Professor of English and Africana Studies at the University of Connecticut. She has published widely on American literature, race, and visual culture, and her last book was *The Illustrated Slave: Empathy, Graphic Narrative, and the Visual Culture of the Transatlantic Abolition Movement, 1800–1852* (2017). She is presently at work on a book about Henry Box Brown, who mailed himself from slavery to freedom in 1849 in a large postal crate.

M. GIULIA FABI is Associate Professor of American literature at the University of Ferrara, Italy. She is the author of *Passing and the Rise of the African American Novel* (2001), which was selected as an Outstanding Academic Book by *Choice Magazine*. She is the editor of the Penguin Classics edition of W. W. Brown's *Clotel* (2004) and has contributed to several volumes, including *Jim Crow, Literature, and the Legacy of Sutton E. Griggs* (2013), *Recovering Five Generations Hence* (2013), *Approaches to Teaching Nella Larsen* (2016), and *African American Literature in Transition, 1900–1910* (2021). She is currently working on the critical edition of Sutton E. Griggs's *Pointing the Way* and completing a manuscript on African American speculative fiction during the Harlem Renaissance.

STEPHANIE FOOTE is the Jackson and Nichols Chair of English at West Virginia University. She is the author of *Regional Fictions* (2001) and *The Parvenu's Plot* (2014) and the editor, with Elizabeth Mazzolini, of *Histories of the Dustheap: Waste, Material Cultures, Social Justice* (2012). With Stephanie LeMenager, she is the cofounder and coeditor of *Resilience: A Journal of the Environmental Humanities*. She is currently working on *The Art of Waste*, a project about waste and literature. Her work has been supported by fellowships from the NEH, the Mellon Foundation, the National Humanities Center, and the Carnegie Foundation.

P. GABRIELLE FOREMAN is a poet's daughter turned literary historian. She is the founding faculty director of the Colored Conventions Project and the Paterno Chair of Liberal Arts at Penn State, where she codirects the new Center for Digital Black Studies. She is the author or editor of four books and collections. Her new work includes *The Colored Conventions Movement: Black Organizing in the Nineteenth Century*, a coedited collection.

SARAH E. GARDNER is Distinguished University Professor of History at Mercer University. She is the author of *Blood and Irony: Southern White Women's Narratives of the Civil War, 1861–1937* (2004) and *Reviewing the South: The Literary Marketplace and the Southern Renaissance, 1920–1941* (2017). She has published articles and essays on nineteenth- and twentieth-century American literary and cultural history.

JOHN GRAMMER is Professor of English at the University of the South, where he also directs Sewanee's interdisciplinary program in Southern Studies. He is the author of *Pastoral and Politics in the Old South* (1997) and of essays appearing in *American Literary History*, *Sewanee Review*, *Oxford American*, and other periodicals.

EDWARD LARKIN is Professor of English and Material Culture Studies at the University of Delaware. He is the author of *The American School of Empire* (2016) and *Thomas Paine and the Literature of Revolution* (2005).

STEPHANIE LI is the Lynne Cooper Harvey Distinguished Professor of English at Washington University in St. Louis. She is the author of six books, including the award-winning *Something Akin to Freedom: The Choice of Bondage in Narratives by African American Women* (2010) and *Playing in the White: Black Writers, White Subjects* (2015). Her work has also appeared in *Callaloo*, *American Literature*, *SAIL*, *Legacy*, and *SAQ*.

JEEHYUN LIM is Associate Professor of English at the University at Buffalo, The State University of New York. She is the author of *Bilingual Brokers: Race, Literature, and Language as Human Capital* (2017) and coeditor of *Looking Back on the Vietnam War* (2016). Her current book project examines the Korean War in American literature and visual culture. With John Young, she is also coediting a volume of essays on twentieth- and twenty-first-century US short fiction for the MLA Options for Teaching series.

GESA MACKENTHUN teaches American Studies at Rostock University, Germany. Her books include *Metaphors of Dispossession: American Beginnings and the Translation of Empire* (1997), *Fictions of the Black Atlantic* (2004), and the coedited volumes *Decolonizing "Prehistory": Deep Time and Indigenous Knowledges in North America* (with Christen Mucher, 2021) and *Sea Changes: Historicizing the Ocean* (with Bernhard Klein, 2004). She currently researches the transatlantic history of enclosures, evictions, and ecocide.

KORITHA MITCHELL is the author of the award-winning book *Living with Lynching* (2011), editor of the Broadview Edition of Frances E. W. Harper's 1892 novel *Iola Leroy* (2018), and author of *From Slave Cabins to the White House: Homemade Citizenship in African American Culture* (2020). She is a professor of English at Ohio State University and a Society of Senior Ford Fellows (SSFF) board member. On Twitter, she is @ProfKori.

PAULA M. L. MOYA is the Danily C. and Laura Louise Bell Professor of the Humanities and Burton J. and Deedee McMurtry University Fellow in Undergraduate Education at Stanford University. Her books include *The Social Imperative: Race, Close Reading, and Contemporary Literary Criticism* (2016) and *Learning from Experience: Minority Identities, Multicultural Struggles* (2002). Coedited collections include *Doing Race: 21 Essays for the 21st Century* (2010), *Identity Politics Reconsidered* (2006), and *Reclaiming Identity: Realist Theory and the Predicament of Postmodernism* (2000).

KINOHI NISHIKAWA is Associate Professor of English and African American Studies at Princeton University. He is the author of *Street Players: Black Pulp Fiction and the Making of a Literary Underground* (2018), and he is currently writing *Black Paratext*, a history of modern African American literature and book design. His essays have appeared in *PMLA, American Literary History, MELUS, Chicago Review*, and other journals.

CLAIRE PARFAIT is Professor Emerita at Sorbonne Paris Nord University. Her research focuses on African American historiography and print culture. Among others, she coedited *Writing History from the Margins:*

African Americans and the Quest for Freedom (2016), *Une anthologie d'historiens africains-américains, 1855–1965* (2018), and *Creative Margins: Afro-descendant and Indigenous Intellectuals in the Americas of the 19th and 20th Centuries* (2020).

LUZ M. JIMÉNEZ RUVALCABA is a PhD candidate in the Program in Modern Thought and Literature at Stanford University. Her research and teaching interests lie at the intersection of literary criticism, comparative ethnic studies, and critical feminisms. Her interdisciplinary research agenda attends to the poetics of trauma and the sociohistorical formations of intimate violence.

SIOBHAN SENIER is Professor of English and Chair of the Department of Women's and Gender Studies at the University of New Hampshire. She is the editor of *Dawnland Voices: An Anthology of Indigenous Writing from New England* (2014) and the website dawnlandvoices.org; her most recent monograph is *Sovereignty and Sustainability: Indigenous Literary Stewardship in New England* (2020).

MIN HYOUNG SONG is Professor of English at Boston College. He is the author of several books, including *Climate Lyricism* (2022), in addition to numerous journal articles and book chapters. He is also the general coeditor of the four-volume series Asian American Literature in Translation and coeditor of *Cambridge History of Asian American Literature* (2015), as well as the former editor of *Journal of Asian American Studies*.

DERRICK SPIRES is Associate Professor of Literatures in English and affiliate faculty in American Studies, Visual Studies, and Media Studies at Cornell University. He specializes in early African American and American print culture, citizenship studies, and African American intellectual history. His first book, *The Practice of Citizenship: Black Politics and Print Culture in the Early United States* (2019), traces the parallel development of early black print culture and legal and cultural understandings of US citizenship. His work on early African American politics and print culture appears in *African American Review, American Literary History,* and edited collections on early African American print culture, time and American literature, and the Colored Conventions movement. His research has been supported by fellowships from the National Endowment for the Humanities, the American Antiquarian Society, the Library Company of Philadelphia, Oberlin Archives, the

Social Science Research Council, and the UNCF/Mellon-Mays and Ford Foundations.

MELANIE B. TAYLOR is Professor of English and Native American Studies at Dartmouth College. She is the author of the monographs *The Indian in American Southern Literature* (2020), *Reconstructing the Native South: American Indian Literature and the Lost Cause* (2011), and *Disturbing Calculations: The Economics of Identity in Postcolonial Southern Literature, 1912–2002* (2008) and is the editor of *The Cambridge History of Native American Literature* (2020) and a Norton Critical Edition of William Faulkner's *Light in August* (2022). She serves as executive editor for the journal *Native South*.

KIARA M. VIGIL (Dakota/Apache heritage) is Associate Professor of American Studies at Amherst College and a council member for the Native American and Indigenous Studies Association. She was the Jan Cohn Fellow and Lecturer in American Studies for Trinity College in 2020. She is the author of *Indigenous Intellectuals: Sovereignty, Citizenship, and the American Imagination, 1890–1930* (2015) and numerous articles and essays in peer-reviewed journals and books.

MAURICE WALLACE is Associate Professor of English at Rutgers University–New Brunswick. He is the author of *Constructing the Black Masculine: Identity and Ideality in African American Men's Literature and Culture, 1775–1995* (2002) and coeditor with Shawn Michelle Smith of *Pictures and Progress: Early Photography and the Making of African American Identity* (2012). His latest work is *King's Vibrato: Modernism, Blackness, and the Sonic Life of Martin Luther King Jr.* (2022).

EDLIE L. WONG is Professor of English at the University of Maryland, College Park. She is the author of *Racial Reconstruction: Black Inclusion, Chinese Exclusion, and the Fictions of Citizenship* (2015) and *Neither Fugitive nor Free: Atlantic Slavery, Freedom Suits, and the Legal Culture of Travel* (2009).

Acknowledgments

Any attempt to study race in American history reminds one of the necessity of collaborative work, and I could not have completed this project without the help of a number of people. Above all, I am grateful to the contributors, from whom I've learned so much. Working with the outstanding scholars represented in this volume has been a great honor, and I will continue to benefit from their work.

I am grateful beyond measure to Ray Ryan at Cambridge University Press for suggesting this project and for working with me through all of its stages. Through Cambridge, I also had the pleasure of working with Edgar Mendez, who was a great help as I worked on this project.

I'm indebted to and grateful for my colleagues at the University of Delaware. Dean John Pelesko has been very supportive as I've worked on this project while serving as chair of the English Department, and I continue to learn and benefit from my astounding colleagues in the English Department and beyond. UD has provided an incredibly supportive environment for this work – both as it pertains to this book and as it pertains to all of the institutional work called for, directly and indirectly, by its essays.

My first research assistant for this project, Jessica Thelen, has been a great help in putting together the final formatted essays for this volume. In addition to formatting and identifying errors and questions to address, Jessica has been an ideal and challenging reader for the volume, and if the volume finds other such knowledgeable and searching readers after publication, I will consider myself very fortunate. At the very end, I benefited from the help of a second research assistant, Darbyshire Witek, who put together the manuscript's final version.

Finally, I'm grateful beyond words for the support of my wife, Denise Eno Ernest. She makes all things possible.

Introduction

John Ernest

Race is central to American history. It is, or should be, impossible to understand the United States without attending carefully to how race has been defined and deployed at every stage of the nation's history. From the 1790 Naturalization Act, which limited naturalization to "free white persons," to the Trump presidency, race has been at the center of American cultural life – both shaping and shaped by economic practices and priorities; influencing where people live and what opportunities they are likely to encounter; serving as a key variable in local, state, and national elections; serving as the ominous subtext of the legal system and policing methods; and guiding government policies and social practices. Although our educational system has almost miraculously managed to isolate and contain much of US racial history into discrete and settled textbook chapters, it is difficult to imagine American history without accounting for the effects of the system of slavery, Indian removal, the Dred Scott decision, the Indian Appropriations Act, the Chinese Exclusion Act, Japanese incarceration, or other racist projects in American history that shaped how the system works – who has control over space, governance, and power. Every aspect of American culture, from the Electoral College to the history of sports and entertainment, has been almost immeasurably influenced by the determination of the white population to define and guard the borders of whiteness and to subordinate and control all those beyond those borders.

Given this history, even a basic and consistent definition of race can be difficult to manage. US history has fostered not a single definition of race but instead multiple definitions, and multiple communities and cultural traditions. For instance, the concept of race used to justify slavery is not the same concept used by African Americans in the nineteenth century for the purposes of promoting Northern communities, working toward rights and opportunities, or engaging in abolitionist activities. To be sure, African Americans had to deal with white America's understanding of race – but it

I

is also true that, over time, white America has had to deal with African American conceptions of race, if only through ongoing efforts to deny, suppress, or appropriate black culture. As Toni Morrison has written,

> for three hundred years black Americans insisted that "race" was no usefully distinguishing factor in human relationships. During those same three centuries every academic discipline, including theology, history, and natural science, insisted "race" was *the* determining factor in human development. When blacks discovered they had shaped or become a culturally formed race, and that it had specific and revered difference, suddenly they were told there is no such thing as "race," biological or cultural, that matters and that genuinely intellectual exchange cannot accommodate it.[1]

Of course, such divisions – traditions of oppression fostering and eventually encountering traditions of collective self-definition – are not limited to black and white America. From the earliest colonial encounters, race defined the experiences across the contested lands that would eventually become the United States, and when immigrant groups later arrived on the nation's shores, they quickly found themselves part of the nation's increasingly complex racial struggles.

American literature is, in many ways, the forum through which this complex history has been not only represented but actually crafted and negotiated. It is one of the primary forums through which racial caricatures and white supremacist ideology have been promoted, and it has provided a forum for communities thus degraded by the dominant culture to develop collective identities capable of withstanding such attacks. American literature has always been engaged in the creation, reinforcement, and popularization of racial images, and it has been engaged as well in attempts by various racially defined communities to create and promote a collective identity capable of addressing this contested racial space. Some of the most influential works by white American writers have revealed volumes about the need for alternate traditions of writing. One can, in fact, put together a rather direct literary genealogy that includes Harriet Beecher Stowe's *Uncle Tom's Cabin* (1852), Albion Tourgée's *A Fool's Errand* (1879), Thomas Dixon, Jr.'s *The Leopard's Spots* (1902) and *The Clansman* (1905), Margaret Mitchell's *Gone with the Wind* (1936), Harper Lee's *To Kill a Mockingbird* (1960), and William Styron's *The Confessions of Nat Turner* (1967). Included in this series of deeply influential novels (and the plays, films, and cultural artifacts that grew out of them) are well-intentioned but limited attempts to address racial injustice, joined with, and complexly intertwined with, fervent attempts to promote white supremacist fears and aggressions. One can learn a great deal about white and black American attitudes about race by attending to the history represented in and by these novels, plays, and films. And while racial thought in America has often been reduced to a black–white binary, other literary traditions and cultural communities – most prominently but not exclusively, Native American, Asian American, and Latinx – have similarly developed not only modes of literary resistance to the pressures of a white supremacist culture but also stories and rhetorical traditions shaped by cultural identities developed over time. American literature is the story of such overlapping and contesting representations of this chaotic social and political landscape of US racial history.

In short, American literature, seen through the framework of US racial history, would lead one to various literary and ideological communities, various modes of representation, various motivations behind those representations, and various tensions among all of the strands of racial thought working with and against one another. The story of the presence of race in American literature is not a simple story but a decidedly messy one – and much of the story has to do with how the different literary traditions work with and against one another.

Race in American Literature and Culture addresses the centrality of race in American literature by foregrounding the conflicts across different traditions and different modes of interpretation. The essays included in this volume explore the unsteady foundations of American literary history, examine the hardening of racial fault lines throughout the nineteenth century and into the twentieth, and consider various aspects of the multiple literary traditions that emerged from this fractured cultural landscape.

The volume makes no claims to full historical coverage, either of American literary history in general or of the specific literary traditions that emerged within that larger framework. The point is not to identify each major movement (e.g., the Harlem Renaissance) or to explore the fallout from each major text (e.g., the responses to William Styron's *The Confessions of Nat Turner*). Instead, the essays in this volume offer reflections on the implications of the modes of representation, the challenges of interpretation, and the dynamics of the different literary traditions that emerged in resistance to a white supremacist culture. The essays offer frameworks for reading different texts from different traditions, interpretive methods that account for relevant but often neglected cultural histories, reconsiderations of what constitutes the literary, and demonstrations of the need for more expansive understandings of literary history. In this way, this volume attempts to cover what cannot be covered in simple linear fashion – a series of traditions fed by different cultural streams, driven by different currents, and directed into different rivers before becoming part of the larger oceanic mass we call American literary history.

Indeed, the volume works both with and against strict chronology, so as to highlight the lasting impact of developments early in the nation's history. *Race in American Literature and Culture* is decidedly weighted toward, though not at all restricted to, the nineteenth and early twentieth centuries. These were the years that saw the development of the fundamental dynamics of US racial history – particularly the development of an increasingly explicit white supremacist dominant culture, shaping stories to marginalize and control what writers presented as foreign or threatening others. At first, in the time of Alexis de Tocqueville, race in American culture was seen as a contest between three races – white, red, and black – an envisioned play of contending forces (and of different understandings of history and civilization) that shaped numerous works of literature. But the Spanish influence on American culture and literature had been profound from the beginning, and by the end of the century, the Chinese Exclusion Act signaled a broader world of perceived threats to the imagined white republic. Through the century, various ethnic groups, the Irish dominant among them, grappled with concepts of racial identity, as well as with the challenges and compromises involved in acquiring limited access to the privileges of whiteness.

By the twentieth century, the marginalized communities had developed their own cultural centers with their own literary traditions and their own protocols for representation and interpretation. These literary and cultural communities – these ontological and methodological centers – developed both in resistance to the dominant culture and in search of ways for living fully on terms other than those prescribed by the dominant culture. These traditions offer important entrances into understanding the larger story of "race in American literature." It is not their purpose to carry the weight of promoting an understanding of race in American history, culture, or literature – and white American literature, which is arguably the most prominent and most problematic of the traditions that involve race, cannot be ignored simply in favor of more focused and more ultimately uplifting stories about this challenging area of American literary and cultural history. The point, then, isn't simply that mainstream understandings of the American literary tradition failed to account adequately for the presence of African American, Native American, Asian American, or Latinx authors and reading communities. The point wasn't simply a matter of exclusion from, inclusion in, or marginalization within the dominant story of

American literary history. The development of various literary traditions in the United States was as much a question of methodology as of presence, involving questions of what constitutes literature, what constitutes an appropriate understanding of the historical or cultural context for understanding literature, and even of how language functions and what kind of cultural weight certain words, images, or narrative lines carry. Recovering and promoting works in a range of cultural traditions was one thing, but establishing the means by which these works might receive just readings was quite another.

The essays in this volume place readers in this chaotic process of literary and cultural development – caught up in a story, as it were, already in progress. It is not the purpose of any essay to introduce readers to a specific critical perspective informed by race or a specific literary tradition; rather, this volume attempts to represent the intellectual life and the methodological priorities of various literary traditions, traditions driven by a common history that is experienced differently by different cultural participants. These various traditions combining to form American literary history involve both matter and method, recovering texts and determining appropriate approaches to texts. Shaping these traditions are different perspectives on American history, different understandings of what literature is and why we might be invested in it, and different conceptions of reading communities. This volume presents these traditions already in progress, allowing readers glimpses into cultural priorities, textual challenges, and interpretive methods that indicate a tradition, while also being mindful that each tradition requires total immersion – and, one might say, commitment – if one is to approach an understanding of the tradition as a palpable history and still-living presence for its readers. Together, the essays might not add up to a coherent narrative, a history of race in American literature and culture, but they will lead the reader to the questions, the tensions, and the innumerable narrative lines that are fundamental to that larger story.

Organization

For those looking for a more straightforward account of racial dimensions of US literary history, some very good studies exist, though much work remains. Aside from the important scholarship that accompanied the development of the African American, Native American, Asian American, and Latinx literary traditions, a search for scholarship that considers race as a defining dynamic in mainstream American literary

history might well lead one to 1993 and the publication of two foundational studies: Eric J. Sundquist's *To Wake the Nations: Race in the Making
of American Literature* and Toni Morrison's *Playing in the Dark: Whiteness
and the Literary Imagination*. Following the transcultural, interracial line of
analysis in these works, one might turn to such groundbreaking scholarship as Valerie Babb's *Whiteness Visible: The Meaning of Whiteness in
American Literature* (1998), Anna Brickhouse's *Transamerican Literary
Relations and the Nineteenth-Century Public Sphere* (2004), and Robert
Levine's *Dislocating Race and Nation: Episodes in Nineteenth-Century
American Literary Nationalism* (2008) – and then to more recent studies
like Brook Thomas's *The Literature of Reconstruction: Not in Plain Black
and White* (2017) or Mark C. Jerng's *Racial Worldmaking: The Power of
Popular Fiction* (2018). While there are not many sustained studies of race
in American literature, and fewer still that extend beyond black–white or
other binaries, the work that has been done is promising, firmly establishing the need for more scholarship on the dynamic presence of race in a
complex literary history.

Beyond attempts to consider interracial dynamics in American literature
is the scholarship that focuses on the different literary traditions that have
emerged from this history. Considerations of these traditions have been
represented in the dominant anthologies for the field: the *Norton Anthology
of American Literature* and the *Heath Anthology of American Literature*, the
former focused on major authors and texts, and the latter focused on
multicultural developments and negotiations. But even before these dominant anthologies were published, anthologies devoted to specific traditions
were both following from and guiding scholarship. We have long benefited
from such pioneering anthologies as *The New Cavalcade: African American
Writing from 1760 to the Present* (1971), *The Way: An Anthology of
American Indian Literature* (1972), and *Aiiieeeee! An Anthology of Asian
American Writers* (1974), or from the more recent *Herencia: The Anthology
of Hispanic Literature of the United States* (2001). There are scholarly
monographs, handbooks, and volumes of essays to support these related,
often overlapping, but still discrete fields, and editions of individual works
from all of these fields continue to flow in and out of print. There was
a time when a study like Vernon Loggins's *The Negro Author: His
Development in America* (1931) was rare and isolated in its approach to
American literary history, but now such studies operate at the center of the
different branches of this history – not always read by those in the other
branches, or even by those who claim authority over the field as a whole,
but still driving important scholarly and literary study.

Race in American Literature and Culture operates, in effect, at the intersection of these two primary approaches to the considerations of the influence of race in the development of American literary and cultural history. In the early sections of this volume – "Fractured Foundations," "Racial Citizenship," "Contending Forces," and "Reconfigurations" – the essays focus on the cultural construction of race. In his consideration of race as a systemic operational principle guiding perceptions and understandings, Charles W. Mills has argued that *"white misunderstanding, misrepresentation, evasion, and self-deception on matters related to race* are among the most pervasive mental phenomena of the past few hundred years, a cognitive and moral economy psychically required for conquest, colonization, and enslavement."[2] In many ways, the essays in these early sections focus on this "cognitive and moral economy," both as they shaped writings by white American writers and as they shaped the priorities of writers from the communities defined by and against these dynamics. The essays gathered in the three sections that follow – "Envisioning Race," "Case Studies," and "Reflections and Prospects" – focus primarily on the cultural communities and literary traditions that have emerged from this history, exploring the representational priorities and the interpretive methods central to these traditions.

While this organization will not provide the reader with a continuous or coherent history of race in American literature and culture, it will, I believe, give the reader a valuable introduction to the subject. This is a fragmented narrative, but one might find a kind of fractal unity in the essays that follow, iterative patterns of concerns, themes, and rhetorical strategies – literary history as a Mandelbrot set. Although the essays require, in some ways, a sudden immersion in a specialized area – contemporary Asian American literature, for example – they are accessible to nonspecialists, and they speak to larger concerns that are echoed across the volume. In all, they capture a reality of race presented by Matthew Frye Jacobson in one of the best histories of race in America, *Whiteness of a Different Color: European Immigrants and the Alchemy of Race* (1998). "Race is a palimpsest," Jacobson concludes, "a tablet whose most recent inscriptions only imperfectly cover those that had come before, and whose inscriptions can never be regarded as final. Contradictory racial identities come to coexist at the same moment in the same body in unstable combinations, as the specific histories that generated them linger in various cultural forms or in the social and political relationships that are their legacies."[3] *Race in American Literature and Culture* explores the development of that palimpsest, the writings, the interpretive strategies, and the literary traditions that addressed and reoriented the pressures of race in individual and collective imaginations, the multidimensional story of America told through the pages of its literature.

Notes

1. Toni Morrison, "Unspeakable Things Unspoken: The Afro-American Presence in American Literature," *Within the Circle: An Anthology of African American Literary Criticism from the Harlem Renaissance to the Present*, ed. Angelyn Mitchell (Durham, NC: Duke University Press, 1994), 370.
2. Charles W. Mills, *The Racial Contract* (Ithaca, NY: Cornell University Press, 1997), 19.
3. Matthew Frye Jacobson, *Whiteness of a Different Color: European Immigrants and the Alchemy of Race* (Cambridge, MA: Harvard University Press, 1998), 142.

PART I

Fractured Foundations

Taking in the foundations of American literary history from the earliest publications to the early nineteenth century, the essays in "Fractured Foundations" examine the instability and mutability of concepts of race. Edward Larkin explores "the expansionist white supremacist face of American empire" that "has dominated much of US policy and history since its inception." Establishing what will be a driving concern for most of the essays in this volume, Larkin distinguishes between "two vectors of empire" that form "one of the great paradoxes of American culture: The United States is simultaneously founded on a celebration of difference and the disqualification of certain peoples on the basis of their difference." Katy Chiles builds on this paradox by asking, "Can we be in two times at once?" Placing the work of such writers as Phillis Wheatley, Samson Occom, and J. Hector St. John de Crèvecœur alongside the work of recent scholars, Chiles meditates on the possibility of "thinking about the moment of slavery and settler colonialism as our own contemporary moment and also hope to conjecture about what we might learn when we read what we generally consider 'early American literature' as literature both of its own time and our own." Following the kind of "diachronic" reading Chiles advocates, Gesa Mackenthun observes that "'racial hybridity' is the racist's greatest fear, and US American literature gives abundant expression of this fear." Mackenthun explores "the trope of racial hybridity and the uncertain construction of whiteness through a reading of two New World novels written in light of, and in response to, the Jacksonian Indian removal and the passing of the Fugitive Slave Act, respectively." In her reading of Edgar Allan Poe's *Narrative of Arthur Gordon Pym of Nantucket* (1837) and Maxwell Philip's *Emmanuel Appadocca, or Blighted Life: A Tale of the Boucaneers* (1854), Mackenthun explores the "entanglements between discourses of race with discourses on antiquity as well as a 'Black Atlantic' literary counterdiscourse" that have had a profound influence on the development of American literary history. Together, then, these

9

essays establish some of the dominant themes of the essays collected in *Race in American Literature and Culture*, the ideological formations that shape the understandings of time, space, and cultural possibility represented in American literature. Race emerges in these essays, in other words, not merely as a theme but as a dynamic principle, a functioning variable guiding narrative and rhetorical strategies for depicting the realities, the possibilities, and the fears governing American life in the nation's formative eras.

CHAPTER I

American Empire

Edward Larkin

Despite its well-deserved reputation as an instrument of oppression, a developing American idea of empire would also form the basis of a productive new approach to negotiating difference that remains essential to the United States' political and cultural successes and failures. The desire to build an American empire to rival its European counterparts' global dominions authorized an expansionist policy built simultaneously on the dispossession of Native Americans and the enslavement of black peoples of African descent. At the same time, an administrative vision of empire underwrote much of the thinking about how to structure a system of cooperation among equals to manage the increasingly turbulent relationships between the thirteen states. To secure the union, it would be essential to develop a model of government that could productively manage the significant cultural, economic, and political differences among the new states. Racial and cultural difference thus simultaneously authorized dispossession and enslavement in one strand of American empire and served as the basis for inclusion and collaboration in another. The contradictions and tensions between these two intertwined but ultimately incompatible strands of American thinking about empire have shaped much of the debate about the American experiment in democracy. One by-product of the discontinuities between these two conflicting visions of difference would be the development of theories of race to complement long-standing class- and gender-based rationalizations for exclusion. If the expansionist white supremacist face of American empire has dominated much of US policy and history since its inception, the inclusive undercurrent of the American empire's internal administrative face has consistently provided the basis for an embrace of difference that has slowly (much too slowly!) reshaped thinking about race (and gender). The tension between these two vectors of empire has produced one of the great paradoxes of American culture: The United States is simultaneously founded on a celebration of difference and the disqualification of certain peoples on the basis of their difference.

The competing values of the expansionist and administrative modes of early American empire manifest dramatically in the US Constitution. The rhetoric of freedom and equality that underwrites the embrace of "the People" as the authorizing body of the American government is made possible by a racist and misogynist logic of whiteness that understands citizenship as the purview of propertied white males and produces the perverse calculus of "three fifths of all other persons."[1] Meanwhile, the administrative theory underwriting the US Constitution dictates that diversity and plurality provide an important basis for good government: Both the structural tensions between the three branches of government and the differences between the states – with their heterogeneous cultures, histories, religions, and economies – enforce compromise and collaboration to produce the best solutions. For Benjamin Franklin, Thomas Jefferson, and James Madison, among the most influential architects of the young republic, the contest of ideas brought forward from different points of view provided the essential foundation to the enlightenment quest for "a more perfect union." To the extent that an administrative emphasis on the contest of ideas seeded the document with a strong sense of the value of multiplicity and difference, it was counteracted and contained by a Eurocentric imperial vision that restricted not only participation in the government but also basic humanity to a select group. The distortions created by the contest between these two competing desires would manifest most spectacularly in the math of representation – not just in the obscene calculations designed to balance North and South while disenfranchising enslaved people, but also in Madison's efforts to determine the exact proportion of represented to representative in *The Federalist*.[2] The scientific racism of the eighteenth and nineteenth centuries here finds its mathematical equivalent. The numbers, that is, are not the product of any genuine effort to determine a ratio of representation (as if that were possible to begin with), but rather speak to a political expedience of balancing power and influence between the states, which were already finding it difficult to work together in the absence of the ongoing threat of British aggression. Ironically, the desire to balance between the states is built on a belief that the contest between different approaches to problems will inevitably lead to better solutions.

In literature, the encounter with difference would become a staple of American writing from James Smith and the early Puritan settlers in New England to Catharine Maria Sedgwick, James Fenimore Cooper, Lydia

Maria Child, and other nineteenth-century American writers wrestling with the ongoing systematic enslavement of Africans and African Americans and the forcible displacement of Native American peoples. African American and Native American writers such as David Walker and Samson Occom would draw upon the resources of the language of American empire not only to open a space for their voices to be heard, but also to challenge efforts to limit the range of subjects to be included under the heading of "We the People," a category that continues to evolve to this day.[3] Race, empire, nation, and a series of related concepts were being invented or reimagined during the decades leading up to and following the American Revolution as political thinkers, writers, poets, and ordinary Americans struggled to come to grips with the challenges and opportunities afforded by the break with Great Britain. The attempt to explore and make sense of what might be possible in this new context characterizes the poetry, drama, and novels of the early United States no less than its political works. Writers like Charles Brockden Brown, Phillis Wheatley, Susanna Rowson, James Fenimore Cooper, and William Apess would shape the conversation about race, empire, and equality in the United States just as much as Benjamin Franklin, Thomas Jefferson, or James Madison.

The ironies of early American empire were not lost on Phillis Wheatley, the formerly enslaved poet from Massachusetts, who frequently addresses her verses to transatlantic, multiracial audiences. The ambiguities of empire shape her most famous poem, with the triangle trade providing the key metaphors for "On Being Brought from Africa":

> 'Twas mercy brought me from my *Pagan* land,
> Taught my benighted soul to understand
> That there's a God, that there's a *Saviour* too:
> Once *I* redemption neither sought nor knew,
> Some view our sable race with scornful eye,
> "Their colour is a *diabolic* die."
> Remember, *Christians, Negroes*, black as *Cain*,
> May be *refin'd*, and join th'angelic train.[4]

The poem turns at the midway point, with the "Some" that begins the fifth line registering the first signs of resistance to the imperial narrative of the opening four lines. The seeming endorsement of the benefit of European imperial expansion, coming in the form of exposure to Christianity, in those opening four lines begins to be qualified with the restrictive import of "some." That subtle shift in line 5 leads to a more overt critique in the final couplet where the exhortation to "remember," stated in the imperative voice, now puts the speaker of the poem in the active role, which contrasts with the passive status of the opening line.

The spatial dynamics of empire, as the speaker's body literally and figuratively moves from periphery to center, is accompanied in the poem by a series of metaphors central to the triangle trade that underwrites the economy of empire. Wheatley takes the imagery of sugar production and translates it into the terms of Christian liberation. The same empire that enslaves Africans, then, when properly implemented, the poem asserts, ought to free them. The key moment in that second move is the implied analogy between "Christians" and "Negroes" in line 7. Grammatically, the sequence "Remember, Christians, Negroes, black as Cain" creates an ambiguous set of relationships: Should both Christians and Negroes remember? Are both Christians and Negroes black as Cain? Is *Negroes* an appositive for *Christians*? The work of empire has put Christians and Negroes side by side, such that Africans and African Americans, like Wheatley, can also be Christians. Hence the directness of the closing line, which once again draws on the economy of empire with a metaphor from sugar manufacturing. The refining of sugar cane – in a play, of course, on the biblical Cain – into sugar serves as a metaphor for the salvation afforded through Christianity. Empire here provides the figures of speech for both the forcible movement of the enslaved Africans and the operations of Christian faith. It is both the source of horror and beauty – that is, at least, the twisted logic of the core of the American republic that the poem is designed to expose. In Wheatley's imagination, the objectification of black bodies, here strategically equated with sugar, comes easily. It's not that she approves of it, but simply that it's no surprise. When the poem applies the metaphor to all Christian bodies in the closing couplet, though, it turns the passive "being brought" of the opening line into a universal being saved that applies equally to all bodies, white or black. The transatlantic geography of empire that moves goods and bodies while also transforming bodies into goods becomes a bizarre metaphor for Christian salvation whose logic transforms sinners into the saved.

If for Wheatley the horrors of slavery had become so matter-of-fact that they could be metaphors for Christian redemption, for J. Hector St. John de Crèvecœur the encounter with the violence of slavery instantiates a crisis of representation that interrupts his hero's celebration of transatlantic empire and causes him to doubt the existence of God. Meditating on the clergy's role on plantations, the protagonist and putative author of the letters, Farmer James, wonders:

Is there, then, no superintending power who conducts the moral operations of the world, as well as the physical? The same sublime hand which guides the planets round the sun with so much exactness, which preserves the arrangement of the whole with such exalted wisdom and paternal care, and prevents the vast system from falling into confusion—doth it abandon mankind to all the errors, the follies, and the miseries, which their most frantic rage and their most dangerous vices and passions can produce?[5]

This lamentation appears at the beginning of a long "melancholy reflection" that leads up to Farmer James' first direct experience of Southern chattel slavery when, on his way to pay a visit to a plantation owner, he witnesses an enslaved person who has been placed in a cage and left to be eaten by the birds.[6] Unlike the speaker of Wheatley's poem, Farmer James cannot account for the violence of slavery within his worldview. He is unable to repurpose and process it as metaphor. Farmer James' failure to recognize and process the place of slavery within American empire leads to a moral failure when he does not confront the slaveholder but instead sits and eats at his table and listens to his rationalization of the punishment for the enslaved man in the cage, and the institution of slavery more broadly.

Whereas Wheatley's speaker translates the trauma and dislocation of the transatlantic slave trade into a metaphor for Christian redemption, the spectacle of violence overwhelms Farmer James. In a moment of sublime horror that deprives him of his agency, Farmer James bears witness but cannot act: "I found myself suddenly arrested by the power of affright and terror; my nerves were convulsed; I trembled; I stood motionless, involuntarily contemplating the fate of this Negro in all its dismal latitude."[7] In a textbook description of the sublime aesthetic, Crèvecœur here presents the flip side to the sublime beauty of the "What Is an American?" chapter. The contrast with the optimistic narrative of the vision of "Letter III" could hardly be starker, but the language of race and empire permeates both visions. The glories of the British empire in North America enable the transformation of European peasants: "From this promiscuous breed, that race now called Americans have arisen."[8] Their independence and agency are in part made possible by their distance from the seat of power in London. Ironically, then, Farmer James is deprived of that independence at the moment when he comes face-to-face with his opposite number in Charleston. The entanglement of Farmer James' and this unnamed enslaved person's respective sublime transformations brings the text's celebration of empire to a screeching halt.

Two letters later, in "Distresses of a Frontiersman," the closing letter of the novel, Farmer James' disenchantment reaches its conclusion with the arrival of the American Revolution and the end of the Anglo-American empire that he had earlier credited with creating "a new man, who acts upon new principles."[9] Rather than return to Europe, as Crèvecœur did, Farmer James relocates to the "wilderness" of the west and settles among the Native Americans. There, once again, racial thinking disrupts our hero's hopes for peace. He celebrates the Native Americans for their social cohesion and peacefulness but is ultimately incapable of shedding his prejudices. In spite of the examples he gives of other Europeans who have settled successfully among the Native Americans, and his admiration for their disposition,[10] his fear that his children will become fully assimilated into the tribe, along with his internalized sense of European cultural superiority, impedes him from settling with them long term. The celebration of Native American "peace and concord" contrasts sharply with the "perpetual discordant noise of disputes so common among us."[11] Along with his assumption of the wholeness of the "us" in his differentiation between racialized visions of European Americans and Native Americans, Farmer James also fails to directly recognize the violence perpetrated by white colonial settlers upon Native Americans. On the contrary, what he imagines first is the potential for violence at the hands of Native Americans working on behalf of the American "rebels": "Must I then, in order to be called a faithful subject, coolly and philosophically say it is necessary for the good of Britain that my children's brains should be dashed against the walls of the house in which they were reared; that my wife should be stabbed and scalped before my face; that I should be either murthered or captivated?"[12] Here, the Native Americans become instruments of the American rebels. They are reduced to a violent nature unleashed by the Revolution. That version of Native American racial and cultural identity is contingent upon the historical omission of Anglo-American violent dispossession and contrasts sharply with Farmer James' actual experience of living among them.

What we see in this chapter, then, is a conflict between Farmer James' unthinking assumptions about Native Americans and his actual experience of living among them. Tragically, but all too typically, he is unable to revise his assumptions. The Revolution has rendered him incapable of rethinking his world because it has rendered reason and the so-called principles of European cultural superiority suspect. Throughout "Distresses," Farmer James swings from one thought to another in a chain of associations and outbursts of emotion that culminate in a prayer in which he pleads for the Supreme Being to "restore peace and concord to our poor afflicted country."[13] In a final twist of irony, then, the prayer reinforces the sense that Farmer James has not internalized the lesson that the "ancient virtues" he clings to are also implicated in the violence and destruction perpetrated by European settlers. It turns out that the idealized arcadian vision of the independent farmer that Crèvecœur and Jefferson celebrated as the foundation of an American utopia requires the violent displacement of another people currently inhabiting those lands. To acknowledge the Native Americans' presence and right to their land would deal a fatal blow to said vision. Therefore, in order to render the Native Americans merely occupants (to borrow Justice Marshall's terms)[14] rather than rightful owners of the land, settlers like Crèvecœur dehumanized Native Americans and reduced their culture to animal instinct. Hence, Farmer James' contradictory account of his family's experiences among them: He cannot accept that the generosity and peacefulness of his family's hosts in the Pennsylvania "wilderness" might be the product of an alternate set of principles – a culture. Instead, he simultaneously marvels at their sense of community and fears his children's absorption into that apparently wonderful community. He wants to have his empire cake and eat it too.

By contrast, in *A Son of the Forest*, the Native American minister, printer, and author William Apess, writing nearly forty years later, uses his autobiography to connect the dots that Farmer James could not.[15] Apess is not limited by the assumptions of European cultural supremacy that prevented Farmer James from recognizing the historical and ideological dynamics shaping the encounter between white settlers and Native American peoples in North America. Apess begins his autobiographical narrative with an attempt to eradicate racial difference: "We are in fact but one family; we are all the descendants of one great progenitor – Adam. I would not boast of my extraction, as I consider myself nothing more than a worm of the earth."[16] Much as Wheatley does in her poem, Apess draws on a shared religious principle – that all humans not only descended from the same person but also have fallen, to overwrite race-based distinctions between whites and other peoples. If economic motives drove the British and American imperial project, racial difference supplied the justification for the exploitation of Africans and the dispossession of Native Americans. By attacking the basis for racial differentiation, Apess and Wheatley expose the economic logic at work in the Anglo-American project in North America. Throughout *A Son of the Forest*, Apess focuses on a series of powerfully entrenched stereotypes about Native Americans that had already obtained the status of racial traits in the early nineteenth century: drunkenness and violence. He dismantles both by reconstructing the history of the encounter between Native Americans and the British in New England to show how white settlers cynically supplied Native Americans with "ardent spirits" for strategic purposes[17] and initiated the violence when they invaded Native American lands, thus prompting violent resistance. Apess asks of the reader: "Suppose an overwhelming army should march into the United States for the purpose of subduing it and enslaving the citizens: how quick would they fly to arms, gather in multitudes around the tree of liberty, and contend for their rights with the last drop of their blood. And should the enemy succeed, would they not eventually rise and endeavor to regain liberty? And who would blame them for it?"[18] Apess does more than pose a hypothetical here; he invokes the rhetoric of the American Revolution to invite white readers to identify with Native Americans and their plight.

Apess returns to this strategy of transposing supposedly Anglo-American values onto Native Americans several years later in his *Eulogy on King Philip* (1836), where he analogizes Metacom, popularly known as King Philip, to George Washington. From 1675 to 1676, Metacom, the son of the Wampanoag chief Massasoit, organized and led an alliance between the Wampanoag, Nipmuc, Pocumtuc, and Narragansett peoples against the New England settlers and their allies, the Mohegans and Mohawks, in a conflict that was widely known as King Philip's War in the eighteenth century. In "Eulogy," which Apess delivered as an oral performance in 1836, he draws a direct comparison between Washington's role during the American Revolution and Metacom's during King Philip's War:

> As the immortal Washington lives endeared and engraven on the hearts of every white in America, never to be forgotten in time—even such is the immortal Philip honored, as held in memory by the degraded yet grateful descendants who appreciate his character; so will every patriot, especially in this enlightened age, respect the rude yet all-accomplished son of the forest, that died a martyr to his cause, though unsuccessful, yet as glorious as the *American* Revolution. Where then shall we place the hero of the wilderness?[19]

Apess thus mobilizes the ostensible principles of the American Revolution to mount a celebration of Philip's accomplishment and advocate for Native American rights. He goes on to retell the history of King Philip's War from a Native American perspective such that the white settlers now come to resemble the British imperial masters they were seeking to overthrow in the Revolution. During the course of the speech, Philip is compared most pointedly to Washington and his role in the American Revolution, including a wonderful moment when Philip's strategic approach exceeds

Washington's decision to cross the Delaware and launch a decisive surprise attack on the British (an event that by 1836 had become firmly entrenched in the mythology of the young republic). But Apess also makes it a point to compare Philip to other imperial military heroes such as Alexander the Great and Napoleon. This celebration of Philip's military brilliance combined with an exposition of the treachery and rapacious behavior of the English colonists in New England is designed to directly counter the standard Anglo-American narrative of conquest in New England, which typically pits the peaceful and innocent religious settlers against the violent and untrustworthy "savages," who routinely violated the terms of treaties and could not be "civilized."

Retelling Philip's history also allows Apess to reassert Native American agency: Philip acts rationally and strategically. He recognizes the long-term threat of the white settlers in New England and seeks to reaffirm Native sovereignty. Rhetorically, however, Apess finds himself in a difficult position. Like Wheatley, he recognizes that challenging the terms of white imperial power in the early United States is futile. A genuine critique of US imperial policy will get him nowhere. Instead, he repurposes the vocabulary and principles of imperial power to animate a celebration of Metacom designed to illustrate Native American character and affirm Native American humanity by analogizing Philip's deeds to American revolutionary leaders and recognized historical military leaders. The desire for freedom and independence that motivates him along with the strategic thinking he employed to attain his goals testify to the inherent worth of Native Americans. Apess hopes his audience, Native American and white readers alike, will understand the text as an effort to underscore the fundamental humanity of Native Americans and thus entitle them to the rights of citizens in the republic. Ironically, then, to prove that Native Americans are human and American, Apess finds himself recovering Metacom in the terms of the very imperialist system that required his death. That Apess recognizes this structural irony is evident both from his use of the name Philip throughout the history and from his reference to him as a martyr. Metacom's martyrdom isn't merely a result of his sacrifice for his people, but his symbolic role in the meta-narrative of American imperialism.

Apess uses his autobiographical narrative, along with other forms of nonfiction writing, to combat the emerging narrative that would become the myth of the vanishing Indian. Writing at the very same time that James Fenimore Cooper was publishing his first few Leatherstocking novels, Apess insists both on the agency of Native Americans, by recovering the causes for their actions in past conflicts with white settlers, and on their ongoing presence in the United States. Once it became evident to thinkers and authors like Cooper that Native Americans possessed a distinct culture and could not be reduced to animals, they had to construct an alternate narrative to justify the United States' policy of Indian removal. The idea that civilizations rose and fell across history and that the once mighty empires of the Native Americans were now in inevitable decline, the stadialist model of history, served this purpose very well.[20] Cooper could thus lament the decline and fall of Native American dominance in the North American continent without turning white European settlers into genocidal mass murderers. Empire, in this meta-historical model, was the natural order of the world. We see this narrative in motion from the very beginning of the Leatherstocking novels in *The Pioneers* (1823).[21]

When we first meet the Leatherstocking, or Natty Bumppo, in *The Pioneers*, he is accompanied by the mysterious Oliver Edwards, whose racial identity remains a mystery for much of the novel. In many ways, the entire novel turns on the question of both Natty's and Oliver's racial identity. Oliver Edwards' appearance alongside Natty makes Marmaduke Temple, the founder of Templeton (a thinly veiled Cooperstown), nervous about his rather suspect claim to the lands where he has been building a settlement. Natty's long association with Mohegan John, also known as Chingachgook (or "the last of the Mohicans"), along with confusion about Edwards' racial identity, inspires Temple to believe that Edwards and Natty are conspiring to challenge his right to the land and reclaim it for the Delaware Indians, from whom it had been acquired.[22] After a much-commented-upon initial encounter that revolves around the question of who has the right to a deer that was killed by Oliver but that Temple claims he shot, which then becomes an argument about the law and the wilderness, Temple and his deputies engage in a series of extralegal measures to attempt to first determine what exactly Oliver and Natty are up to and then scare them off. Temple's doubt about the legitimacy of his title to the land speaks volumes. Were he certain of his claim, none of the dramatic events of the novel would have been necessary. That is, Cooper's plot is structured to raise questions about the legitimacy of the title to these lands and, ultimately, to assert a path to legitimacy.

Cooper's solution to the property question is surprising: The novel ultimately asserts the legitimacy of Oliver's claim through the mechanism of adoption. When the conflict between Temple's forces and Oliver's/ Natty's comes to a crisis, Oliver reveals that he is in fact Edward Effingham, the grandson of Major Effingham who had been granted the lands by none other than Chingachgook/Mohegan John. Temple, through a series of plot points too complicated to rehearse here, had acquired the lands after American patriot forces had confiscated them due to the Effingham family's loyalism. Earlier in the novel, Oliver had asserted his kinship with the Delaware: "Yes! I am proud of my descent from a Delaware chief, who was a warrior that ennobled human nature."[23] Oliver's explanation toward the end of the novel clarifies what he meant by descent:

> Major Effingham was adopted as the son of Mohegan, who at that time was the greatest man in his nation; and my father, who visited those people when a boy, received the name of the Eagle from them, on account of the shape of his face, as I understand. They have extended his title to me. I have no other Indian blood or breeding; though I have seen the hour, Judge Temple, when I could wish that such had been my lineage and education.[24]

Adoption proves a compelling gambit for Cooper: It allows him to work around race while also affirming key racial prejudices of the time. His heroes, Oliver and Natty, are not tainted by Native American blood, as many of his readers would see it, but they can celebrate and represent the values of Native American culture. More importantly for Cooper, they can introduce those values into Anglo-American culture without the risk that they will infect their descendants with the blood of actual Native Americans. The wish that Edward Effingham had benefited from Delaware blood and education thus functions analogously to the myth of the vanishing Indian. Neither can be remedied, but both can be mourned. Homage becomes a kind of escape route that protects him and the reader from asking questions about the legitimacy of racial differences, the actual meaning of blood relations, and the possibility of accepting actual Native Americans as full citizens of the United States.

Without minimizing the horrific ethical calculus of Cooper's logic, we can see that in *The Pioneers*, Cooper avails himself of the logic of empire to absorb some of the values and ideals of Native American culture into the rising US empire. Cooper's approach to incorporating aspects of Native American culture into a racially purified Anglo-American future United States lays bare one of the key challenges of the strange and complicated relationship between race and empire in the early United States: how to reconcile the fundamental heterogeneity of empire with the desire for purity that lies at the core of an emerging white supremacist racial thinking. At its conceptual core, empire prizes the different and other. And, while imperial projects by definition take from other cultures without permission or recompense, it would be a mistake not to recognize that the desire for novelty and difference plays a powerful role in the imperial imagination. Racial hierarchies serve to justify the dispossession of cultures deemed inferior or primitive, but they do very little to dampen the enthusiasm for the encounter with their difference. Sometimes that encounter may take the shape of sublime tales of horror or marvelous encounters with seemingly magical worlds, in others it is captured in objects such as masks or china, and in still others in the shape of a taste like cinnamon or curry. This vampiric absorption of other cultures into the early United States, which in *The Pioneers* takes the shape of Natty's and Oliver's respective acquisition of Native American cultural attributes, would shape a longer-term pattern whereby African, Native American, and other cultures would continually be absorbed into what Crèvecœur called the melting pot of American culture, a coinage that would become a cliché of American culture.[25] If this disembodied and amoral celebration of diversity ignores the brutal cost of the American appropriation of other cultures, we should also not miss the seemingly insatiable desire for novelty and variety that amounts to a craving for difference. Cooper bypasses the question of cost simply by removing US agency in the demise of Native Americans: Native Americans were destined to vanish, according to the terrible logic of a cyclical meta-historical theory of the rise and fall of empires; therefore, preserving or absorbing their best qualities into US culture would be the best possible outcome for all parties involved.

Wheatley, Crèvecœur, Apess, and Cooper all illustrate the extent to which the developing concepts of empire and race, perhaps more so than democracy or equality, worked together to give shape to the literatures and cultures of the United States. The questions they tackle in their respective writings were ones that American government officials and politicians were also attempting to negotiate as they outlined the laws governing the young republic. During the Revolution and first few decades of the young republic, much of the energy of American imperialism was directed inward as the states worked out the structure of their relationships and established the foundation for the expansion to come. The idea that government benefits from the inclusion of varied and multiple voices, visible in *The Federalist* and in Jefferson's writings, for example, stems in large measure from an idea of empire as a model of government that could accommodate a heterogeneous population. As Madison suggests in Federalist No. 10, the strength of a republic lies in its variety:

The smaller the society, the fewer probably will be the distinct parties and interests composing it; the fewer the distinct parties and interests, the more frequently will a majority be found of the same party; and the smaller the number of individuals composing a majority, and the smaller the compass within which they are placed, the more easily will they concert and execute their plans of oppression. Extend the sphere, and you take in a greater variety of parties and interests; you make it less probable that a majority of the whole will have a common motive to invade the rights of other citizens; or if such a common motive exists, it will be more difficult for all who feel it to discover their own strength, and to act in unison with each other.[26]

This passage illustrates how a notion of empire as an approach to governing a country made up of a diverse people with varied interests and ideas underwrites much of the US Constitution. Madison and Hamilton refer to the United States as an empire frequently throughout *The Federalist* and borrow from French thinking about "confederated republics" to describe their vision of the US empire. Extending the sphere, both geographic and demographic, was a foundational premise of the United States and the central challenge for much of the thinking behind the founding documents. That extension, of course, involved the acquisition of territory, but, as Madison's thinking in Federalist No. 10 demonstrates, it was also motivated by a belief in the value of a multiplicity of perspectives.[27]

The premise that debate among peoples with different perspectives would lead to the best solutions to social, political, and economic questions just as much as it did to scientific ones was essential to the structure of the early United States. Of course, that embrace of difference primarily took the shape of a need to accommodate the variety of cultures present in the original states, with all their regional differences. Certainly, Madison, a slaveholder, would have assumed this difference to be limited to European whites from various religious, social, and cultural backgrounds, but the logic of difference governing his thinking here provides the foundation for the kind of thinking we see in Wheatley, Apess, and other American writers and thinkers who advocate for diversity as a foundational value of the republic. Nevertheless, the questions about race that simmer just below the surface of the founding documents were also clearly on the minds of early Americans. If the political documents of the era mostly sought to downplay and suppress questions of race, the literature of the day, as we have seen, tackled matters of race head-on. Whether it's Wheatley's poems, Apess' creative nonfiction, or Cooper's novels, the question of how to account for and address the challenges of race in the early United States comes to the foreground. Those questions are always deeply informed by an ambivalent relationship to a notion of empire that both allows for the negotiation of difference and uses difference as a justification for its worst injustices.

Notes

1. Constitution of the United States, Article I, Section 2, Clause 3. National Archives (www.archives.gov/founding-docs/constitution-transcript).
2. See especially Federalist No. 55–57, Publius [Alexander Hamilton, John Jay, and James Madison], in J. R. Pole (ed.), *The Federalist* (Indianapolis: Hackett, 2005).
3. "Preamble," Constitution of the United States.
4. Phillis Wheatley, *Poems on Various Subjects, Religious and Moral* (London: Bell, 1773), 15.
5. J. Hector St. John de Crèvecœur, *Letters from an American Farmer*, ed. Albert E. Stone (New York: Penguin, 1981), 173.
6. Crèvecœur, *Letters from an American Farmer*, 177.
7. Crèvecœur, *Letters from an American Farmer*, 178.
8. Crèvecœur, *Letters from an American Farmer*, 68.
9. Crèvecœur, *Letters from an American Farmer*, 70. The British would, of course, retain a North American imperial presence in Canada, but Farmer James does not relocate to British Canada. In his imaginary, the alchemical process of transforming impoverished Europeans into self-sufficient Americans was specific to the middle Atlantic and New England colonies.
10. Crèvecœur, *Letters from an American Farmer*, 214, 224.
11. Crèvecœur, *Letters from an American Farmer*, 223.
12. Crèvecœur, *Letters from an American Farmer*, 207.
13. Crèvecœur, *Letters from an American Farmer*, 227.
14. In *Johnson and Graham's Lessee* v. *William McIntosh* (1823), Chief Justice John Marshall rules against Native American ownership of ancestral tribal lands, contending that rather than inhabiting the land, Native Americans merely occupy it, which does not constitute a basis for ownership. Library of Congress, US Reports, https://cdn.loc.gov/service/ll/usrep/usrep021/usrep021543/usrep021543.pdf.
15. William Apess, *A Son of the Forest and Other Writings*, ed. Barry O'Connell (Amherst: Massachusetts University Press, 1992).
16. Apess, *A Son of the Forest*, 4.
17. Apess, *A Son of the Forest*, 7.
18. Apess, *A Son of the Forest*, 31.
19. Apess, *A Son of the Forest*, 105.
20. On Cooper and stadialism, see George Dekker, *The American Historical Romance* (New York: Cambridge University Press, 1987).
21. James Fenimore Cooper, *The Pioneers, or the Sources of the Susquehanna; A Descriptive Tale*, ed. James Franklin Beard (Albany: SUNY Press, 1980).

22. I use *acquired* as a neutral term pointedly here because the matter of how the land came into Temple's possession, and into white settlers' possession more broadly, is a crucial one in the novel (and, of course, in early British–American history).

23. Cooper, *The Pioneers*, 143.

24. Cooper, *The Pioneers*, 441.

25. Crèvecœur's specific phrasing: "Here individuals of all nations are melted into a new race of men, whose labours and posterity will one day cause great changes in the world" (*Letters from an American Farmer*, 70). On the history of the idea of the melting pot, see Werner Sollors, *Beyond Ethnicity: Consent and Descent in American Culture* (New York: Oxford University Press, 1987).

26. Madison, Federalist No. 10, 53 (in Pole, *The Federalist*).

27. For a fuller account of the place of empire in the early United States, see Edward Larkin, *The American School of Empire* (New York: Cambridge University Press, 2016).

CHAPTER 2

Synchronic and Diachronic
Race in Early American Literatures

Katy Chiles

Can we be in two times at once? We often try to be in two places at the same time, but I am wondering how, as scholars of race in American literature and culture, we can be in two times simultaneously. Or, to put it another way, can we both pay scrupulous attention to the temporal specificities of racial formation in any particular period of what is sometimes called "American" history *and also* think about race in any given time of that history as absolutely of our own contemporary moment? In what ways can we, in our scholarship, conceive of race as synchronic and diachronic formations and hold both of those formations in our hands at the same time? In what follows, I try to think through what this can look like for my field of study, early American literary and cultural studies. In this essay, I want to demonstrate the importance of analyzing race within the context of its own period, particularly the late eighteenth century in British North America, a moment that bore witness to transatlantic slavery, settler colonialism, and the founding of the US nation-state. As I have argued elsewhere, understanding the unfamiliar and disorienting elements of early American racial thinking allows us to comprehend more fully how early American literatures depict, engage with, and rework concepts of race. Here, after outlining this thinking, I explain how Phillis Wheatley, Samson Occom, and J. Hector St. John de Crèvecœur draw upon it in their writing and how recent literary scholarship has done even more in analyzing natural historical discourses. I then describe ways we might think about race in the antebellum United States more diachronically, as more of a piece with our own present moment. Here, I highlight the work of writers, artists, and scholars who are thinking about the moment of slavery and settler colonialism as our own contemporary moment and also hope to conjecture about what we might learn when we read what we generally consider "early American literature" as literature both of its own time and our own.

***

Although it might strike us as odd today, early Americans living in the British North American colonies and then the new US nation-state thought about race through a multifaceted concept I call *transformable race*.[1] One's racial status was understood to be potentially mutable: It was believed to be an external bodily trait, produced over time by factors from the environment (which could include climate, food, habits, and modes of living) and constantly susceptible to change. Although not universal, this conventional understanding of race differed radically from what would follow it in the nineteenth century, namely, an understanding of race as a biological truth lodged within one's body that then would be signified by one's exterior appearance. We should think about the changeability of race in two ways: first, that sequential time periods have dissimilar ways of conceptualizing racial formation according to different rubrics; and, second, that in the late eighteenth century, the body's racialized features *themselves* were considered to be changeable over time. In concert with the Judeo-Christian story of a single creation, transformable race attributed the development of the several varieties (what were already coming to be called "races" in this historical moment) of the one human species to how external factors impacted the mutable body over time in various places on the planet. If studies of nineteenth-century and later racial formation demonstrate how any given race comes into being in contradistinction to others, a focus on late eighteenth-century transformable race emphasizes how such identities take form through one's potential to metamorphose from one race into another.[2] In early America, one's race was understood to be in relationship to another race that either one had been or was in the process of becoming, a kind of race that is transformable (trans/form/able) because it takes form through its potential to move across.

Historical records abound with this type of thinking in early America. In 1796, Henry Moss, an African American man who appeared to be turning white, became a scientific fascination in Philadelphia. Many natural historians, mostly white men who professed to study the phenomenon of the natural world through a practice of observing and taxonomizing the external traits of both plants and animals, thought Moss to be an accelerated exemplar of the normal formation of one's racial state. Benjamin Rush, member of the American Philosophical Society and signer of the Declaration of Independence, wrote about Moss's transformation in his commonplace book. Moss also drew the attention of Timothy Dwight, minister and president of Yale College, who hosted Moss in his home. Dwight wrote about Moss in his *Travels in New England and New York*, where he also quotes a letter sent to him from "one of [his] pupils,

Mr. Hart, now the minister at Stonington."³ Describing Elijah Wampey Jr., Andrew Carrycomb, Ephraim Pharaoh, and Samuel Adams (all Native men from New England living at the Brotherton settlement on Oneida tribal lands), Hart writes to Dwight, "Among these Indians, I observed the following singular facts, viz., four men whose skin in different parts of their body has turned white. Where the skin is not exposed to the sun, and the change has been of long standing, it has completely lost its natural color and become entirely white."⁴ Taking into consideration both his observation of Moss and Hart's observation of Wampey, Carrycomb, Pharaoh, and Adams, Dwight writes, "From these facts I infer also that the external appearances of the complexion and hair on the human body are not original, nor at all essential to the nature of the body . . .. These appearances, therefore, were not essential, but incidental; not original, but superinduced upon the human constitution. In other words, men are not red, black, nor white, necessarily, but merely as incidental circumstances direct."⁵ Dwight sums up his observations:

> Hence I conclude that the varieties observed in the complexion and hair of the human species furnish no probable argument that they sprang from different original stocks. The three great varieties are white, black, and red . . .. The ordinary course of Providence . . . has wrought the change [described among these men] here. A similar course of Providence is therefore justly concluded to have wrought the change from white to red and to black, or what is perhaps more probable from red to white on the one hand, and from red to black on the other.⁶

And in 1787, Samuel Stanhope Smith, Presbyterian minister and later president of Princeton University, in an address given at the American Philosophical Society, theorized that

> the state of society comprehends diet, clothing, lodging, manners, habits, face of the country, objects of science, religion, interests, passions and ideas of all kinds, infinite in number and variety. If each of these causes be admitted to make, as undoubtedly they do, a small variation on the human countenance, the different combinations and results of the whole must necessarily be very great; and combined with the effects of climate will be adequate to account for all the varieties we find among mankind.⁷

There were, of course, folks who disagreed with this way of thinking; some Indigenous nations advanced a view of the world wherein a Great Spirit created Native, African, and white peoples separately.⁸ In addition, Thomas Jefferson fudged the question of separate creations, advancing his "suspicion only" that "the blacks, whether originally a distinct race, or made distinct by time and circumstances, are inferior to the whites in the endowments both of body and mind."[9] However, what historians such as Winthrop Jordan have also called "environmentalism" was a common way of thinking.[10]

But in addition to what historians have documented, as I have articulated elsewhere, it is also crucially important that literary scholars understand this unusual racial logic. Becoming conversant with transformable race enables us to recognize how writers drew upon and altered this way of thinking – and thus to open up new and exciting interpretations of their literatures. We can understand, for example, how Phillis Wheatley, an enslaved poet writing in Revolutionary-era Boston, uses the word *dye* as a racialized metaphor, something that makes sense within the historical context of the late eighteenth century. In 1744, Virginian John Mitchell wrote in his natural historical text that "all the different People in the World" descended from one original "tawny People" and that humans' colors could change: "As for the black People recovering, in the same manner [as white people], their primitive swarthy Colours of their Forefathers, by removing from their intemperate scorching Regions, it must be observed, that there is a great Difference in the different Ways of Changing Colours to one another: Thus Dyers can very easily dye any white Cloth black, but cannot so easily discharge that Black, and bring it to its first Colour."[11] And in 1786, abolitionist Thomas Clarkson similarly used the term; he claimed that humankind's many varieties of people formed one species, thus making it immoral for any human of one color to claim right over a person of a different one:

> It is evident, that if you travel from the equator to the northern pole, you will find a regular gradation of colour from black to white. Now if you can justly take him for your slave, who is of the deepest die, what hinders you from taking him also, who only differs from the former but by a shade . . . . But who are you, that thus take into slavery so many people? Where do you live yourself? Do you live in *Spain*, or in *France*, or in *Britain*? If in either of these countries, take care lest the *whiter natives of the north* should have a claim upon yourself."[12]

But in Wheatley's hands, the dye metaphor becomes a way not only to draw upon environmentalist thinking but also to assert her own rich skin tone as one of the pigments a Christian God uses to paint the stunning, polychromatic creation of the world and its inhabitants. Using the eighteenth-century spelling "die," she writes in "On Being Brought from Africa to America,"

> Some view our sable race with scornful eye,
> "Their colour is a diabolic die." (5–6)[13]

Deploying the logic of transformable race, wherein her "sable race" *becomes* dark through a metaphorical process of dyeing (from a prior existing state), Wheatley also inverts the devalued, degenerated status most white natural historians associated with blackness by signifying on it with quotation marks and an ironic tone. In "Thoughts on the Words of Providence," Wheatley's poetic voice praises a deity who spreads color throughout natural creation:

> Hail, smiling morn, that from the orient main
> Ascending dost adorn the heav'nly plain!
> So rich, so various are thy beauteous dies,
> That spread through all the circuit of the skies,
> That, full of thee, my soul in rapture soars,
> And thy great God, the cause of all adores. (41–46)[14]

Here, creation, including both the skies and Wheatley herself, is adorned in multicolor splendor, in "rich," "various," and "beauteous dies." Understanding how Wheatley utilizes transformable race enables us to see that Wheatley's dye is not diabolic. It is divine.

A correspondent of Wheatley's, Mohegan leader and Presbyterian minister Samson Occom, retold the biblical account of creation in "To all the Indians in this Boundless Continent," a text written specifically to an Indigenous audience to assert both a spiritual commonality and equality with (white) Christians, along with a specific physical relation shared among all Indian peoples.[15] He also draws upon the logic of transformable race to assert Native sovereignty – the right of Indigenous peoples to political and cultural self-determination as the independent, self-governing entities that they are.[16] Occom composed the sermon while preparing to join a Mohegan migration from their ancestral homes (in what is now called Connecticut) to the Oneida Nation of the Haudenosaunee Confederacy (sometimes called the Iroquois, in what is now termed New York), where the Oneida had been exposed to nativist thinking, what Gregory Dowd calls an "Indian theory of the separate creation."[17] By instead using the Adam and Eve story of creation, wherein the progeny of this original couple spread throughout the world and developed into several human varieties through their exposure to different environments, Occom claims a common ancestry and political equality with all peoples. He also asserts a bodily singularity for Indigenous peoples by stating, "I am an Indian also, your Brother and you are my Brethren the Bone of my Bone and Flesh of my Flesh."[18] His reworking of the apostle Paul's phrase indicates his inclusion in a metaphorical Christian brotherhood and also a physical relationship specific to Native peoples whose somatic differences would have arisen from environmental influence since the singular creation. Occom uses his indigenized Christianity to counter nativist thinking and to assert a radical equality of *"all* Nations of the *Whole* World."[19] As Joanna Brooks points out, Occom frequently uses "the trope of America as a 'boundless continent,'" and here, he emphasizes the "Boundless Continent" as having been and continuing to be Indian Country.[20] Indeed, a petition coauthored by Occom and the other tribal nations joined together at Brotherton ("Brotherton Tribe to the United States Congress") notes that "the great Sovereign of the Universe" placed the "aboriginal Nations of this Great Indian World" on this "Boundless Continent" *first*, which the petition then uses as an argument for Native sovereignty, whether it is exercised at Mohegan, Brotherton, or any other part of the Native space that this "Boundless Continent" was, is, and continues to be.[21]

Attending to the historically-specific idea of transformable race also points up the racialized complexity of the "new American" that Farmer James theorizes in J. Hector St. John de Crèvecœur's *Letters from an American Farmer* (1782). In *Letters*, James, Crèvecœur's fictional agrarian narrator, ascribes to the belief that one's body is impacted by one's environment. When he describes the "new American" who undergoes a "surprising metamorphosis" after his immigration from Europe, Crèvecœur's narrator depicts this alteration as specifically racialized.[22] With the "back settlers," James writes that "it is with men as it is with the plants and animals that grow and live in the forests; they are entirely different from those that live in the plains" (*L* 76). In addition, people are most suited for their original habitats, as James claims that "the same magical power of habit and custom which makes the Laplander, the Siberian, the Hottentot, prefer their climates, their occupations, and their soil to more beneficial situations leads these good people [Nantucketeers] to think that no other spot on the globe is so analogous to their inclinations as Nantucket" (*L* 148). This language that taxonomizes plants and humans according to environmental effects on them recurs in Farmer James's famous Letter III, "What is an American?" The American people, he writes, "are a mixture of English, Scotch, Irish, French, Dutch, Germans, and Swedes. From this promiscuous breed, that race now called Americans have arisen" (*L* 68). While this "new race" comes from a "strange mixture of blood" (*L* 69) of all these white Europeans, the "new race" also "arise(s)" from its rootedness in American soil. Drawing on natural historical ideas about racial formation, Crèvecœur's use of plant

imagery, while certainly a metaphor, also signifies a literal scientific observation. Here, James's American is not a fully formed US citizen, but a
racialized condition (James calls it a "new race") of a British subject who
develops an American whiteness in the "New World." But it is one that
could darken in the colonies. James writes that if "British America . . . does
not afford that variety of tinges and gradations which may be observed in
Europe, we have colours peculiar to ourselves. For instance, it is natural to
conceive that those who live near the sea must be very different from those
who live in the woods; the intermediate space will afford a separate and
distinct class" (*L* 70–71). After all, he says, "Men are like plants; the
goodness and flavor of the fruit proceeds from the peculiar soil and
exposition in which they grow. We are nothing but what we derive from
the air we breathe, the climate we inhabit, the government we obey, the
system of religion we profess, and the nature of our employment" (*L* 71).

In *The Natural History of Sexuality in Early America*, Greta LaFleur
extends and innovates methodologies of reading environmentalist logics in
early American literature. She draws attention to Farmer James's claim
about colonists living on the "frontier":

> Our bad people are those who have degenerated altogether into the hunting
> state. As old ploughmen and new men of the woods, as Europeans and
> new-made Indians, they contract the vices of both . . . . Hunting is but a
> licentious idle life, and, if it does not always pervert good dispositions, yet,
> when it is united with bad luck, it leads to want; want stimulates that
> propensity to rapacity and injustice, too natural to needy men, which is the
> fatal graduation." (*L* 77–78)

Demonstrating that this vision of racial change is imbricated in the
languages of sex, LaFleur writes, "What Crèvecœur's meditation on the
degenerating power of frontier environmental reveals, then, is his implicit
belief that inhabiting degenerating environments can produce specifically
degenerated behaviors, including sexual behaviors . . . . Through the racialization of specific temperaments and dispositions – such as viciousness,
licentiousness, or rapacity – the frontier, for Crèvecœur, becomes a space
where sexual behavior provides the evidence of the racial degeneration that
occurs there."[23] LaFleur's historicized reading of *Letters* demonstrates
Crèvecœur's belief that exposure to the environment of colonial spaces
affects one's racial composition *and* one's "specific moral and characterological dispositions or tendencies."[24]

What LaFleur terms "the sexual politics of racial difference" changes the
way we think of sex and enables her to articulate a "historiography of
sexuality" in early America.[25] Reading a broad archive, LaFleur ultimately

theorizes "sex – without the subject," where sexuality is *not* primarily lodged deep within a human's body. LaFleur opens up exciting ways to think about race in early America and ways of reading early American literature, and *Early American Literature*'s special issue on the "New Natural History"[26] extends this conversation in even more directions. Who knows what other innovative interpretations of this older literature we sometimes think we know so well will be generated by attending to the historical specificities of this period's racialized thinking that appears so different from that which we know today?

***

But what if such exacting, traditional historical specificity comes at a price? As Miles Grier has so insightfully argued, such a tight focus on historical periods (especially those demarcated by mainstream scientific thinking that can mute other discourses, particularly those informing writers of color), while defamiliarizing race in any given period and generating insights into the ways literature imagines and contests race and racial categories, can also limit the way we understand continuing functions of race and racism. Indeed, Grier calls attention to the diachronic – and even multiply temporal – senses of race that an exclusively synchronic snapshot cannot capture, specifically the ongoing and chronic anti-Black racism and settler colonialism that saturate both "early" and "contemporary" "America."[27] Lisa Brooks (Abenaki) likewise encourages scholars to engage multiple Native temporalities that are nonlinear, asking, "What will American literary history look like if we take seriously Indigenous frameworks for reckoning time and conceiving of literature?"[28]

Indeed, a number of writers, artists, and scholars have brought renewed attention to what Christina Sharpe terms the "wake of slavery," a "conceptual frame of and for living blackness in the diaspora in the still unfolding aftermaths of Atlantic chattel slavery,"[29] and to what J. Kēhaulani Kauanui (Kanaka Maoli), building on Patrick Wolfe, notes: "Understanding settler colonialism as a structure exposes the fact that colonialism cannot be relegated to the past, even though the past-present should be historicized."[30] Toni Morrison, of course, most magisterially depicts the ongoing nature of slavery after its ostensible abolition in *Beloved*, and book artist Tia Blassingame's *Settled* and *Harvest* series materially manifest the connection between lethal anti-Black violence embedded in both slavery and contemporary police brutality. And a number of thinkers, scholars, and activists from Michelle Alexander to Eduardo Bonilla-Siva to Ava DuVernay to Ian

Baucom to Bryan Stevenson to Alicia Garza, Patrisse Cullors, and Opal Tometi have troubled the celebratory and easy slavery-to-emancipation-to-civil rights narrative that would tempt folks to believe either that we live in a postracial world or that things are "much better" for people of color in this country than they "used to be," by instead emphasizing chronologies that track shifts from slavery to Jim and Jane Crow to mass incarceration.[31] Critical race theory teaches us that race and racism are central and continuous – not exceptional – aspects of American life. Even as racial ideologies may change over time, ongoing white supremacy necessitates that and enables racism to mutate in such a way that allows it to be perpetuated continually in various forms.

Native thinkers relatedly call attention to the ongoing structure of settler colonialism, wherein the attack on Native sovereignty, land, and knowledges did not end in some earlier period but continues to this day. Both Audra Simpson (Mohawk) and Glen Coulthard (Yellowknives Dene First Nation) problematize contemporary notions of state "recognition" of Natives as part and parcel of settler colonialism. Here, settler states expect Indigenous people to exhibit a kind of Native-ness defined by settler-colonial epistemologies in order to gain settler state recognition – and, thus, rights – as Native. Simpson theorizes a "refusal" that "interrupts" this paradigm, and Coulthard advances an "alternative politics of recognition" articulated by Native peoples themselves.[32] In *Our History Is the Future*, Nick Estes (Lower Brule Sioux Tribe) places the Native protest against the Dakota Access Pipeline at Standing Rock into the "long tradition of Indigenous resistance" to settler colonialism.[33] Contemporary poet Joy Harjo (Mvskoke) also bears witness to ongoing settler colonialism, and as Mishuana Goeman (Tonawanda Band of Seneca) points out, Harjo responds to how settler colonialism maps Native lands by remapping Native space in writing.[34] The poem of Tanaya Winder (Duckwater Shoshone Tribe), "Love Lessons in a Time of Settler Colonialism," places the increasing numbers of Native women who are missing or have been murdered squarely within this structure. She writes:

> From Industrial Schools to forced assimilation, genocide means re-
> moval of those who birth nations – our living threatens. Colonization
> has been choking
>
> us for generations.[35]

Her "love lessons" are for her daughters, whom she teaches not only that "Colonialism's bullet sits cocked" but also that "they are vessels of spirit, air to lungs expanding; this world cannot/breathe without us." Here,

Winder's "girls" and other Native women experience "danger in being seen, our bodies are targets/marked for violence," a gendered violence produced by ongoing settler colonialism.

Conceptualizing race simultaneously as both a synchronic formation and as a diachronic formation can be particularly generative for thinking about, for example, William Apess's *The Indian Nullification of the Unconstitutional Laws of Massachusetts, Relative to the Marshpee Tribe; or, The Pretended Riot Explained.* A Pequot writer, minister, and activist, Apess composed *Indian Nullification* in 1835 as a response to how white Massachusetts citizens were attacking the sovereignty of the Mashpee Wampanoag peoples. *Indian Nullification* absolutely must be understood within its historical context: As an adopted member of the Wampanoag community of Mashpee, Apess protested the treatment of this Native nation by its government-appointed overseers within the broader context of increased pressure on forced removal of the Cherokee and other Indigenous peoples in the southeastern United States, and he reprints and comments upon white newspaper accounts of what some termed the "Mashpee Woodland Revolt" – and what Apess calls "the pretended riot."[36] Apess instead describes a peaceful act of nonviolent protest wherein he and two other Mashpee men stopped white men from logging on Mashpee lands by removing the wood from their wagon, and he details the peaceful Mashpee community meetings that followed.

But even as we understand Apess's *Indian Nullification* as a text produced within the moment of the 1835 attacks on Native sovereignty, we must also understand it as one produced within the moment of attacks on Native sovereignty in our contemporary moment. In fall 2018, the Mashpee Wampanoag Tribe began fighting efforts to disestablish the tribe's reservation. Exercising what Scott Richard Lyons calls rhetorical sovereignty (i.e., the inherent right of Indigenous peoples to represent themselves as they see fit), the Mashpee Wampanoag initiated an extensive outreach campaign as part of this effort, as the tribe produced posters, videos, and social media posts that engaged with and sometimes commented upon the ways various media outlets were telling the story and framing this attack on their rights. This example, of course, should be considered part of other ongoing practices of Mashpee rhetorical sovereignty: first, Wampanoag linguist and MacArthur Fellow Jessie Little Doe Baird, who founded the Wôpanâak Language Reclamation Project, a Wampanoag language revitalization program to preserve the ancestral tongue, and, second, Darius Coombs, Mashpee Wampanoag Cultural and Outreach Coordinator for Education, who serves as a culture-keeper and practices and teaches traditional Wampanoag lifeways among the Wampanoag and the broader public. After years of fighting this recent attack on their sovereignty, the Mashpee Wampanoag Tribe retained their right to self-governance and succeeded in keeping their reservation in trust status. It is a huge achievement; and yet, the work of protecting their land still continues.

Reading Apess's *Indian Nullification* not just alongside the Mashpee Wampanoag's self-produced representations of their fight against this contemporary encroachment on their sovereignty but also *as of the same moment* allows us a deeper appreciation of Apess's formalist techniques. Lisa Brooks (Abenaki) has helped us see Apess's work, coming specifically out of Native space, as "a tool of transformation, an extensive petition designed to effect change in the social, political, and geographic environment,"[37] and Drew Lopenzina has demonstrated that Apess's decision to request that William Lloyd Garrison publish the Mashpee resolutions in the *Liberator* "had set in motion a sure-footed and surprisingly modern media campaign that forced all the issues at Mashpee to a head," the central component of what Lopenzina calls "America's first successful campaign of civil disobedience."[38] To this we can add a sense of Apess's text itself, like the most recent Mashpee outreach, as a multiformat object (*Indian Nullification* is simultaneously a book; an extended editorial; a bricolage of reprinted newspaper articles, legal documents, and letters; and an edited collection) that comments on how other writers were telling and framing this story, produced within a particular instance of settler colonialism in order to exercise and preserve Mashpee sovereignty by reasserting Mashpee rights. It also presents scholars with an opportunity to put our knowledge about history to good use in our moment: to support the Mashpee in their ongoing work because we understand the role the Mashpee have played in "American" history, to affirm and amplify Mashpee statements about the importance of their nation and its sovereignty, and simply to #standwithmashpee. Thinking synchronically and diachronically gives us a chance not only to reinvigorate our understandings and interpretations of the literatures produced about the *then*, but also to direct our knowledge into attempting an intervention, even a small rupture, in the *now*.

Notes

I thank Kelly Wisecup and Darius Coombs for invaluable feedback on this essay.

  1. Katy L. Chiles, *Transformable Race: Surprising Metamorphoses in the Literature of Early America* (New York: Oxford University Press, 2014). See also Katy L.

Chiles, "Becoming Colored in Occom and Wheatley's Early America," *PMLA* 123.5 (2008), 1398–1417.

2. On this type of oppositional logic, see Toni Morrison, *Playing in the Dark: Whiteness and the Literary Imagination* (New York: Vintage Books, 1993); Eric Lott, *Love and Theft: Blackface Minstrelsy and the American Working Class* (New York: Oxford University Press, 1993); David Roediger, *The Wages of Whiteness: Race and the Makings of the American Working Class*, revised ed. (London: Verso, 1991); and Philip J. Deloria, *Playing Indian* (New Haven, CT: Yale University Press, 1998).

3. Timothy Dwight, *Travels in New England and New York*, ed. Barbara Miller Solomon (Cambridge, MA: Belknap Press of Harvard University Press, 1969), Vol. III, 126.

4. Quoted in Dwight, *Travels*, 126.

5. Dwight, *Travels*, 128.

6. Dwight, *Travels*, 128.

7. Samuel Stanhope Smith, *An Essay on the Causes of the Variety of Complexion and Figure in the Human Species. To Which Are Added Strictures on Lord Kaims's "Discourse, on the Original Diversity of Mankind"* (Philadelphia: Aitken, 1787), 62–63.

8. On what he terms "nativist" Indians, see Gregory Dowd, *A Spirited Resistance: The North American Indian Struggle for Unity, 1745–1815* (Baltimore: Johns Hopkins University Press, 1992).

9. Thomas Jefferson, *Notes on the State of Virginia: The Portable Thomas Jefferson*, ed. Merrill D. Peterson. (New York: Penguin Books, 1977), 192–93.

10. For more on environmentalist thinking, see Winthrop Jordan, *White over Black: American Attitudes toward the Negro, 1550–1812* (Baltimore: Penguin Books, 1968). See also John Wood Sweet, *Bodies Politic: Negotiating Race in the American North, 1730–1830* (Baltimore: Johns Hopkins University Press, 2003); Bruce Dain, *A Hideous Monster of the Mind: American Race Theory in the Early Republic* (Cambridge, MA: Harvard University Press, 2002); and Joanne Pope Melish, *Disowning Slavery: Gradual Emancipation and "Race" in New England, 1780–1860* (Ithaca, NY: Cornell University Press, 1998).

11. John Mitchell, "Essay upon the Causes of the Different Colours of People in Different Climates, M.D. Communicated to the Royal Society by Mr. Peter Collinson, F. R. S." *Philosophical Transactions* 43 (1744–45), 148.

12. Thomas Clarkson, *Essay on the Slavery and Commerce of the Human Species, Particularly the African* (London: J. Phillips, George-Yard, Lombard-Street, and sold by T. Cadell, In The Strand, and J. Phillips, 1786), 185–86, emphasis in original.

13. Phillis Wheatley, *Poems on Various Subjects, Religious and Moral: Complete Writings*, ed. Vincent Carretta (New York: Penguin, 2001), 13.

14. Wheatley, *Poems*, 27.

15. At least two other somewhat related and complementary creation stories occur in Mohegan literatures. One, recorded in Melissa Tantaquidgeon Zobel's *The Lasting of the Mohegans*, was recited by Witapanoxwe / Walks

With Daylight (also known as James Weber), a Lenni Lenape Medicine Man, to Mohegan Medicine Woman Gladys Tantaquidgeon:

> In that place, there was nothing at all times above the earth. At first, forever lost in space the Great Manitou [or Gunche Mundu] was . . . He made the sun, the moon and the stars . . . . Then the wind blew violently and it cleared and the water flowed off far and strong. And groups of islands grew newly [atop the domed back of a giant turtle whom we call 'Grandfather']¹ and there remained.
> ¹: Bracketed inserts are Mohegan additions to the Lenni Lenape Creation Story. (7)

Another exists in the Mohegan Sun Casino, where a mural depicts a man growing from a tree. *The Secret Guide*, a tourist-directed history of the Mohegan nation produced by the Mohegan Tribe and edited by Tantaquidgeon Zobel, addresses this mural in the section "Mohegan Creation Story": "To the left of the Tree of Life, is a large mural depicting the Mohegan Creation Story. The story is told as such; after the Earth was created long ago, a tree grew in the middle of the Earth. The root of the tree sent forth a sprout beside it, and there grew the first man. Then the tree bent over its top and touched the Earth, and there shot another root, from which came forth another sprout, and there grew the first woman" (29). Instead of asking which story is *the* Mohegan origin story, it might suit us better to inquire what *is* a Mohegan origin story. Most likely Occom would claim a Mohegan origin story is one told by a Mohegan, for a Mohegan purpose. Additionally, all these stories have much in common: the emphasis on the natural world, the presence of a single Creator, and the importance of the relationship of the tree to human life. As Caroline Wigginton has pointed out about the many petitions Occom penned during the 1760s–1780s, Occom often used the imagery of the "Sacred Tree" from Mohegan oral history in his writings, something Wigginton notes "spread[s] an Indigenous Christianity" (36). Here, we might consider this less a "replacement" of traditional Mohegan origin stories with a Christian one and more an indigenized Christianity. See Melissa Jayne (Fawcett) Tantaquidgeon Zobel, *The Lasting of the Mohegans, Part I: The Story of the Wolf People* (Uncasville, CT: Mohegan Tribe, 1995), 7; Caroline Wigginton, "Extending Root and Branch: Community Regeneration in the Petitions of Samson Occom," *Studies in American Indian Literatures* 20.4 (2008), 24–55; and Melissa Tantaquidgeon Zobel, *The Secret Guide* (Uncasville, CT: Little People Publications, 1998).

16. On the vast topic of Native sovereignty, see Joanne Barker, ed., *Sovereignty Matters: Locations of Contestation and Possibility in Indigenous Struggles for Self-Determination* (Lincoln: University of Nebraska Press, 2006); Jodi A. Byrd, "Introduction to Indigeneity's Difference," *J19: The Journal of Nineteenth-Century Americanists* 2.1 (2014): 131–36; Scott Richard Lyons, "Rhetorical Sovereignty: What Do American Indians Want from Writing?" *CCC* 51.3 (2000): 447–68; and Robert Allen Warrior, *Tribal Secrets: Recovering American Indian Intellectual Traditions* (Minneapolis: University of Minnesota Press, 1995).

17. Dowd, *Spirited Resistance*, 21.
18. Samson Occom, "To all the Indians in this Boundless Continent," *The Collected Writings of Samson Occom, Mohegan: Leadership and Literature in Eighteenth-Century Native America*, ed. Joanna Brooks (New York: Oxford University Press, 2006), 196.
19. Occom, "To all the Indians," 197, emphasis added.
20. Brooks, editorial footnote, "To all the Indians," 196.
21. Samson Occom, "Brotherton Tribe to United States Congress," *The Collected Writings of Samson Occom, Mohegan: Leadership and Literature in Eighteenth-Century Native America*, ed. Joanna Brooks (New York: Oxford University Press, 2006), 149.
22. J. Hector St. John de Crèvecœur, *Letters from an American Farmer and Sketches of Eighteenth-Century America*, ed. Albert E. Stone (New York: Penguin, 1986), 69. Further references to this edition will be cited parenthetically as *L*.
23. Greta LaFleur, *The Natural History of Sexuality in Early America* (Baltimore: Johns Hopkins University Press, 2018), 43–44.
24. LaFleur, *Natural History*, 43.
25. LaFleur, *Natural History*, 4, 9.
26. *Early American Literature*, special issue, "New Natural History" 54.3 (2019).
27. Miles P. Grier, "Literature in the Key (and Time) of Science," *Criticism* 59.3 (2017): 491–94.
28. Lisa Brooks, "The Primary of the Present, the Primary of Place: Navigating the Spiral of History in the Digital World," *PMLA* 127.2 (2012): 308–16.
29. Christina Sharpe, *In the Wake: On Blackness and Being* (Durham, NC: Duke University Press, 2016), 2.
30. J. Kēhaulani Kauanui, "'A Structure, Not an Event': Settler Colonialism and Enduring Indigeneity," *Lateral* 5.1 (2016), https://csalateral.org/issue/5-1/forum-alt-humanities-settler-colonialism-enduring-indigeneity-kauanui/. See also Patrick Wolfe, *Settler Colonialism and the Transformation of Anthropology: The Politics and Poetics of an Ethnographic Event* (London: Continuum International, 1998).
31. Michelle Alexander, *The New Jim Crow: Mass Incarceration in the Age of Colorblindness* (New York: New Press, 2010); Eduardo Bonilla-Siva, *Racism without Racists: Color-Blind Racism and the Persistence of Racial Inequality in America*, 5th ed. (New York: Rowman & Littlefield, 2017); Ava DuVernay, *13th: From Slave to Criminal with One Amendment* (Netflix, 2016); Ian Baucom, *Specters of the Atlantic: Finance Capital, Slavery, and the Philosophy of History* (Durham, NC: Duke University Press, 2005); Bryan Stevenson, *Just Mercy: A Story of Justice and Redemption* (New York: Spiegel & Grau, 2015); https://eji.org; and https://blacklivesmatter.com/about/our-co-founders/.
32. Audra Simpson, *Mohawk Interruptus: Political Life across the Borders of Settler States* (Durham, NC: Duke University Press, 2014), 11. Glen Coulthard, *Red Skins, White Masks: Rejecting the Colonial Politics of Recognition* (Minneapolis: University of Minnesota Press, 2014), 18.

33. Nick Estes, *Our History Is the Future: Standing Rock versus the Dakota Access Pipeline, and the Long Tradition of Indigenous Resistance* (New York: Penguin Random House, 2019).

34. Mishuana Goeman, *Mark My Words: Native Women Mapping Our Nations* (Minneapolis: University of Minnesota Press, 2013), 119–56.

35. Tanaya Winder, "Love Lessons in a Time of Settler Colonialism," *Poetry* June 2018.

36. William Apess, *The Indian Nullification of the Unconstitutional Laws of Massachusetts, Relative to the Marshpee Tribe; or, The Pretended Riot Explained.* In *On Our Own Ground: The Complete Writings of William Apess, a Pequot,* ed. Barry O'Connell (Amherst: University of Massachusetts Press, 1992), 166–274.

37. Lisa Brooks, *The Common Pot: The Recovery of Native Space in the Northeast* (Minneapolis: University of Minnesota Press, 2008), 164.

38. Drew Lopenzina, *Through an Indian's Looking Glass: A Cultural Biography of William Apess, Pequot* (Amherst: University of Massachusetts Press, 2017), 12. See also Jean M. O'Brien, *Firsting and Lasting: Writing Indians out of Existence in New England* (Minneapolis: University of Minnesota Press, 2010), 181–83; and Maureen Konkle, *Writing Indian Nations: Native Intellectuals and the Politics of Historiography* (Chapel Hill: University of North Carolina Press, 2004), 119–31.

CHAPTER 3

Protean Oceans
Racial Uncertainty in Arthur Gordon Pym and Emmanuel Appadocca

Gesa Mackenthun

It is somewhat remarkable, that, at a time when knowledge is so generally diffused, when the geography of the world is so well understood – when time and space, in the intercourse of nations, are almost annihilated – when oceans have become bridges – the earth a magnificent hall – the hollow sky a dome – under which a common humanity can meet in friendly conclave – when nationalities are being swallowed up and the ends of the earth brought together – I say it is remarkable – nay, it is strange that there should arise a phalanx of learned men – speaking in the name of *science* – to forbid the magnificent reunion of mankind in one brotherhood. A mortifying proof is here given, that the moral growth of a nation, or an age, does not always keep pace with the increase of knowledge, and suggests the necessity of means to increase human love with human learning.

Frederick Douglass, "The Claims of the Negro Ethnologically
Considered" (1854)

Frederick Douglass is writing these lines at a historical moment in which scientific racism arose concurrently with abolitionism, preparing the scientifically grounded justification of social inequality that haunts us to this day. An unstable and fractured category,[1] racial whiteness was invented as part of what Jacobson calls an "alchemy of race";[2] in the nineteenth century, its cultural work consisted in reserving economic, political, and moral privilege to the existing social elite whose racial denomination would, always in complex conversation with religious and linguistic discussions, move from "Anglo-Saxon" to "Aryan" to "Caucasian."[3] The collusion of science with slavery and colonialism throughout the nineteenth and far into the twentieth century is one of the darkest consequences of Enlightenment rationalism.[4] Its ideological reverberations are felt in the present, with the World Wide Web facilitating global racism to translate its inhuman fantasies into bloody deeds.

The greatest fear of white supremacism, as the manifestos of the mass murderers at Utøya, Norway (2011), and Christchurch, New Zealand

41

(2019), make clear, is the so-called Great Replacement of a racially white population by a nonwhite and, in the worst case, Muslim population. Arguably, this master narrative of racial victimization is the key to white supremacism's continuing relevance as a political ideology. White racists frequently imagine this population exchange – this "Umvolkung" in the lingo of German right-wing groups – to be accomplished by the more fertile reproductive activity of the "dangerous races" coupled with reproductive reluctance on the part of whites – a scenario in which the sexual behavior of women is crucial. What white supremacists often neglect, biologically speaking, is the gradual merging of populations into one another, either by violence imposed on women or by female choice and consent. Arguably, the acceleration of ethnic crossing is a greater threat to racial purism than the existence of other "pure" races as long as they keep their geographical distance. "Racial hybridity" is the racist's greatest fear, and US American literature gives abundant expression of this fear.

This chapter will analyze the trope of racial hybridity and the uncertain construction of whiteness through a reading of two New World novels written in light of, and in response to, the Jacksonian Indian removal and the passing of the Fugitive Slave Act, respectively. It will illustrate entanglements between discourses of race with discourses on antiquity as well as a "Black Atlantic" literary counterdiscourse that explores the economic and social undercurrents of racial slavery – a form of labor that could only continue to exist because of the imaginary "scientific" construction of a "natural" hierarchy within mankind. Understanding the racial pathology of Jacksonian and antebellum America is so important because, as Morrison and Stewart, referring to David Brion Davis, assert, "these decades constituted seismic moments in the reshaping of the republican state, ... the shock waves from which still reverberate disturbingly into our time."[5]

Since its invention in the eighteenth century, the scientific classification of races was confronted with the problem that humans reproduced across color lines, whether voluntarily or as a result of colonialism's asymmetries of (sexualized) power. Colonialism's "tense and tender ties"[6] effactually produced an increasingly mixed-ethnic population. Frederick Douglass and William Wells Brown comment on white males' use of black women for both sexual gratification and the increase of the slave labor force by way of systematic breeding.

White supremacism's problem is thus less the replacement of one "race" for another but what Darwin calls the "graduation" of populations into one another in consequence of Western colonialism, which takes place through transcultural sexual unions. While most literary "hybrids" – from

Cooper's *Last of the Mohicans* and Brown's *Clotel* all the way to Faulkner's *Absalom! Absalom!* – are the result of white males "seducing" nonwhite women, transcultural relations have become more reciprocal, adding misogynist hate to race hate in contemporary racist ideology.

This chapter concentrates on two literary works of the fractured Black Atlantic world that represent and explore this cultural pathology. Both Edgar Allan Poe's *Narrative of Arthur Gordon Pym of Nantucket* (1837) and Maxwell Philip's *Emmanuel Appadocca, or Blighted Life: A Tale of the Boucaneers* (1854) feature ethnically "hybrid" and culturally protean figures – sons of white men and nonwhite women – investing them variously with the aesthetics of horror (Poe) and tragic revenge (Philip). Both novels exhibit, and toy with, the ethnic ambivalence of their cross-blood characters and the cultural uncertainty that this represents.[7] They reveal the much greater cultural uncertainties of Jacksonian and antebellum Atlantic America. In the first section, I will show how *Arthur Gordon Pym* exhibits white supremacism's fear of losing control to nonwhite agents, coupled with an anxiety about the superiority of the Western epistemic system. The cultural work of Philip's novel consists of investigating and romancing the violence of transatlantic racial capitalism. Both texts are "fractured" in various ways: structurally, diegetically, epistemologically, and in terms of their characters' fractured identities. The "racial" anxiety and the rebelliousness they articulate allows us to regard them as foundational fictions of the Black Atlantic.

Arthur Gordon Pym begins as a tale of adolescent maritime adventure whose various rites of passage – from life burial and shipwreck to cannibalism, exciting discoveries, savage attacks, and a final race to the Southern Pole and into the embrace of a superhuman white figure – are entangled with numerous observations and reflections on scientific and political topics, such as Poe's parody of Western settlement in Pym's description of the penguin and albatross rookeries, or his pseudo-anthropological description of the tribe of completely black inhabitants that the European discoverers encounter on the Antarctic island of Tsalal. Pym's crossblood companion, Dirk Peters, unites within himself features of what Tocqueville describes as America's three "races" – he is the "ferocious-looking" son of an Upsaroka Indian woman from the Black Hills and a white fur trader while phenotypically resembling a racist parody of an African American:

> Short in stature – not more than four feet eight inches high – but his limbs were of the most Herculean mold. His hands, especially, were so enormously thick and broad as hardly to retain a human shape. His arms, as well

as legs, were *bowed* in the most singular manner . . . . His head was equally deformed, being of immense size, with an indentation on the crown (like that on the head of most Negroes), and entirely bald.[8]

Peters' face is broad-mouthed and thin-lipped, with his teeth exceedingly long and protruding. The initial semblance of constant merriment caused by this extraordinary physique would be superseded, Pym asserts, by "a shuddering acknowledgement" that "the merriment must be that of a demon" (*Pym* 85). Pym's attitude toward Peters changes over the course of the novel from initial repulsion by Peters' ugliness to admiration of his great strength to effeminate dependency on him when Peters rescues Pym from a fall caused by failure of nerve after a series of unfortunate events on Tsalal. At the end, Pym subsumes Peters among the only "white" survivors of the savage attack (*Pym* 212).

I agree with scholars who, noticing the absurd color dualism of Poe's novel, observe that *Pym* is above all a case study of the pathology of whiteness itself.[9] Toni Morrison famously argued in 1992 that "no early American writer is more important to the concept of American Africanism than Poe" and that the mode of gothic romance used in such texts as *Pym* is "an exploration of anxiety imported from the shadows of European culture" as well as of homemade fears of "being outcast, of failing, of powerlessness."[10] Whether unconsciously or deliberately deployed (as Robert Levine argues),[11] it has to be conceded that the racial anxiety articulated in Poe's texts exceeds the discourse on the Africanist presence in the United States. Betsy Erkkila critiques Morrison's "exclusive focus on the shaping presence of 'American Africanism' in the constitution of American national identity," arguing that "there were other races, cultures, and nationalities that vied for geopolitical space and presence in writing and naming America."[12] While Morrison is correct with her subtle, psychoanalytically inspired readings of the "uncanny" racial presences in American literary classics, it is equally important to grasp the transnational and transcultural aspects of these textual presences, as well as their economic dimensions. *Pym* is, as Teresa Goddu observes, a "narrative of racial convertibility"[13] not limited to any specific ethnicity or national territory.

Throughout the novel, Poe not only exaggerates and parodies but also reiterates the Enlightenment compulsion to classify nature, including human beings.[14] Initially referred to as a "hybrid" (*Pym* 93, 102, 106, 124), the figure of Dirk Peters subverts the homogeneity doctrine of this racial logic while his physical strength and intelligence contradict contemporary race theorists' assumptions about the physical and mental weakness of "hybrids" – all the way to infertility.[15]

Peters' counterscientific resilience invites analysis of how the novel represents scientific thinking as an ideological element in asserting white cultural superiority toward people of color. It also merges discourses about black resilience with that of indigenous people. The interactions between the crew of the *Jane Guy* and the Tsalalians – obviously both black and autochthonous to the island – condense and "convert" (in Goddu's terms) textual representations of well-known encounters between white explorers or colonizers and indigenous people, for example, the documents on the third voyage of Cook and his death on Hawaii and Washington Irving's narrative of the eruption of violence at Astoria off Vancouver Island in 1811, including the explosion of the ship *Tonquin*.[16] In both of these cases, the natives are referred to as treacherous, duplicitous, and unreadable, similar to the inhabitants of Tsalal, whose chief bears the telling name "Too-wit." Their wittiness is ill matched by their hysterical fear of everything white – possibly a projection of American culture's own hysteria about losing its racial purity, for instance, by conquering too many "southern" brown-skinned peoples at once. After the "savages" prove witty enough to defend themselves against the white strangers' inroads by causing a rock avalanche to kill most of them, Pym and Peters are confronted with the unthinkable possibility that Tsalal had once been a civilized place. They find themselves in a system of subterranean caves, a place that reminds Pym "of those dreary regions marking the site of degraded Babylon." They behold what seem at first sight the remnants of ancient buildings, "huge tumuli, apparently the wreck of some gigantic structures of art." But at a second glance, Pym authoritatively decides that "no semblance of art could be detected" (*Pym* 230). Moreover, they discover "a range of singularly looking indentures" in the cave wall that "might have been taken for the intentional, although rude, representation of a human figure standing erect, with outstretched arm," whereas others, in Peters' opinion, resembled "alphabetical characters." Pym contradicts this "idle opinion," regarding them "to have been the work of nature" (*Pym* 225).

In his final "Note," Poe the editor authoritatively declares that after extensive philological examination, the inscriptions must be identified as the product of humans, consisting of the Ethiopian verbal root "to be shady," the Arabic verbal root "to be white," and the Egyptian word meaning "the region of the south," ending his reflections with the enigmatic sentence "*I have graven it within the hills, and my vengeance upon the dust within the rock*" (*Pym* 241–42).

As Dana Nelson remarks, the editor's acceptance of the inscriptions and stone formations as the work of human beings, contradicting Pym's previous claims to the opposite, destabilizes Pym's colonial self-image.[17] This conflict between the two narrators, which reveals the arbitrariness of their scientific interpretations, is reinforced by the general *grayness* of the vapor at the South Pole (which anticipates the "grayness" of the fog surrounding the *San Dominick* in Melville's *Benito Cereno*) (*Pym* 236, 237). The presence of (white) flakes of marl at the island's geological and ancient historical center invites the interpretation that the black Tsalalians had replaced an older population that, while both its ethnic identity and its belief in the oppositionality of "white" and "shady" remain indeterminate, at least did not shy away from using a white rock for its inscriptions.

Poe's "Note" dismisses Pym's previous claim about the noncultural origin of the mysterious petroglyphs while gesturing to contemporary discussions of cases of "savage" writing in North America and elsewhere. The presence on Tsalal of quasi-biblical messages evokes theories of ancient transatlantic cultural diffusion circulating in learned magazines at the time Poe wrote his novel. It also implies that Tsalalian culture degenerated from a once-powerful civilization (possessing the arts of writing and prophecy) to the utterly savage state in which Pym and his companions find them. Such a conclusion would reflect knowledge of the transitoriness of empires, sparked by Gibbon's extremely successful *Decline and Fall of the Roman Empire* (1776–88) and Constantin de Volney's popular treatise *Ruins* (1796), as well as the discovery of ancient ruins of bygone civilizations in places like Egypt, Jordan, and Yucatan.

The larger epistemic context of Poe's racial fantasy concerns the position that Anglo-American civilization was thought to inhabit in a world-historical framework. Young America's pervasive discourse of newness (Emerson's "American Scholar"; Manifest Destiny) was conspicuously coupled with equally strong attempts to construct a collective ancient past whose traces would not be lost in vague tribal memories. The historical roots of Anglo-American settler colonialism were not easy to determine, and promoters of historical "firstness" were haunted by the specter of belatedness. While Poe was drafting his novel, three contemporary topics caught the attention of American intellectuals: the discussion about the meaning of petroglyphs on the so-called Dighton Rock near Fall River, Massachusetts; the discovery in 1831 of a skeleton in armor close to the rock; and the long-announced publication of Christian Rafn's multilingual *Antiquitates Americanae* in 1837, in which the Danish scholar seeks to prove that the medieval Norsemen Thorfinn Karlsefne and Leif Eriksson had landed at Cape Cod, near enough to the mysterious rock and skeleton to allow for a connection.[18] Rafn's publication was the culmination of his concerted effort to interpret the Icelandic sagas as evidence for a Norse colonization of New England. While the Norse discovery theory had been in the public sphere since the late eighteenth century, Rafn's book was the first systematic claim with a precise geographical reference to New England/Cape Cod, arguing that the rock inscription was a reference to Thorfinn's landing.[19] The "scientific" analysis of the skeleton accordingly regarded it as the remains of an ancient Norse because of the copper plates found together with it.[20] Rafn's thesis circulated throughout the 1830s in US magazines, including ones edited or contributed to by Poe,[21] where it sat next to speculations about the racial identity of the moundbuilders whose cultural link to present-day Native Americans was the subject of controversy.[22] In other words, *Antiquitates Americanae* burst into an intellectual arena that was already saturated with speculations about the racial past of the continent, denying great antiquity to the tribes who were presently dispossessed and deported while seeking more European claimants for historical firstness in the hemisphere. Joseph Moldenhauer, who has established a connection between the final section of *Arthur Gordon Pym* and the Norse campaign, regards Poe's interpretation of the Tsalalian petroglyphs as the most obvious connection between the Norse colonization debate and the novel.[23] The ominous writing on the cave wall is an "ornate" reference to another facet of America's discourse about race: the feverish search in American society for ancient evidence of a racially acceptable first settlement. The Norse figured among other cultural-geographical groups as candidates for ethnic whiteness and became the favorite of white supremacism at the end of the nineteenth century and beginning of the twentieth century. While the inscriptions in *Pym*, referring to "regions in the south" and speaking pseudo-biblically of "vengeance" (*Pym* 241–42), allude to the contemporary fear of slave revolts,[24] they also refer to the epistemic dilemma of establishing a rule of whiteness on the continent while disavowing the ancient presence of America's indigenous population, including the denial of indigenous forms of writing.[25]

Hidden behind the mysterious allusion to black "vengeance," *Arthur Gordon Pym* negotiates contemporary attempts to invent a "white" prehistory in North America that preceded the arrival of Columbus by 500 years and that discursively effaced the much longer presence of the indigenous population. The establishment of this "white" cultural heritage significantly rests on the epistemic power of reading and writing, and Poe's novel

savagely documents the limits of this power: messages scribbled with
blood, the incapacity to decipher the petroglyphs or to "read" the social
performance of the Tsalalians, Pym's – and Poe's – final inability to
decipher the superhuman white figure appearing at the South Pole. If
colonial power and legitimacy are established through the control of
writing (as in the legal justification of Indian removal), the novel attests
to a nervous incompetence about not being able to read the writing of
nonwhite cultural texts.

Mimetically if not diegetically, Poe employed the mode of romance in
Arthur Gordon Pym – a mode, as Toni Morrison asserts, that offered itself
particularly well for exploring racial anxiety.[26] It is also best suited for
articulating the various forms of cultural overdetermination that the novel
performs – especially its direct link between allusions to the transatlantic
slave trade (including a carnivalesque slave ship revolt) and the maritime
exploration of the Pacific Ocean. Poe wrote the novel in explicit support of
journalist Jeremiah Reynolds' lobbying for a Pacific exploring expedition
that was realized in the year of the book's publication when the massive US
Exploring Expedition of Charles Wilkes departed from Chesapeake Bay
(1838–42). In spite of his imperialist bravado, Poe's invention of a
fantastic, protean, and, as Wilson Harris suggests, "schizophrenic" sea[27]
identifies him as the bard of the dissolution of racial and masculine
superiority lurking behind every rock and wave of white patriarchal
scientific self-assertion.[28]

A protean sea is also at the heart of the first Caribbean novel of the Black
Atlantic, the pirate romance *Emmanuel Appadocca or Blighted Life* (1854)
by the Trinidadian creole writer Maxwell Philip. Like *Pym*, it features a
crossblood figure, this time the protagonist Emmanuel Appadocca, a figure
as tragic, lonely, and charismatic as if sprung from Byron's poetic work-
shop. Appadocca represents the growing population resulting from slave
masters' practice, as Frederick Douglass writes, "to administer to their own
lusts, and make a gratification of their wicked desires profitable as well as
pleasurable."[29] Assuming himself to be the product of such a union,
Douglass predicts the "downfall of slavery by the inevitable laws of population" because "a very different-looking class of people are springing up at
the south, and are now held in slavery, from those originally brought to this
country from Africa." The scripture-based justification of slavery, Douglass
contends, loses all logic in light of this demographic development.[30]

The pirate novel's tragic hero, an illegitimate son of a British plantation
owner and a Trinidadian mulatto woman, takes revenge on agents of
colonialism, particularly his father, who abandoned him together with

his mother. His "blighted life" is meant to condemn the enormous crime inflicted upon people of African descent throughout the Americas. A self-declared avenger of the victims of the slave-based Atlantic system's economic and sexual exploitation, Appadocca plows the Caribbean in a highly technologized ship like an oceanic version of Robin Hood and redistributes the goods from captured merchant ships to the poor inhabitants of the islands. Like Cooper's Red Rover, Appadocca and his crew live at sea; indeed, their radical resistance would dissolve if they went on land and exposed themselves to the superior military force of Britain. Of course, this lonely guerilla battle cannot be victorious in the long run; Appadocca is defeated in the end – although neither by the clumsy British warship that chases him nor by a storm at sea but by a self-declared fate that orders him to commit suicide after having accomplished his personal revenge.

Published in London in 1854, *Emmanuel Appadocca* reacts on the political situation in the United States after the passing of the Fugitive Slave Act (1850),[31] as well as on literary texts written in light of this juridical violation of human rights principles. Appadocca shares the element of racial hybridity coupled with superior intelligence with George Harris; his seaborne rebellion is reminiscent of Douglass' novella "The Heroic Slave" (1853); and his mother's fate shares that of the women characters in *Clotel* (1853). While the protagonist's promethean sense of cosmic purpose bears traces of Melville's Ahab, it also anticipates other black or racially hybrid maritime rebels like Melville's Babo and Verne's Captain Nemo.

The protagonist is described as young, handsome, almost femininely delicate, and of a light olive complexion that "showed a mixture of blood, and proclaimed that the man was connected with some dark race, and in the infinity of grades in the population of Spanish America, he may have been said to be of that which is commonly designated Quadroon."[32] Appadocca leads an authoritarian regime on board his ship, maintaining a mysterious nimbus about his person. His racial hybridity is doubled by that of his "motley crew" (*EA* 27), whose multicultural composition is reminiscent of that of the *Pequod* in *Moby-Dick*. Appadocca's ship, too, shares qualities with the *Pequod*: The "Black Schooner," whose long, low hulk evokes the slave revolt on the *Amistad* (1839), is at once a guarded castle with long, secret passages and a carnivalesque high-tech machine whose power of disguise plays havoc with the unsuspecting Englishmen. With ship, crew, and captain representing protean power, Philip features the high seas as the only place where this power can rule; on land, Appadocca's powers wither away, hemmed in by domestic law and colonial practice. Imprisoned on the ship of his antagonist, a British navy captain, he involves the captain's son, his boyhood friend Charles, in a discussion on national identities, the moral basis of his piratical activities, and the situation of the colonial world. He replies to Charles' predictable self-identification as "an Englishman, and an English officer" by saying, "'And I . . . am an animal, – sub-kingdom, *vertebrata*, genus *homo*, and species, – 'tropical American': naturalists lay my habitat all over the world, and declare me omnivorous" (*EA* 122). This parody of the language of scientific racism is preceded by a radical critique of modern capitalism and its impact on nonwhite people and the poor. Indigenous inhabitants, Appadocca rants, "are driven after the destruction of their cities, to roam the woods, and to perish and disappear on the advance of their greedy supplanters." Intent on avoiding labor, a "fashion springs up" to kidnap "the straggling and weakest portions of a certain race" deemed fit for physical labor,

> load them with irons, [and] throw them into the cruel ordeal of the 'middle passage', to test whether they are sufficiently iron-constituted as to survive the starvation, stench, and pestilential contagion which decide the extent of the African's endurance, and fix his value. This my dear friend is an abstracted idea of the manner in which the world turns. (*EA* 113–14)

His acute analysis of the logic of racial capitalism provides him with the rationale for defending his own Robin Hood–like activities (*EA* 115). To Appadocca, the most pernicious human cost of slave-based capitalism is white men's exploitation of disenfranchised women like his own mother and their abandonment of their offspring. Educated as a member of the mulatto elite in Paris, Appadocca tells Charles how he was thrown into absolute poverty when his mother died. He observes the same patriarchal irresponsibility at the heart of the colonial world in London, where he saves a young woman from committing suicide for not being able to feed her illegitimate child (*EA* 101–2). The scene of female victimization at the heart of the British empire is remarkable for its aesthetical contrast between a Wordsworthian idealization of the British capital coupled with a Blakean description of its human misery.

Appadocca's massive critique of the slave-based Atlantic system is introduced with a demonstration of his astronomical expertise; he scribbles a series of "algebraical figures" on the ship's cabin wall: a mathematical calculation that allows him to predict the natural disaster that will eventually coincide with his death (*EA* 97). Like Ahab, Appadocca is presented as a prophet-like scientific genius. Unlike Ahab, he traces his superior knowledge to his African roots, a "race, which is now despised and oppressed" but among whom

> speculation took wing, and the mind burst forth, and, scorning things of earth, scaled the heavens, read the stars, and elaborated systems of philosophy, religion, and government: while the other parts of the world were either enveloped in darkness, or following in eager and uncontemplative haste the luring genii of riches. Commerce makes steam engines and money – it assists not the philosophical progress of the mind. (*EA* 116)

Making a sharp distinction between the sciences and the humanities, Philip evokes the contemporary trope of African splendor and the intellectual debate about the African origins of the ancient civilization of Egypt propagated by Volney and others, a discourse that also left its trace in Melville's Black Atlantic novels.[33] Appadocca's praise of Africa as the origin of knowledge shares a discursive site with Frederick Douglass' concurrent argument to the same effect (see this chapter's epigraph). In his 1854 address "The Claims of the Negro Ethnologically Considered," Douglass confronts the racial polygenism of Samuel George Morton's *Crania Americana* (1839) with the historical fact that Egypt was "one of the earliest abodes of learning and civilization, ... defying, with a calm front[,] the boasted mechanical and architectural skill of the nineteenth century."[34] He reminds his Northern listeners that "the ancient Egyptians were not white people; but were, undoubtedly, just about as dark in complexion as many in this country who are considered genuine Negroes," and he continues in critiquing racial scientists for their disavowal of intelligence to black people. His explanation for this denial is as true today as it was then: "It is the province of prejudice to blind; and scientific writers, not less than others, write to please, as well as to instruct, and even unconsciously to themselves, (sometimes), sacrifice what is true to what is popular."[35]

Emmanuel Appadocca is a counterhegemonic novel that explores the gendered and class-related inequalities at the center of Atlantic racial capitalism frequently hidden by the scientific discourse of race. Especially its writing scene forms a literary counterpoint to Poe's scientific "hoax" while standing Poe's nervous top-heavy discourse on antiquity and nonwhite knowledge from its head on its feet. It establishes itself on various levels as a key text of Atlantic antebellum abolitionism, together with Black Atlantic novels like Douglass' "The Heroic Slave" and Martin Delany's *Blake* (1861).

William Cain calls *Emmanuel Appadocca* a "multicultural, polyphonic, 'Atlantic' book that challenges, even as it capitalizes upon, traditional notions of what a 'national' literature is and includes."[36] Cain accordingly argues that Philip's novel splendidly fits into Gilroy's paradigm of the Black Atlantic as a diasporic, rhizomorphic "counterculture of modernity"[37] – a culture to which definitions of individual and collective racial identities are crucial. These definitions, as both novels demonstrate, are tied to theories about ancient civilizations, knowledge, and migrations: The colonial invention of antiquity is inseparable from contemporary constructions of race and gender, while the presence of the art of writing functions as a key marker of cultural authority (which is why it was denied to slaves).

Arthur Gordon Pym and *Emmanuel Appadocca* allow us two enlightening glimpses at the ideology investing the expansion of slavery and of racial capitalism in the period between the Indian removal and the Civil War. *Arthur Gordon Pym*'s geographical hybridity may appear aesthetically fractured but effectively illustrates the continuities between Atlantic slavery and Pacific exploration – a knowledge about the intricate dependencies of "slavery" and "freedom" that Herman Melville would explore further in *Moby-Dick* and in *Benito Cereno*. It illustrates the cultural anxiety that inevitably accompanied a historical iniquity of such magnitude. As Toni Morrison so aptly phrases, whiteness as ideology was "formed in fright" – an insight she sees articulated in Melville's *Moby-Dick*.[38] Philip's novel is the cosmopolitan response to Poe's schizophrenic ocean in that it spells out the human cost of an economic paradigm based on greed and social inequality. Both texts call attention to the contribution of colonial science to legitimating such a process, its blindness to social facts, and its failure to formulate a positive foundation of a future society beyond color lines.

In their different ways, both novels diagnose the racial dimension of Atlantic colonialism. They gesture to the conspicuous denial of historical continuity to nonwhite people whose traces colonial discourse was busy erasing from the historical record. The cultural ties of contemporary nonwhite populations were effectively severed from their more "refined" ancestral cultures while Euro-Americans were nervously seeking to construct a continuous past for themselves by way of establishing historical links to idealized versions of ancient empires whose torch of civilization traveled from east to west: the colonial master narrative of *translatio imperii et studi*. Such constructions express a festering uncertainty about the epistemic superiority of "white" civilization. Both novels discussed in this chapter demonstrate the fractured nature of the narrative of westward-traveling knowledge.[39] The search for ancient migrants "white" enough to serve as colonial progenitors – from Phoenicians to Norse to Anglo-Saxons – was accompanied by the invention of racial taxonomies whose cultural work consisted in denying historical coevalness to nonwhite populations. Early anthropology's classification systems, as Douglass and Darwin aptly criticized, were oblivious to colonial realities. They effectively contaminated American society's minds with ideologies of cultural homogeneity, purity, and some races' natural tendency to extinction while denying the fact, stated by Douglass in the epigraph, that all humans – and all nonhumans too – are related to one another. Thus, the racial science of the antebellum period prepared the ideological ground for the toxic theory of social Darwinism whose century-old competition with the ideals of cosmopolitan humanism presently reaches a new climax, for example, in the form of genetically based racial identitarianism[40] coupled with the still powerful myth of indigenous "extinction."[41]

White supremacism's hysteria about "white genocide" turns on a fear of dark-skinned men invading "white" bloodlines through white women's wombs. As Faulkner so masterfully showed in *Absalom! Absalom!*, white supremacism would even tolerate incest because kings did it too, breeding cultural parochialism through endogamous procreation. The hysteria about miscegenation betrays white supremacists' fear of being *themselves* measured and found intellectually wanting. In its obsession with myths of ancient origin, first discoveries, the racial identity of ancient remains, and the illegibility of ancient scripts, supremacist discourse articulates a remarkable anxiety about Euroamerican historical belatedness and epistemic ignorance. Early Black Atlantic literary texts show the grotesqueness and the horror of this culturally deaf and monological ideology whose wrath about its own lack of cultural creativity turns into deadly violence with uncanny regularity.

Notes

1. Theodore W. Allen, *The Invention of the White Race*, 2 vols. (London: Verso, 1994–97).
2. Matthew Frye Jacobson, *Whiteness of a Different Color* (Cambridge, MA: Harvard University Press, 1998), 15.
3. Colin Kidd, *The Forging of Races* (Cambridge: Cambridge University Press, 2006), esp. chapter 6, "The Aryan Moment."
4. See Reginald Horsman, *Race and Manifest Destiny: The Origins of American Racial Anglo-Saxonism* (Cambridge, MA: Harvard University Press, 1981); William Stanton, *The Leopard's Spots* (Chicago: University of Chicago Press, 1960); Robert Young, *Colonial Desire: Hybridity in Theory, Culture and Race* (London: Routledge, 1995); and Stephen Jay Gould, *The Mismeasure of Man*, rev. ed. (New York: Norton, 1996).

5. Michael A. Morrison and James Brewer Stewart, "Introduction," in Michael A. Morrison and James Brewer Stewart (eds.), *Race in the Early Republic* (Lanham, MD: Rowman & Littlefield, 2002), 2–3.

6. Ann Laura Stoler, "Tense and Tender Ties,"in Ann Laura Stoler (ed.), *Haunted by Empire* (Durham, NC: Duke University Press, 2006), 23–70.

7. "Crossblood": I'm using Gerald Vizenor's terminology, aware of the racist connotations of "blood."

8. Edgar Allan Poe, *The Narrative of Arthur Gordon Pym of Nantucket*, ed. Harold Beaver (1837–38; Harmondsworth: Penguin, 1975), 84. Hereafter referred to in text as *Pym*.

9. See especially Dana Nelson, *The Word in Black and White: Reading "Race" in American Literature, 1638–1867* (New York: Oxford University Press, 1992), chapter 5. "White" is one of the least stable categories in scientific racism, fluctuating (historically, between authors) from types like Greek to Germanic, to Anglo-Saxon to Norse, finally condensed in the collective "Caucasian." White is the ethnicity that, being the definer of others, did not have to define itself in any stable way. For a recent survey, see Kidd, *The Forging of Races*, 9–17.

10. Toni Morrison, *Playing in the Dark: Whiteness and the Literary Imagination* (London: Picador, 1992), 32, 36–37.

11. Robert Levine, "Reading Slavery and Classic American Literature," in Ezra Tawil (ed.), *The Cambridge Companion to Slavery in American Literature* (Cambridge: Cambridge University Press, 2016), 137–52. *Pym*, I argue, is located both within and outside the cultural pathology.

12. Betsy Erkkila, *Mixed Bloods and Other Crosses: Rethinking American Literature from the Revolution to the Culture Wars* (Philadelphia: University of Pennsylvania Press, 2005), 105.

13. Teresa A. Goddu, *Gothic America: Narrative, History, and Nation* (New York: Columbia University Press, 1997), 84.

14. Goddu, *Gothic America*, 85.

15. See, for example, Robert Young's discussion of the discourse of hybridity in nineteenth-century racial biology (*Colonial Desire*, chapter 1).

16. Washington Irving, *Astoria*, ed. Edgeley W. Todd (1836; Norman: Oklahoma University Press, 1964), 113—16. See Harold Beaver's comment in the old Penguin edition of *Pym*, 264–65.

17. Nelson, *Word in Black and White*, 104.

18. Annette Kolodny, *In Search of First Contact: The Vikings of Vinland, the Peoples of the Dawnland, and the Anglo-American Anxiety of Discovery* (Durham, NC: Duke University Press, 2012), 151–54.

19. Joseph J. Moldenhauer, "*Pym*, the Dighton Rock, and the Matter of Vinland," in Richard Kopley (ed.), *Poe's Pym: Critical Explorations* (Durham, NC: Duke University Press, 1992), 75–94, at 84.

20. Kolodny, *In Search of First Contact*, 151–54.

21. Moldenhauer, "*Pym*," 85.

22. Roger G. Kennedy, *Hidden Cities: The Discovery and Loss of Ancient North American Civilization* (London: Penguin, 1994), 236–37.

23. Moldenhauer, "*Pym,*" 93.

24. Joan Dayan, "Romance and Race," in Emory Elliott (ed.), *The Columbia History of the American Novel* (New York: Columbia University Press, 1991), 89–109, at 97.

25. Only one critic notes the resemblance of the inscriptions with "the figures which the Indians paint on the smooth side of their buffalo skins" (Edward Everett, in Moldenhauer, "*Pym,*" 87). George Catlin reported similar observations (Kolodny, *In Search of First Contact*, 25).

26. Morrison, *Playing*, 36.

27. In his fascinating attempt to read *Pym* back into a pre-Columbian mythology of carnivalesque twinship, Harris identifies Pym's first ship, the *Grampus*, as a symbolic slave ship; Goddu makes similar claims about the ghost ship that the survivors of the mutiny encounter. Wilson Harris, "The Schizophrenic Sea," in *The Womb of Space: The Cross-Cultural Imagination* (Westport, CT: Greenwood Press, 1983), 99–108, at 104; Goddu, *Gothic America*, 85.

28. Poe's mastership in deconstructing masculine self-confidence is deployed in his stories about mentally and physically fragile male characters haunted by dominant women – as in "Ligeia," "Berenice," and "The Black Cat."

29. Frederick Douglass, *Narrative of the Life of Frederick Douglass, an American Slave*, ed. David W. Blight (1845; Boston: Bedford/St. Martin's, 1993), 40.

30. Douglass, *Narrative*, 41.

31. In his preface, Philip directly refers to the Fugitive Slave Act.

32. Maxwell Philip, *Emmanuel Appadocca, or Blighted Life: A Tale of the Boucaneers*, ed. Selwyn Cudjoe (1854; Amherst: University of Massachusetts Press, 1997), 23–24. Hereafter referred to in text as *EA*.

33. See Carolyn Karcher, "The Riddle of the Sphinx: Melville's 'Benito Cereno' and the *Amistad Case*," in Robert F. Burkholder (ed.), *Critical Essays on Herman Melville's "Benito Cereno"* (New York: G. K. Hall, 1992), 196–229.

34. Frederick Douglass, "The Claims of the Negro Ethnologically Considered," in Philip Foner (ed.), *Selected Speeches and Writings* (1854; Chicago: Lawrence Hill Books, 1999), 282–97, at 288.

35. Douglass, "Claims," 289.

36. William Cain, "Introduction," *EA* ix.

37. Paul Gilroy, *The Black Atlantic: Modernity and Double Consciousness* (Cambridge, MA: Harvard University Press, 1993), 4.

38. Morrison, *Playing*, 18.

39. Erkkila reads the image of Poe's Raven perching on top of the "pallid bust of Pallas" as indicative of this fear (*Mixed Bloods*, 125).

40. Jonathan Kahn, "Forensic DNA and the Inertial Power of Race in American Legal Practice," in Keith Wailoo, Alondra Nelson, and Catherine Lee (eds.), *Genetics and the Unsettled Past* (New Brunswick, NJ: Rutgers University Press, 2012), 114–42.

41. Thus, Jean M. O'Brien diagnoses a "toxic brew of racial thinking" in New England trickle-down extinction discourse that led non-Indians of Native Americans in nineteenth-century New England (and elsewhere) to deny the ethnic survival of their indigenous neighbors, against tangible counterevidence. This terminal (and "terminationist") blindness, produced by the powerful master narrative of the "vanishing Indian," has had massive effects on the legal situation of indigenous groups until today. *Firsting and Lasting: Writing Indians out of Existence in New England* (Minneapolis: University of Minnesota Press, 2010), xv.

PART II

Racial Citizenship

At base, the story of race is the story of community and belonging, of insiders and outsiders, of those recognized by the law as citizens and those recognized by the law as outsiders, claimants at most, those whose rights American citizens are not bound to respect. The question of citizenship, accordingly, loomed large in the courts and in American literature, as those excluded from the pale of official recognition wrote their way into conceptions of community and citizenship that would account for their lives and serve as a challenge to assumptions and practices of the dominant population. This is the subject of Derrick Spires's exploration of African American print culture before the Civil War, a time when African American communities developed their own schools, churches, and other cultural institutions – and built as well concepts of citizenship. "Critics from Phillis Wheatley and David Walker to Henry Highland Garnet and Frances E. W. Harper," Spires observes, "interrogated the fictions of race underwriting white citizenship in content and form." Building on this insight, Spires argues, these and other writers "claimed literature as a citizenship practice that could rewrite America's racist codes, not just in protest, but also for self-care and repair." Koritha Mitchell builds on this analysis by highlighting Spires's comment that this writing was done "not just in protest." The recognition of citizenship involves not just writing practices but also reading practices – and when we read just to find protest writing, we distort and dismiss a great deal of what made communities vibrant and vital. "Believing widely accepted interpretive frameworks obscure more than they illuminate," Mitchell states, "this essay argues for a reading practice attuned to what has actually formed African American culture: homemade citizenship." Focusing on a text long associated with protest, Henry Box Brown's narrative of enslavement and escape, Mitchell calls for us to challenge our own reading practices, the assumptions and practices that shape what we look for and what we find in literature. "When one understands homemade citizenship," Mitchell argues, "protest can be appreciated more in proportion to how it actually functions in African American history and culture. People of African descent have always been much more focused on creating possibility for themselves and each other than in protest." Finally, Edlie Wong notes that issues of citizenship could not be selectively applied, and that the attempt to suppress one racial group inevitably extended out to others. As she states the case, "The legal construction of black and white civic identities necessitated the invention of another racialized alterity." Taking us from the time before the Civil War to the 1880s, Wong argues that "by emphasizing Chinese difference as a 'race' reclassified by the Chinese Exclusion Act (1882) as 'aliens ineligible to citizenship,'" the courts hoped to "combat the sentiment of alienism directed against black Americans in the wake of Reconstruction." In effect, the courts placed different racial groups in a kind of competitive disorder – racialized differently from one another and in comparison with one another. Wong examines these attempts to control both racial identities and concepts of citizenship as they played out in literary works by Chinese American writers at the turn of the century – "a large and wide-ranging body of journalism and short fiction that addressed the complex politics of citizenship, immigration law, and transnational migration." Like African American writers before them, these writers composed communities and reimagined the dynamics of citizenship, recognizing the extent to which race itself operated according to the dynamics of narrative and rhetoric.

CHAPTER 4

"Faithful Reflection" and the Work of African American Literary History

Derrick Spires

Nineteenth-century African American literary history and literary histories offer nuanced assessments of racism and race as technologies of power central to US citizenship in practice.[1] They articulated the foundations of racist ideas in white identity politics and power, recognizing that racism was always on the verge of collapsing under its own contradictory weight and that it required ongoing violence for stability. With an eye toward Western history in general and US slave society in particular, they noted, as Sylvia Wynter would later posit, that racism was the mechanism by which Europeans positioned "Western bourgeois" "Man" as if he constituted the human. "The word 'white,'" Frederick Douglass argued in 1854, is "a modern term in the legislation of this country" that "has sprung up within the period of our national degeneracy."[2] Racism produced white citizens and white citizenship and underwrote the sense that the "white" was self-evident, that, as Supreme Court Justice John McLean argued in dissent to *Dred Scott* v. *Sandford* (1857), the government was "not made especially for the colored race" (532), even if it ultimately recognized their citizenship claims.[3]

Black citizens rejected this premise. In convention addresses and proceedings, fiction, poetry, sketches, and other forms, they indexed and intervened in this race making and the development of white citizenship. They forced white America to formalize and codify racial exclusions in law and to define and redefine citizenship so that it would not – could not – include black people. And they recognized that literature and literary history were technologies central to racism's production and practice. Critics from Phillis Wheatley and David Walker to Henry Highland Garnet and Frances E. W. Harper interrogated the fictions of race underwriting white citizenship in content and form. They demonstrate that while black citizens "experienced, recognized, and lived subjection," they "did not *simply* or *only* live *in* subjection and *as* the subjected."[4] Within, through, alongside, despite, and against racism, nineteenth-century black intellectuals claimed literature as a citizenship practice that could rewrite America's racist codes, not just in protest, but also for self-care and repair.[5]

African American literary history, conceived as both the histories of African American literature and the writing of literary history and aesthetic criticism by African Americans across time, invites us to think about black writing as a collective practice of a literary citizenship that rejected the antiblack terms – the unfaithful reflections – white power set out.[6] Carrie Hyde has defined *literary citizenship* as "a symbolic allegiance to the imaginative realm of the 'republic of letters'."[7] To the notion of allegiance, black writers add an insurgent impulse that, depending on the writer and the context, seeks to transform, disrupt, refuse, and/or rupture this imagined republic. Black writers frame this participation less as a retreat from or in distinction to "real" politics, but rather as a necessary extension of the everyday work required to create and sustain democratic citizenship practices.

This essay sketches this field from the nineteenth century through two concepts I take from Garnet and Walker: "faithful reflection" and the "spirit of inquiry." It asks: What would it mean for American literature and American democracy to represent black citizens faithfully? What would faithful representation mean for racism as structure and ideology? How have black writers theorized, invoked, and used the literary as a form of critical inquiry? Garnet and others ground faithful reflection in a democratic ethos antithetical to the racial capitalism animating US citizenship in its historical and current form. The spirit of inquiry assumes the power to ask questions and seek answers, a power often denied the black citizens whom literary history often treats as objects of study. It invokes the epistemological and methodological challenges black subjects and Black Studies have historically foregrounded. The history I offer here does not flow chronologically. Instead, I follow concepts that appear asynchronously across time as much as they were revised and revived over time. After grounding the essay's framework through Garnet and Walker, I trace these complementary practices through Wheatley's imagination and literary critical responses that draw on her to visualize black literary history's generative work.

Speaking in the halls of Congress in 1865 at the Civil War's conclusion, Garnet leveled a full-throated demand for emancipation, citizenship, and the franchise, telegraphing the Reconstruction amendments' unfolding over the next decade. And yet, Garnet reminded his listeners that legal changes were only part of the reparative process:

The good work which God has assigned for the ages to come, will be finished, when our national literature shall be so purified as to reflect a faithful and a just light upon the character and social habits of our race, and the brush, and pencil, and chisel, and Lyre of Art, shall refuse to lend their aid to scoff at the afflictions of the poor, or to caricature, or ridicule a long-suffering people.[8]

Garnet's prophesy articulates how the law (one mode of formal politics) and literature (one mode of informal politics) function in tandem.[9] Literature did more than mirror white citizenship; it was a mechanism for cultivating and practicing it. It simultaneously catered to white audiences eager for antiblack and white supremacist representations and generated a taste for them. It shaped the public's sense of who had the unqualified right of access and belonging to the state and whose access might be legal but ran counter to a sense of right.

Literature and literary history, then, constitute one of the borders of belonging defining citizenship.[10] The *sense* of right and history, even more than legal history, underwrote both McClean's support for black citizenship as well as Chief Justice Roger Taney's ignoring evidence of black citizenship (voting, military service, state law, Constitutional Convention records, etc.) to argue African-descended people were "so far inferior that they had no rights which the white man was bound to respect." Without citing them explicitly, both opinions invoke ideologies reinforced and cultivated through "Bobolition Broadsides" of the early nineteenth century, blackface minstrelsy, Edward Clay's caricatures of black urban life, and scientific treatises like Thomas Jefferson's *Notes on the State of Virginia* ("the blacks, whether originally a distinct race, or made distinct by time and circumstances, are inferior to the whites in the endowments both of body and mind"),[11] to name just a few examples.

By contrast, a "national" literature, Garnet posits, has a role to play in reconstructing a just nation and dismantling white supremacy by engaging actively and intentionally in *faithful reflection* and in its corollary, faithful representation. Reflect: "To display as if in a mirror; to reproduce, esp. faithfully or accurately; to depict. Also, more generally: to reveal (an underlying reality or cause); to make manifest, express."[12] Garnet's phrasing points to the words printed on the page as well as the craft of composition and reading. To reflect faithfully suggests attention to structure and history. Writers, especially white writers, Garnet implies, should reflect faithfully – that is, diligently and in good faith – on US racism. This faithful reflection should lead to a more just literature, which would indicate and promote a more just democracy.[13] Faithful reflection entails range, commitment to truth and rigor, and consistency. It is method and ethos.

At the same time, black writers cultivated their own national literatures to reflect the United States as they hoped it would become, to reflect critically its present shortcomings, and to reflect a black national consciousness operating within, alongside, and against the functionally white republic. As literary historians from William G. Allen to Radiclani Clytus have argued, black literature and literary criticism was a venue for black citizenship work, even as and especially when more formal methods, including voting, jury service, and office holding, were being stripped away.[14] This national literature offered African Americans faithful reflections of themselves, by themselves, and for themselves within a world premised on antiblackness. "Our warfare lies in the field of thought," the Committee on a National Press famously reported at the 1847 National Convention of Colored People.[15] For many, this work would carry the double duty of representing – reflecting – the race's intellectual capacity within a world republic of letters and speaking to its own subjective artistic standards and aspirations.

Finally, "reflect" has roots in the sciences: to "fold back a flap" of tissue to "expose underlying structures," as Jefferson and others imagined themselves doing when they read immutable biological differences into skin they described as black.[16] "Whether the black of the negro resides in the reticular membrane between the skin and scarf-skin, or in the scarf skin itself," Jefferson posits in a speculative reflection of black skin, the difference "is fixed in nature," resulting in an unattractiveness (to him, he claims) that suggests a more fundamental inferiority.[17] Disguised as sensory empiricism, Jefferson reframes racism – his exercise of power and profit from black bodies – into race – an ideologically and institutionally enforced antiblack ontology – which allows him to claim simultaneously the power to see beneath (to reflect) black skin and characterize that same skin as an "immovable black veil" refusing legibility.[18]

Garnet's faithful reflection, then, is not a passive activity and cannot be reduced to counter-representation. Rather, faithful reflection is a critical exercise that concerns epistemology (historical, literary, scientific, political) and the ramifications of what gets reflected, by whom, and how. At the same time, faithful reflection requires white America to come to terms with itself. Inasmuch as Garnet calls for a literature that refuses to rely on antiblackness for substance, getting there requires an inquiry into the white American imaginary as it is.

Walker, Garnet's literary mentor, places this inquiry work at the center of his *Appeal ... to the Colored Citizens of the World*. *Appeal* – first published in 1829, revised and published in a third edition in 1830, and reprinted by Garnet in 1848 with his "Address to the Slaves of the United States" – understands literary history and criticism as public practices and collective, public goods based in the power to question and inquiry as propulsion and rupture. Walker's questions prod black citizens toward revolution even as they rupture racism's false premises. This power and methodological intervention, a precursor to Black Studies, enables Walker's more aggressive rhetorical maneuvers.[19] Thinking about Walker's work as public textual criticism animated by a "spirit of inquiry" allows us to situate *Appeal* as an early work employing the methods of faithful reflection in the service of literary history.[20]

Walker presents his *Appeal* in order "to awaken in the breasts of my afflicted, degraded and slumbering brethren, a spirit of enquiry and investigation respecting our miseries and wretchedness in this *Republican Land of Liberty!!!!!*" (4–5).[21] Addressed to "My dearly beloved Brethren and Fellow Citizens" of the world and of the United States, the *Appeal* takes black citizenship as self-evident (Walker does not argue *for* black citizenship; he assumes it) and outlines the conditions under which black citizens emerge from rhetorical invocation to material practice. The "republican land of liberty" in italics followed by exclamation points indicates both the site of investigation and an attitude of skepticism tending to incredulity toward how that site has historically reflected itself. More than the "truth" of Walker's assertions throughout the *Appeal*, this spirit suggests an ethics and black citizens' power to collect data and judge as subjects of history rather than its objects. It's a call to engage in the intellectual labor necessary to understanding and ultimately breaking racial capital's chains, the "miseries and wretchedness" Walker invokes throughout his articles.

What happens when a black investigator inhabits the position and assumes the practice of inquiry? What kinds of arguments can one make when, instead of trying to show that black people are *as enlightened* as Europeans, one instead begins with the premise that Europeans do not, in fact, have the definitional power over the human they claim? Walker offers one example of the results early in Article I: "The whites have always been an unjust, jealous, unmerciful, avaricious and blood thirsty set of beings, always seeking after power and authority. – We view them all over the confederacy of Greece, where they were first known to be anything, (in consequence of education) we see them there, cutting each other's throats" (20). Walker shifts focus from lifting Africans out of a biologically determined racial condition to reframing how we read European history. He moves from the degradation of blackness to an affirmation of blackness as an aesthetic and moral standard. To do so, Walker simultaneously repositions Europeans as global criminals and defines the human so that it reflects faithfully free and enslaved Africans' historical and political needs.

Walker's framing brings white citizenship into focus as the problem to be solved. ("*What for the best good of all shall we do with the White people?*" William J. Wilson asks thirty years later.)[22] He gives special attention to Jefferson, because of Jefferson's status as the Declaration of Independence's key author and because *Notes* offered a fitting synecdoche for the disingenuous nature of race talk in American letters (17). Walker calls on "each of my brethren, who has the spirit of a man, to buy a copy of" *Notes* "and put it in the hand of his son" so that they might develop their own critiques of the text. Noting that white allies have already deconstructed Jefferson's claims, Walker nevertheless cites the necessity that they be "refuted by the blacks *themselves*" (18) in print, an echo of *Freedom's Journal's* first editorial: "We wish to plead our own cause" (1827). In other words, Walker calls for a school of black literary criticism and positions *Notes* – along with history writ large – as one of its most visible objects of study. Black liberation requires radically restructuring "every level of society" – political, economic, spiritual, and cultural – toward a more faithful representation of the human that displaces and exposes "Man" as an exercise in colonial power. Walker's inquiry scaffolds the imaginative scholarly work of rebuilding his readers' conception of the world.

Black citizens were only part of this restructuring. As much as black citizens needed to identify the structural causes of "wretchedness," white citizens needed to take responsibility for their professed philosophies or risk ruin. Throughout, the *Appeal* charges white citizens with reading their own works – the Declaration of Independence, the Christian Bible, and so on – and repairing the damage they have caused. Walker puts white America on trial: "See your Declaration Americans!!! Do you understand your own language?" (85). He quotes the Declaration extensively, using typography as an exegetical guide: "ALL MEN ARE CREATED EQUAL!! that they *are endowed by their Creator with certain unalienable rights*; that among these are life, *liberty*, and the pursuit of happiness!" (85).[23] The jeremiadic question is key: "Will you wait until we shall, under God, obtain our liberty by the crushing arm of power? Will it not be dreadful for you?" (79). Walker transforms Jefferson's language – "And can the liberties of a nation be thought secure when we have removed their only firm basis, a conviction . . . that these liberties are of the gift of God? That they are not to be violated but with his wrath?" (*Notes* 173) – replacing Jefferson's vengeful God with black revolutionaries acting through God's sanction. Even as Walker credits Jefferson with authoring the Declaration, then, his inquiry offers a more faithful reflection of its implications.

The spirit of inquiry Walker invokes neither emerges from nor results in calm reflection (only); it rises from a righteous anger. Claiming this anger publicly did generative work for Walker's black readers, then and now. This anger, Tara Bynum reflects, "asks me to return to what's normal, what's right, and what's mine."[24] In these spaces, Walker's anger recalls Jesus of Nazareth's flipping tables to protest abuses of sacred spaces. For Walker, Europeans have turned creation into a market in the service of their own abnormal avarice, and any faithful observer should feel compelled to flip tables. In the face of white recalcitrance, this anger becomes fire burning away racism's more superficial psychic ploys and transforming (but not erasing) its deeper wounds. As Phillis Wheatley's writing and those who followed her illustrate, this work preceded Walker's text and would continue well after him.

Wheatley theorizes inquiry and faithful reflection just as modern racial categories were calcifying. Wheatley's demand in "On Being Brought from Africa to America" to "Remember, *Christians*, *Negros*, black as *Cain*,/May be refin'd, and join th' angelic train," narrates an order to reject race as marker of hierarchical difference.[25] Though not writing in terms of state citizenship and having produced most of her published work as an enslaved British subject, Wheatley was nevertheless speaking in the idiom of rights, membership, and access. Her meditations on understanding and imagination telegraph the shift from enslaved subject to liberated citizen at a time when her white counterparts were invoking enslavement as a metaphor for mental, political, and economic oppression – often without addressing or in contrast to chattel slavery.[26]

In claiming their share in God's kingdom while also reclaiming blackness as valuable sable from white supremacy's "scornful eye," Wheatley's speakers position themselves as worthy of earthly care and entitled to equality and justice. Theirs was not a rhetoric or deferral. As Bynum astutely notes in relation to Wheatley's correspondence with Obour Tanner, Wheatley's invocation of mercy, salvation, and fellowship "names a happiness that she wants to feel on Earth" and that her writings outline through a "liberatory and love-based theology."[27] This both/and approach to spirituality and collective action in the present anticipates black feminist criticism and black womanist theology, both of which emphasize action in the material world as key elements of spirituality.[28] The radical possibilities of love emerge as a method for doing the "good work" (following Garnet) of claiming earthly rights for their "sable race" – current and potential members of the "angelic train" – to happiness and fulfilling lives.

On these terms, "On Being Brought" ruptures an imaginary in which "heathen," "black," and intellectually inferior were becoming synonymous:

> 'Twas mercy brought me from my *Pagan* land,
> Taught my benighted soul to understand
> That there's a God, that there's a *Saviour* too:
> Once I redemption neither sought nor knew.
> Some view our sable race with scornful eye,
> "Their colour is a diabolic die."
> Remember, *Christians*, *Negros*, black as *Cain*,
> May be refin'd, and join th' angelic train.

The opening couplet emphasizes the speaker's capacity "to understand" while the following couplet posits that the speaker's understanding reveals a law-giving God, and also a redeeming Saviour. The italicized *Saviour* – reference to both the Christian messiah and one who liberates mind and body – over the God of law merges spiritual and physical enslavement, enlightenment, and the responsibility of a Christian community to embrace ostensible strangers. The speaker *understands* that race – "a diabolic die" – functions as a pretense for scorn. Those questioning their humanity pose such questions in bad faith. Instead, the speaker mobilizes a radical, love-based imagination: The good Christian acts toward others as a neighbor, as those who "may be," rather than waiting for some recognizable signal of belonging.

As with Garnet and Walker, the question and the imagination – the power of mental transport and speculation, the power of inquiry and reflection – anchor Wheatley's thought. Wheatley's "On Imagination" claims for the speaker the power "To tell her glories with a faithful tongue" (7), to engage in faithful reflection and inquiry. The imagination's "soft captivity" (12) leads to discovery and motion:

> Imagination! who can sing thy force?
> Or who describe the swiftness of thy course?
> Soaring through air to find the bright abode,
> Th' empyreal palace of the thund'ring God.

Imagination frees the speaker to examine the celestial realm where "God," slanted with abode as a "goad," compels further flights of controlled fancy.[29] Wheatley's roving subject characterizes this liberation in the form of questions rendered rhetorical in the implied answer: "who can sing thy force?" they ask. Who can offer a faithful reflection? "I can," the poem proclaims. Where "On Being Brought" narrates the speaker's coming to understand their power and possibility, "On Imagination" demonstrates the world-making force this understanding marshals.

Wheatley's imagination, however, is not simply inward facing. It should lead to just action. As Edward Cahill notes, Wheatley's speaker has mastered the dialectic of aesthetic liberty within self-restraint so that they are "also able to persuade and command the consent of others through aesthetic performance."[30] Such is the case in Wheatley's "To the Right Honorable William, Earl of Dartmouth." The poem signifies ruthlessly on how revolutionary-era thinkers deployed "slavery" as a political metaphor without attending to enslavement as a material and economic practice of brutality.[31] The speaker hails Dartmouth as a liberator – a savior carrying the soft captivity of representative government: "While in thine hand with pleasure we behold/The silken reins, and *Freedom's* charms unfold" (7–8). Wheatley contrasts this rule through consensus to "the iron chain,/Which wanton *Tyranny* with lawless hand/Had made, and with it meant t' enslave the land" (17–19). Lest readers miss the doubling of political liberty and emancipation, the poem pivots through inquiry and a call to reflection:

> Should you, my lord, while you peruse my song,
> Wonder from whence my love of *Freedom* sprung,
> Whence flow these wishes for the common good,
> By feeling hearts alone best understood,
> I, young in life, by seeming cruel fate
> Was snatch'd from *Afric's* fancy'd happy seat:
> What pangs excruciating must molest,
> What sorrows labour in my parent's breast? (20–27)

Some questions ought not need to be asked, but Wheatley's speaker recognizes how racism defamiliarizes basic axioms, such as an enslaved person's deep love of freedom. The poem's play on "God" and "goad" in the last couplet ("And bear thee upwards to that blest abode,/Where, like the prophet, thou shalt find thy God" [42–43]), a repetition of the same rhyme in "On Imagination," reinforces this urgency and aligns emancipation with divine directive. This speaker is Wheatley's "Ethiop," who assumes the power to judge and who warns Dartmouth and others that they risk falling short of God's glory even if they obtain earthly notoriety, especially when such "fleeting fame" (38) requires maintaining a racist regime.[32]

Subsequent writers outline a literary historical tradition that turns on questions posed less as an indication of absence and more as an invocation of Wheatley's insistent presence. They call our attention to Wheatley as "not simply a racial or literary symbol," as Honorée Jeffers puts it, "but a human being who lived and loved while making her indelible mark on history."[33] Critics from William J. Wilson and Frances E. W. Harper to Alice Walker and June Jordan read Wheatley and reflect – as in fold back the surface to expose – a sense of the human that racism attempted to dye white.[34] Wheatley becomes both representative from a black republic of letters and representative of the tensions of black creative life in a slave society.

Wilson's sketch of Wheatley, for instance, counterposes two senses of "reflect," one biological and one literary critical, and finds the latter more reliable. He features Wheatley's "head" in the Afric-American Picture Gallery, an imagined gallery where his pseudonymous persona, Ethiop, itself reminiscent of Wheatley, browses art expressing the breadth and depth of black aesthetics and history. The series, published in the *Anglo-African Magazine* across 1859, makes good on Ethiop's mission set forth in *Frederick Douglass's Paper* to "have a glass of our own" to represent black life and to counter the "system of *puff, boast* and *brag*" white Americans generated to exaggerate their own achievements (July 30, 1852). The gallery is both display and training ground, a space where one might come on a ramble for entertainment or study and where "the careful observer and the thinker" might find "much that is valuable and interesting" (53).[35] Initially, Ethiop describes Wheatley's "head" in ethnological terms to situate her in an intellectual pantheon: "The facial angle contains full ninety degrees; the forehead is finely formed, and the brain large; the nose is long, and the nostrils thin, while the eyes, though not large, are well set." "The whole make-up of this face," Wilson concludes, "is an index of healthy intellectual powers, combined with an active temperament, over which has fallen a slight tinge of religious pensiveness" (218).

The sketch draws on this ethnological description only to set it aside in favor of the more "complex [meditation] on being, subjectivity, and existence," characteristic of what Britt Rusert has theorized as fugitive science.[36] Wilson subordinates ethnology's epistemological grounding – the sense that physiology could "index" intelligence and creativity – to literary history, calling on readers to "scrutinize [Wheatley] more closely through her career and her *works*" to "find her truly an extraordinary person" (218). The italics on works (plural) emphasizes Wheatley's craft and counterposes her works – her writing – against her physiology and the conditions of enslavement under which she produced it:

> Stolen at the tender age of seven years from the fond embraces of a mother whose image never once faded from her memory, and ferried over in the vile slave ship from Afric's sunny clime to the cold shores of America, and sold under the hammer to a Boston merchant – a delicate child, a girl, alone, desolate; a chilly, dreary world before her, a chain on her feet and a thorn in her bosom, and an iron mask on her head, what chance, what opportunity was there for her to make physical, moral, or mental progress? (218)

Wilson's sketch offers a literary historical inquiry composed not of indominable manhood as proffered in classic slave narratives, but of creativity in the midst of vulnerability and injury. Instead of the benevolent enslavers featured in Margaret Odell's *Memoir and Poems of Phillis Wheatley* (1834), Wilson's Wheatley carries "an iron mask on her head," signaling the enslavers' implements of physical torture and the pressure of Anglo-American antiblackness weighing on the child's psyche (218).[37] Yet, Wheatley does not create in isolation. Her "works" include "extensive and elegant epistolary correspondence" with "friends and acquaintances" (218). Where James Weldon Johnson would pronounce in 1922 that Wheatley "never found out her true relation to life and to her surroundings," and J. Saunders Redding would express a critical consensus in 1968 that Wheatley's poetry demonstrates a "sense of abnegation and self-pity," Wilson anticipates more recent scholarship: He shows Wheatley's embeddedness in a rich social world and claims her figure as "one of the finest in the collection" (217).[38]

Wilson's initial reflection primes the sketch's thesis, which, in line with the genre's tendencies, appears near its conclusion: "What one of America's paler daughter's contemporary with her, with all the advantages that home, fortune, friends and favor bring—what one ascended so far up the hill of just fame at any age" (218). Wilson might have had in mind contemporaneous accounts premising Wheatley's fame on her blackness – as a curiosity – rather than on literary merit.[39] Readers, then and now, took Wheatley as an index for assessing African-descended people's intellectual capacity, or, as does Johnson, a test case for how enslavement left African-descended people bereft of a culture. Wilson, however, reframes Wheatley's literary accomplishment as an indictment of whiteness and as a foundation for black literary cultures.[40]

Wilson's omitting Jefferson and others' racist accounts, opting instead to center Wheatley's life and the lessons it offers, intervenes in a literary historical sensibility that often positions critiquing Jefferson as the point from which black writing emerges. The result can (unintentionally) subordinate black writing as a reaction to whiteness, rather than as a collection of writing that, Frances Smith Foster reminds us, black people produced out of a need "to speak to and for themselves about matters they considered worthy of written words" (715). Wilson stakes a similar position. By valuing creative blackness over destructive whiteness, Wilson changes the inquiry's texture and the results it can produce.[41] Jefferson and others were, after all, responding to Wheatley and the expressive cultures she, Ukawsaw Gronniosaw, and others represented, not the other way around.

"What then are we to make of Phillis Wheatley, a slave, who owned not even herself" but who "kept alive, in so many of our ancestors, the notion of song?" Alice Walker presses in "In Search of Our Mothers' Gardens."[42] Frances Harper proffers one answer while emphasizing the power of writing-as-inquiry. Jenny, a character in Harper's "Fancy Etchings," a series begun in the *Anglo-African* (1859–60) and continued in the *Christian Recorder* (1873–74), calls writing "a revelation": "I learned from it that I had power to create, and it gave me faith in myself" (April 24, 1874). It gives her the means to (re)define a more satisfying self. Jenny, like Wheatley before her, turns this imagination outward, as she sets out to become "the poet of my people."[43] Over a century after Harper's "Fancy Etchings," Audre Lorde would distill this principle: "poetry is not a luxury," but rather an "honest exploration" of "our feelings" – a spirit of inquiry – that leads us to "language [that] does not yet exist" and that makes new realities thinkable and actionable.[44] The notion of song Alice Walker invokes through Wheatley, then, is no small thing. This vision of black writing reverberates across African American literary history. The song and African American literature by extension, to return to Garnet's 1865 speech, both indicate and shape possibility.

Notes

1. Thanks to John Ernest, who provided feedback on an earlier version of this essay. This account of African American literary history draws on Catherine Clay Bassard, *Spiritual Interrogations: Culture, Gender, and Community in Early African American Women's Writing* (Princeton, NJ: Princeton University Press, 1999); John Ernest, *Chaotic Justice: Rethinking African American Literary History* (Chapel Hill: University of North Carolina Press,

2009); Brigitte Fielder and Jonathan Senchyne, eds., *Against a Sharp White Background: Infrastructures of African American Print* (Madison: University of Wisconsin Press, 2019); Frances Smith Foster, "A Narrative of the Interesting Origins and Somewhat Surprising Developments of African-American Print Culture," *American Literary History* 17.4 (2005), 714–40; Eric Gardner, "African American Literary Reconstructions and the 'Propaganda of History,'" *American Literary History* 30.3 (2018): 429–449; Elizabeth McHenry, *Forgotten Readers: Recovering the Lost History of African-American Literary Societies* (Durham, NC: Duke University Press, 2002); and Lara Cohen and Jordan Alexander Stein, eds., *Early African American Print Culture in Theory and Practice* (Philadelphia: University of Pennsylvania Press, 2012).

2. Frederick Douglass, "The Kansas-Nebraska Bill," in Philip S. Foner (ed.), *Frederick Douglass: Selected Speeches and Writings* (Chicago: Lawrence Hill Books, 1999), 299.

3. This essay understands race and racism through Charles W. Mills, *The Racial Contract* (Ithaca, NY: Cornell University Press, 1997); John Ernest, *Chaotic Justice: Rethinking African American Literary History*; Ruth Wilson Gilmore, "Race and Globalization," in R. J. Johnston, Peter J. Taylor, and Michael J. Watts (eds.), *Geographies of Global Change: Remapping the World*, 2nd ed. (Malden, MA: Blackwell, 2002); Ibram X. Kendi, *Stamped from the Beginning: The Definitive History of Racist Ideas in America* (New York: Nation Books, 2016); James Brewer Stewart, "Modernizing 'Difference': The Political Meanings of Color in the Free States, 1776–1840," *Journal of the Early Republic* 19.4 (1999), 691–712; and Sylvia Wynter, "Unsettling the Coloniality of Being/Power/Truth/Freedom: Towards the Human, After Man, Its Overrepresentation – An Argument," *CR: New Centennial Review* 3.3 (2003), 257–337. See also work on gradual emancipation, including Erica Armstrong Dunbar, *A Fragile Freedom: African American Women and Emancipation in the Antebellum City* (New Haven, CT: Yale University Press, 2008); Leslie M. Harris, *In the Shadow of Slavery: African Americans in New York City, 1626–1863* (Chicago: University of Chicago Press, 2003); and Joanne Pope Melish, *Disowning Slavery: Gradual Emancipation and "Race" in New England, 1789–1860* (Ithaca, NY: Cornell University Press, 1998).

4. Christiana Sharpe, *In the Wake: On Blackness and Being* (Durham, NC: Duke University Press, 2016), 4.

5. I elaborate on this premise in Derrick R. Spires, *The Practice of Citizenship: Black Politics and Print Culture in the Early United States* (Philadelphia: University of Pennsylvania Press, 2019). See also Audre Lorde, *A Burst of Light: And Other Essays* (1988; New York: Ixia Press, 2017), 130; and Eve Sedgwick, *Touching Feeling: Affect, Pedagogy, Performativity* (Durham, NC: Duke University Press, 2003), 128.

6. My understanding of black "theorizing" is shaped by Barbara Christian, "The Race for Theory," *Cultural Critique* 6 (1987), 51–63. See Carrie Hyde, *Civic Longing: The Speculative Origins of U.S. Citizenship* (Cambridge, MA:

Harvard University Press, 2018), for a similar discussion of literary citizenship.

7. Hyde, *Civic Longing*, 18.

8. Henry Highland Garnet, *A Memorial Discourse* (Philadelphia: Joseph M. Wilson, 1865), 87.

9. As Gene Jarret notes, distinguishing between the two venues should not be taken as a hierarchy in which either form takes precedence over the other. See Gene Jarret, *Representing the Race: A New Political History of African American Literature* (New York: New York University Press, 2011), 9–10. I frame the question slightly differently in terms of state-sanctioned and unofficial citizenship practices in *Practice*.

10. See Barbara Welke, *Law and the Borders of Belonging in the Long Nineteenth Century United States* (Cambridge: Cambridge University Press, 2010).

11. Thomas Jefferson, *Writings* (New York: Library Classics of America, 1984), 270.

12. "Reflect, v.," in *OED Online* (Oxford University Press), accessed December 28, 2019, www.oed.com/view/Entry/160912.

13. See also Ernest, *Chaotic*, 1–11.

14. See, for instance, William G. Allen, *Wheatley, Banneker, and Horton* (Boston: Daniel Laing, Jr., 1849); Radiclani Clytus, "Visualizing in Black Print: The Brooklyn Correspondence of William J. Wilson Aka 'Ethiop,'" *J19: The Journal of Nineteenth-Century Americanists* 6.1 (2018), 29–66; Foster, "Narrative"; and Henry Louis Gates, *Figures in Black: Words, Signs, and the "Racial" Self* (New York: Oxford University Press, 1987).

15. National Convention of Colored People and Their Friends (1847; Troy, NY), "Proceedings of the National Convention of Colored People and Their Friends; held in Troy, NY; on the 6th, 7th, 8th, and 9th of October, 1847," Colored Conventions Project Digital Records, accessed March 30, 2020, https://omeka.coloredconventions.org/items/show/279.

16. "Reflect," *OED*.

17. Jefferson, *Writings*, 269.

18. As Barbara Fields and Jane Fields note in *Racecraft: The Soul of Inequality in American Life* (London: Verso, 2012), "Disguised as race, racism becomes something Afro-Americans are, rather than something racists do" (97).

19. Hortense Spillers's "The Crisis of the Negro Intellectual: A Post-Date," *Boundary 2* 21.3 (1994), 65–116, informs my understanding of inquiry as "rupture."

20. See McHenry's *Forgotten* for a discussion of the "importance of claiming public voice" through print (27) in Walker's *Appeal*; and Melvin Rodgers's "David Walker and the Political Power of the Appeal," *Political Theory* 43.2 (2015), 208–33, for a discussion of how Walker uses the "appeal" genre to frame his argument for black citizenship.

21. All quotes are from Walker's "Third and Last Edition" (Boston: David Walker, 1830), Documenting the American South, https://docsouth.unc.edu/nc/walker/walker.html.

22. William J. Wilson, "What Shall We Do with the White People?" *Anglo-African Magazine* (February 1860), 45.

23. On Walker's typography, see Marcy J. Dinius, "'Look!! Look!!! At This!!!!':
The Radical Typography of David Walker's *Appeal*," *PMLA* 126.1 (2011),
55–72. See also Jacqueline Bacon, "'Do You Understand Your Own
Language?' Revolutionary 'Topoi' in the Rhetoric of African-American
Abolitionists," *Rhetoric Society Quarterly* 28.2 (1998), 55–75; and Mia Bay,
"'See Your Declaration Americans!!!': Abolitionism, Americanism, and the
Revolutionary Tradition in Free Black Politics," in *Americanism: New
Perspectives on the History of an Ideal*, eds. Michael Kazin and Joseph A.
McCartin (Chapel Hill: University of North Carolina Press, 2006), 25–52.

24. Tara Bynum, "Why I Heart David Walker," *J19: The Journal of Nineteenth-
Century Americanists* 4.1 (2016), 13.

25. Bassard has described "On Being Brought" as Wheatley's "highest poetic
achievement" (45), especially in the context of a speaker meditating on "the
twin processes of racialization and acculturation" (45) and "issues of epistemology within a terrain of global power relations" (46). All citations are from
Phillis Wheatley, Complete Writings, ed. Vincent Caretta (New York: Penguin
Classics, 2001). On Wheatley and the language of racialization, Christianity,
and the "language of survivorship," see Bassard, *Spiritual Interrogations*, 29–57.
On Wheatley's poetics and citizenship, see Hyde, *Civic Longing*; and Edward
Cahill, *Liberty of the Imagination: Aesthetic Theory, Literary Form, and Politics in
the Early United States* (Philadelphia: University of Pennsylvania Press, 2012).

26. See Cahill, *Liberty*; Peter A. Dorsey, "To 'Corroborate Our Own Claim':
Public Positioning and the Slavery Metaphor in Revolutionary America,"
American Quarterly 55.3 (2003), 353–86; Manisha Sinha, "To 'Cast Just
Obliquy' on Oppressors: Black Radicalism in the Age of Revolution,"
William and Mary Quarterly 64.1 (2007), 149–60; Eric Slauter, "Neoclassical
Culture in a Society with Slaves: Race and Rights in the Age of Wheatley,"
Early American Studies: An Interdisciplinary Journal 2.1 (2004), 81–122; and
Rafia Zafar, *We Wear the Mask: African Americans Write American Literature,
1760–1870* (New York: Columbia University Press, 1997).

27. Tara Bynum, "Phillis Wheatley on Friendship," *Legacy* 31.1 (2014), 44, 45.

28. See Delores S. Williams, *Sisters in the Wilderness: The Challenge of Womanist
God-Talk* (Maryknoll, NY: Orbis Books, 1993).

29. Cahill, *Liberty*, 60.

30. Cahill, *Liberty*, 60.

31. I discuss these concepts in terms of neighborly citizenship in *Practice*. See also
Sarah Knott, *Sensibility and the American Revolution* (Chapel Hill: University
of North Carolina Press, 2009); and Joycelyn Moody, *Sentimental
Confessions: Spiritual Narratives of Nineteenth-Century African American
Women* (Athens: University of Georgia Press, 2001).

32. For a discussion of this poem's publication history, see Joseph Rezek, "The
Print Atlantic: Phillis Wheatley, Ignatius Sancho, and the Cultural
Significance of the Book," in Stein and Cohen, 19–39.

33. Honorée Jeffers, *The Age of Phillis* (Middletown, CT: Wesleyan University Press, 2020). John Ernest, Rian Bowie, Lief Eckstrom, and Britt Rusert take up "Phillis Wheatley" and the circulation of the famous frontispiece portrait in "Visionary History: Recovering William J. Wilson's 'Afric-American Picture Gallery,'" in Fielder and Senchyne, 233, 238n21–22. Samantha Pinto's *Infamous Bodies: Early Black Women's Celebrity and the Afterlives of Rights* (Durham, NC: Duke University Press, 2020) offers an insightful discussion of Wheatley's "celebrity" and subsequent constructions of "race, Enlightenment ideas of human rights, and the rise of freedom as the locus of meaningful political subjectivity" (26).

34. While Gates's speculative account of Wheatley's trial is important to her resurgence in literary history, Alice Walker's black feminist criticism, in particular, is responsible for bringing Wheatley back into the cultural consciousness. See Alice Walker, *In Search of Our Mothers' Gardens: Womanist Prose* (New York: Houghton Mifflin Harcourt, 2004); and June Jordan, "The Difficult Miracle of Black Poetry in America or Something Like a Sonnet for Phillis Wheatley," *The Massachusetts Review* 27.2 (1986), 252–62. For a key nuancing of the "trial" narrative, see Joanna Brooks, "Our Phillis, Ourselves," *American Literature* 82.1 (2010), 1–28. For more recent critical engagements with Wheatley via poetry, see Jeffers, *Age of Phillis*; Drea Brown, *dear girl: a reckoning* (Gold Line Press, 2015); and Tiana Clark, *I Can't Talk about the Trees without the Blood* (Pittsburgh: University of Pittsburgh Press, 2018).

35. Scholarship on "Afric-American Picture Gallery" and Wilson has grown exponentially. For a representative sample, see Erica Ball, *Living an Antislavery Life: Personal Politics and the Antebellum Black Middle Class* (Athens: University of Georgia Press, 2012); Ernest, *Liberation*; Ernest, Bowie, Eckstrom, and Rusert, "Visionary History"; Eckstrom and Rusert, "Introduction," *Just Teach One: Early African American Print*, http://jtoaa .common-place.org/welcome-to-just-teach-one-african-american/introduc tion-afric-american-picture-gallery/; Spires, *Practice*; and Ivy G. Wilson, *Specters of Democracy: Blackness and the Aesthetics of Politics in the Antebellum U.S.* (New York: Oxford University Press, 2011).

36. Britt Rusert, *Fugitive Science: Empiricism and Freedom in Early African American Culture* (New York: New York University Press, 2017), 5.

37. See also William G. Allen's *Wheatley, Banneker, and Horton* and William C. Nell's *Colored Patriots of the American Revolution* (Boston: Robert F. Wallcut, 1855). For critiques of Odell's *Memoir*, see Caretta, *Complete Writings*, 175–76; Jeffers, *Age of Phillis*, 167–89; and Bassard, *Spiritual Interrogations*, 33–34.

38. James Weldon Johnson, *The Book of American Negro Poetry* (New York: Harcourt, Brace, 1922), xxx; J. Saunders Redding, *To Make a Poet Black* (College Park, MD: McGrath, 1968), 9. On Wheatley's social world, see Bynum, "Phillis," 41–45.

39. Sarah J. Hale's *Woman's Record: or Sketches of All Distinguished Women* (New York: Harper & Brothers, 1853), for instance, claims *Poems*'s "worth arises

from the extraordinary circumstance that they are the productions of an *African woman*" (553, italics original).

40. Martin R. Delany's sketch of Wheatley in *The Condition, Elevation, Emigration, and Destiny of the Colored People of the United States* follows a pattern similar to Wilson's: "she, though young, was . . . one of the brightest ornaments among the American literati" (196). In *Martin R. Delany: A Documentary Reader*, ed. Robert S. Levine (Chapel Hill: University of North Carolina Press, 2003).

41. A similar focus informs Fred Moten's *Black and Blur* (Durham, NC: Duke University Press, 2017).

42. Alice Walker, "In Search of Our Mothers' Gardens" [1972] in Walker, In Search of Our Mother's Gardens, 237.

43. For more on the "Fancy Etchings" series, see Frances Smith Foster, *A Brighter Coming Day: A Frances Ellen Watkins Reader* (New York: Feminist Press, 1990), 37–39 and 223–232; "Excerpts from 'Fancy Etchings,'" in *Who Writes for Black Children? African American Children's Literature before 1900*, eds. Katharine Capshaw and Anna Mae Duane (Minneapolis: University of Minnesota Press, 2017), 318–22; "Sketching Black Citizenship on Installment after the Fifteenth Amendment," in *African American Literature in Transition, 1865–1880: Black Reconstructions*, ed. Eric Gardner, African American Literature in Transition (Cambridge: Cambridge University Press, 2021), 17–48; Rynetta Davis, "National Housekeeping: (Re)Dressing the Politics of Whiteness in Nineteenth-Century African American Literary History," in Gardner, 72–86; and Stephanie Farrar, "Stories of Citizenship: The Rise of Narrative Black Poetry during Reconstruction," in Gardner, 49–71.

44. Audre Lorde, "Poetry Is Not a Luxury," in *Sister Outsider: Essays and Speeches* (Trumansburg, NY: Crossing Press, 1984), 37–38.

CHAPTER 5

Beyond Protest

Koritha Mitchell

Scholars, teachers, and general readers are encouraged to operate as if race is relevant only when discussing people of color. However, literature full of white characters is about race. As important, when one's bookshelves are full of texts by white authors, that is very much about race. Moreover, race shapes white-authored texts in myriad ways. It might manifest as unremarked-upon assumptions that whiteness is the norm, the most expansive representation of human experience. Or, it might emerge in the form of caricatures of anyone who is not white. Race in white-authored texts might manifest in the condescension of liberal good intentions or in the direct promotion of a white supremacist state. Functioning as a category of classification, race shapes human experience, including that of those who racialize others while pretending race is irrelevant to their own experience.[1] There's an equal amount of variation in how works created by African Americans engage the demographic category of race. Unfortunately, when black-authored texts grapple with race, readers ignore the dynamism of the endeavor and view it as simplistic resistance, as rebellion against norms. Even so skilled an artist and critic as James Baldwin all but dismissed Richard Wright's *Native Son* by labeling it a "protest novel."

Whether one agrees or disagrees with Baldwin's assessment of *Native Son*,[2] the dismissal is worth examining because it sheds light on how everyone is encouraged to approach works that feature nonwhite people, especially those by nonwhite authors. Because cultural productions that privilege whiteness are treated as neutral, creations that do not revolve around whiteness are regarded as biased. If a work does not take whiteness for granted, then its importance presumably lies in how it compares to art that addresses "universal" issues. That is, if a composition treats whiteness as racial, not universal, it is interpreted as a shallow response based on a narrow perspective incapable of gleaning more complex "human" concerns. Nevertheless, Baldwin operated as if Wright could have avoided being read as limited, biased, and reactionary by representing African American life with more human complexity. Baldwin did not seem to consider how reading practices determined what people saw in *Native Son*.

Believing widely accepted interpretive frameworks obscure more than they illuminate, this essay argues for a reading practice attuned to what has actually formed African American culture: homemade citizenship. When one understands homemade citizenship, protest can be appreciated more in proportion to how it actually functions in African American history and culture. People of African descent have always been much more focused on creating possibility for themselves and each other than on protest.

What Baldwin wanted to see in Wright's work has always shaped African American art and literature; dominant habits simply make recognizing it difficult. Baldwin insisted upon the need for cultural production that depicts the complexity of how African Americans have managed to survive and thrive in a racist country, and he made his case by saying Wright had failed to do it. *Native Son* falls short, Baldwin insists, because "a necessary dimension has been cut away"[3]: namely, "the relationship that Negroes bear to one another, that depth of involvement and unspoken recognition of shared experience which creates a way of life."[4] Baldwin argues that such complexity perpetually goes missing from American representations, so most believe that, in black life, "there exists no tradition, no field of manners ... such as may [sustain a people]."[5] However, Baldwin declares, "the fact is not that the Negro has no tradition but that there has as yet arrived no sensibility sufficiently profound and tough to make this tradition articulate."[6] He continues, "for a tradition expresses, after all, nothing more than the long and painful experience of a people; it comes out of the battle waged to maintain their integrity."[7] That is, "out of their struggle to survive."[8] In contrast to the legibility of "the Jewish tradition," Baldwin claims, "this sense of how Negroes live and how they have so long endured is hidden from us."[9] As I will demonstrate, however, African Americans have always left abundant evidence that is hidden only when one embraces reading practices that dull perception.

I contend that African American culture is best understood as an ongoing community conversation *about success* that produces *homemade citizenship*. Because black success so often inspires violence, the community conversation is constantly defining and redefining achievement. In order to pursue success, African Americans debate not only the strategies for attaining it but also its very contours and parameters. They debate how one will even know if one has achieved, and as they engage in this process, African Americans create a citizenship that is homemade. Often denied basic ingredients, like safety, by the land of their birth, they cultivate a sense of belonging and achievement that does not depend on civic inclusion; it is a belonging with recourse beyond the nation-state.[10]

To recognize homemade citizenship, scholars, teachers, and general readers must look through the lens of achievement. Doing so reveals that black-authored texts orient themselves toward racial self-affirmation, but that does not keep them from acknowledging white violence. Noticing relentless white violence does not distract them from their goals, and their primary goal is rarely protest. Black people pursue and achieve success, white aggression emerges to counter their progress, and then violence becomes part of any accurate portrait of African American communities. The portrait does not exist to protest racist violence.

Put another way, African American traditions emerge from the individual and collective tendency to engage in racial self-affirmation in the midst of grappling with violence. The customs of African-descended people in the United States spring from the habit of affirming oneself while never ignoring the fact that the resulting success will invite aggression as often as praise. Because hostility has shaped black experience, African Americans could not survive and create a culture without grappling with violence as part of their inheritance. As Baldwin understood, "the Negro has been formed by this nation, for better or for worse, and does not belong to any other . . . . The paradox – and a fearful paradox it is – is that the American Negro can have no future anywhere, on any continent, as long as he is unwilling to accept his past. To accept one's past – one's history – is not the same thing as drowning in it; it is learning how to use it."[11] What does it mean to use African American history? Baldwin devoted much of his life to answering that question. Influenced by his insights, I offer my own, with an eye toward shifting the way audiences approach works by members of marginalized groups, especially African Americans.

The reactionary nature of mainstream culture became clear to me when I realized that black-authored lynching plays of the 1910s and 1920s – plays written in the midst of white violence – do not primarily protest; instead, they showcase black success.[12] The scripts focus on admirable black homes. With access to these intimate spaces before, during, and after the lynching, one sees that mobs most often targeted black men not because they were criminals but because they were successful heads of household in traditional nuclear families. Indeed, because these homes cohere, the scripts can detail their mutilation. The mob's attack can be shown to wreak havoc precisely because, in the absence of violent intervention, there is so much harmony. Forced to cope afterward, communities grapple with the brutal message: Accomplished black people had forgotten their "proper" place in American society. Their deaths therefore serve as a warning to survivors: *Know your place!* Black-authored lynching drama shows how mobs attack African American success while insisting it never existed – insisting, in fact, that black communities are full of criminals, specifically rapists who target white women. Such assertions would have been unnecessary if African Americans had been less successful. Black people had to be cast as rapists and whores, as criminals and deadbeats, because they were proving to be anything but.

Understanding why violence emerged, African Americans had no problem remarking upon its arrival without being distracted by it, and this was the case long before the 1910s and 1920s, when lynching plays were published. Studying black print culture beginning in the 1780s, literary historian Derrick Spires finds that African Americans' efforts were oriented "not simply as a response to white oppression but as a matter of course in the shaping of their own communities and in the process of meeting their own political, social, and cultural needs."[13] They were determined "to not cede key political concepts [such as citizenship and civility] to those who would use them to restrict freedom, access, and reparative justice."[14] No matter how vehemently the United States and white Americans insisted they did not belong, African Americans acted on a firm belief in black citizenship. They proceeded from the premise that "practicing citizenship made citizens."[15]

Analytical approaches to black literature and art will help or hinder recognition of the evidence forebears left about not only what was most important to them but also how they sustained themselves and each other in the pursuit of what was most important. Again, African American culture is best understood as a community conversation about success that produces homemade citizenship, and cultural production is an access point to that ongoing, multivalent conversation. Because they so deliberately contribute to discussions that sustain black people in the midst of violence, those who are both artists and critics prove to be especially powerful guides. Poet and scholar Evie Shockley gestures toward the kinds of practices I prioritize when examining African American culture – practices of racial self-affirmation in the midst of grappling with hostility. Her description of academia applies to black people's experiences in the United States more generally:

> I am neither homeless nor at home in the academy; rather, I am making-myself-at-home. "Making-myself-at-home" is both a state of being and a process in which I am ongoingly engaged. I am doing what I can ... to make the place where I find myself feel like a home (for myself and for my students) by acting like (not pretending, but behaving as if) the academy is ours. We've been invited in. The situation is often hospitable. But you don't have to be invited into your own home.[16]

Because black presence in the United States has been shaped by kidnapping and 250 years of slavery, this is not quite home, so black people are always making themselves at home; what they can grasp is not quite citizenship, so they are always making citizenship from scratch. If African Americans were already home and already accepted as citizens, they wouldn't have to work so hard and so continuously at making themselves at home. But, of course, the effort is also continuous because other Americans (and American laws and public policies) counter even the smallest signs of black success and nearly every assertion of black belonging. *Making-oneself-at-home* therefore means pursuing accomplishment while acknowledging that one does so in an environment that answers one's victories with violence.

Practices of making-oneself-at-home come to the fore when looking through the lens of achievement, and this approach proves especially illuminating when applied to works, such as slave narratives, that readers presume exist to protest injustice. Using the *Narrative of Henry Box Brown* as a case study, this essay demonstrates the power of reading with an eye toward accomplishment. Published in England in 1851, it is Brown's account of how he escaped slavery by mailing himself from Virginia to Pennsylvania, as well as what he endured that motivated him to devise and execute that remarkable plan. Brown's narrative proves animated by a commitment to defining, redefining, and pursuing success while knowing victories inspire violence. At the same time that it primarily represents self-affirmation, Brown's narrative identifies the hostility that so often answers black success.

Brown's life story is one of a march toward accomplishment; white violence enters the narrative because white people insist upon interrupting his journey. In fact, black domestic space becomes important in Brown's account because that's where the nation's reactionary antiblackness most reveals itself. When introducing what will precipitate experiences that would justify simple protest, Brown leads with his sense of himself. Highlighting his goal-oriented self-conception, he reports: "I now began to think of entering the matrimonial state."[17] As Brown sets about achieving the goal of marrying Nancy, he encounters the violence of white people's unjust power, which he represents as an interruption. Brown reports, "We made it up to get married, but it was necessary in the first place, to obtain our masters' permission, as we could do nothing without their consent."[18] In a culture structured to keep nonwhite people subordinated, when African Americans succeed at finding a companion of their choice, a hostile answer stands at the ready: *What matters is white consent, not yours.*

When obtaining permission, Brown does not expect to buy his or Nancy's freedom, but he wants and receives assurance that Nancy's enslaver will not sell her and thereby separate the couple. When Brown's enslaver makes similar assurances, the couple marries, but before they had been together "above twelve months," the man who had promised not to sell Nancy does precisely that.[19] Nancy's new enslaver, Mr. Colquitt, is cruel but Brown says Colquitt's spouse is more so and underscores why: "She used to abuse my wife very much, not because she did not do her duty but because, it was said, her manners were too refined for a slave."[20] It is the evidence of success, the possession of refined manners, that makes Nancy a target. Given this reality, the details Brown next offers prove significant. If the "mistress" finds intolerable the achievement of a refined demeanor, then performing a loving role sparks particular fury. Brown says she "could not bear to see [Nancy] nursing her baby and used to wish some great calamity to happen to my wife."[21] It is one thing for black women to care for white children, but caring for their own inspires enraged resentment because the nation requires their subordination. Indeed, to insist that black women are more on the level with cattle than with people, enslaved women are said to be incapable of a mother's love. As legal scholar Dorothy Roberts explains, "American culture reveres no Black madonna. It upholds no popular image of a Black mother tenderly nurturing her child,"[22] and this tendency began in slavery.

Readers know Nancy continues to embody the triumph that infuriates her "mistress" because Brown reports that "eventually she was so much displeased with my wife that she induced [her husband] to sell her."[23] The sale is a bloodless form of violence in response to black achievement, and the narrative represents it as such. Black self-affirmation propels the story Brown tells, and white violence emerges to interrupt its forward movement.

Knowing Nancy is to be sold, a white man named Cottrell approaches Brown with a deal – if Brown gives him the $50 he needs to meet the asking price, "he would prevent her from being sold away from me"[24] – and the depiction of this conversation proves revealing. Brown not only highlights his suspicions; he also emphasizes that he had stated them outright: "I asked him if I did advance the money what security I could have that he would not sell my wife as others had done."[25] Brown makes unmistakable his motivation – love for his wife and the desire to remain close to her. Cottrell responds with claims about Christianity, and Brown offers a direct quotation: "He said to me 'do you think if you allow me to have that money, that I could have the heart to sell your wife to any other person but yourself, and particularly knowing that your wife is my sister and you my brother in the Lord; while all of us are members of the church? Oh! no, I never could have the heart to do such a deed as that.'"[26] While Cottrell's words hover alongside Brown's fear of separation from his wife, self-affirmation continues to take precedence. Brown explains his logic in terms that emphasize his own sense of worth, his bond to his wife, and his sober judgment about the violence of American Christianity. Brown hands over the money, "not that I had implicit faith in his promise, but that I knew he could purchase her if he wished whether I were to assist him or not, and I thought by thus bringing him under an obligation to me it might at least be somewhat to the advantage of my wife and to me."[27]

Knowing how successful Brown has been in cultivating strong bonds of love with his wife and children, Cottrell weaponizes this knowledge. He makes Brown's intimate connections into vulnerabilities. As soon as he owns Brown's wife and children, he further enriches himself by requiring Brown to house them and not only supply all their needs but also pay him for allowing them to live with Brown, rather than with him. Brown again proves aware of the reactionary quality of white supremacy by labeling Cottrell "a monster tyrant, making light of the most social ties"[28] In noting Cottrell is attacking "the most social ties," Brown underscores that such aggression would be impossible if Brown had not succeeded in nurturing these bonds against the worst odds. This personal example has broad implications because African Americans' dreadful odds are enforced by legally sanctioned slavery. While white Americans erase black love by claiming African Americans have weak familial ties, they use those very ties to wield unjust power.[29] Domination and subordination do not simply endure; they are continually enforced. Further, active subordination would be unnecessary if those who are said to be incapable of domestic success actually were.

"Monster tyrant" highlights white people's investment in preventing African Americans from enjoying achievement, but Brown foregrounds this dynamic while keeping the reader aware of his highest priority: finding ways to grasp gradations of success. Because outright accomplishment will not be permitted, Brown works hard at making adjustments. Even as Cottrell refuses to let him enjoy the home he's paying exorbitantly for, Brown actively reconciles himself to the situation. Cottrell sees nothing but profit because he owns Brown's wife and children while Brown supplies their food and lodging. Despite this unjustly favorable arrangement, Cottrell won't let the family live in peace. Nevertheless, Brown recalibrates his conception of achievement to tolerate conditions. He confesses, "[I might] have managed to live in a kind of a way if we had been let alone here."[30] Even as he actively adjusts in an effort to be happy with that level of domestic success, his tormentor responds with more bloodless violence so that achievements, no matter how small, cannot be enjoyed. Brown reports, "He no sooner saw that we were thus comfortably situated, than he said my wife must do some of his washing."[31]

Adjustments continue and Brown records the effort: "Still we felt ourselves more comfortable than we had ever been before."[32] Because family members keep recalibrating their definition of success in order to focus more on themselves than on the violence they encounter, they have a little peace despite paying Cottrell "whenever he called for it – whether it was due or not."[33] Brown adapts to the aggression because he focuses on his truest goal: being with his wife and children.[34] When a day arrives that Brown cannot pay, Cottrell declares, "I want money, and money I will have,"[35] precipitating Brown's anguish at having his family taken away.

Again, the narrative primarily affirms African American life even as it records the violence that intrudes upon it. The anguish leading up to the family's separation fills the passage with evidence of affection: Brown's "poor wife burst into tears," loved ones linger in "mutually embracing each other," and parents pause in "fondly pressing our little darlings to our bosoms."[36] For anyone reading with an eye toward achievement, Brown states the case strikingly: "I felt that life had joys worth living for if I could only be allowed to enjoy them."[37] He has created a life with much that makes him happy and gives him a sense of purpose, and that accomplishment keeps attracting hostility from white people whom the United States has empowered to terrorize at will.

Brown has consistently stomached being robbed of "the greater portion of my earnings" because doing so means "I could enjoy myself with my family about me while I listened to the pleasing prattle of my children, and experience the kindness of a wife, which were privileges that every slave could not enjoy."[38] As he considers all he has done to navigate a terrain made rocky by white aggression, Brown reminds the reader that he has not placed faith in American Christianity but has dealt with Cottrell on the only terms that might matter to a "tyrant": money. Because he knows white men do not hold themselves to Christian standards, believing in Christianity means recognizing *in himself* admirable attributes not found in those the country deems "superior" to him. He understands that dealing with white men in the realm they have created, the nonspiritual social and political realm, does not inspire them to make promises on which he can depend. Nevertheless, when he engages them in that sphere, he understands how little the treatment he receives says about him. As Baldwin would assert generations later, "what [white Americans] believe, as well as what they do and cause you to endure, does not testify to your inferiority but to their inhumanity and fear."[39] Because Brown's financial deal with Cottrell had been "*on the expressed condition that he should not sell [my wife] to any person but myself*,"[40] Cottrell's betrayal is particularly vicious and Brown marks it as such.

As the text emphasizes cruelty, it underscores that US culture is shaped by a disregard for its own standards. No matter how much black people measure up to what the country claims to respect, their subordination is always in order. Meanwhile, no matter how little white people fulfill the country's stated standards, their power to subordinate will not be hampered.

Cottrell will have his way, so Brown's wife and children sit in jail awaiting removal to North Carolina, and in all his heartbreak, Brown operates based on love and in ways that assert his conception of himself as husband and father. He tries to provide for his family's physical needs, just as he does when they are at home.[41] Also, he tries five times to have his loved ones purchased by someone who will prevent their departure.[42]

Readers do well to notice the racial self-affirmation inherent in this behavior and Brown's recounting of it. The narrative preserves evidence of Brown's deep affection; his words and deeds express who he is and what his family means to him. He is recording the truth of his experience in a society that insists enslaved people's behavior means something else (when their actions are acknowledged at all). Brown affirms himself as well as other enslaved people with similar struggles and other African Americans who are free but who work on behalf of those in bondage out of a spirit of kinship.

While his text does all this work of racial self-affirmation, it also acknowledges reactionary white aggression. The first four rejections from would-be buyers who could keep his family nearby surely feel like terrible blows, but Brown ends this part of his story with an especially brutal fifth.

With tears in his eyes, he returns to his enslaver to request help again, now more desperate than before. He asks him "to advance the smallest portion of the 5000 dollars I had paid him."[43] The response? Besides refusing, "[my *christian* master] even told me that I could get another wife and so I need not trouble myself about that one."[44] Without pausing, "I told him those that God had joined together let no man put asunder, and that I did not want another wife, but my own whom I had loved so long."[45] The suggestion that enslaved people have no preferences about life partners constitutes discursive violence, placing African Americans on the level of animals that presumably mate indiscriminately.[46]

This aggressive attempt at leveling must be seen as a reaction to black success. After all, Brown requests assistance because he has attained something he wants to preserve, giving his "master" reason to remind him of his "proper" place as anything but a recognized head of household. When Brown rejects the denigration of his marriage bond by affirming the meaning he attaches to his family and home, his "*christian* master" answers with hostility because Brown dares to know his family's value on a scale not dictated by mere mortals. Brown reports, "The mentioning of the passage of scripture seemed to give him much offence for he instantly drove me from his house saying he did not wish to hear that!"[47] Brown's clarity about his family's worth outside slavery's logic does not save him from pain, but he depicts his clarity as a victory that inspires oppressors to inflict a very particular type of punishment. With his enslaver determined to humble him, Brown cannot free his loved ones from jail. Brown's narrative lays out the reverberating consequences: "My agony was now complete, she with whom I had travelled the journey of life *in chains*, for the space of twelve years, and the dear little pledges God had given us I could see plainly must now be separated from me for ever, and I must continue, desolate and alone, to drag my chains through the world."[48]

When the moment of separation arrives, Brown's account evinces self-regard and black love through both words and deeds. Brown and his family enact their conceptions of themselves not by resisting white violence and trying to prove white people wrong, but by affirming themselves and each other. For instance, "My wife, under the influence of her feelings, jumped aside; I seized hold of her hand while my mind felt unutterable things, and my tongue was only able to say, we shall meet in heaven!"[49] He continues, "I went with her for about four miles hand in hand, but both our hearts were so overpowered with feeling that we could say nothing, and when at last we were obliged to part, the look of mutual love which we exchanged was all the token which we could give each other that we should yet meet in heaven."[50] The heartbreak Brown records results from white violence bent on putting in check every victory of the enslaved and every assertion of belonging – even belonging within one's own family. This scene ends the longest chapter in the narrative, arguably revealing what Brown most longed to share by writing his life story.

Just as he makes unmistakable the reactionary nature of white violence, Brown exposes the role Christianity plays in producing harsh realities. Directly before offering the details that lead to his family separation, Brown devotes an entire chapter to "the state of the churches in slave countries."[51] Given that a Christianity chapter lays the groundwork for the one in which Brown's marriage is targeted, Brown's portrait of another marriage proves significant. Before his own marital trouble, which is caused by white people, Brown witnesses the problems of a couple deemed "superior" by the law of the land. Brown shares that Mr. Colquitt, whose wife abuses his wife, Nancy, had become gravely ill. Fearing for his life, he asks the enslaved people on his property to pray for his health. When he gets better, his wife teases him about having relied on these lowly creatures. Mr. Colquitt denies having asked for prayers. Aiming to prove his wife wrong, he questions each enslaved laborer and punishes those who corroborate his wife's version of events. Brown reports, "He whipped every one of them which said he had prayed as Mrs. Colquitt had stated."[52] Furthermore, "he seemed wishful to whip me also, but, as I did not belong to him, he was deprived of the pleasure of paying me for my services in the manner, in which others had been rewarded."[53] Here, Brown underscores the irony of black experience with the language of "reward." Doing well and doing something good will inspire aggression, not safety. Achievements require violent responses that keep black people in their "proper" place.

The scene in which Brown and his wife walk four miles holding hands in sorrow actually begins with Brown's having prayed for an enslaver. Colquitt cannot whip Brown, but "determined that I should suffer too, . . . he proceeded to sell my wife."[54] Thus, the narrative highlights two forms of black success that prompt retaliation: the victory of cultivating earthly love bonds and that of feeling connected to a higher power. Conceiving of themselves as children of God allows African Americans to move in the world in ways that are not simply reactions to white "dominance." By focusing on a realm beyond white people's reach, African Americans demonstrate that whiteness is not actually dominant and does not determine everything. As cultural critic Carrie Hyde demonstrates, especially for those denied legal protections, "the comparative concept of a 'higher law' provided a powerful and flexible political framework for developing notions of citizenship."[55] Brown's narrative gestures toward this framework's sustaining power.

Colquitt denied relying on enslaved people's prayers because if a group is inferior, needing its help casts doubt on the validity of one's elevated status. When readers understand that white hostility reacts to black achievement, it becomes clear that a connection with God is worth punishing because it suggests that the enslaved live more Christian lives than the Americans who claim to have built their society on it. As the personification of reactionary white aggression, Colquitt seems to see precisely that writing on the wall.

Christianity's importance to the story Brown tells comes to the fore again once Brown is alone and assumes he will never have an earthly reunion with his family. Brown's narrative continues to detail the effort of defining and redefining success, and the adjustments Brown makes begin to revolve around individual liberty. Brown shares the story of a white friend, a fellow Christian who suddenly feels convicted while singing in a church he knows supports slavery. The friend vows to sever his ties, and Brown proclaims, "I too made up my mind that I would be no longer guilty of assisting those bloody dealers in the bodies and souls of men; and ever since that time I have steadfastly kept my resolution."[56] This decision gives meaning to Brown's experiences in the absence of his wife and children, and it inspires new plans of action: "I now began to get weary of my bonds; and earnestly panted after liberty."[57] Navigating life without his loved ones, the urge for freedom becomes impossible to ignore. He resolves to take "full possession of all that freedom which the finger of God had so clearly written on the constitutions of man, and which was common to the human race; but of which, by the cruel hand of tyranny, I, and millions of my fellow-men, had been robbed."[58] Indeed, "I was determined that come what may, I should have my freedom or die in the attempt."[59] When deprived of his family, he remains connected to white friends and black community members. These connections inspire him to contribute to efforts that honor his awareness of his value and that of others who are treated as if their God-given agency can be denied for social, political, and economic convenience.

Holding on to his self-conception and aligning with others who acknowledge it, Brown not only escapes bondage but also writes this narrative – preserving evidence of his self-affirmation in the midst of violence. Brown's tale "became almost immediately one of the most celebrated stories of liberation in the history of American enslavement."[60]

It commanded attention largely because of the way he gained freedom. Weighing approximately 200 pounds and standing about 5'8", Brown had himself mailed from Richmond, Virginia, to Philadelphia, Pennsylvania, in a box measuring "three feet one inch wide, two feet six inches high, and two feet wide."[61] These extraordinary circumstances made his story best known for the box and its dimensions. Given the risks he took and the discomfort he embraced, there was no denying that his was a "heroic struggle against the odds," and it succeeded in "giving a face, a story, and a driving spirit to the abstract concept of freedom."[62]

Giving flesh to abstraction may be what Brown's narrative does best. The power of performance distinguished this heroic tale and made it suitable for panorama displays, lectures, and traveling exhibitions. By maximizing embodied practices both inside and outside the text – not only his actions but also his written and spoken words – Brown claimed belonging within his family, within his community, and within the nation that actively rejected him. Indeed, performance empowered the *Narrative of the Life of Henry Box Brown* to extend "beyond the priorities of antislavery persuasion [to become] an iconic presence in American culture."[63]

Truly understanding how African American cultural production shapes US culture requires recognizing the mainstream commitment to attacking black success and negating assertions of black belonging. If James Baldwin had focused on the reactionary quality of dominant discourses and practices, he might not have used *Native Son* to make the odd declaration that "there has as yet arrived no sensibility sufficiently profound and tough to make [the Negro] tradition articulate."[64] African American art does not protest injustice so much as white-authored injustice reacts to the achievement of groups it is committed to marginalizing.

Despite the unusual method Brown used to emancipate himself, the story his narrative most focuses on telling revolves around his family and all they meant to him. Because it tells this dynamic truth, Brown's narrative "deserves something more than fascination and celebration,"[65] and because Brown preserved his experience in the archive and repertoire of the community conversation, it is available for posterity to appreciate that "something more." Literary historian John Ernest suggests, "this remains a narrative in search of an audience, and ... with something to say even to today's readers."[66] As I have shown, this is true for all works by members of marginalized groups because they await being examined through the lens of achievement.

Notes

1. Nell Irvin Painter, *The History of White People* (New York: W. W. Norton, 2010).
2. Baldwin himself revised his assessment of the novel after Wright's death, admitting that although he still believed his engagement "was the greatest tribute I could have paid him," Wright "had never really been a human being for me, he had been an idol. And idols are created in order to be destroyed" (*Nobody*, 256, 257). See James Baldwin, *Nobody Knows My Name* [1961], in *James Baldwin: Collected Essays*, ed. Toni Morrison (New York: Library of America, 1998), 131–285.
3. James Baldwin, *Notes of a Native Son* [1955] in *James Baldwin: Collected Essays*, ed. Toni Morrison (New York: Library of America, 1998), 27; hereafter cited as *Notes*.
4. *Notes*, 27.
5. *Notes*, 27.
6. *Notes*, 27.
7. *Notes*, 28.
8. *Notes*, 28.
9. *Notes*, 28.
10. Social contract theory holds that individuals agree to be governed in exchange for protection of their person and property. This has never held for African Americans. One of endless examples: the ease with which unarmed black people are killed today and the courts fail to hold anyone accountable.
11. James Baldwin, *The Fire Next Time* [1963] in *James Baldwin: Collected Essays*, ed. Toni Morrison (New York: Library of America, 1998), 333; hereafter cited as *Fire*.
12. Koritha Mitchell, *Living with Lynching: African American Lynching Plays, Performance, and Citizenship, 1890–1930* (Urbana: University of Illinois Press, 2011).
13. Derrick R. Spires, *The Practice of Citizenship: Black Politics and Print Culture in the Early United States* (Philadelphia: University of Pennsylvania Press, 2019), 7.
14. Spires, *Practice of Citizenship*, 14.
15. Spires, *Practice of Citizenship*, 3.
16. Evie Shockley, remarks on *Black Art Matters: African American Scholar/Artists Creating Home within the Academy and the Arts* roundtable (American Studies Association Annual Conference, Denver, CO, November 2016).
17. Henry Box Brown, *Narrative of the Life of Henry Box Brown, Written by Himself* [1851], ed. John Ernest (Chapel Hill: University of North Carolina Press, 2008), 71; hereafter cited as Brown.
18. Brown, 71.
19. Brown, 72.
20. Brown, 72.

21. Brown, 72.
22. Dorothy Roberts, *Killing the Black Body: Race, Reproduction, and the Meaning of Liberty* (New York: Vintage, 1997), 15.
23. Brown, 72.
24. Brown, 74.
25. Brown, 74.
26. Brown, 74.
27. Brown, 74.
28. Brown, 75.
29. This resonates with these findings: "White people benefited by exploiting black romantic love that propelled most free people's desperate moves to petition to be enslaved for the sake of their families, all the while denying those relationships' legitimacy and standing when they did not serve white interests"; see Tera W. Hunter, *Bound in Wedlock: Slave and Free Black Marriage in the Nineteenth Century* (Cambridge, MA: The Belknap Press of Harvard University Press, 2017), 117.
30. Brown, 75.
31. Brown, 75.
32. Brown, 75.
33. Brown, 75.
34. For more on the history of these priorities among enslaved people, see Hunter, *Bound in Wedlock*.
35. Brown, 75.
36. Brown, 75–76.
37. Brown, 76.
38. Brown, 76.
39. *Fire*, 293.
40. Brown, 76–77, original emphasis.
41. Brown, 77.
42. Brown, 77–79.
43. Brown, 79.
44. Brown, 79.
45. Brown, 79.
46. Literary examples abound, including the scene on page 37 of *Incidents in the Life of a Slave Girl*. See Harriet Jacobs, *Incidents in the Life of a Slave Girl* [1861], eds. Frances Smith Foster and Richard Yarborough (New York: W. W. Norton, 2019).
47. Brown, 79.
48. Brown, 79.
49. Brown, 81.
50. Brown, 81.
51. Brown, 69.
52. Brown, 74.
53. Brown, 74.
54. Brown, 74.

55. Carrie Hyde, *Civic Longing: The Speculative Origins of US Citizenship* (Cambridge, MA: Harvard University Press, 2018), 13.
56. Brown, 82.
57. Brown, 82–83.
58. Brown, 83.
59. Brown, 84.
60. John Ernest, "Introduction: The Emergence of Henry 'Box' Brown," in *Narrative of the Life of Henry Box Brown, Written by Himself*, ed. John Ernest (Chapel Hill: University of North Carolina Press, 2008), 2; hereafter cited as Ernest.
61. Brown, 85.
62. Ernest, 2, 1.
63. Ernest, 3.
64. *Notes*, 27.
65. Ernest, 32.
66. Ernest, 32.

CHAPTER 6

Affiliated Races

Edlie L. Wong

From Slavery to Birthright Citizenship

On a hot and muggy summer day in 1854, nearly 600 abolitionists gathered in Harmony Grove in Framingham, Massachusetts, for a Fourth of July rally that would become celebrated in the annals of American antislavery. A platform decorated with an "American flag hung ... Union down, draped in black" set the mood.[1] The Massachusetts Antislavery Society sponsoring the rally had just faced two major setbacks. Roughly a month earlier, Congress passed the Kansas-Nebraska Act, which repealed the 1820 Compromise and opened the western territories to slavery. Closer to home, state and federal authorities had seized Anthony Burns in a highly public effort to enforce the Fugitive Slave Law. A failed interracial abolitionist rescue effort turned Burns into a cause célèbre. Police, cavalry, and artillery companies were called upon to manage the protesting crowds as Burns was conducted from the Boston courthouse to the city wharf and then back to Virginia. In the now canonized address from the rally, "Slavery in Massachusetts," Henry David Thoreau emphatically proclaimed: "The law will never make men free; it is men who have got to make the law free."[2] Now over twenty years into the antislavery struggle, abolitionists like William Lloyd Garrison and his supporters saw no future in either the Union or the Constitution that bound it together.

This radical abolitionist outlook was perhaps most powerfully represented by an act. At the conclusion of a rousing opening speech, Garrison held aloft a copy of the US Constitution, condemned it as "the source and parent" of the atrocities of slavery, and lit it on fire.[3] "So perish all compromises with tyranny!" Garrison exclaimed, as the Constitution turned to ash.[4] In the face of some "hisses and wrathful exclamations," black abolitionist Charles Lenox Remond defended Garrison, claiming the gesture "in the name of three million slaves, with whom he was identified by complexion."[5] Remond further reminded the audience that "not only were the colored people outlawed under the American Constitution, but every man on that platform."[6] In short, the Constitution ensured the wholesale subjugation of black Americans and criminalized the abolitionists who sought their freedom. It was rightfully burned.

This dramatic act remains one of the most defining scenes in the history of American antislavery. For Garrison, it was the culmination of nearly twenty years of antislavery legal thinking.[7] In 1840, the publication of James Madison's record of the *Debates in the Federalist Convention of 1787* confirmed what abolitionists like Garrison had long acknowledged. Slave interests played a significant role in shaping the Constitution, and the document recognized, if it did not explicitly sanction, the legal status of chattel slavery in the nation.[8] Wendell Phillips further popularized this historical necessity thesis after he compiled all the extracts from Madison's *Notes* having to do with slavery and published them in 1844 as *The Constitution: A Pro-Slavery Compact*.[9] Abolitionists and proslavery ideologues alike focused on the ambiguous wording of the infamous constitutional clauses pertaining to taxation and representation (Three-Fifths Clause), fugitive labor rendition (Fugitive Slave Clause), and "migration and importation" (1808 Sunset Clause) as evidence of the framers' "original intent."

Debates over the US Constitution as either proslavery or antislavery also fueled the ideological rift between Garrison and his equally famous former protégé, Frederick Douglass, who refused to interpret the Constitution as a "slaveholding instrument."[10] Garrison, however, believed that emancipation would require the evisceration – if not the utter elimination – of the Constitution itself, as symbolized by his dramatic gesture at Framingham. As slavery expanded across the nation, Garrisonian abolitionists saw freedom and civil rights as positively antithetical to the law and Constitution. Proslavery ideologues like John C. Calhoun helped solidify this abolitionist position when he claimed constitutional sanction for slavery in his widely circulated 1849 "Address of the Southern Delegates in Congress."[11] According to Hoang Phan, by 1854, when Garrison burned the Constitution, jurists, politicians, and activists on either side of the slavery controversy had begun to accept the Constitution's slavery-sanctioning "original intent" as a critical commonplace.[12]

The Civil War and the end of slavery facilitated a radical reorientation toward the Constitution. Reconstruction legislators faced the uncomfortable yet broadly acknowledged fact that the Constitution had countenanced slavery. The chief architects of the Reconstruction Amendments understood that the preservation of the Constitution and the Union that it bound together required its reaffirmation as "the bulwark of antislavery legal principle and the prerequisite for freedom," argues Deak Nabers.[13] The Fourteenth Amendment set out to guarantee and secure civil freedom through the *reassertion* of the nation's Constitution, the selfsame document that Garrison had destroyed as a "polluted and blood-stained instrument."[14] The amendment conferred citizenship on black Americans, who had been denied citizenship in *Dred Scott* v. *Sandford* (1857). According to Chief Justice Taney's ruling, blacks had not been embraced in the word "citizen," and the 1790 Naturalization Act served as a wholesale "repudiation of the African race" as "alien" to "the political family of the United States."[15] The new amendment also went further to establish the territory of one's birth or *jus soli* as the basis for political membership in the nation or birthright citizenship. "In language that transcended race and region," the Fourteenth Amendment, according to Eric Foner, "challenged legal discrimination throughout the nation and changed and broadened the meaning of freedom for all Americans."[16]

However, the expansive possibilities of the Fourteenth Amendment were relatively short-lived as Republican strife, public outcries, and a worsening depression helped Democrats achieve electoral dominance in the 1870s.[17] The federal judiciary assumed authority over the interpretation and enforcement of the new amendment. Shortly after ratification, Justice Samuel Miller's oft-critiqued 5–4 majority ruling in the *Slaughterhouse Cases* (1873) began to restrict the scope of the Reconstruction Amendments. He insisted that the Fourteenth Amendment had not expanded the definition of national citizenship for *all* Americans. It simply accorded black Americans certain rights already enjoyed by whites. As a consequence, the *Slaughterhouse* ruling maintained state authority over the regulation of the civil rights of US *citizens* and refused to subordinate state to federal citizenship.[18] In subsequent cases, including *United States* v. *Cruikshank* (1876) and the Civil Rights Cases (1883), the Supreme Court further limited the federal and state protection of black American civil rights. As Jeannine DeLombard has argued, these cases, following the *Slaughterhouse* ruling, debated the "applicability of the Reconstruction Amendments beyond the immediate context of slavery, emancipation, and abolition."[19] Slavery and abolition became the ready prism for interpreting the Reconstruction Amendments and apprehending their limited operation in the present.

Subsequently, Justice Henry Billings Brown relied heavily on the Slaughterhouse Cases as precedent in *Plessy* v. *Ferguson* (1896), which upheld the constitutionality of racial segregation in the United States. According to Brown's 7–1 majority ruling, the "proper construction" of the Thirteenth and Fourteenth Amendments was "first called to the attention of this court in the *Slaughterhouse Cases*."[20] By 1900, when Pauline Hopkins serialized *Contending Forces: A Romance Illustrative of Negro Life North and South*, it had become apropos of the era for her noble race-man Will Smith to proclaim, "the Constitutional amendments are dead letters."[21] Smith's skepticism was amply justified by judicial rulings that narrowed the federal protection of the nation's new citizens while expanding corporate power and supporting, in DeLombard's words, "capital's war against labor."[22] By Brook Thomas's count, 312 of the 607 Fourteenth Amendment cases brought before the Supreme Court by 1911 concerned corporations, whereas only 30 involved the rights of racial minorities.[23]

As the federal courts began to limit the scope of the Reconstruction Amendments and the expansion of federal power, anti-Chinese ideologues and nativists began advancing new immigration and naturalization legislation that restricted legal entry into the United States and challenged birthright citizenship. For example, the new 1870 Naturalization Act expanded race-based naturalization rights to "aliens of African nativity" and "persons of African descent," despite Charles Sumner's more radical proposal to strike the word *white* from the "free white persons" enumerated in the original 1790 Naturalization Act.[24] Similar anxieties over Chinese immigrants had made their way into the earlier congressional debates over the Fourteenth Amendment. Pennsylvania Senator Edgar Cowan expressed concern over extending birthright citizenship to the children of Chinese immigrants, playing up fears of the Chinese overrunning the Pacific Coast states.[25] His anxieties over birthright citizenship anticipate the 1898 federal case against Wong Kim Ark. The federal government, which prosecuted the unsuccessful case against Wong, alleged that his birth on US soil did not make him a citizen because his immigrant parents (as Chinese subjects) remained under Chinese jurisdiction even while in the United States.

As Carrie Hyde has argued, the term *citizen* "conjures some of the most persistent fantasies of US politics: the promise of inalienable rights, the sovereignty of self-governance, and the dream of democratic equality."[26] Yet, this American dream of inclusion has long derived its cultural significance from the threat of political exclusion.[27] These countervailing forces might be found in Justice John Marshall Harlan's oft-celebrated lone dissent from the *Plessy* majority. Harlan rejected racial "caste" legislation as antithetical to the Fourteenth Amendment; yet, his more expansive formulation of freedom and citizenship drew another exclusionary line between black and white citizens and Chinese aliens deemed politically inassimilable to the nation. In his words:

> There is a race so different from our own that we do not permit those belonging to it to become citizens of the United States .... I allude to the Chinese race. But, by the statute in question, a Chinaman can ride in the same passenger coach with white citizens of the United States, while citizens of the black race in Louisiana, many of whom, perhaps, risked their lives for the preservation of the Union ... are yet declared to be criminals, liable to imprisonment, if they ride in a public coach occupied by citizens of the white race.[28]

The legal construction of black and white civic identities necessitated the invention of another racialized alterity.[29] By emphasizing Chinese difference as a "race" reclassified by the Chinese Exclusion Act (1882) as "aliens ineligible to citizenship," Harlan sought to combat the sentiment of alienism directed against black Americans in the wake of Reconstruction. He forged a vision of a more liberal citizenship on what Claire Jean Kim describes as the "field of racial positions," in which subordinate groups are at once "differently racialized" and "racialized in comparison with one another."[30] Harlan's dissent reminds us that the ideology of racial exclusion has long defined the limits of community and the boundaries of US national belonging.

The short yet unsettled path from the Fourteenth Amendment to *Plessy v. Ferguson* led to complex developments within US immigration and naturalization law and border control policies. The passage of the 1875 Page Act and the Chinese Exclusion Acts represented, as legal scholar Mae Ngai argues, "the most complete race-based legal exclusion from citizenship since *Dred Scott*," leading to the creation of the "Asiatic Barred Zone" in the twentieth century.[31] The Page Act ushered in this period of restrictive immigration control, as Congress banned from entry certain "undesirable" immigrants, including convicted felons, contract laborers from "China, Japan, or any Oriental country," and "lewd and immoral" women intended for prostitution.[32] In practice, the Page Act severely interdicted the entry of Chinese women, thus preventing family formation and the reproduction of birthright citizens. It ensured a supply of temporary male laborers. In 1882, the first of several increasingly strict Chinese Exclusion Acts followed. It stipulated a class-based racial exclusion barring the entry of Chinese laborers with the exemption of the "superior classes" of merchants, teachers, students, and tourists, and it further banned all Chinese from naturalization to US citizenship.[33] In *Chae Chan Ping* v. *United States* (1889), the Supreme Court upheld the validity of Chinese racial exclusion. The ruling portrayed Chinese immigration as a national security threat and rooted its regulation in "a doctrine of inherent sovereign powers." It delegated to the legislative and executive branches plenary power or absolute authority over immigration.[34]

By the end of the century, the Chinese Exclusion Acts and federal rulings on Chinese immigration cases completed the redefinition of the Asiatic as the categorically excluded. The nation's first raced and classed immigration and naturalization ban helped stabilize the meaning and value of citizenship at the very moment when the federal judiciary began limiting the compass of the Fourteenth Amendment. The enforcement of these new laws transformed non-elite migrants into improperly documented or undocumented immigrants, subject to deportation.[35] For example, the 1888 Scott Act retroactively cancelled the identity certificates that had once permitted Chinese legal residents to travel abroad and return, abruptly stranding 20,000–30,000 outside US borders.[36] Barred from legal entry, many attempted to return by way of Canada and Mexico, establishing smuggling routes that were used well into the twentieth century. As historian Erika Lee notes, "The first immigrants to be excluded from the United States, Asians became the first undocumented immigrants."[37] Federal efforts to defend the nation against this unauthorized and subsequently criminalized population "established the country's first border security policies and practices."[38] Chinese exclusion policies produced new forms of racialization that shaped perceptions of undocumented border crossers as unwanted and criminal illegal aliens. They also launched a new regime of immigrant identification and registration regulations that continues today.

Contrasting Views: Wong Chin Foo and Edith Maude Eaton

The remainder of this essay explores two lesser-known Asian American writers who contributed to the cultural imagination of citizenship as the federal court and new immigration laws reshaped its meaning. The late nineteenth and early twentieth centuries witnessed an enormous expansion in local, state, and federal regulation of immigration and immigrant life.[39] The life and writings of Wong Chin Foo (1847–98), like those of fellow Chinese North American journalist Edith Maude Eaton (1865–1914), better known as Sui Sin Far, span the volatile political contexts of Reconstruction, the Gilded Age, and the Progressive Era. Among the earliest Asian American writers to publish in English, Wong and Eaton produced a large and wide-ranging body of journalism and short fiction that addressed the complex politics of citizenship, immigration law, and transnational migration. They took advantage of the heterogeneity of the periodical form, experimenting with different genres of short- and serial-form writing, from travelogues of American Chinatowns, editorials, manifestoes, satirical sketches, and correspondences to essays on various topics.

Wong and Eaton often positioned themselves as North American ambassadors of Chinese culture, yet recent biographies reveal that they diverged on the issue of undocumented immigrants, especially as public concerns grew over the criminal entry of "contraband Chinese."[40] Wong spent some of his later life as an informant for immigration officials (with a brief appointment as a Chinese inspector) while Eaton witnessed (if not participated in) her family's growing involvement in the smuggling of undocumented Chinese into the United States from Canada.[41] As Wong began to limit his political advocacy to the narrow scope of citizenship and the nation-state, Eaton espoused a more capacious human rights–based approach to transnational migration. Publishing in the 1890s, Eaton was one of the earliest writers to address the complex motivations or push factors that structured illegal networks of border crossing and labor smuggling.[42] Her short fiction and journalism sought out alternatives to territorialized citizenship, insisting on the fundamental "right to have rights."[43]

As Eaton noted in her journalism and stories, illegal border crossings and the expansion of transnational networks of labor smuggling were both a product of and response to racializing immigration law. They also became the focus of sensationalized media attention. Editorial cartoons from *The San Francisco Illustrated Wasp*, the most widely read magazine west of the Rocky Mountains, began depicting the so-called "coolie immigrant" as the archetype for the racialized illegal alien who undermines the social, economic, and territorial integrity of the nation. The racialized imaginings of Asiatic "coolie" labor as unfree and coerced became a powerful rhetorical touchstone for later policies on race, national security, citizenship, and immigration. For example, President Theodore Roosevelt's 1905 annual address cited the example of the "Chinese coolie" as the archetype of the unwanted immigrant.[44] The visual language of the *Wasp* drew upon and reconfigured this Orientalist binary of unwanted coolies versus desirable immigrants to facilitate the association of *all* Chinese newcomers with illegal entry. George Frederick Keller's "Hard

Pushing" (1881) depicts California Senator John Franklin Miller, an outspoken proponent of Chinese exclusion, attempting to stem the rising tide of "coolie immigration" (see Figure 6.1).[45] Such images emphasizing the fortification of US borders strike an uncanny note with recent calls to build a wall along the US–Mexico border under the Trump administration (see Figure 6.2).

The repeated images of Asiatic figures breaching US border walls attribute a monstrous agency to the "coolie immigrant" that effaces the evolving role of immigration policies in the creation of undocumented border crossers. In two of the most discussed *Wasp* cover illustrations, "Now Shut the Back Gate" (1888) and "The Back Door" (1889), cartoonist Solly Walter luridly centers the figure of the Asiatic illegal alien in the transformation of the United States into a gatekeeping nation (see Figures 6.3 and 6.4). As Jean Pfaelzer has documented, the most extreme violence against the Chinese occurred *after* the Exclusion Act, which validated nativist ideologues who blamed these immigrants for undercutting wages and lowering living standards for American workingmen.[46] Elliott Young further argues that the growth of immigration bureaucracy after 1882 further centralized the "disciplining and punishing functions" that were once the prerogative of these vigilante mobs.[47] Complementary images, these two caricatures chart how the state strengthened its role in regulating immigration (allegorized in Uncle Sam's wielding the bat of "frontier justice") through the transformation of the Chinese labor migrant into the dehumanized Asiatic coolie (snake) and unwelcome criminal illegal alien.

Public anxieties over "contraband Chinese" helped transform the US immigration system into a racializing technology of national fortification, as immigration bureaucracy grew in manpower and assumed extraordinary legal power to enforce and police borders. It also made newly undocumented immigrants even more vulnerable to unfair informal and contract labor relations (or the "coolie" servitude) that these laws were purported to prevent in the first place. From 1882 to 1920, official estimates record 17,300 undocumented Chinese migrants entering the United States through Canada and Mexico.[48] In visual and print media, the widely disseminated Yellow Peril threat of this illegal "coolie immigration" erased distinctions between banned labor migrant and exempted "merchant" elite even as enforcement of the law increased disparities between the elite and non-elite. This Janus-faced process heightened class tensions within migrant communities and influenced the direction of early Asian American politics and writing.

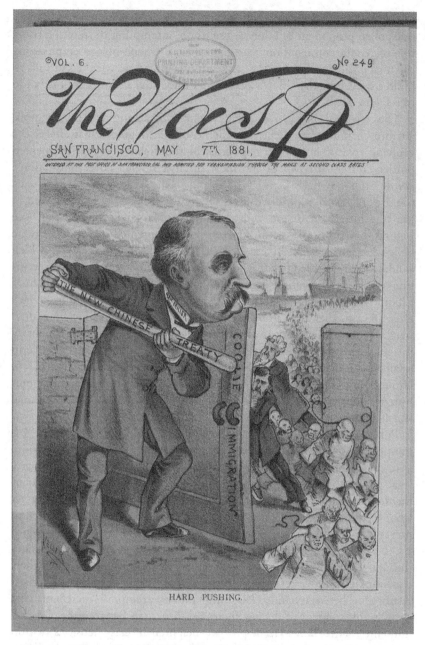

Figure 6.1   George Frederick Keller, "Hard Pushing." *Wasp* 6 (January–June 1881),
https://oac.cdlib.org/ark:/13030/hb18700107/?layout=metadata&brand=oac4

Figure 6.2   George Frederick Keller, "The Chinese Question: The Remedy Too Late."
Wasp 7 (July–December 1881), http://content.cdlib.org/ark:/13030/hb1j49n4h9/?
layout=metadata

Wong was an outspoken critic of Chinese exclusion, best remembered as the founder of the first Chinese American newspaper in New York and the Chinese Equal Rights League (1892). Arriving in San Francisco in 1873, Wong reportedly fled China as a political refugee. In 1893, John Weber, New York's first Commissioner of Immigration, recruited Wong to help control the smuggling of undocumented Chinese and opium into the country, which had become the sensationalized stuff of yellow journalism and melodramas. Wong was later "sent to Boston with instructions to run down certain Chinese merchants, who were engaged in importing their countrymen by way of Canada."[49] His investigation uncovered political corruption and graft, and his career was cut short after he publicly accused several high-ranking customs officers of taking bribes in Chinese inspection operations.[50] Wong numbered among the handful of Chinese informants and interpreters hired by immigration officers to assist in their efforts. Complex figures, these immigrant power brokers, as historian Lisa Mar has argued, were variously perceived as benevolent community representatives and compromised collaborators in league with a racist nation-state.[51]

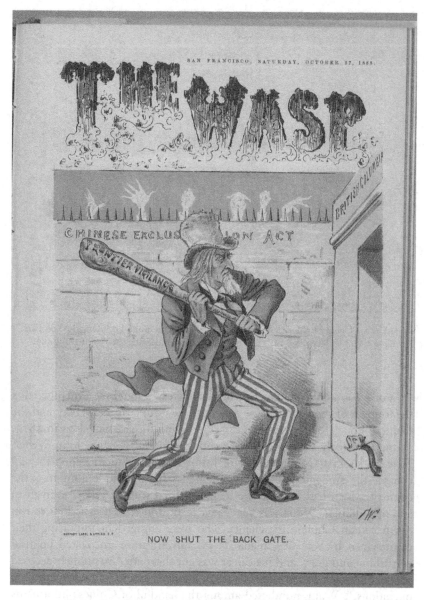

Figure 6.3   Solly Walter, "Now Shut the Back Gate." *Wasp* 21
(July–December 1888), https://oac.cdlib.org/ark:/13030/hb3290029p/
?brand=oac4&layout=metadata

Figure 6.4   Solly Walter, "The Back Door. The wily Chinese sneaking over the Northern frontier." *Wasp* 23 (July–December 1889), https://oac.cdlib.org/ark:/13030/hb1f59n4fm/?brand=oac4&layout=metadata

As Chinese exclusion became a permanent feature of his adopted country, Wong's political commitments and ad hoc journalism gradually shifted from crusading against the exclusion of Chinese labor migrants to advocating for the citizenship and naturalization rights of Chinese legally in the United States.[52] Wong numbered among a small group of Chinese immigrants who had managed to naturalize to citizenship before the Chinese Exclusion Act. In 1874, a Michigan circuit court granted Wong's petition for naturalization, although his legal status as a US citizen was later challenged by nativist demagogues like Denis Kearney and not recognized by the federal government.[53] Wong's 1891 passport application was denied because a State Department official declared that "no Chinaman is entitled to a passport," and Wong later faced charges of voter registration fraud.[54] In a letter reprinted in the *Pittsburgh Dispatch*, Wong referenced Edward Everett Hale's popular tale in describing his condition of statelessness: "I have just discovered that I am the only individual in New York that has no country . . .. A man without a country, kicked out of China, disowned by the United States."[55]

In the print public sphere, Wong sought to decouple the controversial topic of Chinese immigration from the issue of naturalization and citizenship. However, his efforts often reinforced the social hierarchies and asymmetries of power between elite Chinese American merchants and non-elite or undocumented immigrants. Wong's ethnographic piece, "High and Low Life in China" (1893) reminds readers that "any man who goes from one nation into another for the purpose of gain, without the necessary capital is either a serf or a slave."[56] Associated with criminality and unlawful entry, these servile laborers – whom Wong collectively refers to as the "Chinese coolie" – shape popular perceptions of Chinese immigrants as low-wage workers, the nation's "house-servants," "laundrymen," and "farmers."[57] American officials, Wong maintains, have unfairly "excluded from the United States great scholars, noble patriots, eminent scientists . . . [i]n their zeal to shut out [this] shameless element."[58] By the 1890s, Wong had embraced the raced and classed stratifications established in the original Exclusion Act and began limiting his advocacy to the merchant elites. His rhetoric reaffirmed the United States as an idealized nation of immigrants by highlighting the socioeconomic value of *legal* immigration in ways that encouraged the continued marginalization and criminalization of undocumented migrants. Wong's writings espoused a binary paradigm of inclusion/exclusion, which, as Hyde argues, "preserves the incorporative telos of the American Dream by equating citizenship with political self-realization."[59]

Like Wong, Eaton was a prolific writer, and her uncollected journalism and short fiction address the complex networks of transnational labor migration in ways that complement her only published book, *Mrs. Spring Fragrance and Other Stories* (1912), a collection of Chinatown tales for which she is most recognized. Often developed from her journalistic sketches and reports, Eaton's stories, spanning both humor and tragedy, encompass elite and non-elite, legal and undocumented aliens, allowing readers rare glimpses into the tense relations of collaboration and antagonism within these immigrant networks and communities. Eaton's pursuit of journalistic work took her from Montreal to Kingston, San Francisco, Seattle, and Boston.[60] Her characters trace similar circum-Atlantic and cross-continental routes of movement and migration. Crossing and recrossing the US–Canadian border during the era of Chinese exclusion, Eaton most likely passed as "white" as she traveled through US immigration and border control checkpoints. Her ethnographic journalism similarly recounts the various routes by which Chinese migrants found their way to North America. These accounts often blur the distinctions between "legal" and "illegal" immigration that Wong stressed in his later political activism. One piece published in the *Los Angeles Express* (1903) introduced readers to "Mrs. Sing, the most prominent Chinese woman in Los Angeles," who was "[k]idnapped as a little child from her parents in China ... [and] ... brought to this country by her captors."[61] She later escaped through the intervention of Christian benefactors who educated her. She married a prominent Chinese merchant and became the mother of "ten bright children," birthright citizens in the United States. The girl who had been illegally trafficked into the United States was now an exemplary Chinese American.

Eaton's writings draw critical attention to the ways that racialized immigration policies helped create and sustain transnational labor smuggling, undocumented immigration, and the shadow economy. They also express a deep skepticism toward forms of civic longing that shape the politics of national identification and imagined citizenship.[62] In her oft-cited essay, "A Plea for the Chinaman" (1896), Eaton stresses transnational labor migration as an essential component of the global integration of national economies. In her words, Chinese labor migration "affect[s] the material interests of this country ... and in various branches of agriculture and manufacturing [provides] a source of wealth to those who employ him."[63] Undocumented border crossing and illegal entry serve a globalizing economy that depends on the "cheap" and easily deportable foreign labor supply that racially restrictive immigration and naturalization law creates.[64] By asking readers to consider immigrants' complex relationship to the state, Eaton illuminates the complementary and agonistic links forged between emerging globalization, the territorialization of state power, and US immigration law. As Douglas Massey has argued, globalization feeds off of state-sanctioned efforts to restrict immigration, strengthen national sovereignty, and enforce territorial boundaries even as it erodes "the power ... of nation states to control transnational movements of labor as well as of capital, goods, and information."[65] Eaton's writings, dating from the 1890s, had long called attention to the political-economic conditions facilitating transnational labor migration irrespective of state regulations and border control. "As long as they are allowed to do the washing of the nation," she proclaimed, "they seem to care not who makes the laws."[66]

Eaton's accounts of labor smuggling and illegal border crossing serve as important corollaries to her more familiar Chinatown stories dramatizing the impact of racializing immigration restriction and exclusion laws on the domestic lives of "legal" Chinese immigrants in the United States. Her sentimental plots emphasize themes of familial separation, "self-deportation," and failed immigration in short narratives that also center Chinese figures as agents in and interpreters of their experiences in the United States. First published in William Hayes Ward's New York *Independent*, Eaton's oft-anthologized tale "In the Land of the Free" (1909) most powerfully adapts sentimental tropes to critique the abusive administration of US immigration law. The story begins with the return of a Chinese mother to the United States after giving birth while on a visit to China. The Chinese merchant Hom Hing eagerly awaits his family's return. However, immigration inspectors detain the child, claiming, "'We cannot allow the boy to go ashore.'"[67] They proceed to enforce the strict letter of the law against the Chinese parents, for "the boy has no certificate entitling him to admission to this country," taking him into custody until they "hear from Washington."[68] A stray remark muttered by one of the inspectors, "'I don't like this part of the business,'" speaks to the regularity of family separation as a procedural norm of Chinese immigration administration.[69] Hom Hing's repeated protestation, "'He is my son,'" elicits the rote response, "'We have no proof.'"[70] The Immigration Bureau transfers the child to a Christian mission where "white women" care for him. The parents suffer though ten long, desperate months and legal fees that deplete their resources until the document came at last – "the precious paper which gave Hom Hing and his wife the right to the possession of their own child."[71] However, the force of US immigration law continues to mark the long-sought-after reunion. Separation had turned mother into a stranger, and the story ends with the child's rejection of his mother: "'Go'way, go'way!' he bade his mother."[72] Eaton's stories of failed legal immigration offer profound critiques of US border control policies and make legible the normalizing racial violence that attended US nation and empire building under the aegis of Christian benevolence, tutelage, and uplift. In a complementary fashion, her accounts of smuggling and undocumented entry begin to bring human rights considerations to bear upon immigration.

These writings humanize the mass-mediated figure of the criminalized, undocumented border crosser by centering the perspectives of the "smugglers and the smuggled." Unlike her sentimental tales of "legal" immigration, Eaton often used humor to subvert xenophobia and nativist discourses that fixated on undocumented immigrants as national security threats. In a piece published in the *Montreal Daily Star*, she wrote with unmistakable sarcasm:

> The infinite plans taken by the Chinese to get into Canada and the United States suggest a passion for America life which one would not have expected of them. They lose sleep in devising methods of evading the restrictive laws. The underground railway, by which the slaves used to escape into Canada, is nothing to the modern inventions of the Chinese for climbing tariff walls and creeping under the wire fences of Christian civilization. They are always at it, showing their devotion to America in a hundred ways, with a pathetic persistence. Still they are not popular.[73]

Eaton recasts the sensationalized association of Chinese immigrants or "coolies" with slavery and involuntary servitude. In a series of dizzying reversals, she analogizes undocumented border crossers to the fugitive slaves who once defied unjust law and the Constitution – Garrison's "blood-stained instrument" – by escaping into Canada. In "evading the restrictive laws," undocumented migrants chart an equally clandestine – if inverse – route from Canada to the United States. Exposés such as Julian Ralph's "Chinese Leak" (1890) for *Harper's New Monthly Magazine* offered shocking accounts of human smuggling and the "lawless practice [s] . . . from one end of the border to the other" for public consumption. In contrast, Eaton's journalism and stories playfully humanized the participants, showing sympathy for smugglers and their criminal "freight," according to Mary Chapman.[74]

By highlighting the idea of the border as a "social fiction," Eaton's writings stress human agency and the inventive resistance of undocumented immigrants against the territorialization of state power.[75] Chapman's biographical recovery efforts suggest that the Eaton family participated in these smuggling networks in Montreal. Eaton's father, Edward, was twice arrested for smuggling undocumented migrants into the United States.[76] Newspaper reports sensationalized him as a "'kingpin' in Montreal's Chinese smuggling community, one of the two 'most skillful men at the business' and 'one of the old school in this line' whose 'hairbreadth escapes … fights with officers and … struggles … with the Chinamen in [his] charge would fill a volume.'"[77] In this vein, Eaton's stories often center the productive contradiction of smugglers and the smuggled as outlaws and cultural heroes who find collective empowerment through the subversion of unjust laws. For example, "The Smuggling of Tie Coe" (1900) characterizes a white smuggler named Jack Fabian, who numbered "[a]mongst the daring men who engage in contrabanding Chinese from Canada into the United States" as an "unimmortalized Rob Roy."[78] In the story "Woo-Ma and I" (1906), a Eurasian character joins the "smugglers of Chinamen" as a way of asserting control over her life after suffering betrayal and abandonment by her bigoted white lover.[79] In another subversively humorous tale, Eaton depicts a Chinese labor migrant named Tian Shan who takes great "pleasure" in "running backwards and forwards across the border."[80] She may have based this character on interviews with Wah Lee, a Chinese laborer who worked in eastern Canada and the United States and was "smuggled backwards and forwards across the line whenever the fancy pleased him."[81] The smugglers and undocumented migrants featured in Eaton's stories and journalism embrace a different sense of territoriality. They challenge the legitimacy of immigration restrictions as a curtailment of freedom. In contrast to Wong's politics of territorialized citizenship, Eaton advanced a human rights understanding of immigration that stressed the right to free movement and open borders, anticipating the rhetoric of immigration activism today.[82] The "Chinaman is as much a human being as those who presume to judge him," she insisted, "and if he is a human being, he must be treated like one."[83]

"No Human Being Is Illegal"

The Citizenship Clause remains one of the most contested aspects of the Fourteenth Amendment. Revisionist right-wing interpretations of the clause have surfaced periodically in the past few decades, corresponding with xenophobic shifts in US popular opinion during periods of economic and political uncertainty. The idea that "a nation without borders is not a nation" served as one of the core tenets of Donald Trump's Make America

Great Again! platform.[84] His policy paper on immigration also called for the end of birthright citizenship, portraying it as "the biggest magnet for illegal immigration."[85] In interviews, Trump repeatedly challenged the citizenship of those born to undocumented immigrants on US soil, referring to them as "anchor babies." His views have reinvigorated efforts to restrict automatic citizenship at birth and renewed calls for the reinterpretation of the Fourteenth Amendment.

Opponents to birthright citizenship challenge the idea of ascriptive citizenship represented in the principle of *jus soli*. Following Peter Schuck and Rogers Smith's argument in *Citizenship without Consent: Illegal Aliens in the American Polity* (1985), these efforts to unsettle the supposedly settled law of *United States* v. *Wong Kim Ark* (1898) assert that *jus soli* or birthright citizenship is a feudal remnant of English common law, deriving from *Calvin's Case* (1608), an ascriptive principle incompatible with republican citizenship based on consent.[86] They contrast *jus soli* to the idea of consensual or contract-based citizenship. However, as Gerald Neuman has argued, contract-based citizenship is not a new concept. It "realized its most dangerous potential in the Dred Scott decision," which positioned black Americans outside the constitutional compact.[87] In Taney's words, the Constitution identified "the negro race as a separate class of persons . . . not regarded as a portion of the people or citizens of the Government then formed."[88] Contemporary opponents of birthright citizenship likewise argue that the nation did not consent to the presence of undocumented aliens in the United States. Therefore, the children born of undocumented aliens are not subject to US jurisdiction and should not be granted automatic citizenship at birth.

Perhaps it should come as no surprise that such revisionist interpretations of the Citizenship Clause often rely upon the narrow contextualism first modeled in Miller's *Slaughterhouse* ruling. Take, for example, the posters featuring the slogan "The 14th Amendment and Civil Rights was for Blacks Not Illegals!" from a July 2010 counterdemonstration at a SB 1070 protest rally against Major League Baseball's plan to hold the All-Star Game in Phoenix.[89] Arizona's controversial SB 1070 was considered the most restrictive contemporary anti-illegal immigration measure until the executive orders on border security and interior enforcement under the Trump administration.[90] In 2012, the Supreme Court struck down three key provisions but upheld the most controversial aspect of the law, which required police officers to verify the status of suspected illegal immigrants, clearing a path for racial profiling and rights abuses against Latinos, Asians, and all others presumed to be criminally "foreign." In an echo of Harlan's

Plessy dissent, the counterprotest slogan marshals the paradoxical logic of "inclusive exclusion" to redraw the boundaries of American identity and belonging as the coexistence of citizens and noncitizens becomes an increasingly fixed feature of our society.[91]

Immigration law is governed by the central premise that the government owes nothing to aliens except the privileges that it explicitly grants to them, unlike the constitutional rights accorded to citizens.[92] US immigration policies have long emphasized issues of securitization driven in part by anxieties around protecting territorial sovereignty and control over borders.[93] As a consequence, immigration issues have been recast as a problem of "law and order," with little thought to human rights considerations or their negative impact on the exercise of fundamental rights.[94] In response, immigration activists have begun embracing human rights discourse, emphasizing the idea, attributed to Holocaust survivor and novelist Elie Wiesel, that "No Human Being Is Illegal."[95] As Crystal Parikh argues, human rights "provide deeply meaningful methods of political and moral imagining, especially for subjects whose recognition by the state is tenuous, if not altogether foreclosed."[96]

As migration becomes a permanent structural feature of Western democracies, immigration activists insist that the subjects of humanitarian campaigns lie not elsewhere, but among us. These efforts also ask us to reconsider how the concept of citizenship has become the measure of equality and inclusion in immigration debates. The figure of the criminalized "illegal immigrant" remains a ready foil for the citizen – its "silent double," in Ngai's words, shoring up fantasies of national belonging as our civil liberties face increasing erosion.[97] By centering the stories of noncitizens and the undocumented, Eaton's early writings represent a lesser-known yet important contribution to our understanding of US citizenship. At the dawn of an earlier century, she asked, as we ask today, how are we to regard those who work, live, and create families and communities among us, yet whose claims upon rights and belonging remain uncertain and the subject of political debate?[98]

Literature, broadly conceived, offers us a unique vantage on this conflicted and evolving history of US citizenship. The literature that emerged as a product of these historical tensions also served as useful modes of critical investigation. In addition, this literature performed important reparative work, forging connections across the rifts and divides of race-, gender-, and class-based law and policies. From the antebellum struggle over slavery to contemporary debates over birthright citizenship, the writers discussed in this chapter model the power of literature to humanize populations that are otherwise objectified in legal and political discourse. In 1854, Thoreau urged, "it is men who have got to make the law free."[99] Eaton later recast this maxim in the context of US immigration and naturalization law and border control policies. Her surprisingly prescient stories suggest alternative freedoms and ways of living within and beyond the nation-state that continue to challenge and provoke us today.

Notes

1. "The Meeting at Framingham," *Liberator* (July 7, 1854), 106.
2. Henry David Thoreau, "Slavery in Massachusetts: An Address Delivered at the Anti-Slavery Celebration at Framingham, July 4th, 1854," *Liberator* (July 21, 1854), 116.
3. "The Meeting at Framingham," 106.
4. "The Meeting at Framingham," 106.
5. "The 'Covenant with Death,'" *Liberator* (July 21, 2854), 114; and "The Meeting at Framingham," 106.
6. "Proceedings at the Anti-Slavery Celebration at Framingham, July 4, 1854," *Liberator* (July 14, 1854), 1.
7. Deak Nabers, *Victory of Law: The Fourteenth Amendment, the Civil War, and American Literature, 1852–1867* (Baltimore, MD: Johns Hopkins University Press, 2006), 1.
8. Nabers, *Victory*, 6.
9. Hoang Phan, *The Bonds of Citizenship: Law and the Labors of Emancipation* (New York: New York University Press, 2013), 120.
10. Frederick Douglass, "The Constitution of the United States: Is It Pro-Slavery or Anti-Slavery?" (1860), reprinted in C. Bradley Thompson, ed., *Anti-Slavery Political Writings, 1833–1860* (New York: Routledge, 2015), 144–58.
11. Phan, *Bonds*, 2.
12. Phan, *Bonds*, 112.
13. Nabers, *Victory*, 194, viii.
14. Nabers, *Victory*, viii, and "The Meeting at Framingham," 106.
15. Hoang Gia Phan, "'A Race So Different': Chinese Exclusion, the *Slaughterhouse Cases*, and *Plessy v. Ferguson, Labor History* 45.2 (2004), 133–63, 134.
16. Eric Foner, *Reconstruction: America's Unfinished Revolution, 1863–1877* (New York: Harper & Row, 1988), 257–58.
17. Foner, *Reconstruction*, 527, 529.
18. Jeannine DeLombard, "The Novel and the Reconstruction Amendments," in *The American Novel, 1870–1940*, eds. Priscilla Wald and Michael Elliott (Oxford: Oxford University Press, 2014), 74.
19. DeLombard, "The Novel," 75.
20. Brook Thomas, ed., *Plessy v. Ferguson: A Brief History with Documents* (Boston: Bedford/St. Martin's, 1997).

21. Pauline Hopkins, *Contending Forces: A Romance Illustrative of Negro Life North and South* (New York: Oxford University Press, 1988), 297.

22. DeLombard, "The Novel," 76.

23. Brook Thomas, *The Literature of Reconstruction: Not in Plain Black and White* (Baltimore, MD: Johns Hopkins University Press, 2017), 13.

24. Joshua Paddison, *American Heathens: Religion, Race, and Reconstruction in California* (Berkeley: University of California Press, 2012).

25. Foner, *Reconstruction*, 258; and Gerald Neuman, *Strangers to the Constitution: Immigrants, Borders, and Fundamental Law* (Princeton, NJ: Princeton University Press, 1996), 170.

26. Carrie Hyde, *Civic Longing: The Speculative Origins of US Citizenship* (Cambridge, MA: Harvard University Press, 2018), 3.

27. Hyde, *Civic Longing*, 181.

28. Thomas, *Plessy*, 58.

29. Phan, "'A Race,'" 133.

30. Claire Jean Kim, "The Racial Triangulation of Asian Americans," *Politics & Society* 27 (1999), 105–38, 107.

31. Mae M. Ngai, "Birthright Citizenship and the Alien Citizen," *Fordham Law Review* 75 (2007), 2521–30, 2523.

32. Kornel Chang, "Enforcing Transnational White Solidarity: Asian Migration and the Formation of the US-Canada Boundary," *American Quarterly* 60.3 (2008), 671–96, 679.

33. Edward J. W. Park and John S. W. Park, *Probationary Americans: Contemporary Immigration Policies and the Shaping of Asian American Communities* (New York: Routledge, 2005), 4.

34. Phan, "'A Race,'" 150, 152; and Mae M. Ngai, *Impossible Subjects: Illegal Aliens and the Making of Modern America* (Princeton, NJ: Princeton University Press, 2004), 11, 12.

35. Claudia Sadowski-Smith, "Unskilled Labor Migration and the Illegality Spiral: Chinese, European, and Mexican Indocumentados in the United States, 1882–2007," *American Quarterly* 60.3 (2008), 779–804, 780.

36. Grace Delgado, *Making the Chinese Mexican: Global Migration, Localism, and Exclusion in the US-Mexico Borderlands* (Palo Alto, CA: Stanford University Press, 2012), 77.

37. Erika Lee, *The Making of Asian America: A History* (New York: Simon & Schuster, 2015), 192.

38. Lee, *The Making of Asian America*, 192.

39. Erika Lee, "Immigrants and Immigration Law: A State of the Field Assessment," *Journal of American Ethnic History*, 18.4 (1999), 85–114, 86.

40. Julian Ralph, "The Chinese Leak," *Harper's New Monthly Magazine* (December 1, 1890), 515–25.

41. Scott D. Seligman, *The First Chinese American: The Remarkable Life of Wong Chin Foo* (Hong Kong: University of Hong Kong Press, 2013), 235–37; Mary Chapman, "Introduction" in *Becoming Sui Sin Far: Early Fiction,*

Journalism, and Travel Writing by Edith Maude Eaton, ed. Mary Chapman (Montreal: McGill-Queen's University Press, 2016), xiii–lxxvi.

42. Claudia Sadowski-Smith, *Border Fictions: Globalization, Empire, and Writing at the Boundaries of the United States* (Charlottesville: University of Virginia Press, 2008), 48.

43. Crystal Parikh, *Writing Human Rights: The Political Imaginaries of Writers of Color* (Minneapolis: University of Minnesota Press, 2017), 4.

44. Theodore Roosevelt, "Fifth Annual Address" (December 15, 1905), www .presidency.ucsb.edu/ws/index.php?pid=29546, accessed March 1, 2018.

45. Mae M. Ngai, "Western History and the Pacific World," *Western Historical Quarterly* 43.3 (2012), 282–88, 288.

46. See Jean Pfaelzer, *Driven Out: The Forgotten War against Chinese Americans* (Berkeley: University of California Press, 2008).

47. Elliott Young, *Alien Nation: Chinese Migration in the Americas from the Coolie Era through World War II* (Chapel Hill: University of North Carolina Press, 2014), 129.

48. Lee, *The Making of Asian America*, 192.

49. Seligman, *The First Chinese American*, 236.

50. Seligman, *The First Chinese American*, 236.

51. Lisa Rose Mar, *Brokering Belonging: Chinese in Canada's Exclusion Era, 1885–1945* (Oxford: Oxford University Press, 2010), 4.

52. See Hsuan L. Hsu, "Wong Chin Foo's Periodical Writing and Chinese Exclusion," *Genre* 39.3 (2005), 83–106.

53. Seligman, *The First Chinese American*, 187.

54. Seligman, *The First Chinese American*, 187, 190–91.

55. Seligman, *The First Chinese American*, 189.

56. Wong Chin Foo, "High and Low Life in China," *The Colorado Magazine* 1.4 (1893), 356–59, 356.

57. Wong, "High and Low Life in China," 356–59, 356.

58. Wong, "High and Low Life in China," 356–59, 356.

59. Hyde, *Civic Longing*, 8.

60. Dominika Ferrens, *Edith and Winnifred Eaton: Chinatown Missions and Japanese Romances* (Champaign: University of Illinois Press, 2002), 185–86.

61. Amy Ling and Annette White-Parks, eds., *Mrs. Spring Fragrance and Other Writings* (Champaign: University of Illinois Press, 1995), 202.

62. Hyde, *Civic Longing*, 9.

63. Mary Chapman, ed., *Becoming Sui Sin Far: Early Fiction, Journalism, and Travel Writing by Edith Maude Eaton* (Montreal: McGill-Queen's University Press, 2016), 85.

64. Lee, *The Making of Asian America*, 197.

65. Douglas S. Massey, "Foreword," in *Smuggled Chinese: Clandestine Immigration to the United States*, by Ko-Lin Chin (Philadelphia: Temple University Press, 1999), ix–xiii, xii.

66. Edith Maude Eaton, "Chinese Visitors," *Montreal Daily Star* (July 6, 1895), reprinted in Chapman, *Becoming Sui Sin Far*, 58.

67. Sui Sin Far [Edith Maude Eaton], *Mrs. Spring Fragrance and Other Writings*, eds. Amy Ling and Annette White-Parks (Champaign: University of Illinois Press, 1995), 94.

68. Far, *Mrs. Spring Fragrance*, 94.

69. Far, *Mrs. Spring Fragrance*, 94.

70. Far, *Mrs. Spring Fragrance*, 94.

71. Far, *Mrs. Spring Fragrance*, 101.

72. Far, *Mrs. Spring Fragrance*, 101.

73. Eaton, "Chinese Visitors," 58.

74. Mary Chapman, "Introduction," in *Becoming Sui Sin Far: Early Fiction, Journalism, and Travel Writing by Edith Maude Eaton*, ed. by Mary Chapman (Montreal: McGill-Queen's University Press, 2016), xiii–lxxvi, xxxviii.

75. Patrick Ettinger, *Imaginary Lines: Border Enforcement and the Origins of Undocumented Immigrants, 1882–1930* (Austin: University of Texas Press, 2010), 7, 8.

76. In 1896, he was arrested for smuggling three Chinese from Montreal to upper New York State in the bottom of a lumber wagon. Twenty years later, Edward was again arrested for conspiring to smuggle Chinese into the United States (Chapman, "Introduction," xxvi).

77. Chapman, "Introduction," xxvi.

78. Edith Eaton, "The Smuggling of Tie Coe," in *Mrs. Spring Fragrance*, ed. Hsuan Hsu (Toronto: Broadview Press, 2011), 133.

79. Edith Eaton [Sui Sin Far], "Woo-Ma and I," *The Bohemian* 10 (January 1906), reprinted in Chapman, *Becoming Sui Sin Far*, 196.

80. Eaton, "Tian Shan's Kindred Spirit," in Hsu, *Mrs. Spring Fragrance*, 155.

81. Edith Eaton [Sui Sin Far], "The Chinese in America, Part III," in Ling and White-Parks, *Mrs. Spring Fragrance*, 247.

82. Parikh, *Writing Human Rights*, 40.

83. Edith Eaton [E.E.], "A Plea for the Chinaman: A Correspondent's Argument in His Favour," *Montreal Daily Star* (September 12, 1896), reprinted in Chapman, *Becoming Sui Sin Far*, 89.

84. "Trump Make America Great Again! Immigration Reform That Will Make America Great Again," retrieved February 6, 2019, from https://assets .donaldjtrump.com/Immigration-Reform-Trump.pdf.

85. "Trump Make America Great Again!"

86. Peter H. Schuck and Rogers M. Smith, *Citizenship without Consent: Illegal Aliens in the American Polity* (New Haven, CT: Yale University Press, 1985).

87. Neuman, *Strangers*, 167.

88. *Dred Scott v. Sandford*, 60 US 393, 416, 407 (1856).

89. Ed Hornick, "Is the Next Immigration Fight Over 'Anchor Babies'?" CNN .com (April 28, 2011), www.cnn.com/2011/POLITICS/04/28/anchor.baby/ index.html, accessed February 6, 2019.

90. In 2016, Arizona announced the end to its practices of requiring police officers to demand the papers of individuals suspected of being illegal immigrants in a settlement with the National Immigration Law Center and other immigrants' rights groups that brought suit after passage of SB 1070.

91. Devon W. Carbado, "Racial Naturalization," *American Quarterly* 57.3 (2005), 633–58, 638.

92. Lucy Salyer, *Laws Harsh as Tigers: Chinese Immigrants and the Shaping of Modern Immigration Law* (Chapel Hill: University of North Carolina Press, 1995), 250.

93. Ruth Rubio-Marin, "Introduction: Human Rights and the Citizen/Noncitizen Distinction Revisited," in *Human Rights and Immigration*, ed. Ruth Rubio-Marin (Oxford: Oxford University Press, 2014), 1–18, 2.

94. Rubio-Marin, "Introduction," 2.

95. Lauren Gambino, "'No Human Being Is Illegal': Linguists Argue Against Mislabeling of Immigrants," *The Guardian* (December 6, 2015), www.theguardian.com/us-news/2015/dec/06/illegal-immigrant-label-offensive-wrong-activists-say, accessed November 16, 2021.

96. Parikh, *Writing Human Rights*, 1.

97. Ngai, *Impossible Subjects*, 230.

98. Martha S. Jones, *Birthright Citizenship: A History of Race and Rights in Antebellum America* (Cambridge: Cambridge University Press, 2018), 15.

99. Thoreau, "Slavery in Massachusetts," 116.

PART III

Contending Forces

It is not surprising that the period following the Civil War would be a decisive and divisive era in American literary history, representing regional tensions and imagined national reunions, and not only representing but actively promoting white racial fantasies and fears. Writers representing every racial community in the United States worked to account for the complex possibilities and heightened racial tensions that followed the war – the possibility of hope joined with the very real presence of a white reign of terror, with lynching becoming an increasingly visible reality nationwide. The essays in this section offer an overview of some of the writers who responded to the possibility of a new nation emerging from the Civil War, along with the traces of the old nation pressing for ongoing struggles and racial domination. Sarah E. Gardner guides us into this troubled era by focusing on a group of prominent black and white writers who searched "for a narrative capable of accounting for the uncertainties and possibilities of their time." Most were unable to find or imagine such a narrative, but their inability to do so is itself revealing, as Gardner explains in an essay that explores the work of writers who tried "to imagine a different future, one that broke with the nation's history of continued abrogation of the principles laid out in the Declaration of Independence." John Grammer brings us to a different group of writers, white Southerners who were deeply invested in addressing the place of race in the recon-structed United States. Their approaches were driven from a range of social visions, from a belief in equal social and political rights to openly white supremacist control. The literature that resulted from this ideological spectrum through which Grammer carefully guides us produced some of the most lasting and damaging stereotypes of African Americans ever committed to the printed page, supporting visions of the terms of national social order that are still troubling America's political climate today. In effect, both Gardner and Grammer explore issues of belonging – how to think of the national community – and Stephanie Foote extends that exploration to regionalism, with writers "trying to work through ideas about who belongs to a particular region or place, and who had the right to define and speak for it." For Foote, regionalism can involve "limits" and "regulations," as well as "methods of exclusion and . . . fantastical, never-fulfilled promises." But regionalism can also offer ways of challenging established ideas of community. Indeed, Foote is interested in "how regional literature imagined race and how black writers found in its form and its conventions a way to enter the literary conversation." Race is central to this genre, Foote argues, in ways that complicate our under-standing of not only specific regions but also the concepts of national identity that both contain and, in some ways, are contained by regional visions. As Gardner, Grammer, and Foote all demonstrate, such national visions were deeply dependent on how race was represented in literature, and how narratives of the national community accounted for that systemic racial dynamic.

CHAPTER 7

Reconstructing Race

Sarah E. Gardner

In early February 1866, Charles Sumner, the indefatigable radical Republican senator from Massachusetts, delivered a lengthy speech on equal rights by noting Congress's obligation to enact legislation designed to "'effectuate legitimate objects.'"[1] The "legitimate object" to which Sumner referred was the abolition of slavery. And if ever a constitutional provision needed teeth, the Thirteenth Amendment was it. The Civil Rights Act, which Congress had passed but President Andrew Johnson had vetoed, signaled one indication of Congress's commitment to immediate and uncompensated emancipation. But it alone was insufficient. Freedom needed to be backed up with political power. Congress need not consider another constitutional amendment; it merely needed to protect the one it had with "appropriate legislation." On this point, the Constitution was certain. What's more, Republicans had the might of Union victory behind them. As Sumner explained, "Even if the text were doubtful, the war made it clear." For nearly eight decades, the Constitution had "been interpreted for slavery." No more, Sumner declared: "From this time forward it must be interpreted, in harmony with the Declaration of Independence, so that Human Rights shall always prevail." The Constitution's commitment to equal rights represented the war's greatest victory. "It is nothing less than the Emancipation of the Constitution itself," Sumner proclaimed (27).

Here, Sumner pushed for a particular reading of the Confederacy's downfall, one that sought to reconcile the contradictions inherent in the nation's founding. By turning to an "emancipated" Constitution that now aligned with the principles set down in the Declaration of Independence, Sumner demanded justice predicated on an ethic of human rights.

More than two decades after Sumner delivered this address, Frances Ellen Watkins Harper, the nation's foremost black woman activist, called out the federal government for its failure to make good on its promise to protect its citizens from lynch mobs. "A government which can protect

and defend its citizens from wrong and outrage and does not is vicious,"
she accused. "A government which would do it and cannot," she decried,
"is weak." The cause is immaterial. Whether by viciousness or weakness,
Watkins Harper charged, there is "a lack of justice, and where this is
wanting, nothing can make up the deficiency."[2]

At the time Watkins Harper issued her indictment at a meeting of the
National Council of Women in 1891, she had been active in race and
gender politics for more than three decades. She is perhaps best known for
her 1892 novel *Iola Leroy, or Shadows Uplifted*, which, among other things,
countered the racialized tropes of late nineteenth-century plantation fiction that celebrated an imagined harmonious and organic relationship
between enslaver and enslaved.[3] Watkins Harper understood the ways in
which the Civil War and Reconstruction were sites of significant narrative
contests, and she participated in these literary clashes throughout the
second half of the nineteenth century. These battles were carried out in
scores of novels and in hundreds of stories published in popular magazines,
writings that are arguably central to any understanding of American
literary history but usually are represented by only a few canonical Civil
War novels, such as Stephen Crane's *Red Badge of Courage* (1895),
Thomas Nelson Page's *Red Rock* (1898), and Thomas Dixon Jr.'s *The
Clansman: A Historical Romance of the Ku Klux Klan* (1905).

These later writings, joined with exuberant efforts to mark the landscape
with monuments and the calendar with commemorative ceremonies, did
much to shape how Americans understood the Civil War and the possibilities for the nation following that harrowing episode. Race is at the
center of the many such writings, sometimes overtly, but almost always in
the background, the shadowy presence behind the reconciliation of white
Northerners and Southerners. Well before the moonlight and magnolia
school of Civil War fiction exerted its death grip on the postwar literary
imagination, however, an earlier contest waged that sought to set the terms
of the debate. Its participants were largely unsuccessful, for different
reasons and to greater or lesser degrees. Their missteps, their uncertainty,
and their unwillingness to see what Sumner pressed all Americans to see
highlight the reluctance, even among the most well intentioned, to sub-
scribe to Sumner's interpretation of the war's meaning.

The literary works of Rebecca Harding Davis, Louisa May Alcott,
William Wells Brown, and Frances Ellen Watkins Harper reveal their
search for a narrative capable of accounting for the uncertainties and
possibilities of their time. Each understood that genre, venue, and audience mattered. They used the literary marketplace strategically to influence

a collective, but still inchoate, understanding of the war's meaning. But their visions differed. Harding Davis was at best ambivalent. Alcott was steadier in her convictions, but the imperatives of the publishing world sometimes intruded on her literary imagination. Brown and Watkins Harper were more sure-footed, but even Brown's vision had its limits. This essay traces their attempts to imagine a different future, one that broke with the nation's history of continued abrogation of the principles laid out in the Declaration of Independence.

"Life in the Iron Mills," published in April 1861, earned Harding Davis her literary reputation. Championed by the luminaries of New England's literary set and pursued by publishers, Harding Davis accepted an exclusive seven-year contract, which she did not honor, with *The Atlantic Monthly*, the nation's premier literary journal. She initially welcomed the recognition the invitation signaled. Still, the fit between the author and the editorial board was not a neat one. As Susan Goodman has written, to Harding Davis, New England's literati "had a surprising innocence – not entirely benign."[4] As Harding Davis later recalled in her reminiscences, "While they thought they were guiding the real world, they stood quite outside of it, and never would see it as it was."[5] On no position was this disconnect more pronounced than on that of abolitionism, which the journal's founders championed but Harding Davis considered reckless. For Harding Davis, this question of who was inside history and who was out, who had the authority to narrate that history and who did not, and who had the courage to see and who looked away became a central concern of her Civil War–era fiction.

In 1862, Harding Davis penned three short stories for *The Atlantic Monthly* – "John Lamar," "David Gaunt," and "Blind Tom" – set during the Civil War. Each story, in greater or lesser measure, advances an argument about the war's origins and its ruinous effects. Harding Davis's narrators lay blame for the carnage squarely and equally with hotheaded secessionists and fiery abolitionists, whose irresponsible rhetoric and unyielding positions precipitated war. Too, each contends that war's destruction and devastation are total and complete, regardless of political loyalty. And each exposes slavery as a dehumanizing and brutal institution that had no place in the American republic.

Harding Davis credited her literary vision to the time she spent in both the slaveholding South and the free North. During the first half of the Civil War, Harding Davis lived in occupied territory; her house in Wheeling, Virginia, had a direct view of the Union Army's headquarters. Recently, scholars have highlighted her early life on the "borderlands." As one critic has observed, "The Civil War border states, much like today's border cultures, were a site where the lifeblood of two worlds merged to form a third country."[6] Harding Davis phrased it differently. She never suggested the contested region formed its own culture. But she did argue that it gave her a particular worldview, upon which she drew heavily to comment on the contemporary political and social scene.[7]

Like many antislavery advocates, Harding Davis was, in the words of Harris, "imperfect in her own attitudes about race" (292). That is putting it kindly. If she had found the magazine's editorial board naïve in its view of the war's causes, she shared its understanding of race. As Stephen Knadler argues, during the Civil War era, *The Atlantic Monthly*'s articles and short fiction "tended repeatedly to identify in the current national crisis the 'birth' of a new nation purified and united in its representative [i.e., Anglo-Saxon] character."[8] The final scene in "David Gaunt" illustrates this point, making clear that Harding Davis was more concerned about the liberation of western Virginia from the thralldom of the Confederacy than she was about the emancipation of the four million enslaved. The story's protagonist, Theodora, "is a half-Abolitionist herself," the narrator declares. She "knows her State will soon be free."[9] For Theodora, then, the reforging of the (white) republic centered on the states' liberation from slavery's tyrannical hold, not on the emancipation of the enslaved (420). Put another way, Harding Davis, like so many of her contemporaries, "imagined the Civil War as," in historian Elizabeth Varon's terms, "a war of deliverance, waged to deliver the South from the clutches of a conspiracy and to deliver to it the blessings of free society and of modern civilization."[10]

But emancipation of the enslaved came, and shortly after the war had ended Harding Davis began writing a novel about Reconstruction, titled *Waiting for the Verdict*. Harding Davis thought she understood what was at stake in the Civil War. She was less sure about Reconstruction. Harding Davis's initial willingness to contemplate the dehumanizing effects of two of the most powerful developments in mid-nineteenth-century America, namely, industrialization and mechanized warfare, contrasts sharply with her attempt to make sense of a world nearly ripped asunder. By 1867, Davis's gaze no longer penetrates; instead, it looks askance, diverted from the vexing questions that plagued a reconstituted nation. The very subject invited her to sit in judgment. And at the most fundamental level, the novel asked her to consider the nature of justice, who arbitrates it, and who is granted or denied it. Indeed, the novel's title signals to readers Harding Davis's inability to hold up her end of the bargain.

The novel's plot is complicated, at times convoluted. Davis needed a wide cast of characters, a variety of settings, and familiar themes of disguised and mistaken identities, forces inexorably bringing people together and pulling them apart, and convenient deaths when the direction in which the novel was headed proved uncomfortable. Davis approached the questions that faced the nation but then retreated, writing herself out of the morass by falling back on tropes familiar to mid-nineteenth-century readers.

One example will suffice. Sap, a young mulatto slave, is purchased and then freed and educated by a Quaker woman, passes for white, renames himself John, and becomes a prominent Philadelphia surgeon. His position is threatened when Nathan, an escaped slave and John's long-lost brother, finds himself on John's operating table. In Harding Davis's eyes, John has two choices: kill his brother in order to protect his identity or acknowledge his lineage and accept his fate as a black man in Civil War–era America. The internal struggle lasts for five pages. "Why should he voluntarily drag the fate of his race upon him," John wondered. While gazing upon the sleeping Nathan, however, "the two paths of life opened clearly before him, and he made his choice. . . . 'Better be Sap in shambles," he said, than the trickster I have made of John Broderip." Whatever else happened in life, "in his soul he faced God, at last, an honest man."[11]

John's decision affects those around him, perhaps most especially the white woman whom he courted. More questions confront John. "What should he do with these treasures of luxury or art in this intolerable solitude to which he was hereafter condemned?" the narrator asks. "What should he do with the habits and tastes which he had painfully gained? He looked at the yellow skin of his wrist with a fierce loathing. It was an iron mask, that shut him in from all the hopes, the ambitions, the enjoyments of other men" (313). John could not answer these questions because Rebecca Harding Davis couldn't answer them. Better just to kill him off, which she does by having John enlist in the Union Army and dying heroically in battle. Doing so allowed Harding Davis to suggest that African Americans played a significant role in securing their own freedom, an important argument to make in 1867. But Harding Davis used John's heroic death to avoid other, perhaps more troubling, questions that centered on the black man's place in postwar America and whether freedom necessitated equality in public and private affairs. John had been poised to propose to a white woman before he was reunited with Nathan. Could Harding Davis have countenanced an interracial union? Could America? Rather than tackle the questions squarely, Harding Davis falls back on the trope of the tragic mulatto, albeit in a revised form. She had sacrificed John for the sin of slavery, but there is no sense of atonement. And by the novel's last paragraph, she had abdicated all responsibility, laying blame at the nation's doorstep: "Broderip, in his grave yonder, has not saved his people from their balked, incomplete lives. The country which he and they have served is still silent, while they stand waiting for its verdict" (361).

Rebecca Harding Davis had struggled mightily to pen a magnum opus but could not quite pull it off. The critical and ironic distance that marked her early writing was largely (although not wholly) absent in her novel. Harding Davis's failure to pen the novel she had envisioned had less to do with audience and plot than with her inability to imagine what postwar America should look like. She had understood war's carnage. But her understanding of emancipation was both narrow and cautious, and that kind of reading – one that was widely shared – undercut the kind of political work that abolitionists sought to achieve.

The limits of Harding Davis's literary vision become all the more apparent when read alongside the short fiction of Louisa May Alcott. In early 1860, in the wake of John Brown's Raid at Harpers Ferry and his subsequent trial and execution, Alcott finished drafting "M. L., An Abolitionist Tale." The story tells of a white woman who willingly, knowingly marries the mixed-race son of a Cuban planter and "a beautiful Quadroon."[12] Randall Fuller argues that "Louisa's new story was designed to shock the prudent."[13] Alcott, it seems, thought differently. *The Atlantic Monthly* refused to publish the story because, in Alcott's words, "'it is antislavery and the dear South must not be offended.'"[14] More than delicate sensibilities were on the line.

Alcott took her story elsewhere, eventually publishing it in the *Commonwealth*, a Boston abolitionist newspaper, in 1863. If Alcott could not place her story in the purportedly abolitionist literary monthly *The Atlantic*, admittedly the more prestigious publication, then the uncompromising *Commonwealth* was the more suitable venue. An editorial that ran in the paper's second issue simultaneously celebrated the eagerly anticipated preliminary Emancipation Proclamation and made clear the paper's stance: "[L]et us thank God for the opportunity, and ... by the purity of our own souls that the meanness and hypocrisy of seventy-five years, always increasing and always failing of its object, shall stop here; that not only the dear, grand old republic of our fathers shall be saved, but that it shall be saved most especially that it may do the justice which it ought from the first to have done, for dear justice's sake."[15] The *Commonwealth*, like Sumner three years later, had appealed to an ethic of human rights. So, too, had Alcott in her "abolitionist interracial romances." It is these stories, Sarah Elbert concludes, that Alcott's "boldest statements for human rights" appeared.[16]

To be sure, the story is a race melodrama, complete with disguised identities, denied patrimony, families ripped asunder, and secrets exposed. Paul, the formerly enslaved son of the Cuban planter, knows he must confess to his beloved Claudia the full story of his lineage, even though he fears her response. "Now, seeing what I have been, knowing what I desired to be, remembering mercifully what I am," he concluded, "try my crime and adjudge my punishment." He need not have worried. "Pride, and fear, and shame had dropped away," the narrator explains, leaving [Claudia's] purer passion free" (21). Warned of "social suicide" and "tormented" with "entreaties" and "reproaches," Claudia firmly rejects the limited vision of her friends and neighbors, accepting instead an ethic that "welcomed all humanity to its broad church" (27). Even Fuller conceded that Alcott's bold literary imagination envisioned "the slow unraveling of racial prejudice, the redemption of America through interracial love" (126). The nation, however, was hardly prepared to accept such a tale unless it "end [ed] in tragedy" (127).

If tales about interracial love were taboo, stories about heroic African American soldiers did sell, at least in some circles. Like Harding Davis, the formerly enslaved William Wells Brown also wrote about the sacrifice of black troops to the Union war effort. Unlike Harding Davis, however, Brown need not wait for the verdict. Acutely aware that white America had already passed judgment, Brown sought to expose the hollowness of the nation's narrow reading of Union victory by writing a new narrative of the war.

In 1867, the same year that *Waiting for the Verdict* appeared in serial form, Brown reworked his 1853 novel *Clotel: or, The President's Daughter*, for a third time. The first and most well-known version offered a fictionalized account of Sally Hemmings and her two daughters, fathered by Thomas Jefferson. Originally published in London, *Clotel* sought to expose the violence wrought by slavery; in particular, it highlighted the horrors of the domestic slave trade. Brown first revised his novel, which appeared as *Miralda: or, The Beautiful Quadroon*, for Thomas Hamilton's *Weekly Anglo-African* from December 1860 to March 1861. A few years later, amidst the Civil War's bloodiest campaigns, Brown "repackaged" his revised novel as *Clotelle: A Tale of the Southern States*, this time as a dime novel for abolitionist James Redpath's "Books for Campfire" series. As Sara

N. Roth has observed, the three iterations were thus pitched to different readerships at "critically different times" – British reformers during the 1850s, "black New Yorkers during the secession crisis and Union soldiers, primarily white men, at the height of the bloody Civil War."[17] In 1867, Brown rewrote his novel yet a third time, now targeted to a postwar reading audience, appending to the wartime edition additional chapters that centered on an African American soldier's contribution to Union victory.

By the time Brown published the re-revised novel, he had already embarked on a project that served a similar purpose. Six months earlier, Brown had published *The Negro in the American Rebellion*. Brown confessed his "desire to preserve for future reference" the part played by the enslaved and free people of color in "suppressing the Slaveholders' Rebellion."[18] Knowing his credibility was on the line, Brown carefully explained his methodology. "In collecting facts connected with the Rebellion," he explained, "I have availed myself of the most reliable information that could be obtained from newspaper correspondents, as well as from those who were on the battle-field." He thanked the officers and the enlisted men "of the several colored regiments" who furnished him with "detailed accounts of engagements" (v–vi.) Brown thus emphasized not only his work plan but also the reliability of his sources, even if they often remain unattributed. In so doing, he positioned himself as a collator and an interpreter of the evidence. As John Ernest has noted, Brown had "deliberately mixed documentary and non-documentary sources." In an effort "to address white supremacist culture's persistent misrepresentation of African-American experience, Brown amplified the documentary practice of antebellum Abolitionist newspapers," Ernest explained, "which had frequently reprinted articles from other papers, sometimes without comment so as to allow readers to sift truth from reportorial framing."[19] Brown never was interested in scrupulous documentation. Nor was he particularly interested in evaluating evidence. He was, however, interested in having his say.

Taken together, these two works sought to write African American men into the national narrative about Union victory. Brown had made a number of significant revisions to the subsequent editions of *Clotel(le)*, including the creation of Jerome, a slave purchased by Clotelle's owner. Unlike the mulatta women who occupy much of this novel, Jerome was "of pure African origin, was perfectly black, very fine-looking, tall, slim, and erect as anyone could possibly be." More than aesthetically pleasing, Jerome was "brave and daring, strong in person, fiery in spirit, yet kind and true in his affections, earnest in his doctrines."[20] What had been absent in the original text, a heroic slave, was now present. And what was important for the intended audience of the 1860–61 edition – African American subscribers to the *Weekly Anglo-African* – and for the Union soldier readers of the 1864 dime novel edition became critical to the imagined readers of the 1867 edition.

In all three of the subsequent editions, Jerome had condemned the chattel principle that governed American slavery and offered a powerful defense of liberty. Prophetically, he announces that the day will soon come when "the negro will learn that he can get his freedom by fighting for it" (65). Brown had written this scene during the secession crisis of 1860–61. Although he could not anticipate the formation of the US Colored Troops, he could, along with many of his fellow abolitionists, hope for that day. The scene remained in the 1864 and 1867 editions. It is only in the last edition, however, that Jerome realizes that prophecy.

Jerome and Clotelle, now wealthy and free, arrive in occupied New Orleans just as General Benjamin Butler issues "General Order 63," which calls into service of the federal government a battalion of African American soldiers. Jerome enlists immediately. "The Native Guard did good service in New Orleans and vicinity," readers are told, "until ordered to take part in the siege at Port Hudson." Brown says little about the siege itself. He was more concerned with excoriating the commanding officer who sent Jerome, along with more than a dozen other black men, to his death. "There was," Brown wrote, "one scene, closing the first day's attack . . . which, while it reflects undying credit upon the bravery of the negro, pays but a sorry tribute to the humanity of the white general who brought the scene into existence." The commanding officer ordered four men – four black men – to retrieve the body of a fallen US soldier. Because the body was positioned "directly under the range of the rebel batteries," the four men "were all swept down by the grape, canister, and shell . . . let loose by the enemy." Three more times the commanding officer ordered four men to retrieve the body. In this last effort only two men were killed. "Of these," Brown told, "one was Jerome," "the hero of our story." His death was gruesome and, Brown suggests, utterly unnecessary. Jerome's "head was entirely torn off by a shell. The body of the deceased officer having been rescued, an end was put to the human sacrifice" (105–6).

Brown had devoted considerably more space to the siege at Port Hudson in his study of African American participation in the Civil War. The sentiment was similar but amplified. The men of the First Regiment, Brown explained, "were composed mostly of freedmen, many whose backs still bore the marks of the lash, and whose brave hearts beat high at the thought that the hour had come when they were to meet their proud and unfeeling oppressors." When confronted with the question of whether anything other than the slaughter of African American soldiers had been accomplished, Brown answered with a resounding yes. "The self-forget-fulness," he asserted, "the undaunted heroism, the great endurance of the negro . . . created a new chapter in American history for the colored men" (172). As in *Clotelle*, Brown readily acknowledged the pervasive racism that had infected the ranks of white Union soldiers. To emphasize this point, Brown concluded the chapter with the admonition that "humanity should not forget, that, at the surrender of Port Hudson, not a single colored man could be found alive" (175–76).

But that sacrifice served a greater good, namely, Union victory coupled with emancipation. Brown concluded his chapter on Port Hudson not with the slaughter of African American troops but with the effusive praise offered by the Northern press that Brown had strung together at the end of the chapter. Brown froze this moment in time. Harding Davis had, if only briefly, contemplated the uncertainty that followed the heady optimism of Union victory. Neither she nor the characters who populate her novel can imagine a path forward. But Brown never makes it that far. Instead, he stops with noble sacrifice and Northern recognition of African American participation in the war effort. Unable to imagine a new future and unwilling to acknowledge the limits of Northern support for Reconstruction, Brown suspends time in this moment of possibility that has yet to be fully realized.

Two years later, Frances Ellen Watkins Harper published *Minnie's Sacrifice* as a serialized novel in the *Christian Recorder*, the official organ of the African Methodist Episcopal (AME) Church. The paper began publishing under that banner in 1854 with the mission to disseminate "religious knowledge and general intelligence among the colored people in all parts of this country."[21] Her decision to publish in the *Recorder* thus says a great deal about her intended audience, for it signals her commit-ment to the black press and to black readers.[22] As literary scholar Frances Smith Foster argued, Watkins Harper did not intend her serialized novels "to convert and convict readers outside of the African American culture." *Minnie's Sacrifice* thus "speak[s] about and to African Americans them-selves" (xxviii).

Like Harding Davis, Alcott, and Brown, Watkins Harper borrowed from established literary themes, including that of the "tragic mulatto." *Minnie's Sacrifice* centers on two light-skinned enslaved children, Louis and Minnie, both of whom were the offspring of a white enslaver and his slave. Both children were independently sent North by sympathetic Southerners who found their presence on Southern plantations unsettling. Eventually, their racial identities are discovered, and the two characters are forced, again independently, to decide whether they should pass as white or cast their lot with the race assigned to them by law. Fortune brings Minnie and Louis together. The two marry and, after the war, return to the South in order to work on behalf of their race.

Unlike Harding Davis's character, Sap/John Broderip, Minnie never agonized over her decision. To Louis's mother, Minnie confesses, "having passed most of my life in white society, I did not feel that the advantages of that society would have ever paid me for the loss of my self-respect, by passing as white when I knew I was colored; when I knew that any society, however cultivated, wealthy, or refined, would not be a social gain to me, if my color and not my character must be my passport to admission. So," she continues, "when I found out that I was colored, I made up my mind that I would neither be pitied nor patronized by my former friends, but that I would live out my own individuality and do so for my race, as a colored woman" (72). Harding Davis might have assumed that African Americans lived "balked, incomplete lives." Watkins Harper most assuredly did not.

Minnie dies at the end of the novel, but she is not the martyr figure sacrificed to expiate the sins of the nation. She dies because America is a violent place for African Americans. Louis survives, but he is not particularly sanguine about the nation's future. "The times were evil," Watkins Harper wrote near the end of the novel, "and the days were very gloomy." She then catalogued the myriad ways in which the United States had abandoned African Americans. Louis tried to buoy the spirits of the freedmen whom he counseled: "We must trust and hope for better things" (86). But the words sounded hollow to his ears. The federal government proved powerless to stem the violence in the defeated South. If mob rule reigned, then perhaps American civilization had failed. And yet Louis continued. "Life with its solemn responsibilities still met him; its earnest duties still confronted him, and though he sometimes" longed to join Minnie in death, he "knew it was his work to labor and wait" (89). Labor and wait. Louis understood that change could not come without human action. But he also knew that change would not come quickly. And so Louis would "labor and wait until peace . . . should descend where carnage had spread ruin around, and freedom and justice . . . should reign triumphant where violence and slavery had held their fearful carnival of shame and crime for ages" (90).

Watkins Harper concluded her story by directly addressing readers of the *Christian Recorder.* "The lesson of Minnie's sacrifice is this," she explains, "that it is braver to suffer with one's own branch of the human race ... than to attempt to creep out of all identity with them ... for the sake of personal advantages" (91). *Minnie's Sacrifice* is a cautionary tale, one that promoted racial solidarity, self-help, and faith in God as the only path to justice.

Throughout the 1860s, Charles Sumner still held out hope that the nation would make good the principles articulated in the Declaration of Independence. In no other time had the nation been better positioned to commit fully to an ethic of human rights than the immediate postwar period, Sumner believed. But that moment was threatened by measures that sought to circumscribe the meaning of freedom. One of the proposed modifications of what would become the Fourteenth Amendment included a provision that allowed for the denial of the right of suffrage based on race or color. Sumner was incensed. "After the lapse of genera-tions, when our obligations have increased," he railed, "at an epoch of history when mankind are more than ever before sensitive to the claims of human rights—and when among ourselves there is more than ever before a desire and a duty to fulfill all the promises of the Declaration of Independence, we are invited to make the Constitution slap the Declaration of Independence in the face."[23] Should Congress adopt this measure, Sumner accused, "you will be little better than the Harpies who defiled the feast that was spread. The Constitution is the feast spread for our country," Sumner wailed, and members of Congress were poised to insert "a political obscenity" in it (6).

Sumner had repeatedly advocated an interpretation of the Constitution that was predicated on the Declaration as a way out of the world both created and exposed by the Civil War. Harding Davis resisted that narra-tive framework. So too did Brown, who seemed to embrace a transactional form of justice: Black men die for the nation and the nation rewards us for our service. But even he seemed skeptical of such a reading. Both *Clotel(le)* and *The Negro in the American Rebellion* suggest that Brown distrusted any stable narrative framework but nonetheless insisted on being a part of the conversation. Alcott imagined sympathy and love could foster an ethic of human rights, a proposal more radical than anything put forward by Sumner. Watkins Harper used her Reconstruction-era fiction to call on the African American community to secure its own future. Her vision most closely aligned with Sumner's. And like Sumner, she feared that white Americans could not interpret their historical moment. "[S]lavery had cast such a glamour over the Nation," she wrote in her 1892 novel *Iola Leroy; or, Shadows Uplifted*, "and so warped the consciences of men, that they failed to read aright the legible transcript of Divine retribution which was written on the shuddering earth, where the blood of God's poor children had been as water freely spilled."[24] But she held out hope. Watkins Harper wrote *Iola Leroy* for a broad audience, believing it would serve its purpose if it fostered "in the hearts of our countrymen a stronger sense of justice and a more Christianlike humanity."[25] The legible transcript is still waiting to be read.

Notes

1. Charles Sumner, "The Equal Rights of All; The Great Guarantee and Present Necessity, for the Sake of Security, and to Maintain a Republican Government" (Washington, DC: Congressional Globe Office, 1866), 27.
2. Frances Ellen Watkins Harper, speech, in Rachel F. Avery, ed., *Transactions of the National Council of Women of the United States, Assembled in Washington, D.C. on Feb. 22–25, 1891* (Philadelphia: J. B. Lippincott, 1891), 87.
3. See Koritha Mitchell, "Introduction," in *Iola LeRoy, or Shadows Uplifted* by Frances E. W. Harper, ed. Koritha Mitchell (Peterborough, Ontario, Canada: Broadview Press, 2018), 27.
4. Susan Goodman, *Republic of Words: The Atlantic Monthly and Its Writers, 1857–1925* (Lebanon, NH: University Press of New England, 2011), 18. Subsequent references to this work are given in the text.
5. Rebecca Harding Davis, *Bits of Gossip* (Boston: Houghton Mifflin, 1904), 37–38. Subsequent references to this work are given in the text.
6. Gloria Anzadula, quoted in Sharon M. Harris, "The Anatomy of Complicity: Rebecca Harding Davis, *Peterson's Magazine*, and the Civil War," *Tulsa Studies in Women's Literature* 30 (2011), 292. Subsequent references to this work are given in the text.
7. See Harding Davis, *Bits of Gossip*, 165–66.
8. Stephen Knadler, "Miscegenated Whiteness: Rebecca Harding Davis, the 'Civil-izing' War, and Female Racism, *Nineteenth-Century Literature* 57 (2002), 79–80.
9. [Rebecca Harding Davis], "David Gaunt," *The Atlantic* 10.60 (1862), 420.
10. Elizabeth R. Varon, *Armies of Deliverance: A New History of the Civil War* (New York: Oxford University Press, 2019), 2.
11. Rebecca Harding Davis, *Waiting for the Verdict* (New York: Sheldon & Company, 1868), 304. Subsequent references to this work are given in the text.
12. Louisa May Alcott, "M. L.," in *Louisa May Alcott on Sex, Race, and Slavery*, ed. Sarah Elbert (Boston: Northeastern Press, 1997), 17. Subsequent references to this work are given in the text.

13. Randall Fuller, *The Book That Changed America: How Darwin's Theory of Evolution Ignited a Nation* (New York: Viking, 2017), 122. Subsequent references to this work are given in the text.

14. Alcott, quoted in Elbert, "Introduction," x.

15. Moncure Daniel Conway, "The Question of War," *Commonwealth*, 1.2, (September 13, 1862), 2.

16. Elbert, "Introduction," x.

17. Sarah N. Roth, *Gender and Race in Antebellum Popular Culture* (New York: Cambridge University Press, 2014), 220, fn. 32. See also Lara Langer Cohen, "Notes from the State of Saint Domingue: The Practice of Citation in Clotel, in *Early African American Print Culture*, eds. Lara Langer Cohen and Jordan Alexander Stein (Philadelphia: University of Pennsylvania Press, 2012), 161–77.

18. William Wells Brown, *The Negro in the American Rebellion: His Heroism and His Fidelity* (Boston: Lee and Shepard, 1867), v. Subsequent references to this work are given in the text.

19. See John Ernest, "The Negro in the American Rebellion: William Wells Brown and the Design of African American History," in *Literary Cultures of the Civil War*, ed. Timothy Sweet (Athens: University of Georgia Press, 2016), 59.

20. William Wells Brown, *Clotelle; or, the Colored Heroine: A Tale of the Southern States* (Boston: Lee and Shepard, 1867), 57–58. Subsequent references to this work are given in the text.

21. Elisha Weaver, quoted in Eric Gardner, *Black Print Unbound: The Christian Recorder, African American Literature, and Periodical Culture* (New York: Oxford University Press, 2015), 74.

22. Frances Ellen Watkins Harper, *Minnie's Sacrifice; Sowing and Reaping; Trial and Triumph: Three Rediscovered Novels by Frances E. W. Harper*, ed. Frances Smith Foster (Boston: Beacon Press, 1994), xxx. Subsequent references to this work are given in the text.

23. "Speech of the Hon. Charles Sumner of Massachusetts, on the Proposed Amendment to the Constitution Fixing the Basis of Representation; Delivered in the Senate of the United States Senate, March 7, 1866" (Washington, DC: Congressional Globe Office, 1866), 6. Subsequent references to this work are given in the text.

24. Frances E. W. Harper, *Iola LeRoy; or Shadows Uplifted*, ed. Koritha Mitchell (Peterborough, Ontario, Canada: Broadview Press, 2018), 72.

25. Harper, *Iola Leroy*, 251.

CHAPTER 8

Out of the Silent South
White Southerners Writing Race during the Long Reconstruction

John Grammer

I

The essay was called "The Silent South."[1] In it, the white New Orleans writer George Washington Cable – beloved for fictional works like *Old Creole Days* and *The Grandissimes* – extended the increasingly bold political argument about the South that he had been developing for about a decade. Almost alone in his region, Cable had called for the full legal and political equality of black Southerners. The claim of "The Silent South" was that a substantial part of the region's white population quietly agreed with him and, when they emerged from the stunned silence that had befallen them since the defeat of the Confederacy in 1865, would speak for a future of racial equality.

His confident claim about a progressive silent majority in the South was soon discredited by events. But the essay remains notable, especially for the way it begins. Cable recalls the bronze statue of Robert E. Lee that towered over New Orleans. This monument honored a Confederate warrior whose personal virtues Southerners revered and even Northerners tended to admire. But it did more: "lifted far above our daily strife of narrow interests and often narrower passions and misunderstandings," Cable explained, the statue "symbolizes our whole South's better self, that finer part which the world not always sees; unaggressive, but brave, calm, thoughtful, broad-minded, dispassionate, sincere, and, in the din of boisterous error around it, all too mute."[2] In "The Silent South," Cable attempted a kind of ventriloquism, supplying a voice for the mute bronze effigy of the white South's representative man. His essay tried to say what the region itself would say had it not been struck dumb by the traumas of war and Reconstruction.

Most white Southern writers in the years between Reconstruction and the early twentieth century were attempting something similar, giving voice to a people who, though voluble enough before the war, had fallen

133

into inarticulate bewilderment since Appomattox. What would the South say, especially about its defining circumstance, the racial situation?

As C. Vann Woodward has argued, the answer was not immediately obvious:

> In most parts of the South ... race relations during Reconstruction could not be said to have crystalized or stabilized nor to have become what they later became. There were too many cross currents and contradictions, revolutionary innovations and violent reactions.[3]

Though this process ended with the firm establishment of segregation and white supremacy, that conclusion did not seem inevitable in the 1860s, 1870s, 1880s, or even 1890s. The issues needed to be worked out, not only by political and judicial bodies but also in the minds of Southern people and the writers who tried to speak for them.

II

One of the first discoveries they made was that their region needed two voices, not one. The South could be made articulate only through a dialogue between voices represented as black and white. Much would depend on how those voices spoke and what they were allowed to say. Consider, for instance, one of the first Southern writers to try to represent such a racial dialogue, "the boy poet of Mississippi," Irwin Russell (1853–79). Inspired by the dialect verse of Robert Burns, he wrote poems in the voices of enslaved people such as the ones he had known as a child in Port Gibson, Mississippi, and by 1876 was publishing these in *Scribner's Monthly* (whose fascination with the South enabled much of the writing this essay will discuss). "Christmas-Night in the Quarters" (1878) was the most celebrated.

The poem describes Johnny Booker's Ball, a celebration by plantation slaves, who have been excused from labor because it is Christmas. In form it is a medley of voices: Several black speakers are introduced, then periodically interrupted, by a white narrator. Its energy arises almost entirely from the contrast between their racialized voices. The white speaker, self-consciously literary, strains for Augustan wit:

> Some take the path with shoes in hand,
> To traverse muddy bottom-land;
> Aristocrats their steeds bestride—
> Four on a mule, behold them ride![4]

But his pretentious archaism is really just the foil for the much more artful and inventive speech of the slaves, as when their spiritual leader, Brother Brown, asks God for a preemptive dispensation covering any sins that might be committed during the frolic:

> Remember, Mahsr,—min' dis, now,—de sinfulness ob sin
> Is pendin' 'pon de sperrit what we goes and does it in;
> An' in a righchis frame ob min' we's gwine to dance an' sing,
> A-feeling' like King David, when he cut de pigeon-wing...[5]

Soon the white speaker is lamenting that "[i]n this our age of printer's ink," educated people such as himself can speak only as books have taught them to, treating arbitrary regulations like the rules of grammar as though they were the dictates of Nature. The participants in the frolic, on the other hand, are "untrammeled" and "unrestrained."[6] The ultimate expression of black expressive freedom, and the most often anthologized part of Russell's poem, comes toward the end, when host Johnny Booker takes up a heretofore unheard instrument, enjoining an earlier musician to silence:

> Go 'way, fiddle! Folks is tired o' hearin' yu a-squawkin'.
> Keep silence fur yo' betters!—don't you heah de banjo talkin'?[7]

The lines that follow are a homemade myth about the origins of the banjo – but Russell, himself a banjo player, knew that the instrument's true origins were in Africa, and that it had reached the United States partly by way of revolutionary Haiti.[8] When the banjo silences the violin, the imaginative and possibly subversive challenge of African voices and cultures to European ones has gone as far as it can in Russell's poem.

How far is that? What exactly are we hearing when the banjo begins talking? Russell's conflation of black voices and black music may remind us of Eric Sundquist's claim that "[t]he problems of transcribing black language and black music are not, in fact, separable in the evolution of African American culture."[9] Russell's poems began appearing at nearly the same time that the Fisk Jubilee Singers emerged, performing a version of the vocal music of the enslaved. Both projects offered white audiences the chance to "overhear" a culture that usually lived out of earshot; both undoubtedly involved some pandering to racist expectations, inviting a measure of friendly condescension. But what else did they do? Does Russell's poetry, for instance, involve what Sundquist calls "the counterpossibility ... that black language was also the sign of a secret world kept out of range of the middle-class mind," a language that, "[i]n Ralph Ellison's powerful metaphor, ... spoke on 'lower frequencies'"?[10]

Russell's poems are probably too slight, and his career too short, to support any firm answer. After all, the stakes of "Christmas Night's" implied contest between black and white voices are cultural, not political; the white speaker's cheerful concession of black supremacy in imagination is enabled by his own unquestioned authority in other matters. On the other hand, the poem's unmasking of linguistic conventions – which seem natural but are exposed as arbitrary – might imply a similar vulnerability in other conventions claiming the authority of Nature, such as the ones governing race relations. In Russell's poem, freedom speaks with a black voice, not a white one. But the implication is left undeveloped in a poem that doesn't mind being taken as mere entertainment.

III

Thus, Russell's early effort to break the Southern silence (like the simultaneous efforts of Joel Chandler Harris of "Uncle Remus" fame, which a longer essay would treat in detail) might be considered tentative or transitional approaches to what came to be known, interchangeably, as "the Southern question," "the Negro question," or "the race question." When white Southern writers started attempting definitive answers, they needed more authority than the poem or sketch could give them. These Southerners may have been among the first American writers to recognize the cultural authority once held by verse would now belong to the novel. Most of them learned it in the same hard way, from an antebellum novel that – as Virginia writer Thomas Nelson Page conceded in an 1892 essay – had "touched the heart of Christendom," "overruled the Supreme Court of the United States, . . . abrogated the Constitution," and thus "contributed more than any other one thing to [slavery's] abolition."[11] The power of *Uncle Tom's Cabin* was something that no postbellum Southern writer could afford to ignore. They needed their answers to carry the kind of authority *Uncle Tom* had. They needed to touch hearts as well as change minds; they might need to overrule the Constitution and the Supreme Court as well. Harriet Beecher Stowe had shown them that it was possible, in the right kind of extended fiction, to do all that.

One way to think about the novels produced by white Southerners during the thirty years after Reconstruction is to employ the taxonomy the historian Joel Williamson developed in his classic study of Southern racial ideology, *The Crucible of Race*. White Southerners who addressed the issue after Reconstruction, Williamson argues, sorted themselves into three broad groups: Liberals, who felt that the role of black Southerners in the postwar world was uncertain and who were open to certain kinds of racial equality; Conservatives, who claimed a paternalistic affection for the formerly enslaved but were willing to tolerate them only as recognized subordinates; and Radicals, unapologetic racists for whom black Southerners had no legitimate place at all.[12] Each school of thought, as it happens, produced its own big book, its *Uncle Tom*–like attempt at a comprehensive and unanswerable statement.

The most prominent partisan of the "Liberal" position was George Washington Cable, who – after placing several New Orleans stories in *Scribner's* – undertook writing his first novel, *The Grandissimes*, in 1879. It would be a historical romance, set in New Orleans at the fateful moment in 1803–4 when the French colonial city passed into the control of Americans – but also a kind of period-dress allegory for Cable's own moment: "It was impossible that a novel written by me then should escape being a study of the fierce struggle going on around me," Cable recalled later. "I was still very slowly and painfully guessing out the riddle of our Southern question."[13] The novel's newly arrived Americans are in effect victorious Yankees; its proud, reactionary Creoles represent unregenerate Confederates; and its central consciousness, the idealistic but naïve merchant Joseph Frowenfeld, a recent immigrant who tries to read "the book . . . of New Orleans," is a version of Cable himself.[14]

The Grandissimes incorporates two distinct plot lines, loosely related but both about a community coming to terms with historical trauma. The more prominent of these, an entirely white story, concerns the ancient quarrel between two Creole families and its happy resolution by a marriage between the heroic and handsome scion of the Grandissimes and a beautiful widow of the deGrapions. This romance plot and the historical episode unfolding behind it – New Orleans's grudging accommodation to American rule – move forward in predictable tandem as enmity gives way to reconciliation and a comic ending. Cable's editors at *Scribner's* loved it, as did readers once it began appearing in 1879.

Nearly all the interest *The Grandissimes* has for us today, however, concerns what might be called its "second story," a network of subordinate plots that all concern the troubled racial situation of French Louisiana. These plots address the brutal legacy of slavery, the ambiguous status of formerly enslaved people, and the rigid and irrational workings of the color line. At the heart of this second plot is a story everyone in New Orleans seems to know, though they spend half the book withholding it from Joseph Frowenfeld and thus from the reader. It concerns their recent and traumatic memories of Bras Coupé, the gigantic and fearless African who was enslaved by members of the Grandissime family during the last years of French Colonial rule. The details of Bras Coupé's story – his physical and moral impressiveness, his impulsive assault on his enslaver and the terror it struck in the white population, his temporary freedom in the swamps, and his eventual capture, horrible mutilation, and death – preoccupy every significant character in the book.

But the novel does not locate all its traumas in the past or confine them to the institution of slavery. In *The Grandissimes* that problem lives not only in the community's half-repressed memories but also in the experiences of several present-day characters. The most important of these is Honoré Grandissime, a wealthy, Paris-educated gentleman whom Cable calls "the f.m.c." – the free man of color. The designation is needed to distinguish him from another character, the unquestionably white hero of the novel, who is *also* named Honoré Grandissime. The two are half-brothers, sons of the same father, who fell in love with a quadroon woman, fathered a child with her and gave that child his name, but then was forced by his family into a legal marriage with the mother of the white Honoré. The doubling of these characters italicizes the arbitrariness of the conventions that assign them to utterly different spheres of society: the white brother standing as its first citizen, and his identically cultivated sibling a barely tolerated pariah. We first hear of the f.m.c. as the guest who was slapped and expelled from a ball by a white man darker than himself. He finds a warmer welcome at Joseph Frowenfeld's shop, but he vanishes silently whenever a white customer enters. Though a prominent landlord, he communicates with his white tenants only in writing, his ghostly near-invisibility earning him the narrative tag "the rent-spectre."[15] A specter indeed, a ghostly reminder of inherited wrongs, as the bizarre workings of the color line are the ghostly survivals of slavery.

Cable's editor at *Scribner's* did his best to talk him out of this "second story." "Too much local color," Robert Underwood Johnson warned, by which he meant "descriptions of local ancestors and characters not necessary to the story which distract from the plot—the tendency to tell all the truth ... in other words a historical tendency."[16] As is often the way in conversations about the South, "history" here was code for race: Johnson meant that he and his readers wanted the white story of reconciliation, not the multiracial story of unresolved historical trauma. History, yes, but not the kind that tells "all the truth": a kind of remembering that depends on a kind of forgetting.

But Cable refused to grant his book or his readers such comforting amnesia. His refusal took the form of a pattern of allusions to *Uncle Tom's*

Cabin. The white Honoré Grandissime, for instance, recalls another idealistic young Creole who faced the task of righting historic wrongs – then shrank from it: "I can't turn knight-errant, and undertake to redress every individual case of wrong in such a city as this," Stowe's Augustine St. Clare confesses.[17] But Cable's Honoré, who literally enters the novel on horseback, is just the sort of knight-errant to undertake this redemptive task, trying single-handedly to resolve the conflicts in both the novel's racialized stories. After befriending the newly arrived Americans and reconciling with his ancient enemies, the deGrapions, he shocks his family by joining the f.m.c. in a business partnership known as "Grandissime Brothers." But if this revision of St. Clare grants him the energy and purpose the original tragically lacked, Cable does not thereby rescue his story about "the Southern question" from tragedy. Other migrants from Stowe's novel ensure this. Palmyre, a quadroon former slave, is as murderous as Simon Legree's mad concubine Cassy, attempting to assassinate her former enslaver on the streets of the city. But she does not experience any of the miraculous redemption that Cassy finds after the sacrificial death of Uncle Tom. Though she inherits sufficient wealth to leave New Orleans, Palmyre's benefactor is the tragic free man of color, who has committed suicide after a lifetime of exclusion and disappointment and despite his white brother's belated acknowledgment. And Bras Coupé is the double of Stowe's Scipio – a heroically rebellious slave who assaulted his overseer, fled to the swamps, was recaptured, and then converted to Christianity by a kind master. But Cable's heroic slave, tortured to death after a nearly identical rebellion, memorably refuses such assimilation; when the priest administering last rites asks him, "do you know where you are going?" he defiantly gasps, "to Africa."[18] Cable's allusions to *Uncle Tom's Cabin* emphasize his thematic departures from it. Thanks to its "second story," *The Grandissimes* refuses to be what Stowe's novel – with its miraculous reunions and resurrections, its reversals of tragic history – unapologetically is: a redemptive prophecy of American racial history. For Cable, such redemption occurs only in his white reconciliation romance – within, that is, the fantasy, monochromatic South his editors wished he'd stuck with.

There are, of course, Bras Coupé's last words. These, we might say, extend the rather tentative promise made by Irwin Russell's black banjoist – that a defiant Africana identity might be *heard* over the din of both white oppression and Christian sympathy. It is telling, though, that these four gasped syllables, *to Africa*, are the only memorable speech by a black character in Cable's novel. This isn't because the others lack tragic stature:

Palmyre in her rage and the f.m.c. in his sad dignity have equal moral authority. But they are linguistically helpless: Fluent only in French, they must now communicate in English, the mandatory language of commerce and the only language of their sympathizer, Frowenfeld; caught between the tongue of their old exploiters and that of their would-be redeemers, both are effectively silenced. Black voices in *The Grandissimes* are choked, halting, inhibited. Frowenfeld and Honoré can speak Cable's liberal ideals resonantly, but their voices alone cannot enact them. With racial dialogue thwarted, the novel ends with "the riddle of our Southern question" still unguessed.

Cable's doubtful take gained some plausibility just three years later, in 1883, when the US Supreme Court ruled in "the Civil Rights Cases." The Court found that the US Civil Rights Law of 1875, which had forbidden racial discrimination in public accommodations such as restaurants and streetcars, was unconstitutional: The Fourteenth Amendment had only forbidden discrimination by the government itself, leaving private enterprises free to follow local custom. The decision left "the Southern question" exactly where Cable's novel had: undecided and to be determined only by the consciences of Southern whites. His response came in his civil rights essays, the first of which appeared in *Century* magazine (the reborn *Scribner's*) in 1885. "The South stands on her honor before the clean equities of the issue," Cable wrote in "The Freedman's Case in Equity." "It is no longer whether constitutional amendments, but whether the eternal principles of justice, are violated. And the answer must—it shall—come from the South."[19]

IV

Of course he was right, and he hadn't long to wait. In fact, a year before it published "The Freedman's Case," *Century* had introduced the world to Thomas Nelson Page, the young Virginian who would emerge as the leading spokesman for the South's "Conservative" position. "Marse Chan," his first fictional effort, is the sad story of a noble-hearted Virginia boy, scion of a proud old family, who regretfully followed his state into the Confederacy and died in battle moments after receiving a letter from the belle back home, agreeing to marry him. We hear all this from his former slave Sam, who eagerly praises young Chan, his family, and the entire plantation system, to a visitor from the North: "Dem wuz good ole times, marster—de bes' Sam ever see!"[20] Though this utopia has been lost, its reputation is permanently secured by Sam's elegiac testimony.

That voice wrung infinite pathos out of white Southern trauma, touching the hearts of readers across the country (Thomas Wentworth Higginson, a militant abolitionist who had led a black regiment in the Union Army, was reportedly moved to tears).[21] *Century* eagerly solicited more of Page's stories and finally, through its book-publishing arm, Scribner Brothers, gathered them in Page's first book, *In Ole Virginia* (1887). A career had been launched and a literary formula established: the powerful compound that was formed when white pathos met black dialect, when white and black tears flowed together. Page had learned it, of course, from *Uncle Tom's Cabin*.

Page knew he must attempt his own big book, and by 1889 he had begun writing his first and – despite its many flaws – his most successful novel.[22] Finally published in 1898, *Red Rock* concerns the aristocratic Gray family and their struggle to resist Reconstruction and retain their ancestral plantation, Red Rock. At times, the book reads like the most wooden of allegories: What can one say about a novel that includes a parasitic carpetbagger named "Leech," a judge named "Bail," and an accountant named "Ledger"? Even the characters who rise above allegorical personification stall out at the level of cliché: dashing cavaliers and beautiful belles, virtuous yeomen who know how to defer to their aristocratic betters, virtuous ex-slaves who know how to defer to all white people, and morally confused *arrivistes* of both races who have never learned, and must be firmly taught, how to defer at all. They are joined by a white Confederate Uncle Tom, noble Dr. Cary, who sacrificially dies from exhaustion while trying to bind the wounds of his stricken Southern world.

But this is as it must be for the novel Page needed to write. For the narrative and political goal of *Red Rock* is not, as in *The Grandissimes*, to discover an unknown good, a racially just society. Rather, it is to *recover* a fully known though temporarily forgotten good, a hierarchical society in which everyone has, deserves, and accepts his or her place. Original or dynamic characters would be very unwelcome in such a narrative. The essential premise of the novel, as of the politics behind it, must be that identity and social placement are fixed and readily knowable. But what *is* one's place, and how can it be discerned?

The issue had become salient in the United States just two years before Page published *Red Rock*, when the US Supreme Court ruled in *Plessy* v. *Ferguson*. Homer Plessy was a black New Orleans man who had tested a new state law requiring segregated accommodations on railroad trains. He boarded a white car and, by prearrangement, was arrested for refusing to yield his seat. The issue in *Plessy* was whether the Fourteenth Amendment permitted a state to mandate separate, nominally "equal," accommodations for black and white citizens. The court held that the amendment had not required the integration of the races because "legislation is powerless to eradicate racial instincts or to abolish distinctions based upon physical differences."[23]

The trouble was that the differences between Plessy and the white passengers around him were not, or at least not visibly, "physical." Plessy was a man of mixed race who could easily pass for white; in order to be arrested, he had to identify himself as black to the unsuspecting conductor. How were "racial instincts" to assert themselves when the "physical differences" that assigned people to their social and physical places could be nearly invisible?

This seems to have been Page's major question in *Red Rock*, a novel short on action and even shorter on character development, whose principal scenes are nearly all moments of *recognition*. The book begins on an evening before the Civil War, when a party of Northern travelers in the "Red Rock district," lost in the darkness, are met by a Southern gentleman, Dr. Cary. He assures them that they will be welcomed for the night "at every house in the State" and certainly at the nearest, Red Rock. Then Dr. Cary explains to his traveling companions that the lost man he has spoken to, though invisible in the darkness, is "a gentleman by his voice," thus a worthy recipient of the region's hospitality.[24] The Southerners who welcome Major Welch and his party to Red Rock immediately affirm Dr. Cary's judgment, and the visitors in turn quickly recognize the nobility of their hosts; soon interregional friendships, and eventually romances, are formed that help turn the plot for the next 500 pages. And so it goes throughout the novel: The worthy characters of all classes and both regions, white and black, are able to *recognize* one another, to place one another socially, almost instantaneously.

The conflicts in the novel arise because, in the topsy-turvy world created by Reconstruction, disruptive characters, like Homer Plessy, keep trying to invade social and physical spaces that are properly beyond them. Hiram Still, once a mere overseer, becomes the temporary owner of Red Rock, evicting the Gray family. His despicable son "Washy" somehow becomes a doctor. Jonadab Leech of the Freedman's Bureau awards himself the spurious rank of "captain" because his job permits him to command troops. The formerly enslaved Moses exhorts his fellows to become voters and confesses even larger ambitions for himself: "I'm jest as good as any white man, and I'm goin' to show 'em so. I'm goin' to marry a white 'ooman and meck white folks wait on me."[25] Moses's ambition to "show" his detractors, to compel recognition of his merit, is the single and endlessly reiterated motive of every villain, white and black, in the book.

At one time, such pretentious antics would have been merely comic, a kind of cakewalk, easily exposed by genuine aristocrats like the Grays and the Carys. In several early scenes, we watch these worthies effortlessly humble their inferiors, often merely by "stiffening" or flaring a single nostril. But such social aikido has lost much of its effectiveness amid the democratic scramble of Reconstruction. Who can testify on behalf of the old hierarchies?

The author of "Marse Chan" knew the answer to this question. When Dr. Cary is hauled before "Captain" Leech on a frivolous charge, he must call on one of his old "servants" – of course named Tom – to corroborate his innocence. Tom is happy to oblige: "Yas, suh—I'll groberate ev'y wud you say—'cus I wuz dyah."[26] A bit later Leech and his minions invade Red Rock itself, supposedly searching for illicit weapons. The white mistress bears the insult in stoic silence, but another old "servant," Mammy Krenda, happily functions as the southern *id*, lashing out furiously at the invaders:

> "Yaas, I know jet what sort you is," she said, mockingly: "you is the sort o' houn'-dog that ain't got sperit enough to fight even a old hyah, let alone a coon. . ."[27]

Happy resolution of the novel's convoluted plot requires, for reasons too complicated to explain, a marriage between its white southern hero Steve Allen and his northern girlfriend Ruth Welch. But how can Ruth know that Steve is a worthy suitor? The necessary assurance, on which everything in *Red Rock* depends, comes from "Old Peggy," Steve's mammy, who pointedly informs the Yankee girl that he is "good 'nough for anybody. . .I held him in dese arms when he wa'n't so big. . .and I knows."[28] In *Red Rock*, Page imagines an infinitely virtuous society, rightfully ruled by white aristocrats, whose survival paradoxically depends on the dialect-speaking voices of its lowliest members. For a time, as in "Marse Chan," Page's black characters give the South its only voice.

In the end, of course, the novel's white aristocrats recover their voices, using them to expose the pretensions of the unworthy and restore, almost unchanged, the timeless order represented by Red Rock plantation. The novel can end when it has solved what the Atlanta journalist Henry Grady, in what became the South's quasi-official rebuttal to Cable's civil rights essays, had called the problem of "assortment": the establishment of a stable hierarchy that alone can permit the members of diverse races, classes, sexes, and regions to live together in what we are assured will be permanent harmony.[29]

V

The radical answer to "the Southern question" began appearing just four years after *Red Rock*, when Thomas Dixon Jr. (1864–1946) decided to become a novelist. The energetic North Carolinian had already run through brief careers as a lawyer, Baptist minister, graduate student in politics (Woodrow Wilson was a classmate), and public lecturer. It was during one of his lecture tours that he watched a play based on *Uncle Tom's Cabin*. He found it such an insult to his region that he immediately began crafting the rebuttal that would keep him occupied from 1902, when his first novel, *The Leopard's Spots*, appeared, until 1915, when his second, *The Clansman*, was filmed as *The Birth of a Nation*. *The Leopard's Spots* actually borrowed characters from Stowe – Simon Legree became a carpetbagger – but it was *The Clansman* (1905) that comprehensively stated Dixon's answer to "the Southern question."

Like *Red Rock*, *The Clansman* takes place mostly in the South during Reconstruction. The Cameron family of Piedmont, South Carolina, struggle to resist the injustices imposed by federal authority and now-empowered former slaves. Meanwhile, Congressman Austin Stoneman, the Radical Republican author of all those injustices, moves to Piedmont for his health, bringing his adult son and daughter. The congressman watches with perverse delight as his program turns the antebellum world upside down: Former slaves hold all political power while white men are whipped, chained, and have "no rights a negro need respect."[30] Meanwhile, his son, Phil, and daughter, Elsie, befriend the locals and, naturally, fall in love with the Cameron siblings, Margaret and Ben (the novel's hero and an eventual Ku Klux Klan leader). The outrages of Reconstruction multiply, culminating in the rape of young Marion Lenoir by the brutal ex-slave Gus, until the white community finally reacts in a spasm of righteous violence. As in *Red Rock*, the novel ends with the restoration of white supremacy and the expected interregional marriages.

But Dixon's Reconstruction isn't quite Page's. It is, for one thing, much simpler; whereas Page tries to sort his characters into a complex hierarchy of social ranks, Dixon recognizes only two, white and black. In *The Clansman*, race is the most fundamental human reality; acknowledging its primacy is each person's most urgent spiritual imperative.

Most in need of enlightenment on the matter is Congressman Stoneman, the only character in the novel granted any real complexity. Based on Thaddeus Stevens, with a bit of Milton's Satan thrown in, Stoneman is a brilliant, visionary, even poetic soul but also a damaged one, prone to the "Blue Devils" of depression and crippled by a birth defect, his club foot symbolizing his alienation from normal – that is, white – life.[31] So he has cultivated intimate relationships with several people of color, above all the mysterious Lydia Brown, "a mulatto, a woman of extraordinary animal beauty and the fiery temper of a leopardess," who keeps his house, screens his visitors, and apparently controls him with her erotic power.[32] Stoneman's tireless campaign to impose black rule on the South has wrecked his health, but upon examining him his physician is baffled by the physical and psychological symptoms he presents. Declaring his patient "the deepest mystery I've yet encountered," he nonetheless offers a prescription: "[Y]ou have but three months to live unless you go South and find a new life."[33]

The doctor's instinct is right. In Dixon's novel, the South functions as a vast sanatorium for the victims of racial confusion, a pathology that has apparently reached epidemic proportions in postbellum America. In fact, the real plot of *The Clansman* – notwithstanding its perfunctory courtships and its lurid scenes of black violence and white revenge – is the story of the racial rehabilitation of all its white characters, particularly the Northern visitors, an account of their slow movement toward the epiphany young Phil Stoneman will announce late in the book: "I am a white man."[34]

The other main difference between *The Clansman* and *Red Rock* is that the former is a much quieter book, with dialogue carrying very little thematic weight. Dixon's was mainly a visual imagination; his most urgent meanings are often communicated by silent tableaux, moments when the narrative momentarily freezes the characters in symbolically resonant postures, as when two enormous black men carry Stoneman, his face white with pain, into the Senate for the impeachment of Andrew Johnson.[35] Parts of *The Clansman* read as though Dixon were already planning the silent movie version. The crucial scenes – the rape of Marion and the Klan's mobilization for revenge – are notably silent. Gus snarls only a few guttural words before "the claws of the beast sank into the soft white throat."[36] And the Klan's retaliation is accomplished "without a word, save the whistle of [their leader], the crack of his revolver, and the hoofbeat of swift horses moving like figures in a dream."[37] There is nothing to discuss in either scene: Gus's crime is the product of racial instinct, not thought, and the wordless action of the Klan simply "revealed the unity of the racial life of the people."[38] It is by observing or participating in these actions, not by discussing racial politics, that the book's white characters are brought to acknowledge their true identities.

The novel is not, however, utterly silent. Its opening scene describes a "fair girl ... playing a banjo and singing" to a wounded Confederate soldier in a hospital bed.[39] The music seems to have a tonic effect on Ben Cameron, reminding him of home, so he asks Elsie Stoneman to play his favorites, and she obliges "[w]ith a deft, sure touch and a soft negro dialect."[40] Strangely, banjo music runs as a faint and intermittent sound-track through the first two-thirds of The Clansman, doing more or less what it does in "Christmas Night": voicing the Africana strain in a multiracial Southern life. But that voice becomes, in Dixon's novel, an increasingly menacing thing. "Bring Elsie and her guitar," Mrs. Lenoir will finally tell Ben. "I don't like the banjo."[41] After Gus's assault on young Marion, she and her mother stand on the brink of Lover's Leap, deciding whether to commit suicide, when "floating up from the river valley came the music of a banjo in a negro cabin, mingled with vulgar shout and song and dance."[42] With a shudder, they both jump. By this time, "America's African instrument" (as banjo historian Laurent Dubois calls it) has become simply the audible signature of "the Black Curse," as Phil has learned to call it, the only blight in the Southern garden.[43] The remainder of the novel will be engaged in purging that curse, silencing the instrument Irwin Russell had joyously summoned back in 1878.

VI

Near the beginning of the white South's postwar conversation about race, George Washington Cable had tried to imagine the as-yet-unheard voice of the region's best self, speaking in measured tones for racial equality, emanating somehow from the statue of Robert E. Lee that stood above his native city. The conversation might be said to have been resolved when a much grander Lee monument was installed high above another Southern city. In January 1924, the sculptor Gutzon Borglum, later famous for Mount Rushmore, was ready to reveal the beginning stage of what would eventually be the largest of all Confederate monu-ments, carved into the granite face of Stone Mountain above Atlanta. Stone Mountain had been the scene of another notable event not quite ten years before: the dramatic refounding of the Ku Klux Klan, inspired in part by The Clansman and timed to coincide with the Atlanta premiere of The Birth of a Nation. The 1924 unveiling might be considered the last phase of Thomas Dixon's triumph and George Washington Cable's defeat. Stone Mountain historian David Freeman recounts the scene: Borglum spoke briefly and then the veil, an enormous American flag, was lifted. The assembled crowd – "the South," for that moment – was briefly silent one last time, awed by what they saw: General Lee's enormous head, hovering uncannily disembodied over yet-uncarved rock. Then "applause, screams, cheers, and even Rebel yells echoed off the mountain in a thunderous din."[44] No calm voice of reason spoke for the South's better self. No banjo music was heard.

Notes

1. George Washington Cable, "The Silent South," in *The Negro Question*, ed. Arlin Turner (Garden City, NJ: Doubleday Anchor Books, 1958), 85.
2. Cable, "The Silent South," 86–87.
3. C. Vann Woodward, *The Strange Career of Jim Crow* (New York: Oxford University Press, 1955), 25.
4. Irwin Russell, "Christmas Night in the Quarters," in *Library of Southern Literature, Volume 12*, eds. Edwin A. Alderman and Joel Chandler Harris (Atlanta: Martin & Hoyt, 1907), 4608–15, lines 13–16.
5. "Christmas Night," lines 88–91.
6. "Christmas Night," lines 58, 68, 73.
7. "Christmas Night," lines 183–84.
8. See Laurent Dubois, *The Banjo: America's African Instrument* (Cambridge, MA: Belknap Press of Harvard University Press, 2016).
9. Eric Sundquist, *To Wake the Nations: Race in the Making of American Literature* (Cambridge, MA: Belknap Press of Harvard University Press, 1993), 310.
10. Sundquist, *To Wake*, 312.
11. Thomas Nelson Page, "The Negro Question," in *The Old South* (New York: Charles Scribner's Sons, 1905), 303.
12. Joel Williamson, *The Crucible of Race: Black-White Relations in the American South since Emancipation* (New York: Oxford University Press, 1984), 5–6.
13. Cable, "My Politics," in *Essays*, 15.
14. George Washington Cable, *The Grandissimes* (New York: Penguin Books, 1988), 103.
15. Cable, *Grandissimes*, 62.
16. Robert Underwood Johnson, quoted in Barbara Ladd, *Nationalism and the Color Line* (Baton Rouge: Louisiana State University Press, 1996), 43.
17. Harriet Beecher Stowe, *Uncle Tom's Cabin* (New York: Penguin Books, 1981), 328.
18. Cable, *The Grandissimes*, 193.
19. Cable, "The Freedman's Case in Equity," 81.

20. Thomas Nelson Page, "Marse Chan," in *In Ole Virginia* (Chapel Hill: University of North Carolina Press, 1887), 10.

21. Jay B. Hubbell, *The South in American Literature* (Durham, NC: Duke University Press, 1954), 801.

22. Page published a children's book, a fictionalized memoir called *Two Little Confederates*, in 1888.

23. *Plessy v. Ferguson*, 163 US 537 (1896), 551.

24. Thomas Nelson Page, *Red Rock: A Tale of Reconstruction* (Ridgewood, NJ: Gregg Press, 1967), 17.

25. Page, *Red Rock*, 291.

26. Page, *Red Rock*, 112.

27. Page, *Red Rock*, 125.

28. Page, *Red Rock*, 362.

29. Henry Grady, "In Plain Black and White: A Reply to Mr. Cable," *Century Magazine* (April 1885).

30. Thomas Dixon, *The Clansman* (New York: Triangle Books, 1941), 289.

31. Dixon, *The Clansman*, 57.

32. Dixon, *The Clansman*, 57.

33. Dixon, *The Clansman*, 185, 180.

34. Dixon, *The Clansman*, 329.

35. Dixon, *The Clansman*, 170–71.

36. Dixon, *The Clansman*, 304.

37. Dixon, *The Clansman*, 342.

38. Dixon, *The Clansman*, 341.

39. Dixon, *The Clansman*, 3.

40. Dixon, *The Clansman*, 12.

41. Dixon, *The Clansman*, 300.

42. Dixon, *The Clansman*, 306.

43. Dixon, *The Clansman*, 282.

44. David B. Freeman, *Carved in Stone: The History of Stone Mountain* (Macon, GA: Mercer University Press, 1997), 75.

CHAPTER 9

Neighborliness, Race, and Nineteenth-Century Regional Fiction

Stephanie Foote

I

Late nineteenth- and early twentieth-century regional literature was famously devoted to elaborating the daily life of small towns, villages, and households in geographically distinct areas of the United States, taking as its object the affective and cultural intricacies of the local, the minor, and the quotidian. Regional narratives lingered nostalgically over the rhythm of local village life even as they dissected the workings of those communities with the precision of the anthropological studies emerging at the same moment as well as with the rich descriptiveness of realist literature. The kind of regional literature celebrated in its own era, and rediscovered by feminist critics after it was dismissed by mid-twentieth-century critics as merely "quaint" or "minor," is generally thought of as written by white women, who did indeed create some of its most widely read and critically esteemed texts. But the story of how regional writing was forgotten and recovered, as well as a close look at some of the texts themselves, reminds us that the genre most often associated with small New England towns was, in ways big and small, trying to work through ideas about who belongs to a particular region or place, and who had the right to define and speak for it.

The question of what it meant to belong to a local and national community was central to the political and cultural landscape of the period. The late nineteenth century saw an unprecedented rise of immigration and the emergence of various laws aimed at restricting immigration from China, Japan, and eastern Europe. It witnessed the rise of urban and labor unrest, various populist and progressivist movements, and the emergence of an industrial economy and concentration of wealth in the hands of an oligarchic few. And perhaps most importantly, the late nineteenth century was the period of Reconstruction and its violent cultural, juridical, and political afterlives. For writers in its moment, and for critics in ours, regional literature offers a privileged vantage point for understanding how gender, class, nationality, and especially race were understood as matters of local and national belonging in the late nineteenth and early twentieth century.

Regional literature, sometimes called local color fiction, was among the most important and critically esteemed genres of the late nineteenth and early twentieth century. Championed by periodical editors like William Dean Howells, regional literature came to national prominence at the same moment as the genre of realism, and it drew on many of realism's formal qualities. The genre evolved from early to mid-nineteenth-century tall tales, but it refined tall tales' exaggerated, often comical depiction of dialect speech and local customs by integrating them into realism's emphasis on richly described interior lives and social worlds. And like the realist fiction with which it shared its narrative structure and strategies, late nineteenth- and early twentieth-century regional fiction appeared in and was reviewed in nationally circulated periodicals like *The Atlantic*, which in turn meant that it addressed and reached an educated, middle-class audience for whom taste and cultural knowledge were important signs of its class identity.[1]

Although regional writing was popular in its own day among cultured urban readers, by the early part of the twentieth century, when critics began to consolidate the canon of US literature and to establish a national literary tradition, regionalism was consigned to the status of a minor literature. By the 1970s and 1980s, feminist critics turned their attention to how the canon of literature had been shaped in a way that excluded women, and they found in regional fiction a genre that had allowed women to both enter the literary marketplace as writers, as well as imagine a kind of belonging that was analogous but not identical to national citizenship. They argued that the genre had been effectively feminized because it seemed to deal only with small, local concerns; it appeared elegiac and nostalgic, and though it shared formal strategies with realism, the period's dominant genre, its focus on socially marginal people and places ensured that it would occupy a marginal part of literary history. Critics like Marjorie Pryse, Judith Fetterley, Elizabeth Ammons, and Sandra Zagarell demonstrated the tautological quality of this literary historical judgment, pointing out that the logic underwriting the classification of regionalism as a "minor" genre drew on and affirmed the marginal quality of its subjects.[2]

Following their lead, a new group of scholars returned to the genre and argued that late nineteenth-century regional writing crystallized the period's most pressing social issues. Critics like June Howard, Philip Joseph, Tom Lutz, Stephanie Foote, and Richard Brodhead, among others, demonstrated how regional writing negotiated ethnicity and immigration, how it produced nonnormative versions of gender and sexuality, how it engaged with the economic and cultural exchanges of imperialism, and how it brokered a cosmopolitan cultural imaginary, as well as how the genre itself provided access to writers who had been excluded from the literary marketplace.[3] As I have argued elsewhere, the rediscovery of the genre, and of the idea of the local's relationship to the national and global, has made regionalism one of the great comeback stories of US literary history.[4]

In this essay, I ask particularly about how regional literature imagined race and how black writers found in its form and its conventions a way to enter the literary conversation. Race, I argue, is central to the genre, and it provides us with a way to look at debates over who counted as a person and a citizen of a particular place. I want to centralize race as a category by returning to the key word "community," which feminist critics used to put pressure on the genre, but I do not want to use the term in any ideal way; indeed, I wish to focus precisely on its limits and its regulations, on its methods of exclusion and its fantastical, never-fulfilled promises. Here, I follow the work of more recent critical regionalists like Krista Comer, Sean Goudie, and Tom Lutz, and understand that the community that regionalism was thought to imagine and that drew the attention of the feminist critics who recovered it was always imbricated in both global and imperial concerns, as well as deeply structured by racial and ethnic exclusions.

I want, paradoxically, to look at the "big picture" of race and regionalism – as well as at the history of critiquing the genre – by concentrating on its smallest, most meticulous representation of what it means to belong to or inhabit a region. Though regional fiction often defines its regions reasonably carefully – texts might be about a small village or an island in Maine, about a small town in Tennessee or the Midwest – it was marketed in more generic ways by publishers as about New England or the South. But individual texts tended to work by uniting a more abstract sense of regional belonging and a more precise one, representing the working of a single household, or street, or neighborhood as an emblem of a larger or smaller unit of geographic and social belonging. In this reading, regional literature's primary mechanism of sociability is neighborliness. But how far can such a small category take us if we are looking at large social issues?

II

Neighborliness as a daily practice is customary and local, a quotidian art of social interaction generated by the accident of physical proximity. Neighborliness demands continual negotiation between privacy and social interaction, between the commonality of shared interests and the sovereign interior of a home. It can – and in some sense *must* – tolerate difference that cannot be entirely assimilated to a more abstract ideal of "who we are" in a community, and it provides a more nuanced way than community to look at the dialectics between strangers and natives, and at the unspoken but customary obligations people owe to one another.

Regional fiction is especially attentive to the idea of neighborliness, and it asks us to see it as a material and micropolitical practice that is nonreproductive but nevertheless gendered, as well as a kind of labor that is both material and legislative rather than always affective. In this sense, neighborliness gives us a way to imagine the social work of regional fiction outside the conventional models of family or nation, or even the vague though quite productive sense of "place" that has helped critics open up the genre to broader questions of political interaction. Most usefully, neighborliness in regional texts functions outside of what we might think of as affective attachments; that is, the imperative to be a good neighbor is actually stronger in the face of antipathy than it is in the context of affection. Neighborliness is not merely about care; it's legislative and requires that actors meet in the field of judgment. Who has need and who should meet it? Who deserves help and who does not? To whom does a town or village owe something? How do we balance the claims of individuals against the needs of the community as a whole? Neighborliness is here impersonal and indifferent to the people who will come to be its objects.

Neighborliness is also a critical term for race studies for more obvious reasons. If neighborliness is about how physically proximate people must learn to accommodate one another's right to be part of the polity, it is haunted by the fact that geographic dispossession is one of the founding national gestures of the United States. In the broadest strokes, this includes the appropriation of native land, the enslavement of people of color, and the restriction of immigration for people not considered to be white. But those gestures, enshrined in national mythology as a triumphant settlement of the continent, are also unofficially and often officially legislated by more local practices: the dumping of waste in areas inhabited by people of color; the restriction of rights to own land or vote; the redlining and segregation of cities, towns, and neighborhoods. All of these make any idea of neighborliness seem an odd topic. And yet, it is precisely the fact that neighborliness is such a high value in a genre that offered black writers access to the most conventional form of high literary culture that makes it so interesting. Neighborliness is the genre's most consistent strategy of negotiating the claims of regional outsiders, and it is a strategy designed to meditate on the limits of quotidian forms of belonging. But it is also a strategy that seems to arise as an unspoken consensus, somewhere beneath the juridical debates about place that focus on ownership or the daily negotiations of something like family responsibilities.

The ambivalence of neighborliness is what makes it so important for understanding how regional literature thinks about race. At exactly the moment regional literature was trying to imagine new forms of belonging, the claims of which were somewhere between juridical and social, so too was the United States trying to work through race and citizenship. The emergence of the particular kind of regionalism that attained cultural consecration and became in turn the entry into authorship for writers coincided with the period in the United States known as Reconstruction, particularly the debates around the Thirteenth, Fourteenth, and Fifteenth Amendments to the Constitution, which sought to formalize the enfranchisement and political participation of people of color. As Jeannine Marie DeLombard writes, the literature of the period, particularly the realist literary tradition, understood the role of race as a matter of obligation and "mutual accountability," and she argues that it drew on an attempt to transform debates about the meaning of national belonging into terms that were more defined and affective.[5] But we see too that progressive white writers like Albion Tourgee and George Washington Cable as well as black writers like Charles Chesnutt and W.E.B. DuBois recognized and tried to address the distinction between social belonging and legal enfranchisement. That distinction, for them, was precisely the space where claims to local, embodied, place-based belonging were most incendiary, most likely to fail claimants of color. That space, too, fell under regional literature's brief.

If we turn to one of the classic texts of regional fiction for a moment, we will see that the legislative aims of neighborliness are most often expressed in the practical work of daily living. Sarah Orne Jewett's 1900 story "The Foreigner," which though published separately continues the narrative of her 1896 *The Country of the Pointed Firs*, is about a Creole woman brought to Dunnet Landing in Maine to live among people she does not know and who don't like her "outlandish" ways. Mrs. Todd, who recalls the story, says that her mother told her, "I want you to neighbor with that poor lonesome creatur',"[6] but Almira Todd finds it rough going. She argues that you can't neighbor with someone who seems to like "other ways better'n our'n."[7] Of course, that, as the story tells us, is who you must neighbor with, for the mere fact of living there means that Mrs. Captain Tolland, as she is called after her marriage to the Maine sea captain, has a material claim on the town. The fact that Almira Todd does end up "neighboring," as the text calls it, with Mrs. Captain Tolland provides material benefit to her. Mrs. Todd inherits all of Mrs. Captain Tolland's fortune (which can't ultimately be found) but more importantly ends up learning certain medical and culinary proper-ties of herbs, knowledge that actually ends up helping her maintain her status as the center of her own community.

"The Foreigner" is less about the triumph of neighborliness as an ideal than it is an indictment of a community that can't really assimilate out-siders. Yet the story is actually about a model of neighborliness that emerges in distinction from more common models of belonging. The first model, of course, is familial – the story opens with Mrs. Todd's fear and then relief that during a big storm her mother has company, and is framed by the company of the stranger-turned-friend represented by the text's narrator. But that familial model is undone by the fact that merely marrying "the foreigner" does not make Mrs. Captain Tolland part of the Dunnet Landing community, for her marriage is the result of a neighborliness gone wild. That, of course is the Atlantic shipping trade that undergirded the US empire, which is the other model of neighborli-ness in the text, one here structured by race all the way through. And thus, this classic regional text is critical for our understanding of how race haunts regional literature in its entirety; as Sandra Zagarell, Patrick Gleason, and I have all argued, it deliberately introduces racial difference into the world of the region, using it as both the bedrock of Dunnet Landing as well as the limit of that town's sense of obligation to "outsiders."[8]

The model of neighborliness here, then, is a deliberate searching for some middle ground in which the domestic and the political claim can be balanced in a given location at a given moment, something we see recur in the work of other women regional writers, in particular, Mary Wilkins Freeman. Freeman's villages are peopled by eccentrics who are only marginally assimilated, and many of them are women who have never married or who have somehow been left behind by more conventional social arrangements.

A look at her collected short stories reveals that the idea of neighborli-ness is the practice that makes possible the idea of community or place precisely because neighboring requires both judging and acceptance at once. That is, neighboring almost always has an expressly legislative function, and what it mainly does is help to draw boundaries between different social actors, adjudicating their claims on various kinds of scarce goods like food or wood or housing. But perhaps most importantly, neighborliness counterintuitively helps to keep some people entirely separate from the village or town while still belonging to it. Freeman's stories, especially those collected in *A New England Nun*, often focus on women with no families: spinsters and widows who are making their way in the world without having to throw themselves on the charity of their neighbors. For them, neighborliness is expressed in the villagers' judgment that they should be left alone – not sent to the poor house, not evicted from their hovels, not forced to marry, not sent away to kin. Neighborliness encodes an obligation to respect their autonomy, and to see it as a constitutive part of a social organization that does not merely take its brief from the reproductive unit of the family.

Similarly, George Washington Cable's 1880 novel *The Grandissimes* is organized around the function of neighborliness, but because it deals with the complexity of race relations after the Civil War in New Orleans, the novel's meditation on neighborliness as a kind of impersonal local government makes clear that neighborliness as an ideal and as a practical structuring device works only when race is not at issue. In other words, the abstract ideal of neighborliness, which in regional fiction works as an impersonal virtue that does not need to consider the particularity of a given neighbor, is radically altered in the face of the substantive legal inequalities of race.

The novel follows a family in which there are two Honoré Grandissimes, one white and one a free man of color, and it is narrated from the perspective of Joseph Frowenfeld, who has moved to New Orleans from the North. Like much post-Reconstruction fiction, it thematizes how the North and South can reconcile their cultures and their economies, and it is filled with narrative exposition, rendered in the kind of dialect to which readers of regional fiction had become accustomed, in which local characters attempt to explain those differences to Joseph Frowenfeld.[9] In this sense, the novel has an overtly national agenda – what will it mean for Louisiana, and especially the Creole city of New Orleans, to be absorbed and assimilated into a standard national culture? Those arguments are staged for and directed to Frowenfeld, a stranger to the South, to New Orleans, and to the lived reality of racial difference and racial coexistence.

The Grandissimes is not – at least thematically – a notably different novel from many other works of Southern regional fiction that attempted to portray the faded nobility of Southern culture and the ultimate necessity of national reconciliation. Such novels and stories were endemic during Reconstruction, usually inventing a version of a chivalrous, romantic South that never existed, a version in which the structuring element of racial violence is at best converted into a paternalistic fantasy and at worst simply erased. Such novels imagine the nation as a family, or as an extended all-white neighborhood, and the reunion of that family comes at the expense of people of color. In the most virulent case – Thomas Dixon's *The Clansman* – it comes as the result of simultaneously demonizing and terrorizing black characters.

The viciousness of Dixon is a close cousin to the benevolent paternalism of the romantic New Southern regional novels, so when Cable structures the events of his novel around a family with white *and* black members in a city in which racial categories, customs, and laws are quite distinct from those of the United States, he is making what for the time was a serious argument about the role of race in fictions about place and identity. His black characters underwrite the plot and catalyze the events, and he does not spare his reader the violence with which Clemence and Bras-Coupé's claims to belonging are met by white characters. Clemence especially – as the neighborhood fixture, singer of witty songs, inventor of rhymes, seller of baked goods – occupies an uneasy role in demonstrating both the racial exclusion that organizes New Orleans as well as the consequences of attempting to take her place as a member.

Here, the example of the tensions of local belonging and customs organized through neighborliness are both foregrounded and critiqued. It is not simply that in New Orleans the black and white members of the Grandissime family are quite literally neighbors, sharing the same name, occupying the same streets, and, in an ironic turn of events, renting houses from one another. It is that the question of national belonging, allegorized by local color fiction as a question of family belonging or regional belonging, is always experienced on the ground, through a set of shared daily practices. What, Cable asks, are the obligations people owe to one another? What does the ideal of neighborliness have to hide and what values does it have to commit to in order to operate as both a value and a form of governance? What are its limits? These questions were not simply part of Cable's narrative strategy for his novel. As a passionate advocate for political and social recognition for people of color, Cable tried to make a distinction between "civil relations" and "social relations," arguing that civil relations should be impersonal and legal. He hoped that such an impersonal, legal relationship would allow white people, especially white Southerners, to understand that social relations between the races should necessarily follow.[10]

III

Those limits are of special interest to regional writers of color. Let's take, for example, perhaps the most well-known black local color writer, Charles Chesnutt, who famously disdained the genre and yet found his greatest success in it. Chesnutt was not the only black local color writer in the heyday of regional writing, but he was among the most successful, and his career as a regional writer is among the most instructive for how race and region intersected in the literary marketplace. Chesnutt's ability to enter the literary marketplace was the product, as Richard Brodhead has argued, of his deliberate and creative manipulation of the genre's formal and thematic conventions.[11] In 1899, he published two short story collections, *The Conjure Woman* and *The Wife of His Youth and Other Stories of the Color-Line*. The stories in *The Conjure Woman* are organized around the figure of Uncle Julius, who lives on a post–Civil War plantation that has been bought by a white Northerner and his wife. Julius, once a slave on the plantation, speaks in dialect, while the stories are narrated in standard English and are organized from the position of the Northerners who see in Julius a culturally familiar figure. To them, he might as well be a character in a novel. As John and his wife, Annie, try to find a way to build a life in Reconstruction North Carolina, as well as improve Annie's health, Uncle Julius visits them and regales them with stories of pre–Civil War life.

Literary critics have lingered over the stories, demonstrating that Chesnutt used them to gain access to the literary marketplace by riffing on the formal elements of regional writing, thus finding a way to publish his works in the premier literary journal of his day. Critics similarly point out that Chesnutt, who had long sought to publish more serious work about the color line, turned the genre to his own ends. His use of Uncle Julius can be seen as a response to Joel Chandler Harris's Uncle Remus stories (1880), which featured a gentle black man telling folk stories to a young white boy. Chesnutt's iteration of this scenario fed audience hunger for the authentic voice and narrative of black characters, while also sharply critiquing that hunger.

To take the most obvious example of that critique, though Harris's stories attempted to use some of the "authentic" stories he had heard while living in the South as a newspaperman, thus preserving real folk tales, he placed them in a frame in which the transmission of those stories was untroubled by the legacy of racial violence in the post-Reconstruction South. Chesnutt, on the other hand, used that same framing device, which in its broadest sense was standard in almost all regional writing. But he did not use "authentic" stories as the basis for Uncle Julius's stories, emphasizing instead Julius's creative use of narrative as the basis for his local claim to belonging to the place that John and Annie had purchased.

If we think about this through the ideal of neighborliness, we see a concerted meditation on regional writing's strategy of legislating inclusion and exclusion, especially around the issue of race and its relationship to property. If we look at the framing device of each of the stories in *The Conjure Woman*, we can see this in action. Uncle Julius stops by John and Annie's newly bought plantation house, at first to welcome them to the neighborhood, and eventually to pass along neighborly advice. Annie and John find him at turns amusing, and although John doubts the veracity of his stories, Julius usually finds a way to direct their actions so that he gets something he wants, or holds on to some proprietary activity John and Annie's presence threatens. Julius's strategy is to tell John and Annie stories about the plantation's past, folk stories or ghost stories. Some of them, as Brodhead has pointed out, are searingly violent, such as the haunting of Tennie, and some are seemingly more innocent.[12] Yet each of them aims to preserve a traditional way of using land or resources, keeping them from the private ownership and use of the new tenants and placing them firmly back in the domain of something more like the commons.

But this further underscores something about race and neighborliness — it is underwritten, as Julius's stories point out, by a shared assumption that goods and obligations should be distributed equally across a given community. If in work by writers like Mary Wilkins Freeman or Sarah Orne Jewett the needs of the neighbor are of prime consideration for the community, even if those needs have to be insisted on, even if the neighbors are rude or unlikable, Chesnutt's stories reveal that contract is always underwritten by the assumption of shared whiteness. The introduction of race requires, as Chesnutt's Julius understands, the need to trick his white neighbors into being neighborly.

Chesnutt's revelatory critique of the core value of regionalism is perhaps, then, a way to understand the relationship between his early regional fiction, which brought him the status of professional authorship, and *The Marrow of Tradition*, his 1901 novel about the Wilmington race riots. Chesnutt's journals and his correspondence with literary figures like

William Dean Howells and George Washington Cable reveal that he had struggled to find venues for his stories, and he felt thwarted by the fact that audiences seemed to only want to read local color stories. It had been difficult for him to place his novel *The House Behind the Cedars*, and in *The Marrow of Tradition*, he not only castigates the fragility of the legal civil rights putatively guaranteed to black citizens, but he also exposes the social contract of neighborliness, or what Cable called "social" rather than civil equality, as founded on whiteness. Regional fiction, in Chesnutt's penultimate novel, is entirely underwritten by racial inequality.

IV

The regional writing I have focused on in this essay is that particular version of the genre that was most fully elaborated in the late nineteenth century, but the conventions of local color writing proved remarkably enduring, especially for writers of color, for whom regional writing in the modernist period and in the Harlem Renaissance provided a mechanism to elaborate the various kinds of belonging – to the literary field, to literary and cultural traditions, to geographic place, to the long histories of disenfranchisement and enslavement. Writers like Jean Toomer and Zora Neale Hurston found in the genre, and its core value of neighborliness, a way to represent the extraordinary violence of black life, in part by understanding neighborliness as a false political promise. In a text like *Cane*, for example, the literary convention of neighborliness is stretched to its violent limit and exposed as a fictional conceit. Here, Toomer draws on the histories of lynching, dramatizing how quickly the tenuous "neighborliness" of a world structured by white supremacy and segregation could be weaponized against black bodies.

I close this essay not with a plea for neighborliness, but a caution against its blandishments. I have argued that one of the ways we can understand the role of race in regional fiction is by looking at how it brokered the representation of regions to a larger national audience, converting matters of politics into matters of cultural belonging. And I have argued, too, that the professionalization of expertise about local cultures meant that writers of color could use the genre's ambivalent relationship to authenticity to their own ends. But I have mainly argued that we can follow the thematic cues of regional writing, which focuses its attention precisely on the small and local, to their logical end by focusing on the ideal of neighborliness. Neighborliness is an intimate and personal relationship, and yet it must maintain an element of impersonality and impartiality in order to bear the weight of social proximity. It is the element of shared community that bears most closely on shared physical proximity, and it thus cuts across the laws governing how to share official space. And yet, as we have seen, neighborliness – and its impersonal intimacies – is precisely where the official stories about race and the unofficial narratives about who gets to claim to belong can intersect most explosively. Eve Dunbar has recently argued that region is an especially powerful lens through which to understand black writing in the United States, in part because its generic demands overlap with the evolution of black writing that resisted and critiqued the very fictions of place that seemed to keep black writers in the position of regional local informant or cosmopolitan exile.[13]

Neighborliness, deployed in the hands of late nineteenth-century writers and taken up by the Harlem Renaissance writers who adapted regionalism's strategies, was the site by which a range of claims – from expertise about culture to professional authorship to political membership – could be advanced. But we might also say that race relations in the United States are often cast as versions of regional fiction – that is to say that when larger systemic racial injustices are identified, it is all too easy for white people to deny them by pointing to the particularities of their local culture. They have black friends, or black neighbors. They do not understand themselves as having racist thoughts. They might even say that they do not even "see color." Even the most liberal thinkers have a tendency to exempt themselves from the problem of race on the grounds that they have also suffered based on their grandparents' ethnicity, or their gender, or their class. These forms of discrimination are not negligible, and they are not unimportant. And it is certainly true that race is not a uniform category that every person of color inhabits in the same way, as theorists of intersectionality have pointed out. But a concentration on the local can overlook larger structural injustices and narrative patterns. Neighborliness here is a version of civility that seeks an abstract commitment to things as they are. But that abstract commitment, as nearly all regional writers argue, collapses in the face of racism.

By looking at neighborliness, then, I do not argue that it is some idealized social form, or that neighborliness is so capacious and virtuous that everyone can benefit from it. It's often quite brutal in its daily operations. We might see it as a corollary to Carrie Tirado Bramen's recent work on "niceness" as the prized national category that hides its violence under the veneer of civility and innocent gestures of sociability.[14] But I do mean to say that there is something in it that is provisional in multiple senses – that is, it is a temporary and local solution to problems of governance that leave some out and draw some in, and that its aim is to provide, just for a moment, some reasonable solution to a real social problem of survival. In this sense, neighborliness as a strategy navigates a scalar problem of governance between the small unit of the family and the big unit of the government of a village, town, or region. And it also helps us to see again what is interesting about regional fiction as it neighbored next to the more well-known realists in the literary canon, and as it provided a way for writers to make a living from towns and villages that, on the one hand, sustained them and, on the other hand, left them to their own devices.

Notes

1. For more on the print cultural history of regionalism and its relationship to realism, see Nancy Glazener, *Reading for Realism: A History of a US Literary Institution, 1850–1910* (Durham, NC: Duke University Press, 1997), especially the chapter "Regional Accents."
2. Central texts in the feminist recovery of regional literature include Elizabeth Ammons, "Going in Circles: The Female Geography of Jewett's Country of the Pointed Firs," *Studies in the Literary Imagination* 16 (1983), 83–92; Judith Fetterley and Marjorie Pryse, *American Women Regionalists, 1850–1910* (New York: Norton, 1992); Sandra Zagarell, "Country's Portrayal of Community and the Exclusion of Difference," in *New Essays on the Country of the Pointed Firs*, ed. June Howard (Cambridge: Cambridge University Press, 1994); and Judith Fetterley and Marjorie Pryse, *Writing out of Place: Regionalism, Women, and American Literary Culture* (Champaign: University of Illinois Press, 2005).
3. See, for example, Philip Joseph, *American Literary Regionalism in a Global Age* (Baton Rouge: Louisiana State University Press, 2007); Richard Brodhead, *Cultures of Letters: Scenes of Reading and Writing in Nineteenth-Century America* (Chicago: University of Chicago Press, 1993); Stephanie Foote, *Regional Fictions: Culture and Identity in Nineteenth-Century American Literature* (Madison: University of Wisconsin Press, 2001); Tom Lutz, *Cosmopolitan Vistas: American Regionalism and Literary Value* (Ithaca, NY: Cornell University Press, 2004); June Howard, "Introduction: Sarah Orne Jewett and the Traffic in Words," in *New Essays on the Country of the Pointed Firs*, ed. June Howard (Cambridge: Cambridge University Press, 1994); June Howard, *The Center of the World: Regional Writing and the Puzzles of Place-Time* (Oxford: Oxford University Press, 2018); Samaine Lockwood, *Archives of Desire* (Chapel Hill: University of North Carolina Press, 2015).
4. Stephanie Foote, "The Cultural Work of American Regionalism," in *A Companion to the Regional Literatures of America*, ed. Charles L. Crow (Oxford: Blackwell, 2003).

5. Jeannine Marie DeLombard, "The Novel and the Reconstruction Amendments," in *The Oxford History of the Novel in English: US Fiction, 1870–1940*, eds. Priscilla Wald and Michael Elliott (Oxford: Oxford University Press, 2014), 69–85. DeLombard writes that "novels published at the end of this era indicate that an important cultural effect of the Reconstruction Amendments was to translate the official, constitutional language of rights into civil law's idiom of responsibility and dignity. Intensifying the novel's generic predisposition to probe the most intimate spaces of personal and domestic life, the recent turn of American fiction to ever more elusive interior realms enabled the realist novel to privatize and denationalize questions of accountability left unresolved by the Civil War" (72). See also Edlie Wong's discussion of custom versus law, the very distinction that Plessy relied on, and which Chesnutt attempts to use in his fictions. Edlie Wong, "Plessy and the Novel," in *The Oxford History of the Novel in English: US Fiction, 1870–1940*, eds. Priscilla Wald and Michael Elliott (Oxford: Oxford University Press, 2014).

6. Sarah Orne Jewett, *Novels and Stories*, ed. Michael Davitt Bell (New York: Library of America, 1994), 540.

7. Jewett, *Novels and Stories*, 540.

8. See Stephanie Foote, *Regional Fictions*; Sandra Zagarell, "Country's Portrayal of Community"; and Patrick Gleason, "Sarah Orne Jewett's 'The Foreigner' and the Transamerican Routes of New England Regionalism," *Legacy* 28.1 (2011), 24–46.

9. For more on dialect and regional writing, see Gavin Jones, *Strange Talk: The Politics of Dialect Fiction in Gilded Age America* (Berkeley: University of California Press, 1999).

10. George Washington Cable, *"The Silent South" Together with "The Freedman's Case in Equity" and "The Convict Lease System"* (New York: Charles Scribner's Sons, 1885), 53.

11. Brodhead, *Cultures of Letters*. See especially his chapter on Chesnutt, "'Why Could Not a Colored Man?' Chesnutt and the Transaction of Authorship."

12. See Richard Brodhead, "Introduction," in Charles Chesnutt, *The Conjure Woman and Other Conjure Tales*, ed. Richard Brodhead (Durham, NC: Duke University Press, 1993).

13. Eve Dunbar, *Black Regions of the Imagination: African American Writers between the Nation and the World* (Philadelphia: Temple University Press, 2012).

14. Carrie Tirado Bramen, *American Niceness: A Cultural History* (Cambridge, MA: Harvard University Press, 2017).

PART IV

Reconfigurations

Because race is systemic, marking access to economic opportunity, social networks, cultural authority, and political power, the pressures to assimilate, either by force or by choice, are enormous, to the extent that various conceptions of assimilation, self-identification, and resistance became a major preoccupation in the literature of the late nineteenth century well into the twentieth century. The essays in this section, "Reconfigurations," explore the literature of the racial borderlands, the pressing calls for assimilation, and the politics of racial and cultural passing. Exploring stories of African Americans capable of passing for white, M. Giulia Fabi argues that the writers of these stories "deployed the trope of passing to capitalize on the subversive implications of crossing the ostensibly 'natural' racial dichotomies." In this way, they "exposed the sociopolitical construction of 'race'" and called for "more egalitarian racial epistemologies." Approaching the racial boundaries from a different perspective, John Alba Cutler asks, "What language should a writer use to represent a community that finds itself in between cultures?" Cutler observes that "Latinx writers understand assimilation to refer to many other things besides . . . 'straight-line' assimilation: the inevitable dynamism that results when groups come into contact over long periods of time, or the creative adaptation that individuals make of behaviors or forms from the dominant culture, or the efforts of a dominant society to integrate ethnic communities." Addressing this broad understanding of interracial influences and exchanges, Cutler argues that "above all, Latinx writing attends to the uneven power dynamics that govern the broad swath of choices and experiences that go under the name of assimilation." Adopting a similarly nuanced understanding of assimilation, Kiara M. Vigil observes that "by the turn of the twentieth century, Native peoples from the Americas had developed strategies not only for resisting their forced 'assimilation' into white culture but also for sharing national and regional debates concerning citizenship and race." Surveying the lives and works of four prominent

Native intellectual leaders, Vigil presents "a story of a complex intellectual culture shaping an equally complex expressive culture, a story similar to other literary traditions that have emerged from American literary history." Cari Carpenter takes this line of analysis further still, focusing on Northern Paiute author and activist Sarah Winnemucca Hopkins's relationship with the white educational reformer Elizabeth Peabody, a relationship central to Winnemucca's efforts "to establish a school for the Paiutes that would avoid the assimilationist violence often associated with white-run schools for Native Americans." Following this story, Carpenter contends, "gives us a way of thinking about Native American literature more broadly." In the final essay in this section, Mita Banerjee brings these considerations of racial ambiguity and belonging to a legal point, exploring a "remarkable moment in US legal history in which the law, for a period of time that would span seven decades, came to doubt its own categories." The exploration leads Banerjee to a study of "the parallel development of naturalization policies and literary naturalism, addressing the ways in which literature was used to both open and police the boundaries of citizenship."

CHAPTER 10

Passing

M. Giulia Fabi

As both theme and literary strategy, passing figures prominently in African American fiction from its very beginning. The literary trope of passing is rooted in the historical realities of the racial and sexual exploitation of slavery, as well as in the legal fiction of the one-drop rule.[1] The classic passing figure is legally black because of being genealogically connected with African Americans, however remotely, and somatically light-skinned enough to be read as white. The invisibility of the passer's ancestry destabilizes rigid attempts at pseudo-biological racial classification like the one-drop rule, foregrounding their artificiality and hegemonic uses. African American writers deployed the trope of passing to capitalize on the subversive implications of crossing the ostensibly "natural" racial dichotomies invoked to legitimize social institutions like slavery and, later, segregation. They exposed the sociopolitical construction of "race" and thereby articulated alternative, complex, counter-hegemonic, and more egalitarian racial epistemologies.

When William Wells Brown chose a female passer as the eponymous protagonist of the first known African American novel, *Clotel; or, The President's Daughter* (1853), mixed-race characters (then variously termed "mulattos," "quadroons," or "octoroons") were already established, popular, sensationalistic, and in many ways stereotyped characters in European and mainstream American literature.[2] Their narrative fate, most often tragic, was presented as rooted in their in-between status as supposedly neither black nor white and in a presumed genetic incompatibility that ultimately reasserted the very racial dichotomies that their mixed-race background and, in the case of passers, their status as "white negroes" called into question.

Well aware of both its popularity and its problematic uses even in American abolitionist fiction,[3] early African American novelists like Brown and Frank J. Webb adapted and radically revised the tragic mulatta and mulatto character by articulating a black-centered racial imaginary that infused the theme of passing with profound political relevance.[4] Their privileged focus is on characters who are not only of mixed heritage, but so light skinned as to be able to cross the color line. Their literary representations of the trope of passing question the legibility of both blackness and whiteness and induce a more critical awareness of the instability of supposedly biological racial differences, highlighting instead the sociocultural apparatus (e.g., law, custom, pseudoscientific discourses, economic and political institutions, long-standing stereotypes) that creates and perpetuates racial hierarchies. To explore race as a sociocultural construct, for instance, Brown plays with color(s) in a variety of ways, also presenting characters who are legally white but somatically dark. Gender intersects with race in crucial ways, as well, and cross-dressing represents a strategy that complements and enables passing.[5] Importantly, the sociocultural apparatus reproducing and manipulating racial classifications includes language as well, since the possibility of passing requires blending into the mainstream aurally, as well as visually. Thus, the narrative use of standard English itself becomes politicized as another disguise of the passer that exposes unequal access to education as a crucial means of racial oppression (e.g., the notorious laws that prohibited teaching slaves how to read and write).

By exploding the assumed causal connection between blackness and tragedy, African American writers opened up new narrative trajectories beyond the tragic mulatto and mulatta stereotype. In early African American fiction, passers are most often rebellious figures who succeed in challenging, escaping, or helping others to escape from slavery. Even in those cases when the all-but-white characters do meet with an untimely death, their tragic fate is presented clearly as the consequence not of some innate flaw, but rather of prejudice and oppressive social institutions (e.g., slavery, discrimination, or even segregation in the "free" North, as in the case of Webb's 1857 *The Garies and Their Friends*, set in Philadelphia).[6] The story of individual passing thus embodies a broader political critique of the structural racism historically inherent in American democracy, of the contradictions between its founding libertarian ideals and its oppressive legal and social practices. Literary representations of the passer's option of crossing racial lines do not emphasize the individual freedom of performing different identities but rather, as in Webb's novel, the artificial rigidity of racial hierarchies, thematizing the dramatically different and unequal social destinies of "blacks" and "whites."

In early African American fiction, passing also operates as a literary strategy informed by a keen awareness of prevailing literary stereotypes and the determination to undermine them from the inside, in order to enable more complex racial imaginaries and modes of reading. The sensationalistic prominence of the passer serves as a cloaking device to introduce the slave community as a new, forceful protagonist of American literature. The lives, aspirations, and adventures of a large and diversified group of visibly black characters surround those of the all-but-white protagonists, connecting their individual disruptiveness with the collective ethos of resistance of an entire community that shares not only a history of oppression in the new world, but also a culture.

Whereas passing as a theme pushes the boundaries of arbitrary, but nevertheless operative and prevailing, racial dichotomies, passing as a literary strategy enables a radical experimentation with novelistic conventions. Infusing the novel with his inside knowledge of the brutality inherent in the racialized ideology and power structures of slavery, Brown, for instance, challenges assumptions of the linear ordering of events through the multiplication of characters and subplots. In the process, he deliberately disrupts and frustrates the reader's expectations in ways that compel a more critically self-aware reading mode. He unsettles his audience, making them experience some of the sense of powerlessness and overwhelming uncertainty that characterizes slave life (as encapsulated in the "To-Day a Mistress, To-Morrow a Slave" plot pattern).[7]

Addressing both a black and a white audience, Brown promotes the creation of a black counter-public sphere by surreptitiously increasing the centrality of the slave community and presenting blackness not solely as a condition, but as a consciousness rooted in shared historical experiences, cultural traditions, and the ethos of resistance of African Americans in the New World. When read within this celebratory black-centered narrative context, the individual crossing of racial classifications on which passing relies acquires subversive political valence when it is thematized or, as in the case of many ante- and postbellum novels, when it is relinquished in favor of a voluntary belonging to the African American community.

After the Civil War and the abolition of slavery, the rise of Jim Crow[8] segregation confirmed the continued importance of organized African American resistance, and literature reaffirmed its function as a means both of community building and of counterhegemonic contest over the public sphere. Especially in light of the increasing limitations imposed on the newly acquired franchise of African American men, the printed word operated as a crucial means to oppose the prevailing discourses of segregation and white supremacy, as testified by the proliferation of African American periodicals and publishing houses.

Black Americans did not have to wait for the institutionalization of segregation in 1896 to realize that legal emancipation needed to be accompanied by a cultural change in mainstream prejudiced notions of race that had yet to occur. At the very beginning of the Reconstruction period (1865–77), this sober awareness characterizes the closing mild optimism of Brown's 1867 revision of *Clotel*. The all-but-white heroine, who returns to the United States from Europe with her visibly black husband, Jerome, to help in the Civil War effort, becomes a war widow and eventually opens a school for the freedmen to help in the new postwar effort to improve the condition of former slaves.[9] The famous abolitionist poet, orator, and novelist Frances E. W. Harper presents an even more cautionary tale in her serialized novel *Minnie's Sacrifice* (1869).[10] In Harper's novel, both the hero and the heroine are former unwitting passers who, upon discovering their African American ancestry, relinquish passing and in the postwar period move south to uplift the freedmen. Unlike Brown's heroine, Minnie is killed by a group of white racists. Both her death and her husband's closing determination to continue the fight for racial equality offer an early indictment of the violent white supremacist regime that would triumph in the era of Jim Crow.

The rise of segregation was accompanied and legitimized by the upsurge of virulent stereotypes and pseudo-Darwinian racist discourses. In this context, the subversive potential of passing as a means to question the enforced rigidity of racial boundaries was put to activist use in all-but-white Homer Plessy's legal challenge to segregation in transportation. The consequent 1896 *Plessy v. Ferguson* Supreme Court ruling that upheld the constitutionality of "separate but equal" public facilities, thereby effectively institutionalizing segregation, testifies to the virulence of racial prejudice at the turn of the twentieth century and provides a national context to appreciate the complexity of post-Reconstruction African American literary representations of the trope of passing.

Despite the momentous changes in their legal status and, consequently, in the rights they could legitimately demand, when the century turned to its close and black American history reached its nadir, the cultural battles African Americans had fought in the antebellum period proved a source of inspiration and took on new relevance as African Americans faced the "new slavery" of Jim Crow.[11] The literary trope of passing played a crucial role in the "battle of images"[12] in which African American writers engaged in order to popularize an alternative, empowering racial imaginary, challenging the racialized stereotypes that not only prevailed in the gross caricatures of mulattos by plantation fiction writers like Thomas Nelson

Page or Thomas Dixon, but also residually infused the more sophisticated portrayals of passing characters by William Dean Howells or Mark Twain.[13]

Post-Reconstruction African American writers exposed and defied the biased logic of such long-standing stereotypes both directly and indirectly. Sutton E. Griggs, for instance, thematized explicitly the absurdity and tragic consequences of Viola Martin's belief in pseudoscientific arguments against race mixing in *Imperium in Imperio* (1899).[14] At the same time, the revisionary and experimental uses of passing as a literary strategy enabled a sharp critique of the culture of segregation. At the turn of the twentieth century, during the "black woman's era," African American women writers took up the challenge to the tragic mulatta stereotype and the related confining discourses on race and gender it mobilized. The intersection of race, gender, and class had already appeared in the antebellum period, in the aforementioned episodes of cross-dressing. However, in the post-Reconstruction period, the emphasis lay more forcefully in a redefinition and expansion of women's sphere and of their role as representatives for the entire black community.

African American women writers such as Frances E. W. Harper and Pauline E. Hopkins privileged the focus on family and genealogy characteristic of the trope of passing to explore the gender-specific history of white sexual abuse of black women in slavery and freedom, as well as to question masculinist discourses. Through their use of this trope, they presented blackness as a choice, rather than an imposed social destiny, as a conscious preference for the counterhegemonic values of the African American community that often takes literary form in the quest for the formerly enslaved mother.[15] They offered models of self-reliant, educated, working African American new women and advanced a forceful critique of the sexual double standard by articulating alternative narrative closures of survival for sexually abused heroines.[16] Even when death befalls the heroine, as in the case of *Of One Blood* (1902–3), Hopkins presents the story of incest leading to the tragic fate of the passer as a loss of cultural and historical memory (both of Africa and of slavery), thereby offering a warning against and capturing the worried sense of the possible loosening of ties within post-Reconstruction African American communities that, despite discrimination, possessed somewhat greater mobility and were becoming internally more stratified.[17]

As in the antebellum period, passing served as a literary trope that both required and aimed to teach self-consciously critical modes of reading literature and, by extension, reality. African American authors devised multilayered textual strategies to reach the deeply divided audiences of Jim Crow America. Centering on the deceptiveness of visual appearances, passing prompts readers to question them, engage more attentively with the process of reading, and readjust their expectations in light of unexpected narrative challenges. African American writers continued to deploy the high visibility and established literary role of the all-but-white character as a screen to introduce new figures in American literature, unsettling established racial epistemologies of blackness and popularizing a more complex racial imaginary. Alongside the title passing heroine, for instance, Harper presents Lucille Delany, a determined teacher and successful school administrator "of unmixed blood," who embodies the ideal new woman.[18] Hopkins introduces possibly the first African American female detective, Venus, in her serialized saga of passing, *Hagar's Daughter* (1901–2).[19] Besides the more traditional all-but-white protagonist, Regenia Underwood, McHenry Jones's *Hearts of Gold* (1896) features another heroine, the enterprising stenographer Lucile Malone, in a novel focusing on the brutal realities of the convict lease system that at the time were being neglected or misrepresented by the mainstream press.[20] Griggs chooses elderly, uneducated, vernacular-speaking Uncle Jack as the central consciousness and civil rights activist in *Pointing the Way* (1908), where he presents multiracial passing beyond black and white and questions the legibility of race against ostensibly self-explanatory appearances by having his all-but-white heroine disguise herself as a Chinese woman.[21]

In the case of Amelia E. Johnson's and Edward A. Johnson's novels at the turn of the twentieth century, passing was not thematized but rather narratively performed by the authors, who deliberately gave no explicit indication of the ethnic background of their characters. These racially indeterminate figures would "generally be translated as white" by mainstream readers, to quote Barbara Christian,[22] but they also allowed for a different reading by cultural insiders cognizant that the authors were well-known figures in African American circles. For Amelia E. Johnson, the first African American writer to publish Sunday School novels for the important American Baptist Publication Society of Philadelphia, the choice of racially indeterminate protagonists in *Clarence and Corinne; or, God's Way* (1890) was strategic to foreground the poverty and marginalization in urban environments as societal, rather than specifically African American, problems.[23] For Edward A. Johnson, who was an outspoken activist for black rights and the author of textbooks like *A School History of the Negro Race in America from 1619 to 1890* (1890),[24] the racially indeterminate protagonist of his utopian novel *Light Ahead for the Negro* (1904) offers a model conversion to the goals of greater racial and social equality that characterize a future American nation where segregation is in the process of being eliminated.[25] Crossing the racial divide enforced by Jim Crow also in the literary realm, writers like Paul L. Dunbar and Charles W. Chesnutt wrote novels centering on white life.[26] In *The Colonel's Dream* (1905), for instance, Chesnutt's systematic adoption of the circumscribed narrative point of view of a liberal racist, Colonel French, enables a dissection from the inside of the regime of Jim Crow segregation prevailing both north and south.

The pervasive irony that dominates *The Colonel's Dream*, leading the attentive reader to appreciate how unfounded the Progressive era optimism voiced by Colonel French is, will become a characterizing feature of the Harlem Renaissance. The modernist poetics of that period profoundly transforms the trope of passing, repurposing it to address the changed circumstances of migration, mass urbanization, and the contrast between the democratic rhetoric of US interventionism in World War I and the continuing assault against the basic civil rights of black American citizens at home. James Weldon Johnson's *The Autobiography of an Ex-Colored Man* represents a crucially transitional text in the use of passing as both theme and literary strategy. Published anonymously in 1912 to little critical notice, it was originally mistaken as a real autobiography. In the 1927 reprint, instead, both the author's name and the book's fictionality were disclosed, and Johnson's revisionary deployment of the trope of passing exerted a strong influence on Harlem Renaissance writers.[27]

On the one hand, the radical unreliability of the first-person narrator and his own expressed regret and sense of inadequacy following the decision to pass permanently in order to avoid the harshness of segregation reassert, by contrast, earlier uses of passing to celebrate blackness. The significance of passing, or rather of its relinquishment, as a conscious statement of preference for black culture was present also in the contemporaneous work of other Harlem Renaissance authors like Walter White or Jesse Fauset.[28] On the other hand, Johnson's pervasive irony and his use of parody and intertextuality to multiply the echoes and guide the interpretation of the central character and the plot, as well as his focus on the Ex-Colored Man's internalized white supremacism as the cause, rather than the result, of his decision to abandon his mother's people effected a dramatic shift in the conceptualization of passing as a trope.

This shift comes to beautifully complex fruition in Nella Larsen's *Passing* (1929). Larsen multiplies the possible forms of (un)conscious physical and ideological passing in order to emphasize the constructedness of the mulatta as a literary trope and advance a far from monolithic understanding of blackness that foregrounds its intraracial diversification and intersection with gender and class.[29] Her sophisticated modernist aesthetics enables an in-depth psychological portrayal of female characters. Larsen filters the gendered experience of race through her radical focus on Irene Redfield's circumscribed point of view, delving into her doubts, assumptions, denials, desires, frustrations, and ambitions in ways that question even those clear-cut oppositions that Irene herself would like to uphold in order to legitimize the wisdom of her life choices as a true race woman. From this vantage point, *Passing* can be seen as a sequel to *Iola Leroy* that challenges Harper's voluntaristic happy ending. Irene's own statement of preference for the black community, in fact, does not save her from the gendered oppression of her life with her doctor husband. Her choice of blackness does not even protect her from being initially taken in by those popular mainstream versions of the tragic mulatta as a hopeless in-between who feels neither black nor white that Clare evokes in order to gain Irene's sympathy and enter into her life.

Through a rich web of intertextual references to other literary heroines, including W.E.B. Du Bois's Zora,[30] Edith Wharton's Ellen Olenska and Pauline and Nona Manford,[31] Harper's Iola Leroy and Lucille Delany, and Francis Scott Fitzgerald's Daisy Buchanan,[32] as well as through Irene's perception of her own conflicted ambivalence toward Clare, Larsen also offers a meta-narrative exploration of different conceptualizations of womanhood. The reading challenge she poses culminates at the end of the novel in an ironic proliferation of differently tragic mulattas: At the party organized by the Freelands, Clare's staging of the revelation scene characteristic of the trope of passing backfires and becomes a reality that leads to her death; Irene's survival promises no escape from her devastating marriage; and racist John Bellew's discovery of his wife's secret places their daughter Margery in the classic traumatic position of the unwitting passer who learns belatedly about her mixed-race background. As Irene's husband notes, to understand passing fully would require "know[ing] what race is," but the complexity of Larsen's novel preempts that possibility, revealing the intrinsic inadequacy of any such definition.[33]

The use of passing to expose the sociocultural construction of racial identities takes a powerfully satiric turn in George S. Schuyler's *Black No More* (1931).[34] Through the generic science fiction frame of African American doctor Junius Crookman's invention of a treatment that transforms blacks into ultrawhites and thereby occasions a mass passing of African Americans, Schuyler ridicules the dominant pseudoscientific stereotypes and racial hierarchies of the segregation era. At the same time, he foregrounds the socioeconomic uses of racial differences, however arbitrary in their definition. In the ironic closing reversal, when it is discovered that former blacks have become a few shades whiter than whites, the latter decide to get suntanned in order to reassert a visible difference as the basis for their social privilege. The ultimate satiric thrust, however, is that African American protagonist and master trickster Max Disher (aka Matthew Fisher) goes through all of these chromatic transformations and eventually passes among the new tanned elite.[35]

This critical play with multiple reversals also characterizes Langston Hughes's 1956 short story "Who's Passing for Who?"[36] The first-person narrator, who describes himself as a writer and "a member of a minority race," recounts an episode that took place during the Harlem Renaissance at a club where he and some friends were trying to shock three slumming whites with tales of passing. Initially, Hughes's story seems to confine the relevance of the theme of passing to the past, through both its setting and its explicit references to Nella Larsen and James Weldon Johnson, whose *Autobiography of an Ex-Colored Man* the narrator and his "dark bohemia[n]" friends (164) have not read, "because we paid but little attention to the older colored writers—but we knew it was about passing for white" (165). However, with a surprising and ironic closing twist, the story reasserts the classic use of the trope of passing to question superficial assumptions on racial identity. In the end, Hughes involves the reader in the suspense of unsolved racial indeterminacy, as the narrator cannot ultimately discern whether the "light-colored people" (166) he has been spending the evening with are in fact African Americans passing for white or, instead, whites passing for blacks who are passing for white.

Hughes's meta-narrative play with the supposed pastness of passing, his Janus-like backward- and forward-looking approach, captures in many ways the contested and continued significance of this trope to the present day. The legislative changes caused by the Civil Rights Movement, including the *Loving* v. *Virginia* Supreme Court ruling that in 1967 proclaimed the unconstitutionality of laws against interracial marriage, and the increased flexibility of racial classifications that the possibility of marking multiple racial categories in the 2000 US Census seemed to promise have been invoked to question the present relevance of passing. However, scholars have argued that, despite its announced diminished significance, in the late twentieth and early twenty-first centuries, the trope of passing remains a crucial means to explore the shifting epistemologies of race and at the same time challenge how racialized boundaries, however artificial, continue to be societally oppressive.

Contemporary novels emphasize intraracial and multiracial dynamics, building on the intersectionality of race, class, gender, and sexuality that has historically characterized the literary trope of passing and giving it increased visibility. Indeed, the intertextual conversations that contemporary authors establish with the earlier tradition of novels of passing pay homage to the importance of this trope in American literature. Not unexpectedly, passing features in historical novels set in the nineteenth century – such as J. California Cooper's *Family* (1991),[37] Colson Whitehead's *The Underground Railroad* (2016),[38] Ralph Ellison's *Three Days before the Shooting* (2010),[39] and Barbara Chase-Ribaud's *The President's Daughter* (1994) – which dialogues intertextually with Brown's *Clotel* by recuperating his focus on the offspring of Thomas Jefferson and his slave Sally Hemings.[40] The history of intricate and often secret mixed-race genealogies linked with the passing trope appear in Toni Morrison's *Song of Solomon* (1977) as well, pointing to the weight of the past on the characters' self-definition in the present.[41]

Passing also enables explorations of a more recent history. Danzy Senna's *Caucasia* (1998), for instance, explores the legacy of the Civil Rights and Black Power movements through the point of view of the biracial adolescent first-person narrator, Birdie Lee, who can pass for white and is obliged to pass for Jewish when her WASP mother, who has been politically active in radical circles and is afraid of being arrested, decides to go underground.[42] Birdie's *Bildung* goes through various attempts to fit into different racialized contexts that foreground the intersections of race, gender, class, and sexuality. Senna rewrites the post-Reconstruction narrative focus on the passer's search for the mother, which was metonymic of the preference for the black community, into Birdie's quest for her visibly black sister, Cole, from whom she has been divided after their parents' separation. Senna intertextually points to the earlier tradition of passing novels by referring explicitly to Nella Larsen and evoking themes from her fiction. Birdie's father's decision to move to Brazil is motivated by the hope of finding a place of greater racial equality, a hope that also appeared in Larsen's *Passing*, where it constituted an important cause of the marital unhappiness that led to the final tragedy. Senna's focus on how this emigration proves short-lived and disappointing, but nevertheless contributes to breaking up the family along color lines in ways for which Birdie's father does not take responsibility, calls new attention to and offers retrospective insight into the oppressive gender dynamics of Larsen's novel.

Contemporary African American fiction also shows the continued uses and adaptations of passing as a literary strategy. The classic deployment of passing and racial indeterminacy as strategies to instill more consciously critical modes of reading acquires a postmodern twist in Colson Whitehead's and Toni Morrison's works. In Whitehead's *The Intuitionist* (1999),[43] as Michele Elam has noticed, the "narrative slippage between genres enacts one of the challenges of passing that is thematized in the novel itself: the call . . . to reconsider and remake acts of interpretation."[44] In her short story "Recitatif" (1983)[45] and her novel *Paradise* (1997), Morrison does not disclose the racial background of the central characters.[46] This narrative choice involves readers in a process of attempted decoding of the background of the characters that, by becoming self-conscious, prompts a critical questioning of the criteria, or the commonplaces, used to define racial identities. To quote Juda Bennett, "by refusing to solve the mystery of racial identity," Morrison "remaps the passing dynamic onto reader and character, effectively creating a metafictional narrative."[47]

In the twenty-first century, then, the tradition of novels of passing exceeds the antiquarian interest as a legacy of the past and lives a new life in multiethnic and mainstream literature, as well as in a variety of media contexts.[48] In contemporary fiction, aesthetic experimentation continues to mold the deconstruction of the interpretive frameworks informing racialized forms of discrimination. Passing is thereby being repurposed to confront the paradoxes of the "new Jim Crow" and challenge present-day contradictions between the rhetoric of postracialism and the persisting violent realities of inequality.[49] By complicating and destabilizing superficial epistemologies of "race" and exposing their oppressive social consequences, the trope of passing retains its relevance as a malleable literary strategy of cultural and political intervention.

Notes

1. The literary trope of passing has a real-life basis in the sociological phenomenon of passing that Martha J. Cutter, in her study of advertisements for runaway slaves, has traced back to the early eighteenth century ("'As White as Most White Women': Racial Passing in Advertisements for Runaway Slaves and the Origins of a Multivalent Term," *American Studies* 54.4 [2016], 73–97). In this essay, I focus specifically on the literary trope and foreground the tradition of novels of passing that continues to the present day. This tradition highlights the oft-underestimated artistry, literary self-awareness, and long-term influence of pre–Harlem Renaissance African American writers.

2. William Wells Brown, *Clotel; or, The President's Daughter* (1853; New York: Penguin, 2004).

3. See, for instance, Harriet Beecher Stowe's *Uncle Tom's Cabin* (1852; New York: Penguin, 1986) and Lydia Maria Child's "The Quadroons" (1842; in *Fact and Fiction: A Collection of Stories* [New York: C. S. Francis, 1847], 61–76).

4. Julia Collins also deserves to be mentioned, though her serialized novel *The Curse of Caste; or The Slave Bride* (1865; New York: Oxford University Press, 2006) remained unfinished.

5. In Brown's novel, Clotel passes for white and also as a man in order to acquire more mobility in her search for her daughter. Brown may have been inspired by the famous real-life story of fugitive Ellen Craft, who fled from slavery in 1848 by passing as a white man. Conversely, Clotel's daughter Mary saves her beloved George by helping disguise him as a woman in order to escape from prison.

6. Frank J. Webb, *The Garies and Their Friends* (1857; New York: Arno Press, 1969).

7. "To-Day a Mistress, To-Morrow a Slave" is the title of Chapter xv of Brown's *Clotel*.

8. The very phrase "Jim Crow," which has become a synonym for racial segregation, evokes a form of passing, in this case for black. As a song and dance, it was popularized by blackface performer T. D. Rice.

9. See William Wells Brown's *Clotelle; or, The Colored Heroine: A Tale of the Southern States* (1867; Miami: Mnemosyne, 1969).

10. Frances E. W. Harper, *Minnie's Sacrifice* (1869), in *Minnie's Sacrifice, Sowing and Reaping, Trial and Triumph: Three Rediscovered Novels by Frances E. W. Harper*, ed. Frances Smith Foster (Boston: Beacon Press, 1994), 1–92.

11. Paul L. Dunbar, "To the South: On Its New Slavery," in *Lyrics of Love and Laughter* (New York: Dodd, Mead and Co., 1913), 151–52.

12. Barbara Christian, *Black Women Novelists: The Development of a Tradition, 1892–1976* (Westport, CT: Greenwood Press, 1980), 25.

13. See, for instance, William Dean Howells's *An Imperative Duty* (1891; New York: Harper & Brothers, 1893) and Mark Twain's *Pudd'nhead Wilson* (1894; New York: Penguin, 1969).

14. Sutton E. Griggs, *Imperium in Imperio* (1899; New York: Arno Press, 1969).

15. See, for instance, Frances E. W. Harper's *Iola Leroy or Shadows Uplifted* (1892; Boston: Beacon Press, 1987).

16. See, for instance, Pauline E. Hopkins's *Contending Forces: A Romance Illustrative of Negro Life North and South* (1900; New York: Oxford University Press, 1988).

17. Pauline E. Hopkins, *Of One Blood; Or, the Hidden Self*, in *The Magazine Novels of Pauline Hopkins* (1902–3; New York: Oxford University Press, 1988), 441–621.

18. Harper, *Iola Leroy*, 199.

19. Pauline E. Hopkins, *Hagar's Daughter*, in *The Magazine Novels of Pauline Hopkins* (1901–2; New York: Oxford University Press, 1988), 1–284.

20. McHenry Jones, *Hearts of Gold* (1896; Morgantown: West Virginia University Press, 2010).

21. Sutton E. Griggs, *Pointing the Way* (1908; New York: AMS Press, 1974).

22. Barbara Christian, "Introduction," in *The Hazeley Family*, by Amelia E. Johnson (New York: Oxford University Press, 1988), xxvii.

23. Amelia E. Johnson, *Clarence and Corinne; or, God's Way* (1890; New York: Oxford University Press, 1988).

24. Edward A. Johnson, *A School History of the Negro Race in America, from 1619 to 1890* (rev. ed., 1911; New York: AMS Press, 1969).

25. Edward A. Johnson, *Light Ahead for the Negro* (1904; New York: The Grafton Press, 1975).

26. See Paul L. Dunbar's *The Uncalled* (New York: Dodd, Mead, and Co., 1898), *The Love of Landry* (New York: Dodd, Mead, and Co., 1900), and *The Fanatics* (New York: Dodd, Mead, and Co., 1901), and Charles W. Chesnutt's *The Colonel's Dream* (New York: Doubleday, Page, & Co., 1905), as well as Chesnutt's rediscovered *A Business Career*, *Rainbow Chasers*, and *Evelyn's Husband*, which were not published during his lifetime.

27. James Weldon Johnson, *The Autobiography of an Ex-Colored Man* (1912; New York: Norton, 2015).

28. See, for instance, Walter White's *Flight* (1926; Baton Rouge: Louisiana State University Press, 1998) and Jessie Redmon Fauset's *Plum Bun* (1928; London: Pandora Press, 1985).

29. See the differences between Irene Redfield, who passes only occasionally; Clare Kendry, who passes permanently and has a virulently racist white husband; Gertrude Martin, whose husband and family know about her passing; and Margery Bellew, Clare's daughter, who is possibly unaware to the end of the novel of her mixed racial background. Scholars like Jacquelyn Y. McLendon and Deborah E. McDowell, respectively, have also explored forms of ideological passing in the novel, such as Irene's adoption of mainstream bourgeois definitions of womanhood and the subtext of Irene and Clare's homoerotic desire. Clare's self-absorption, self-pity, and tendency to blame others in order to rationalize her own convenient choices recall Johnson's ex-colored protagonist.

30. See W.E.B. Du Bois, *The Quest of the Silver Fleece* (1911; Boston: Northeastern University Press, 1989).

31. See Edith Wharton's *The Age of Innocence* (1920; New York: Penguin Classics, 1996) and *Twilight Sleep* (1927; New York: Scribner, 1997).

32. See Francis S. Fitzgerald's *The Great Gatsby* (1925; New York: Penguin Classics, 2000).

33. Nella Larsen, *Quicksand and Passing*, ed. Deborah E. McDowell (New Brunswick, NJ: Rutgers University Press, 1986), 185.

34. In these same years, the tragic mulatto trope appears in the racially undefined protagonist of William Faulkner's *Light in August* (1932; New York: Vintage Classics, 2000).

35. Schuyler's white-to-black passing has literary antecedents in Ignatius Donnelly's *Doctor Huguet* (Salem, MA: Higginson Book Company, 1891).

See also the short story "Lex Talionis," originally published by Robert W. Bagnall in 1922 in *The Crisis* and recently reprinted by Eurie Dahn (*African American Review*, 51.4 [2018], 279–87).

36. Langston Hughes, "Who's Passing for Who?" in *The Collected Works of Langston Hughes*, ed. R. Baxter Miller (Columbia: University of Missouri Press, 2002), vol. 15, 163. Further references to the story appear parenthetically in the text.

37. J. California Cooper, *Family* (New York: Doubleday, 1991).

38. Colson Whitehead, *The Underground Railroad* (New York: Doubleday, 2016).

39. Ralph Ellison, *Three Days before the Shooting* (New York: Modern Library, 2010).

40. Barbara Chase-Ribaud, *The President's Daughter* (New York: Crown, 1994). In 1998, the story of Jefferson's mixed-race slave children was proven by DNA evidence.

41. Toni Morrison, *Song of Solomon* (New York: Alfred A. Knopf, 1977).

42. Danzy Senna, *Caucasia* (New York: Riverhead Books, 1998).

43. Colson Whitehead, *The Intuitionist* (New York: Anchor Books, 1999).

44. Michele Elam, *The Souls of Mixed Folk: Race, Politics, and Aesthetics in the New Millennium* (Stanford, CA: Stanford University Press, 2011), 119.

45. Toni Morrison, "Recitatif," in *Confirmation: An Anthology of African American Women*, ed. Amiri Baraka and Amina Baraka (New York: Morrow, 1983), 243–61.

46. Toni Morrison, *Paradise* (New York: Alfred A. Knopf, 1997).

47. Juda Bennett, "Toni Morrison and the Burden of the Passing Narrative," *African American Review* 35.2 (2001), 213.

48. Among the monographs and essay collections that have recently focused on the contemporary cultural relevance of passing, see Suzanne W. Jones's *Race Mixing: Southern Fiction since the Sixties* (Baltimore, MD: Johns Hopkins University Press, 2004); Elam's *The Souls of Mixed Folk*; Julie Cary Nerad's *Passing Interest: Racial Passing in US Novels, Memoirs, Television, and Film, 1990–2010* (Albany: State University of New York Press, 2014); and Mollie Godfrey and Vershawn Ashanti Young's *Neo-Passing: Performing Identity after Jim Crow* (Chicago: University of Illinois Press, 2018).

49. Michelle Alexander, *The New Jim Crow: Mass Incarceration in the Age of Colorblindness* (New York: New Press, 2010).

CHAPTER II

Beyond Assimilation

John Alba Cutler

Introduction

It's difficult to think of a more common preoccupation of Chicanx and Latinx writing than assimilation, or a more durable one.[1] Beginning with such nineteenth-century writers as Maria Amparo Ruiz de Burton and José Martí and continuing through such luminaries of the twentieth- and twenty-first-century canon as Américo Paredes, Piri Thomas, Sandra Cisneros, and Julia Alvarez, Latinx writers have repeatedly dramatized complex questions of cultural change and loyalty. What language should a writer use to represent a community that finds itself in between cultures? How can an individual maintain loyalty to her community when the pursuit of educational or economic opportunities requires her to leave it behind? When do choices about language, dress, or behavior signify cultural betrayal?

Scholars often characterize Latinx writing as anti-assimilationist, but that is true only in a narrow sense. If we understand assimilation to mean something like "the eventual loss of attachment to one's country of origin and the disappearance of the ethnic distinctiveness of immigrants," then it is accurate to describe Latinx writing as anti-assimilationist, especially when that idea is held up as a choice for migrant or ethnic communities to make.[2] But Latinx writers understand assimilation to refer to many other things besides this version of "straight-line" assimilation: the inevitable dynamism that results when groups come into contact over long periods of time, or the creative adaptation that individuals make of behaviors or forms from the dominant culture, or the efforts of a dominant society to integrate ethnic communities. Above all, Latinx writing attends to the uneven power dynamics that govern the broad swath of choices and experiences that go under the name of assimilation.

We might compare, for instance, famed journalist Tom Brokaw's recent use of the term with an example from Américo Paredes's novel *George*

Washington Gómez (1990). In a segment on NBC's *Meet the Press* on January 27, 2018, Brokaw responded to a discussion about immigration policy by declaring, "I also happen to believe that the Hispanics should work harder at assimilation. That's one of the things I've been saying for a long time. You know, that they ought not to be just codified in their communities but make sure that all their kids are learning to speak English, and that they feel comfortable in the communities."[3] Brokaw's comments indicate the staying power of a particular idea about assimilation in American culture, what sociologists refer to as "boundary-crossing assimilation." As Richard Alba and Victor Nee describe it, "boundary crossing corresponded to the classic version of individual-level assimilation: someone moves from one group to another without any real change to the boundary itself."[4] For Brokaw, the onus is on "Hispanics" to make certain choices about language and social integration in order to cross the boundary into Americanness.

Responses to Brokaw's comments were vociferous, if predictable (the journalist issued a swift apology). Some commenters defended the right of Latinx communities to maintain their cultural distinctiveness. Others pointed out that Latinx immigrants acquire English at roughly the same rate as immigrants from other parts of the world, essentially noting the irony that efforts Latinx communities have already made to assimilate have not yet resulted in their full incorporation as Americans. As *Washington Post* columnist Theresa Vargas puts it, "People touted their degrees and their accomplishments online, asking if that made them assimilated enough. They also spoke of what their families had given up to be seen as American. Was that sacrifice enough? Would anything be enough?"[5] What many Latinxs perceive, in other words, is that their difference from "Americanness" persists despite their initiative in attempting to cross the boundary. This is the condition that Tanya Golash-Boza describes as "racialized assimilation," foregrounding race as a conspicuous absence in traditional assimilation sociology.[6]

As a concept, racialized assimilation helps make sense of how Guálinto – the inimitable protagonist of Paredes's *George Washington Gómez* – experiences the persistence of Mexican difference in the borderlands of South Texas. "In school Guálinto/George Washington was gently prodded toward complete Americanization," the narrator observes.

> But the Mexican side of his being rebelled. Immigrants from Europe can become Americanized in one generation. Guálinto, as a Mexicotexan, could not. Because, in the first place, he was not an immigrant come to a foreign land. Like other Mexicotexans, he considered himself part of the land on

which his ancestors had lived before the Anglotexans had come. And because, almost a hundred years before, there had been a war between the United States and Mexico, and in Texas the peace had not yet been signed.[7]

The description of Americanization in *George Washington Gómez* obviously differs from the boundary-crossing assimilation that Brokaw and his detractors debated. For one thing, the term *Americanization* marks the text's 1930s provenance, before *assimilation* became the predominant term for describing the same process.[8] The passive construction describing European immigrants "becoming Americanized" makes it difficult to discern whether the immigrants themselves are choosing to assimilate, or whether the process is somehow happening to them. And for the narrator of *George Washington Gómez*, that's the point. It doesn't matter whether you choose to assimilate or not. What's important is the historical determination of your difference. For Mexican Americans in South Texas, assimilation on the European immigrant model is nonsensical, since it would deny not only their longstanding residency in the region but also the history of cultural conflicts between Anglos and Mexicans there.

The passage also points at another important feature of assimilation, which is its endorsement by a state institution – the school. *George Washington Gómez* poses an almost paradigmatic example of the school as an ideological state apparatus, to use Louis Althusser's term, functioning "massively and predominantly ... by the ideology of the 'ruling class.'"[9] Althusser describes ideological state apparatuses as sites of intense class conflict; in *George Washington Gómez*, that conflict maps onto race, with middle-class and elite white and "Spanish" students fighting in multiple ways against working-class and poor Mexican students. The discourse of Americanization becomes a way of covering over this conflict, forgetting Texas's violent history and encouraging students to acquiesce to the norms and values of Anglo-American culture.

George Washington Gómez anticipates later Chicanx and Latinx critiques of assimilation, noting how the discourse fails to account for histories of racialization that defy the telos of integration and harmonious coexistence. In addition, as I show in this essay, a range of Latinx writing demonstrates a different blind spot in assimilation sociology: namely, the way that it neglects the inextricability of gender and sexuality from cultural identity. Finally, as I show in the concluding section, Latinx writing encourages us to attend to the role of the state in facilitating or impeding the integration of immigrant and racialized groups. In the last thirty years, immigration policy has been a particular, often violent obstacle for the integration of

Latinx migrants, resulting in a situation where many Latinx migrants paradoxically assimilate without being assimilated. Assimilation sociology was once a discourse centering primarily on cultural citizenship, but in the absence of legal citizenship, contemporary Latinx writing suggests that cultural citizenship is not enough.

Racialized Assimilation, Gender, and Sexuality

Hardly anyone agrees on what *assimilation* means. Some people use it to describe a set of choices that immigrants make to adopt the cultural values and practices of their host society. Other people use it to describe a more or less inevitable process of adaptation that happens to immigrant groups over the course of generations. Still others use the verb in its transitive sense to describe the efforts of the host society to fully integrate new-comers. Each of these different ideas carries the potential for value judg-ments in a broad range of areas, including language, dress, food, and politics. Despite the lack of a popular consensus about the meaning of the word, as Catherine Ramirez notes, "Assimilation has long functioned as the *telos* in narratives about the American experience and as an organiz-ing rubric in US immigration history, the social sciences, particularly sociology, and public policy."[10]

Due in large part to the influence of the Chicago school of sociology, over time academics and the general public have arrived at some agreement over the basic parameters of assimilation, including what it is *not*. Consider the following three examples:

1. Robert E. Park's entry on "Assimilation, Social" in *Encyclopedia of the Social Sciences*: "Assimilation is the name given to the process or processes by which peoples of diverse racial origins and different cultural heritages, occupying a common territory, achieve a cultural solidarity sufficient at least to sustain a national existence."[11]
2. Nathan Glazer and Daniel Patrick Moynihan's book *Beyond the Melting Pot: The Negroes, Puerto Ricans, Jews, Italians, and Irish of New York City* (1963): "The initial attributes of [New York ethnic] groups provided only one reason why their transformations did not make them all into the same thing. There was another reason—and that was the nature of American society itself, which could not, or did not, assimilate the immigrants fully or in equal degree."[12]
3. Then-candidate Donald Trump's rejoinder to Jeb Bush in a 2015 Republican debate: "We have a country where to assimilate,

you have to speak English, and I think that where he was, and the way it came out didn't sound right to me. We have to have assimilation to have a country."[13]

These statements concur on one thing: that the scale of assimilation is essentially national. Even in the case of Glazer and Moynihan, whose book is explicitly about New York City, the issue isn't the degree to which ethnic groups have assimilated to New York or Northeastern regional culture, but rather to *American* society. Indeed, Park's conception of assimilation – which would become the endpoint of his influential theory of the race relations cycle – imagines assimilation as a sine qua non for the possibility of national existence, forming the basis for the way that later generations of sociologists would approach the topic.

These three statements also agree that as a process, assimilation concerns *solely* nationality or ethnicity, neglecting various other factors that might influence an individual's identity, such as gender, sexuality, dis/ability, or social class. To be fair, sociologists since Park and the Chicago School have always shown interest in the ways that race and religion affect assimilation, but as Glazer and Moynihan's work demonstrates, there are limitations to assimilation sociology's historical engagement with race, while gender and sexuality have always been sidelined.[14] Surely, though, experiences of cultural change affect various aspects of identity. As Latinx writing shows again and again, what it means to be Mexican or Puerto Rican or Cuban or American is always bound up with what it means to be a Mexican *man* or a Puerto Rican *woman* or queer or trans or disabled and so forth.

This is certainly the case in *George Washington Gómez*, where Guálinto's conflicted cultural identity is routed through various avatars of Mexican and American masculinity. Many scholars have commented on Paredes's description of Guálinto's conflicted self as "a divided personality, made up of tight little cells independent and almost entirely ignorant of each other, spread out all over his consciousness, mixed with one another like squares on a checkerboard."[15] Ramón Saldívar, for example, understands this passage as evidence of the vexed ideological conflict of the US–Mexico borderlands, where "the dialectic we encounter ... depends on the centrality of an ongoing dialogue between contending discourses, opposed in contra-diction, that cannot be resolved in one voice and thus has no equivalent in other conceptual systems."[16] Saldívar notes that Mexican gender ideology is one of the contending discourses structuring Guálinto's identity. To build on that observation, we might note that American gender ideology is equally at play:

> George Washington Gómez secretly desired to be a full-fledged, complete
> American without the shameful encumbrance of his Mexican race .... It
> was he it was [*sic*] who fought the British with George Washington and
> Francis Marion the Swamp Fox, discovered pirate treasure with Long John
> Silver, and got lost in a cave with Tom Sawyer and Becky Thatcher. Books
> had made him so. He read everything he could lay his hands on. But he also
> heard from the lips of his elders songs and stories that were the history of his
> people, the Mexican people. And he also fought the Spaniards with
> Hidalgo, the French with Juárez and Zaragosa, and the Gringos with
> Blas María de la Garza Falcón and Juan Nepomuceno Cortina in his
> childish fancies.[17]

Here we see the opposition of contending discourses, just as Saldívar
describes it, and the careful distinction between the symbolic capital of
Anglo-American written discourse versus the oral storytelling of Mexican
folk discourse. Just as important, the opposition isn't between abstract
versions of Americanness and Mexicanness but between ideals of American
and Mexican masculinity.[18] In this, Paredes's novel resembles other canonical works of Latinx literature, such as José Antonio Villarreal's *Pocho*
(1959), Piri Thomas's *Down These Mean Streets* (1967), and Junot
Díaz's *The Brief Wondrous Life of Oscar Wao* (2008).

Cuban American writer Achy Obejas illuminates how thoroughly
sexuality also affects identification and assimilation in her short story
"We Came All the Way from Cuba So You Could Dress Like This?"[19]
The story consists of the unnamed narrator's recollections of her family's
processing by the Immigration and Naturalization Service after arriving as
refugees from Cuba in 1963, alternating with reflections about how her life
has changed in the three decades since their migration. Whereas her
parents wholly embrace the United States as an alternative to what they
see as the decline and chaos of Cuba under Castro's communist regime,
the narrator resists conservative jingoism and questions whether the world
can be simply divided into good and evil the way it was presented to her as
a child. For the narrator, however, this is not simply a matter of national or
ethnic identity, as becomes clear in the complicated ways her queerness
affects her sense of self.[20]

In Obejas's story, an initial encounter with sexual difference in the
processing center, when a volunteer quotes suggestive verses to her from
the Song of Songs in the Bible, leads to a lifetime of anxiety about the
political significance of the narrator's erotic attachments. She connects
the blond doll she is given in the processing center as a child with a series
of blond boyfriends and "yellow-haired lovers," including a boy from a

military academy "who subscribes to Republican politics like my parents" and a girl named Martha whose boyfriend throws her out after discovering their affair and who later takes up with "a Kennedy cousin still in the closet who has a love of dogs, and freckles sprinkled all over her cheeks."[21] In these various affairs, sexuality as an axis of identification intersects with national and cultural identification. The story provides some cues that we might see the narrator's sexuality itself as a site of acculturation, where the sexual revolution of the 1960s liberates her from the strictures of some other existence – hence, the narrator's affairs with white men and women, as well as the intimation that her first sexual encounter with a Cuban woman might not have been possible under the constraints of the revolutionary government in Cuba. Yet Cubanness continues to signify intimacy to the narrator in essential ways. She contrasts the "ooohhh oooohhhh ooooooohhhhhhhh" of her white lovers with the "*Aaaaaayyyyyaaaaaayyyyaaaaay*" of her Cuban lover and describes the latter encounter in such rich, loving detail that it is clear the encounter gives her some elemental connection that was lacking in her previous affairs.[22] The sexual encounter enacts a reverse acculturation, where the Spanish *Aaaaaayyyyyaaaaaayyyyaaaaay* – one fluid expression that begins with a capital letter – communicates genuine passion in a way that the English *ooohhh*, uncapitalized and broken over three separate exclamations, cannot.

The convergence of cultural authenticity and sexuality in Obejas's story has a startlingly close analogue in Sandra Cisneros's short story "Bien Pretty," in which the narrator, an artist named Lupe, carries on a love affair with a Mexican pest control worker named Flavio Munguía. A middle-class Chicana from California, Lupe struggles with feelings of inauthenticity in San Antonio, where she has taken up a post as an art director for a community cultural center. She initially meets Flavio, a working-class Mexican migrant, when he comes to treat her apartment for pests, but after conscripting him to pose for a painting, she begins an affair with him. "*¡Ay!* To make love in Spanish," Lupe croons, "that language murmured by grandmothers, those words that smelled like your house, like flour tortillas, and the inside of your daddy's hat, like everyone talking in the kitchen at the same time, or sleeping with the windows open."[23] As in Obejas's story, Spanish for Lupe, signified in the exclamation *¡Ay!*, returns her to a sense of authenticity she feared she had lost. This passage follows close on the heels of Lupe's confession that she was a product of her "American education," suggesting that Spanish is not hers the way it is Flavio's.[24] Yet the intense intimacy signaled by her description of Spanish in this passage suggests just the opposite – that regardless of fluency, Spanish represents for her a true mother tongue.

Neither the narrator of "We Came All the Way from Cuba So You Could Dress Like This?" nor Lupe in "Bien Pretty" rejects assimilation per se. In Obejas's short story, the narrator follows the lead of her college activist friends and becomes a hippie, defying her parents in the process. Lupe confesses almost constant anxiety about her own distance from true Mexicanness, an anxiety that Flavio exploits to maintain his masculine privilege. (He conceals the fact that he's married, for example.) But the stories do not do anything so simplistic as support assimilation. Like *George Washington Gómez*, they invite us to attend to the complexity of cultural identification – to the ways that language, gender, and sexuality all inflect what it means to belong to a culture, especially a culture under threat of disappearance.

Assimilation without Citizenship

None of the three statements that I cited at the beginning of the previous section mention the state explicitly, yet it's worth noting that both the state and, more abstractly, the nation are central players in the way immigrant, racial, and/or ethnic groups experience assimilation. Certainly, these statements are intensely interested in the threat that failures of assimilation pose to national life. Park asserts that some assimilation at least is necessary to "sustain a national existence," and before he became president, Trump declared that "we have to have assimilation to have a country." In both these cases, determining how assimilation happens and, more importantly, what role the state has to play in facilitating – or perhaps coercing – the process is a matter of preserving the nation.[25] Park's sociological studies of assimilation in the wake of the Immigration Act of 1924 were meant to influence state policy in the direction of anti-racism. Trump's support for assimilation was part of a larger consolidation of support among nativist elements of American conservatism. But perhaps the link between the state and assimilation discourse is nowhere more evident than in the long career of Daniel Patrick Moynihan, who moved from a tenure-track position at Syracuse University to a series of appointments in the Kennedy, Johnson, and Nixon administrations before serving four consecutive terms in the US Senate. While serving as Assistant Secretary of Labor, Moynihan put his academic training to work to issue the report *The Negro Family: A Case for National Action* (1965), a study of the roots of black poverty that would influence state welfare policy for decades, and which, as I've shown elsewhere, has its roots in assimilation sociology.[26] As these examples suggest, assimilation is not merely an abstract, cultural discourse; it is deeply embedded in institutions of power.

As Latinx literature shows, myriad cultural forces act on individuals and groups that might influence their assimilation, but perhaps nothing so determines an individual's ability to assimilate as her citizenship status. This is where it becomes important to define the word *assimilation* carefully. If we were following the popular understanding of boundary-crossing assimilation, then it would present something of a contradiction to say that an individual might assimilate without being assimilated – that she might speak English, eat at McDonald's, listen to American popular music, read *Vogue*, and watch the latest superhero movie, and yet not be fully assimilated into American life, unable to travel freely, unable to pursue her education to the fullest extent possible, unable to secure the job or career she desires. This is the paradox of assimilation without citizenship, a process that Catherine S. Ramírez describes as "differential inclusion," whereby "a person or a social group assimilate[s] or is assimilated as a distinct, constitutive, and subordinate other."[27]

To explore this paradox, it may be helpful to adjust our language. The sociologist Milton M. Gordon makes a distinction in his classic book *Assimilation in American Life* (1965) between acculturation, or a "change of cultural patterns to those of the host society," and other types of assimilation, including "attitude reception assimilation," or the "absence of prejudice," and "behavior reception assimilation," or the "absence of discrimination."[28] Though it may seem outdated, importantly, this schema reminds us that assimilation is not a one-way process – it requires something of the host society as much as it does of migrants or ethnic groups. As Golash-Boza points out, this is precisely the situation of many Latinxs, who "face discrimination and who are not perceived to be white," and consequently are perceived as not being fully American.[29] Though for Gordon and Golash-Boza, interpersonal relationships are the primary site of potential discriminatory encounters, the state plays an enormous role in reinforcing boundaries against Latinx assimilation. Despite individuals' best efforts to assimilate, as Tomás R. Jiménez has shown, "legal status can mark a hard boundary defining insiders and outsiders."[30]

"(Citizen)(Illegal)," the title poem of José Olivarez's 2018 book, centers on the idea of assimilation without citizenship. The speaker of the poem is a citizen but his parents are not, and so the poem asks whether something of their precarious position inheres in him:

> Mexican woman (illegal) and Mexican man (illegal)
> have a Mexican (illegal)-American (citizen).
> is the baby more Mexican or American?
> place the baby in the arms of the mother (illegal).
> if the mother holds the baby (citizen)
> too long, does the baby become illegal?[31]

As is apparent in this first stanza, the poem lends both designations, "illegal" and "citizen," symbolic weight beyond the legal status they denote. It is not *illegal* to be Mexican, and yet part of the cultural logic of the contemporary immigration regime is the way it racializes Mexicans and other Latinxs through the prism of illegality. Published at the height of public outcry over family separations at the US–Mexico border in 2018 and a renewed debate about birthright citizenship, "(Citizen) (Illegal)" is especially trenchant. It implies that we cannot escape racialization internal to the United States as long as entry into the country is policed via race.

Another way of putting it would be to say that Olivarez's poem demonstrates how illegality has become affixed to Mexicanness in such a way that it precludes full assimilation, even in cases where individuals (like the poet) are legal citizens. This is now a standard feature of the modern border enforcement regime, as Nicholas DeGenova has argued: "Enforcement proclivities and prerogatives, and the statistics they produce . . . have rendered 'Mexican' as the distinctive national/racialized name for migrant 'illegality.'"[32] This racial formation has both symbolic and material consequences for Mexicans and other US Latinxs, who encounter discrimination in all regions of the country. It also results in situations where individuals are left in a kind of cultural limbo, not belonging to the nation they have always called home, but now removed from the national culture of their parents. The final stanza of Olivarez's poem asks:

> if the boy (citizen)(illegal) grows up (illegal) and can only write (illegal)
>   this story in English (citizen), does that make him more
>   American (citizen) or Mexican (illegal)?[33]

These lines ache with the poet's self-doubt, the possibility of regret, and a hint of shame about the poetic project. The title of the poem surfaces with its echo of Spanish syntax, the "illegal" stubbornly attaching to "citizen," seemingly adhering fast in the meeting of the opening and closing parentheses separating the words. Americanness is no compensation for a loss of language and culture, especially when that Americanness always socially signifies as lacking.

Javier Zamora's "June 10, 1999," the final poem in his debut collection *Unaccompanied* (2017), similarly dramatizes this impasse. The poem begins with the speaker remembering the first time he rode in an airplane, a trip that triggered memories of his immigrant journey from El Salvador to the United States as a teenager: "first day inside a plane I sat by the window / like when I ride the bus / correction when I rode buses / below the border."[34] From the beginning, the poem establishes two layers of retrospection: the poet looking back on his first experience in an airplane, which was itself a moment of looking back on his immigrant journey. Only a surface-level connection exists between the two journeys in the act of looking out the window. Where the airplane journey mostly passes without incident, the immigrant journey – which consists of multiple attempts to cross the border through the desert at night – is fraught with danger. These scenes of danger and trauma precede and inflect the speaker's acculturation in the poem. The paradox of assimilation without citizenship in essence begins even before the speaker's acculturation, since his experience of presence in America is founded on a trauma.

The poet's traumatic introduction into America compounds with this lack of documents to produce abiding shame. As in Olivarez's poem, that shame becomes confused with a different kind of shame, as the speaker reflects on what poetry signifies in the context of his acculturation:

> in public again writing at the corner
> so people can't see line breaks
> so they think I'm essayist
> maybe I'm ashamed
> maybe I don't want them reading this
> that was not part of *Mi Vida Gringa*
> *Mi Vida Gringa* not the movie I paid to see then
> on that ceiling
> but I still haven't exited in protest
> haven't been kicked out
> for not having a valid ticket
> I sneaked in bought the popcorn drank the Coke[35]

The speaker locates his shame in two places at once: in the idea of poetry, and in the way his American life fails to correspond to his idea of what he thought it would be. Of course, the two ideas are bound up with one another – the fact that he's writing poetry is one of the things that makes his life different from what he might have hoped. (At the end of this section of the poem he reflects: "I was supposed to be lawyer / businessman soccer player / Mom and Dad said / someone of value."[36]) Thus, the poem ties together two moments of deception – hiding his poetry and sneaking into the movie theater – the latter serving as a metaphor for being in the country without documents, or a "valid ticket." Both are sources of shame.

It's worth reflecting on what kind of shame the poem might be expressing. The opening stanzas, where the speaker seems mortified by the idea of other people reading his poetry, correspond to what scholar Gillian White describes as "lyric shame," referring to "shame experienced in identifications with modes of reading and writing understood to be lyric, especially as these have been determined by a diffuse 'New Critical' discourse by now so thoroughly absorbed as to seem natural."[37] The hegemony of New Critical discourse is essential to White's idea of lyric shame since it "contributed to a view of lyric poems as expressive objects that 'speak' to the reader without, paradoxically, the reader's need to understand anything of the history of the work's production, reception, or circulation."[38] To build on White's work – which focuses on such canonical US poets as Elizabeth Bishop, Anne Sexton Bernadette Mayer, and James Tate – we might think about the history of this work's production as essentially the history of undocumented migration followed by a particular kind of acculturation. The poet's shame here is not essentially about the uselessness or detachment of the lyric but rather about how it marks both his misacculturation – becoming a poet rather than, say, a businessman or soccer player – and his continued state of nonbelonging in the United States.

Gender and sexuality continue to permeate these instances of acculturation-without-assimilation, as Valeria Luiselli's short memoir *Tell Me How It Ends: An Essay in Forty Questions* (2017) demonstrates. The memoir recounts Luiselli's experience translating for mostly Central American children in US immigration court, a service she begins performing while waiting for her own green card to be processed. As part of this work, Luiselli is tasked with asking the children a series of forty questions that the US government uses to adjudicate asylum claims. If the children answer the questions "right" – that is, if their answers add up to a convincing asylum claim – then they will be able to obtain legal representation. One day Luiselli interviews two young indigenous girls from Guatemala who are unable to provide a satisfactory account of their situation.

For children of that age, telling a story – in a second language, translated to a third – a round and convincing story that successfully inserts them into legal proceedings working up to their defense, is practically impossible.

But how does the story about those girls end? My daughter asks.

I don't know how it ends, I say.

She comes back to this question often, demanding a proper conclusion with the insistence of very small children:

But what happens next, Mama?

I don't know.[39]

Luiselli's sense of desperation at the thinness of the Guatemalan girls' story syncs up with her own identity as a mother. The daughter's desire to know what happened to "those girls" implies that she identifies with them as surely as we are invited to identify her with them. It may be that the memoir thus depends on a certain version of feminine vulnerability and helplessness to evoke the pathos of the situation, but it also does so rather uncomfortably, by putting Luiselli's position of privilege in tension with her inability to resolve the plot. *Tell Me How It Ends* presents us with a portrait of what Jiménez would describe as "*relational* assimilation," but construed negatively here, whereby Luiselli's ability to assimilate is narratively inextricable from her *in*ability to assimilate the children she interviews.[40]

These texts by Olivarez, Zamora, and Luiselli represent only the latest in a wave of literature exploring the dilemma of undocumented Latinxs since the militarization of the border began in earnest in the 1990s. In works such as Luis Alberto Urrea's *The Devil's Highway* (2002), Reyna Grande's *Across a Hundred Mountains* (2006), and Cristina García's *A Handbook to Luck* (2007), as Marta Caminero-Santangelo has shown, Latinx writers "have increasingly turned their attention to the topic of the undocumented in the years following the implementation of Operation Gatekeeper and the IIRIRA."[41] It would be a mistake to think of these texts as centering primarily on an international problem, however – a problem of immigration policy solely. Like the texts I have been discussing in this essay, each of these novels has a genealogy in Latinx literature that thematizes the contradictions and anxieties of assimilation. They build on that legacy by returning us to the state as one of the primary agents of (or, alternately, obstacles to) assimilation, the institution perhaps most fundamentally responsible for determining whether changes in culture result only in trauma or enable something like human flourishing. In the end, that's what narratives of assimilation are really seeking – not just belonging, but something more lasting and vital – the chance to choose the life one wants to live.

Notes

1. In this essay, I have adopted the terms *Chicanx* and *Latinx* to reflect current preferences for broad linguistic inclusion. I do so recognizing that debates continue about the political stakes and historical accuracy of these terms. For more, see Richard Rodriguez's excellent essay "X Marks the Spot," *Cultural Dynamics* 29.3 (2017), 202–13.

2. Tanya Golash-Boza, "Dropping the Hyphen? Becoming Latino(a)-American through Racialized Assimilation," *Social Forces* 85.1 (2006), 30–31.

3. Antonia Noori Farzan, "Tom Brokaw Apologizes after Saying 'Hispanics Should Work Harder at Assimilation,'" *Washington Post*, January 28, 2019, www.washingtonpost.com/nation/2019/01/28/tom-brokaw-apologizes-after-saying-hispanics-should-work-harder-assimilation/?utm_term= .902d3b1c1642.

4. Richard Alba and Victor Nee, *Remaking the American Mainstream: Assimilation and Contemporary Immigration* (Cambridge, MA: Harvard University Press, 2003), 60.

5. Theresa Vargas, "The Real Question at the Center of the Brokaw Backlash: What Does It Take to Be American Enough?" *Washington Post*, January 30, 2018, www .washingtonpost.com/local/the-real-question-at-the-center-of-the-brokaw-back lash-what-does-it-take-to-be-seen-as-american-enough/2019/01/30/3b40b52a-24b8-11e9-ad53-824486280311_story.html?utm_term=.4a9748022e1c.

6. Golash-Boza, "Dropping the Hyphen," 34.

7. Americo Paredes, *George Washington Gómez* (Houston, TX: Arte Público, 1990), 148.

8. *George Washington Gómez* was written between 1936 and 1940, but Paredes lost the manuscript and moved on to other projects. After finding the manuscript in the 1980s, Paredes agreed to let Arte Público publish the novel, but only on the condition that it appear unrevised, as much a historical document as anything else. For more on the novel's publication history, see Ramón Saldívar, *The Borderlands of Culture: Américo Paredes and the Transnational Imaginary* (Durham, NC: Duke University Press, 2008).

9. Althusser, *Lenin and Philosophy and Other Essays*, trans. Ben Brewster (New York: Monthly Review, 2001), 98.

10. Catherine S. Ramírez, "Assimilation," in *Keywords for Latina/o Studies*, eds. Deborah R. Vargas, Nancy Raquel Mirabal, and Lawrence La Fountain-Stokes (New York: New York University Press, 2018), 14.

11. Robert E. Park, "Assimilation, Social," *Encyclopedia of the Social Sciences*, eds. Edwin R. Seligman and Alvin Johnson (New York: Macmillan, 1930), 281.

12. Nathan Glazer and Daniel Patrick Moynihan, *Beyond the Melting Pot: The Negroes, Puerto Ricans, Jews, Italians, and Irish of New York City*, 2nd ed. (Cambridge, MA: MIT Press, 1970), 14.

13. Nick Gass, "Trump Explains Why He Attacked Bush for Speaking Spanish," *Politico*, September 16, 2015, www.politico.com/story/2015/09/2016-gop-debate-donald-trump-jeb-bush-spanish-213748.

14. I have written elsewhere about the history of assimilation sociology and its blind spots regarding race, gender, and sexuality. See John Alba Cutler, *Ends of Assimilation: The Formation of Chicano Literature* (New York: Oxford University Press, 2015).

15. Paredes, *George Washington Gómez*, 147.

16. Saldívar, *The Borderlands of Culture*, 159.

17. Paredes, *George Washington Gómez*, 148.

18. It's interesting that whereas the Mexican examples Guálinto encounters are all examples of warrior masculinity from nationalist conflicts, the American examples include a wider range of masculine behaviors, including adventure and ingenuity. This might speak to why Guálinto eventually elects to pursue Americanness so wholeheartedly.

19. Achy Obejas, "We Came All the Way from Cuba So You Could Dress Like This?" In *We Came All the Way from Cuba So You Could Dress Like This?: Stories* (Minneapolis: Cleis Press, 1994), 113–31.

20. The narrator declines to name her sexuality. She details sexual encounters with both men and women, so she could be bisexual, but her encounters with men could also have occurred while she was closeted. I've elected to describe her as queer to account for this ambiguity.

21. Obejas, "We Came All the Way from Cuba," 115–16.

22. Obejas, "We Came All the Way from Cuba," 115–16.

23. Sandra Cisneros, "Bien Pretty," in *Woman Hollering Creek* (New York: Vintage, 1991), 153.

24. Cisneros, "Bien Pretty," 153.

25. Antonio Viego offers a compelling account of what he describes as the "coercive mimeticism" endemic to the "culture of assimilation in North America" (*Dead Subjects: Toward a Politics of Loss in Latino Studies* [Durham, NC: Duke University Press, 2007], 70). The history of coerced assimilation as represented by such shameful historical episodes as the Indian boarding schools should give us pause when evaluating what the role of the state should be regarding assimilation. See David Wallace Adams, *Education for Extinction: American Indians and the Boarding School Experience, 1875–1928* (Lawrence: University Press of Kansas, 1995).

26. See John Alba Cutler, *Ends of Assimilation: The Formation of Chicano Literature* (New York: Oxford University Press, 2015), 118–52.

27. Catherine S. Ramírez, *Assimilation: An Alternative History* (Oakland: University of California Press, 2020), 15.

28. Milton M. Gordon, *Assimilation in American Life: The Role of Race, Religion, and National Origins* (New York: Oxford University Press, 1965), 71.

29. Golash-Boza, "Dropping the Hyphen," 52.

30. Tomás R. Jiménez, *The Other Side of Assimilation: How Immigrants Are Changing American Life* (Oakland: University of California Press, 2017), 12.

31. José Olivarez, *Citizen Illegal* (Chicago: Haymarket, 2018), 3.

32. Nicholas DeGenova, "Migrant 'Illegality' and Deportability in Everyday Life," *Annual Review of Anthropology* 31 (2002), 436.

33. Olivarez, *Citizen Illegal*, 3.
34. Javier Zamora, *Unaccompanied* (Port Townsend, WA: Copper Canyon, 2017), 79.
35. Zamora, *Unaccompanied*, 89.
36. Zamora, *Unaccompanied*, 89.
37. Gillian White, *Lyric Shame: The "Lyric" Subject of Contemporary American Poetry* (Cambridge, MA: Harvard University Press, 2015), 2.
38. White, *Lyric Shame*, 2.
39. Valeria Luiselli, *Tell Me How It Ends: An Essay in Forty Questions* (Minneapolis: Coffee House, 2017), 66.
40. Jiménez, *The Other Side of Assimilation*, 11.
41. Marta Caminero-Santagelo, *Documenting the Undocumented: Latino/a Narratives and Social Justice in the Era of Operation Gatekeeper* (Miami: University Press of Florida, 2016), 7.

CHAPTER 12

Native Reconfigurations

Kiara M. Vigil

> The status of the immigrant who came to America because he willed
> to do so and had an end in view, the status of the slave who was
> forced to come, and the status of the American native who was here,
> in their original form, all differ. It is one thing to say, 'I came because
> I desired to rule,' another thing to say, 'I came because I was
> compelled to serve,' and quite another thing to say, 'I was here and
> this continent was mine.'
> – Arthur C. Parker (Seneca), "Problems of Race Assimilation
> in America" (1916)

By the turn of the twentieth century, Native peoples from the Americas
had developed strategies not only for resisting their forced "assimilation"
into white culture but also for sharing national and regional debates
concerning citizenship and race. Understanding this work requires an
entrance into the broad range of Native American activist and expressive
culture, which highlights the limitations of a narrow understanding of
American literary history. Using collective cultural biography as an analytical framework to connect the work of four prominent Native intellectual
leaders – Charles Eastman, Carlos Montezuma, Gertrude Bonnin, and
Luther Standing Bear – to a wider network of Indian people who used
their work to suggest reimaginings of American history, I argue, enables a
redefinition of early twentieth-century intellectual traditions.[1] What
emerges is a story of a complex intellectual culture shaping an equally
complex expressive culture, a story similar to other literary traditions that
have emerged from American literary history. Arthur C. Parker's criticism
of the assimilationist logics underlying US colonial policies and cultural
practices lays bare the different ways that Native and non-Native peoples
contended with a nationalist discourse, which sought to define citizenship
in racialized terms. As an interlocutor of Eastman, Bonnin, and
Montezuma, Parker's discussion of the problems of race and assimilation
in the United States illustrates the shared interests this network of Native

intellectual producers expressed in their writings, public appearances, and political reform activities during the dawn of the twentieth century. Their voices collectively shaped how Native and non-Native publics thought about citizenship and the place of Indigenous peoples in American culture.

In *Indigenous Intellectuals: Sovereignty, Citizenship, and the American Imagination, 1880–1930* (2015), I consider the different political and cultural spaces in which Native writers, from a later generation, grappled with citizenship. I emphasize how these Native intellectuals used their published writings and spoken performances as cultural sites of resistance to counter the encroachment of white ideologies and cultural practices.[2] Drawing on the work of Jean O'Brien, who argues that "dual citizenship" operated as an early form of Indigenous resistance during the early nineteenth century, I trace the ways that Native intellectuals from a later period took up the promises of American citizenship while simultaneously embracing Native notions of sovereignty. Just as earlier writers, like William Apess, personified the revolutionary idea "that Indians could both exercise self-determination as Indian peoples and become citizens,"[3] a later generation of Indigenous intellectuals, such as Eastman, Montezuma, Bonnin, and Luther Standing Bear found their own ways to use writing and performance to exercise their rights as Native citizens.

Native intellectuals used personal narratives to position themselves as speakers on behalf of a wider Native public, to represent Indian Country almost as a distinct nationality, in the hopes of unsettling dominant discourses concerning fitness for citizenship within the United States that were intimately tied to race. They eagerly participated in shaping American culture in order to reshape national narratives that had disavowed the roles Native people ought to play within the United States.[4] Much of this discussion of citizenship, assimilation, race, and the strategies Native peoples used to navigate the contours of these definitions demonstrates the limits being placed on them by settler colonialism. In this context, Native forms of resistance engender the "third space of sovereignty," defined by Kevin Bruyneel.[5] Eastman and Montezuma, as well as Bonnin and Standing Bear, found ways to work within this "supplemental space," given how their cultural and political work often existed along the boundaries, rather than the inside or outside, of the American political system, and by extension, the emerging "canon" of American literature. Their work pushed against these boundaries "exposing both the practices and the contingencies of American colonial rule."[6] Before considering specific examples of how Native cultural producers responded to these limits, and their efforts to operate within the "third space of sovereignty,"[7]

I turn to how settler colonialism is constructed within the United States; how it is "a structure, not an event";[8] and how it intersects with understandings and articulations of race and racialization that impact both Native and Black communities.

In the United States, ways of thinking about race have their roots in both the institution of slavery and settler-colonial policies. Patrick Wolfe's study of settler colonialism engages deeply with what he terms "elementary structures of race" through examples, across time and space, which illustrate the ways race can be understood as a social construct. Most importantly, Wolfe argues that race making operates in contingent struggles over land, labor, culture, and power. As a discourse, race is also a distinctly European phenomenon and "constitutes an ideology in the purest of senses."[9] During the early nineteenth century, racial discourse for Native and Black peoples took different, but linked, forms, with the logic of blood quantum used to define Indian identity and the "one-drop" rule as a measure of blackness. Working in tandem, blood quantum suggested that any intermixing with non-Natives would threaten the stability of Indian identity and with it any claims to land title would be less justified. For African Americans, the inverse proved to be the case, given that any portion of black "blood" meant one was Black and therefore less entitled to freedom and any other aspects of white civilization. These became foundational racial principles for maintaining white supremacy and a settler logic to eliminate the Native. As Wolfe asserts, "settler colonialism destroys to replace."[10] In this case, white blood has the "capacity to breed Nativeness out, a biogenetic extension of frontier homicide,"[11] which most Americans experience through the pervasive discourse of the Vanishing Indian.[12]

Throughout the nineteenth and twentieth centuries, popular narratives regarding western conquest in the United States concluded that Native people were doomed to disappear either through warfare, disease, death, or intermarriage and assimilation – while Black Americans became, at the same time, ever more visible through hypodescent. James Fenimore Cooper's *Leatherstocking Tales* (1823–41), especially the second installment, *The Last of the Mohicans* (1826), was among the first popular narratives to promote the idea of the Vanishing Indian. Prior to an important shift in federal Indian policy during the late nineteenth century with the General Allotment Act of 1887, there were vast removals of Native communities from along the Atlantic coast and southeastern states as another form of dispossession. Unlike removal, which forced Native peoples to abandon their homelands and move westward, the later policy of "allotment" sought to break up the common ownership of tribal lands in order to encourage the assimilation of Natives into American society as individual titleholders, which resulted in any "unallotted" lands being sold for white settlement.[13] During the antebellum era, as the Cherokee and others migrated westward, formerly Native-occupied lands became open for plantation slavery. While Native people were told they were less "Indian" if they intermarried with whites, the inverse proved to be the case for African Americans. The "one-drop" rule encouraged the reproduction of blackness so that an enslaved population would persist – available to work the lands once held by Native nations. As Justin Leroy argues, it is impossible to have a full picture of American history without considering the intersections between colonization and slavery. "Settler colonialism is a logic of indigenous erasure that has developed and sustained itself through anti-blackness. Anti-black racism, in turn, has overcome the setbacks of emancipation and the black freedom struggle by calling upon discourses of secularization and militarized occupation with roots in colonialism."[14]

Over time, the concept of "blood quantum" was constructed to manage Native populations as a way of measuring Indigenous claims to identity, which worked alongside fictional narratives that perpetuated the Vanishing Indian. Established in the nineteenth century, the federal Indian policy of blood quantum was a method the government used to both measure and fix "Indianness."[15] The degree to which one could be counted as an Indian determined whether one could be allotted land once held in common by the tribal nation. Today, the Bureau of Indian Affairs enables individual Native people to apply for a CDIB card, or a "certificate of degree of Indian blood." The first item on this application notes: "Your degree of Indian blood is computed from lineal ancestors of Indian blood who were enrolled with a federally recognized Indian tribe or whose names appear on the designated base rolls of a federally recognized Indian tribe."[16] This application, as recent DNA tests also demonstrate, is connected to a long history of outsiders working to define the terms by which Native people might understand and express their identity. Kim TallBear, an associate with Red Nation Consulting and a member of the Sisseton-Wahpeton Oyate in South Dakota, has written extensively on the problematics involved with DNA testing for determining Native identity. "Like 'blood quantum' DNA is an imperfect answer to the cultural question. Neither a higher blood quantum nor DNA can guarantee greater cultural attachment," she writes.[17] The politics surrounding blood quantum as a colonial policy originate in the nineteenth century but remain significant for several reasons: First, it had direct effects on Indian communities, and, second, the "blood" discourse created during this period had to be confronted by a later generation of Native intellectuals who became public representatives for Indianness. Ramifications were critical since the "less" Indian one might be, then the less entitled one is to landownership. As federal officials first created rolls to define the terms of Native identity, they did so with this in mind. The process of allotment worked to dispossess Native peoples of more of their land by not only drawing strict lines to divide Native from non-Native people, according to the logics of blood quantum, but also by breaking up communally held lands into smaller and smaller parcels. Any parcel left "unallotted" would be open for settlement by non-Natives. Blood quantum as a discourse aimed to delimit the terms for defining Indian identity, not according to cultural politics, belonging, and kinship, but according to race.

For Eastman, Bonnin, Montezuma, and Standing Bear, published writings and private correspondence became the critical terrains through which they voiced interpretations of history and culture, in the hopes of situating Native politics more prominently in American modernity, and they used these venues to challenge dominant understandings of Indian identity as a purely racial category. Invitations to speak for a range of non-Native audiences enabled them to re-present Native perspectives and to talk back to some of the ways Indian peoples and cultures had been misrepresented in the past.[18] They took up terms related to "blood" that came from colonial policies, like the measurement of blood quantum, and considered how they might refute the Vanishing Indian storyline that suggested colonization was complete. They argued for social and political inclusion in tandem with more cosmopolitan perspectives, which reflected the fluidity of both culture and identity. What their actions demonstrate, when viewed as part of a collective formation of texts and activities, is the expansion rather than the contraction of Indian Country during the early twentieth century. So despite allotment and forced assimilation and acculturation, Native peoples sought ways to resist incorporation into America because they did not want to disappear. Rather, they argued for fuller visibility and representation in terms of political and social structures.

Charles Eastman became a leader and champion for Native issues during this period and, due to his publishing, was the most well-known figure among this early cohort of Native intellectuals. As Eastman published books and gave public talks that celebrated his Dakota upbringing, he highlighted the necessity of including Indian history in the foundation of the United States as a nation. He used the platform created by public desires to consume "ethnic" texts and performances by Native people, who many believed were "vanishing," to argue for citizenship. Much of Eastman's views, at least initially, appeared to favor so-called assimilation. Read carefully, his arguments supporting "citizenship" denote one way that Native people could achieve enhanced visibility by having their voice heard as part of the body politic, which did not mean giving up tribal sovereignty.

On February 16, 1914, Eastman spoke at the Montauk Club of Brooklyn to an all-white, all-male audience. Newspaper reports celebrated the festivities of this "Memorable Sportsmen's Evening," highlighting their guest dressed "in full regalia of a Sioux chieftain." Although Eastman was described as "an added attraction" for the club, he used the opportunity to criticize wanton killing of game for the sake of sport.[19] This appearance, like the vast majority that Eastman was paid to give during the early twentieth century, required an appearance in "full regalia," and reports of this "costume" emphasized that he was a "real Indian" *because* he was a "full blooded Sioux." Although Eastman's writings presented more nuanced and complicated articulations of Native identity, these public performances traded on audiences' desires to consume Indianness as acts of imperialist nostalgia.[20] For Eastman, these presentations were supplements to a fairly modest income as a writer who had to support a wife and six children. So Eastman played dress-up to engage his audiences' expectations and then spoke back in ways that disrupted what was expected.[21] Encapsulating the strategic and accidental elements shaping his larger educational mission, his lecture performances and writings revealed his deep familiarity with the narrative imaginaries that defined Indianness. Indeed, many of the representations of Eastman's performances reflect his strategic choices – serving as advertisements for his work and leaving a lasting impression of his success as an Indian intellectual who performed his role both with and against expectations.[22]

The majority of Eastman's published writings reflect an ethos for Native identity that is best expressed in *The Indian Today: The Past and Future of the Red American* (1915). This text is not aimed at young adults like so many of Eastman's other books, nor is it purely autobiographical, like *Indian Boyhood* (1902) and *From the Deeps Woods to Civilization* (1916); rather, it is an account of other Native cultural producers and leading political reformers. In it, Eastman reflects on the Native as a philosopher and "a noble type both physically and spiritually" who embodies what he so often aimed to do with his public appearances. The subtlety of his prose gestures to the visual effects of wearing, or not wearing, "regalia," as Native leaders offer the wisdom of a "true child of nature" without "the garb of deception and pretence[sic]."[23] By strategically straddling the demands of Indian Country for better representation in American society with a popular imagination that embraced romantic portrayals of Natives as already doomed to disappear, Eastman continually pushed back against the tide of white civilization that displaced indigenous claims to land and culture in the United States. Eastman's second autobiography, *From the Deep Woods to Civilization*, offers readers a chance to imagine a future in which Native people remain in the United States as citizens, but not without a critique of the capitalist undercurrent that he understands as driving settler colonialism since the founding of the nation. He writes, "I am an Indian; and while I have learned much from civilization, for which I am grateful, I have never lost my Indian sense of right and justice. I am for development and progress along social and spiritual lines, rather than those of commerce, nationalism, or material efficiency. Nevertheless, so long as I live, I am an American."[24] His language strategically balances competing versions of history and understandings, with both settler-colonial and Dakota origins.

On October 5, 1912, Carlos Montezuma gave an address at the annual meeting of the Society of American Indians, a pan-tribal political reform group that was the first of its kind. His talk, "The Light on the Indian Situation," touched on issues like military service and citizenship, which were primary concerns for SAI members. Five years later, his writing appeared in *Wassaja*, his self-published newsletter, which addressed an even wider and more diverse Native reading public, reminding them that "all men are treated on an equal footing" and that human rights for Indians in America must be upheld. Montezuma was interested in reforming, if not dismantling, the Bureau of Indian Affairs and more generally in reshaping how most Americans viewed Indian people.[25]

In addition to these published pieces, the dominant mode of writing that Montezuma used to remain actively connected to Native performers, activists, and political leaders throughout his lifetime was epistolary culture. For him, letters were material goods that produced intellectual theses and frameworks for understanding his perspective on race and citizenship. Looking at examples from his correspondence, it is possible to trace some of the political and cultural networks that he accessed, created, and maintained.[26] Montezuma's writings were addressed to non-Native and Native consumers of print culture, and *Wassaja* in particular offered him a space to issue calls to action as well as shape the terms of debate when it came to major issues facing Native people in the United States. The tenor of his personal letters and editorial pieces reflects the emergence of a pan-Indian public sphere, which both diverged from and converged with American representative democracy.[27] One of the most prolific correspondents of Montezuma, who frequently commented on the future of Indians in America, was Richard H. Pratt. He is noteworthy, if not infamous, for being the creator and headmaster of the Carlisle Indian Industrial School in Pennsylvania. Known for coining the school's slogan, "Kill the Indian, Save the Man," Pratt maintained an impressive number of friendships with leading Native figures. On May 22, 1909, Pratt sent a letter to Montezuma with the hope that educated Indians might have the power to change federal policy. Although education was the means through which Pratt enacted change, he also embraced the notion of blood quantum, along with all the problems associated with it. In another letter to Montezuma, Pratt confirms this perspective, when referring to the work of Rev. Coolidge, "being like yourself, a full-blooded Indian, highly educated, his views are entitled to the most serious consideration." "Pratt's sentiments link discourses of the body with the mind by reconciling Indian blood with education. He also participates in a discussion of assimilation, a process he thought necessary for Native people to incorporate themselves into American culture. Pratt defines citizenship through a careful combination, rather than a synthesis, of an 'authentic' Indian subjectivity tied to blood quantum, with a right to speak based on one's educational background."[28] The kind of hailing that Pratt's letter instantiates was not out of the ordinary for Montezuma and other Native intellectual leaders during this period.

Having to contend with allies who wanted to "uplift" Indians through mechanisms like education while simultaneously referring to their Native identity in terms of blood only confirmed that disciplinary paternalism lay behind the projects being framed as uplift or assimilation. Beth Piatote links disciplinary paternalism to the "restructuring of Indian economies" through the "reassignment of labor, and reshaping of gender roles" that she argues "extended from the paired workings of allotment and boarding schools." Through her study of competing legal and literary representations of home, family, and nation in Native American culture, she defines *disciplinary paternalism* as follows: "Indian policy advocates and the law understood surveillance and violence as regrettable but necessary features of the assimilation process. Because of the assumed alignment of father and ward, such measures against Indians could be understood only as being for their own good."[29] With this framework in mind, Pratt's celebration of the twinned facets of education and full-bloodedness make total sense.

Montezuma, like many of his other Native interlocutors during this period, understood what was motivating Pratt's commentary. These Native intellectuals grew weary of Pratt's emphasis on race as a biological fact and industrial education, at a school like Carlisle, as the solution for solving problems facing Native peoples as *a race*. For most Native leaders, learning to read and write were more important than training in black-smithing and any other outmoded skills promoted by Carlisle. Circulating throughout Indian Country, to many non-Native subscribers, Montezuma printed articles, letters, and cartoons that criticized racial uplift projects like Pratt's in *Wassja: Freedom's Signal for the Indians.*[30]

In print from 1916 to 1922, *Wassaja* emerged out of Montezuma's home-base in Chicago and circulated throughout rural reservation communities in the Southwest, Great Lakes, and the Great Plains. Featuring letters from readers, the paper was an important node in the network of Native epistolary and print culture, since it enabled Native people to engage with one another in public discussions regarding pan-tribal issues, such as policy and education, as well as local concerns, such as land rights and reservation management. Furthermore, since *Wassaja* included a multitude of genres, from prose to poetry as well as liturgy and parody it reflected an increasingly multifaceted and diverse spectrum of tastes for its readers. Montezuma's use of political cartoons and allegories, like his inclusion of parody and sarcasm, suggests his criticism was taken seriously but was also clear and lighthearted. Readers could experience, in Native terms, Montezuma's disavowal of the popular misrepresentations of "the Indian" that figured prominently in other public arenas.[31]

The imposition of both spatial and temporal boundaries by the United States as a colonial state on Native peoples is a dominant feature of settler logic always already aimed at restricting expressions of tribal sovereignty. The pages of *Wassaja* offer Native engagements with these boundaries and an American political discourse that is intent on limiting Native agency. Bruyneel describes the *Third Space of Sovereignty* as a way of understanding how legal and political institutions operated alongside "temporal boundaries" concerning "narratives of economic and political development, cultural progress, and modernity."[32] This approach is useful for analyzing and understanding the complicated relationship between the United States and its Indigenous inhabitants. Much of what Bruyneel uncovers are the limits being imposed on Native actors given political discourses aimed at constraining tribal sovereignty, treaty rights, Indigenous identity, and political expressions. Montezuma uses *Wassaja* to work within the "third space" of sovereignty that Bruyneel identifies. Given the "limited nature of tribal sovereignty" through the imposition of colonial rule that seeks to "limit the ability of Indigenous people to define their own identity and develop economically and politically on their own terms," Native political actors have to work across "American spatial and temporal boundaries, demanding rights and resources from the liberal democratic settler-state while also challenging the imposition of colonial rule on their lives."

Bonnin's representational politics offer a different example for how a Native woman, as a writer and reformer, actively contested the limits imposed on her because of colonial rule. She is part of a Native female intellectual history that features writers like Sarah Winnemucca, S. Alice Callahan, and E. Pauline Johnson, who, like earlier generations of activists, sought equality and enfranchisement given the broken treaties they witnessed. Bonnin and her contemporaries embraced "dual citizenship" and "rhetorical sovereignty" as strategies that enabled them to situate Indigenous spaces as independent from the United States, and at a moment when tribal nations were not necessarily being treated fairly or viewed through the paradigm of a nation-to-nation relationship with the United States.[33] Bonnin's writings demonstrate the different strategies Native intellectuals used to negotiate modernity and foster cross-cultural conversation and political change. Bonnin's first public appearance, in 1896, featured an essay she penned for a speech contest, sponsored by Earlham College where she was a student. In "Side by Side" she invokes a racial discourse of imperialism to strategically argue for Indian peoples' freedoms and inclusion into the body politic.[34] In the writings and speeches that followed, Bonnin emphasizes historical events to confront racist attitudes that she repeatedly experienced. She creates links between Americanness and Indianness that allow her to claim separateness from American society, while simultaneously asserting her desire for an equal share of the American future that has so long been denied Indian people. The themes in "Side by Side" appear as she describes "our claim to a common country." This phrasing reflects her negotiation of a set of expectations that cast Native people outside of modernity and the nation, separated by biological inferiority (too primitive to be part of the present or the future), and yet also ripe for assimilation (physically adjacent by permission). Temporally, Native people are understood as pacified and defeated, so they might live "side by side" with white settlers and immigrant groups being similarly interpellated into a system of Americanization. "Side by Side" is just one example of Bonnin's representational politics in a written and spoken text. It was important not only because of the arguments she made but also because she presented them as a public speaker.[35]

By 1919, while Bonnin served as the general editor for *The American Indian Magazine*, she published "America, Home of the Red Man." As the quarterly journal for the Society of American Indians, Bonnin's essay reached a diverse audience of Native reformers and their non-Native allies.[36] Her article plays with an association between "home" and "nation" to make a claim for Indian citizenship. Using allegories to enliven and inspire her fellow Native activists, she suggests ways for reconsidering what "home" means for Native people who live under the threat of US settler nationalism.[37] Alternating between first and third person, the essay's narration describes a "chance encounter" between Native and non-Native travelers going west by train. The Native woman in the story wears a service pin for her husband, "a member of the great Sioux Nation" who "is a volunteer in Uncle Sam's Army." This image gestures toward "dual citizenship" in a way that is reminiscent of Bonnin's earlier speech in "Side by Side," and it encourages the reader to wrestle with how to reconcile Native military service with the fact that Natives were not citizens. More strangeness ensues, as a "pale-faced stranger" responds to the woman, saying: "You are an Indian! Well, I knew when I first saw you that you must be a foreigner." The stranger soon fades into the background and readers must confront the idea that Native people are both foreign and domestic according to the colonial state. The story continues, and Bonnin's argument emerges more clearly driven by the idea that "the Red Man of America loves democracy and hates mutilated treaties."[38]

Like Eastman's speeches, and Montezuma's polemical writings that circulated in *Wassaja* and *The American Indian Magazine*,[39] Bonnin's essay worked within and against racial logics that continually positioned Natives as the Other against which American identity was constructed.[40] Through the "third space of sovereignty," she, like many of her interlocutors, crafted a persona and argument that resisted the logics of blood quantum and erasure, which were foundational to settler colonial policies and practices. By the 1930s, these approaches took different forms as Native performers, such as Luther Standing Bear, confronted a proliferation of misrepresentations produced by Hollywood films that reimagined western conquest and Indianness.

Luther Standing Bear was among the first graduating class of the Carlisle Indian Industrial School. After several decades of struggling to make a living, among his people at Pine Ridge and Rosebud in South Dakota, and as a live performer for William "Buffalo Bill" Cody's Wild West traveling troupe, he finally settled in Los Angeles, California. While employed as a film actor, Standing Bear produced several autobiographical portraits of

Lakota life, which were published as four books between 1928 and 1934. During this time, he also worked alongside other Native actors and white supporters to found the National League for Justice to American Indians in 1931. Built by urban and cosmopolitan Natives, from different tribal-national backgrounds, the league was concerned with improving the working conditions of Native actors living in Hollywood and providing education and social welfare programs for their families.[41] As an activist, writer, and performer, Standing Bear's cultural work showcased the persistent and pernicious effect of racialized thinking on Native people that for him appeared most prominently in film. His first book, *My People the Sioux*, pushed back against these kinds of misrepresentations. Standing Bear writes in his preface, "I trust that in reading the contents of this book the public will come to a better understanding of us, I hope they will become better informed as to our principles, our knowledge, and our ability. It is my desire that all people know the truth about the first Americans and their relations with the United States Government."[42] This text, as well as the others Standing Bear authored, celebrates his contributions to modern America as a Native man.

Among Standing Bear's writings about race and representation are details from his work as a "show Indian." As he recounts working under William Cody, one incident reflects the intimacy involved in this sort of occupation, and the racial politics of the moment. While Standing Bear and his family appeared as part of Cody's "Wild West," his wife gave birth to their daughter. Cody was quick to capitalize on the presence of an Indian infant to promote his show. Such a notion was hardly new. From the earliest exhibitions, through the 1893 World's Fair in Chicago and the Wild West era, children and infants offered showmen a powerful marketing hook. Audiences gained an opportunity (not always taken) to humanize Indian people though the harmlessness and "uncultured" nature of children who had yet to be socialized into Native and white worlds. Children and infants offered possibilities for viewers to imagine individual development rather than social evolutionary destiny – and their "performances" contributed to the cultural underpinnings of policies (including a Carlisle education) that focused on the individual, rather than the community. Of course, babies did not perform. They simply were. Such a context did not allow Native everydayness to be other than performative. They were always already signifying racial possibilities and destinies, gender hierarchies (considering that Cody approached Luther – not Luther's wife – about exhibiting the baby), and class dynamics.[43]

In this setting, Standing Bear may have bristled at the suggestion, even felt rage at being asked, but he acquiesced given the economic gain. This aspect of his decision seems clear given the way he describes the event.

> My wife sat on a raised platform, with the little one in the cradle before her. The people filed past, many of them dropping money in a box for her. Nearly every one had some sort of little gift for her also. It was a great drawing card for the show; the work was very light for my wife, and as for the baby, before she was twenty-four hours old she was making more money than my wife and I together.[44]

Such earning potential carried with it the baggage of colonialism and white supremacy, as their performance reinforced a market to see Indianness on display. The sideshow experience was not wholly dissimilar from Cody's offer to patrons to come "backstage," so they could meet and mingle with *real* Indians who were featured performers in his shows. In these instances, Native actors could decide the degree to which they were still performing according to certain racialized scripts. For Standing Bear, the sideshow offered an occasion to both *play* Indian and play *with* Indianness, as it muddled the usually clear division between the viewed and the viewer since it was clothed neither in the accoutrements of myth nor the spectacle of reenactment, but rather the messy reality of poverty.[45] Much of the popularity of Cody's shows traded on the "facts" he advertised in his programs and the suggestion that these were "reenactments" of historical events, which included some Native people who had firsthand experiences on the battlefield. Standing Bear's writings recall these moments to celebrate his talents and his labor, pointing both to the opportunities and limits associated with a life based on ethnic performance that operated within "the third space" of sovereignty.

By tracing a few examples of literary work produced by the first generation of Native intellectuals, who contended with ongoing efforts to dispossess Natives of their lands, cultures, and histories, this chapter highlights how these texts responded to assimilation projects that were developed out of boarding schools, allotment, and the promise of American citizenship. Many of their writings, public appearances, collective actions, and modes of performance illustrate the kinds of debates taking place across Indian Country. Today, similar discussions are occurring that relate to how Native people determine and define the boundaries of ethnic identity and tribal citizenship. Then and now, Native people confronted derogatory racialized representations and essentialisms, which they engaged and refuted through their published writings, public speeches, and activist efforts. Including this Indian-based dialogue as a core facet of American literary history pushes at the boundaries of the field and many of its underlying assumptions concerning what constitutes literature and America.

Notes

1. I define collective cultural biography in Kiara M. Vigil, *Indigenous Intellectuals: Sovereignty, Citizenship, and the American Imagination, 1880–1930* (Cambridge: Cambridge University Press, 2015), 11–15.
2. Vigil, *Indigenous Intellectuals*, 15.
3. Jean O'Brien, *Firsting and Lasting: Writing Indians Out of Existence in New England* (Minneapolis: University of Minnesota Press, 2006), 145.
4. Vigil, *Indigenous Intellectuals*, 17.
5. Kevin Bruyneel, *The Third Space of Sovereignty: The Postcolonial Politics of US-Indigenous Relations* (Minneapolis: University of Minnesota Press, 2007), xvii.
6. Bruyneel, *The Third Space of Sovereignty*, xvii.
7. Bruyneel, *The Third Space of Sovereignty*, 21.
8. Patrick Wolfe, "Settler Colonialism and the Elimination of the Native," *Journal of Genocide Research* 8.4 (2006), 387–409.
9. Patrick Wolfe, *Traces of History: Elementary Structures of Race* (London: Verso, 2016), 7.
10. Wolfe, "Elimination of the Native," 388.
11. Wolfe, *Traces of History*, 4.
12. Brian Dippie, *The Vanishing American: White Attitudes and US Indian Policy* (Lawrence: University Press of Kansas, 1991).
13. For more on the history of allotment policy, see C. Joseph Genetin-Pilawa, *Crooked Paths to Allotment: The Fight over Federal Indian Policy after the Civil War* (Chapel Hill: University of North Carolina Press, 2012).
14. Justin Leroy, "Black History in Occupied Territory: On the Entanglements of Slavery and Settler Colonialism," *Theory & Event* 19.4 (2016), 8.
15. Vigil, *Indigenous Intellectuals*, 19–20.
16. "Bureau of Indian Affairs Certificate of Degree of Indian or Alaska Native Blood Instructions," OMB Control #1076-0153, www.bia.gov/sites/bia.gov/files/assets/public/raca/online_forms/pdf/CDIB_1076-0153_Exp3-31-21.pdf.
17. Kim TallBear, "Can DNA Determine Who Is American Indian?" *Indian Country Today* (December 3, 2003), https://newsmaven.io/indiancountrytoday/archive/tallbear-can-dna-determine-who-is-american-indian-EkvpMM7fUES2Zht3ARyZQA/.
18. Frederick E. Hoxie, *Talking Back to Civilization: Indian Voices from the Progressive Era* (Boston: Bedford/St. Martin's, 2001).
19. Vigil, *Indigenous Intellectuals*, 72–73.

20. Renato Rosaldo, "Imperialist Nostalgia," *Representations* 26 (1989), 107–22. Rosaldo defines imperialist nostalgia as mourning or longing for that which one has had a hand in destroying. For settlers in the United States, this mourning often takes the form of celebration and embrace of primitivist aesthetics viewed as essential characteristics representing Native ethnic identity.

21. Philip J. Deloria, *Indians in Unexpected Places* (Lawrence: University Press of Kansas, 2004).

22. Vigil, *Indigenous Intellectuals*, 75.

23. Vigil, *Indigenous Intellectuals*, 83.

24. Charles Eastman, *From the Deep Woods to Civilization* (Boston: Little, Brown, 1916), 195.

25. Vigil, *Indigenous Intellectuals*, 103.

26. Vigil, *Indigenous Intellectuals*, 103.

27. Vigil, *Indigenous Intellectuals*, 104.

28. Vigil, *Indigenous Intellectuals*, 113.

29. Beth Piatote, *Domestic Subjects: Gender, Citizenship, and Law in Native American Literature* (New Haven, CT: Yale University Press, 2013), 14.

30. Vigil, *Indigenous Intellectuals*, 116.

31. Vigil, *Indigenous Intellectuals*, 118.

32. Bruyneel, *The Third Space of Sovereignty*, xiii.

33. Vigil, *Indigenous Intellectuals*, 167.

34. Vigil, *Indigenous Intellectuals*, 170.

35. Vigil, *Indigenous Intellectuals*, 170.

36. Hazel Hertzberg, *The Search for an American Indian Identity: Modern Pan-Indian Movements* (Syracuse: Syracuse University Press, 1971). This text provides the first thorough history and examination of the "Society of American Indians."

37. Vigil, *Indigenous Intellectuals*, 185.

38. Vigil, *Indigenous Intellectuals*, 186.

39. *The American Indian Magazine* also published Montezuma's speech "Let My People Go" in 1916. Vigil, *Indigenous Intellectuals*, 141.

40. Philip J. Deloria, *Playing Indian* (New Haven, CT: Yale University Press, 1998), 37.

41. Vigil, *Indigenous Intellectuals*, 234–35.

42. Luther Standing Bear, *My People the Sioux* (1928; Lincoln: University of Nebraska Press, 1975), xvi.

43. Vigil, *Indigenous Intellectuals*, 259.

44. Standing Bear, *My People the Sioux*, 266.

45. Vigil, *Indigenous Intellectuals*, 260.

CHAPTER 13

Dispossessions and Repositionings
Sarah Winnemucca's School as Anti-Colonialist Lesson

Cari Carpenter

> I attribute the success of my school not to my being a scholar and a
> good teacher but because I am my own Interpreter, and my heart is
> in my work.
>
> – Sarah Winnemucca Hopkins[1]

With these words, Northern Paiute author and activist Sarah
Winnemucca Hopkins stakes her claim in the linguistic landscape of the
late nineteenth-century colonialist regime. Winnemucca (Thocmetony)
dealt early on with the repercussions of US colonialism. After her birth
around 1844, she spent her early years living with the Northern Paiutes –
the Numa, as they call themselves – in the stretch of the Great Basin now
known as Nevada. As a member of the band known as the Kuyuidika-a
(Eaters of the Cui-ui, an ancient fish in Pyramid Lake), Sarah was only a
young girl when non-Natives began to enter Northern Paiute territory;
diseases and other calamities followed. Martha C. Knack and Omer
C. Stewart report that two-thirds of the Paiute population was killed
during this period.[2] Unlike her grandfather, who told a traditional story
about whites as the tribe's "long-looked for brothers" who had once been
separated from them, Sarah Winnemucca increasingly focused on resistance.[3] In April 1870, she wrote a letter to Indian Commissioner Ely
Samuel Parker calling for the humane treatment of the Indians. The letter
was printed in a number of publications, including *Harper's Weekly*. In
the letter, she adopted the tone of her future missives, detailing agents'
abuse of power and declaring that if the Indians were well treated, they
would become "educated" in English and non-Native ways. But she
rejected the whites' description of the Northern Paiutes; as she writes,
"the savage, *as he is called to-day*, will be a law-abiding member of the
community fifteen or twenty years hence."[4] For Winnemucca, to become
educated in English did not mean endorsing a view of assimilation
wherein Native cultures were denigrated.

What follows, a close study of Sarah Winnemucca, is an example of Native American literary history, which requires something more than identifying novels, poems, or other literary works by Native American authors and placing them neatly in an established tradition. Rather, it demands our attention to the broad field of writing in which Native Americans engaged in resistance and self-definition. This is a body of literature that engages with a complex and often contested cultural history, often leading to a number of writings, from letters to legal documents, that guide us into histories that have been obscured or misrepresented. This essay focuses on a seemingly singular but important example of that cultural work, Winnemucca's self-narrative *Life Among the Piutes: Their Wrongs and Claims* (1883). Winnemucca's book draws us into her relationship with the New England educational reformer Elizabeth Peabody, who hosted many of her speeches in New England and contributed to her school, as well as Winnemucca's attempts to establish a school for the Paiutes that would avoid the assimilationist violence often associated with white-run schools for Native Americans. Following this book into this history gives us a way of thinking about works of Native American literature more broadly, and the histories that led to their emergence – their *necessity* – in a nation determined to control the voices and destinies of Native Americans across the country.

Winnemucca's self-narrative *Life Among the Piutes* offers readers a key to some of the central issues of Native American literary history in the nineteenth century. A collection of both autobiographical information and drafts of lectures she delivered across the country arguing for Indigenous rights, it touches on several of the tensions experienced by Native American writers in the period. Readings of the self-narrative have often exposed colonialist assumptions about this Native American woman and her life work.[5] Just as some have tended to see feminism as white women's mode of thought, certain scholars have questioned the degree to which white editor Mary Mann or her sister, educational reformer Elizabeth Peabody, influenced, or even wrote, Sarah Winnemucca's book.[6] A close look at this book indicates, however, that Winnemucca is the one directing the lesson. In a time in which most whites believed Native Americans had no educational system of their own, Winnemucca devotes an entire chapter of her self-narrative to detailing the education that Northern Paiute children traditionally receive. Winnemucca's book teaches a certain kind of feeling for Native Americans, a feeling that directly challenges the sentiments of those who were used to controlling the education of Native children. It would thus be a mistake to read her efforts as assimilationist; while she is clearly familiar with (and prepared to incorporate) certain white traditions, her interpretation of her school exemplifies her sense that Northern Paiutes have an admirable model of education. In other words, to become educated at her school is not to "become white." Winnemucca's school, a combination of Northern Paiute traditions and Elizabeth Peabody's feminist-minded educational philosophy, was a powerful counterpoint to the US boarding schools of the time. In keeping with Maureen Konkle,[7] who has argued that scholars have not paid adequate attention to the political autonomy of Native peoples – assuming instead that they have been "incorporated" into the United States – I see Winnemucca's school as one example of that autonomy. And though the nineteenth-century United States was marked by Indigenous dispossession of all sorts – not least of which was their control over the education of Native American children – newspaper articles written by and about Winnemucca indicate how she was able to reposition herself as a central figure in the classroom. The fact that this repositioning occurred alongside Elizabeth Peabody does not lessen its anti-colonial effect; indeed, it makes us reconsider dominant assumptions about "disempowered" Native Americans.

Given Winnemucca's endorsement of education as a means of empowering Northern Paiutes, what would it mean for her to "interpret" her work at one of the only American Indian–run boarding schools of the time? In interpreting, or taking control of her narrative, Winnemucca both authored *Life Among the Piutes* and taught at a unique Indian school. Although little attention has been paid to this school, it was a remarkable institution – not only for the Native American children who attended it, but also as an example for Indigenous scholars today.[8] Winnemucca's interpretation of her feminist, anti-colonialist school is apparent in several features, I argue: the centrality of the mother figure; the emphasis on Native American languages, traditions, and cultures; and the role of the Native American woman – the interpreter – as educator.

Following a chapter of *Life Among the Piutes* on the initial interactions between whites and her Northern Paiute tribe is a chapter aptly titled "Domestic and Social Moralities," which begins simply, "Our children are very carefully taught to be good."[9] This is phrased in the present tense, with the sense that this is not what whites teach them, but how they are traditionally instructed. When Winnemucca presents white influence as only detrimental to their education, their morality and goodness are moved to past tense: "Oh, with what eagerness we girls used to watch every spring for the time when we could meet with our hearts' delight, the young men, whom in civilized life you call beaux."[10] The result is a rather sly equation of civility and immorality. Winnemucca goes on to discuss the extensive moral education Northern Paiute children receive in terms of the treatment of others, the prohibition of swear words, courtship and marital rites, and the Festival of Flowers, in which young girls get flower-based names.

Winnemucca's school involved craft activities directly related to the land. As she mentions in the chapter "Domestic and Social Moralities," "the Indian children amuse themselves a great deal by modeling in mud. They make herds of animals, which are modelled exceedingly well, and after setting them up, shoot at them with their little bows and arrows. They also string beads of different colors and show natural good taste."[11] This lesson is mentioned in a later newspaper article about Winnemucca's school: "One form of art is also native to them, and that is modeling in mud, in which they excel, making animals and other playthings."[12] In encouraging them to "model in the mud," Winnemucca not only advanced a traditional Paiute craft but also helped her students think of the land – their land – as a place of learning. The footnotes of *Life Among the Piutes* make obvious the melding of Winnemucca's school and Peabody's vision: "Indian children really get an education of heart and mind, such as we are beginning to give now to ours for the first time. They are taught a great deal about nature; how to observe the habits of plants and animals."[13]

The Paiute mother and grandmother take center stage in this chapter, though partly for a sobering lesson of the deleterious effects of colonialism. As Winnemucca writes, "My people have been so unhappy for a long time they wish now to *disincrease*, instead of multiply. The mothers are now afraid to have more children, for fear they shall have daughters, who are not safe even in their mother's presence."[14] Here Winnemucca makes clear, even subtly, the threat to Northern Paiutes of sexual assault by white men, something they never had to fear in the precontact period. Again, if learning needs to happen, it is not the Northern Paiute children who most need a lesson.

As the chapter continues, further detailing gender, courtship, and political rites, the tense switches back to present, as if to signal that these traditions continue despite the presence of whites. So instead of the Native American who is frozen indelibly in the past, we have one who is very much alive and persisting despite the intrusion of whites. The white editors "intrude" at this moment with a much kinder footnote, pointing out that "in one of her lectures, Mrs. Hopkins spoke of other refinements and manners that the Indian mother teaches her children; and it is worthy the imitation of whites."[15] So, too, it seems, would be Winnemucca's comments on the political power of Northern Paiute women: "The women know as much as the men do, and their advice is often asked. We have a republic as well as you."[16] Again, the book actively repositions student and teacher, so that the white reader is made to view Northern Paiute governance as more egalitarian than her own.

The significance of the maternal figure is evident throughout *Life Among the Piutes*. Early on, Winnemucca makes reference to the "first mother" (not father, interestingly) "of the race," and throughout she uses the title of "mother" to denote appreciation for an authority figure.[17] The white teacher at Malheur is referred to as "the white lily mother," and Winnemucca herself takes the title as the book continues.[18] Elizabeth Peabody's kindergarten model shared an emphasis on the mother figure as a critical part of the classroom; as a line from her essay "The Piutes: The Model School of Sarah Winnemucca" reads, "The literary work is alternated with outdoor exercises in helping on the farm, planting, weeding, sometimes digging. The school is thus an enlarged home, of which she is the recognized mother."[19] The idea of the teacher as a "recognized mother" is reminiscent of Paula Gunn Allen's essay "Who Is Your Mother? Red Roots of White Feminism." According to Gunn Allen, the Laguna Pueblo see the mother as far more than just a woman with a child:

> At Laguna Pueblo in New Mexico, "Who is your
> mother?" is an important question. At Laguna,
> one of several of the ancient Keres gynocratic
> societies of the region, your mother's identity is
> the key to your own identity .... Of course, your
> mother is not only that woman whose womb formed and
> released you—the term refers in every individual
> case to an entire generation of women whose
> psychic, and consequently physical, "shape" made
> the psychic existence of the following generation
> possible.[20]

The maternal figure is a feature of much Native American feminist theory, from assertions of "mother earth" to the figure who tells cultural stories and is a source of ethnic inspiration.

Life Among the Piutes makes clear there was space here – at least as Winnemucca imagined it – for female power. When she participates in a horseback rescue of her father during the Bannock War, she initially defers when they ask her advice, saying, "You are men, you can decide better than

I can."[21] Yet when they insist that she knows the country better than they do, she slips easily into a leadership role, suggesting the performativity of her earlier protest. Newspaper articles about the school suggest it too was less restrictive than most government boarding schools, where girls were taught domestic lessons while boys were schooled in vocation.[22] As one article reports, just as the girls make shirts from cloth sent by Winnemucca's Eastern friends, "the boys, wanting to do all that the girls did, have also become expert and can make shirts."[23] Such an activity, which allowed girls and boys to pursue the same kind of education, would not exist at the typical US boarding school.

Winnemucca's Peabody Institute, which first opened in late 1884 or early 1885, serves as a marked contrast to the typical American off-reservation boarding school. Carlisle, the prototype for these schools, was established in 1879 by William Pratt, who employed his military experience in every aspect of the institution. Carlisle itself evolved from Ft. Marion, the penal institution at Saint Augustine, Florida, that was used to house and "educate" Plains Indians from the Cheyenne, Kiowa, Comanche, Arapaho, and Caddo tribes who had been involved in the Red River Wars. Carlisle, with its military discipline, discouragement of Native languages and traditions, and strict gender segregation, was an epitome of the colonialist boarding school. While boarding schools were quite diverse, at worst they were devastating, disease-ridden, soul-crushing institutions that sought, in Pratt's infamous words, "to kill the Indian and save the man."[24]

As Winnemucca often told the media, she herself had very little formal education. She had avoided the government boarding school; she first learned English during her stay with the Ormsby family in Genoa, Nevada, whom she describes as kind and generous with their books. The one formal educational experience she had was in a San Jose convent after her grandfather's death. In *Life Among the Piutes*, Winnemucca reports that her stay there was cut short by parents who did not want an Indian attending school alongside their children.[25] And as the second chapter of *Life Among the Piutes* details, Winnemucca had a rich tribal education early on. The Peabody Institute was not her first teaching experience; she had taught at Fort Malheur, the Yakima Reservation, and Fort Vancouver. As Anne Ruggles Gere notes, Winnemucca was one of the first Native teachers of the time and thus constitutes an important (and underexamined) part of nineteenth-century US history. Winnemucca and other Native women teachers were challenged, Gere argues, by various aspects of US education such as pay inequality, the decision in 1881 that federally funded schools could not teach Native American languages, and the racist sense that Indigenous people were "savages" who did not belong in the classroom. The patriarchal culture of the educational system made Native women's experiences even more difficult: "Frequently they turned to teaching because they needed money, but just as frequently they received less pay than their white colleagues, were summarily replaced by white family or friends of Indian agents, or arbitrarily transferred from one school to another with no consideration for the economic hardships such moves entailed."[26] In starting her own biracial school and arguing it was equal or even superior to the US model, Winnemucca challenged the racist, sexist system at its core.

An important ingredient of Winnemucca's success was her collaboration with the Easterner Elizabeth Peabody, an early architect of the kindergarten educational model. Elizabeth Peabody's confidence in Indigenous capacity was due, at least in part, to the time she spent with Winnemucca in 1883, when the Paiute leader stayed in her Boston home during her lecture tour. Seeing the collaborative nature of their relationship as a dynamic pairing in which each influenced the other, rather than the "ward and guardian" relationship assumed by most whites at the time, is in fact an important repositioning that Winnemucca's writing requires. Peabody's life, which stretched over the nineteenth century, illustrates the changes in women's status over those years. Peabody was fortunate to have a mother who was a very influential teacher; it was her rigorous school that the young Elizabeth attended. She also enjoyed private lessons from her father, who taught her Latin and inspired her to learn ten other languages.[27] She went on to pursue private lessons from people like Ralph Waldo Emerson and to advance her own teaching career. Peabody's work establishing the kindergarten movement in the United States reflects her belief in the power of maternal love: the idea that women could be permitted to transcend the home if they, in effect, made a home of school. Women, she believed, "are always in maternal relation to society" even if they aren't actually mothers.[28] This ideology suited an independent woman who at the same time did not seek to mount an overt challenge to existing gender roles.

The etymology of kindergarten – humans as plants – fit well with Winnemucca's model, exemplifying one way the two philosophies coincided. Peabody called for the kindergarten to encourage children to grow organically through both physical play and spiritual music and art.[29] Winnemucca's school incorporated such beliefs throughout, including outside activities, song, and crafts. *Life Among the Piutes* illustrates the idea of the school best understood as a consolidation of Native languages and traditions and Euro-American philosophies of education: one which, above all else, offered a central place for women.

The school Winnemucca created both contrasted the US model and complemented Peabody's vision for kindergarten in specific ways. First, it included multiple languages, from English to Northern Paiute. Winnemucca herself spoke five languages and had obvious respect for multilingualism. Because her school operated with private funding, she could ignore the 1881 prohibition against bilingualism – though, of course, ignoring it also meant she could not get those badly needed federal funds. Second, she was committed to keeping children close to their parents and their wider family.

In its focus on what she called a "green arbor," suggesting horticulture and other natural subjects, Winnemucca's school differed from the curriculum of most of the country's boarding schools. Mary Stout offers the daily schedule of the Haskell Institute, from the 5:30 a.m. rising bell and military drill to the 9:15 p.m. taps.[30] In contrast, Winnemucca's school included Native storytelling – a direct contrast to the government boarding school, which would never have included such traditional teachings. This provided the children with an anti-colonial narrative, which the children wrote throughout their landscape:

> She gave them always the initiative in conversation, as the kindergartens do their children, asking each to say something in Piute, and then telling them how to say it in English, writing in chalk upon the blackboard for them to imitate the leading words, and then find them in the books. She says they never forget these words, but write them all over fences in [L]ovelocks, and tell their meaning in Piute to their parents, delighting to display their acquisitions.[31]

In this sense, the children were encouraged to see English (and Northern Paiute) as "acquisitions" of their own. This is reminiscent of Simon Ortiz's argument that English can itself be considered a Native language:

> The indigenous peoples of the Americas have taken the language of the colonialists and used them for their own ends. Some would argue that this means Indian peoples have succumbed or become educated into a different linguistic system and have simply forgotten or have been forced to forsake their native selves. This is simply not true.[32]

What Ortiz (and Winnemucca) describes is itself a repositioning of the English language as a possession – and tool – of Native Americans, which profoundly challenges the colonial sense of their disempowerment.

Early descriptions of the school envision it in Euro-American terms but also demonstrate the promise of Winnemucca's Paiute leadership. The school, originally a "no-be," a traditional house made of branches that provided sufficient shelter in the summer months, was set on a 150-acre farm given to her brother Natchez Overton by ex-Governor Leland Stanford of California in the spring of 1885. In October 1885, Peabody gave Winnemucca $350 to support the construction of a physical school. With farming supplies and food donated by Easterners, Natchez and Sarah were able to make "two tents, one for him and his family of seven children and one for herself with the addition of the "green arbor" for a school-room."[33] The school thus becomes an ideal place, at least in the East Coast newspaper, for the Native American: He or she is saved from "wandering" by a generous gift of land to "improve" by farming.

Winnemucca's distinctive vision of the school quickly became evident. Her brother Natchez, in a kind of miniaturized version of allotment, divided his farm into six ten-acre farms to six homeless Paiutes. Sarah planned for these men to form the governing council, "with equal voice for their own self-education in material affairs and social union" -- thus exerting a definitive authority in tribal affairs.[34] Although this suggests men would dominate the governing council, Winnemucca assumes a position somewhat like that of the Haudenosaunee/ Iroquois clan mother who selects – and has the power to remove – male leaders. Additionally, she gathered them each day for public worship, which also served for English lessons. By the end of 1885, Winnemucca's only need was a house with room for the lodging of white teachers. Winnemucca, displaying the rhetorical acumen that Malea Powell first described, initially presents the school as an idyllic community with land for the Indians, Christianity, and room for white teachers.[35]

The promise of the school as an anti-colonial enterprise is reflected in other newspaper articles. An article from a Nevada newspaper reports that the students were learning quickly, able to read and write after only six weeks. As the *Silver State* announces in the summer of 1886, the students were advancing rapidly in orthography, primary arithmetic, spelling one-syllable words, numerals, and the singing of hymns. The article stresses the surprising progress made by the children, adding that "the Piute Princess is certainly entitled to great credit for the interest she is taking in their education. The Indian Bureau should do something toward assisting this remarkable woman in her very laudable undertaking."[36] Winnemucca points to good interpreters as the key to a successful school: those who are not tools of the agent. "I attribute the success of my school not to my being a scholar and a good teacher but because I am my own Interpreter, and my heart is in my work."[37] In these terms, the Native American woman determines the direction of her school, a truly anti-colonial move. Peabody echoed this sentiment: "Self-education is the only complete education, and it can be accomplished only when children are made happy from the beginning, as *she* makes her scholars."[38] Education is thus not the sole province of the whites; rather, it is a tool that she has secured for the good of her people. Winnemucca's most significant repositioning comes soon after, when she makes the case that she should be placed in charge of a new Native American boarding school in the area. Here, she mentions her ability to speak five languages, read, and write, not to boast, "but simply to show you what can be done."[39] Some might consider the following lines an indication of her move to assimilate:

> A few years ago you owned this great country; to-day the white man owns it all, and you own nothing. Do you know what did it? Education. You see the miles and miles of railroad, the locomotive, the Mint in Carson, where they make money. Education has done it all. Now, what it has done for one man it will do for another. You have brains same as the whites, your children have brains, and it will be your fault if they grow up as you have. I entreat you to take hold of this school, and give your support by sending your children, old and young, to it, and when they grow up to manhood and womanhood they will bless you.[40]

Yet this passage is significant for its endorsement of a particular kind of education that goes against the colonialist mindset of the United States; here, it is through the figure of a Native American woman that the school offers a way for Native children to gain equal standing with whites. The newspaper then makes the case that the Indian Department should fund a Native American school in Nevada with Sarah as its head: an efficient enterprise, it argues, that would inspire the sympathy of all "right-minded people."[41] It is essential, the article argues, that the teacher be Indian herself, for this way she can increase the confidence of her Native students and overcome the usual "great gulf" between a white teacher and Indian students:

> The pupils must often despair of ever approximating the learning which they believe came as naturally to the white man as the color of his skin. But when an Indian teacher like Sarah can say to them: 'I learned this, I am an Indian, and you are as good as I am. What I learned is as possible and as easy to you,' there must be in it a superior encouragement.[42]

This model demonstrated a rare investment in racial (and gender) equity that would undoubtedly be threatening to many white men. To read this simply as a statement of Winnemucca's desire to turn Natives into whites assumes that any kind of education is white when, in fact, hers was particularly Northern Paiute. If we grant that Native education exists, and thus to become educated is not to become white (or even less Indian), we see the power of Winnemucca's school.

In December 1886, Peabody, in an illustration of her advocacy for Winnemucca's anti-colonialist, feminist cause, embraced Winnemucca's call to create a government school of which she was in charge. Arguing that *Life Among the Piutes* should be read for a true knowledge of this remarkable woman and her tribe, Peabody offered to send, postpaid, a copy of such to any one sending $1 to her address at Jamaica Plain, Massachusetts. The money thus received would make the "nest egg of a new fund to enable Sarah to renew her grand enterprise of making a normal school (for that is what she was doing) of Indian teachers of English."[43] Thanks in part to this call, Winnemucca got enough money to reopen with 21 students. The schedule was four hours a day for literary work, and the rest for farming. Peabody refers to a well-spelled, spontaneously written letter from one of Sarah's students, an eleven-year-old girl who couldn't speak one word of English a year before. Drawings from other children reveal a "good eye for drawing, and prove what has been stated, that the Indian's inherent love for nature will unconsciously aid him when put to this kind of work."[44]

Winnemucca was faced with the ultimate challenge to her anti-colonial model in April 1887, when a group of Northern Paiute students were taken by Superintendent Davis to enroll in a government school in Grand Junction, Colorado.[45] In language that sounds progressive even today given the chaos and inhumanity of parent–child separation at the southern border, Winnemucca resisted, saying that "she had no control over them, and that he must consult their parents.[46] In other words, she felt it was not her place, but the family's, to decide where a child should be educated – a challenge to the US officials' assumption that Native children could be sent to whichever institution the white adults wished. As one article reads, she "found on the farm a school, which shall not be, as is usual, a farce, nor, like the schools of Hampton and Carlisle, have the inevitable effect of separating and estranging parents and children, but shall educate both together."[47]

Frustrated with this development and determined to raise more funding to support her school, Winnemucca returned to the East Coast to collect donations, undoubtedly finding the most sympathetic crowds in Peabody's milieu. Meanwhile, Peabody renewed her call for Winnemucca to be placed at the head of a government school. Yet dispossession forces continued; in June 1887, the *Reno Evening Gazette* ran the most negative account of Winnemucca and her school, an account that serves to indicate the prejudice she faced from the white "Indian reform" movement. The article claims, in response to the Grand Junction school controversy, that Superintendent Davis was set to leave the next day with "at least forty recruits for his excellent school."[48] He would bring more, the reporter notes, but for Natchez and Sarah, the "idolized friend" who "interposed a veto" out of the "outrageous" desire to educate her people rather than to have the government do so.[49] The article in which these quotes appear is significant for its articulation not only of the degree to which Winnemucca's school was seen as contrary to the US government, but also the threat Winnemucca herself seemed to pose to that government. According to Peabody, at its height in November 1887, 400 students clamored to be taught by Winnemucca. Lacking sufficient funds, however, the school was ultimately not sustainable and closed soon after.[50]

As *Life Among the Piutes* and the nineteenth-century newspaper articles and letters teach us, then, there was an alternative to the colonialist boarding school. Winnemucca's school becomes a kind of case study that demonstrates the power of an education that embraced Native languages, pride in Native traditions, and the importance of women. Likewise, Winnemucca's collaboration with Elizabeth Peabody should signal her influence on a woman who was herself a key educator in the United States. As Winnemucca demonstrated, her model of Native education was successful in its time as a decolonizing mission. Keeping her school in mind, we should consider other examples of such autonomy in Native American literature and culture. Although Winnemucca's school did not have the legacy it deserved, it is an exceptional alternative to the nineteenth century story of dispossession that we have come to know so well.

Notes

1. Cari M. Carpenter, and Carolyn Sorisio, eds., *The Newspaper Warrior: Sarah Winnemucca Hopkins's Campaign for American Indian Rights, 1864–1891* (Lincoln: University of Nebraska Press, 2015), 261.
2. Martha C. Knack and Omer C. Stewart, *As Long as the River Shall Run: An Ethnohistory of Pyramid Lake Indian Reservation* (Berkeley: University of California Press, 1984), 83.

3. Sarah Winnemucca Hopkins, *Life Among the Piutes: Their Wrongs and Claims*, Vintage West Series (1883; Reno: University of Nevada Press, 1994), 3.

4. Carpenter and Sorisio, *Newspaper Warrior*, 39, emphasis added.

5. Following most scholars, I refer to her as "Sarah Winnemucca" for consistency from here on, although after her marriage to Hopkins she adopted his surname in addition to her own. Also note that the title of Winnemucca's book misspells *Paiute*; the *a* is left out in the original.

6. Georgi-Findlay and Steward question the degree to which Mary Mann influenced the text. As Georgi-Findlay notes, a letter that Mann wrote to a friend suggests that she may have made more changes than she admits to in the preface. I have found no evidence to support this claim. Zanjani notes that a letter by Mary Mann in which she comments on Winnemucca's manuscript "definitively settles the issue." See Brigitte Georgi-Findlay, "The Frontiers of Native American Women's Writing: Sarah Winnemucca's *Life among the Piutes*," in *New Voices in Native American Literary Criticism*, ed. Arnold Krupat (Washington, DC: Smithsonian Institution Press, 1993), 222–52; and Julian H. Steward and Erminie Wheeler-Voegelin, *The Northern Paiute Indians*, United States Indian Claims Commission, Garland American Indian Ethnohistory Series, Paiute Indians 3 (New York: Garland, 1974), 36. See also Sally Zanjani, *Sarah Winnemucca* (Lincoln: University of Nebraska Press, 2001).

7. Maureen Konkle, *Writing Indian Nations: Native Intellectuals and the Politics of Historiography, 1827–1863* (Chapel Hill: University of North Carolina Press, 2004), 7.

8. Since neither *American Indian* nor *Native American* is a more preferred term in Native American Studies scholarship, I use the two interchangeably.

9. Hopkins, *Life Among the Piutes*, 45.

10. Hopkins, *Life Among the Piutes*, 46.

11. Hopkins, *Life Among the Piutes*, 57.

12. Carpenter and Sorisio, *Newspaper Warrior*, 253.

13. Hopkins, *Life Among the Piutes*, 52.

14. Hopkins, *Life Among the Piutes*, 48.

15. Hopkins, *Life Among the Piutes*, 51.

16. Hopkins, *Life Among the Piutes*, 51.

17. Hopkins, *Life Among the Piutes*, 45.

18. Hopkins, *Life Among the Piutes*, 117.

19. Carpenter and Sorisio, *Newspaper Warrior*, 280.

20. Paula Gunn Allen, "Who Is Your Mother? Red Roots of White Feminism," *Sinister Wisdom* 25 (1984), 34–46, at 34.

21. Hopkins, *Life Among the Piutes*, 156.

22. Clifford E. Trafzer, Jean A. Keller, and Lorene Sisquoc, *Boarding School Blues: Revisiting American Indian Educational Experiences* (Lincoln: University of Nebraska Press, 2006), 179. A student newspaper at Carlisle indicates the gendering of printing. Photographs of the student printers display young men

only until 1895. In May 1888, a Pueblo student wrote in the *Red Man*, "I think printing is as appropriate a trade for girls as it is for boys .... I hope it may happen that girls will learn to print. I don't think printing is any harder than washing."

23. Carpenter and Sorisio, *Newspaper Warrior*, 280.
24. A conversation on April 26, 2019, with Jim Gerencser, college archivist at the Carlisle Indian School Digital Resource Center at Dickinson, convinced me that Carlisle may have actually been one of the best government Indian schools given Pratt's need to maintain a good reputation. Gerencser could cite few cases of physical punishment, though it did on occasion occur. Importantly, Gerencser said Carlisle – like any school – changed over its almost four-decade history; in his words, "Carlisle is at least 8,000 different stories," given that he estimates that at least 8,000 students were enrolled there. He describes three main periods: The first is the early era of the nineteenth century, which was probably the most traumatic to students given the culture shock. Although Pratt did not encourage the speaking of Native languages, evidence suggests it wasn't entirely prohibited; for example, a school newspaper was named *Eadle Keatah Toh* from 1879 to 1882. A "middling" period existed from 1890 to 1905, during which time Carlisle's relevance decreased somewhat. From 1905 to 1918, there were more attempts to include Native traditions with the work of people like Ho Chunk artist Angel DeCora. At this time, given that there were several other schools modeled after Carlisle, most of the students who came to Carlisle were already somewhat assimilated. Many students expressed a desire to attend Carlisle, considering it the "Harvard" of Indian schools. A congressional investigation in 1914 focused on mismanagement; Pratt, who had left in 1905, continued to be critical of successor Moses Friedman. For more information, see carlisleindian.dickinson.edu/.
25. Hopkins, *Life Among the Piutes*, 70.
26. Anne Ruggles Gere, "Indian Heart/White Man's Head: Native American Teachers in Indian Schools, 1880–19," *History of Education Quarterly* 45.1 (2005), 38–65, at 45–46.
27. Bruce A. Ronda, *Elizabeth Palmer Peabody: A Reformer on Her Own Terms* (Cambridge, MA: Harvard University Press, 1999), 10.
28. Ronda, *Elizabeth Palmer Peabody*, 349.
29. Ronda, *Elizabeth Palmer Peabody*, 37.
30. Mary Stout, *Native American Boarding Schools* (Santa Barbara, CA: ABC-CLIO, 2012), 48–49.
31. Carpenter and Sorisio, *Newspaper Warrior*, 279–80.
32. Simon Ortiz, "Ethnic Literature and Cultural Nationalism," *MELUS* 8.2 (1981), 7–12, at 10.
33. Carpenter and Sorisio, *Newspaper Warrior*, 252–53.
34. Carpenter and Sorisio, *Newspaper Warrior*, 256.
35. See Malea Powell, "Rhetorics of Survivance: How American Indians Use Writing," *College Composition and Communication* 2.1 (2002), 396–434.

36. Carpenter and Sorisio, *Newspaper Warrior*, 261.

37. Carpenter and Sorisio, *Newspaper Warrior*, 261.

38. Carpenter and Sorisio, *Newspaper Warrior*, 281.

39. Carpenter and Sorisio, *Newspaper Warrior*, 262.

40. Carpenter and Sorisio, *Newspaper Warrior*, 262–63.

41. Carpenter and Sorisio, *Newspaper Warrior*, 263.

42. Carpenter and Sorisio, *Newspaper Warrior*, 263.

43. Carpenter and Sorisio, *Newspaper Warrior*, 266–67.

44. Carpenter and Sorisio, *Newspaper Warrior*, 267.

45. On April 27, the *Silver State* reports that "twelve young Paiutes" left for Grand Junction with Superintendent David, accompanied by Dave Numaga and his brother John Numaga (Carpenter and Sorisio, *The Newspaper Warrior*, 314).

46. Carpenter and Sorisio, *Newspaper Warrior*, 271.

47. Carpenter and Sorisio, *Newspaper Warrior*, 256.

48. Carpenter and Sorisio, *Newspaper Warrior*, 272.

49. Carpenter and Sorisio, *Newspaper Warrior*, 272.

50. The fact that Winnemucca spent seventh months, between June 1887 and January 1888, visiting relatives in Baltimore suggests the school was closed that spring, before her departure. It is possible that the school survived into 1888, but Carolyn Sorisio and I were unable to find any reference to its existence in the newspaper record after March 1887.

CHAPTER 14

"White by Law," White by Literature

Naturalization and the Constructedness of Race in the Literature of American Naturalism

Mita Banerjee

From the very beginning, race was central to the definition of Americanness as such. As Matthew Frye Jacobson argues, "Citizenship was a racially inscribed concept at the outset of the new nation: by an act of Congress, only 'free white' immigrants could be naturalized."[1] Naturalization was hence tied to race from the very beginning. At the time the statute was made, however, it seemed to be entirely clear who was white and who was not. As Ian Haney López notes, the 1790 statute was explicitly designed to exclude both black slaves and Native Americans. Then, the phrase "free white persons" seemed completely unambiguous, but the lawmakers of 1790 would come to be haunted by their own assurance about the certainty of whiteness. Toward the end of the nineteenth century, the United States was the destination for unprecedented waves of immigration. Immigrants from Ireland, Sicily, China, India, Syria, and Greece came in search of a new beginning, all wanting to become naturalized. This desire for naturalization, however, put lawmakers in a dilemma. These lawmakers, whose predecessors had been able to distinguish between "whiteness" and "nonwhiteness" with such remarkable ease, now found themselves at a loss. They were confronted with all kinds of hues and shades of potential whiteness that the makers of the 1790 statute could never have anticipated. Whiteness, as historian Jacobson notes, suddenly came in all shades and colors. To use Jacobson's memorable metaphor, American judges suddenly found themselves confronted with "whiteness of a different color."[2] The immigration waves of the late nineteenth century sparked off, as Jacobson puts it, an "odyssey" of whiteness.[3]

What interests me in this chapter, then, is the remarkable moment in US legal history in which the law, for a period of time that would span seven decades, came to doubt its own categories. What emerged from this period of uncertainty is a series of court cases that seem both intriguing and bizarre for a number of reasons. The so-called racial prerequisite cases took place from 1878 to 1954. Their sole aim was to decide which group of immigrants was white and which was not. Because whiteness was the racial prerequisite for naturalization, petitioners had to prove in a court of law that they were white and, hence, deserved to be naturalized. It was in this legal moment of uncertainty, then, that the judges presiding over the racial prerequisite cases acknowledged their own confusion. As Judge Lorenzo Sawyer, Chief Justice of the Supreme Court of California, noted, "The very words 'white person' . . . constitute a very indefinite description of a class of persons, where none can be said to be *literally* white, and those called white may be found in every shade from the lightest blonde to the most swarthy brunette."[4]

What makes the racial prerequisite cases so interesting from today's point of view is that they revealed, with glaring obviousness, that "racial categorization," to use López's words, "finds its origins in social practices."[5] Both the judges and the petitioners were entirely unsure about which category or criterion to resort to in order to demonstrate whiteness. What ensued was a veritable hit-and-miss definition of race. Petitioners would resort to all kinds of explanations in order to demonstrate their whiteness, from skin color to cultural behavior to dress code. Whiteness was not so much something that could be seen, but something that could and had to be *performed* before the judiciary. Syrian petitioner Tom Ellis, for instance, was able to convince the court of his whiteness by dressing appropriately for the court hearing. As Jacobson observes, "in identifying Ellis as [white], the judge . . . could have been referring to any of a number of things . . . – Ellis's social bearing, his proficiency in English, his dress, his manner, his style, his demeanour."[6] The racial prerequisite cases, then, constitute a moment that we might call the interregnum of racial definition – the moment when one system has ceased to apply and another has not yet been found. In this historical moment, immigrants could refer to their *cultural* behavior in order to demonstrate their whiteness. Culture could hence become the arbiter of whiteness. If indeed race is not a biological fact but a cultural category, petitioners only had to strike the right cultural code to convince the judiciary of their own whiteness.

White by Literature

Remarkably, the judges calling for help in this moment of racial uncertainty resorted not only to the notion of common sense, but also the terrain of literature. As Judge Sawyer notes in *In re Ah Yup* (1878), naturalization needs to take into account the popular understanding of the term "white person": The words "white person" ... in this country, at least, have undoubtedly acquired a well settled meaning in common popular speech, and they are constantly used in the sense so acquired in the literature of the country, as well as in common parlance.[7]

Literature, in this context, would of course not only have meant literature in an aesthetic sense, but also would vaguely have referred to any piece of writing. Yet, for the purposes of this essay, I would like to refer to literature in a very specific sense. What is so remarkable about the period of the racial prerequisite cases, I argue, is that in the terrain of American literature, the legal debate on naturalization was *paralleled* by the literature of naturalism. What, then, are we to make of this parallelism between naturalism and naturalization? As I will try to illustrate in the paragraphs that follow, naturalistic literature in its musing about the "color" of whiteness bears a remarkable resemblance to the legal naturalization debate that took place in the courts at the exact same time that naturalization unfolded.

The Proof Is in the Pudding: The Case of the Chinese Cook in Frank Norris's *The Octopus*

Mapped onto the terrain of literature, the logic of the racial prerequisite cases may in fact have surprisingly similar correlates in naturalistic fiction. First, the racial prerequisite cases expose us to immigrant cultures that had hitherto been entirely unknown to the American public. This public, through the records of the racial prerequisite cases, now became exposed to the cultural specificities and complexities of Christian culture in Syria, to Hindu religion in India, and to marriage practices in Bohemia. Far-flung regions from all over the globe suddenly converged in US court-houses. Similarly, naturalistic literature now confronted American readers with the *immigrant cultures* that had come to people its cities. In the pages of naturalistic literature, these immigrant cultures unfolded. The logic of their unfolding, however, is strikingly similar to the logic defining legal debates: What takes place in the literature is exactly what, at the exact same time, is taking place in the court. What may cause the *reader* to sympathize with a given immigrant group may cause the judge to naturalize a petitioner from this same immigrant group. How, then, does an immigrant protagonist "become white"[8] in a court of literature? What criteria does he resort to in order to "earn his whiteness"?[9]

In this context, the question of narrative perspective may be of particular importance. From whose perspective is the story of immigration and naturalization told? Within a given narrative, some literary petitioners may not be able to represent themselves, and consequently they might not earn the reader's sympathy. Such is the case in Frank Norris's novel *The Octopus*. The story at first seems to have nothing at all to do with naturalization. What matters, rather, is the farmers' fight against the all-encompassing power of the railroad, which, like an octopus, threatens to engulf their lives. Far from anyone's petition for citizenship, *The Octopus* seems to be an anti-capitalist manifesto. If there are cultural associations in *The Octopus*, then they are white cultural associations. The natural instinct, the harmony between the soil and its tenant, and the common sense of the farmers are deeply interwoven here. "Color" seems to be entirely absent from *The Octopus*; if there is immigration at all, it is present only in the lily-white beauty of the male characters' love interests. But why, we may ask in this context, should the narrative insist that the blond giants who till the earth in *The Octopus* are immune to color, to the extent that when exposed to the sun, they do not even acquire a tan? "[Harran] was blond," we are told, "and incessant exposure to the sun, instead of tanning him brown, merely heightened the colour of his cheeks."[10] In Norris's novel, there are two antidotes to the corrupt capitalism whose tentacles threaten to engulf the white farmers[11]. First, their rootedness in the soil is seen as a counterbalance to the capitalist estrangement of labor. Second, this rootedness in the soil is balanced by an equally self-contained domesticity.

Yet, who, we may ask, makes this domesticity possible? Who lays the table in the early morning hours when Norris's protagonists sit down at the table that has already been made? This is the novel's sole reference to "color": "Soon after this [the guest] took himself away, and Derrick's Chinaman came in to set the table."[12] I would like to blow this seemingly innocent, entirely marginal scene deliberately out of proportion by arguing that this may in fact be a petition, albeit a highly truncated one, by a Chinese petitioner for American citizenship. Historically, the first racial prerequisite case ever to be held in a US court was the petition by a Chinese claimant, Ah Yup (1878). If indeed the nameless "Chinaman" in Frank Norris's *The Octopus* were read as the fictional equivalent of Ah Yup, what criteria would this petition rely on? In the racial prerequisite cases, a claimant's work ethic, his industriousness, might well earn him naturalization. This was the case, for instance, for many Syrian applicants. As Sarah Gualtieri notes, "Syrians were able to offer evidence of their economic success, including their acquisition of property, as proof of their ability to perform whiteness – to do what successful white people were expected to do."[13] In *The Octopus*, then, the Chinese cook can be said to resort to the same argumentative strategy employed by Syrian petitioners in the racial prerequisite cases: He, too, demonstrates his industriousness.

Moreover, it could be argued that the unnamed Chinese servant demonstrates in Norris's naturalistic novel not just his impeccable work ethic but also his domestic fitness. The way in which he lays the table, in other words, proves his nuanced familiarity with white domesticity. The same is true of his cooking:

> The Chinaman had made a certain kind of plum pudding for dessert, and Annixter, who remembered other dinners at the Derrick's, had been saving himself for this, and had meditated upon it all through the meal. No doubt, it would restore all his good humour, and he believed his stomach was so far recovered as to be able to stand it.[14]

If naturalization depends on the cultural compatibility of an immigrant petitioner with US mainstream culture, Norris's Chinese servant clearly proves that he has indeed mastered the cultural codes of whiteness. As the narrative perspective implicit in this passage indicates, however, the Chinese servant – despite his meticulous way of laying the table and his delicious cooking – is not given a proper hearing in the first place. The narrative's gaze in the cited passage is by no means on the cook, but on his employer's guests. Yet, the fact that they "remembered other dinners at the Derrick's"[15] nonetheless implies that the cook's culinary accomplishments are always excellent. If his cooking is proof of the Chinese servant's "cultural bearing," then, the plum pudding shows the extent of his familiarity with white cultural codes. He prepares a dessert appropriate for the occasion; and it is his culinary diplomacy that may be essential for his employer's political strategy of convincing his guests to take anti-capitalist action. The proof of the Chinese cook's fitness for naturalization, then, may in fact be in the pudding.

However, the judges would not be content with merely inspecting the Chinese cook's work environment. They would want to see not where the cook works, but where he *lives*. The racial prerequisite cases can be said to be obsessed with immigrant domesticity. Behind the curtain, behind the closed door of immigrant homes, what bizarre cultural rituals, what immoral scenarios, might be taking place? It was for this reason that the judges would inquire into the petitioner's marriage, his family arrangements, his customs. As Tamara Nopper notes, "A series of acts passed between the 1880s and 1920 excluded several Asian ethnicities from entry, permanent settlement, or naturalization . . . .. Other policies regulated gender and sexual norms among immigrants by identifying certain acts such as homosexuality, polygamy, prostitution and child-bearing as either immoral or racially threatening."[16] In one particular instance in the racial prerequisite cases, the petition by a Syrian applicant, Farras Shahid, was turned down on a couple of counts: first, because he did not speak the language, but second, because he was taken to be a believer in polygamy. Interestingly, Shahid's answers may have left the court in doubt as to whether he really believed in polygamy or simply did not understand the question. Yet, in any case, what is remarkable with regard to the criteria for naturalization is that the reference to polygamy – and, implicitly, to alternative family structures as well – works against an immigrant's claims to naturalization.

Outside the courts and similarly judging immigrants' "fitness for citizenship,"[17] women missionaries ventured into immigrant homes to assess their moral standards. In this context, and in the context of both *In re Ah Yup* and *The Octopus*, it may be interesting to note that women missionaries went into Chinatown homes in order to determine the moral fitness of Chinatown's inhabitants. To the extent that Chinese homes "passed" the self-appointed inspectors' test, this was seen as a form of conversion. As historian Nayan Shah notes, "In a style reminiscent of sensationalist journalists and public health investigators, [women missionaries] detailed the precarious journey of conversion for missionary-report readers."[18] It is crucial to note here that the "inspection" of immigrant homes comprised a number of parameters at once. First, the inspection was a probing, by the women missionaries, into Chinese moral codes: How many parties lived in the home? Was there a nuclear family structure? Second, what was at stake were the hygienic standards of these immigrant homes. In this as in many other contexts, hygiene, modernization, and "civic fitness" were closely intertwined. As Natalia Molina puts it, toward the end of the nineteenth century, "Cleanliness became something more than a way to prevent epidemics and make cities liveable – it became a route to citizenship, to becoming American."[19] Third, and perhaps more surprisingly, the appropriateness of the "décor" was also assessed. The décor may in fact be seen as the equivalent of the "cultural bearing" that petitioners had to evince in the courts of law. As Nayan Shah notes, the expulsion of Chinese décor from the immigrant home was seen both as a cultural conversion and proof of the immigrants' hygienic knowledge. According to Shah,

> The moment of conversion was marked by the intolerance of the Chinese woman for dirty habitations and signified by the cleansing and redecoration of her apartment. In conversion narratives the movement from "darkness" to "light" consciously mixed spiritual and medical meanings.[20]

Like the claimants in the racial prerequisite cases, then, Chinese immigrant wives had to come up with their own strategy in order to pass the inspection.

Crucially, Chinese immigrants were keenly aware of the moral and hygienic standards that would be expected of them by the self-appointed inspectors of immigrant morality and domesticity. In order to pass the inspection, then, Chinese immigrant wives and their husbands resorted to a remarkable strategy: They kept two living rooms: one to live in and one to show to the missionaries. As Shah describes,

> In several instances, Chinese husbands took the initiative to convert the material circumstances of their homes, and they instructed their "wives and children to appear in order and cleanliness." . . . Ironically, the special room was "locked and only opened" for missionary visits. The room did not reflect changes to the everyday life of the Chinese family, but it demonstrated the commitment of this merchant to appear to assimilate to American material culture and social conduct.[21]

In this feat, Chinese immigrants proved a remarkable cultural competence: They understood the logic of naturalization to the fullest, and they perfectly knew what it meant to act *white*. The same, we might argue, might hold true of the unnamed cook in Norris's novel: Just like the Chinese immigrant wives, the cook knows how to keep a white house and how to prepare US mainstream food. He, too, would pass the inspection. And he, too, might keep two living rooms or kitchens, one for himself and another one to show to the judges and the missionaries' wives.

Yet how, we may ask, did Ah Yup's case end? And what, in the end, is Norris's judgment about the naturalizing of the Chinese cook? It may be interesting to note that in the end, both petitions fail. Ah Yup's petition is turned down because, according to Judge Sawyer, "a native of China, of the Mongolian race, is not a white person."[22] Thus, the presiding judge ultimately decided in favor of racial classification, dismissing Ah Yup's cultural behavior or "social bearing."[23] And, for the same reason, the unnamed Chinese cook's claim in *The Octopus* fails as well. Even if, in the latter case, the literary judiciary had favored "social bearing" and an excellent work ethic over racial classification, the Chinese cook would still not have stood a chance since, in Norris's novel, the Chinese cook is not even allowed to speak. His petition for citizenship is truncated because he remains a marginal character, an extra in Norris's naturalistic novel. Even if his housekeeping skills demonstrate that he indeed knows how to keep house, the literary inspector never even bothers to look at the Chinese cook's home.

Irish Homemakers and Pathetic Blue Ribbons:
Stephen Crane's *Maggie*

Domesticity is also at the core of Stephen Crane's novella *Maggie*. Remarkably, the Irish, at the turn of the twentieth century, were said to be on the verge of naturalization. As Ignatiev notes, the Irish were "probationary whites": "[W]hile the white skin made the Irish eligible for membership in the white race, it did not guarantee their admission; they had to earn it."[24] Even if in legal terms they did not have to prove their whiteness in court, the Irish were nevertheless *culturally* suspect. In a remarkable study, Noel Ignatiev retraces the journey of how, historically, the "Irish became white."[25] What, however, of the literary journey of the Irish into whiteness? If indeed it is true that, like the racial prerequisite cases, naturalistic novels grant a hearing to all kinds of immigrant petitioners, it comes as no surprise that the Irish, too, feature prominently in naturalistic fiction. Yet, here as in the actual racial prerequisite cases, there may be a gradation of degrees of naturalizability. While the Chinese cook is not quite given a hearing in Norris's *The Octopus*, the Irish do get a fair trial in Stephen Crane's *Maggie*. In the court of literary naturalization, I would argue, Maggie's journey into whiteness begins with the fact that the petitioner has turned from a marginal character into a protagonist. Even if Maggie eventually fails (in a sense that I will explain below), she may nevertheless come close to naturalization. Maggie's journey into whiteness begins with her rebellion against her dysfunctional environment and family life. As the narrative opens, the Irish home does not bode well for the naturalization of the Irish. Their dysfunctionality, violence, and alcohol abuse render them unfit for whiteness. On all counts, Maggie's portrayal of Irish domesticity is the picture of absolute dysfunctionality:

> As the father and children filed in she peered at them. "Eh, what? Been fightin' agin!" She threw herself upon Jimmie. The urchin tried to dart behind the others, and in the scuffle the babe, Tommie, was knocked down. He protested with his usual vehemence, because they had bruised his tender shins against a table leg. The mother's massive shoulders heaved with anger. Grasping the urchin by the neck and shoulder she shook him until he rattled . . .. At last she tossed him into a corner where he limply lay weeping.[26]

Maggie's journey into whiteness, then, begins with her revolt against her surroundings. This revolt, in turn, takes the shape of proper domesticity.

As in the case of the Chinese living room, the remaking of the Irish home in terms of American whiteness starts with the décor. Maggie's journey into whiteness begins with her loathing of her home's inappropriate furnishings.

In disgust, she contemplates a "clock, in a splintered and battered oblong box of varnished wood, [which] she suddenly regarded as an abomination."[27] In what the narrative portrays as a painstaking but pathetic attempt at escaping her surroundings and rising above her circumstances, Maggie tries to ameliorate the sordidness of the Irish living quarters. As in the case of the Chinese immigrant wives, Crane's narrative makes clear that Maggie's disgust at her surroundings is not just a matter of taste, but has a distinct "medical" connotation: It is a revolt against her mother's immigrant taste as much as about her lack of hygiene. Maggie's attempt at "sanitizing" the Irish home is thus a matter of taste (in the sense of what Jacobson terms "cultural bearing"), hygiene, and morality at one and the same time:

> Turning, Maggie contemplated the dark, dust-stained walls, and the scant and crude furniture of her home . . . . The almost vanished flowers in the carpet pattern, she conceived to be newly hideous. Some faint attempts which she had made with blue ribbon to freshen the appearance of a dingy curtain, she now saw to be piteous.[28]

Seen in terms of the naturalization logic of the late nineteenth century, then, the reference to dust is far from accidental here. The fact that Maggie is able to identify dust as an "abomination" (one of many such abominations in the Irish home) marks her as a "hygienically fit" potential citizen.

In terms of naturalization and its logic, this scene is far from trivial. Like the Chinese immigrants' wives, Maggie knows how to keep house, and she knows how to keep a *white* house. The "piteous blue ribbon" says as much. Unlike the Chinese wives, however, Maggie does not keep two living rooms but one. The fact that she sets out to restore domestic morality and that she strives to remake the family's sole living room in the image of whiteness and white domestic respectability proves her "fitness" for citizenship.[29] The tragedy of Crane's novel, of course, is that Maggie ultimately fails to escape from her dismal surroundings. Having been abandoned by Peter, her lover, she resorts to becoming a prostitute. Yet, in the end, her moral sense triumphs over the sordidness and moral corruption of her environment. Paradoxically, Maggie becomes white by committing suicide. Her suicide becomes the ultimate proof of her moral fitness, and hence of her deserving American citizenship.

Whiteness as Christianity in Upton Sinclair's *The Jungle*

In the literary court cases that I have examined so far, then, Upton Sinclair's *The Jungle* (1906) may be the most illustrative. With regard to an immigrant group successfully seeking naturalization, Sinclair's Lithuanians may in fact come closest to such an achievement. This may be the case because in contrast to *The Octopus* and to some extent to *Maggie*, Sinclair's Lithuanians are allowed to submit a complete naturalization case. *The Jungle*, after all, is not a novella, but a full-fledged novel. While *Maggie* as a novella remains an abridged version of the Irish petition for citizenship, *The Jungle* is a highly nuanced account of Lithuanian immigrant life. What is only hinted at in Maggie and her failed attempt to decorate the dysfunctional Irish home with a ribbon comes full circle in the Lithuanians' revolt against the surroundings they have been forced to inhabit. What is a matter of choice for Maggie's mother (the filth that Mary Murphy seems to revel in) is a matter of coercion in *The Jungle*. When his wife is lying in childbirth, Jurgis revolts against the lack of hygiene that characterizes not only the quarters he is forced to live in but also that which the German midwife displays. Significantly, the first image we get of the German impostor at the medical practice of midwifery is from Jurgis's perspective. Jurgis's disgust at the woman's sight is clearly apparent here:

> He had a glimpse of her, with a black bottle turned up to her lips. Then he knocked louder, and she started and put it away. She was a Dutch woman, enormously fat – when she walked she rolled like a small boat on the ocean . . .. She wore a filthy blue wrapper, and her teeth were black.[30]

Added to Mme Haupt's lack of personal and dental hygiene, there is a lack of moral decency. As the narrative goes on to specify, once again from Jurgis's perspective: "She took off her wrapper without even taking the trouble to turn her back to Jurgis, and put on her corsets and dress. Then there was a black bonnet which had to be adjusted carefully, and an umbrella which was mislaid."[31] The midwife's superfluous search for her umbrella, then, is the ultimate proof of her medical misconduct: By the time they arrive at Jurgis's home where his wife, Ona, is lying in labor, it is already too late. At this moment, in a striking overlap with the capitalist critique in Frank Norris's *The Octopus*, the German midwife turns out to be not just unhygienic and unethical, but also ruthlessly capitalistic:

> At this moment she chanced to look around, and saw Jurgis. She shook her finger at him. "You understand me," she said, "you pays me dot money yust de same! It is not my fault dat you send for me so late. I can't help your vife . . .. I haf tried all night, and in dot place vere it is not fit for dogs to be born . . .. She will die, of course," said the [midwife], angrily. "Der baby is dead now."[32]

Jurgis's own moral sentiment, then, is spelled out by the novel on all levels: It is a hygienic sentiment that marks Jurgis both as civically fit and as modern. It is a moral emotion and feeling of human decency that make him despair over his wife's plight and his own moral dilemma. Eventually, Jurgis attacks his Irish employer, who, by coercing his wife into sexual favors in order for Jurgis to be able to keep his job, turns out to be the Lithuanian family's undoing. However, when Jurgis is sent to prison, it is not, the novel makes clear, because he is a criminal; it is because of his ultimate attempt at saving his wife from the corrupt Irish employer.

In *The Jungle*, arguably, the whiteness of the Lithuanians is proved by the novel's pitting their case against that of other immigrant petitioners. In *The Jungle*, the Lithuanians, it could be argued, are naturalized on the back of the Irish (the corrupt Irish employer) and the Germans (the disgusting midwife). Similarly, the logic of contrast was also central to some of the racial prerequisite cases. There, too, a claimant could earn naturalization by debunking the case made by petitioners from other immigrant groups. In his 1922 petition for naturalization, a Japanese claimant, Takao Ozawa, used racial science as a case in point. According to López,

> Taking the "white person" requirement literally, Ozawa argued that to reject his petition would be "to exclude a Japanese who is 'white' in color." In support of this proposition, Ozawa quoted in his brief to the Court the following from different anthropological observers: "in Japan the uncovered parts of the body are also white"; "the Japanese are of lighter color than other Eastern Asiatics, not rarely showing the transparent pink tint which whites assume as their own privilege"; ... [they] are whiter than the average Italian, Spaniard, or Portuguese."[33]

Ozawa's strategy is thus to establish his own whiteness by demonstrating the nonwhiteness of other petitioners for naturalization. Similarly, even if Sinclair's narrative is not referring to skin color but to cultural demeanor, the same strategy is used in *The Jungle* in order to establish the Lithuanian protagonist's whiteness. Jurgis deserves to be naturalized as a white American citizen, the novel implies, because he is morally superior to his Irish employer and hygienically and ethically superior to the German midwife.

The ultimate proof of Jurgis's whiteness, however, may not be his moral sentiment, but his religious conviction. Even though, as a Lithuanian, Jurgis would have been orthodox, and hence not fully compatible with the Protestantism of US mainstream culture, the narrative at this crucial moment downplays inter-Christian differences to focus on the spirit of Christianity as such:

But then he made out a melody in the ringing; there were chimes . . .. (For) fully a minute Jurgis lay lost in wonder, before, all at once, the meaning of it broke over him – that this was Christmas eve! Christmas Eve – he had forgotten it entirely! There was a breaking of flood-gates, a whirl of new memories and new griefs rushing into his mind. In far Lithuania they had celebrated Christmas . . .. It was too far off for Santa Claus in Lithuania, but it was not too far for peace and good will to man, for the wonder-bearing vision of the Christ-child.[34]

It is at this moment that the journey of the Lithuanians into whiteness is complete. Where the Chinese cook's respectable domesticity is evidenced only through his behavior at work, and where Maggie ultimately fails to keep house, Sinclair's Lithuanians prove their fitness for citizenship on all levels: through their moral decency, their knowledge of hygiene, and their religious sentiment. Where George Dow told the court that he came from the region where Jesus Christ was born and hence failed to refer to his own religious denomination, Jurgis assures the American public that he, too, is Christian.

As this chapter has tried to demonstrate, the parameters of naturalization are thus strikingly similar for both the racial prerequisite cases and the "case" of naturalistic literature. Both in literature and the courts, many different groups appear and (implicitly or explicitly) petition for naturalization. In the framework of the racial prerequisite cases, the court has to separate the wheat of whiteness from the chaff of nonwhiteness. Similarly, it can be argued that in naturalistic literature, too, immigrant characters as potential petitioners for citizenship are made to file before a white American readership and make their claim to whiteness. In the cases of both literature and the law, however, it is not entirely clear what precisely the criteria for "whiteness" may be. Anything ranging from dress code to demeanor to language and religion may earn the petitioner naturalization. Where for the Chinese cook in Frank Norris's *The Octopus*, even the proof of his (American) cooking is not enough, Maggie almost succeeds in proving her whiteness by choosing an appropriate décor, and by being revolted by her unhygienic Irish surroundings. Finally, Jurgis Rudkus, the Lithuanian protagonist in Upton Sinclair's *The Jungle*, proves his whiteness on all counts at once: He is hygienically fit and morally superior, and he is Christian.

Yet, despite these remarkable parallels between literature and naturalization, there may be one crucial difference between the court of law and that of literature. In the legal hearings for naturalization, petitioners themselves drew up their own strategy for proving their whiteness. In the literary court hearings, on the other hand, it is the novel's author who masterminds the cases that unfold inside the pages of his text. If the Chinese cook fails to win his naturalization, in other words, it is because it is Norris who has devised his naturalization strategy for him. Yet, it is here that we may want to consider not just the "double bind" between society and the law[35] but also the double bind between society and literature as well. Literature, too, both reacts to social change and helps to reinforce categories that already exist in society. Seen from this perspective, if *The Octopus* does not grant the Chinese cook a hearing, the narrative can be seen to reinforce an ignorance of Chinese cultural complexity that may also have characterized the social order.

By the mid-twentieth century, the racial categories that had been so destabilized at the turn of the nineteenth century had once again solidified in the courts of law as much as, perhaps, in those of literature. What remains, however, is a remarkable period both in legal and in literary history. As the remarkable parallel between naturalism and naturalization reveals, this was a period when the mechanisms of the construction of race were suddenly interrupted, their machinery hampered by an unprecedented proliferation of shades of whiteness. In periods when, as today, we may believe in the certainty, even the "naturalness," of racial definitions, we may do well to revisit the moments of racial uncertainty. To look closely at such periods, this chapter has tried to suggest, may cause us to doubt what we believe to be natural, what we hold to be "common sense." As the twenty-first century opens, at a time when racial and cultural differences seem to be more recalcitrant than ever, leading to new polarizations, the solace of uncertainty may be more necessary than ever. Far from being a destabilizer of culture, uncertainty may in fact be an antidote to cultural fundamentalisms of all kind. In trying to understand and remember the constructedness of race in the twenty-first century, we may hence do well to revisit nineteenth-century literary and legal imaginaries. Seen from this perspective, the literature of naturalism and the racial prerequisite cases for naturalization may be far from obsolete.

Notes

1. Matthew Frye Jacobson, *Whiteness of a Different Color: European Immigrants and the Alchemy of Race* (Cambridge, MA: Harvard University Press, 1999), 13.
2. Jacobson, *Whiteness of a Different Color*, passim.
3. Jacobson, *Whiteness of a Different Color*, 4.
4. Jacobson, *Whiteness of a Different Color*, 227, italics added.

5. Ian Haney López, *White by Law: The Legal Construction of Race* (New York: New York University Press, 1996), 6.
6. Jacobson, *Whiteness of a Different Color*, 239.
7. López, *White by Law*, 5.
8. Noel Ignatiev, *How the Irish Became White* (New York: Routledge, 1995), 3.
9. Ignatiev, *How the Irish Became White*, 59.
10. Frank Norris, *The Octopus: A Story of California* (1901; New York: Penguin, 1986), 8.
11. Colleen Lye, "American Naturalism and Asiatic Racial Form: Frank Norris's *The Octopus and Moran of the 'Lady Letty*,'" *Representations* 84.1 (2003), 78.
12. Norris, The Octopus, 99.
13. Sarah Gualtieri, *Between Arab and White: Race and Ethnicity in the Early Syrian American Diaspora* (Berkeley: University of California Press, 2009), 3.
14. Norris, *The Octopus*, 102.
15. Norris, *The Octopus*, 102.
16. Tamara Nopper, "Eugenics," in *Anti-Immigration in the United States: A Historical Encyclopedia*, ed. Kathleen Arnold (Santa Barbara, CA: Greenwood, 2011), 192.
17. Natalia Molina, *Fit to Be Citizens? Public Health and Race in Los Angeles, 1879–1939* (Berkeley: University of California Press, 2006), x.
18. Nayan Shah, *Contagious Divides: Epidemics and Race in San Francisco's Chinatown* (Berkeley: University of California Press, 2001), 112.
19. Molina, *Fit to Be Citizens*, 2.
20. Shah, *Contagious Divides*, 112.
21. Shah, *Contagious Divides*, 112–13.
22. López, *White by Law*, 54.
23. Jacobson, *Whiteness of a Different Color*, 238.
24. Ignatiev, *How the Irish Became White*, 59.
25. Ignatiev, *How the Irish Became White*, passim.
26. Stephen Crane, *Maggie: A Girl of the Streets, and Selected Stories* (New York: Signet, 1991), 7.
27. Crane, *Maggie*, 23.
28. Crane, *Maggie*, 23.
29. Molina, *Fit to Be Citizens*, passim.
30. Upton Sinclair, *The Jungle* (1906; New York: Signet, 1980), 209.
31. Sinclair, *The Jungle*, 212.
32. Sinclair, *The Jungle*, 217.
33. López, *White by Law*, 81.
34. Sinclair, *The Jungle*, 182.
35. López, *White by Law*, 14.

PART V

Envisioning Race

The concept of race has often relied on visual features – visible distinctions between people that have been viewed as markers of fundamental differences, signs of collective affiliations that can be classified in terms of racial differences. Those visual markers became increasingly less reliable over the course of the nineteenth century, to the point that the American legal system developed methods for determining one's racial identity when that identity could not be visually determined. Accordingly, when we encounter actual images in print culture or references to images in literary works, or when we encounter literary works that envision the American racial landscape, it becomes important to think about what and *how* we are being drawn to see race, and from what vantage point. Martha J. Cutter sets the stage for this section by drawing us into "an archive of visual images" used "to protest slavery and claim US citizenship for a group of Black individuals who previously had been denied it." Focusing on a wide variety of sources, Cutter explores the ways in which images reveal both actual and ideal interracial relationships, and the extent to which these images promoted a concept of shared citizenship. Maurice Wallace, on the other hand, takes us into a more "fraught logic obtaining between seeing and being (black) between 1839 and 1889," examining the "new proto-photographic technology" and its uses during this period. Addressing references to photographic images in one of the most influential novels of the nineteenth century dealing with race, Harriet Beecher Stowe's *Uncle Tom's Cabin*, Wallace's essay "explores the spectacle cast of race in nineteenth-century American literature and culture," including the pseudoscientific craftings and applications of such spectacles. Melanie B. Taylor approaches the visual field from a geographical perspective, arguing that the American South, "the primal site of the US plantation, and with it the birth of racial capitalism in the American context, fundamentally relies on the irrelevance and erasure of Indians." But this erasure of Indians requires such efforts "to implicate, resurrect, indict, and appropriate their substance at nearly every turn" that, "as a result, 'Indians' are simply everywhere and nowhere in the Southern narrative." Taylor's essay draws us far into the twentieth century, and Paula M. L. Moya and Luz M. Jiménez Ruvalcaba continue this turn to the contemporary, and extend the geographical frame considerably, arguing that American racial literature is best understood in an international context. Focusing on the British writer Bernardine Anne Mobolaji Evaristo as "one of a cohort of contemporary fiction writers, in the U.S. and abroad, who are self-consciously pushing the boundaries of content and form," Moya and Ruvalcaba examine a world revealed by "the absence of something that both is and is not there." Accounting for an approach to representation utilized by such writers as "Toni Cade Bambara, Leslie Marmon Silko, Toni Morrison, Helena Maria Viramontes, Marlon James, Louise Erdrich, and Tommy Orange," Moya and Ruvalcaba explore "decolonial literary techniques designed to redress the historical lack of representation, and misrepresentation, of the ethnoracial communities from which they come." In all, this section addresses the ways in which racial cultures develop technologies of vision – literary and otherwise – that shape how we locate ourselves geographically, historically, and socially, and the ways that literature works either to enforce or liberate us from those acquired habits of seeing.

CHAPTER 15

Picturing Race
African Americans in US Visual Culture before the Civil War

Martha J. Cutter

After television images and photographs circulated of Colin Kaepernick "taking a knee" during the national anthem in 2016, President Donald Trump reacted angrily, saying not only that NFL owners should fire players who protest the national anthem but also that "maybe [Kaepernick] should find a country that works better for him."[1] Trump's comments seem to highlight the tenuous nature of the idea of African Americans as belonging within the United States and to reinforce the way that visual images can be used to support both progressive and conservative causes.[2] "I am not going to stand up to show pride in a flag for a country that oppresses black people and people of color," said Kaepernick in one interview;[3] in another, he commented: "I couldn't see another hashtag Sandra Bland . . . Hashtag Tamir Rice . . .. At what point do we take a stand as a people and say this isn't right?"[4] In contrast to Trump, Kaepernick viewed his protest – caught in photographs and on film – as taking a clear-cut stance against injustice.

The presence of race in American culture – and in visual representations of its citizens, noncitizens, and marginalized citizens – is sometimes arranged to highlight victorious struggles for freedom over the overwhelming machinery of racial oppression. Yet the Kaepernick incident shows that the realm of the visual is a heavily inflected one, and that it is often controlled by the dominant culture and the mainstream media. There is no simple story, here, about an athlete being fired from his job due to a president's casting him as "un-American," for although Kaepernick never played in the NFL again, he received a lucrative contract with Nike, and now, a different image of him – his face with the words "Believe in something, even if it means sacrificing everything. #JustDoIt" – circulates in advertisements for Nike products.[5] Has Kaepernick resisted the silencing of his initial protest via his presence in such Nike ads? Yet in these advertisements, Kaepernick's mouth is closed, and the words are stamped onto his face like a logo. "Visibility is a trap," comments philosopher Michel Foucault,[6] and this seems to be particularly the case for individuals who do not control the terms under which the visual comes to have force and meaning in US culture. Is the visual ever a realm in which racialized individuals can find a "voice," belonging, citizenship, freedom, and power?

This essay will focus on examples from the past in which Anglo-Americans and African Americans utilized an archive of visual images to protest slavery and claim US citizenship for a group of Black individuals who previously had been denied it.[7] Of course, historically, the question of what US citizenship might entail for African Americans is a vexed one; many historians and legal theorists argue that during much of the nineteenth century, only whites were seen as being capable of attaining full citizenship rights on a federal level.[8] This essay argues that one goal of picturing race in the nineteenth century via illustrated books, almanacs, print publications, paintings, pamphlets, and photographs was not just to show the harms of slavery, but also to promote empathy between black and white inhabitants of the United States; moreover, some of these illustrations attempt to confer a type of symbolic citizenship onto African Americans, whether free or enslaved, that could be taken into the postbellum era.

Yet especially before the war, the illustrated documents discussed in this essay often replicated binaries in which African Americans were objects of the gaze and continually in need of a white viewer's assistance. White abolitionists tended to invoke empathy but also rely on a certain degree of abjectification of African American bodies in their visual works, whereas works by some African Americans undermined ideas of empathy in favor of a construct of African Americans as producers of visual texts in which they exhibited agency and self-determination. The visual works created by African Americans, moreover, often challenged the idea that such texts delivered a single message; they were instead multivalent products of particular historical controversies that gave off multiple messages about the complexity of African American subjectivity, both under slavery and in freedom.

Harnessing the Power of the Image to End Slavery: White Abolitionists and the Construction of Empathy

Before the start of the Civil War, white abolitionists were determined to harness the great power of the visual to protest the inhumanity of slavery and create empathy for the enslaved. Charles C. Green, who authored an illustrated, book-length antislavery poem called *The Nubian Slave* (1845), argues that the "application of Pictorial Art to Moral Truth is capable of producing a great, and as yet, almost untried Force."[9] Such a goal is evident in the famous antislavery icon created in England by Josiah Wedgwood in 1787 that came to be known as "the supplicant slave"; this image featured a kneeling, enchained man looking up to a white individual, saying "Am I Not a Man and a Brother?" The popularity of this icon – which treats the enslaved as a pathetic, unfinished self, in need of a white viewer's sympathy – cannot be overstated; in England and the United States, it was stamped onto abolitionist membership certificates, sugar bowls, hair ornaments, aprons, patch boxes, or other cultural artifacts.[10]

Beyond employing such imaging, in the United States a number of prominent white abolitionists utilized illustrated books to protest slavery's inhumanity and promote empathy. Such books were a powerful instrument in the abolitionist visual arsenal because stories could be twined around images to guide a reader toward a particular interpretation or political standpoint. In 1852, the full version of Harriet Beecher Stowe's *Uncle Tom's Cabin* was published, and it contained illustrations, many of which would become famous and inspire a legacy of films, vases, dolls, shows, musicals, and performances that would last well into the 1970s. But even before this outpouring of visual images regarding slavery, many white abolitionists strove to harness the interactive potential of words and images.

One early example of such an endeavor is Jesse Torrey's illustrated book, *A Portraiture of Domestic Slavery, in the United States* (1817). In one picture, Torrey's illustrator draws an almost ethereal image of an enslaved woman who attempts to kill herself by jumping from a third story window; the woman hangs in the air, caught in a liminal space between life and death, freedom and slavery.[11] She suffers grave injuries from her fall but does not die, and when Torrey interviews her she clarifies that family separation – a powerful theme that Stowe will also invoke – was the root of her desperation. Crucially, Torrey believes that the picture in his text, when combined with the woman's "unvarnished story," will force the reader to "delineate [her sorrow] with the mental pencil (quill), and then view the picture from his own hand." Torrey advocates for the power of internal visual delineation of this woman's story (the "mental quill") to create a type of embodied empathy: He challenges anyone not to have a "humid eye" after mental explication of her story.[12]

Yet for Torrey, empathy is just the first step; action is next. Another image from Torrey's text depicts the author taking down in his notebook the stories of several people who have been kidnapped into slavery. In a

The Author noting down the narratives of several free-born people of colour who had been kidnapped.

Designed and Published by J. Torrey Jr. Phila. 1817.

Figure 15.1   Jesse Torrey's *Portraiture of Domestic Slavery in the United States*
(1817, between pages 46 and 47). Caption reads: "The Author noting down the
narrative of several free-born people of color who had been kidnapped."
Google Books, public domain

sense, this is a meta-picture (or a picture about a picture) because a drawing
of the author writing what will (in a future moment) become the book a
reader holds appears in the author's book; the temporal gap of these meta-
pictures makes a reader focus on how processes of reading, writing, and
storytelling might create empathy and action (see Figure 15.1).

   In this illustration, Torrey and the man who has been kidnapped face
each other; the man speaks while Torrey silently writes; a mother and two
children sit in the corner. This is a respectful and somber image that
attempts to instate the dignity and humanity of these individuals. Torrey
notes in his text that by writing about these captives, he is able to liberate
them via his legal actions; he takes his written account of them to a judge
and eventually they are freed. What seems important is the movement into
activism that he models via his pictures and words – a movement into
action (and perhaps empathy) in which he wants readers to engage.

   However, while Torrey states that such individuals as the ones that he
manages to liberate are "men, women, and children, whose freedom and
moral rights, are guaranteed by our national and state constitutions," he

stops short of incorporating them as citizens within the body politic of the United States.[13] The fiery abolitionist George Bourne, on the other hand, uses his illustrated antislavery work *Picture of Slavery in the United States of America* (1834) to emphasize both the citizenship and humanity of the enslaved. In one illustration from his book, for example, Bourne depicts the torture of an enslaved man, but he explicitly (and in defiance of the law) calls this individual a "citizen" (see Figure 15.2).

Figure 15.2 calls the tortured man an "American Citizen," and in so doing it attempts to create empathy between the reading viewer and the enslaved. Yet the image itself – which shows a man being whipped brutally while tied to the ground – fosters an idea of the enslaved as debased, low bodies, incapable of resistance. Bourne does try to turn visual attention toward the (white) free citizen-torturer, who stands in the middle of the picture. However, as Teresa Goddu argues, in this illustration the enslaved man is "literally tied to the landscape and always embedded in it," whereas the slaveholder has access to an "aerial view," establishing his visual and literal power as "perspectival" and panoramic.[14] On the other hand, the text surrounding this image attempts to deconstruct this hierarchy, and it is therefore crucial to consider the symbiotic message achieved by the words and illustration together. The passage is narrated by a white man born in Virginia, "amid slaves," who has become an ardent abolitionist after seeing (while he was a boy) this particular scene of torture.[15] In other words, the debasing image within the text is meant to promote not so much pity in a viewer, but a movement into empathy and antislavery activism.

Other famous white abolitionists tried to use pictures to inculcate ideas of the humanity of the enslaved. As previously mentioned, Stowe's *Uncle Tom's Cabin* was published in 1852 with illustrations. The illustrations in the novel – created by Hammatt Billings – are circumspect and attempt to evoke empathy in a viewer. One of the most famous and remade illustrations in the 1852 edition was titled "Little Eva Reading the Bible to Uncle Tom in the Arbor" (see Figure 15.3).

This is an intimate portrait, carefully etched, of the young child, Eva, helping Tom to understand the biblical passage they are reading.[16] Eva's touching of Tom, and her clear empathy with him, is meant to signal to a reader that they too should feel empathy for Tom. Yet what does it mean that a little child – a young girl – must teach Tom to understand the Bible? And what does it mean that a viewer's eyes are first directed to Eva, who sits in the center of the picture, with her finger upraised? A reader may be drawn to feel empathy for the saintly child and to learn from her how to empathize with the enslaved. Like Torrey, Stowe's text uses an illustration

Torturing American Citizens.   Page 129.

Figure 15.2 "Torturing American Citizens," from George Bourne, *Picture of American Slavery* (1834, between pages 128 and 129).
Google Books, public domain

LITTLE EVA READING THE BIBLE TO UNCLE TOM IN THE ARBOR Page 65.

Figure 15.3   Illustration from Harriet Beecher Stowe, *Uncle Tom's Cabin*
(1852, vol. 2, between pages 62 and 63). Illustrator Hammatt Billings. Google
Books, public domain, www.google.com/books/edition/Uncle_Tom_s_Cabin/
gTw7045TBdgC?hl=en&gbpv=1

to guide the reader toward empathy, but this empathy is troubling because
the equality of the enslaved with the viewer is never directly demonstrated.

Beyond these books, visual culture as a whole tended to depict the
enslaved via modes of abjection. For example, several illustrations in the
1838 *American Anti-Slavery Almanac* portray images of enslaved torture.
We learn, for instance, of "the slave Paul," who "finally hung himself, that
he might not again fall into the hands of his tormentor." Even in death,
however, Paul's body does not escape brutalization, because the drawing
shows buzzards eating out his eyes and tearing apart his flesh.[17] Images of
the torture of half-naked, enslaved women also were omnipresent within
the pages of such print publications.[18]

Yet not all white illustrators within US visual culture pictured the
enslaved as passive, tortured, or evading slavery only in death. In 1849,
Henry Box Brown escaped from slavery in Richmond, Virginia, to freedom in Philadelphia, Pennsylvania, via a large postal crate in which he
mailed himself, and Brown was often pictured coming up safely out of his
box. In one lithograph from 1850 by Samuel Rowse, for instance, Brown's
miraculous escape and rebirth is emphasized via the caption of this work:
"The Resurrection of Henry Box Brown from slavery."[19] Escape is also the
subject of Eastman Johnson's painting *A Ride for Liberty – The Fugitive*

Slaves (ca. 1862). Johnson's painting is based on an incident he witnessed of a family fleeing from slavery during a Civil War battle in Manassas, Virginia, sometime in 1862 (see Figure 15.4). The family grouping draws a viewer's attention, and perhaps promotes empathy, as they make a break for Union lines in the chilly predawn light. As Hugh Honour notes: "Johnson fused the galloping horse, child, man, and woman with a baby in her arms, silhouetted against the sky, into a forceful image not so much of flight as of liberty."[20] The mother looks back worriedly over her shoulder, perhaps suggesting that someone is in pursuit of the family, but the main focus seems to be their willingness to claim freedom, on their own terms and in their own way, despite the risks.

Black Abolitionists and the Remaking of Visuality

Before the war, Black abolitionists (many of whom were former slaves) also crafted a visualization of African Americans that focused on their heroism; again, illustrated books were central to this imaging. Like Torrey's, Bourne's, and Stowe's works, such books tended to use words and images to impel readers toward either empathy or action. One of the earliest illustrated slave narratives was penned by Moses Roper in 1837; Roper, a light-skinned US-born man, had escaped from slavery in 1834, and he published *A Narrative of the Adventures and Escape of Moses Roper, from American Slavery* in 1837 in Britain and in the United States the following year. While Roper's book does sometimes depict enslaved torture, it also tends to emphasize resistance and movement into freedom. For example, in one image Roper flees his master on horseback, and he looks heroic and powerful.[21] What is imperative to notice about Roper's text is the way the interaction between its pictures and words script modes of agency and resistance onto African American enslaved bodies; indeed, Roper's text as a whole emphasizes multiple points at which the master's control over the body of the enslaved individual is undermined. Moreover, Roper could and did "pass" as white, and in the text's drawings, his racial identity as a "Black" man being tortured is not always clear; his book therefore at times pictorially undermines divisions demarcating black and white bodies, suggesting that the tortured form of the enslaved could be anyone's body. Perhaps because of this, the corporeality of the white reader may become entangled in some way with the body of the enslaved via such blurring mechanisms.

Frontispiece portraits also were a way that formerly enslaved individuals claimed a free subjectivity, and this feature is common in works by Phillis

Figure 15.4 Eastman Johnson, *A Ride for Liberty—The Fugitive Slaves* (ca. 1862). Brooklyn Museum. www.brooklynmuseum.org/opencollection/objects/495

Wheatley, Olaudah Equiano, Moses Roper, and others. Such portraits provided a type of authenticity to the narrative that white readers demanded, but they also served other purposes. One of the most interesting of these portraits is Henry Bibb's, which appears in his heavily illustrated account of his life in slavery and escape, *Narrative of the Life and Adventures of Henry Bibb* (1849).[22] Intriguingly, Bibb includes a frontispiece portrait that contains (below it) a small cartoon of his figure fleeing from slavery (see Figure 15.5).

The portrait at the top of the page shows Bibb as a composed, literate individual (with his hand on a book), and his flowing signature appears underneath this carefully crafted portrait. However, the cartoon below this image, which depicts Bibb as a fugitive slave, seems to undermine this dignified picture because it portrays Bibb with his hands in the air, running through darkened streets, with this caption: "Stop the runaway! Where is he! Daniel Lane after Henry Bibb in Louisville, Kentucky. The object was to sell Bibb in the slave market but Bibb turned the corner too quick for him and escaped." The cartoon mocks the discourse of the master with its frantic exclamation points ("Stop the runaway! Where is he!"); in fact, Bibb never was recaptured. Bibb appears to slip free from the master (at least linguistically), as his cartoon figure flees toward the left side of the image, yet does he also slip free visually, because he is not captured here? This double image also manifests knowledge that the fugitive slave or ex-slave exists in a liminal space, somewhere between slavery and freedom. The top portrait's intention might be to draw a reader in and encourage empathy with the "real" man, Henry Bibb, yet the cartoon underneath it seems to reject this empathetic move via irony and caricature. Taken together, these images present a multivalent and complex picture of African American subjectivity, implying that these identities cannot be easily captured, contained, or controlled.

Black abolitionist print publications also used illustrations to present multifaceted versions of African American identity that might (again) both draw a reader in but also reject the idea that the reader had fully comprehended the subjectivity of the enslaved. For example, perhaps in response to a controversial header for William Lloyd Garrison's journal *The Liberator* (1831–65), which made use of the supplicant slave image, Frederick Douglass's journal, *The North Star* (1847–51), had a masthead showing an enslaved man running away on his own, with this phrase: "Right is of no Sex—Truth is of no Color—God is the Father of us all, and we are all Brethren."[23] The phrase "we are all Brethren" forces a reader to see the enslaved as equal, yet the masthead image – of a solitary man following the North Star – emphasizes separation between a white and

Engraved by P.H. Reason

Henry Bibb

he runaway where is he $5. R^e Reward for him

...and lane after Henry Bibb in Louisville, Kentucky June 1848
...object was to sell Bibb in the slave market but Bibb turned
...corner too quick for him & escaped

Figure 15.5   Frontispiece to some versions of Henry Bibb, *Narrative of the Life and Adventures of Henry Bibb*, 2nd ed. (1849), with double portrait. *Top*: copper engraving by Patrick Henry Reason. *Bottom*: wood engraving (artist unknown).
Google Books, public domain

Black reader; the man pictured stands alone in a pool of light, with his back to the viewer. As explored below, Douglass was fully aware of the power of pictures to create both positive and negative portraits of African American identity. Scholars have argued that Douglass was one of the first individuals to use photography as a public relations instrument – and that he often used photographs of himself to inspire others and create dignity for his race.[24] Yet Douglass's relationship with the visual realm was complex, as he full well understood its power to give dignity to his race but also caricature and surveil African Americans.

Douglass was the most photographed US individual in the nineteenth century, and the archive of images of him that exists is vast.[25] Yet in most of these images, Douglass refuses to smile for the camera, in part because he believed that visual renditions of African Americans often caricatured or debased them. In a speech from 1854, for instance, Douglass denounces the illustrations of African Americans in scientific treatises; he writes that while "the European face is drawn in harmony with the highest ideas of beauty, dignity, and intellect ... [t]he negro ... appears with features distorted, lips exaggerated, forehead depressed—and the whole expression of the countenance made to harmonize with the popular idea of negro imbecility and degradation."[26] As regards photography, he believed that it could help others see a truer (if not exactly true) reality of their image. Due to the advent of photography, he writes, "Men of all conditions and classes can now see themselves as others see them and as they will be seen by those [who] shall come after them."[27]

In daguerreotypes (an early form of photography) of Douglass – the vast majority of which he controlled by picking a photographer and deciding which images would be circulated – he carefully crafts an image as dignified, heroic, and powerful. In a daguerreotype from 1852, for example, taken in Akron, Ohio, by Samuel J. Miller (see Figure 15.6), Douglass is elegantly dressed and coifed, and he wears a stylish, richly brocaded vest; such imaging distances him from his enslaved origins and from the stereotypical drawings so often replicated in advertisements for runaway slaves.

Yet in this image, Douglass's brow is furrowed and one eye is even in partial shadow; perhaps the darkness that covers part of the right side of his face is meant to invoke those individuals who still reside in the darkness of slavery proper. Douglass appears almost angry, and this image can be contrasted with the more genteel frontispiece portrait of Bibb, in which Bibb looks calm and even benign. The stare with which Douglass fixes the reader here seems to attempt to galvanize the reader into action not via empathy, but via righteous indignation.

Figure 15.6   Daguerreotype of Frederick Douglass, 1852, by Samuel J. Miller.
www.artic.edu/artworks/145681/frederick-douglass. 1996.433. Used courtesy of
Art Institute of Chicago

In a rare and unusual move, in a photograph of Douglass from
1893 taken in his home study in Washington, DC, he turns his back to
the viewer, as if refusing the visibility that he had tried to use in his fight
for the freedom of his race.[28] At this point – in 1893 – the United States
had entered what historians term the *nadir*: the worst period in US history
for African Americans in terms of lynching, other acts of illegal violence,
the enfranchisement of Jim Crow segregation, and the retrenchment of
many of the voting reforms put into place during Reconstruction.[29] In the
1893 photo, Douglass's turned back may signal pessimism toward the idea
that African Americans would ever have full citizenship, as well as a
rejection of the visual as a progressive mode that could enact lasting
political change.

A somewhat wary attitude toward visuality is also evident in Sojourner
Truth's marketing of images of herself. Drawings and photographs of

Truth sometimes contained a motto she had fashioned: "I sell the shadow to support the substance." Some critics argue that *shadow* in this formulation can be understood as physical race, so she engages in a "race trade" in which images of herself became marketable items, things that could be bought and sold.[30] But this phrase is enigmatic, and we must remember that Truth sells a simulacrum or photographic shadow of herself; viewers may believe they "own" the real Sojourner Truth, but her substance, her soul, her essential self remains her own. In a trickster-like fashion, Truth plays with the idea that people believe they own other people, either via slavery or photographs of them. Visibility may indeed be a trap, but it appears that her motto complicates this idea by implying that the "real" Truth (the substance of her identity) is not caught in her photographs; her real self exists somewhere beyond, or perhaps outside of, this visual domain.[31]

Moreover, Truth often manipulates symbolic items in her photos, knitting in one, for example (and thereby alluding to her domestic and womanly status). And in a photograph taken sometime between 1863 and 1865, she wears a small daguerreotype of her grandson, who was a prisoner of war at James Island, South Carolina (see Figure 15.7). Truth is elegantly attired in a polka-dot dress that appears to be made of a costly material, and she confronts viewers directly, looking into their faces. She seems to be asking not so much for pity, sympathy, or empathy from the viewer, but for equality. She may have lost a grandson (at this time, she did not know where he was; he had been captured by rebel soldiers and would survive, but Truth only knew that he was missing). She asks the viewer to understand her sacrifice for her country. Moreover, her inclusion of a grandson who is fighting on the Union side demands a type of recognition of his (and perhaps her own) symbolic citizenship. Yet the picture-within-the-picture of her grandson gives this photograph meta-pictorial elements and makes a viewer aware of the artificiality of the photographic domain. Perhaps by including this image within her photograph, Truth seeks to ask the viewer to reflect on the power of photography not only to convey "reality," but also to act as an instrument of creativity, artifice, and visual control.

Douglass and Truth use their photographs to demand recognition of their personhood, dignity, and (at times) symbolic citizenship. As formerly enslaved human beings, they had a commanding moral force, especially during the Civil War era. Indeed, photographs of all kinds were used to protest slavery; mixed-race children were exhibited to show that even "white"-looking people were enslaved; the deeply scarred back of a formerly enslaved man named Gordon who had become a Union solider was

Figure 15.7   Carte de visite of Sojourner Truth with a photograph of her grandson, James Caldwell, on her lap (ca. 1863–65), www.loc.gov/pictures/item/2017648645/. Library of Congress

photographed to show the horror of slavery; and Wilson Chinn, a branded
and scarred formerly enslaved man, even went back into a steel head collar,
manacles, and leg irons to convey his cruel mistreatment while enslaved.[32]
Such photographs protest the mistreatment of the enslaved, but they may
visually as well as symbolically re-enslave these individuals. What pictures
of African Americans in freedom exist, beyond the facts of enslavement,
fugitivity, and torture? As Jasmine Cobb notes, the archive of images
picturing freedom is more limited than the one that depicts enslavement,
especially in the early and mid-nineteenth century.[33] Yet some images
do exist.

Picturing Freedom

Knowing full well the ways in which their image as enslaved men and
women dominated the visual imaginary of the United States, some African
Americans crafted quieter and more genteel images. A daguerreotype from
the 1850s creates a portrait of middle-class gentility, showing a woman in
an elegant dress with lace collar, her hair carefully styled, and jewelry on
her hands and wrists. Her left elbow rests lightly on a book, symbolizing
her literacy. But what is perhaps most striking about this image is the
expression on this woman's face (see Figure 15.8).

In this daguerreotype, there is something self-protective in her facial
expression, and it is difficult for a viewer to know what she is thinking;
further, her neatly folded and draped arms suggest self-containment and
self-possession. Under slavery, women were often objects of the gaze and of
a kind of pornographic torture;[34] even after slavery, many African
American women were assumed to be on view for a male (and white)
prurient viewer. Yet this quiet image seems to resist such objectification by
its careful, composed, and even enigmatic tone.

Moreover, during the 1850s, photographs of enslaved African
Americans had been commissioned and displayed by the scientist Louis
Agassiz in an ethnographic, racist manner that featured nude African
American men and women.[35] Portraits of African Americans created in
freedom should be seen as a substantial and antithetical corrective to such
an othering, ethnographic gaze.[36] The woman in the 1850s daguerreotype
presents an entirely decorous and self-contained image, one that stands in
stark contrast to the many illustrations of slavery and torture that have
existed throughout US history and the ethnographic work that both
pictured and debased its heavily racialized subjects.

Figure 15.8   Daguerreotype portrait of an unidentified woman (ca. 1850). P.9427.15, https://digital.librarycompany.org/islandora/object/Islandora%3A65644?solr_nav%5Bid% 5D=d58ceca7b3c5e16d6814&solr_nav%5Bpage%5D=0&solr_nav%5Boffset%5D=126. Used courtesy Library Company of Philadelphia

Conclusion

US visual culture as a whole often pictured African Americans for a variety of political purposes and to cultivate empathy, but such imaging could replicate psychological or physical enslavement. White abolitionists themselves were often unable to imagine African Americans in anything other than abject terms. Black abolitionists such as Bibb, Douglass, and Truth used visual images to complicate flat portrayals of African American identity, and also to play with the notion that such imaging created truth and captured their subjectivity. Their sophisticated work with the image exists as a kind of radical counterpolitics to the dominant culture's practice of surveilling the bodies of the enslaved; the visual work of Bibb, Douglass, Truth, and others undermines the idea that reality has been captured in these images via meta-pictures, trickster-like ghosting of the "real" self, cartoons that pun on the idea that the fugitive can be captured at all, or quiet, dignified poses that refuse to generate a sense of interiority. It seems, then, that these early visual practitioners know something that contemporary individuals such as Kaepernick must also comprehend: Within a racist society, there is no neutral gaze, no way of using visibility to create a unidimensional politics or poetics of resistance, truth, or freedom. Power comes, then, not from trying to create truth, but from conceptualizing the visual image itself as a sort of performative façade – a second skin that individuals could slip into and out of, as they sought not freedom per se, but destabilization of the limiting racist visual modes that endeavored to confine them.[37]

Notes

1. P. R. Lockhart, "Trump Praises NFL Anthem Rule, Says Kneeling Players 'Maybe Shouldn't Be in the Country,'" *Vox*, May 24, 2018, www.vox.com/2018/5/24/17389288/donald-trump-nfl-kneeling-protest-national-anthem.
2. Even more glaringly, on July 14, 2019, Trump stirred controversy when he tweeted that four women of color who are House representatives – Ilhan Omar, Alexandria Ocasio-Cortez, Rashida Tlaib, and Ayanna S. Pressley – should "go back" to "the totally broken and crime infested places from which they came"; a day later he tweeted: "IF YOU ARE NOT HAPPY HERE, YOU CAN LEAVE!" All of the women are US citizens, and three were born here. https://twitter.com/realDonaldTrump (July 14, 2019; July 15, 2019).
3. Steve Wyche, "Colin Kaepernick Explains Why He Sat during National Anthem," *NFL*, August 27, 2016, www.nfl.com/news/colin-kaepernick-explains-why-he-sat-during-national-anthem-0ap3000000691077.
4. Tim Keown, "Colin Kaepernick Is a Real American," *The Undefeated*, October 4, 2016, https://theundefeated.com/features/colin-kaepernick-is-a-real-american/.
5. Michael Errigo, Rick Maese, and Mark Maske, "Colin Kaepernick to Star in Nike's 'Just Do It' Campaign," *Washington Post*, September 4, 2018, www.washingtonpost.com/news/early-lead/wp/2018/09/03/colin-kaepernick-is-now-the-face-of-nikes-just-do-it-campaign/. Nike, of course, has been known since the 1990s for its brutal exploitation of Brown and Black workers in third world countries.
6. Michel Foucault, *Discipline and Punish: The Birth of the Prison*, trans. Alan Sheridan (New York: Vintage, 1995 [1977]), 200.
7. Recent scholarship on the visualization of slavery, abolition, and race in the nineteenth century is too vast to list here, but key works include Marcus Wood, *Blind Memory: Visual Representation of Slavery in England and America, 1780–1865* (New York: Routledge, 2000); Shawn Michelle Smith, *Photography on the Color Line: W. E. B. Du Bois, Race, and Visual Culture*

(Durham, NC: Duke University Press, 2004); Simon Gikandi, *Slavery and the Culture of Taste* (Princeton, NJ: Princeton University Press, 2011); Maurice Wallace and Shawn Michelle Smith, eds., *Pictures and Progress: Early Photography and the Making of African American Identity* (Durham, NC: Duke University Press, 2012); and Deborah Willis and Barbara Krauthamer, *Envisioning Emancipation: Black Americans and the End of Slavery* (Philadelphia: Temple University Press, 2013).

8. See Jeannine DeLombard, *In the Shadow of the Gallows: Race, Crime, and American Civic Identity* (Philadelphia: University of Pennsylvania Press, 2012), 52; and Matthew Frye Jacobson, *Whiteness of a Different Color: European Immigrants and the Alchemy of Race* (Cambridge, MA: Harvard University Press, 1998).
9. Charles C. Green, "Prospectus," *Liberator* 15.12 (1845), 48, http://fair-use.org/the-liberator/1845/03/21/the-liberator-15-12.pdf.
10. See Martha J. Cutter, *The Illustrated Slave: Empathy, Graphic Narrative, and the Visual Culture of the Transatlantic Abolition Movement, 1800–1852* (Athens: University of Georgia Press, 2016), 1–5.
11. See the image between pages 42 and 43 of Jesse Torrey's *Portraiture of Domestic Slavery in the United States* (Philadelphia: Jesse Torrey 1817), Google Books, www.google.com/books/edition/A_Portraiture_of_Domestic_Slavery_in_the/iFoSAAAAIAAJ?gbpv=1.
12. Torrey, *Portraiture of Domestic Slavery*, 43–44, 59.
13. George Bourne, *Picture of Slavery in the United States of America* (Middletown, CT: Edwin Hunt, 1834), 45, 59, internet archive, archive.org/details/pictureofslaveryoobour/page/n9/mode/2up.
14. Teresa A. Goddu, "Antislavery's Panoramic Perspective," *MELUS* 39.2 (2014), 18.
15. Bourne, *Picture of Slavery*, 128, 129.
16. Harriet Beecher Stowe, *Uncle Tom's Cabin*, 2 vols. (Boston: Jewett, 1852), 2, 84.
17. See *American Anti-Slavery Almanac*, vol. 1.3 (April 1838), 12, Samuel J. May Antislavery Collection, Cornell University, http://dlxs.library.cornell.edu.
18. See, for example, "The Flogging of Females" in *Anti-Slavery Record*, vol. 1.10 (October 1835), 109, Google Books, https://books.google.com/books?id=_vISAAAAYAAJ&printsec=frontcover&source=gbs_ge_summary#v=onepage&q&f=false.
19. For more on Brown and to view a copy of this lithograph, see Martha J. Cutter, "Will the Real Henry 'Box' Brown Please Stand Up?" *Common-Place* 15.1 (2015), http://common-place.org.
20. Hugh Honour, *The Image of the Black in Western Art*, vol. IV, part 1, ed. David Bindman and Henry Louis Gates Jr. (Cambridge, MA: Belknap Press, 2012), 192.
21. See Moses Roper, *Narrative of the Adventures and Escape of Moses Roper, from American Slavery*, 2nd British ed. (London: Darton, Harvey, and Darton, 1838 [1837]), 43, Google Books, https://books.google.com/books?id=BmE6AAAAcAAJ&printsec=frontcover&dq=editions#v=onepage&q=editions&f=false.

22. Henry Bibb, *Narrative of the Life and Adventures of Henry Bibb, an American Slave, Written by Himself*, 2nd ed. (New York: Henry Bibb, 1849), Google Books, www.google.com/books/edition/_/Pfv6uWVYciQC?hl=en&gbpv= 1&pg=PT1&dq=Narrative+of+the+Life+and+Adventures+of+Henry+Bibb, +an+American+Slave,+Written+by+Himself. For more on Bibb, see Cutter, *Illustrated Slave*, 152–73.

23. *The North Star* was published from 1847 to 1851. It is not clear whether all issues had this illustrated masthead, but some definitely did; see *North Star*, June 20, 1850, p. 1, Library of Congress, www.loc.gov/exhibits/african/ afam006.html#obj2.

24. This argument about Douglass's photography has been made most recently by John Stauffer, Zoe Trodd, and Celeste-Marie Bernier in their introduction to *Picturing Frederick Douglass: An Illustrated Biography of the Nineteenth Century's Most Photographed Man* (New York: Norton, 2015), ix–xxviii.

25. Many of these photographs are collected in Stauffer, Trodd, and Bernier, *Picturing Frederick Douglass*.

26. "The Claims of the Negro Ethnologically Considered: An Address Delivered in Hudson, Ohio, on 12 July 1854," in *The Frederick Douglass Papers*, series 1, vol. 2, ed. John W. Blassingame (New Haven, CT: Yale University Press, 1982), 510.

27. Frederick Douglass, "Pictures and Progress," in Stauffer, Trodd, and Bernier, *Picturing Frederick Douglass*, 165.

28. See Stauffer, Trodd, and Bernier, *Picturing Frederick Douglass*, 69.

29. This term was coined by Rayford Logan in 1954 (see *The Betrayal of the Negro, from Rutherford B. Hayes to Woodrow Wilson*, reprint ed. [Boston: Da Capo Press, 1997]).

30. Augusta Rohrbach, "Shadow and Substance: Sojourner Truth in Black and White," in *Pictures and Progress*, ed. Wallace and Smith, 96.

31. According to Nell Irvin Painter, Truth "sat for at least fourteen photographic portraits . . . between 1863 and about 1875"; see Nell Irvin Painter, *Sojourner Truth: A Life, A Symbol* (New York: Norton, 1996), 198. Also see Darcy Grimaldo Grigsby, *Enduring Truths: Sojourner's Shadows and Substance* (Chicago: University of Chicago Press, 2015).

32. See "Rebecca, Charley & Rosa, slave children from New Orleans" (ca. 1864), www.loc.gov/resource/ppmsca.11234/; "Gordon as he entered our lines" (1863), www.loc.gov/resource/cph.3b44593/; and "Wilson Chinn, a branded slave from Louisiana" (1863), www.loc.gov/resource/ppmsca.57689/.

33. See Jasmine Nichole Cobb, *Picture Freedom: Remaking Black Visuality in the Early Nineteenth Century* (New York: New York University Press), 2015.

34. See Mary A. Favret, "Flogging: The Anti-Slavery Movement Writes Pornography," in *Romanticism and Gender*, ed. Anne Janowitz (Cambridge: Brewer, 1998), 19–43.

35. See Mandy Reid, "Selling Shadows and Substance," *Early Popular Visual Culture* 4.3 (2006), 285–305.

36. See the Library of Congress's Gladstone Collection of African American Photographs at www.loc.gov/collections/gladstone-african-american-photo graphs/.
37. I draw here on ideas from Anne Anlin Cheng's *Second Skin: Josephine Baker and the Modern Surface* (New York: Oxford University Press, 2013 [2011]).

CHAPTER 16

"The Man That Was a Thing"
Uncle Tom's Cabin, *Photographic Vision, and the Portrayal of Race in the Nineteenth Century*

Maurice Wallace

This essay explores the spectacle cast of race in nineteenth-century American literature and culture by way of highlighting an impulse in white writing at mid-century to represent black figures according to a cultural materialism that had its genesis in the invention of the daguerreotype in 1839. Specifically, I am interested in the diffractive cultural force of daguerreotypy on nineteenth-century US literary and visual portrait cultures and, more specifically, on the visual politics of race in American expressive practice. Differently put, I pursue here a fraught logic obtaining between seeing and being (black) between 1839 and 1889 that the new proto-photographic technology would both answer back to and blindly abet, for example, in Harriet Beecher Stowe's 1852 *Uncle Tom's Cabin*. This cross-purposive (il)logic, simultaneously personifying and objectifying, is central to the trigonometry by which race, slavery, and personhood come to be portrayed relationally in literary history. At stake in this inquiry is not only a renewed contemplation of the social consequentiality of early photography as art and science on the writing mind in the nineteenth century, but a reconsideration of the broadly epistemic problem of discriminating between person and thing, an entanglement Stowe captured in the first, provisional subtitle she announced for her work, "Or, The Man That Was a Thing." In Stowe, emblematically, both the literary and the dialectical effects of racialized vision on the question of human being follow from a strange technology of words and thought that granted the slave not only "two bodies" in early American legal history, as Stephen M. Best keenly argues,[1] but admitted of him two rival *beings* – one personalistic (or, more precisely, im*person*ating) and the other held, enjoyed, possessed, *thingly*. Their difference is not so much born of a contradiction between ontologies as it is obscured by a categorical contraction willed by law, if copied by literature.

Race, Law, and the Problem with Personhood

The Universal Declaration of Human Rights (1948), the International Covenant on Civil and Political Rights (1954), and the American Convention on Human Rights (1978) would all seem to affirm Hannah Arendt's 1949 avowal, repeated in 1951 in *The Origins of Totalitarianism*, that the first basic right of the human being is the right to be possessed of rights. That "[e]veryone has the right to recognition as a person before the law," as the Universal Declaration of Human Rights asserts,[2] however, is no guarantee of the protections so decreed, as is proven again and again over the history of the modern world. The world community, in fact, is crowded with human subjects who clearly are *not* inherently persons in the protected sense inasmuch as they are not claimed by any law whatever giving rise to a recognizable political community. They are refugees, asylees, nomads, slaves, and other stateless actors existing in extralegal suspension, just outside the statist logic of the global political and social order. Without personhood's legal coverture, these outlaw subjects might just as well be among the dead. Unfortunately, this narrow application of personhood's meaning in law extends beyond the law, coming to pose a problem not only for the unprotected but for the concept of personhood itself as well.

The problem with personhood is not that it isn't, and hasn't been, as universally available to the human family as the ostensible equivalency of *person* and *human* in everyday speech has pretended; it is law's ongoing worrying of personhood's *formal* delineation.[3] But if personhood "has long been, if not a juridical question, then at least a juridified one," as Sheryl N. Hamilton argues,[4] it has never been, I hasten to add, nor could it ever be, I maintain, altogether extricated from its further entanglements in philosophy, sociology, religion, biology, ethics, and aesthetics. The law's express adjudications of who is or is not a person may pass conceptually as straightforward and pretend to unimpeachable authority on the question, but beneath the veil of its vanities, the law is far less certain about its judgments than its authority performs. "The fact is," writes legal scholar Linda Bosniak, "that the category of person is historically constructed, and there has been persistent debate about the boundaries of the category, up to the present period."[5] Today, as in earlier times, personhood is – to borrow a phrase – a "fugitive property," no more under the law's conceptual mastery in contemporary legal debates about the constitutional standing of corporations, fetuses, cyborgs, and great apes, say, than it was when James Wilson and Roger Sherman, two of the founding fathers and leading jurists of the Revolutionary era, proposed the Three-Fifths Compromise to the 1787 US Constitutional Convention. From the first, racial slavery in particular posed a problem for, if it was not the very basis of, personhood's political definition.

Stephen Best's *The Fugitive's Properties: Law and the Poetics of Possession* amplifies this point with expert subtlety. His study's specific discernment of what John Plotz has characterized as "the unsettling transformations of *people into things* under the new legal dispensation of Gilded Age America"[6] nuances the racial problem of personhood by attending to the complications and logical contradictions inhering to the slaves' condition under the law as juridified "things." According to Best,

> At the beginning of the [nineteenth] century, legal fictions pictured property, ideally, as absolute dominion over "things," as the right to a tangible parcel with clear boundaries. William Blackstone is the jurist largely responsible for the popularization of this fiction, for ... he takes property ... to encompass all things "as contradistinguished from persons." ... Courts perceived the concept of property to rest inevitably in the nature of things, and thus a certain "objectness" provided the premise from which ownership could be deduced with certainty.[7]

If *The Fugitive's Properties* seems an especially cogent deconstruction of personhood in American legal history with its concern for the categorical liminality of enslaved subjects between the protections of personhood and their standing as things, then that which *The Fugitive's Properties* was to come to theorize in literary criticism, a zealous Harriet Beecher Stowe rendered 150 years earlier in fiction. Indeed, Stowe's *Uncle Tom's Cabin* is essential to Best's review of the predicaments of law, property, and personhood in the ante- and postbellum periods. But it is the particularity of Stowe's preoccupation with the visual calculus of race and being animating this conceptual tangle that this criticism is about, being concerned above all else with a certain revolution in visual representationalism unfolding contemporaneously with the most intense flashpoints of legal debate about racial slavery and the physiognomic conceits of personhood in the white imagination. Specifically, the popularization of the daguerreotype as an evidentiary form of doubly scientific and moral knowledge could not but assert a deep and defining influence on the nineteenth century's culture of letters and on *Uncle Tom's Cabin*, more precisely, as a paradigmatic musing on personhood's confounded logics.

What I have called "the problem with personhood" in nineteenth-century legal thought, in particular, owes its puzzlements and perplexities – its tortured logics of white self-interest, on the one hand, and radical democracy, on the other – to the vaunted knowledge claims of a prior sophistry passing for objective science among the elite and intellectual classes of the day. Scientific polygenism was contrived to prove the speciational difference of racial blackness from the white and yellow races. Among its votaries, that difference was purported to be picturable under a photographic gaze. In fact, the nineteenth century's baldest attempt to show proof of the polygenist argument photographically was made only a few months before Stowe proposed *Uncle Tom's Cabin* to the editor of the anti-slavery *National Era* newspaper. It was not speciation, though, that the fifteen ill-famed slave daguerreotypes attributed to Harvard scientist Louis Agassiz turned out to visualize, finally. Rather, the circumstances of the daguerreotypes' making in the Columbia, South Carolina studio of photographer J. T. Zealy and their obscurity as lost objects forgotten for over a century to a storage cabinet in the Harvard Peabody Museum of Archaeology and Ethnology point up, above every other consideration, a *thingly* condition outside of species that Stowe seemed to have desired most to underline. Importantly, she would use her own version of what critic Michael Chaney has called "camera tactics" to do so.[8]

The Camera and the Slave

Months ahead of the first appearance of *Uncle Tom's Cabin* in the *National Era*, Agassiz's several daguerreotypes of five enslaved men and two enslaved women, all immodestly posed in varying degrees of undress, put the slave on spectacular "scientific" display. In some detail, Brian Wallis explained in 1995:

> The fifteen daguerreotypes are divided into two series. The first consists of standing, fully nude images showing front, side, and rear views. This practice reflected a physiognomic approach, an attempt to record body shape, proportions, and posture .... The second series was more tightly focused, showing the heads and naked torsos of three men and two women. This series adhered to a phrenological approach, emphasizing the character and shape of the head.[9]

Appearing in the first and second series, one subject, identified as "Jem, Gullah, Columbia, SC," is pictured staring back blankly at Zealy's camera staring "scientifically" at him. A note accompanying a second daguerreotype of Jem identifies him further as "belonging to FW Green, Columbia, SC." In 1850, Green was the proprietor of the Red Bank Cotton Factory of Lexington, South Carolina, and owner of twenty-three slaves. It is unclear whether Jem served Green in or near Green's Columbia residence, or closer to the Red Bank factory in Lexington some fifteen miles to the west. Wherever he worked, what *is* clear is that Green's house was mere blocks from Zealy's second-story Main Street studio in 1850. By then, Zealy was "an artist already . . . favorably known, not only in the State [sic] but throughout the country."[10] Certainly, Green could not have missed Zealy's studio; probably Zealy knew Green by reputation.

A year later, in 1851, Zealy built a new studio across town in the Granite Range community. The new space was "fitted up with great taste and elegance."[11] An elegant piano, a large skylight, and an outsized camera for panoramic outdoor views set the new studio apart. Both Brian Wallis and Molly Rogers have imagined the striking incongruity of Zealy's new studio and the abject condition of the enslaved subjects whose daguerreotype pictures he made, both of them envisioning the slaves' amazement at seeing so much opulence displayed in the photographer's new place.[12] I want to imagine a more foundational shock to the seven corralled slaves than Wallis and Rogers do, however, one that underscores the very categorical crises slavery created. If the affective experience of being photographed in the flesh included shock at all, Zealy's captive subjects might have been much less "stunned by the colors and the textures"[13] on the walls and floors of Zealy's studio as they might have been by the arrestive power of *the thing* before him (and many other things besides), hailing them into their own thingly condition such that the camera and the slaves would seem to confront one another in an unblinking standoff. By attending to the lived practice of daguerreotypy and its material accoutrements and not just to the representational politics of that practice, one may discern not only the precise ways the enslaved man or woman was seen by Zealy, or the polygenesists like Agassiz seeing what Zealy (imagines he) sees through his camera, but also the captive him- or herself seeing in the camera's lens what the camera sees seeing him or her as one thing among all the other things in Zealy's possession. Theorist Bill Brown offers one way at least – thing theory – of helping us see this paradox of seeing seeing, the camera's seeing and the slave's, more clearly.

In his discerning *A Sense of Things: The Object Matter of American Literature*, Brown argues usefully that

> Even as the prose fiction of the nineteenth century represents and variously registers the way commodity relations came to saturate everyday life, so too (despite those relations or, indeed, intensified by them) this fiction demonstrates that the human investment in the physical object world, and the mutual constitution of human subject and inanimate object, can hardly be reduced to those relations.[14]

Following Brown's familiarly Weberian notion of "the mutual constitution of human subject and inanimate object" and the understated social relations between things in commodity culture secondary to it, I maintain that Agassiz's daguerreotypes, far from merely enacting a perverse *still*-life survey, reflect a *transitional* one instead – reflect a liminality, in other words, "between the sphere of man and the sphere of the object," as Czech thinker Jiří Valtruský has written.[15] "As can be seen," Valtruský explains, "the sphere of the live human and that of the lifeless object are interpenetrated, and no exact limit can be drawn between them."[16] Thus does Stowe's *Uncle Tom's Cabin* too disclose a general cultural condition in stark historico-materialist terms. In *Uncle Tom's Cabin*, as in Zealy's studio, the slave's hypostatic cross-condition as person and nonperson, possessive individual and individual possession, human-made "half-thing" – Heidegger's phrase – by "the mysterious character of the commodity-form" – Marx's – is vividly portrayed (i.e., daguerreotyped) in its fungible, mixed condition.

Like few other nineteenth-century American prose writers, Stowe appeared to understand the puzzlings of personhood as a function of juridical and commercial confusions (or, let us say, *conveniences* instead?) between the slave as vendible property with no claim to the issue, profit, or prerogatives of his or her captive body, and the slave as, at root, an impersonation made subject to the law by a force of law that it demands of itself in order to know itself as law. *Uncle Tom's Cabin* portrays this "weighing of person and property—the limited recognition of the slave as person, to the extent that it [does] not interfere with the full enjoyment of the slave as thing" – as a violence "commensurate with the exercise of property rights," to borrow Saidiya Hartman's words, "and essential to the making of perfect submission" that the force of (slave) law commands.[17] In Stowe's novel, I mean, what Hartman casts as "the law's selective recognition of slave personhood,"[18] which I tend to view as the slave's impersonating or impersonative personhood, follows, it would seem, from not only an historical legal tension, as Best shows above, but equally from a materialist (il)logic animating popular visual discourse (viz., the daguerreotype portrait) in the antebellum period as well.

"The Man That Was a Thing": Picturing Uncle Tom

Though not widely discussed this way, *Uncle Tom's Cabin* could hardly have escaped the cultural and commercial boon of early photographic technology as the novel was taking shape in a series of short magazine sketches late in 1851. By then, daguerrean science was nearly a decade old, and its demand in Europe and the United States was vast and frenzied. So powerful was its charm in the world, especially in the United States, that daguerreotypy not only "represented photography in America," as Alan Trachtenberg observed, but it also "represented America itself, picturing the nation in a manner unlike any other media before or since, photographic or otherwise."[19] It is one thing to say that "the nation achieved a simply astonishing collective visibility" by means of the daguerreotype, however; it is quite another to claim that the daguerreotype "taught countless people, practitioners and audiences, the value of a certain kind of quick, incisive seeing . . .. [I]t taught, by necessity, a kind of seeing that might lead to art."[20] Trachtenberg undoubtedly had in mind the expressive possibilities of the daguerreotype itself, its silvery capture of an ever more discriminating practice of observation. Yet this very seeing, penetrating and Whitmanesque, "might lead" to a kind of literary daguerreotyping too. Stowe, at least, seemed to trust that possibility. Early in *Uncle Tom's Cabin*, she put the work up to a restrained trial. Though an actual daguerreotype of Eva and St. Clare appears several chapters in, it is on the introduction of Uncle Tom himself that a photographic urgency comes abruptly upon Stowe. "[A]s he is to be the hero of our story," she explains, "we must daguerreotype [Uncle Tom] for our readers"[21] (27). In the picture of him that follows, a sketch properly daguerrean in its calculus to construct out of the bare facts of Tom's form and appearance a reliable characterological indexicality, Stowe styles "Mr. Shelby's best hand," as what a more recent vintage of American vernacularity would call, suggestively, *a specimen*.

> He was a large, broad-chested, powerfully made man, of a full glossy black, and a face whose truly African features were characterized by an expression of grave and steady good sense, united with much kindliness and benevolence. There was something about his whole air self-respecting and dignified, yet united with a confiding and humble simplicity. (27)

Although it is not especially difficult to imagine a picture like Stowe's in a physical, rather than ekphrastic form, and, visualizing it, apprehend Tom's broad chest and shining complexion as the technical effects of framing, perspective, and/or lighting, for the nineteenth-century viewer these were also the effects, captured by camera, of an essential interiority inclined in advance toward "good sense . . . kindliness and benevolence." But the daguerreotype did not so much externalize an interior mien as it interpolated the dignity of its subjects. Stowe's description of Tom's size and deportment, in other words, repeats the daguerrean fallacy: The camera reveals nothing hidden; the details of Tom's physical form and appearance ("He was a large, broad-chested, powerfully-made man, of a full glossy black, and a face whose truly African features ...") follow from, and are seen through, a prior decision about his essential honor. The daguerreotype was thus, in a way, an instrument of fiction well before fiction, in its novelistic embodiment, appropriated photography's materiality, and cultural (il)logic to novelistic ends. Stowe's investments in daguerreotypy were deeper and more intimate than its fictional utility alone, however.

Not unlike the camerical fascination of her contemporaries, Nathanial Hawthorne and Frederick Douglass, Stowe was charmed by "chemical pictures," as daguerreotypes were then being called. According to Marcy Dinius, the daguerreotype afforded readers of early African American and antebellum abolitionist literature "what would have been understood as a detailed, lifelike, and accurate representation of both the experience of slavery and the slave's identity as ... an actual person."[22] Dinius imagines Stowe as "exploiting" the cultural power of the daguerreotype for its universal trustworthiness to represent the real in unmediated mimesis, "validating the novel's representation of slavery and ... developing [a] powerful affective attachment" between Uncle Tom and Stowe's reading audience.[23] Still, skeptics of the daguerreotype's deep and "affective" influence on *Uncle Tom's Cabin* and its reading public might accuse Dinius with making a proverbial mountain out of a molehill of just two mere mentions of the daguerreotype in Stowe's copious novel. And yet, according to visual historians Floyd Rinhart and Marion Rinhart, the years 1847–50 *were* the critical years of expansion for the daguerreotype in the United States, two modest mentions notwithstanding.[24] An 1849 *Godey's Lady's Book* article observed how the daguerreotypists were "limning faces" that year "at a rate that promises soon to make every man's house a Daguerrean Gallery ... In our great cities, a Daguerreotypist is to be found in almost every square; and there is scarcely a county in any state that has not one or more of these industrious individuals busy at work." So ubiquitous was this "industrious" band of professionals "at work in 'catching the shadow' ere the 'substance fade,'" in fact, that "now," wrote the *Godey's* contributor, "it is hard to find a man who has not gone through the 'operator's' hands from once to a half-a-dozen times." Every man, it seemed, displayed "the shadowy faces of his wife and children" proudly from ornate pocket-sized cases.[25] The daguerrean turn missed no one. In Maine as much as Mississippi, Americans of all stripes were rapt by its heliographic magic.

It hardly surprises, then, that Stowe's original vision for the novel she would pitch to the *National Era* would be "limned" (to recall *Godey's*) in the language of daguerrean desire. She envisioned *Uncle Tom's Cabin*, she'd disclose to the *National Era* editor, as "a series of sketches which give the lights and shadows of the 'patriarchal institution.'"[26] In terms well suited to the work of the professional portraitist, Stowe committed herself to "show[ing] the best side of *the thing*, and something," she added, "faintly approaching the worst."[27] If, further down in her letter to Gamaliel Bailey, Stowe declared that her compulsion to tell the story of Uncle Tom, cribbed heavily from *The Life of Josiah Henson* (1849), was not that felt by a writer but "that of painter," it is in the interest of advancing a metaphor, *painting,* for "the most lifelike and graphic manner" of representation in her métier, or *writing.* Communicating other than a simple identification with the portrait painter, Stowe *wills to paint.* And in 1851, to paint "in the most lifelike and graphic manner," it turns out, meant to daguerreotype.

At mid-century, the relationship of painting to photography was a vexed one, as Marcus Root, a prominent Philadelphia daguerreotypist, lay bare in *The Camera and the Pencil; Or, the Heliographic Art, Its Theory and Practice in All Its Various Branches; E.g. Daguerreotypy, Photography, &C,* an 1864 defense of daguerreotypy (called "heliography" by Root) as an artistic, rather than mechanical, activity. Allowing that some who have approached the daguerreotypist's task, namely, "those itinerant portrait-painters, who anticipate the death of their victims, by destroying every trait of *life-likeness* in the faces they *execute,*"[28] Root nevertheless argued that

> when we come to the expression—that something which reveals the soul of the sitter, the individuality which differences him from all beings else—we find an antagonism between the two classes [i.e., the mechanical and the artistic portraitists], as decided as between a living man and the wooden image of a man. As the mechanic can but put together dead materials, his work must needs be lifeless. The artist, on the contrary, creates, and into his work he "breathes the breath of life," and it "becomes a living soul."[29]

Root was keen to see that daguerreotypy held an exalted status in the expressive arts, that it was not viewed merely in light of its "mechanical and chemical appliances,"[30] as he would refer to the "lifeless" side of its execution and outcomes. "Why (I queried with myself) should not Heliography be placed beside Painting and Sculpture, and the Camera be held in like honor with the Pencil and the Chisel?" he wanted to know.[31] Root's faith in the creative powers of daguerreotypy – powers Root's own words figure as religious – surely reflected the evangelical attitudes of others as well, Stowe not least among them. In confessing to Bailey, "My vocation is simply that of painter," Stowe not only evoked a sense of the creative divine in her work's pursuit ("vocation" being inextricably tethered to Christian discourse until the twentieth century, evidently)[32] but also pointed up an intimate relation between painting and writing that Root's treatise helps us see more clearly by juxtaposing the daguerreotypist's camera to the painter's "pencil," by which he means, we'd say, the painter's brush. This, the homology in his reflexive question above plainly reveals. In pursuing "painting" as a religious imperative and aesthetic objective, at once, Stowe's portrait of *Uncle Tom's Cabin* proleptically realizes Root's hope for the honor of daguerreotypy by showing how, through the "various dispositions of light and shadow"[33] obtaining to photographic forms, the pencil-as-stylus might portray her novel's hero with camerical realism and, moreover, painterly dignity.

Try as she might to portray the Christ-like forbearance of Uncle Tom as "the best side" of slavery's evil, however, Stowe could not elude entanglement in the gaming of race and personhood she was seeking to expose to the light of faith and moral compunction. For in "daguerreotyping" Tom narratively, inadvertently Stowe fell into, and reproduced, Zealy's briar patch of black binomial being. By *black binomial being*, I mean to improvise upon Lindon Barrett's concern for that allusion of "binomial being" in the title of Olaudah Equiano's 1989 *Interesting Narrative of the Life of Olaudah Equiano, or Gustavas Vassa, the African, Written by Himself,* according to which Barrett came so smartly to consider the "irregularity by which racial blackness conflates with textuality" to materialize "an anomalous figurative rendition of the human being" – which I formulate as *impersonation* above – "that, at once, ... seems to [also] forfeit the figurativeness of human being," Barrett concludes – in its distinctly *thingly* cast, I add, seconding him.[34] We might say that by virtue of what Barrett calls "the Atlantic lineaments of race," Stowe's Uncle Tom shares binomial being with Equiano inasmuch as his name and the premise of his personhood, which the interchangeability of "painting" and "daguerreotyping" to Stowe is intent upon underlining, are similarly threatened by the book's ghosting subtitle: "The Man Who Was a Thing." Against the true-to-life background of the life and fugitive adventures of Rev. Josiah Henson, whom some of Stowe's severest critics have called "the real Uncle Tom" for certain intertextual liberties taken with *The Life of Josiah Henson,* the name Uncle Tom, like that of Olaudah Equiano, marks a "suspension between two ... epistemological orders."[35] Uncle Tom has *two* names, the sign of a split condition that Barrett describes as a "rendition of the human being" that "forfeit[s] the figurativeness of human being" at one and the same time. In *Uncle Tom's Cabin*, Uncle Tom exists in the transverse and between of opposing categories of legal ranking and being: person and thing. The condition of black binomial being in Stowe is the condition of being irresolvably binary in the structural order of white antebellum life and black racial experience.

Race, Slavery, and the Double Bind of Being

Arbitrary as it sounds, Stowe's will to daguerreotype Tom in the hope of portraying him in light of "the great and the good, the heroes, saints, and sages," in Root's words, hardly brings any resolution at all to the double bind of double being-for-others as a provisional person and a commodity-object under the law. As Zealy's example helps show, to take the picture of Tom that Stowe is committed to "painting" for her readers in stark black and white is to hold Tom doubly captive, despite Stowe's intentions. Daguerreotyped, Tom is hardly made a person by Stowe's ekphrasis. He would seem, instead, to realize a "glossy black" impersonation of the object-being of that very "portrait of General Washington" hung upon the wall of the cabin he shares with Aunt Chloe. Twice framed, then, by the categorical confusion between personhood and possession that the daguerreotype as a seeing of seeing and chattel object occasions, Tom's doom is sealed from the first. Introduced as "an uncommon fellow," "good, steady, sensible, pious," invoked alongside "everything [Mas'r Shelby] had—money, house, horses" (8), Tom's exceptionalism arises out of the surprise that the *thing* might also, appearing human, be pressed into service as a proxy for Shelby within the very economy (if not in the very trade) that metamorphosed the slave into commodity form. "Why, last fall," Shelby boasted, "I let him go to Cincinnati alone, to do business for me, and to bring home five hundred dollars" (8). Shelby believes in Tom implicitly. "I trust you, because I think you are a Christian—I know you wouldn't cheat" (8). His confidence in Tom notwithstanding, as Shelby's proxy in business, Tom's (non)personhood is always already fraudulent. He is allowed to pass for a person only insofar as he is constrained to stand in for Shelby by Shelby in his master's business dealings. Tom is not only "Mr. Shelby's best hand," then, but, like the figure of self-making recursivity in Dutch painter M. C. Escher's iconic lithograph a century later,[36] the "hand" that is/authors its own condition of possibility as it/he conducts Shelby's business an arm's length away from, while also on behalf of, the master as slaveholder. Tom, thus, enacts a cross-classificatory impersonation in two senses. He both plays the part of the devoted bondsman who "wouldn't cheat" or "make tracks for Canada" (8) *and* invests into the uncertain being of that role the air of personhood, despite his slave status, necessary for efficaciously representing Shelby's proprietorial interests as he constitutes and is appointed to advance or protect said interests simultaneously. Stowe places the burden of responsibility for this doubling of Tom's being-for-others in property and personation squarely at the law's feet:

> [O]ver and above the scene [of plantation paradise] there broods a portentous shadow—the shadow of *law*. So long as the law considers all these human beings, with beating hearts and living affections, only as so many *things* belonging to a master,— . . . so long as it is impossible to make anything beautiful or desirable in the best regulated administration of slavery. (14–15, emphasis in original)

The law may bind slave to master as one of "so many *things*," but it is the "*shadow*" it casts that recalls, not so coincidentally, the photographical bind of F. W. Green's Jem and Tom alike, abject objects of a singular camerical gaze intent upon opposing conclusions about the slave's properties. I mean, in Zealy's daguerreotype of Jem (whose visual reproduction here I refuse) and Stowe's daguerreotyping of Tom, the slave's *two* bodies are projected from the dual and dueling play of their daguerreotype studies. The one body is physical, enfleshed, and violently instrumentalized according to slavery's material and symbolic objectives. The other is virtual, approaching spectrality, impersonating – in Hegelian dialectics, the slave's shadow to the lord's substance. The problem of personhood arising out of this proto-Duboisian *twoness* that the invention of race in America has engendered, therefore, is a problem not for Uncle Tom alone, or the enslaved men and women facing Zealy's daguerreotyping camera, but for nineteenth-century thought itself, for the fictions of classification, category, science, and the social sciences, and for law, visual culture, and literature.

Perhaps more than any of her contemporaries, Harriet Beecher Stowe wrestled mightily with this conceptual quandary. *Uncle Tom's Cabin* portrays the black slave's precarious personhood (which is to say, the impersonating or impersonative personhood of the enslaved subject) as following from an historical legal tension and a materialist (il)logic animating popular visual discourse as well. Stowe's concern to novelistically sound the abyss between human personhood and the "unique species of 'living property'" posited by Stephen Best reflects the binomial being of the enslaved not as persons debased into property so much as property nominally impersonated in the interest of impersonation's serviceability to aspirational democracy (in the rhetorical sense, at least) and Southern interests. Following Stowe, we might regard the slave as having once had being a "half-thing," then—a peculiarity painfully precise in its apprehension of the (il)logic of race and chattel slavery in America. *Uncle Tom's Cabin*, like few other works of nineteenth-century American fiction portraying race, through straining badly to see clearly, could not *not* see this being (as) a problem.

Notes

1. See Stephen M. Best, *The Fugitive's Properties: Law and the Poetics of Possession* (Chicago: University of Chicago Press, 2004).
2. Universal Declaration of Human Rights, adopted December 10, 1948, by the United Nations General Assembly, www.un.org/Overview/rights.html.
3. And yet, no sooner than the fundamentally legal foundation of personhood comes into plainer view do its imbrications formally and historically in philosophy and science also become equally apparent.
4. Sheryl N. Hamilton, *Impersonations: Troubling the Person in Law and Culture* (Toronto: University of Toronto Press, 2008), 9.
5. Linda Bosniak, "Persons and Citizens in Constitutional Thought," *International Journal of Constitutional Law* 8.1 (2010), 12.
6. John Plotz, "Can the Sofa Speak? A Look at Thing Theory," *Criticism* 47:1 (2005), 117.
7. Best, *The Fugitive's Properties*, 31.
8. Michael Chaney, "Mulatta Obscura: Camera Tactics and Linda Brent," in *Pictures and Progress: Early Photography and the Making of African American Identity*, eds. Maurice O. Wallace and Shawn Michelle Smith (Durham, NC: Duke University Press, 2012), 109.
9. Brian Wallis, "Black Bodies, White Science: Louis Agassiz's Slave Daguerreotypes," *American Art* 9.2 (1995), 45.
10. H. H. Snelling, ed., "Gossip," *The Photographic Art-Journal* 2.6 (1851), 376.
11. Snelling, "Gossip," 376.
12. Wallis, "Black Bodies," 60n13; Molly Rogers, *Delia's Tears: Race, Science, and Photography in Nineteenth-Century America* (New Haven, CT: Yale University Press, 2010), 213–14.
13. Rogers, *Delia's Tears*, 213.
14. Bill Brown, *A Sense of Things: The Object Matter of American Literature* (Chicago: University of Chicago Press, 2003), 5.
15. Jiří Valtruský, "Man and Object in the Theater," in *A Prague School Reader on Esthetics, Literary Structure, and Style*, ed. Paul Garvin (Washington, DC: Georgetown University Press, 2007), 86.

16. Valtruský, "Man and Object in the Theater," 86.

17. Saidiya Hartman, *Scenes of Subjection: Terror, Slavery and Self-Making in Nineteenth-Century America* (New York: Oxford University Press, 1997), 97, 86.

18. Hartman, *Scenes of Subjection*, 97.

19. Alan Trachtenberg, "The Daguerreotype: American Icon," in *American Daguerreotypes: From the Matthew R. Isenburg Collection*, eds. Richard S. Field, Robin Jaffee Frank, et al. (New Haven, CT: Yale University Art Gallery, 1989), 15.

20. Trachtenberg, "The Daguerreotype," 16.

21. Harriet Beecher Stowe, *Uncle Tom's Cabin*, ed. Jean Fagin Yellin (1852; New York: Oxford University Press, 1998), 27. Subsequent references are to this edition and shall be indicated parenthetically in the text above.

22. Marcy J. Dinius, *The Camera and the Press: American Visual and Print Culture in the Age of the Daguerreotype* (Philadelphia: University of Pennsylvania Press, 2012), 128.

23. Dinius, *The Camera and the Press*, 135.

24. See Floyd Rinhart and Marion Rinhart, *The American Daguerreotype* (Athens: University of Georgia Press, 1981).

25. T. S. Arthur, "The Daguerreotypist," *Godey's Lady's Book* 38 (1849), 352.

26. Robert Forrest Wilson, *Crusader in Crinoline: The Life of Harriet Beecher Stowe* (Philadelphia: Lippincott, 1941), 259.

27. Wilson, *Crusader in Crinoline*, 259, emphasis added. Although it is likely that "the thing" was a reference to "the 'patriarchal institution,'" "the thing" cannot be easily disassociated from the man who was a thing in Stowe's original subtitle.

28. Marcus A. Root, *The Camera and the Pencil; Or, the Heliographic Art, Its Theory and Practice in All Its Various Branches; E.g. Daguerreotypy, Photography, &C* (Philadelphia: Root, Lippencott, Appleton, 1864), xv, emphasis in original.

29. Root, *The Camera and the Pencil*, 32.

30. Root, *The Camera and the Pencil*, xiv.

31. Root, *The Camera and the Pencil*, xv.

32. This seems to be what a fast study of the history of *vocation* in the *Oxford English Dictionary* and Max Weber's *The Protestant Ethic and the Spirit of Capitalism* (1930) reveals. See Chapter 3 in Weber, "Luther's Concept of the Calling" and, especially, the chapter's first note. Max Weber, "Luther's Concept of the Calling," *The Protestant Ethic and the Spirit of Capitalism*, trans. Talcott Parsons (New York: Routledge, 1992), 39–50, 154–57n1.

33. Root, *The Camera and the Pencil*, 34.

34. Lindon Barrett, *Racial Blackness and the Discontinuity of Western Modernity*, eds. Justin A. Joyce, Dwight A. McBride, and John Carlos Rowe (Urbana: University of Illinois Press, 2014), 50.

35. Barrett, *Racial Blackness*, 53.

36. The 1948 lithograph goes by the title "Drawing Hands."

CHAPTER 17

Locating Race

Melanie B. Taylor

> If white is the color of mischief, then these white walls, this little
> house of marble we hide behind, willing the man with his notebook
> to find someone else to follow. We hide, kin to bone, to tuft of fur
> caught in the chain-link fence, to everything under the snow: tooth,
> grass, a skunk's belly bloated and facing heaven .... Didn't we hope
> something else might rise from the snow and rock us to sleep? Rock
> us long past the dreaming of what we had lost.
> – Janet McAdams, *Seven Boxes for the Country After* (2016)

A telling moment in the introduction to *A Listening Wind* – a recent
collection of southeastern Native American literature – exemplifies the
confounding tradition of locating race and ethnicity in the US South.
Editor Marcia Haag summarizes a hoary critical debate – one of many
"academic tiffs" that break out in such contested historical terrain – over
the cultural origins of the Uncle Remus stories. At its most stark, the query
centers on "whether the Negroes borrowed the tales from the Indians or
whether the Indians borrowed the tales from the Negroes."[1] Scholars of
African, Cherokee, and Saponi folklore have variously and vigorously
claimed the animal tales, and indications of likely cross-pollination or
syncretism are reduced to verdicts of "appropriation" from one culture or
another. Haag subtly adjudicates in favor of the tales' primarily Native
roots, and while she cautions against "chasing the chimera 'authenticity,'"
she nonetheless suggests that Indigenous texts are distinctive: "It is the
changed perception of themes, the emphasis of some kinds of relationships
and the diminishment of others, the place of humor, and so many other
sublime differences that make these tales Native American."[2]

Aside from Haag's pointed reference to "humor," the other cited traits
are slippery – vague invocations of "sublime differences," difficult to
pinpoint or articulate. The sovereign critical impulse nonetheless persists
and abounds – nationally, to be sure, but pointedly in the US southeastern context, where "southern" identity is marked implicitly as white or

black, and where Native Americans struggle either to locate or to remove themselves. Inclusion in southern spaces is never, for the region's embattled others, a comfortable or uncomplicated task; and the compulsion to define one's culture over and against an injurious white monolith triggers pageants of reverse essentialisms and exceptionalisms that can be both damaging and illogical in the face of irrefutable hybridity. There, the deep genealogical traffic between African and Native groups has frequently been cause not for celebration but for antagonism; one need look no further than the purging of freedmen from Cherokee tribal rolls for an example of such internecine hostility.[3] Within academia, more recent altercations have surfaced between Afropessimists and Indigenous scholars, both of whom deny the kinship of the other: Whereas Afropessimist thought essentially classes all nonblack agents – including Indians – as inherently "*anti*black," settler colonial studies models likewise assert that all non-Indigenous actors – including blacks – must be settlers.[4] As critics such as Iyko Day and Glen Sean Coulthard have usefully suggested, we are better served to pursue anti-exceptionalist frames of analysis that embrace a more complex, dialectical model for the growth of the American nation-state, one predicated on the inextricability of land and labor as the linked, paradigmatic grounds for the genocidal subsuming of *both* Indigenous and African elements.[5] Together, the conjoined histories of both black and Indian exploitation serve to destabilize the primarily material instigators – not just the secondary racializations – undergirding white proprietorship. As Annie Olaloku-Teriba puts it, we ought to "see 'race' not as an anchor, but as a mystification conjured to weather crises of legitimacy."[6]

Indeed, fictions of racial difference are the true chimeras in the southeastern context, where motivated constructs of "race" trump Indians' legal and community-based metrics of identity, and where one-drop hysteria has been used inversely to either confirm blackness or invalidate Indigeneity. *A Listening Wind* predicates its curation on such fictions, focusing on tribal narratives and languages that appear as "different" and as untouched by colonial interference as possible. Somewhat oppositely, another anthology of southeastern Indian writing published several years earlier – *The People Who Stayed* – endeavors to delineate how one might be "Indigenous *through* one's Southernness, and not in spite of it."[7] The editors even choose to organize the collection by subregion and state, contra the strategic impulse that Eric Gary Anderson has outlined, in which "American Indian literature and criticism that has to do with the South often does without 'the South' as an explanatory category, focusing instead on particular southeastern tribal nations or on intellectual paradigms—such as Native American literary separatism—that, for obvious reasons, do not rely on non-Native notions of regionalism."[8] The methodological divergence is, on the one hand, specific to the South's penetrating histories of both enfolding and erasing Indians from its perverse economies; desires to reclaim, reorient, and reject are thus understandably fluid, competing impulses in the aftermath of such processes. As critics, we work feverishly to draw attention to obscured Indigenous traces and persistence in the South, even as many Indians would rather not be identified with such spaces. But the sovereign state of mind cannot ultimately overcome the material state of *being* in a deterministic region like the South. Indeed, the most honest approach may lie in a reckoning with what Anderson deems "literary-historical messiness,"[9] an acknowledgment that the crucible of southern history – marked densely by the often overlapping traffic of Removal, plantation slavery, Reconstruction, and occupation – has indissolubly bound the experience of white, black, and Indian in ways that we simply cannot disentangle.

Indeed, I have previously made the provocative claim that "Indians" and "southerners" – categories of meaning and being constructed alike by settler colonialism and racial capitalism – find uncanny kinship in their shared experience of defeat, dispossession, and internal colonization. As a result, both groups have developed contemporary identities invested in principles of sustained community, regional or tribal sovereignty, ecological stewardship, and debt and reparations (construed as a spiritual as well as material phenomenon). Consequently, perhaps the most frequently deployed tropes in the literatures of both groups relate to tradition, history, and place – often rendered as idealized concepts ruptured by regional and colonial traumas and invasive, extractive economies. Such priorities explain a pervasive insistence on "locating" identity, as tenancy forms the baseline principle for the coherence of region or tribe, respectively. As Rose Powhatan puts it, "I'm living in a country with the curious distinction that your tribe can be changed and you can be erased from the Book of Life when you change your address. Move off the reservation and you cease to be Indian. You're dead. You never existed."[10] This is a phenomenon that plagues the "country" writ large, though it occurs in the South with particular force: Here, Indians have either been *re*located – hence made extinct as either Indians or southerners – or they have been subject to the racial conscriptions of local histories and juridical processes. For Indians remaining in the South, one's geographical location determines one's racial identification as well: Powhatan and others have described the phenomenon known as "document" or "paper genocide" by which post-Removal Natives were frequently made casualties of biracial classification schemes – listed as either black or white – or of federal recognition policies that refuse to acknowledge surviving tribes. It requires "constant vigilance," Powhatan observes, "if you intend to be a survivor."[11]

In American Indian terms, "survival" (or the more frequently cited Derridean term "survivance," commandeered by Anishinaabe writer and critic Gerald Vizenor to denote active tribal presencing) implies a willed immunity to the geographical, political, and economic coordinates that define the settler state and overwrite tribal precedence. Such invocations of sovereignty function mainly as intellectual or artistic aspirations rather than lived conditions. The bracing distinctiveness of the South is its magnification of racial separatism and intersectionality all at once – a clash that further highlights the anomalous position of the Indian, banished strategically from an intimate biracial order, and yet locked permanently and in fact produced within those genealogies. Put another way, the primal site of the US plantation, and with it the birth of racial capitalism in the American context, fundamentally relies on the irrelevance and erasure of Indians – and yet it continues to implicate, resurrect, indict, and appropriate their substance at nearly every turn, making them an indelible (if functionally illegible) component of a racialized economy. As a result, "Indians" are simply everywhere and nowhere in the southern narrative.

Indians in the (Plantation) Cupboard

Indeed, there is a long-standing misconception that Indians do not exist in the South after the Removal efforts of the 1830s; while the so-called Trail of Tears fundamentally evacuated the traditional homelands of many of the (again) so-called Five Civilized Tribes, many individuals escaped Removal – hiding out in the hills or in plain sight, as participants in the reigning plantation economy – and remnant tribes have steadily rebuilt grounds for sovereignty and self-determination since. But while the myth of eradication is powerful, so too is the romantic fiction of its motivations – to clear tribal lands for the invigoration of a plantation economy that utterly alienated and excluded Native predecessors. In fact, Indians are banished from the plantation only ideologically: Their strategic dispossession was and is both a material and a conceptual necessity, indeed, but its execution relies on the strategic assembly of an apocryphal Indigenous subjectivity innately unsuited for the usefulness or coherence of a labor-based and extractive economy.

In current invocations of the "Plantationocene" – an expansion of the
Anthropocene thinking that has shifted environmental and political theory
(with the humanities following suit, albeit more slowly) – scholars are now
grappling with the notion that the development of the plantation complex
in the New World radically restructured not just the mechanics of economic production but social, juridical, and ontological history. Moreover,
as Kris Manjapra has argued, this "destructive, cellular form that metastasized from the Caribbean across the Global South *after* abolition,
creating ... a global 'plantation arc'" long outlives the period of emancipation.[12] Indians exist in such models primarily as erased subjects, yoked
to land that needed to be repurposed for settler needs, and recoverable only
in appropriated, fetishized forms. To be sure, Indigenous expropriation
and absence is both a material and discursive reality. Yet increasingly,
historians such as Tiya Miles, Claudio Saunt, and Theda Perdue have
uncovered vast evidence of southeastern Indians' early integration within
regional economic development, and in particular their adoption of chattel
slavery to fuel their agronomic enterprises. In keeping with an expanding
historical consciousness of chattel slavery beyond the South and throughout colonial America, historians in recent years have examined
slaveholding among Indian tribes in the Deep South, Southwest, Great
Lakes, Pacific Northwest, Midwest, and beyond.[13] Whereas many critics
would like to soften such discoveries by suggesting that Indian slaveholding was less mercenary and its masters "kinder and more lenient," as
Barbara Krauthamer puts it, most historians have concluded that Indian
slaveholding was typically just as violent and coercive as among their white
comrades and competitors.[14]

This new historiography forces us to contextualize more carefully and
soberly the traces of Indigeneity that have long suffused the literary
histories of both white and black southerners. For whites in particular,
the resurrection of an Indigenous ancestor has served both to authenticate
settlement claims and to deny their own material motivations in the
process. In a 1996 Southern Focus Poll, Theda Perdue and Michael
Green report, "40 percent of Southerners claimed Native ancestry ...
[which is] considerably more than the 22 percent who claim descent from
a Confederate soldier."[15] The fabled Pocahontas has been perhaps the
most frequently claimed of such predecessors among southern families,
particularly the so-called First Families of Virginia – an elite community
that still proudly traces its lineage to Pocahontas and John Smith/Rolfe
and their triangulated, romantic fiction of national settlement. This
mythology deepened during the Civil War, when Pocahontas buttressed

a threatened white nativist mythology and attendant feelings of cultural inferiority. Indeed, one Virginia cavalry dubbed itself "The Guard of the Daughter of Powhatan," complete with Pocahontas's image on their battle flag.[16] Such mythologies betray the slippery conceit of Indigeneity as a "race," a mechanism by which to paradoxically invigorate whiteness. As Mick Gidley and Ben Gidley put it, "as long as they have been in the Americas, white people have been escaping the mapped and policed world of the European empires, 'running to the hills,' 'going Indian.'"[17] Indeed, such antiestablishment proclivities were seductive to white southerners keen to mystify their material investments in chattel slavery and, increasingly, to lambast the industrial incursions that supplanted it.

Well into the twentieth century, Indians have served the regional imaginary as noble allies in humanism and anti-commercialism. Writers such as Stark Young, Allen Tate, Eudora Welty, Caroline Gordon, and William Faulkner frequently invoke Indigenous characters and themes as part of their anti-modern apparatus.[18] Throughout *I'll Take My Stand*, the 1930 collection of manifesto-type essays by the so-called Nashville or Vanderbilt Agrarians, many of the authors style themselves overtly as "natives" and the northern carpetbaggers as "invaders";[19] nearly all claim an Indigenous kinship with a preindustrial world and a commitment to preserving both a landscape and a culture under siege.[20] Perhaps most unnervingly, the Indigenous ally has often been resurrected to serve a white nationalist cause, manifested perhaps most plainly by the Alabama segregationist Forrest (Asa) Carter, who presented himself as a Cherokee in his counterfeit autobiography, *The Education of Little Tree* (1976); the volume charmed and fooled readers for nearly two decades, when it was discovered to be a hoax and was reclassified as fiction (but continued to be read, taught, and applauded for some time thereafter). Ultimately, Carter's act of appropriation is less interesting than the public's willingness to blindly ingest its highly romanticized content. As Michael Marker put it, "Perhaps the move from Klansman to New Age guru is not as much of a shift as we would like to think. Both roles offer the chance to provide simplistic answers to troubling and intricate questions."[21] More recently, the much-publicized crises of the Anthropocene have redoubled the utility of the Indian as a figure of salvation, one that might both deliver and redeem an ecologically minded and exploited rural South. Wendell Berry's prescient 1968 essay "A Native Hill" surveys his Kentucky homelands as crippled by historical and industrial transgressions, and he elevates the original Native inhabitants as angels of ecological salvation: "Surely there could be a more indigenous life than we have," he muses.[22]

In most white southern literature, Indigeneity is just such an aspirational quotient – a state of mind and an affirmation of otherworldly
substance and value increasingly imperiled by modernity. Paradoxically,
the same sentiment can often be observed in African Americans' invocations of Native kinship, both biological and spiritual. In Patrick Minges's
curation of a number of Works Progress Administration (WPA) interviews
with former slaves, the theme of African–Native heritage and kinship is
paramount and proudly proclaimed – the phenomenon of the "Black
Indian" having been sutured in the long history of the plantation complex
throughout the Americas.[23] Even today, as African American scholar
Willard Johnson attests, "by far, the majority of African American families
I know, or that I have come into contact with and have worked with, claim
to have an Indian connection. A majority, by far. Some scholars have
argued that maybe up to two-thirds, or even three-quarters of black
Americans have some Native blood tie." Johnson admits that few
African Americans directly acknowledge the fact that their Indigenous
ancestry is a by-product of slavery – of being owned by Indian masters.
Instead, the relation is often left "fuzzy" and romanticized, and for an
important reason: Indian kin are "the origin of the only reparations,
actually, Blacks have gotten in terms of land. The 'forty acres and a
mule . . .' never came from the Federal Government. The only forty acres
blacks ever got came from the Indians."[24] The ironic gift is not just
material but spiritual – a way for the post-emancipated black worker to
enliven and reroot within poisoned landscapes and economies that effected
what Orlando Patterson, Frank Wilderson, and others have deemed the
slave's permanent "social death."

Alice Walker – a writer who identifies as both African American and
Cherokee – dramatizes the heady tangle of such dispossessions and reparations in her 1976 novel *Meridian*, about an eponymous black female
protagonist. Meridian's family lives on formerly Indian land, a farm
allotted to her great-grandfather after emancipation, complete with a
Serpent Mound where Meridian's grandmother – a woman tellingly
named "Feather Mae" – had periodic bouts of ecstasy that Meridian
inherits. On the mound, she feels herself "a dot, a speck in creation, alone
and hidden . . . surrounded by the dead."[25] Meridian's father inhabits the
land differently, his perhaps literal kinship undone by insurmountable
guilt: "That mound is full of dead Indians," he mourns. "Our food is
made healthy from the iron and calcium from their bones. . . . We were
part of it, you know . . .. Their disappearance."[26] He tries unsuccessfully to
give the land back but botches the transaction, offering the deed to a

random Cherokee proxy just passing through. There is no return from such histories, Walker avers, nor are contemporary Indians suitable vessels for receiving the remainders of a metastasized socioeconomic order. Indeed, the state of Georgia seizes the farm from Meridian's family, leveling the mound to create a public park that African Americans are not permitted to visit; the double eviction underscores the reiterative vacancies of the post-emancipation, indeed the post–civil rights context.

Walker's novel refuses to identify her African Americans explicitly as part-Indigenous, as they clearly seem to be, rendering their kinship a "fuzzy" and finally valueless by-product of such coiled histories and redundant dispossessions. To subtly underline her point, in a short chapter called "Gold," Meridian recalls a childhood discovery on that same land: a bar of bullion "so thickly encrusted with dirt that even when she had washed the metal it did not shine through. Yet she knew the metal was there, because it was so heavy." It is a ponderous metaphor for what lies buried in the South's unquiet soil – a sublime, invisible token of value that turns out to be unserviceable. And so, she reinters it, digging it up again periodically simply "to look at it. Then she dug it up less and less . . . until finally she forgot to dig it up."[27] The mode of re-presencing Indigeneity in these post-plantation contexts amounts to just such a process: first a "look," which implies and perhaps manufactures vitality, followed frequently by a reburial and a kind of autonomic repression. This brand of "forgetting" is an apt metaphor for the "fuzzy" invocations of Black–Indian intimacy and rivalry in the Old South, what William Loren Katz once deemed a "hidden heritage"[28] – one made significantly more visible in the work of scholars of both African and Indigenous history – including Jack Forbes, Kim Tallbear, Tiya Miles, Christina Snyder, and Shona Jackson – and further contoured by literary scholars and art historians, such as Gabrielle Tayac, Keely Byars-Nichols, and Sharon Holland. But the push and pull of kinship haunts these alliances as well, emerging as competing marginalizations – a plight that very much includes the colonization of the South under Reconstruction and the perceived assault on whiteness. Southerners from every coordinate on the plantation map have grown hungry for ways to both claim and repudiate their very identities within the perverse economies that invented them.

In the work of Virginia writer Belle Boggs, we find ourselves in a teeming watershed of these coeval histories: a revelatory space between the Mattaponi Indian reservation and the Mattaponi River itself – a waterway formed by the mingling of three separate streams, and thus a metaphor for the fluid cohesion of the red, black, and white groups that have long cohabited in rural Virginia. But while her work is inherently generative, she acknowledges the gravitational impulse toward reburial; in the opening vignette to her 2010 short story collection, *Mattaponi Queen*, an art teacher has collected artifacts for a still life assignment: "a beautiful little hand-blown glass bottle, an arrowhead, a Confederate belt buckle, a bone toothbrush without any bristles." All of the items came from her own backyard; "How did you find those things anyway? her husband wanted to know. I dug around a little, she said, remembering descending the sloping sides into the hole's cooler air, brushing away the layers and layers of leaves and scraping the damp clay ways with her fingers. Next time you'll likely find a copperhead, he said."[29] Obscured by "layers and layers" of history is the weighty evidence of the region's suggestive abutments: a work of art; a Confederate icon; a Native weapon; and a bald, unusable tool to cleanse and purify it all. It is the task of the student and the artist to make sense of the juxtaposition – copperheads and all.

(E)racing Indigeneity

Such contexts necessarily complicate and perhaps fatally undermine the project of Indigenous southern "survival," which simply cannot occur as a sovereign, exceptional mode of existence in the dense legacies of southern economic history. Though plenty of separatist projects do exist and perform important work to buttress and build tribal continuity and coherence nationwide – many of them highlighted and celebrated elsewhere in this volume – the southern context provides a unique vista for a bleaker but finally rewarding navigation of the textures of intersectionality or of cultural loss and absence. Importantly, such work acknowledges the slippery casts of racial predetermination that overshadow Indigenous sovereignty, even as its practitioners work to carve alternative spaces – sometimes mapped and constrictive, but often placeless or abstract landscapes of deep, unrecoverable loss. As Cherokee writer Cynthia Kasee puts it starkly, "To understand the 'race memory' of the Indian removals, if you're not Indian, try picturing yourself as a Jew visiting Auschwitz or a Cambodian survivor returning to Pol Pot's killing fields."[30] Having grown up mainly in Cincinnati, Kasee acknowledges the irreparable aporia of southeastern Removal: "To be a descendant of a removed tribe is to be homesick for a place you've never been," she avers.[31] Kasee's declaration here echoes what N. Scott Momaday famously (and controversially) termed the "memory in the blood" of all Native peoples, a willful assertion of innate, genetic knowledge that defies histories of brutal erasure, racial dilution, and transformation.[32]

Such tropes embrace a paradox: a proud claim on absence and ineffability, a memory made of desire rather than experience – a "blood" that is not a measurable or juridical metric but what Chadwick Allen calls an "authenticating genealogy."[33] Elsewhere, Allen has called for replacing institutionalized forms of race for Indigenous peoples with a more nuanced "blood/land/memory complex" that has both material and spiritual significance.[34] As North Carolina Cherokee poet MariJo Moore puts it in a poem about her Appalachian home, "Memories unfold from around these / glorious ancestral mountains / ... close enough to smell / but not close enough to touch / just close enough to taste / but never close enough to touch."[35] Twice, Moore affirms that the body might bear witness to an otherwise ungraspable past, situated in tangible landscapes yet unable to be touched. These lived, corporeal experiences may sometimes descend into wish fulfillment, assertions of fullness and certainty without corroboration; but just as often, they can be intrepid envoys into the realities of sublime subjugation and loss – something the body senses, either in ecstasy or suffering, but cannot name or own. As Alabama Creek poet Janet McAdams muses in one of her rare, direct meditations on her southernness, the "land called 'Indigenous'" may exist only "on the map of my body." But which part, she wonders? Littlest finger, long left leg, hidden heart? The answer is slippery in a place "where Indianness is simultaneously sentimentalized and ignored": "this is real life," she concludes, "which is inexact, messy."[36]

For McAdams, the racialized Indigenous body is a sentient but ultimately imperfect vehicle for carrying one's identity into the twenty-first century, for mapping the vast coordinates of loss. Instead, she locates both "Indian" and "Southern" in the sometimes unplaceable terrain of her poetry, rarely set in the South – or anywhere identifiable – with strategic intent. The effect is not universalizing per se, but a way of understanding local heritage and racial identity together as a particularized entry point into histories that are damagingly, devastatingly real. She is quick to explain that although the South itself rarely appears directly in her work, its imprint is everywhere: "Our deepest metaphors are the furniture, language, oxygen of that other world, the 'unacknowledged' world," she asserts. "It is a life's work to understand them. It is the lifework of a poet to write them down."[37] McAdams's writings offer a seemingly bottomless archive of such metaphors: in her poetry collections *The Island of Lost Luggage* (2000), *Feral* (2007), and *Seven Boxes for the Country After* (2016), as well as her lyrical novel *Red Weather* (2012). In all of these, she returns repeatedly to motifs of history, haunting, excavation, and the porous boundaries between humans, animals, and the worlds they share – worlds that variously invent, sustain, and undo us.

In *Feral*'s final poem – "Earth My Body Is Trying to Remember," McAdams's speaker both addresses and invokes "Earth" – at once the space of loss suffered by the Indigenous southerner, and the interlocutor in the process of remembering:

> We were born but born too young to remember.
> The land they took us from, the mothers' milk dried up,
> every womb a dried-up
> crackle of flesh. Earth my body
> is trying to remember.
> Child-That-Was, don't try to remember, but lean back
> into this place outside history.
> Lean into the bright color climbing the stone wall
> as if violet against grainy white or pale blue crocuses
> were the end of the story.

McAdams deftly reminds us that contemporary Indigenous subjects do not automatically harbor innate memory of their intimacy with land; history itself is the rupture, setting in motion a perverse settler colonial logic of dispossession predicated precisely and paradoxically on the Indians' unitary relationship with the land. Paradoxically, to rupture that metonymy becomes a decolonizing gesture of sorts, a way of inhabiting a new geography "outside history." Once taken, the land ceases to be a nutritive subject and is rendered instead a desiccated mother. In the compressed grammar that elides "Earth" and "my body," this peculiarly southern amnesia is both invoked and shattered: the body is "trying to remember" not just earth but its own substance, a doubly foiled quest. The Indigenous body's fatal land-based value is underscored: "They chipped away at us, / hammered us out like gold." More than bodies, Indigenous subjects "were cell and stone and field, the sky: / Stars pulled down from their wandering."[38] This is, could be, "the end of the story" – but in fact, it is a haunting tautology.

This futility haunts not just McAdams's poetry but so much southern and Indigenous literature. Can there be such a place "outside history," or a new and "bright color" to counterpoise the "grainy white" of the "stone wall" (read: *Stonewall*)? Perhaps not – but poets like McAdams offer us arresting views into pasts and presents that are bracingly messy and disarmingly real. In the final prose poem of her most recent collection, *Seven Boxes for the Country After* (2016), she offers a vision of a stripped-down future at a mythical waypoint:

We undress behind a screen in a small room in the space between countries. They search our pockets, tossing it all in a box marked THINGS, half full with false teeth, a tangled wig, a book losing the old skin of its binding. They search our folds, our stories, peeling away wrist scars, the doctor's thumbprint on a vein in my neck, from the year I tried to sleep all winter. Calluses rubbed by bad shoes, a hangnail, a false tooth, the twisted veins of your ropey arms. They take: our shoes, our pockets, the hole from the lobe of your left ear, the skin that sifts like snow in cold weather. They take until we are tender as babies, until we have nothing left to declare.[39]

Poets like McAdams offer visions of Indigenous futurity that are, quite literally, raw: Her speakers are scarred, depleted, barren things hovering "between" rather than within countries and communities. Yet somehow she finds grace and newness in such stories, which slough off their "old skin" and cast off the "THINGS" that drown us – who we are and what we own functioning together as our tickets into a country that will "take," press, and wound rather than nourish and deliver. To have "nothing left to declare" is to be without a passport into a South that so deeply imprints and supplements the body; there is mourning in the loss but also, perhaps, embryonic hope for new beginnings, stories, and skins.

Indeed, the best new work in southern literary and critical studies alike attempts, in many ways, to flee its moorings. In 2008, scholar Leigh Anne Duck called for a "Southern studies without 'The South'" – the only way, she averred, that we might evade "the realm of our most basic assumptions,"[40] which range from gross aberrance to flagrant romanticism. Accordingly, the editors of a new, pathbreaking volume on *Keywords in Southern Studies* attest that doing southern studies in the twenty-first century might be summed up as a charge to resist the monolith in all its dimensions: It is about "thinking geographically, thinking historically, thinking relationally, thinking about power, thinking about justice, thinking back."[41] What gets produced in these spaces of local intersectionality and global interconnectivity are more supple and subtle articulations of identity and belonging, of region and race – a space where, according to one of *Keywords'* contributors, we may finally find ourselves "more precisely articulating the disruptive knowledge of subalterns," and with a better ability "to glean from the history of colonization and slavery the means by which the colonized and enslaved have improvised alternative visions of freedom and justice."[42] These are soaring prospects and projects, undertaken by some of today's most capable critics, and they are vital for moving forward as a discipline and as a nation; but as the region's texts and bodies remind us, such "thinking back" can also entail a journey not away from but into the structures of enslavement – to the basic ordering impulses of all human organizations and interrelations that precede settlement, slavery, Removal, segregation, and the multiple disenfranchisements of difference.

Notes

1. Alan Dundes, quoted in Marcia Haag, ed., "Introduction," in *A Listening Wind: Native Literature from the Southeast* (Lincoln: University of Nebraska Press, 2016), xiii–xxxii, at xxvii.
2. Haag, "Introduction," xxviii. Haag gives an overview of the various critical positions in the debate but does not mention the work of black-Indian literary theory – such as that by Jonathan Brennan, notably, *When Brer Rabbit Meets Coyote: African-Native American Literature* (Champaign: University of Illinois Press, 2003), which asserts a distinctive literary tradition emerging from communities of mixed African and Native descent.
3. The enmity between many Indians and descendants of former slaves has reached a nadir in recent decades, with the Cherokee Nation's use of blood politics to legally expel nearly 3,000 black freedmen from tribal rolls – an act overturned by a US district court in 2017 in a decision citing the "lesser known" fact "that both nations' chronicles share the shameful taint of African slavery" and characterizing freedmens' citizenship status as a kind of reparations owed them by the Cherokee Nation. See *Cherokee Nation* v. *Nash*, 267 F. Supp. 3d 86 (D.D.C. 2017), https://ecf.dcd.uscourts.gov/cgi-bin/show_public_doc?2013cv1313-248.
4. For some of the most influential articulations of these positions, see Patrick Wolfe, "Recuperating Binarism: A Heretical Introduction," *Settler Colonial Studies* 3.3/4 (2013), 257–79; and Frank B. Wilderson III, "Gramsci's Black Marx: Whither the Slave in Civil Society," *Social Identities* 9.2 (2003), 225–40.
5. See Iyko Day, "Being or Nothingness: Indigeneity, Antiblackness, and Settler Colonial Critique," *Critical Ethnic Studies* 1.2 (2015), 102–21; and Glen Sean Couthard, *Red Skin, White Masks: Rejecting the Colonial Politics of Recognition* (Minneapolis: University of Minnesota Press), 2014.
6. Annie Olaloku-Teriba, "Afro-Pessimism and the (Un)Logic of Anti-Blackness," *Historical Materialism* 26.2 (2018), 108–9.
7. Janet McAdams, "From *Betty Creek: Writing the Indigenous Deep South*," in *The People Who Stayed: Southeastern Indian Writing after Removal*, eds. Geary Hobson, Janet McAdams, and Kathryn Walkiewicz (Norman: University of Oklahoma Press, 2010), 251–56, at 253. Subsequent references to selections from this anthology will be rendered as *TPWS*.
8. Eric Gary Anderson, "On Native Ground: Indigenous Presences and Countercolonial Strategies in Southern Narratives of Captivity, Removal, and Repossession," *Southern Spaces* (August 9, 2007), https://doi.org/10.18737/M7PC8K.

9. Eric Gary Anderson, "Native," in *Keywords for Southern Studies*, eds. Scott Romine and Jennifer Rae Greeson (Athens: University of Georgia Press, 2012), 166–78, at 175.

10. Rose Powhatan, "Surviving Document Genocide," in *TPWS*, 23–28, at 23–24.

11. Powhatan, "Surviving," 24–25.

12. Kris Manjapra, "Plantation Dispossessions," in *American Capitalism: New Histories*, eds. Sven Beckert and Christine Desan (New York: Columbia University Press, 2018), 361–88, at 363.

13. See, for instance, James F. Brooks, *Captives and Cousins: Slavery, Kinship, and Community in the Southwest Borderlands* (Chapel Hill, NC: University of North Carolina Press, 2011); Leland Donald, *Aboriginal Slavery on the Northwest Coast of North America* (Berkeley: University of California Press, 1997); Carl J. Ekberg, *Stealing Indian Women: Native Slavery in the Illinois Country* (Champaign: University of Illinois Press, 2007); Robbie Ethridge and Sheri M. Shuck-Hall, eds., *Mapping the Mississippian Shatter Zone: The Colonial Indian Slave Trade and Regional Instability in the American South* (Lincoln: University of Nebraska Press, 2009); Alan Gallay, *The Indian Slave Trade: The Rise of the English Empire in the American South, 1670–1717* (New Haven, CT: Yale University Press, 2001); Alan Gallay, ed., *Indian Slavery in Colonial America* (Lincoln: University of Nebraska Press, 2009); Pekka Hämäläinen, *The Comanche Empire* (New Haven, CT: Yale University Press, 2008); Barbara Krauthamer, *Black Slaves, Indian Masters: Slavery, Emancipation, and Citizenship in the Native American South* (Chapel Hill, NC: University of North Carolina Press, 2013); Tiya Miles, *Ties That Bind: The Story of an Afro-Cherokee Family in Slavery and Freedom* (Berkeley: University of California Press, 2016); Tiya Miles, *The House on Diamond Hill: A Cherokee Plantation Story* (Chapel Hill, NC: University of North Carolina Press, 2010); Celia Naylor, *African Cherokees in Indian Territory: From Chattel to Citizens* (Chapel Hill, NC: University of North Carolina Press, 2008); Andrés Reséndez, *The Other Slavery: The Uncovered Story of Indian Enslavement in America* (Boston: Houghton Mifflin Harcourt, 2016); Robert H. Ruby and John A. Brown, *Indian Slavery in the Pacific Northwest* (Spokane, WA: Arthur H. Clark, 1993); Brett Rushforth, *Bonds of Alliance: Indigenous and Atlantic Slaveries in New France* (Chapel Hill, NC: University of North Carolina Press, 2012); Claudio Saunt, *Black, White, and Indian: Race and the Unmaking of an American Family* (New York: Oxford University Press, 2005); Christina Snyder, *Slavery in Indian Country: The Changing Face of Captivity in Early America* (Cambridge, MA: Harvard University Press, 2010); Fay A. Yarbrough, *Race and the Cherokee Nation* (Philadelphia: University of Pennsylvania Press, 2008); Gary Zellar, *African Creeks: Estelvste and the Creek Nation* (Norman: University of Oklahoma Press, 2007).

14. Krauthamer, *Black Slaves, Indian Masters*, 57.

15. Theda Perdue and Michael D. Green, *The Columbia Guide to American Indians of the Southeast* (New York: Columbia University Press, 2001), 147.

16. Honor Sachs, "How Pocahontas – the Myth and the Slur – Props Up White Supremacy," Wickedlocal.com, October 16, 2018, www.wickedlocal.com/opinion/20181016/opinion-how-pocahontas—myth-and-slur—props-up-white-supremacy.

17. Mick Gidley and Ben Gidley, "The Native-American South," in *A Companion to the Literature and Culture of the American South*, eds. Richard Gray and Owen Robinson (Malden, MA: Blackwell, 2004), 171.

18. By far the most thorough study of the Native traces in modern southern fiction, Annette Trefzer's *Disturbing Indians* (Tuscaloosa: University of Alabama Press, 2009) examines how William Faulkner, Caroline Gordon, Andrew Lytle, and Eudora Welty responded to Indigenous histories in order to better understand their identities as both southerners and Americans.

19. John Crowe Ransom, "Reconstructed but Unregenerate," in *I'll Take My Stand: The South and the Agrarian Tradition*, by Twelve Southerners (Baton Rouge: Louisiana State University Press, 1978), 23; Herman Clarence Nixon, "Whither Southern Economy?," in *I'll Take My Stand*, 193.

20. Ransom, "Reconstructed," 20; John Gould Fletcher, "Education, Past and Present," in *I'll Take My Stand*, 99–100; Nixon, "Whither Southern Economy?," 183.

21. Michael Marker, "The Education of Little Tree: What It Really Reveals about the Public Schools," *Phi Delta Kappan* 74.3 (1992), 226–27.

22. Wendell Berry, "A Native Hill," *Hudson Review* 21. 4 (1968–69), 628.

23. Patrick Minges, ed. *Black Indian Slave Narratives* (Winston-Salem, NC: John F. Blair, 2004).

24. Transcription of the National Congress of American Indian's 57th Session, "Exploring the Legacy and Future of Black/Indian Relations," November 14, 2000, http://web.mit.edu/wjohnson/www/kiaanafh/NCAI_pdf_Transcript.pdf.

25. Alice Walker, *Meridian* (New York: Washington Square, 1976), 59.

26. Walker, *Meridian*, 54–55.

27. Walker, *Meridian*, 52.

28. William Loren Katz, *Black Indians: A Hidden Heritage* (New York: Atheneum, 2012).

29. Belle Boggs, *Mattaponi Queen* (Minneapolis: Graywolf Press, 2010), 5.

30. Cynthia Kasee, "Homecoming," in *TPWS*, 180–82, at 180.

31. Kasee, "Homecoming," 182.

32. Momaday first deploys the concept in his award-winning novel *House Made of Dawn* (New York: Signet, 1968) and returns to it in later works, such as "The Man Made of Words," in *Indian Voices: The First Convocation of American Indian Scholars* (San Francisco: Indian Historian Press, 1970), 49–84.

33. Chadwick Allen, "Blood (and) Memory," *American Literature* 71.1 (1999), 93–116, at 94.

34. See Chadwick Allen, *Blood Narrative: Indigenous Identity in American Indian and Maori Literary and Activist Texts* (Durham, NC: Duke University Press, 2002).

35. MariJo Moore, "In These Mountains," in *TPWS*, 177.

36. McAdams, "From *Betty Creek*," 256.

37. McAdams, "From *Betty Creek*," 256.

38. Janet McAdams, "Earth My Body Is Trying to Remember," in *Feral* (Norfolk, UK: Salt, 2007), 76.

39. Janet McAdams, *Seven Boxes for the Country After* (Kent, OH: Kent State University Press, 2016), Kindle edition.

40. Leigh Anne Duck, "Southern Nonidentity," *Safundi* 9.3 (2008), 329.

41. Scott Romine and Jennifer Rae Greeson, "Introduction," in *Keywords for Southern Studies*, eds. Scott Romine and Jennifer Rae Greeson (Athens: University of Georgia Press, 2016), 4.

42. Shirley Elizabeth Thompson, "Creole/Creolization," in *Keywords for Southern Studies*, 141–54, at 153.

CHAPTER 18

De-forming and Re-making
Bernardine Evaristo's Girl, Woman, Other *and the Multifocal Decolonial Novel*

Paula M. L. Moya and Luz M. Jiménez Ruvalcaba

In a hauntingly lovely scene in Bernardine Evaristo's Booker Prize–winning novel, *Girl, Woman, Other,* the character Amma describes what she saw when she and her friend Dominique visited the legendary lesbian club The Gateways shortly before it ceased operations. Describing the visit as a "pilgrimage," Amma is suffused with nostalgia for her "younger days" as she remembers taking a trip to a place, and thus a time, when enjoying oneself as a lesbian required secrecy, and cross-dressing as a man was remarkable. Although the club was not a prominent feature of Amma's youth, since she came of age after its heyday, Evaristo's decision to have the fictional Amma visit the real historic locale is notable for its documentary value. As a private club for lesbians that operated for over fifty years, "The Gates" was the longest running of its kind. Hip and trendy during the 1960s, the club eventually fell victim to the politicization of gay and lesbian identities and the gentrification of its Chelsea, London neighborhood. But if Evaristo's decision to have Amma visit the space is notable, even more important is the way she renders the visit. We see the dimly lit space, the two middle-aged women in men's suits and haircuts standing at the bar "looking as if they'd walked straight out of the pages of *The Well of Loneliness,*" and the "two very old and very small women, one in a black suit, the other in a forties-style dress" who dance "cheek-to-cheek" to Dusty Springfield's tune "The Look of Love."[1]

In transporting her readers to The Gateways, Evaristo makes visible an obscured and in some ways painful past—one in which lesbians lived and loved and enjoyed each other's company outside the view of a censorious public.[2] But more important is a presence called out by the absence of something that both is and is not there. In evoking the enchantment that attends the two elderly female lovers, Evaristo posits the existence of a thing – a spinning, glittery disco ball – that is not in the club. She writes: "and there wasn't even a glittery disco ball spinning from the middle of the ceiling, sprinkling stardust on to them."[3] The brilliance of writing the disco ball into the scene by emphasizing its absence is that Evaristo creates in the reader's mind an image of two lovers dancing together under a glittery disco ball. For an attentive reader, the two elderly female lovers are at one and the same time dancing together in a dark, drab club that has seen better days, and also the central figures in a magical scene whose dancing is consecrated by sprinkles and stardust. Here, Evaristo deploys the resources of literary fiction to document an obscured historical past while harnessing the imagination to reshape an understanding of that past. She understands that if she wants to make positive change in the direction of social justice, she must first imagine that change. In the manner of the decolonial thinker and writer Frantz Fanon, Evaristo initiates a "cycle of freedom" by acknowledging while also "going beyond the historical and instrumental given."[4]

Evaristo is one of a cohort of contemporary fiction writers, in the United States and abroad, who are self-consciously pushing the boundaries of content and form to go "beyond the historical and instrumental given." Like Evaristo, writers such as Toni Cade Bambara, Leslie Marmon Silko, Toni Morrison, Helena Maria Viramontes, Marlon James, Louise Erdrich, and Tommy Orange, among others, have cultivated a range of decolonial literary techniques designed to redress the historical lack of representation, and misrepresentation, of the ethnoracial communities from which they come. Key among these techniques is the use of a multifocal narrative structure – one that distributes narrative attention and character space more or less equally among a large number of characters and that also pays attention to the networks of interaction and affiliation that connect the different characters to each other.[5] Authors of multifocal decolonial novels understand that the stories readers absorb through literature do not merely reflect reality. Instead, they participate in its constitution. Works of literature shape our understanding, our behavior, and our ability (or inability) to create change in the world.[6] Novels that democratize the space of the novel via an increase in focalizing characters have become more common as writers (primarily of color) seeking to develop a decolonial aesthetic have gained increased access to mainstream publishing venues. But because this generic innovation has not been adequately theorized, we turn here to an examination of the features and goals of the multifocal decolonial novel.

We begin by clarifying some terms. *Decoloniality*, as it has been reflected across feminist fiction, is fundamentally concerned with countermanding the categorical, dichotomous, and hierarchical logic of what sociologist Aníbal Quijano and literary critic Walter Mignolo have called "modernity/coloniality." Usually hailing from, or working within, geographical spaces whose indigenous people have suffered the experience of colonization (i.e., the Caribbean, the Americas, and Africa), decolonial thinkers turn away from what is given to focus elsewhere for the purpose of perceiving anew.[7] Because their starting point is the referential inaccuracy and genocidal logic of a Eurocentric racial imaginary, they observe and critique key aspects of that imaginary – especially the master morality that in the name of "progress" rationalizes both psychic and somatic violence against people of color across the globe. Importantly, decolonial authors understand decoloniality less as a description of our existing social world than as an ethos – one that at a minimum assumes goodwill toward others. Insofar as they reject the subordination or exploitation of others as either a primary goal or an unintended consequence of caring for the self, decolonial authors put their writing into the service of remaking themselves and the social world. Championing relationality, quotidian witnessing, and the necessity of rigorous self-assessment, these writers concurrently make visible and further develop the multiple emancipatory "worlds of sense" that constitute our shared social world.[8] They do so to move toward onto-epistem-ological multiplicity and the development of complex solidarities.[9]

Focalization, for those unfamiliar with the term, is a nimble narratological concept that allows a literary critic to clearly distinguish between the "one who speaks" (the narrator) and the "one who sees" (the focalizer) in a literary text.[10] A text's focalizers serve a necessary mediating function–they provide the prism, the perspective, the angle of vision through which a scene in any given text is presented. As a narratological concept that refers to the representation of perception, focalization describes the relationship between the "agents who perceive" (the focalizers), the "elements perceived" (the focalized objects), and the "visions that are perceived."[11] Attending to the way a text is focalized encourages a critic to register the coordinates of space and time, the emotional state and cognitive capacity, the age, the experience, and the ideological perspective of its various focalizers.[12]

There are a couple of aspects of focalization that merit attention. Although a narrative's focalizers are often linked to specific characters in the story, they can also be situated outside the story – as in the case of an omniscient narrator.[13] Moreover, although a text's focalizers often overlap with its narrators, they can be disjunct. Helena Maria Viramontes' 1995 novel *Under the Feet of Jesus* provides a case in point.[14] The novel features one third-person narrator across the whole of the narrative.

However, this narrator is not omniscient. Instead, it moves into and out of the consciousnesses of four different focalizers. Indeed, one of the novel's distinguishing characteristics is that, instead of focusing on a single protagonist, it features four "major" characters, each of whom takes a turn focalizing the narrative so that the world portrayed literally "changes character" – often from one paragraph to the next. All four characters in this novel about Mexican farmworkers occupy the same "social world" – a world in which they come into contact and interact with each other. But they each perceive and experience it differently, from within distinct worlds of sense. So when the members of the family arrive together at the shack that will be their new home, they each look out onto the world and perceive very different things. An attentive literary critic is able to tell which character is orienting (or focalizing) the narrative by what the character does and sees, and by the adjectives and metaphors used to describe what they perceive.

To wit, Perfecto – older, tired, but ever responsible – is oriented toward utility. When he notices some crates in a corner, he envisions an altar for Petra's religious statues: "Perfecto **inspected** the two-room bungalow, sliding his thick bifocals up to the bridge of his nose. He **rattled** the knob, **stepped** into a **dingy** room with a window facing the porch. The **stink of despair** shot through the **musty** sunlight, and he **knocked** a fist against the window to loosen the **swollen** pane to get some fresh air into the room."[15] Petra, feeling overwhelmed and entrapped, is oriented toward danger. When she looks at her children's bare feet, she imagines the threat of scorpions: "She **watched** Estrella's long legs leap over the tall blades of wild mustard grass, her own legs **shackled** by varicose veins. She **called** for Estrella and **raised a broom** as a threat, **screamed** to her children: —Get back this minute huercos fregados, who do you think you are, corriendo sin zapatos? . . . but her **words netted** in the rustle of the trees."[16] Thirteen-year-old Estrella, younger and less jaded than both, instead perceives adventure and possibility. She looks at a row of eucalyptus trees lining the dirt road and sees "thin **dancing girls** fanning their **feathers**. The breeze **billowed her dress** and for a moment she held her elbows as she watched the mother **swish** the broom against the **mentholated wind** . . . She **couldn't wait** until morning to **investigate** and began **running** again."[17] All of this is conveyed through one third-person narrator. This example illustrates that thinking through focalization when analyzing a multifocal narrative enhances a critic's ability to register the differing physical, psychological, and ideological aspects of each focalizer's world of sense.

Multifocal narratives excel at illustrating the fact that there are always multiple worlds of sense – or domains of intelligibility – that make up a shared social world. They make visible alternative "visions" of the same event, effectively creating the conditions of possibility for readers to compare and judge. By showing the ecological and interconnected nature of the social-natural world, such novels provincialize the so-called universal perspective without falling into epistemological or ontological relativism.[18] Indeed, for authors who explore profound ethical questions through fiction, the advantages of having multiple focalizers within the space of a novel is clear. Attuned as they are to occluded and denigrated interpretations of the social world, decolonial authors turn to multifocal narrative structures to effectively amplify the voices and perspectives of marginalized persons – those persons usually cast as the minor characters whose "case," in the words of literary critic Alex Woloch, has been too often suppressed by novels concerned with filling out the subjectivity of a singular protagonist.[19] In what follows, we will say a few words about *Girl, Woman, Other* (hereafter *GWO*) before laying out in a systematic way the features and goals of the multifocal decolonial novel. We will then return to *GWO* with a close reading of one character, Carole, that illustrates the decolonial imperative put forth by multifocal decolonial novels.

GWO introduces its readers to a variegated world of women/womxn/ wimmin/womyn – some seditious, others acerbic, some insecure, others haughty, and still others who are haughty *because* they are insecure. Published in the UK in 2019, the novel made an immediate splash, sharing the Booker Prize with Margaret Atwood's eagerly awaited novel *The Testaments* (itself a multifocal novel).[20] Hailed by critics as a "beautiful, hilarious and moving homage to what it means to be black and British," *GWO* offers to its readers a view of a social world that has been largely invisible to those outside its bounds. Sensitively rendering the lives and interactions of a network of thirteen characters born in Britain between 1895 and the first decade of the twenty-first century – most of them black, most of them female, and all of them having some amount of African ancestry – the novel examines the contradictory feminisms and contradictory political ideologies that emerge from what is a heterogeneous population.

Frustrated by the invisibility of contemporary black British women in literature and interested in establishing the historical presence of black people in Britain, Evaristo conceives of her writing as a way of "putting presence into absence."[21] She includes in *GWO* a scene in which a theater director tells the character Dominique that she is "wasting his time" when she turns up for an audition for a Victorian drama because "there weren't any black people in Britain then" (7). Evaristo puts the lie to this misconception by including in the novel several interrelated focalizing characters who establish, in concert with one another, a genealogy of black British presence. One is the character of Grace, the daughter of an Abyssinian (Ethiopian) seaman and a working-class English woman. Born in 1895, Grace eventually marries Joseph Rydendale, with whom she has a daughter, Hattie, a character who becomes important both as the great grandmother of the genderfree character Megan/Morgan as well as the biological mother of Penelope, the white woman adoptee who is revealed in the epilogue to have African ancestry as a result of being Hattie's daughter. For the purpose of establishing the historical presence of blacks in Britain, Hattie is important in another way as well. She is the descendant of Captain Linnaeus Rydendale, a laborer's son turned wealthy landowner who made a fortune trading African slaves for sugar in the West Indies. This secret is revealed upon the death of Hattie's father – alongside another family secret. It turns out that Linnaeus had returned to England from Jamaica with a young wife – a merchant's daughter named Eudoré – a woman whose painted portrait, in light of Linnaeus' slave-trading past, reveals her likely African ancestry. Because *GWO* is a character-driven novel rather than a plot-driven novel, narrative coherence is provided by having most of the characters attend, or at least hear about, the opening night performance of a theater production written and directed by the character Amma. Amma holds a place of primacy by virtue of being the first character to be introduced and the last to focalize the novel proper. And as we will note in the discussion below outlining the features and goals of multifocal decolonial novels, granting to one character some sort of primacy is a common strategy pursued by their authors. Allowing one character to be "first among equals" helps orient readers accustomed to having a protagonist.

Although individual multifocal decolonial novels are unique works of art with aesthetic elements that deserve to be analyzed on their own terms, they share important features and goals that distinguish them as part of an emergent genre formation. We turn to those features below, keeping *GWO* as our touchstone. For the sake of clarity, we call out each feature by designating it with a number from 1 to 9. We do this to assist readers in identifying these features in other novels. By (1) eschewing a singular protagonist and (2) distributing narrative attention and character space more or less equally across a large number of characters, multifocal decolonial novels democratize the space of the novel and refuse the idea of minor-ness. *GWO*, for example, distributes narrative attention among thirteen distinct focalizers. In addition, authors of multifocal decolonial novels (3) retell historical narratives with attention to what historians have called "histories from below."[22] They do so to rectify inaccurate representations of people and groups who have been consigned by "official" narratives to the margins, or else assigned the role of villain. Moreover, because these novels (4) present a wide range of characters from ethnoracial communities that have been historically absent from, or underrepresented in, literature, they effectively establish the presence and the heterogeneity of the people who belong to those groups. Evaristo, for example, puts "presence into absence" by including a cleaning person, a white woman who learns late in life that she has African ancestry, a genderfree character, and an Oxford-educated vice president of an investment bank, to name a few.

By (5) including scenes and interactions between characters that either tell about, or show instances of, violence and exclusion based on historically denigrated human characteristics such as race, gender, sexuality, and ability, multifocal novels reveal the processual and evolving nature of the dynamics of subordination.[23] *GWO* features a scene in which Winsome tells her granddaughter about the racism she and her husband faced as a young married couple when they were refused food, shelter, and work as they sought to make a life on the southwest coast of England. Moreover, because the history of nonwhite communities within modernity/coloniality includes a constitutive amount of racial trauma, multifocal decolonial novels (6) maintain a focus on how these traumas are expressed at the individual level. The impetus behind relating the past is not merely to expose past wrongs, but also to find a way forward in the face of trauma. Accordingly, multifocal decolonial novels have a concomitant focus on the rituals of healing that are necessary for reworking the pains of the past into a healthier, more just future.

Finally, because multifocal decolonial novels (7) include a focus on interiority that is dispersed across the several major characters, they make visible the large number of worlds of sense that make up any one social world. Furthermore, by (8) paying sustained attention over the course of the narrative to how the different characters are connected in an evolving network of interactions, they effectively dismantle the idea of the autonomous individual. In *GWO*, the character Penelope, whom readers meet as a mildly racist wealthy white woman who had been adopted as a baby, is revealed in the epilogue to be the daughter of the mixed-race farmer Hattie, who had been forced to give up her baby shortly after birth.

Penelope is also the coworker of Shirley, the employer of Bummi, and the cousin of Megan/Morgan. Shirley, meanwhile, is the daughter of Winsome and the teacher of Carole. These are just a few of the many tangled connections that exist between the characters in *GWO*.

The complex connections between the various characters in *GWO*, as in other multifocal decolonial novels, are not immediately obvious and would be difficult to represent in a compelling way in a novel that centered on just one character. Their connections are revealed bit by bit, over both story time and discourse time, as readers work their way through each character's experiences and preoccupations in the separate focalizing chapters.[24] Importantly, the totality of this information is not available to the characters involved in this network. Much as in the real world, where the web of connections in which people are caught as nodes in an evolving network of relations is only ever partially perceptible to them, so are these characters only tangentially aware of each other. The ability to pull these people together into a legible network of relations turns out to be a privilege accorded by an author to a reader who is situated outside the story. Even so, the reader must work hard to make those connections, and the novel as a whole, legible.

One way that authors of multifocal decolonial novels assist their readers in making sense of a complex network of connections is through (9) the extensive use of paratexts such as epigraphs, sections, titles, prologues, and epilogues. Sections and titles provide a great deal of guidance to readers seeking to make sense of a novel; they help readers keep track of which character is focalizing that section of the narrative and cue readers to attend to how the focalizing character might be related to other characters who have referred to them by name in other parts of the book. In some novels, they also function to call attention to the making of the narrative itself. *GWO*, for instance, consists of five chapters and an epilogue. The first four chapters establish a pattern whereby each chapter is further divided into three subsections titled with the name of a focalizing character. In this way, the novel introduces the assortment of characters whose stories only loosely cohere. Evaristo does something different in the fifth chapter and does so in a way that demonstrates the import of multiple focalizations. Chapter 5, "The After-party," is not titled for a character but instead references the party that follows Amma's opening night performance. The chapter is partially focalized by the only male character (Roland) accorded the privilege of orienting the narrative. But it also includes three "paired" focalizations in which – similar to a two-shot in film – two characters with a shared history meet and converse. Even as the characters speak cordially to each other, Evaristo's narrative takes us into their minds, exposing their most intimate thoughts and undercutting their exchanged pleasantries to reveal their truer – and sometimes rather cruel – opinions of each other. To understand the significance of these paired focalizations, it is worth recalling literary critic Mieke Bal's observation that focalization is "the most important, most penetrating, and most subtle means of manipulation" available to an author of a narrative text.[25] Bal explains that when only one character in an exchange is allowed to focalize, that character has the "advantage as a party in [a] conflict" because it "can give the reader insight into its feelings and thoughts, while the other character cannot communicate anything."[26] The situation is changed completely in the case of a paired focalization. When *both* characters are empowered to influence the sentiments of readers by giving insight into their thoughts and feelings, the narrative inequality that is set up by a single focalization is nullified.

In multifocal decolonial novels, the emphasis on interiority that is dispersed across the major characters allows authors to explore characters from both the inside and the outside – to compare how the various characters are perceived by others with the way they understand themselves. Moreover, the focus on interiority, despite being partial and dispersed, provides authors with the space to develop other kinds of decolonial literary techniques. Evaristo, for example, draws on her background as a poet and director of experimental theater to create a syntactic style she calls "fusion fiction." Heir to modernist stream-of-consciousness narration, Evaristo's style features long, free-flowing sentences with minimal punctuation. Periods appear very rarely; they show up only at the end of the numbered sections that divide each character's titled subsection. Allowing herself to go "all over the place—the past, the present" within each character's head, Evaristo frees herself from diachronic temporal progression.[27]

Lacking the resources of a conventional sentence structure, Evaristo controls the pacing of *GWO* with line breaks and caesuras. *Caesura* is a poetic term used to describe a moment of pause in the logic and flow of the text; whereas a period privileges separation and autonomy, a caesura indicates pause and connection at the same time. Evaristo often uses terminal caesuras that, in conjunction with line breaks, appear most prominently in the representation of the enactment, memories, and long-term psychological effects of rape. Starting in Carole's section, caesuras repeatedly interrupt free-flowing prose to demand a deliberate attention to sexual violence – about which we will say more below. The prose is further arranged into narrative "thought vignettes" that are signaled as distinct by an extra blank space in the text. Some of the thought vignettes are long and rambling while others consist of just a few words arranged on the page in the manner of a prose poem. These syntactic features are put to striking use in the subsection focalized by Carole.

When the reader first meets her, Carole is walking resolutely through London's Liverpool Station on her way to work. With filmic attention, the narrative zooms in from an initial description that narrates her movement across the chaotic station to the details of her most private considerations. Though the passage is marked by a will to saturation – the aural fullness, the crowded platforms, the organized chaos of the "rushing hour" – our analysis is most concerned with the moment in which such saturation dissolves into a precise interiority, deeply personal and marked by what is only hinted at (*GWO*, 113–14). Halfway through Carole's opening thought vignette, a narrative volta floats the idea of suicide: "a body under a train / how *very* inconsiderate" (*GWO*, 114). A rhetorical feature characteristic of the sonnet form that points to an abrupt shift – or "turn" – in meaning, the volta is here taken up by the novel to signal the disruptive shadow of complex sexual trauma. Specifically, the thought of a lifeless body triggers Carole's thoughts of her own possible suicide. This volta's concern with death helps establish her as a character who wavers between despair and restraint.

As the British child of Nigerian immigrant parents, Carole worked hard to overcome the racialized contingencies she faced as a result of growing up in public housing and attending overpopulated and underfunded schools.[28] After her taxi-driving father dies of stress and overwork, Carole is nurtured and protected by her hardworking mother, Bummi, who supports them by cleaning houses. Taught by her mother to "wonder" at maths, Carole at first thrives academically, and even attains the status of "Super Geek of Year 9" before her upward trajectory is abruptly halted (*GWO*, 120). At the age of thirteen and a half, she is brutally gang-raped in a park during an unsanctioned party hosted by her friend LaTisha. Hurting, and fearing that she will be disbelieved or else accused of "gagging for it," Carole internalizes her pain and retreats to her bedroom. Because she "never told a soul," Carole also never fully heals from her trauma, and instead represses her pain (*GWO*, 127). Resolving at last to claw her way out of poverty, she seeks the help of another of Evaristo's focalizing characters, the well-meaning but quite self-involved teacher Mrs. Shirley King. Thus, by the time the reader first meets her, Carole is an attractive and exquisitely groomed young black vice president of an investment bank. A graduate of Oxford, she has married well to a member of English high society whose friendly blond presence at her side helps advance her career. This is the context within which we must consider the disjuncture between Carole's private despair and her outward success.

Carole understands "what it's / like to appear normal but to feel herself *swaying* || just one leap away ... / *swaying* || just one leap away from / eternal / peace" (*GWO*, 114, emphasis added). In this passage, the power of Evaristo's use of caesura becomes evident.[29] *Swaying* appears twice, both times at the end of a line. The first time, the word ends Carole's thought; the second, it stands alone in its own line. The repetition of "swaying" and its placement at a line break emphasizes Carole's vacillation between hopelessness and a constantly recuperated will to live. Instead of allowing Carole to sway toward the certainty of suicide, Evaristo uses caesura to arrest her movement – the pause introduces a process of careful revelation. Even as the novel intimates Carole's past sexual trauma, it tells the truth haltingly so as to not reduce her entire being to the experience of rape. Importantly, as a technique for truth telling, "swaying" evokes the slanted truth of Emily Dickinson's caesural meditations in her poem 1263, "Tell all the truth but tell it slant"; it also hints at a method for reworking the pain of rape for the purpose of moving forward. A closer look at Dickinson's poem suggests how.

Homiletic, Dickinson's poem recommends: "Tell all the truth but tell it slant — / Success in Circuit lies / Too bright for our infirm Delight / The Truth's superb surprise / As Lightning to the Children eased / With explanation kind / The Truth must dazzle gradually / Or every man be blind —." As if heeding Dickinson's instruction that the truth be approached circuitously, Evaristo closes in on the moment of sexual assault with care. "Dazzling" gradually, the narrative conceals even as it reveals. Though it is clear that a past traumatic event underlies Carole's suicidal thoughts, the narrative does not immediately reveal the rape and its iterations as the cause of her distress. Rather, the reader is eased into the "superb surprise" of sexual violence through the details of Carole's survival in the long wake of the assault. Two pages after the idea of suicide is first floated, the novel turns to Carole's chronic insomnia. In light of her unhealed trauma, Carole's bedtime reading practices help distract her from the pronounced disquiet of the night. Resistant to sleep, she loses herself in the "beautiful infinity" of financial modeling; long into the night, she scrutinizes investment plans and moves "hyperactively" across online news sources where she reads international news and their effect on global market conditions (*GWO*, 115–16). As she drags herself "bleary-eyed" to bed, the narrative turns to caesura to prompt the reader to wonder at the "bad things" that "happen / to bad little girls || who || ask || for || it" (*GWO*,

116). *It*, as the reader eventually finds out, stands in for the sexual violence that Carole survives. This "slanted" introduction thus prepares readers to sensitively receive the story of rape; it encourages them to come to the truth slowly, but fully.

The enactment, memories, and long-term psychological effects of rape are marked by the use of terminal caesuras across the whole of *GWO*. Accompanying short, one-word lines that break from each other, caesuras repeatedly interrupt free-flowing prose to demand a deliberate attention to sexual violence. The pause that punctuates every line accomplishes two things simultaneously: First, it suggests the brutal physical force, the thrust, of rape; and second, it distills the experience of rape to its most embodied form. However, in doing so, it emphasizes a paradoxical disembodiment that is also part of a response to rape. With short, pause-ridden lines that appear to heave, Evaristo describes the moment *it* happens to a semi-conscious Carole: "then || her || body || wasn't || her || own || no || more" (*GWO*, 125–26). Foregoing lushness, Evaristo's spare language here exposes the violence done to Carole's body. While this disclosure is significant on its own, it matters also for the connection it makes to another character, LaTisha Jones. The childhood friend who hosted the party where Carole was assaulted, LaTisha is also the character who, years after she and Carole lose touch, is raped by the same man who raped Carole years earlier. When LaTisha's date with Trey turns unexpectedly violent, she is unable to fight him off after he does not heed her pleas to stop his sexual advances. Similar to the syntactic pattern established to represent Carole's assault, LaTisha's rape is depicted in verse, and once again relies on caesura. Alone and confused after the assault, LaTisha returns home "where she spent a long time in the shower / wondering if he'd done anything wrong || or was it her fault" (*GWO*, 211). Caesuras in *GWO* attend to the silent, unaddressed, and relational wound. Whether or not a reader is consciously aware of them, they function as "grief work" that might initiate the process of healing. Importantly, that healing is set into motion only when the sexual violence is denounced, and only as the novel's readers consent to the imperative of decolonial witnessing.

Race does not function solely within a national frame, and within the boundaries of literary conventions lie intersectional realities that both resist and yet call for representation. Evaristo's use of caesuras in *GWO* provides an illustration of how de-forming a conventional taken-for-granted structure (narrative prose organized into conventional sentences) contributes to an author's ability to make visible a kind of content (the existence and trauma of sexual assault) that has been too long ignored and is still often misunderstood. Moreover, her use of caesuras is analogous to the kind of de-forming and re-making of a novel's narrative structure that authors of multifocal decolonial novels are undertaking. Both techniques, at the micro and the macro level, illustrate the onto-epistem-ological import of innovating an older form in the service of providing new content that will allow us all to go beyond the painful past of our specific historical and instrumental givens as we seek to initiate our own cycles of freedom.

Notes

1. *The Well of Loneliness* is a celebrated 1928 lesbian novel by the British writer Radclyffe Hall (London: J. Cape, 1928). Dusty Springfield was an English pop singer and swinging sixties icon with hits like "You Don't Own Me" and "Son of a Preacher Man" that made her a fixture on both the *US Billboard Hot 100* and the *UK Singles Chart*. Springfield was involved in several romantic relationships with women and frequented the Gateways club.
2. Bernardine Evaristo, *Girl, Woman, Other* (New York: Black Cat, 2019), 22–23.
3. Evaristo, *Girl, Woman, Other*, 23.
4. Frantz Fanon, *Black Skin, White Masks*, trans. Richard Philcox (New York: Grove Press, 2009), 205.
5. Novels featuring more than one point of view have been around for almost as long as novels have existed. Multifocal narratives of the sort we are interested in first appeared in the early part of the twentieth century as experimental works of modernist literature. Multifocal decolonial novels can be distinguished by a proliferation of character focalizers, the turn away from a singular protagonist, and a decolonial approach. On character space and the role of the minor character, see Alex Woloch, *The One vs. the Many: Minor Characters and the Space of the Protagonist in the Novel* (Princeton, NJ: Princeton University Press, 2003).
6. This is also the case for adjacent art forms like films, videos, and video games.
7. Exemplary works include Maria Lugones, *Pilgrimages/Peregrinajes: Theorizing Coalition Against Multiple Oppressions* (Lanham, MD: Rowman & Littlefield, 2003); Maria Lugones, "Toward a Decolonial Feminism," *Hypatia* 25.4 (2010), 742–59; Nelson Maldonado-Torres, "The Decolonial Turn," in *New Approaches to Latin American Studies: Culture and Power*, trans. Robert Cavooris, ed. Juan Poblete (New York: Routledge, 2018), 111–27; Walter Mignolo, *The Darker Side of the Renaissance: Literacy, Territoriality, and Colonization* (Ann Arbor: University of Michigan Press, 1995); Walter Mignolo, *Local Histories/Global Designs: Coloniality, Subaltern Knowledges, and Border Thinking* (Princeton, NJ: Princeton University Press, 2012); Aníbal Quijano, "Coloniality and Modernity/Rationality," *Cultural Studies* 21.2–3 (2007), 168–78; Aníbal Quijano, "Coloniality of Power, Eurocentrism, and Latin America," *Nepantla: Views from the South* 1.3 (2000), 533–80; Sylvia

Wynter, "Unsettling the Coloniality of Being/Power/Truth/Freedom: Towards the Human, After Man, Its Overrepresentation – An Argument." *New Centennial Review* 3.3 (2003), 257–337.

8. Lugones describes "worlds of sense" as alternative domains of intelligibility that each have their own sociality, sets of values, characteristic ways of interacting, and particular people who actively inhabit that psychic space. See *Pilgrimages*, 20–26, 85–93.

9. Karen Barad, "Posthumanist Performativity: Toward an Understanding of How Matter Comes to Matter," *Signs: Journal of Women in Culture and Society* 28.3 (2003), 802–31, at 829, offers the neologism "onto-epistemology" to signal a refusal of the divide between knowing and being. On complex solidarity, see Michael R. Hames-García, *Fugitive Thought: Prison Movements, Race, and the Meaning of Justice* (Minneapolis: University of Minnesota Press, 2004), 208–19, and Michael R. Hames-García, *Identity Complex: Making the Case for Multiplicity* (Minneapolis: University of Minnesota Press, 2011), 1–37.

10. See Gérard Genette, *Narrative Discourse: An Essay in Method*, trans. Jane E. Lewin (Ithaca, NY: Cornell University Press, 1980), 161–211.

11. See Mieke Bal, *Narratology: Introduction to the Theory of Narrative*, trans. Christine van Boheemen (Toronto: University of Toronto Press, 1985), 104–10.

12. See Shlomith Rimmon-Kenan, *Narrative Fiction: Contemporary Poetics* (London: Methuen, 1983), 78–87.

13. Omniscient narrators are located outside the story told in the text. They are almost always third-person narrators, but as we discuss below, third-person narration can also be focalized through different characters within the story.

14. For a fuller analysis of the focalization in *Under the Feet of Jesus*, see Paula M. L. Moya, *Learning from Experience: Politics, Epistemology, and Chicana/o Identity* (Berkeley: University of California Press, 1998), 185–200.

15. Helena Maria Viramontes, *Under the Feet of Jesus* (New York: Atria Books, 1995), 8.

16. Viramontes, *Under the Feet of Jesus*, 8–9.

17. Viramontes, *Under the Feet of Jesus*, 9.

18. See Bruno Latour, *Reassembling the Social: An Introduction to Actor-Network-Theory* (New York: Oxford University Press, 2005), for an account of society as an evolving assemblage of natural-cultural forces. See Dipesh Chakrabarty, *Provincializing Europe: Postcolonial Thought and Historical Difference* (Princeton, NJ: Princeton University Press, 2000), for what it means to provincialize the European "universal." For an account of objectivity that acknowledges the unavoidability of interpretive bias, see Paula M. L. Moya, "Introduction: Reclaiming Identity," in *Reclaiming Identity: Realist Theory and the Predicament of Postmodernism*, eds. Paula M. L. Moya and Michael R. Hames-García (Berkeley: University of California Press, 2000); Paula M. L. Moya, *Learning from Experience: Politics, Epistemology, and Chicana/o Identity* (Berkeley: University of California Press, 1998), esp. 49–57.

19. Alex Woloch, *The One vs. the Many: Minor Characters and the Space of the Protagonist in the Novel* (Princeton, NJ: Princeton University Press, 2003), 12–42.

20. *The Testaments* is the sequel to Atwood's 1985 Booker Prize–winning dystopian novel *The Handmaid's Tale*. See Margaret Atwood, *The Testaments* (New York: Doubleday, 2019).

21. In a *Guardian* interview with Sethi, Evaristo explains that after learning about the presence of Africans in Britain during the Roman occupation, she wrote *The Emperor's Babe* (Bernardine Evaristo, *The Emperor's Babe: A Novel* [London: Hamish Hamilton, 2001]). Anita Sethi, "Interview: Bernardine Evaristo: 'I Want to Put Presence into Absence'," *The Guardian*, April 27, 2019, www.theguardian .com/books/2019/apr/27/bernardine-evaristo-girl-woman-other-interview.

22. For a description of the phenomenon, see E. P. Thompson, "History from Below," *The Times Literary Supplement*, 3345 (1966), 279 (*The Times Literary Supplement* Historical Archive, 1902–2014). For an example, see Howard Zinn, *A People's History of the United States* (New York: Harper & Row, 1980).

23. For an explanation of race as a dynamic process, see Paula M. L. Moya, and Hazel R. Markus, "Doing Race: An Introduction," in *Doing Race: 21 Essays for the 21st Century*, eds. Hazel Markus and Paula Moya (New York: Norton2010); and MarYam Hamedani, et al. "RaceWorks Toolkit," (2020), http://sparqtools.org/raceworks/.

24. Story time refers to the time it might take for the events in a story to occur – several minutes, hours, days, or months. Discourse time refers to the amount of time it might take to read, in a text, about those events. The point is that they often diverge. In two pages of text, for instance, a novel can cover several minutes, days, or months in the story. See Seymour Chatman, "Genette's Analysis of Narrative Time Relations," *L'Esprit Créateur* 14.4 (1974), 353–68.

25. Bal, *Narratology*, 116.

26. Bal, *Narratology*, 110.

27. Sethi, "Interview: Bernardine Evaristo."

28. Social psychologist Claude Steele defines an identity contingency as the specific set of responses that a person with a given identity has to cope with in a specific setting. See Claude M. Steele, *Whistling Vivaldi: And Other Clues to How Stereotypes Affect Us* (New York: Norton, 2010), 68.

29. When representing line breaks that are also caesuras, we have decided to make use of double parallel lines (||) instead of a single forward slash (/). Importantly, across *GWO*, not all line breaks are caesuras; Evaristo also writes using enjambment, where lines "run over" from one to the next without pause or punctuation. We represent enjambed lines through the use of a single forward slash (/).

PART VI

Case Studies

The case studies presented here demonstrate the range of research involved in addressing the broad and complex development of literary traditions shaped by US racial history. We begin with an example of the most fundamental and generative research involved in efforts to attend to this history – the work of recovering authors and texts obscured, marginalized, or misunderstood by a dominant culture guided by its own literary and racialized protocols. Claire Parfait gets us started by addressing two examples of the collective biography, one of the most important genres in African American literary history, William J. Simmons's *Men of Mark* (1887) and Henry F. Kletzing and William H. Crogman's *Progress of a Race* (1897). Addressing the publishing histories of these works, Parfait considers the role of print culture in shaping concepts of African American history. José Antonio Arellano is also interested in the relation between literature and history, but he poses a challenging question about the extent to which Mexican American literature can claim to support "Chicano activism focused on the working class." In fact, though, Arellano argues that stories can "function as the cultural arm of a nascent labor movement by enabling a group to recognize its solidarity." Communities come to know themselves – even come to constitute themselves – *as* communities through stories. Arellano considers both the possibilities and the challenges of literary activism so as to "enable those of us who read and teach literature to question what exactly literary activism enables, who and what this activism is for, and what goals it posits as its aim." Considerations of social class and the protocols of literary study occupy Kinohi Nishikawa as well, who reflects on what he calls "the racial underground." Examining a print culture market devoted to sensation, "black sleaze," Nishikawa argues that "black sleaze is important to recover precisely because African American authors were aware of it as a significant, if subterranean, part of the literary marketplace." This is a marketplace that is important precisely because it disrupts our progressive understandings of racial

307

history. "Although self-styled 'outsider' literature is a centuries-old phenomenon," Nishikawa observes, "the conjuncture of race and bad taste is peculiar to post–World War II print culture and the social changes it both registered and responded to. What made the racial underground a contentious market niche was that it reveled in illiberal, antisocial messages precisely while mainstream society was pursuing a liberal, integrationist agenda." Next, Jeehyun Lim draws us into another area where assumptions about social class and the protocols of literary taste are called into question. Lim examines literature in Hawaiian Pidgin, exploring its capacity to have "countercultural and subversive force." Whereas Pidgin has been appreciated as a means "to represent the rich and varied culture of its speakers," Lim argues that "if not always explicitly articulated, the reevaluation of literature in Pidgin by literary critics share with the scholarship on language diversity and linguistic justice an interest in and attunement to the relations of power and language." Anna Brickhouse closes the case studies, focusing on the lingering power of representations of race by offering an intertextual study that reflects on the presence of the nineteenth century in the present. Brickhouse considers Celeste Ng's *Little Fires Everywhere* (2017) as a "novel that thinks about race and American literature across the sweep of time, from Nathaniel Hawthorne's *The Scarlet Letter* (1850) through our own moment and beyond." The result of this consideration is "a meta-literary investigation into the relationship between literary and cultural form and the series of racial entanglements – black and white and Asian – played out in its neoliberal 1990s setting," one that explores the features of postracial form, which soon yield to the tragedy of "color-blindness as the mask of racial violence."

CHAPTER 19

Collective Biographies and African American History
Men of Mark *(1887) and* Progress of a Race *(1897)*

Claire Parfait

In *What Is African American History?* Pero Dagbovie notes that "black biography is one of the oldest genres of black historical writing as well as a popular form of black intellectual history."[1] Within the biographical genre, "collective biographies have been a staple of African American publishing."[2] Indeed, collective biographies – collections of biographical sketches – have played a particularly important role in African American history writing since Robert Benjamin Lewis's 1836 *Light and Truth*. The number of collective biographies penned by African Americans exploded after the Civil War, especially in the last decades of the nineteenth century.[3] The pantheon of eminent men and women proposed in these works evolved over the century, as did the target audiences and the roles collective biographies were meant to fulfill. While a number of scholars have examined antebellum African American history works,[4] late nineteenth-century collective biographies remain relatively unexplored, especially from the point of view of print culture. This essay proposes a case study of two works, *Men of Mark* by William J. Simmons (1887) and *Progress of a Race* by Henry F. Kletzing and William H. Crogman (1897), with a particular focus on their publishing histories.

In the late nineteenth century, a period Rayford Logan has described as the "nadir" in race relations, collective biographies were one of the ways African Americans sought to address degraded race relations, racial stereotypes, and, to a certain extent, the rewritings of American history. Far from being the exclusive domain of African Americans, the genre was very popular then, as Scott Casper demonstrates in *Constructing American Lives*. Yet while mainstream collective biographies could be viewed as a way to reinforce master narratives about the American past, the addition of "neglected individuals and groups" made it possible to "challenge those narratives and suggest alternative interpretations."[5] African Americans used the genre to highlight the progress accomplished since emancipation, and many works bore eloquent titles such as *Men of Mark* (1887), *Negro Stars in All Ages of the World* (1890), *Women of Distinction* (1893), *Noted Negro Women* (1893), *Progress of a Race* (1897), and *One Hundred Distinguished Leaders* (1899). David Blight, in addressing the "'progress of the race' rhetoric" that took hold at the end of the nineteenth century in "African American life and letters," has aptly termed these collective biographies "encyclopedic pep talks."[6]

Late nineteenth-century collective biographies share a number of common points with their predecessors. At a time when history was becoming professionalized, they were still penned by amateur historians, even if some of their authors (like Simmons, the author of *Men of Mark*, and Crogman, the main author of *Progress of a Race*) had a college education. Like earlier versions of the genre, they were a form of militant history, one that meant to set the historical record straight and address the problems of the times their authors lived in. Unlike their predecessors, however, late nineteenth-century works tended to focus on contemporaries and sometimes explicitly addressed a black readership. Moreover, while their publication often depended on their authors' financial involvement, as antebellum works did,[7] a few were issued by white subscription publishers. This is the case of *Men of Mark* (1887) and *Progress of a Race* (1897).

Men of Mark (1887) and *Progress of a Race* (1897): Commonalities and Differences

Both *Men of Mark* and *Progress of a Race* were authored by men whose lives were apt illustrations of the "progress of a race." William J. Simmons (1849–90), the author-compiler of *Men of Mark*, was born into slavery and became a Baptist minister, an educator, and the president of a state university in Louisville, Kentucky. He held high-ranking positions in the Baptist church, edited the *American Baptist*, and was also president of the National Colored Press Association. Simmons's life is in many ways similar to that of the individuals he sketches in his book.

Simmons's book includes only men, as its title indicates, though the work is dedicated to "the women of our race." He intended to write a companion volume devoted to women but died before he was able to. More than a history book proper, Simmons's book is closer to a Who's Who or a dictionary of black biography. Among the 177 sketches in what is a very thick volume (1,138 pages, with more than 100 engravings of the subjects of the sketches), which are not organized according to any recognizable order,[8] a minority – about one-tenth – are neither African American nor contemporaries. They include men who were recurrent features in antebellum works, such as French writer Alexandre Dumas, and hero of the Haitian revolution Toussaint L'Ouverture, as well as Crispus Attucks, Benjamin Banneker, and Nat Turner. The vast majority of the biographical sketches, however, are devoted to contemporaries of Simmons. Ministers – many of them Baptist, like Simmons himself – represent about one-third of the men portrayed, followed by politicians, academics, and newspaper and magazine editors; lawyers, physicians, businessmen, and a motley crowd consisting of a phrenologist, a silk culturist, a couple of photographers, and so on, make up the rest of the biographies.

Men of Mark is both less eclectic and less inclusive in terms of gender, origin, and time period than most antebellum collective biographies because the work was primarily meant to reflect the achievements of African Americans since emancipation. Like earlier works, however, *Men of Mark* includes long quotes taken from various sources, including a great many books, encyclopedias, and newspapers. Simmons seems to have known many of the subjects he sketches, and occasionally he refers to black historians such as George Washington Williams, viewed as "the most eminent Negro historian in the world."[9]

Unlike earlier collective biographies, in which a double audience of whites and African Americans was clearly inscribed in both text and paratext, *Men of Mark* targets an African American audience, in particular black youth. Simmons had been struck by the ignorance of his students with respect to "the work of our great colored men"; he wanted "their lives snatched from obscurity to become household matter for conversation." *Men of Mark* was meant both to provide role models and, by the sheer accumulation of sketches, to demonstrate the almost infinite possibilities open to young African Americans as long as they worked hard. This was reinforced with advice such as "What men have done, others can do. Reader, take courage, go forward; you can and will win."

Men of Mark is resolutely optimistic, perhaps because Simmons himself succeeded against all odds. Yet together with Simmons's uplifting philosophy and upbeat tone, the work also documents the racial violence in the South, with references to lynchings, for instance, and attempts to counter the ongoing rewriting of slavery as benign; for Simmons, there was no question that the system was wrong and Nat Turner was "a heroic 'black John Brown,'" whose violence was justified by that of the system itself.[10]

Progress of a Race was published exactly ten years after *Men of Mark*. By then, the condition of African Americans had further degraded. The 1890s was the worst decade of the century with respect to the number of racially motivated lynchings. The work was announced as the collaboration of two men whose names appear in reverse alphabetical order on the title page, Henry F. Kletzing and William H. Crogman. For African American readers of the time, and perhaps a few white ones, the name Crogman would have sounded familiar. Like Simmons, Crogman (1841–1931) was a fitting illustration of the claim made in the title of the work. Born on the Caribbean island of Saint Martin, he was orphaned at a young age and was a sailor for a few years before he moved to the United States. By 1880, he had become a professor of classical languages at Clark University, Atlanta, which he was later to preside. The African American press praised him as one of the leading black educators. In 1896, Crogman had authored *Talks for the Times*, a collection of various addresses and speeches he had delivered over some thirteen years. The title page bears the mention "Printed for the Author," and the work was most likely self-published.

Henry F. Kletzing was a professor of mathematics in Naperville, Illinois, at what was then called North-Western College, where James Lawrence Nichols, founder of the J. L. Nichols publishing company (which issued *Progress of a Race*) also taught for many years. A close examination of *Progress* indicates that Crogman – whose portrait appears as the frontispiece – was the main author of the work, which borrows abundantly from his earlier *Talks for the Times*, and in which Georgia is disproportionately represented. The recurrent use of the pronoun *we* when African Americans are mentioned tends to confirm the hypothesis that Crogman was the sole or main author of the book, which is introduced by Booker T. Washington, a longtime friend of Crogman's.

Unlike *Men of Mark*, *Progress of a Race* is a mixture of history and collective biography. As the very long subtitle of the work – *The Remarkable Advancement of the Afro-American Negro from the Bondage of Slavery, Ignorance and Poverty to the Freedom of Citizenship, Intelligence, Affluence, Honor and Trust* – indicates, its main objective was to highlight the progress made by African Americans since the end of slavery, a progress "not equaled in the annals of history," and "aid in the work of elevating the Race" by "inducing the multitudes to catch the same spirit of progress that imbues their leaders."[11] The book attempted to assess the current condition of African Americans from a variety of perspectives, which included education, morality, financial worth, health, and so on.

Unlike *Men of Mark*, *Progress* devotes an entire chapter to women and includes whites such as abolitionists William Lloyd Garrison and Wendell Phillips. The African American pantheon in chapter 14, "Noted Personages of the Afro-American Race," has a few eighteenth-century examples, such as Phillis Wheatley and Crispus Attucks, but, like *Men of*

Mark, Progress focuses mainly on contemporaries. All of the characters sketched are American, and the sketches are organized by category. As in *Men of Mark*, ministers account for the largest number of sketches, and while men predominate, 2 of the 12 professors are female, as are 7 of the 11 authors and artists. The preface to *Progress* reveals that the subjects were asked to provide biographical information, and perhaps photographs as well. Other sources include books (George Washington Williams is frequently quoted), newspapers (usually without dates), reports, statistics drawn from the 1890 census, and so on.

Progress is abundantly illustrated, but unlike *Men of Mark*, in addition to its portraits of eminent men and women (in engravings and half-tones), *Progress* provided its audience with many portraits of anonymous characters, including slaves, students in various universities and colleges, workers in a cotton field and in a sawmill, and photographs of buildings such as colleges and universities, private residences, and shops, sometimes with their manager and employees. *Progress* thus offers a snapshot of an entire period, especially in the South and Georgia. The countless individuals and groups that people its pages represent so many answers to the stereotyped representations of African Americans at the time and can be seen as "self-fulfilling accounts of racial unity."[12]

Like *Men of Mark*, *Progress* addressed rewritings of history and the current condition of African Americans in the South. *Progress* is thus openly critical of lynching, segregation, and disenfranchisement. At a time when abolitionists were increasingly seen as misguided fanatics who bore a heavy responsibility in causing the war,[13] Crogman described them as heroes. Similarly, *Progress* wrote against plantation literature with its happy slaves and benevolent masters by emphatically stating that slavery was "a curse"[14] and borrowing heroic escape stories and engravings from William Still's 1872 *The Underground Railroad*.

The question of the target audience for *Progress* is less easily answered than in the case of *Men of Mark*. The inclusion of whites in the work and the introduction by Booker T. Washington, who was both well known and much praised by whites and blacks alike, could indicate the wish to reach a double audience, as does the choice of a white coauthor. The latter point was to become one of the sales arguments used by the publisher for *Progress*.

Publishing Histories

Both *Men of Mark* and *Progress* came out under the imprint of white subscription houses, during the post–Civil War boom in subscription publishing. Subscription publishers sent agents, or canvassers, door-to-door, trying to convince potential buyers to write their names in the blank pages of a canvassing book or prospectus. To entice customers, canvassing books included samples of text, illustrations, and bindings of the work.[15] Although the vast majority of subscription houses do not seem to have published works by African American authors, there were a few exceptions: For instance, Frederick Douglass's third autobiography, *The Life and Times of Frederick Douglass*, came out under the imprint of the Park Publishing Company in Hartford in 1881, and the American Publishing Company, also based in Hartford, which issued many of Mark Twain's works, brought out Joseph T. Wilson's *Black Phalanx* in 1888 as well as John Mercer Langston's *From the Virginia Plantation to the National Capitol* (1894).

The publishing histories of *Men of Mark* and *Progress of a Race* are difficult to trace.[16] In both cases, publishers' archives have apparently disappeared, as has any correspondence from the authors relating to the works. The story has to be pieced together from sources such as city directories, newspaper advertisements and articles, occasional correspondence, and lawsuits.

Men of Mark came out under the imprint of Geo. M. Rewell, of Cleveland, Ohio. Rewell seems to have had a variegated and not altogether successful business career. The Cleveland city directories show that he worked as a clerk for ship chandlers in the late 1870s before becoming a book agent and a publisher. In the early 1880s, he entered a short-lived partnership with another Cleveland publisher, N. G. Hamilton, but by 1884 he was on his own again, specializing in subscription books and engravings. He branched out into other business fields and was a partner/manager in several companies in the late 1880s and early 1890s, including the sign-painting company Rewell and Meier and the Low & Rewell Company, which made mops, dishwashers, and items for carriages such as the "Webster elastic draught for carriages," guaranteed to "remove all horse motion."[17] By the early 1900s, Rewell no longer owned or managed any companies and was listed as a salesman in the city directory. His business ventures manifestly failed, and when his father – a ship captain on the Great Lakes who owned real estate and whose property was valued at some $32,000 – died in 1899, he bequeathed part of his estate not to his son, but to his daughter-in-law: His will states that George had "not been fortunate in business," and any money given him might go straight to his creditors.[18] In spite of his apparent shortcomings as a businessman, Rewell was well known and respected in Cleveland, as evidenced by the many references in the *Cleveland Plain Dealer* to his activities in the Knights of Pythias, a fraternal society in which he held various positions of honor starting in the 1890s.[19]

The career of Rewell as a publisher spanned almost twenty years, from the early 1880s to 1897. What is striking about it, apart from the fact that it was only one of many activities and was always limited in scale, is that from the first he seems to have specifically targeted the African American market.[20] He issued engravings and lithographs with titles such as "Heroes of the Colored Race" and "Colored Chieftains," which he sold by subscription. In the 1880s, these were advertised and praised in African American newspapers like the *Cleveland Gazette*, the *Huntsville Gazette* (Alabama), and the *New York Freeman*. Rewell's imprint appears on an 1882 edition of Douglass's *Life and Times of Frederick Douglass*,[21] but *Men of Mark* seems to have been the only original work issued by the publisher. He may have commissioned it, or Simmons may have approached Rewell, who was in his own way promoting "men of mark" with his "excellent charts of colored men," as the *Cleveland Gazette* noted in its September 25, 1886, issue.

Rewell advertised *Men of* Mark – a "standard work of biography" that was "elegantly bound" in cloth or half-leather – in a limited number of African American papers, but his advertisement in the *New York Age*, for instance, ran for several months in 1888.[22] Rewell specifically targeted African American agents, male or female, to sell the work. African American newspapers announced the publication of *Men of Mark*, occasionally referred to agents selling it,[23] and reviewed the work in glowing terms; the *Washington Bee* admired a book that told the truth about its subjects without "rhetorical exaggeration."[24] The *Cleveland Gazette* highlighted the low price – $3 – of a work with 1,138 pages and 106 illustrations, which would "adorn anybody's table" and which all ought to buy.[25] The book seems to have done quite well, and Simmons prepared a new edition that came out in 1890 and was reissued the following year. The new edition was much shorter than the first, with only 90 sketches and 736 pages. As in the case of the first edition, African American agents, whether male or female, part-time or full-time, were considered particularly suitable for canvassing.[26] The African American press reported on the brisk sale of the new edition and called for more canvassers. When Simmons died in 1890, the *New York Age* observed it was a "calamity to the race," while the Indianapolis *Freeman* noted that Simmons had probably done more for African Americans than any man of his generation save Frederick Douglass and remarked that *Men of Mark* ought to bring

Simmons's widow and children "a small fortune."[27] In the months that followed, the work continued to be sold by agents, but it was also offered as a bonus by the *Freeman*, which pledged to send the book free of charge to anyone who brought in three one-year subscribers or six six-month subscribers.[28] For a similar purpose, the Detroit *Plaindealer* gave away *Men of Mark* and other books, together with sewing machines, carpet sweepers, watches, and air rifles.[29]

Men of Mark quickly became a standard work, and newspapers both referred readers to Simmons's book and borrowed from it. The *Freeman* told his readers: "Read THE FREEMAN to tell what the Negro is doing and must do to better his condition and "Men of Mark" to tell what he has done." This, according to the paper, was "the key to the so-called Negro problem."[30] Contemporaries likewise used it: Irving Garland Penn, for instance, drew on it for his *The Afro-American Press and Its Editors* (1891). Although the work does not appear to have been reprinted until 1968, its enduring importance as an early dictionary of black biography cannot be denied. In his 1965 *Betrayal of the Negro*, historian Rayford Logan noted that of those late nineteenth-century African Americans who gained recognition for one reason or another, a few were unknown because "they were not included in *Men of Mark*."[31] In his preface to a 1968 reprint, Ernest Kaiser observed that without *Men of Mark*, "written when many of the people included were still alive, the field of Negro biography would be infinitely poorer."[32] Two years later, Lerone Bennett, in his own preface to another reprint, claimed that *Men of Mark* was still "a basic text of black biography" and added, "It is a commentary on the state of American biography and a tribute to the vision of author William J. Simmons that this old and enduring classic contains more detailed biographical information on more figures of Afro-American history than any other single book."[33] The afterlife of *Men of Mark* therefore seems to have fulfilled the prediction of Roscoe C. Simmons, who dedicated a copy of the 1890 edition to his sons, with the inscription, "In time to come, dear sons, the stories herein told, will become the basis of fascinating history."[34]

James Lawrence Nichols, whose company issued *Progress of a Race*, was what could be called an accidental, or perhaps more aptly opportunistic, publisher. His early life was difficult: A German immigrant, he was orphaned when a child and had a series of harsh masters. He began selling books door-to-door to earn money to go to college. In 1880, he graduated from North-Western College in Naperville, Illinois, and soon became professor, then head of its Commercial Department. He published his lectures as a book, *The Business Guide*, which his students sold across the country during their vacation to finance their studies. The work was so successful that Nichols founded a publishing house whose catalog initially consisted of that one title, in English and later also in German. He gradually added a few titles typical of subscription publishing, such as religious works, dictionaries, guides to domestic economy, and health and hygiene manuals.[35] Nichols died in 1895 and in his will left the management of the company to a former North-Western College graduate, John A. Hertel, who was in charge of the Toronto branch of the company. The company also had a branch in Atlanta, headed by Austin N. Jenkins.[36] According to Hertel, it was Jenkins, a former book agent, who approached Crogman, planned the work with him, and insisted that there was an audience for this kind of work: "To Mr. Jenkins belongs the honor of suggesting and planning a Negro History, and at his earnest solicitation his publishers issued 'Progress of a Race,' which has been a great success and introduced him as a race publisher."[37]

In the 1890s, Naperville had no African American population, and, unlike Rewell, the Nichols company had never published any books authored by or intended for African Americans. In all likelihood, Hertel accepted Jenkins's proposal on the condition that a white coauthor appear on the title page. Hertel chose Henry Kletzing, one of his former professors at North-Western, to fill that role. Kletzing's main function, if we are to believe the promotional campaign for *Progress*, was to allow the publisher to target a twofold audience of white and black readers in the North and South: "Race prejudice buried," an advertisement loudly proclaimed, a point visually interpreted in an engraving of the two authors shaking hands. While the sales pitch of an 1899 sample book for *Progress* ascribes the work rather generally to "the laborer, mechanic and the professional man," agents were instructed to focus on the "prominent educators," one from each race, one from each section, who had "clasped hands, united their energies, and given to the Negro the best product of their brains."[38] The publishers touted the book as the "most Concise, Complete and Authentic Book on the Negro Race that has ever been Placed on the Market," and sought to entice buyers with the promise of a work that was both "instructive and fascinating." The work was priced at $1.50 in cloth and $2.25 in leather, with gilt edges. Compared to other subscription books of the time, it was relatively cheap.

In the late nineteenth-century, subscription houses had a poor reputation, partly because they tended to sell old material as new, with inflated claims and through aggressive agents.[39] Like Rewell himself and other subscription publishers, Nichols systematically used superlatives in his advertisements for agents, whatever the works for sale. *Progress of a Race* was no exception: in the "Agents wanted" section, Nichols described the work as "the best seller we ever had," noting that a "colored preacher sold 15 at church in 20 minutes," and that "our agent in Charleston sold 53 in a week."[40] The work was mostly promoted in African American papers such as *The Colored American* (Washington, DC), where Nichols's advertisement ran for two months in May and June 1898, but the Nichols company also campaigned for agents in a few mainstream papers. Jenkins, who was in charge of promotion in the South, advertised for agents in the *Dallas Morning News* (March 29 and 31, April 2, 1898) and the *Daily Picayune* of New Orleans (March 27 and 29, 1898). There were only a few such examples, perhaps because they proved ineffective, and on the whole, *Progress* was promoted on a limited scale, especially when compared with the aggressive and long-term campaign the company launched for Booker T. Washington's *The Story of My Life and Work*, which it brought out in 1900.

Like *Men of Mark*, *Progress* was also pushed indirectly, for instance, through passing references to the agents it could be obtained from, providing valuable insights into the identity of agents. The African American paper *Cleveland Gazette* told its readers on December 11, 1897, that "R.E. Ballard is on the road canvassing for 'Progress of a Race.' He has had fair success so far." Agents sometimes placed their own advertisements, as did Thomas Blagburn in the African American newspaper *Iowa State Bystander*. In an advertisement disguised as an article, Blagburn, an African American book agent,[41] touted *Progress* as a "very interesting and useful" book, which "should go into the homes of every family" (October 21 and 28, 1898). The *Colored American* alerted its audience to the arrival of George Adams, a student at Wilberforce, Ohio – one of the historically black colleges – who had made Washington, DC, his home for the summer and was the agent for *Progress*. The editor added that "every colored person of the city should get one of these books from Mr. Adams" (*Colored American*, July 16, 1898).[42]

Reviews were another form of promotion. As in the case of *Men of Mark*, the mainstream press does not seem to have noticed the work, possibly because subscription companies rarely sent out advance copies for reviews. The African American press, however, printed laudatory assessments of *Progress of a Race*. E. E. Cooper, the editor of *Colored American*, who was the subject of a flattering sketch in *Progress* ("[He] is making a name which will be honored when many of our so-called great men will be forgotten"),[43] praised a work devoid of the "gush and brag so common to nearly all books about Negroes by Negroes" and claimed that it was "unquestionably the best book about the Negro that has yet been written." *Progress* offered a "wealth of information hitherto unpublished," which made it "a valuable reference book." [44] The low price was another incentive. At only $1.50, it was money well invested, noted the *Broad Ax* commentator who wished he could afford to send a copy to all colleges and educational institutions in the country.[45]

In the absence of archives, the sales of the work cannot be calculated, nor can the proportion of black and white readers be assessed. Yet *Progress* did sufficiently well to fulfill the prediction Cooper made at the end of his glowing review for the *Colored American*: "It is a book that will live." Indeed, between 1897 and 1929, *Progress of a Race* was regularly revised and enlarged. The names on the title page were modified twice; in 1902, Henry Kletzing was replaced by John William Gibson, another white Naperville teacher. James Lawrence Nichols II, the son of the founder, appeared as the first author in 1920, for an entirely revised shorter edition entitled *New Progress of a Race*. The changes in the work – new chapters on the Great Migration, World War I, and an updated "Who's Who in the Negro Race" – for the first time justified Crogman's position as a second author.

In the years that followed the first publication of the work, Crogman and *Progress of a Race* were often referred to as examples of African American achievements. The book was included in the volumes that were presented at the 1900 Paris World Fair, and the African American press frequently listed it among the works that all African Americans should own, along with books by Douglass, Booker T. Washington, George Washington Williams, W.E.B. Du Bois, Paul Laurence Dunbar, and others.[46] Perhaps because the publisher kept issuing new editions of *Progress of a Race*, the book was not offered as a bonus by newspapers.

The case of *Progress of a Race* confirms Burg and Burkett's claim that by the turn of the century, white publishers realized there was an African American market for books and started to produce works aimed at that sector of the population.[47] In 1897, the same year he wrote the introduction to *Progress of a Race*, Booker T. Washington asked J.L. Nichols whether they might be interested in publishing his autobiography. Wondering why he sent the proposal to such "an obscure house," the editors of the first volume of the *Booker T. Washington Papers* note that Washington was most likely aware that Nichols had many agents and a substantial market in black communities both North and South.[48] The sales of *Progress of a Race* may have been instrumental in his decision.

This initial exploration of late nineteenth-century African American collective biographies is inevitably fragmented, owing to the lack of information as to the arrangements between authors and publishers, among others. However, it shows that they played a part in the struggle over representations and rights, as had earlier works of history by African Americans. Like their predecessors, Simmons and Crogman were activists and wrote history with an agenda. Unlike antebellum works, however, *Men of Mark* and *Progress of a Race* seem to have reached a sizable audience; they were reprinted and, at least in the case of *Progress*, had several revised editions over an extended period of time. While buying cannot be equated with reading, this invites us to reconsider the question of who read and distributed books in the African American communities of the various parts of the United States, both rural and urban, at that time. Much exciting work remains to be done.

Notes

1. Pero Dagbovie, *What Is African American History?* (Cambridge: Polity Press, 2015), 41.
2. John Ernest, "Life Beyond Biography: Black Lives and Biographical Research," *Common-place* 17.1 (2016), http://common-place.org/book/life-beyond-biography-black-lives-and-biographical-research/.
3. John Ernest notes that white abolitionists also produced sketches of prominent African Americans (John Ernest, *Liberation Historiography: African American Writers and the Challenge of History, 1794–1861* [Chapel Hill: University of North Carolina Press, 2004], 63). Postbellum white authors also produced collective biographies of African Americans, for instance, G. F. Richings, *Evidences of Progress among Colored People*, 8th ed. (Philadelphia: Geo. S. Ferguson, 1902).
4. Among scholars who have examined early African American historians within the past two decades are John Ernest, *Liberation Historiography*; Margot Minardi, *Making Slavery History: Abolitionism and the Politics of Memory in Massachusetts* (New York: Oxford University Press, 2010); and Stephen G. Hall, *A Faithful Account of the Race: African American Historical Writing in 19th-Century America* (Chapel Hill: University of North Carolina Press, 2011).
5. Scott E. Casper, *Constructing American Lives: Biography and Culture in Nineteenth-Century America* (Chapel Hill: University of North Carolina Press, 1999), 6.
6. David Blight, *Race and Reunion: The Civil War in American Memory* (Cambridge, MA: Belknap Press of Harvard University Press, 2001), 319, 333.
7. Claire Parfait, "Early African American Historians: A Book History and Historiography Approach. The Case of William Cooper Nell (1816–1874)," in *Race, Ethnicity and Publishing*, ed. Cécile Cottenet (Houndmills, Basingstoke, UK: Palgrave Macmillan, 2014), 29–50.

8. Except in Martin Delany's *Condition, Elevation, Emigration, and Destiny of the Colored People of the United States* (Philadelphia: Published by the Author, 1852), where the sketches are arranged under different headings, such as soldiers, citizens, and businessmen, there is no apparent logic to the organization of biographical sketches in antebellum works.

9. William J. Simmons, *Men of Mark: Eminent, Progressive and Rising* (Cleveland, OH: Geo. M. Rewell, 1887), 549.

10. Simmons, *Men of Mark*, 6, 8, 393, 1036.

11. Henry F. Kletzing and William H. Crogman, *Progress of a Race or The Remarkable Advancement of the Afro-American Negro from the Bondage of Slavery, Ignorance and Poverty to the Freedom of Citizenship, Intelligence, Affluence, Honor and Trust* (Naperville, IL: J. L. Nichols, 1897), preface.

12. Laurie F. Maffly-Kipp, *Setting Down the Sacred Past: African-American Race Histories* (Cambridge, MA: Belknap Press of Harvard University Press, 2010), 233.

13. Timothy Patrick McCarthy and John Stauffer, eds., *Prophets of Protest: Reconsidering the History of American Abolitionism* (New York: New Press, 2006), xiii–xv.

14. Crogman, *Progress*, 143.

15. Michael Winship, "The Rise of a National Book Trade System in the United States," in *A History of the Book in America. Vol. 4: Print in Motion. The Expansion of Publishing and Reading in the United States, 1880–1940*, eds. Carl F. Kaestle and Janice A. Radway (Chapel Hill, NC: American Antiquarian Society and University of North Carolina Press, 2009), 56–77; Lynne Farrington, "'Agents Wanted': Subscription Publishing in America," online exhibition of the Annenberg Rare Book and Manuscript Library, University of Pennsylvania, www.library.upenn.edu/exhibits/rbm/agents/index.html.

16. See also chapter 1 of Elizabeth McHenry, *To Make Negro Literature: Writing, Literary Practice, and African American Authorship* (Durham, NC: Duke University Press, 2021).

17. *Boston Herald*, October 13, 1889, and *Charleston News & Courier*, January 19, 1890, for the draught; *Boston Herald*, February 10, 1890 ("Rewell ratchet mop"); the Rewell-Low Company went into receivership in 1893 (*Plain Dealer*, Cleveland, January 11, 12, 20, 1893; April 18, 1893).

18. *Amelia K. Rewell v. Josie R. Warden et al.*, Ohio Circuit Court Reports – new series, vol. IV, ed. Vinton R. Shepard (Cincinnati: Ohio Law Reporter Co., 1904), 545–56.

19. See, for instance, *Plain Dealer* dated May 4, 1892; May 13, 1900; August 4, 1907; and July 15, 1910.

20. Rare exceptions to this are in 1881, when he advertised for agents to sell a book adapted from British surgeon Pye Henry Chavasse's *Advice to a Wife*, retitled *Man's Strength and Woman's Beauty: A Treatise on the Physical Life of Both Sexes...* (a work "particularly adapted to lady solicitors," *Plain Dealer*, June 28, 1881); in 1887 and 1888, he looked for agents for an anti-Catholic pamphlet entitled *Fifty Years in the Church of Rome*, penned by former

Catholic priest Charles Chiniquy (*Boston Herald*, November 22, 1887; May 17, 1888; among others).

21. A copy at the Library Company of Philadelphia bears the imprint of the publisher, the Park Publishing Company of Hartford, which copyrighted and issued it in 1881, together with other imprints, including Rewell's. Publishers contracted with regional agencies for the distribution of works; see Michael Winship, "Charles Scribner's Sons as Subscription Publishers: The Canvass for Stanley's 'In Darkest Africa' in the Pacific Coast Agency," *Princeton University Library Chronicle* 71.2 (2010), 121–50.

22. See, for instance *New York Age*, July 28, 1888; May 4, 1889.

23. Men are mentioned as well as women, along with a few professors (see *Cleveland Gazette*, June 9 1888; *Washington Bee*, July 14, 1888).

24. "Prof. Lawson on Men of Mark," *Washington Bee*, September 17, 1887.

25. *Cleveland Gazette*, January 7, 1888.

26. *Freeman*, September 20, 1890.

27. *Freeman*, November 15, 1890.

28. *Freeman*, April 5, 1890; the other works were *Webster's Dictionary*, Williams's *History of the Negro Race*, Wilson's *The Black Phalanx*, the *General World Atlas*, and the *Encyclopedia of Human Nature*. The advertisement was repeated in various issues in 1890 and 1891.

29. *Plain Dealer*, May 22 and June 12, 1891.

30. *Freeman*, June 13, 1891.

31. Rayford W. Logan, *The Betrayal of the Negro: From Rutherford B. Hayes to Woodrow Wilson* (New York: Collier Books, 1965), 315.

32. Ernest Kaiser, "Preface," in *Men of Mark* by William J. Simmons (New York: Arno Press/*New York Times*, 1968).

33. Lerone Bennett Jr., "Foreword," in William J. Simmons, *Men of Mark* (Chicago: Johnson, 1970).

34. Houghton Library, Harvard University. Simmons was the nephew of Booker T. Washington.

35. On Nichols and his clever strategies to evade censorship in the latter type of works, see Alicia Puglionesi, "'Your Whole Effort Has Been to Create Desire': Reproducing Knowledge and Evading Censorship in the Nineteenth-Century Subscription Press," *Bulletin of the History of Medicine* 89.3 (2015), 463–90.

36. The college paper, the *North-Western Chronicle*, and Naperville's *Clarion* provide valuable information on Nichols and the company. I am especially grateful to Jennifer Bridge, of Naper Settlement, Naperville, for her help; my thanks also to Mary-Jo Watts for her generosity in sending me valuable material on Nichols, and to Lynne Farrington, Michael Winship, Bryan Ogg, Zachary Bishop, Randall Burkett, and Graham Greer. I am also indebted to many other scholars and curators whom space precludes me from listing here.

37. Prospectus presenting Hertel, Jenkins & Co., ca. 1904, Booker T. Washington Papers, Library of Congress, reel 51.

38. Zinman Collection of Canvassing Books, University of Pennsylvania Library.

39. Keith Arbour, *Canvassing Books, Sample Books, and Subscription Publishers' Ephemera 1833–1951 in the Collection of Michael Zinman* (Ardsley, NY: Haydn Foundation for the Cultural Arts, 1996), introduction.

40. *Dallas Morning News* (white paper), March 31, 1898, repeated. The claim was probably true; in May of the same year, Hertel wrote to Washington that the book was having "a remarkable sale" (Booker T. Washington Papers, Library of Congress, May 23, 1898, reel 141).

41. Des Moines, Iowa, directory for 1898.

42. Hertel tried to get Tuskegee students to sell the work and told Washington that the company employed many students who paid for their education by canvassing books. John A. Hertel to Booker T. Washington, January 18, 1898, Booker T. Washington Papers, Library of Congress, reel 139.

43. Crogman, *Progress*, 570.

44. *Colored American*, June 4, 1898.

45. *Colored American* April 26, 1898, and June 4, 1898; *Broad Ax* (Salt Lake City) January 7, 1899.

46. *Iowa State Bystander*, March 30, 1899; *Washington Bee*, January 28, 1901.

47. Barbara A. Burg and Randall K. Burkett, "Reference Works," in *The Harvard Guide to African American History*, eds. Evelyn Brooks Higginbotham et al. (Cambridge, MA: Harvard University Press, 2001), 26.

48. "Introduction," *Booker T. Washington Papers*, vol. 1: *The Autobiographical Writings* (Champaign: University of Illinois Press, 1972), xvi–xvii.

CHAPTER 20

Aztlan for the Middle Class
Chicano Literary Activism
José Antonio Arellano

During a charged scene in Rudolfo A. Anaya's novel *Heart of Aztlan* (1976), the character Clemente Chávez attends a railroad workers' meeting. Angered by their managers' inattention to the dangerous working conditions claiming employees' lives, and frustrated by their union's complicit failure to intervene, Clemente and the other workers discuss their options. The cacophony of voices offering different strategies – including violent resistance, (new) union organizing, and legal retaliation – threatens to fracture the group into competing factions. The workers quiet down only when a blind bard named Crispín begins to strum his guitar and sing traditional folk songs. They may all disagree about what to do next, but at that moment they exist as a group, listening. As the music affects him, Clemente wonders, "But the strike? The strike and the railroad? What do these stories have to do with that?"[1]

The scene stages one of the most pressing questions concerning the relationship between Mexican American literature and the strand of Chicano activism focused on the working class: What do "stories" have to do with the plight of workers? And the novel as a whole dramatizes an answer. Stories could function as the cultural arm of a nascent labor movement by enabling a group to recognize its solidarity. The function of these stories, and the literature they help constitute, is neither the procurement of policy nor the legislation of tactics. Rather, stories help bring a community into being via a tautology of self-production: a people coming into being via their production of art, the art in turn enabling the people's recognition of itself as "a people." In the novel's last scene, the railroad workers march in unison, proclaiming, "Adelante!" ("Forward!"). Where they are going is left unclear and what they will do once they get there is left unstated, yet the conclusion's forward momentum appears to lead to a utopian, if blurry, horizon.

Were that the end of the story, we might continue to assume that "the people" that Crispín's stories bring together and the "working class" are effectively identical terms. That assumption, however, is complicated by Anaya's prolific body of work, which showcases their ultimate divergence in aims. The following will analyze this complication to reconsider the characterization of Chicano literature as promoting the interests of the Mexican American working class. I start with Anaya because *Heart* tells a relatable story concerning what happens to a Mexican American family when it is forced to change its way of life radically. We might understand this story as a "paradigmatic Chicano narrative" because of this relatability.[2] I argue, however, that the term "Chicano" does not name the various stories involving Mexican Americans; rather, the term implies a *solution* to the delineated problems that such stories convey. This solution centers on a particular conceptualization of culture as made available through self-consciously Chicano literature and art. I will show how the solution as dramatized in this literature became unsustainable during the 1980s, and newer works published since then depict an ongoing ambivalence about the solution's viability. This reconsideration may enable those of us who read and teach literature to question what exactly literary activism enables, who and what this activism is for, and what goals it posits as its aim.

From Labor to Culture

Published in 1976, *Heart of Aztlan* implicitly adduces the events that had taken place a decade prior, in which the playwright Luis Valdez assisted the labor organizing efforts of César Chávez. The bard Crispín can be read as a stand-in for Valdez, whose Teatro Campesino operated as the cultural arm of the effort to organize farmworkers during the mid-1960s. And the novel's central character, Clemente Chávez, could be seen as César Chávez's analog, their names emphasizing the comparison. Teatro Campesino staged Valdez's one-act plays on the back of flatbed trucks situated on the very fields where the migrant fruit and vegetable pickers worked and protested. Workers were invited to fill the acting roles, and the plays were meant to raise the workers' understanding of their situation and solidarity. They learned the value of not crossing the picket lines even as their families faced starvation, and they also learned to connect themselves to a much longer cultural history. One of the imperatives of the Teatro Campesino, according to Francisco Jiménez, was "to inform the Chicano of his rich heritage so as to instill in him pride in his culture."[3] This centuries-long cultural history is evident in Valdez's introduction to *Aztlán: An Anthology of Mexican American Literature* (1972), wherein he claims the Olmecs, Mayans, and Aztecs as Chicano cultural predecessors.[4] Seen in this context, Valdez's style of *indigenismo* and cultural pride can be considered homologous with the activism of labor organizing.

This homology of ethnic culture and labor organizing, however, comes under pressure as Valdéz next writes the play *Zoot Suit* (1978), the local success of which led to its being both staged on Broadway in 1979 and adapted to film in 1981. Valdéz did not "sell out" by turning away from migrant workers in need of a union to appeal to a broader American audience. Instead, his work's trajectory emphasizes what his cultural intervention had always made available: His work makes it possible for the Hollywood movie and Broadway play audiences to feel connected to a larger community even as this connection is more symbolic and affective than practical. Like Anaya's bard Crispín, Valdéz's work makes it possible for the Chicano community to come into being by recognizing itself as such. This brief analysis of Valdéz's example begins to highlight the divergence in aims.

We encounter a similar trajectorial shift in Anaya's novels. Whereas the political drama involving workers and management takes center stage in *Heart*, it is relegated to the margins in Anaya's next novel, *Tortuga* (1979). Considered by Anaya as part of a trilogy that includes *Heart of Aztlan* and his more famous *Bless Me, Ultima* (1972), *Tortuga* tells a related story about a boy (possibly related to the protagonist of *Heart*) who suffers a paralyzing accident and is taken to a hospital for extended therapy. At the hospital, he undergoes a spiritual journey to understand the meaning and purpose of his life. Close to *Tortuga*'s ending, the boy receives a letter from his mother, in which she informs him of two things: "The battle" between workers and management "has continued. It is like a war. Nothing is settled. The workers are without work." And she informs him of the bard Crispín's death. "That is why I am writing. He left you his guitar, the one he would play in the evenings."[5] The news from home interrupts the novel's plot, and the phrase "the workers are without work" dampens the optimism with which *Heart of Aztlan* had ended. While the persistence of both the workers' "battle" and the ancient cultural "stories" could continue to suggest their interconnectedness, *Tortuga*'s plot and the trilogy of which it is a part focus mostly on the continuation of culture at the expense of the depiction of class struggle. The boy will become the bard who relates the stories of a people who are sometimes workers, sometimes not, but always identifiable as "a people." In short, Anaya's novels depict how a cultural tradition can and does persist independently of political concerns and outcomes. Although this tradition could have a temporary rallying effect when used to address localized conflicts, say, between workers and management, such conflicts are but blips along a cosmological timeline.[6]

The Chicano Solution

This is not to say that Anaya's fiction does not attend to historical conditions leading to displacement. Indeed, his novels dramatize how culture can sustain a people battered by economic shifts. In *Heart*, Clemente's family must figure out what life looks like when they are no longer spatially and spiritually anchored by an increasingly unsustainable agrarian way of life. The family is forced to move into a city that cannot sustain Clemente's sense of self. Newly employed, Clemente's daughters begin to assert their independence and question Clemente's authority over their behavior and bodies. Clemente's sons consider the dangerous allure of life on the streets, where respect, money, and diversion appear readily available. When Clemente loses his job at the railroad, he gradually slips into alcoholism and despair because his life "no longer had meaning" (*Heart*, 121). The relocation of the family thus entails a crisis of patriarchy, which the novel parallels with the railroad workers' crisis of unsafe working conditions. As one railroad worker puts it, "the familia without a strong father soon falls apart ... a pueblo without a good leader is not united in its effort to serve the people" (*Heart*, 83). Leadership and patriarchy operate as homologous terms in need of the scaffolding that Crispín's stories could provide. This is why when Clemente reaches the nadir of his despair, he nearly drinks himself to death until he sees "the face of his father" (*Heart*, 121). The approaching figure that looks like his father turns out to be Crispín, who becomes Clemente's spiritual guide, helping him find his purpose. "That is what I need to live!" Clemente comes to discover. "I will search for those signs, I will find that magic heart of our land about which you whisper, and I will wrestle from it the holy power to help my people!" (*Heart*, 123). He comes to realize that the "stories" conveyed through Crispín's songs already reside within him. He learns how to take a psychic journey within himself and tap into his embodied "memory," thereby discovering a long-standing tradition of ancient archetypal myths captured in Mesoamerican – and now Mexican American – storytelling. Stories, and the culture they transmit, enable the rise of a messianic patriarch who will lead his people.

Anaya's writing could function as readers' symbolic spiritual guide, providing them with the archetypal stories that connect them to a way of life, a culture. This culture provides the psychic scaffolding necessary to maintain a sense of their selves as they are continually barraged by a modernized life devoid of a spiritual and agrarian foundation. Like Clemente, readers must learn to search Anaya's texts for "the signs" and interpret their symbolism, an interpretive experience that connects them to a – to our – mythical past. Literature, here, appears to function as a source of both a symbolic (substitute) paternalism to guide us and a metaphorical (metaphysical) essentialism to unite us. The people who make up the "us" share an archetypal "heart," the mythic blood of which pumps through us all. We need only interpret the signs and search within ourselves to find there our spiritually anchoring home, Aztlan.

How this symbolic search will help those in the position of *Heart*'s characters, however, is left to the reader to imagine. One character describes his predicament: "We're in the same pinch all the time just holding our noses above debts so we won't drown, hoping things at the shops don't get worse and hoping el Super doesn't shut off our credit at the store" (*Heart*, 16). These economic problems resulted in part from the shift during the 1970s from a manufacturing-based economy to one of finance and service employment. The situation for manufacturing and railroad employees would only worsen during the 1980s when deregulation became the norm (evident in such acts as the Staggers Rail Act of 1980 and the Northeast Rail Service Act of 1981). While increasing the industry's rate of return, the benefits of deregulation did not amount to job security or workers' well-being. As Judith Stein has argued, the driving assumption during the deregulation of the 1980s was that the advances in the industries' profit would eventually benefit the workers.[7] The motivation behind the Chicano cultural intervention reproduces this metonymic faith: What is good for Clemente will be good for the people he leads.

The ultimate divergence between the function of a mythic culture and the needs of the working class highlights how Chicano literary activism has mostly operated as the psychic support for a growing Mexican American middle class, especially the students who headed to college to improve their class status. Though this may appear as an unfair characterization, we need only turn to Rodolfo "Corky" Gonzales's poem "Yo soy Joaquín" (1967) to see the Chicano intervention placed in relation to upward class mobility. Widely mimeographed and performed during student conferences and student demonstrations, the poem is generally understood as one of the primary works inaugurating the Chicano literary renaissance. Notice how the poem presents the problem it addresses:

> My fathers have lost the economic battle
> and won the struggle of cultural survival.
> And now! I must choose between the paradox of
> victory of the spirit, despite physical hunger,
> or to exist in the grasp of American social neurosis,
> sterilization of the soul and a full stomach.[8]

The "paradox" for a new Mexican American generation, here, centers on the simultaneous desire to achieve upward class mobility while retaining cultural integrity: How can one climb the class hierarchy without selling out? How might one be both economically secure and culturally proud? This way of framing the problem seems to accept the racialization of class but also points to a Chicano solution: the gendered identity declared and enabled by the poem itself.

Professors associated with the Chicano movement thus assumed the responsibility of making visible to their undergraduates the identity enabled by Chicano literature by editing anthologies that provided a forum for neglected voices.[9] The underlying metonymic belief motivating the Chicano literary intervention understands college undergraduates as stand-ins for the much larger percentage of Mexican Americans not in college. The very faith in Chicano literature's liberating potential rests on the belief that a politics of redistribution – through which workers might begin to avail themselves of the profits their labor makes possible – is nested *within* a more primordial politics of recognition. The identity asserted by these anthologies (with titles including *We Are Chicanos*) creates a sense of unity between college students' cultural alienation and workers' labor alienation by suggesting that art expresses both types of experiences simultaneously by uniting them in a shared culture.

Freedom, in this account, is enabled through self-representational acts of resistance against the circulated caricatures of the oppressed. The gains made by social movements in the United States and liberation movements in Africa fueled the momentum leading to the establishment in Berkeley of the first independent Chicano publishing house, Quinto Sol. Through its journal *El Grito*, Quinto Sol offered a venue for articles, poetry, short stories, and visual artists' portfolios, which collectively helped to debunk the existing social scientific mischaracterizations of Mexican "traditional culture." In the social science literature of the time, Mexicans were depicted as "cultureless" or as having a damaging traditional culture that prevented generations of Mexican Americans from achieving individuality, goal orientation, and economic success.[10] In 1969, Quinto Sol published the first anthology of Chicano literature, titled *El Espejo—The Mirror*, with a preface by Octavio

Ignacio Romano-V declaring the importance of self-recognition through self-representation: "To know themselves and who they are, there are those who need no reflection other than their own. Thus ... EL ESPEJO—THE MIRROR. Enough said ... let this book speak for itself, and for the people that it represents."[11] The metonymic power of Chicano literature invoked by the preface does not appear to require any explanatory commentary because it can speak for itself *as* "the people."

"Please, Let Me Tell Your Story."

As the Mexican American population within the United States continued to grow, and as the gendered and often nationalistic parameters of the Chicano identity continued to be challenged, faith in this metonymic substitution waned considerably. Although the term "Chicano" continues to circulate, its use is often associated with a degree of ambivalence that is dramatized in literary works of the 1990s and 2000s. Daniel Chacón's provocatively titled collection of short stories, *Chicano Chicanery* (1996), for example, highlights this ambivalence in the short story "Aztlán, Oregon" – a story whose protagonist is also named Chavez. A few flash-backs throughout the story show how Ben Chavez, an anchorman on the local news, had been a "gang member" without much of a future.[12] As a high school student, Ben is forced to work for a presidential campaign to earn credit for his civics course. Ben picks "an old radical named Marta Banuelos" who had no chance of winning because she had launched her campaign on "a platform telling white people to go back to Europe and leave Aztlán to the Indians" ("Aztlán," 64). While out canvassing for Banuelos, rival gang members surround the younger Ben and threaten to "slice him." In a desperate effort to hold off the assault, Ben begins to recite the Chicano party line he recently learned from Banuelos. He realizes that the Chicano unity he talks about becomes momentarily actualized by his words. So long as he kept talking and they kept nodding, he was safe. And when Ben turns in his essay "on the importance of the Banuelos campaign to Chicano unity, an historical perspective," his teacher declares it the "best paper [he had] ever read on this assignment" ("Aztlán," 68). The incident thus launches two things: Ben's unexpected career as a news anchor (academically motivated, he goes to college and majors in journal-ism) and Ben's political consciousness (*conscientizado*; he understands himself as part of history and a collective).

The story contrasts the idealism of Ben's awakened youth with his present-day complacency, his moderate success leading to at least one

European vacation and a new car. Looking at his naked, flabby body in the mirror, Ben realizes, "He *was* getting fat. Fighting for his people is what he used to be about, but ever since he'd been away from Aztlán, all he took care of was himself" ("Aztlán," 69, original emphasis). So when he has the chance to advance his career (potentially scoring a national news anchor position) by recording "a good feature" on "Hispanic street gangs," his enthusiasm to "tell it like it is" and "say something radical" rejuvenates him ("Aztlán," 72–73). As he looks for people to interview on the street, gang members once again confront him, and he again diffuses their potential hostility by talking to them about Chicano unity:

> I wanna tell it like it is. White people don't know shit about us. I understand why you guys are in gangs, man. It's this *pinche* society, *verdad?* Brown people don't have a chance in this white, racist society . . . I'm just a Chicano, all right? I mean no disrespect to your barrio, all right? I'm here because I need to tell your story. Please, let me tell your story. ("Aztlán," 72)

As he recites the standard Chicano line, he notices how his gold watch and necktie mark a class difference impeding the Chicano unity he is trying to establish. Yet the greatest obstacle to that unity is one gang member's resoundingly clear response to Ben's narrative. After Ben finishes talking, the gang member named Rafa asks, "What the fuck are you talking about?" He is more impressed that Ben appears on television than he is interested in Ben's account of Chicano activism:

> He [Ben] had wanted it to say something radical, but when Rafa [the gang member] got to the heart of what *he* wanted to say, Ben didn't want to hear it. Rafa had a dream of owning a house, having a wife, and kids and "nice things." He had no consciousness of a political struggle, no concept of the Chicano movement. . . . Rafa said that if he could go to college he would want to major in business. He could see himself as a businessman, "making all kinds of money and shit." Whenever Ben tried to get what he thought of society into the interview—whenever he suggested that it was racist and responsible for the condition of Chicanos—Rafa looked at him funny. . . . "Well, I don't know about that," Rafa would say, "but . . ." and he'd continue saying things that hurt Ben to hear. ("Aztlán," 72)

Ben wants the story that gave *his* life meaning to be reaffirmed by the person he is placing as the stand-in for the community. What this person recites instead is the story of wanting to enter into a class that enables material comfort, yet a class that is fractured by the very self-interest that brings it into being.[13] And it is *this* story that not only articulates Rafa's desires but also describes what Ben's life has become.

But how is the reader supposed to *feel* about the waning of the Chicano solution's ability to galvanize a sense of solidarity? Should we lament the waning of this solution, which no longer appeals to a younger generation? If so, readers might consider "Aztlán, Oregon" itself *as* the medium for consciousness raising. Literature and history about Mexican Americans can, with the aid of encouraging teachers, bolster the self-pride necessary to envision personal success. The younger generation has yet to figure out what they want because they have yet to read the books that will show them who they are, books that do *that* by teaching their readers their history. The younger Mexican American generation has lost something like the Chicano narrative; Chicano literature – like *Chicano Chicanery* – can begin to give it back to them. "Aztlán, Oregon" is not unsympathetic to this approach. The plot includes a detail about Ben reading a mystery novel in which the "bad guy" is a caricatured Mexican ("*Señor*, I theenk your time she is up"). Ben dislikes the mystery novels and wants them out of his house. So just as Ben benefited from the political process, he might have also benefited from reading the mystery novels of writers including Lucha Corpi and Manuel Ramos. By providing a much more nuanced depiction of Mexican American characters, such novels could go a long way to correct the problems of stereotyping. If Rafa (the interviewed gang member) had access to this literature, he might (like Ben) gain the self-confidence to imagine a future that defies what others have predicted for him.

Even if readers accept this as a possible interpretation – that what Rafa and those like him need is Chicano literature and Chicano politics – we would still need to explain why the present-day Ben appears so miserable. He, after all, *was* exposed to the Chicano movement. The sense of belonging that this movement induced within him is one that he cannot maintain. Ben tries calling his father (who keeps asking him, incredulously, how much he spent on his car),[14] and he visits small towns "where some Mexican farmers lived just to hear Spanish being spoken" (though he never tries speaking with them).[15] Ben's moderately successful career appears to separate him from his family and the farmers. Perhaps, then, Ben needs to find a community of middle-class Chicanos who would reciprocate the vision he has of himself. He needs to find Aztlán somewhere in Oregon – a place where he might receive the life-affirming recognition he needs. A belief in the Chicano solution could maintain such a group's cohesion and its self-understanding.

Yet "Aztlán, Oregon" highlights this solution's untenability.[16] Readers can hear in Ben's desperate plea – "Please, let me tell your story" – an allegory of the fiction writer's continued insistence to be the conduit for the voice of the people. Chacón's short story allows its readers to consider just what would be gained when a person in Ben's position – advancing his career – places a spotlight on youths at risk. The suggestion that a spotlight on poverty addresses its problems implies that the structural condition of poverty is the product of a fundamental lack of empathy and that an appropriate response to the situation is primarily affective. The story instead suggests that perhaps the material gains will be Ben's alone. Ironically, Ben needs a community more than "the community" he imagines speaking for needs him. Although he can try to improve a people's situation, it is the very effort to improve their lot that gives him his sense of self because "fighting for his people is what he used to be about." Without the community and that effort, he's just a guy, getting fat. This depicted ambivalence points to a diagnosis of the problems affecting Mexican Americans that the Chicano solution's focus on cultural empowerment does not address.

"What Aztlán Is Really All About"

A novel published more than a decade later, Manuel Ramos's *King of the Chicanos* (2010), is also simultaneously nostalgic of Chicano activism while dramatizing a heightened sense of ambivalence about this activism's efficacy. The novel commemorates the rise of the messianic patriarch, the Chicano leader of the people who will usher in their salvation. The plot follows Ramón Hidalgo as he becomes a migrant worker, political organizer, and then Chicano militant activist. The small but real gains of the movement fall short of the envisioned utopian horizon, and Ramón is left disillusioned. No longer enchanted by Chicano politics, Ramón turns to art by opening up a café that functions as a makeshift cultural center. He wonders if by dispensing art to his patrons he has finally found his purpose. By imagining himself as a curator of culture, he can continue to envision himself as a Chicano, as part of a community, because a sense of community coheres when based on shared tastes in art.[17] Art can become a corrective to disillusion because its circulation among a public brings that very public into being.[18] In short, Ramón's small business creates the conditions for Aztlán's possibility. As he puts it, "This could be what Aztlán is really all about."[19]

King of the Chicanos would thus appear to suggest that what a character like Ben in "Aztlán, Oregon" needs is what Ramón discovers. Ben could envision himself as the person who gives gang members (like Rafa)

Chicano literature. This literature would, in turn, provide Rafa with the political consciousness and historical awareness necessary for him to persevere. Indeed, this is why *King of the Chicanos* includes an appended reading list of nonfiction books about the Chicano movement, and why the novel narrates some of the historical events affecting Mexican Americans, which it incorporates by depicting them as part of the protagonist's world-historical life. The novel highlights the merits of this type of cultural, historical education by showing how one of the café's younger customers, Roberto Urban, benefits from Ramón's influence. After being exposed to Chicano literature, Roberto proceeds to go to college and entertains the idea of becoming a lawyer, but he realizes that his passion centers on literature. When Ramón asks him what kind of literature Roberto would write ("Chicano Literature? Or maybe it's Latino Literature these days?"), Roberto responds with a decidedly Chicano answer: "I'm developing a mystery story. A Chicano mystery story ... Back when, during the Movement, there was a killing, and that killing haunted this guy who used to be heavy into the Movement."[20] Describing the very plot of Manuel Ramos's own first mystery novel, *The Ballad of Rocky Ruiz* (1993), Roberto's mystery story could be what someone like Ben in "Aztlán, Oregon" might read at a young age, benefiting his self-perception. (No more "*Señor*, I theenk your time she is up" nonsense.) Roberto is able to publish four collections of poetry that help him secure a position as a "Chicano Studies and English associate professor," his educational experience thus placing him in a position to further benefit a younger generation.[21] Roberto, we might say, has made it, and he can now help others make it too.

The novel qualifies this optimistic Chicano conclusion, however, by depicting Roberto's "Latino" ambivalence. Once Roberto finds the very job that allows him to live the life he wanted – "books and reading and writing were what he valued most" – his poetry takes an introspective turn. He feels ambivalent, publishing a book titled *Mezcla: This Mestizo Thing Has Me All Mixed Up*, the poems of which "poked fun at the author and his attempts to rationalize his existence as a middle-class, middle-aged, successful Latino who still thought of himself as a young, struggling Chicano."[22] The confusion he feels is not simply that of *mestizaje*, which after all could be said to be constitutive of the Mexican American identity as such. (Why should he feel confused about the "mestizo thing" *now*? What changed?) What confuses his sense of self seems to be the result of his new class status, which separates him from the disadvantaged community that gives his identity as a Chicano meaning. Once comfortably situated, Roberto wonders if he could still claim to be "Chicano" insofar as being a Chicano meant representing a struggling community. The novel, here, is less sanguine, suggesting that once Roberto is a part of the university, he is a "Latino."[23]

But why should this be the case? Why not show how Roberto continues to fight for *la causa* within the hallowed walls of academia? After all, one of the primary initiatives of the Chicano movement was the integration of the university, which Chicanos would change from within. Chicanos could update the university's methodologies, in part by debunking a false faith in the objectivity of the social sciences, enabling them to revise facile accounts of Mexican "passivity."[24] They could rewrite the literary histories, thereby helping to create a much richer narrative that does not simply begin with the New England colonies.[25] And by introducing new Chicano voices, the literary representation of Mexican Americans would counteract the reductive caricatures in canonized American literature.[26] Roberto could see himself as clearing a path into the university that younger Chicanos might follow. And just as Ramón, disillusioned with the movement, could find Aztlan in his café/cultural center, Roberto could have reimagined Aztlan *as* the university, the mythical homeland now continually augmented by being refashioned within the nation's centers of higher education. *This* Aztlan could become the homeland for those wanting to reaffirm their Chicano identity by circulating the media that constitute the Chicano public's cohesion; the place where the struggle for publication and tenure *is* the struggle for community; where Chicanos can awaken their students' political consciousness by introducing them to their histories that had been heretofore excluded from their education.

That the novel does not take this route suggests the waning of this form of the Chicano solution, a wane that itself suggests that as long as the goal of struggle continues to be the Chicano integration of the middle class, the resulting ambivalence might be inevitable because the success of this integration (however limited) may not ever be enough. This grim conclusion dampens the optimism of the advocates of Chicano and now Latinx literature. When José F. Aranda calls for a "New Chicano studies" in his aspirationally titled *When We Arrive: A New Literary History of Mexican America*, readers of the work should ask: *Who* constitutes this "*we*"? *Where* exactly are we going? How will we know when we get there? How will literature help us answer these questions? Ilan Stavans, the editor of the *Norton Anthology of Latino Literature* (2010), offers some potential answers. Referring to the monumental Latino *Anthology*, he states, "In the last several decades, Latinos finally have been entering the middle class.

This anthology not only explains the forces behind that economic move but justifies the move. It is a book that all middle-class Latinos need, proof that we've made it: We've arrived."[27] Stavans's celebratory declaration suggests that the gradual inclusion into a class marks the goal that has been centuries in the making and that the relative success of the few counts for the whole. A novel such as *King*, however, depicts the resulting ambivalence of a member of the middle class and his nostalgia for a community of solidarity and shared purpose. This depiction suggests that however comfortable a middle-class existence can be, there is the lurking recognition that it is not the good life that might otherwise be possible.

Notes

1. Rudolfo A. Anaya, *Heart of Aztlan* (Berkeley: Editorial Justa, 1976), 86. I refer to the novel as *Heart* hereafter.
2. Ramón Saldívar uses this phrase when analyzing the novel *Pocho* (1959), which he sees as providing "the paradigmatic Chicano narrative." There are many variations on this story: Mexicans fleeing to the United States in the aftermath of the Mexican Revolution; Mexican Americans displaced from the American Southwest when their agricultural lives are no longer economically viable; Mexican landowners living in California being dispossessed of their land by a government failing to meet its end of the Treaty of Guadalupe Hidalgo; and Mexican and Mexican American migrant workers traveling across the United States in search of meager wages.
3. Francisco Jiménez, "Dramatic Principles of the Teatro Campesino," *Bilingual Review / La Revista Bilingüe* 2.1–2 (1975), 102.
4. Luis Valdez and Stan Steiner, eds., *Aztlán: An Anthology of Mexican American Literature* (New York: Knopf, 1972).
5. Rudolfo Anaya, *Tortuga* (Berkeley: Editorial Justa, 1979), 168.
6. In Anaya's Sonny Baca detective novel series, the dimensions of the ongoing "war" expand until they encompass the very battle between good and evil as such. The drama of that battle is transhistorically cyclical, manifesting itself archetypically.
7. Judith Stein, *Pivotal Decade: How the United States Traded Factories for Finance in the Seventies* (New Haven, CT: Yale University Press, 2010).
8. Rodolfo "Corky" Gonzales, "I Am Joaquín, an Epic Poem, 1967," in *Message to Aztlán: Selected Writings* (Houston, TX: Arte Publico, 2001), 16.
9. Philip D. Ortego, editor of one such anthology, for example, laments the psychological effects of cultural deprivation on Chicanos' self-esteem. Philip D. Ortego y Gasca, *We Are Chicanos: An Anthology of Mexican-American Literature* (New York: Washington Square, 1973), 296.
10. Octavio Ignacio Romano-V, "Minorities, History, and the Cultural Mystique," *El Grito* 1 (1967), 5–11. Octavio Ignacio Romano-V, "The Anthropology and Sociology of the Mexican-Americans," *El Grito* 2 (1968): 13–26.

11. Octavio Ignacio Romano-V, "Preface," in *El Espejo—The Mirror: Selected Chicano Literature* (Berkeley, CA: Quinto Sol, 1969), n.p.
12. Daniel Chacón, "Aztlán, Oregon," in *Chicano Chicanery: Short Stories* (Houston, TX: Arte Público, 2000), 63. Subsequent references are cited in parentheses in the text.
13. The sense of disillusion associated with the rise of the bourgeoisie coincides with that rise, the dissatisfaction emerging coterminously with the undeniable benefits it brought into being. For a relevant account of this dissatisfaction with modernity, see Robert B. Pippin, *Modernism as a Philosophical Problem: On the Dissatisfactions of European High Culture* (Cambridge, MA: Blackwell, 1991).
14. Chacón, "Aztlán," 70.
15. Chacón, "Aztlán," 63.
16. Suppose that a candidate like Marta Banuelos *had* won the election, leading, somehow, to every person of European descent being forced out of "Aztlán." How would this political platform address the structures of impoverishment that would remain, only now operated by people from a different descent? Who or what would "the enemy" be then?
17. See Nicholas Brown's encyclopedic entry on "Aesthetics," in *The Johns Hopkins Guide to Literary Theory and Criticism*, eds. Michael Groden, Martin Kreiswirth, and Imre Szeman (Baltimore, MD: Johns Hopkins University Press, 2005), 7.
18. For an influential account of publics, see Michael Warner, *Publics and Counterpublics* (New York: Zone Books, 2005).
19. Manuel Ramos, *King of the Chicanos: A Novel* (San Antonio, TX: Wings, 2010), 147.
20. Ramos, *King*, 156.
21. Ramos, *King*, 168.
22. Ramos, *King*, 168.
23. Popularized in the 1980s, the more inclusive term "Latino" captures the much-touted value of multiculturalism. It appears in Ramos's novel as something like a polite, inclusive term that erases the specific histories of racialization, political struggle, and economic exploitation among groups as vastly different as "Cubans," "Mexicans," and "Puerto Ricans."
24. See Michael Soldatenko, *Chicano Studies: The Genesis of a Discipline* (Tucson: University of Arizona Press, 2009).
25. See the introduction of Dorothy E. Harth and Lewis M. Baldwin, *Voices of Aztlan: Chicano Literature of Today* (New York: New American Library, 1974).
26. Philip D. Ortego Y Gasca, *We Are Chicanos: An Anthology of Mexican-American Literature* (New York: Washington Square, 1973).
27. "What Defines Latino Literature?" Interview with Ilan Stavans by Chloë Schama, *Smithsonian Magazine*, December 2, 2010, www.smithsonianmag.com/arts-culture/what-defines-latino-literature-73399798/.

CHAPTER 21

The Racial Underground

Kinohi Nishikawa

Frank Marshall Davis was synonymous with Chicago's literary scene in the 1930s and 1940s. A Kansas-born migrant to the city, Davis rose through the ranks of its black newspapers to become executive editor of the Associated Negro Press. His creative skills as a poet were honed through the Federal Writers' Project, part of the New Deal's Works Progress Administration, as well as the South Side Writers Group, a collective of artists and intellectuals who paved the way for what is now known as the Black Chicago Renaissance. Davis published three well-received volumes of poetry in the 1930s and became widely known for his protest verse. He was viewed as a contemporary of and literary equal to Richard Wright.

That all must have seemed a lifetime ago when Davis gave a reading at the Afro-American Historical Society in San Francisco in 1973. It was his first trip back to the continental United States after having moved to Honolulu, Hawaii, in 1948. Although he had picked up newspaper work in the isles, Davis saw his star fade over time, isolated as he was from the civil rights movement sweeping the rest of the nation – which made what one audience member said to him at the reading all the more surprising. In a moment to themselves, an African American bookstore owner referenced a book he suspected Davis had written: "I mean *Sex Rebel: Black*. Although it did not list your name as author, I wracked my brain trying to figure out what other black writer might be in Hawaii. I could think of nobody but you. Then I reread your poetry. I saw the similarities in style and phraseology. I hit it right on the head, didn't I?"[1] In response to the query, Davis confessed he was indeed the man behind the pseudonym Bob Greene, and that he had authored the pornographic autobiographical novel whose parenthetical subtitle was *Memoirs of a Gash Gourmet*. The book had come out in 1968 with the country's leading publisher of sex paperbacks, Greenleaf Classics.

You won't find mention of *Sex Rebel: Black* in Valerie Babb's *A History of the African American Novel*, or in Bernard W. Bell's earlier, more focused study *The Contemporary African American Novel*. Nor does it appear in the Project on the History of Black Writing's list of novels published between 1965 and 1969.[2] Davis's use of a pseudonym may be partially responsible for this oversight. Yet dealing with pen names is a regular feature of literary scholarship, and some of the most famous African American novelists, such as Toni Morrison, are known by their pseudonyms. A likelier explanation for the obscurity of *Sex Rebel: Black* is its pornographic content and the presumed uses for such explicit content. Badly in need of funds, Davis wrote the book as a lurid exposé of interracial sex, partner swapping, and bisexual exploration during an era, the 1930s, that is not typically associated with sexual liberation. Davis's interlocutor notwithstanding, *Sex Rebel: Black* would have been sold to white readers eager to consume fantasies of racial licentiousness *without* having to question their own racial privilege. The book was one of many paperbacks that defined the market for what I elsewhere have termed "black sleaze."[3]

The literary history of what this chapter will call the *racial underground* begins with the rise of black sleaze in post–World War II print culture. Reflecting the basest projections of white fantasy at the precise moment when African Americans were pushing for civil rights is the central irony of this market niche. And though black sleaze was immensely popular, it was also something of a guilty pleasure – explicitly lowbrow, the paperbacks were sold alongside (and meant to be read like) tabloid newspapers and pinup magazines. The smuttiness of sleaze ensured that its popularity went mostly uncommented on, certainly during its time but even more so today, as its titles remain the province of fans and collectors, not scholars and librarians.

Yet as Davis's experience implies, black sleaze is important to recover precisely because African American authors were aware of it as a significant, if subterranean, segment of the literary marketplace. Even though the racial underground flourished in the market for bad taste, it was also popular enough to pay the bills for a struggling writer or professional hack. Against the notion of authorial genius, the racial underground points to an understudied aspect of literary history: the writers who, by necessity or by choice, attempt to mold their output into the most generic categories available.

This is not the only reason to attend to the racial underground. Though black sleaze was a powerful diversion for white readers during the civil rights movement, the racial underground's infrastructure laid the groundwork for the rise of black pulp fiction and related popular print commodities in the age of Black Power. In some cases, the same publishers who had brought out sleaze turned their attention to releasing pulp *by* black authors *for* black readers. The most notable publisher to make this transition was Los Angeles–based Holloway House, a white-owned operation that became virtually synonymous with the racial underground in the 1970s and 1980s. An enduring irony of the post–civil rights period is that the infrastructure of the sleaze period was repurposed to cultivate a popular literary culture for black readers.

This chapter describes and analyzes the shift from black sleaze to black pulp fiction. The history it recounts is not simply one of popular literary taste. Instead, it takes as its subject the underbelly of literary taste as such. Although self-styled "outsider" literature is a centuries-old phenomenon, the conjuncture of race and bad taste is peculiar to post–World War II print culture and the social changes it both registered and responded to. What made the racial underground a contentious market niche was that it reveled in illiberal, antisocial messages precisely while mainstream society was pursuing a liberal, integrationist agenda. By "underground," then, this chapter means not strictly illicit or even subcultural but *oppositional to* the good taste of readers, subjects, and citizens.[4] Exactly who identified with such opposition will emerge as an important factor in tracing how the racial underground changed over the years.

***

Essential to the mid-twentieth-century periodization of the racial underground is the so-called paperback revolution. As a format, the modern paperback book was, according to Beth Luey, not so much a "technological innovation" as a "marketing and selling revolution." Although paperbound books had existed in various manifestations since the nineteenth century, it was not until the founding of Pocket Books and the opening of the New York office of England-based Penguin Books in 1939 that mass-market paperbacks altered the course of publishing history. A postwar economic boom, combined with returning GIs' familiarity with government-issued paperbacks known as Armed Services Editions, fueled a tremendous demand for mass-market literature in the late 1940s and throughout the 1950s. Luey's statistics tell the story: "In 1947 approximately 95 million mass-market paperbacks were sold for slightly more than $14 million. Five years later, 270 million copies were sold for $40 million; in 1959 nearly 286 million copies sold for $67 million." By this last date, paperback sales exceeded hardcover trade sales for the first time, "even though paperbacks were much cheaper than hardcover books."[5]

Thomas L. Bonn, Kenneth C. Davis, Paula Rabinowitz, and others have argued that the paperback revolution instigated a democratizing of letters in American culture.[6] The cheap and handy mass-market format made books that had been prohibitively expensive and designed for upper-class consumption far more accessible to everyday readers. A classic work of literature or a recent best-selling title now could be had for two bits. Moreover, because paperbacks were distributed like magazines, rather than conventional (hardcover) books, one could find them "on newsstands and in drugstores, variety stores, tobacconists, railroad stations, and other locations visited by thousands of people who might never have entered a bookstore."[7] Soon "quality" paperback books seemed to be everywhere, forcing traditional publishing houses to play catch-up in terms of negotiating the market.

As edifying as the paperback revolution sounds, like any innovation in media, the mass-market format was susceptible to baser pleasures. Scholars of the paperback revolution have noted how reprints of even classic literature tended to feature scantily clad women on their covers. Harking back to the pulp and pinup magazine covers of the 1930s and 1940s, respectively, illustrators of paperback covers made no secret of the fact that sex appeal was the order of the day. Less acknowledged, however, is how race intersected with sex on many of these covers.

Interracial sex was a consistent theme in the popular literature of the postwar era. Even hardcover publishers recognized the public's fascination with books that framed the question of racial equality through the taboo on interracial sex. But when these books were reissued by paperback houses, their content was repackaged in ways designed to capture the attention of consumers. That usually meant gaudy illustrations displaying alternately titillating and lurid scenes of racial and sexual exploitation. Jack Woodford and John B. Thompson's *Honey*, for example, originally published by Arco in 1951, was given a complete makeover by Beacon in 1956. The new cover transforms the title into a tagline – "Tawny Flesh—Reckless Lust—And Lips That Were Sweeter Than. . . . . . .HONEY" – and exhibits an illustration of a blond man seizing a young woman of color, whose bust is ready to burst out of her unbuttoned top (Figure 21.1). Priced at 35 cents, the format of this edition was cheap, and so was its appeal to consumer instincts.

Paperback publishers' marketing of interracial sex was more fraught when it came to books dealing with black men accused of violating white women. In 1949, for instance, Chester B. Himes's *If He Hollers Let Him Go* (1945) was reissued by New American Library's popular Signet

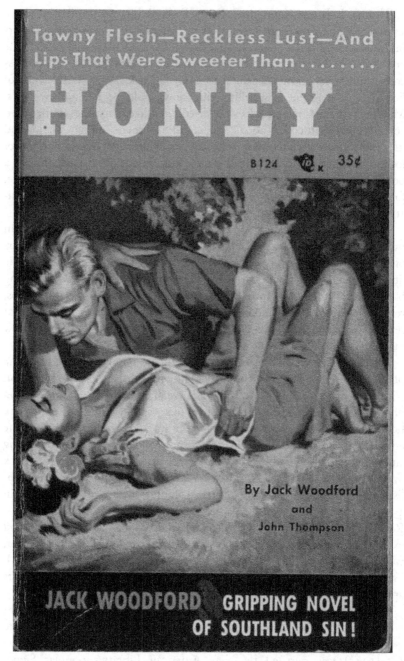

Figure 21.1   Front cover of *Honey*, reprinted by Beacon in 1956. Cover artist unknown

imprint. On the paperback cover, James Avati's illustration practically hails the reader with the accusatory finger Madge Perkins points at protagonist Bob Jones (Figure 21.2). A few years later, in 1952, Avati created a similar scene for the reprint of Erskine Caldwell's *Place Called Estherville* (1949), only this time the white man is shown visiting retribution upon the black male character. In their static, sensationalized display, these illustrations aim not only to put the black man in his place but to sexualize the white woman supposedly in need of defense. This duality is made especially clear in Lou Marchetti's cover art for the 1958 book *Summer Boy* (Figure 21.3), Pyramid's paperback reissue of Walter B. Lowrey's 1953 novel *Watch Night*. Although here the black man's visage elicits a degree of pathos, the outright sexualization of the white woman, posed as if she were a pinup model, redounds on the guilt of the former. These books by Himes, Caldwell, and Lowrey are very different in how they approach the taboo on interracial sex. However, driven by sales, their paperback packaging proved remarkably similar in terms of playing into the dialectic of disgust and desire at the heart of readers' fascination with interracial sex.

The paperback revolution was such a success in the 1950s that authors who had hoped to build respectable careers in the first-run hardcover market soon found themselves selling directly to the paperback houses. This was the case for Curtis Lucas, a black novelist whose urban, hard-boiled style rivaled that of his contemporary Himes. Lucas's career began with the crime novels *Flour Is Dusty* (1943) and *Third Ward, Newark* (1946), both published in hardcover by Dorrance and Ziff-Davis, respectively. Like Himes, Lucas sought to unsettle white readers by confronting racial and sexual taboos, particularly in the context of urban America, where white authors generally feared to tread. But when *Third Ward, Newark* came out in paperback from Lion Books in 1952, Lucas, like Himes, found his main character's perspective displaced by the white gaze. In the cover illustration (Figure 21.4), Wonnie Brown is shown in a state of violation, clinging to a road sign as two white men lurk in the background. The tableau falls underneath the incongruous line, "A NEGRO GIRL GETS THE JOLT OF HER LIFE!" Even here, a book about white sexual exploitation in the North cannot help but render the black female character desirable precisely in her defilement. Little is known about Lucas except that he spent the remainder of his career writing sex-fueled interracial melodramas for Lion (*So Low, So Lonely* [1952], *Angel* [1953], *Lila* [1955]) and Beacon (*Forbidden Fruit* [1953]), the last of which sported a tagline summing up his late output: "SHE WAS WHITE—HE WAS NOT!"

Figure 21.2   Front cover of *If He Hollers Let Him Go*, reprinted by Signet in 1949.
Cover art by James Avati

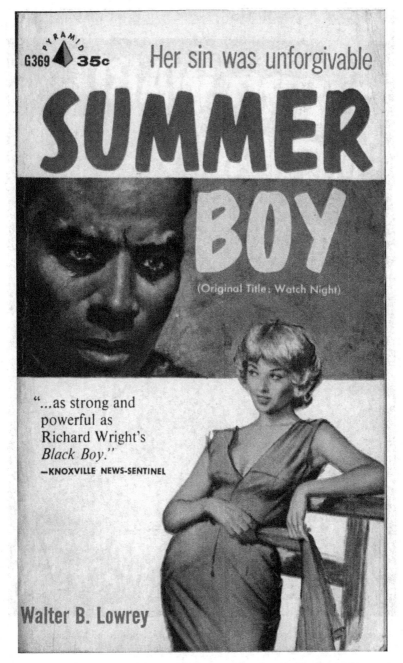

Figure 21.3 Front cover of *Summer Boy*, reprinted and retitled by Pyramid in 1958. Cover art by Lou Marchetti

Figure 21.4   Front cover of *Third Ward, Newark*, reprinted by Lion in 1952.
Cover artist unknown

The trajectory of Lucas's career tracks the emergence of the racial underground in the literary marketplace. Whereas paperback houses had initially cashed in on sexed-up reprints of classic literature or contemporary hardcover books, it soon became clear that they could be even more profitable publishing paperback "originals" that were written specifically for their format. That was the case for Lucas's final four books, but it also applied to Himes's *The Primitive* (1955) and Richard Wright's *Savage Holiday* (1954). The kind of sensationalized storytelling expected of these originals put the squeeze on a generation of black writers. At the same time, it threw open the gates to white readers' fantasies of racial and sexual exploitation. Writing direct-to-paperback, in other words, gave rise to sleaze.

Black sleaze amplified the early postwar years' fascination with the taboo on interracial sex into a veritable print bonanza of racial and sexual stereotypes. San Diego–based Greenleaf Classics, for example, used *Sex Rebel: Black* as a launchpad for publishing a wide range of erotic fiction and sexology studies focusing on interracial sex. In addition to Davis's book, which came out in June 1968, Greenleaf's various imprints released these titles:

Robert Ellis, *White Slaves* (1968)
Lance Baker and Jill Baker (pseud. Jerry Murray), *Black Woman, White Woman* (1969)
C. A. Brown, *White Woman and Black Lovers* (1969)
A. De Granamour (pseud. Paul Hugo Little), *Sally in Black Bondage* (1969)
Kate Lea, *Swaps in Black and White* (1970)
William J. Lambert III (pseud. William Maltese), *Master Black* (1971)
Chad Stuart (pseud. William Maltese), *Blackballed* (1972)
J. X. Williams, *Bartered Black Girl* (1972)

All of these book titles were original to Greenleaf. No respectable hardcover house would publish them, and that, of course, was the point. With the relaxing of US obscenity laws in the late 1960s, publishers like Greenleaf no longer required a hardcover alibi for their output. Now they could aim for straight-up smut. Thus, while mainstream publishing during this time facilitated the phenomenal success of activist black voices such as James Baldwin, Maya Angelou, and Malcolm X, the racial underground plunged into a fantasy world where racial inequities were exactly that which gave frisson to sundry sexual situations. The point was to delight in those inequities, not to change them.

Although contemporary-minded smut was rampant during this period, the racial underground harbored scores of books that rehearsed the previous era's fascination with Southern sexual taboos. This time paperback houses went further back in time, setting erotically charged fiction in the slave era. The fad began with the small-scale, independent publication of Kyle Onstott's *Mandingo* in 1957. This historical novel about slave breeding, filled as it is with dubious suppositions and exploitative scenarios, was an unexpected hit, and the Fawcett paperback edition sold upward of three million copies. The book's popularity keyed Fawcett to the sales potential of a series set at Falconhurst, the fictional plantation where much of the action takes place. Between 1962 and 1988, fourteen books in the series, written by two authors who succeeded Onstott, were published, immersing millions of readers in a fictional universe where the institution of slavery was reduced to a protracted sadomasochist power play. In a turn that should come as no surprise, the success of Fawcett's series spurred other paperback houses to bring out their own slavery-set erotica. Today known as "slavers," these books were widespread throughout the 1960s and, like their smut counterparts, relied on unequal racial scripts to generate readerly interest.[8]

To be sure, the market-driven irreverence of the racial underground afforded the occasional black author the opportunity to publish something that no one else would touch. Davis is a case in point, but a more pertinent example might be Steve Cannon, author of *Groove, Bang, and Jive Around*, released by Maurice Girodias's Paris-based Olympia Press in 1969.[9] The design of the paperback book fit squarely into the racial underground's market for black sleaze (Figure 21.5). But the book itself is something of a benchmark in black avant-garde writing. The novel recounts the misadventures of a black teenage girl in New Orleans, in the process skewering a number of American shibboleths about race, respectability, politics, and freedom. Cannon had been a member of the black experimental writers' group Umbra, and his aesthetic deliberately toed the line between pornography and art. The underground success of *Groove, Bang, and Jive Around* caught the attention of Bay Area writer Ishmael Reed, who loved the book so much that he, Cannon, and Joe Johnson began a joint venture committed to publishing similarly experimental works by writers of color in the 1970s.

Still, it must be reiterated that Cannon's experience was not the norm. In the decade that spanned the civil rights and Black Power eras (1965–75), the racial underground was dominated by white authors churning out voyeuristic, stereotyped fiction for an implied audience of white readers. Encompassing nonmainstream houses (such as Greenleaf)

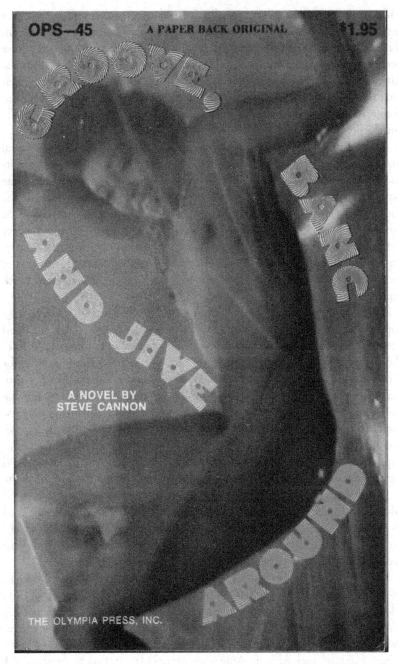

Figure 21.5 Front cover of *Groove, Bang, and Jive Around*, published by Olympia Press in 1969

and corporate firms willing to dip into sleaze (such as Fawcett), this segment of the literary marketplace was a striking riposte to urgent calls for black equality. While race liberals and the intellectual elite may have been hip to Huey P. Newton and Angela Davis, millions of middle-class Americans indulged in fantasies of racial and sexual exploitation. Their lowbrow tastes were "underground" to the extent that few people talked about liking this stuff, whether in the mainstream press or in polite company. But the appeal was there.

Given this history, it may seem surprising that the seeds for the racial underground's turn toward a black readership came from within its conditions of production. That is exactly what happened when one especially market-savvy sleaze enterprise, Holloway House, became the country's leading publisher of black pulp and popular fiction in the 1970s. A comprehensive study of Holloway House, to which this chapter is meant to serve as a corollary, may be found in my book *Street Players*. For the remainder of this section, I survey the company's work as it specifically relates to the transformation of black sleaze into black pulp fiction.

Releasing its first titles in 1961, Holloway House was established to turn copy from two pinup magazines, *Adam* and *Sir Knight* (later renamed *Knight*), into mass-market paperbacks. The entities were integrated under the ownership of Bentley Morriss, a white publicist with a penchant for dredging the bottom of Hollywood's talent pool. Where some pinup magazines, like Hugh M. Hefner's *Playboy*, moved toward an upscale readership, others, like Morriss's holdings, favored a down-market aesthetic that nursed white men's feelings of being victimized by a female-dominated world order. In this segment of the market, pinups and paperbacks alike fostered a misogynistic view of women as either gold diggers or sex workers. At Holloway House, the antisocial views of sleaze were popularized by a handful of hack writers – most notably a Hollywood tabloid and gossip columnist by the name of Leo Guild – who published scores of books between them. These men kept up the illusion of Holloway House drawing on a stable of talent through ghostwriting and pseudonymous authorship.

Holloway House's first African American authors were Robert Beck, an ex-convict who went by the pen name Iceberg Slim, and Robert H. deCoy, a local writer and outspoken activist. Slim's books, *Pimp: The Story of My Life* and *Trick Baby: The Biography of a Con Man*, and deCoy's *The Nigger Bible* (all 1967) were marketed as black sleaze. Although indebted to black urban folklore and African American vernacular stylistics, *Pimp, Trick*

Baby, and *The Nigger Bible* advanced stereotypes about black masculinity that doubled as fantasies of "authentic" manhood for a white readership. Unlike the majority of works of black sleaze that preceded them, Holloway House's titles lent white readers a powerful point of identification with black pimps, confidence men, and seducers. In consciously activating the dialectic of disgust and desire, Slim's and deCoy's male characters were simultaneously reviled as criminals, exploiters, and social outcasts and valorized as "real" men capable of resisting society's feminization.

White men remained Holloway House's target audience in the late 1960s. In 1969, deCoy penned a fictionalized biography of the boxer Jack Johnson, *The Big Black Fire*, while Slim wrote *Mama Black Widow* (Figure 21.6), a cautionary tale of what happens when black men are victimized by overbearing mothers. Holloway House also turned to Guild, one of their most versatile hacks, to script a dubious "true story" titled *The Girl Who Loved Black* (1969). The cover of the book, which features a bare-chested black man staring fixedly at the camera, stands out for potentially appealing to women's or same-sex desire (Figure 21.7).[10] That appeal was not uncommon in sleaze, given that the contemporary sexual revolution threw together a variety of gendered interests in the pursuit of sexual freedom. Ultimately, though, Guild's book was like all other sleaze titles when it came to turning black male sexuality into a fetish for voyeuristic white consumption. (Spoiler alert: the titular "girl" comes out on top in her conquest of the "Negro pimp.")

The boundaries of the racial underground were porous enough such that some sleaze found its way into the hands of black readers. In Holloway House's case, the entrance of Slim's books into urban black neighborhoods provoked skepticism among Black Power's politically conscious elements. In fact, Slim's reception among cultural nationalists and Black Panthers compelled the author to apologize for his reactionary past. Observing the rise of black radicalism at the turn of the decade, Slim wrote a collection of self-flagellating essays titled *The Naked Soul of Iceberg Slim* (1971). The book helped make the case for Slim's "redemptive anachronicity," which compared his criminal past unfavorably to the political ideals of Black Power.[11] Despite such criticism, Slim's fans eventually outnumbered his critics, and the controversy surrounding his books only fueled their popularity among black readers. He was a welcome guest on the Black Power public television show *Black Journal*, and he was frequently quoted in scholarly works about urban black culture. Slim's second book, *Trick Baby*, was even adapted into a blaxploitation movie of the same name. That point of pride was tempered,

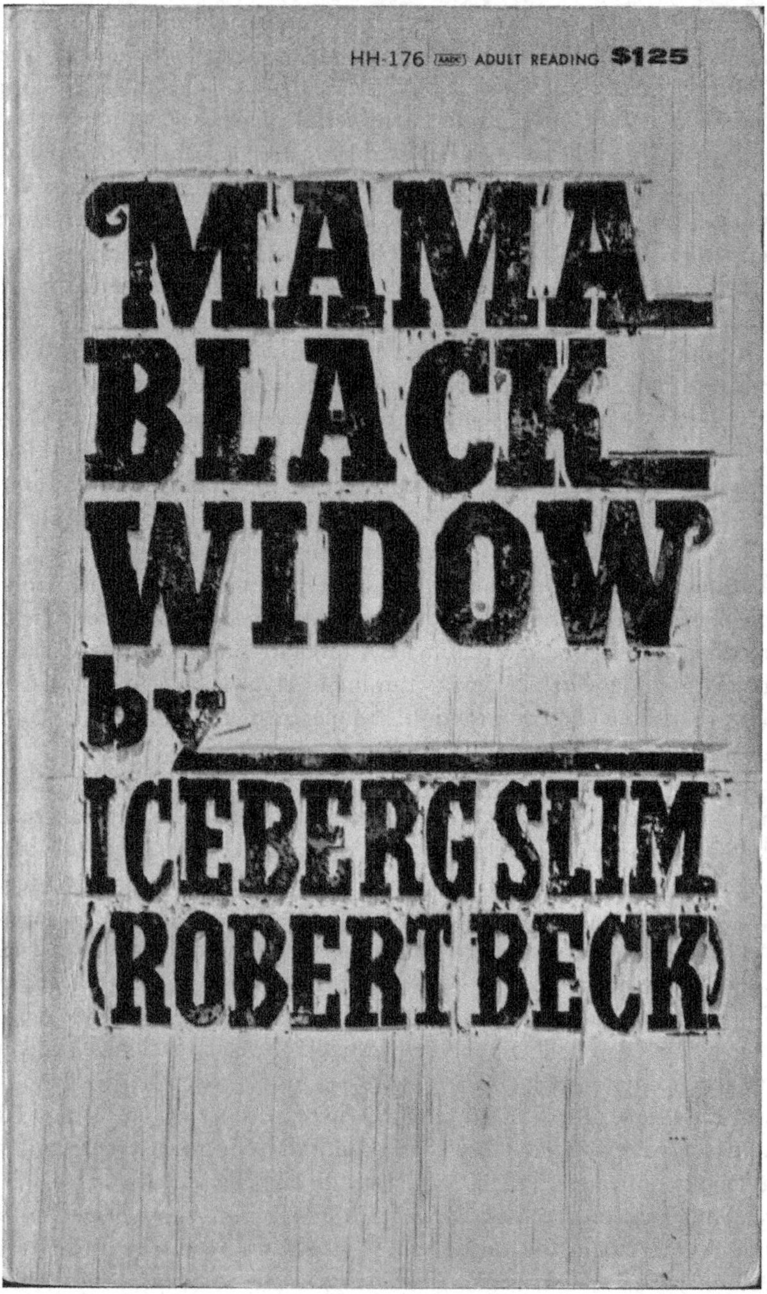

Figure 21.6   Front cover of *Mama Black Widow*, published by Holloway House in 1969. Cover design by Ron Wolin

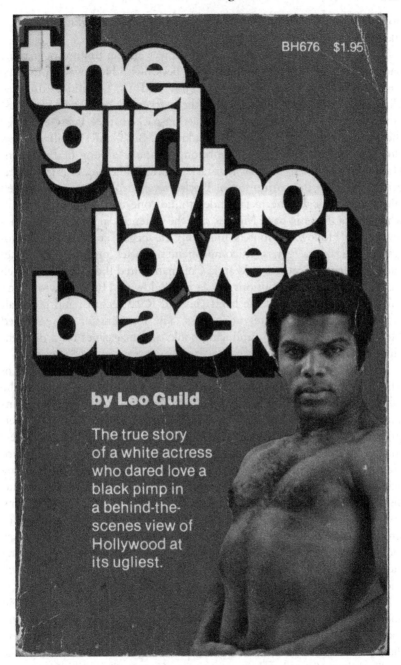

BH676 $1.95

the girl who loved black

by Leo Guild

The true story
of a white actress
who dared love a
black pimp in
a behind-the-
scenes view of
Hollywood at
its ugliest.

Figure 21.7   Front cover of *The Girl Who Loved Black*, reprint featuring
original cover photograph from 1969

however, by the fact that the novel's mixed-race protagonist was portrayed by white actor Kiel Martin.

While Slim stumbled into the Black Power era, an unknown quantity
named Donald Goines began publishing books with Holloway House that
were distinct from sleaze. Between 1971 and 1973, Goines surpassed
Slim's output and set the terms for the market for black pulp fiction.[12]
Goines's books were fast-paced and action-packed; they rarely exhibited
the vernacular flair for which Slim was known. But Goines's ability to hew
closely to genre codes proved enormously popular among black readers.
Harrowing, inner-city dramas that tackled drug addiction, criminal enterprises, and even the corruption of Black Power ideology: Goines's novels
laid a new path for the racial underground, one that was indifferent to
white tastes. For his part, Morriss saw the potential in this market. In a
reversal of Holloway House's founding, he began an all-black pornographic magazine, *Players*, to complement the black pulp fiction Goines
had pioneered. Local writer Wanda Coleman edited the magazine, which
featured literary contributions by James Baldwin, Huey Newton, and
Ishmael Reed; reviews of the latest jazz and R&B records; and pictorials
of women in various states of undress. The founding of *Players* sealed
Morriss's commitment to producing books and magazines for a different
kind of readership.

Around 1973, then, the racial underground bifurcated along the lines of
white and black readers. White readers held on to sleaze, pushing the
subgenre to its absurd limits, whereas black readers finally found a company, Holloway House, willing to publish fast-and-furious books for their
enjoyment. In a clear sign of which of these tracks he thought had the best
chance for success moving forward, Morriss decided to cease most of
Holloway House's white-oriented book operations and put everything
behind what he called "black experience paperbacks." Sleaze was thus
displaced from the catalog in favor of pulp fiction. It was good timing
insofar as the market for sleaze contracted significantly after the main-
streaming of hardcore pornography in the mid- to late 1970s. When sex
suddenly became permissible, sleaze looked like a well-worn tease. Among
independent publishers of the racial underground, Holloway House was
one of the few to survive the era.

By 1975, the real action of the racial underground was happening in
books written by black authors for black readers. Most of these were
coming out of Holloway House, which now specialized in genre fiction
that combined the pleasures of blood-and-thunder sensationalism with the
predictability of tried-and-true formulas. Goines alone published nine

books in 1974 – a remarkable feat considering he was murdered in his Detroit home on October 21 of that year. While the authorship of some of his last novels, including two more published in 1975, is a question newly raised by *Street Players*, the fact that Holloway House consolidated the Goines "brand" in a couple of years cannot be denied.[13]

Goines was just the tip of the iceberg. Holloway House published scores of black writers over the decade, saturating the racial underground's market for pulp fiction. First-time authors flourished at the company. Four installments of Roosevelt Mallory's action series Radcliff came out between 1973 and 1975. James-Howard Readus published *The Black Assassin* and *The Big Hit* in 1975, *Black Renegades* in 1976, and *The Death Merchants* in 1979. Laurence Blaine's nod to Chester Himes's *If He Hollers Let Him Go*, *Black Muscle*, arrived in 1976 (Figure 21.8),[14] followed up by *Sweet Street Blues* in 1978. And Charlie Avery Harris must have been writing at Goines-like speed to witness Holloway House release his six novels between 1976 and 1978.

The undisputed master at writing black pulp fiction was Joseph Nazel. A veteran journalist of Los Angeles' African American newspapers, Nazel took over as editor of *Players* after Coleman had left just over a year into the job.[15] In addition to putting together the magazine, he wrote piles of books for Holloway House in whatever genre you could throw at him. Nazel authored two action serials, one under his own name (The Iceman, eight books, 1974–87) and the other under the pseudonym Dom Gober (James Rhodes, four books, 1974–76). He wrote promiscuously across genres, from horror and mystery to war and conspiracy novels. Long after he had left the helm of *Players*, Nazel even tried his hand at romance, writing under the name Joyce Lezán. Valerie Babb lists close to forty titles for Nazel in her survey of the African American novel.[16] But even this tally doesn't capture the extent of his output. For Nazel was also the man behind the pseudonym Omar Fletcher, who is listed in Babb's work as a separate author, as well as the pen name Amos Brooke, who doesn't appear at all. Adding these pseudonyms to Nazel's count brings him closer to fifty – and that is still without factoring in the numerous biographies of African American personages he wrote for Holloway House.

While many of the books Nazel and other authors produced during this period were entirely safe for mainstream consumption, they remained fixed in the racial underground because of their close association with an urban black reading demographic. These books received coverage in the black press, and some authors became mini-celebrities in their hometowns. But the essentially subcultural circulation of Holloway House's pulp fiction

Figure 21.8   Front cover of *Black Muscle*, published by Holloway House in 1976.
Cover artist unknown

put it in a structurally similar position to sleaze. These were thrilling yet disposable fantasies that, in the view of the mainstream literary market-place, reflected a certain down-market taste.

As judgmental as that may sound, there was reason for black pulp fiction to be cast in this light. In order to tighten his hold on the racial under-ground's black readership, Morriss made sure that Holloway House's books were viewed as the natural complement to *Players* magazine. Indeed, pulp and porn became necessary adjuncts in Morriss's survey of black men's readerly tastes. That may not have been a problem in theory, except the way *Players* was run reinforced the very racial and sexual stereotypes the magazine was supposed to overcome. After Coleman's departure, the magazine experienced a steady decline in quality: models were depicted as slaves and prostitutes; lifestyle features were replaced by coverage of professional sports; and fantasies of urban sophistication were punctuated by reminders of "ghetto" poverty and blight. The magazine's editorial changes couldn't help but have an effect on pulp fiction, for these products were offered alongside each other in black neighborhoods' news-stands, corner stores, and bookshops.

A sign of how much pulp had to contend with porn between 1974 and 1977 can be seen in the following list of Leo Guild's publications:

Cherri Grant, *Swingers Three* (1974)
Leo Guild, *Black Bait* (1975)
Mary Turner, as told to Leo Guild, *Black Champion* (1975)
Dr. Phyllis James, as told to Leo Guild, *The Black Shrink* (1975)
Leo Guild, *Street of Ho's* (1976)
Cindy Kallmer, as told to Leo Guild, *The Senator's Whore* (1976)
Leo Guild, *Josephine Baker* (1976)
Leo Guild, *Cons and Lovers* (1977)
Kelley Eagle, as told to Leo Guild, *Black Streets of Oakland* (1977)

As this list demonstrates, sleaze was never really far from Morriss's staking new ground for black pulp fiction. So long as racial and sexual stereotypes circulated in the magazine, Holloway House's books came perilously close to reanimating a sleaze aesthetic that black authors' embrace of genre fiction was meant to have superseded.

***

By now, it should be clear that although the racial underground was able to make room for black readers' tastes, it never relinquished white ownership of publishing and distribution networks. For all the transformation that occurred between the paperback revolution and Holloway House's closure in 2008, white men exerted near total control over how books made their way into the racial underground. These men treated books as different in format but not in kind to tabloids, gossip rags, pinup magazines, and pornography. The point was always to produce cheap thrills that could be distributed to readers and disposed of by the same with relative ease. Although Holloway House greatly expanded the idea of what such thrills could contain, its white ownership left well-founded doubts about exactly who was profiting from sensationalized representations of race, gender, and sexuality.

The epilogue to this account, however, isn't so bleak. The sheer popularity of Holloway House's books among black readers spurred some of them to flee the prescriptions of the racial underground and create a literature of their own. Teri Woods, for example, was working as a legal secretary in Philadelphia when she decided to add her voice to the pulp pantheon. Donald Goines's masculinism had worn thin after twenty years of shaping the market, but his hard-boiled style of writing pointed Woods to a "new league" of literary authorship. As a result, Woods penned *True to the Game*, a novel about a young black couple who get caught up in the fast life of the drug trade. Woods's manuscript was turned down by multiple publishers. But those rejections did not deter her from reaching her audience. She borrowed some money, taught herself desktop publishing, and printed copies of *True to the Game* under the label Meow Meow Productions (copyrighted 1994, published 1998). She sold 70,000 books from the trunk of her car, pounding the pavement in black communities across the Northeast. Woods then invested the profits in her own publishing company, committed to promoting gritty romances like hers.[17]

Detroit native Vickie Stringer blazed a similar path to literary recognition. While serving a stint in federal prison for interstate drug trafficking, Stringer was inspired by Goines's example of drawing on his life experiences in the criminal underworld to start his own writing career behind bars. She finished a novel, *Let That Be the Reason*, and hoped to find a publisher upon her release. Instead, she received only rejection slips – 26 of them. Not giving up on her manuscript, she borrowed money from a friend, printed copies of the book herself, and sold *Let That Be the Reason* (copyrighted 1999, published 2001) at "car washes, corner stores and hair salons." Although the book enjoyed tremendous success on its own, Stringer, like Woods, saw the need to lift up authors who yearned to share their stories with the world. So she also started her own imprint: Triple Crown Publications, named after her ex-boyfriend's gang.[18]

Woods and Stringer are progenitors of what is now known in the publishing industry as "urban fiction" – hard-boiled romances written by black authors, mostly women, for black women readers. With roots in these do-it-yourself publishing operations, urban fiction has become, in the twenty-first century, a multimillion-dollar segment of the literary marketplace. Houses that once rejected Woods and Stringer now curry favor with black women writers and readers, dedicating specific imprints to urban fiction and other genre fiction. Meanwhile, independent outfits hoping to break into the industry keep sprouting up, adding street-level cachet to the genre's self-definition and readerly appeal.[19]

Hewing closely to formulas that center on *black women's* perspectives on life, love, loss, and redemption, urban fiction is unlike anything produced in the racial underground, even though Holloway House's books lay behind its initial success. But besides its female-oriented content, urban fiction is distinct from black sleaze and "old school" black pulp fiction in that it has always involved a degree of black ownership over its product. While today's corporate interest in the genre is unmistakable, entrepreneurs like Woods and Stringer have found a way to partner with companies to earn a share of profits while having a seat at the editorial table. With urban fiction now a fixture in mainstream publishing, it remains to be seen whether the racial underground has a future – or if it has met its match in black women's popular fiction.

Whatever its fate, the history of the racial underground encourages us to conceive American literary history anew. Today, our sense of that history is indelibly marked by the multicultural turn of the 1990s, which highlighted the creative output of writers, poets, and artists of color. As a result, we are more attuned than ever to the range of literary and cultural expression produced by indigenous, black, and ethnic American subjects. Yet these welcome shifts to our thinking nonetheless have consistently overlooked the underbelly of the literary marketplace. For decades, the racial underground has been a site not simply of popular literary taste but of reading in bad taste. Indeed, far from the idealistic conception of literature as expanding readers' capacity to connect and empathize with others, the racial underground has supplied fare that appeals to readers' extant prejudices. That goes for urban fiction, too, which African American journalist Nick Chiles once dismissed as black women's "smut."[20] Even under black ownership, these literary productions seem too crass, too disreputable, to be given any credence by the most liberal-minded critics.

But who says literature is only that which enlarges, expands, and enlightens? Isn't this conception of literature as antiquated as the belletristic, Eurocentric one that predominated before the 1990s? It is, yet many literary scholars tacitly affirm it by curating their objects in a way that reserves critical significance for highbrow expression. Literary *historians* ought to avoid that tendency insofar as their task is not to use texts to support an extant thesis but to survey the full range of objects that could possibly be included in the category of "literature." And lest they restrict that category for fear of letting in undesirable objects, the history of the racial underground reminds us that many black writers have had to negotiate bad taste in order to get published, and that it's precisely in this market niche where a popular literary culture for black readers has taken root and flourished. To the extent that literary historians recognize the value in recovering these accounts of black authorship and reading, it behooves them to turn their attention to the racial underground.

Notes

1. Quoted in Frank Marshall Davis, *Livin' the Blues: Memoirs of a Black Journalist and Poet*, ed. John Edgar Tidwell (Madison: University of Wisconsin Press, 1992), 346.
2. Valerie Babb, *A History of the African American Novel* (New York: Cambridge University Press, 2017); Bernard W. Bell, *The Contemporary African American Novel: Its Folk Roots and Modern Literary Branches* (Amherst: University of Massachusetts Press, 2005); "Novel Collections: 1965–1969," Project on the History of Black Writing, https://hbw.ku.edu/1965-1969.
3. Kinohi Nishikawa, *Street Players: Black Pulp Fiction and the Making of a Literary Underground* (Chicago: University of Chicago Press, 2018), 75–104.
4. This definition of the underground is meant to update, to a twentieth-century context, the broad parameters of a classic book-historical account of Enlightenment outsider literature. See Robert Darnton, *The Literary Underground of the Old Regime* (Cambridge, MA: Harvard University Press, 1982).
5. Beth Luey, "The Organization of the Book Publishing Industry," in *A History of the Book in America*, vol. 5, *The Enduring Book: Print Culture in Postwar America*, eds. David Paul Nord, Joan Shelley Rubin, and Michael Schudson (Chapel Hill: University of North Carolina Press, 2009), 43, 45.
6. Thomas L. Bonn, *Heavy Traffic and High Culture: New American Library as Literary Gatekeeper in the Paperback Revolution* (Carbondale: Southern Illinois University Press, 1989); Kenneth C. Davis, *Two-Bit Culture: The Paperbacking of America* (New York: Houghton Mifflin, 1984); Paula Rabinowitz, *American Pulp: How Paperbacks Brought Modernism to Main Street* (Princeton, NJ: Princeton University Press, 2004).
7. Luey, "Organization," 43.

8. Two useful surveys of the Falconhurst phenomenon are Earl F. Bargainnier, "The Falconhurst Series: A New Popular Image of the Old South," *Journal of Popular Culture* 10.2 (1976), 298–314; and Paul Talbot, *Mondo Mandingo: The "Falconhurst" Books and Films* (Bloomington, IN: iUniverse, 2009).

9. Like Davis, Cannon is not to be found in Babb, *A History of the African American Novel*, even though the study includes a chapter on pulp and popular fiction.

10. This cover is from the first reprint of the book, but it retains the photographed, bare-chested male who adorns the original printing.

11. Nishikawa, *Street Players*, 107–34.

12. Goines published five novels during these years: *Dopefiend* (1971), *Whoreson* (1972), *Black Gangster* (1972), *Street Players* (1973), and *White Man's Justice, Black Man's Grief* (1973).

13. See Nishikawa, *Street Players*, 188–90, for an examination of Goines's last days and the way Holloway House exploited his death for profit.

14. The switch in implied reader from Himes to Blaine can be seen in this cover, which reverses the power dynamic between a white woman and a black man.

15. On the contentious split between Coleman and the magazine, see Nishikawa, *Street Players*, 166–74, 190–92.

16. Babb, *A History of the African American Novel*, 395–96.

17. Erica Buddington, "A Peek Inside Her Agenda: Teri Woods," *Her Agenda*, October 7, 2013, http://heragenda.com/power-agenda/teri-woods/; "Teri Woods: Author of True to the Game," *New York Beacon*, July 17, 2002.

18. Jonathan Cunningham, "Romancing the Hood," *Detroit Metro Times*, June 22, 2005.

19. Scholarship on urban fiction, alternately known as "street lit" or "hip-hop literature," has lacked a materialist analysis of its development out of black pulp fiction's genre categories but from a discrete, 1990s, early digital-publishing milieu. Too many studies collapse distinctions between, say, Holloway House and contemporary urban fiction. Both this chapter and Nishikawa, *Street Players*, 242–43, 249–50, stand as correctives to this trend and instigations for future work in the field.

20. Nick Chiles, "Their Eyes Were Reading Smut," *New York Times*, January 4, 2006.

CHAPTER 22

Literature in Hawaiian Pidgin and the Critique of Asian Settler Colonialism

Jeehyun Lim

In this essay, I draw on scholarship in sociolinguistics and liberal political theory on language diversity and linguistic justice to examine whether literature in Hawaiian Pidgin can still have a countercultural and subversive force given the criticism of Asian settler colonialism.[1] Literary criticism on literature in Pidgin has focused on demonstrating the capacity of the much-stigmatized language to represent the rich and varied culture of its speakers.[2] In this process, literature in Pidgin has come to be associated with a countercultural position that illuminates the dynamics of social domination. Given this context, the critique of Asian settler colonialism, which assumes Asians to be a settler group in Hawai'i, can be devastating for the identity of literature in Pidgin. I turn to the controversy surrounding Bamboo Ridge, an independent publishing house and journal established by Eric Chock and Darrell H. Y. Lum in 1978, as an opening for exploring the significance of literature in Pidgin in relation to new political and cultural consciousness of the enduring and wide-ranging repercussions of settler colonialism. Summarized best in Chock's 1996 essay "The Neocolonialization of Bamboo Ridge," this controversy hinges on representational politics.[3] While its aim in aspiring to be local literature was to give voice and presence to underrepresented writers from Hawai'i, Bamboo Ridge met with the criticism that their use of the term "local" was appropriative of the indigenous population. To the critics it was, in brief, neocolonial.

In this chapter, I explore the possibilities that literature in Pidgin can be an ally to indigenous rights and claims based on its philosophy of critiquing cultural hegemony. Within Pidgin's guerrilla philosophy, which I discuss below, lies an idea of linguistic justice that does not rely on or borrow from liberal ideas of justice but rather approaches the concept from experiences of linguistic domination. Writers such as Lee A. Tonouchi and Lisa Linn Kanae show that to advocate for and write in Pidgin is to cherish an understanding of the history of the language, of the adversities that led to the language's development, and of living with and challenging the stigmas of a nonstandard, marginal language. Despite its origins in the experiences of Asian plantation workers, Pidgin is not necessarily wedded to a fixed Asian American identity. Rather, Pidgin identity coheres more or less around a collective effort to remember a past of exclusion and to resist assimilation into a way of life that is imposed from the outside.

It should be noted that Bamboo Ridge encountered the critique of Asian settler colonialism on the cusp of literary criticism's turn to affirm literature in Pidgin. Bamboo Ridge's years of work to build a network and a community of writers interested in literary expressions of Hawai'i that do not conform to widely accepted literary portraits of the islands in the continental United States may not have directly caused this turn in literary criticism. Yet the cultural work of Bamboo Ridge exists in a larger system of literary value production to which both writers and critics, as well as the professional networks and organizations for both groups, belong. Does literary criticism's reevaluation of literature in Pidgin imbue it with cultural capital it did not have before? Where does literature in Pidgin stand now in a changing cultural economy of American literature? I ask these questions to raise the point that cultural capital is one of the (invisible) stakes and conditions in the Bamboo Ridge controversy. This is important for the meaning of allyship.[4] My argument that writers like Tonouchi and Kanae open Pidgin's potential to align with and support the movement for indigenous Hawaiians rests on a fluctuating relationship between these individual writers' works and the world of cultural capital within which they reside. In their writings, a critical consciousness based on Pidgin's outsider history and status – its simultaneous belonging and nonbelonging in Hawai'i – enables an identification from the perspective of the excluded. How this critical consciousness will affect and be affected by the cultural capital of literature in Pidgin – still in an emergent stage in my opinion – is something to pay attention to. Will Pidgin's guerrilla philosophy be able to prevent any cultural capital associated with literature in Pidgin from being exclusive or appropriative? My hope is that it would be. But I leave this as an open question.

Pidgin Culture

In the brief opening meditation to *Living Pidgin*, entitled "On Being Pidgin," Tonouchi cites an anecdote from the poet Wayne Westlake, whose collection of poems by local children of Hawai'i, *Born Pidgin* (1979), serves as a model for his own. The anecdote features Westlake

teaching in Hawai'i's Poets-in-the-Schools program. He gives an assignment asking students to use Pidgin, and one student resists, complaining,
"But I don't know how talk pidgin." Westlake recounts, "Before I could
say 'you just did,' another boy across the room shot back: 'eh brah, wat
you mean you no know how fo talk pidgin—you wuz BORN pidgin!'"[5]
This story illustrates at least two aspects of Pidgin Tonouchi emphasizes
throughout *Living Pidgin*. First, Pidgin is already a part of one's identity
even if one may not acknowledge it, as the example of the complaining
student shows. Unlike Westlake's unspoken response – "you just did" –
which would have based the first student's relationship to Pidgin on his
immediate speech, the classmate suggests that their relationship to Pidgin
precedes conscious, intentional recognition. It is not because they speak
Pidgin that they are Pidgin speakers; it is because they themselves are
Pidgin that they speak the language. To deny Pidgin, therefore, is not just
to deny (in this case, incorrectly) what and how you speak but to deny
one's identity.

Second, Pidgin is infused with a democratic ethos that views its speakers
as social equals. The two students in Westlake's class perform a scene of
social struggle over Pidgin as identity. The first student who denies Pidgin
reflects the social prejudices against the language. Before the teacher can
respond, though, the second student voluntarily assumes the role of the
pedagogue. Instead of the imposition of knowledge from the top, a peer-
to-peer dialogue is at the heart of the pedagogy of Pidgin. Tonouchi evokes
this opening anecdote's spirit when he emphasizes egalitarianism in his
discussion of Pidgin later in *Living Pidgin*, proclaiming that "dat willingness to try and undahstand wea da person is coming from, and not being
so quick to judge one noddah person—das da basis of Pidgin" and that
"one of da fundamental values of Pidgin culture should be one respeck for
da Hawaiian culture."[6] As an identity and as a medium of egalitarian social
relations, Pidgin emerges simultaneously as a language well suited for the
cultivation of *demos* – for creating public spaces for conversations between
social equals to take place – and a language of *ethnos* wherein membership
is determined not by choice but by birth.

To attribute both *demos* and *ethnos* to Pidgin may seem like a paradox
when one considers the fact that these terms are seldom used to describe
coextensive or mutually reinforcing relationships. More commonly seen are
different kinds of exclusivity associated with birth-determined group affiliation clashing with demands for inclusiveness. To borrow the well-known
terms used by the literary critic Werner Sollors in his analysis of American
literature, *demos* is about consent and *ethnos* descent.[7] How can Pidgin

claim both *demos* and *ethnos*? Be both inclusive and exclusive? Lisa Linn Kanae's chapbook, *Sista Tongue*, offers an interpretation of the sociocultural history of Pidgin that sheds light on this question.[8] Kanae's poetic meditation is loosely organized around two narratives: a personal narrative where she remembers her brother's struggles with speech when he was young and an account of the sociocultural history of Pidgin that she has learned out of the need to confront the prejudices against the language. Drawing from a number of sociolinguistic studies, Kanae locates the origin of Pidgin – alternately called Hawaiʻi Creole English (HCE) or Hawaii Pidgin English (HPE) in the book per the usage in the sociolinguistic studies – in the conditions of the plantation. In this condensed account, Pidgin is a language that developed out of the interactions between the plantation bosses and the mostly Asian contract laborers. The need for efficient communication between people who spoke different languages called for the creation of a new language. Instead of disappearing after the plantation industry waned, this new language survived due to segregated schools even as Hawaiʻi's evolving relationship with the United States, first as territory and later as state, privileged Standard English and stigmatized Pidgin.

Alongside this account of Pidgin as a language borne out of conditions of exclusion and exploitation, Kanae also charts how Pidgin took on a life of its own as the Asian laborers used it as a language to communicate across their different and varied languages. "Pidgin was the result of a multi-ethnic working class's attempt at solidarity," Kanae emphasizes.[9] If the language intersected with the formation of a pan-ethnic political identity for the laborers, and for their children, Kanae explains, Pidgin meant more than political identity. For the "children who could neither connect ancestrally with their own native culture nor to a relatively foreign mainstream American culture," the hybrid language offered a cultural identity of their own.[10] She cites a sentence from an academic study by Kevin Y. Kawamoto to complete her reflection: "By being 'local' one could maintain a sense of ethnic identity while at the same time identifying with a larger, more encompassing culture."[11] Pidgin as *ethnos*, then, is not so much a language of biological determination but of social formation. The ethnicization of Pidgin comes by way of the formation of a political working-class identity on the part of the Asian laborers and the development of this identity into a culture by their children that is neither like the ethnic culture of their parents nor like the dominant white culture but is rooted in the everyday experiences mediated by Pidgin.

The case for Pidgin as a language for *demos* parallels the case for Pidgin as a language of *ethnos* once ethnicity is understood as neither biological nor fixed but socially produced. From the presentation of Pidgin as a language that enabled working-class solidarity among the plantation laborers, Kanae moves to present Pidgin as a language of resistance. If she begins with speculation about Pidgin's relationship to resistance – "Perhaps Pidgin's perseverance stems from the necessity for resistance" – the speculation soon gives way to a poetic claim on the language: "Resistance is an intrinsic element of Pidgin."[12] The claim rises from Kanae's interpretation of contemporary literature from Hawai'i that generously and boldly employs Pidgin. The writers she lists, including Darell Lum, Eric Chock, and Lee Tonouchi, show a network of writers who share an investment in Pidgin as a literary language and discloses literature in Pidgin as a field in its own right, as Pierre Bourdieu would call it.[13] Pidgin becomes a language of resistance through the shared view and uses of the language as such in this field. Kanae illustrates the cultural politics of an emergent field of literature by the descendants of Asian laborers whereby a language looked down upon by what she calls "institutionalized elitism" is transformed into a language of craft and deliberation.[14] In identifying Pidgin as a language of resistance, Kanae also presents it as a language that holds out the possibility of democratic struggle for the dispossessed and the underrepresented. It becomes a language that performs egalitarian strivings in the face of those who support the concentration of power and resources in the few.

The construction of Pidgin as a language of resistance by the writers in the field makes the charge of literature in Pidgin's complicity with (neo) colonialism all the more troubling. The linguist Tove Skutnabb-Kangas's distinction between indigenous and immigrant languages is helpful in thinking through the discrepancy between the field's self-conception and the critique of Asian settler colonialism. Among other contributions, Skutnabb-Kangas is known for coining the term "linguicism" to draw attention to inequalities that appear along the line of language difference.[15] As someone who has studied language minority groups and criticized the lack of support for language minority students in schools, Skutnabb-Kangas shares with the writers in the field of literature in Pidgin an interest in challenging social domination occurring through language. Here, I refer to a short essay by Skutnabb-Kangas directed to a public audience where she addresses the difficulty of arriving at linguistic justice through bureaucratic multiculturalism. "Indigenous or Immigrant Minorities? Who Is at Greater Risk?" is meant to elucidate bureaucratic multiculturalism's tendency to employ parallelism in managing different groups, erasing from view the operations of power that often establish hierarchies among groups. The answer she offers for the question in the title is simple and straightforward: "Indigenous languages as languages are much more threatened than languages of immigrant minorities."[16] It certainly satisfies the common sense that immigrant languages are still spoken in their countries of origin, whereas indigenous languages are confronted with linguicide. Lest one too hastily dismiss the essay, its query is more important for the way it forces one to see what Skutnabb-Kangas calls "a nested hierarchy of linguistic human rights" than for the question and answer.[17] This "nested hierarchy" is an exercise in seeing the structural relations of power in a society and in recognizing the racial hierarchy connoted in Asian settler colonialism.

The distinction between indigenous and immigrant languages, of course, does not immediately apply to Pidgin and Hawaiian. Pidgin occupies a somewhat undetermined status in Skutnabb-Kangas's categorization of languages. Being a creole language, it is neither an immigrant language nor a dialect.[18] In *Sista Tongue*, Kanae relates Pidgin's defiance of existing language categories to the history of interracial mixing in Hawai'i. A rigid view of boundaries or an adherence to the idea of purity fails to see the significance of both Pidgin and interracial unions.

Yet Kanae also acknowledges that a celebratory embrace of mixing also turns a blind eye to the subtle ways in which certain categories and identities become subject to erasure while others remain socially viable. She notes that while she is of mixed-race ancestry – "My genealogy can be traced back to Japanese pig farmers in Happy Valley, Maui; Chinese and Filipino immigrant plantation workers; and Native Hawaiians from the island of Hawai'i" – the two languages she is fluent in are Standard English and Pidgin.[19] The absence of Hawaiian among her languages is conspicuous. Choosing Hawaiian is a foreclosed option for Kanae, whereas she can still consciously and strategically employ Pidgin.

The foreclosure of Hawaiian, however, still leaves a trace in Kanae's linguistic and literary practice, a trace that can be seen in Pidgin. Her choice to use Pidgin in her creative writing is based on her willing participation in the field of place-based literature, where Pidgin is a language of resistance and is used to "both criticiz[e] and hea[l] the inferiority complexes and self-loathing that was created by cultural elitists."[20] One may argue that her relationship to Pidgin is guided by a principle and philosophy that bring to view the absent language of Hawaiian in her work.

The story of Asian plantation labor in Hawai'i and the sociopolitical marginalization of Asian groups in the islands is certainly part of the history of imperialism in Hawai'i and the Pacific. The same history of imperialism calls for a reckoning with the "nested hierarchy" in the islands wherein indigenous Hawaiians experience a continued loss of rights and land even as social and political acts of redress and rehabilitation create opportunities of uplift for Asian groups. Behind the conflict over the term "local" is a much more complex story of the continued dispossession and nonrecognition of indigenous Hawaiians and a rise in Asian American representation in Hawai'i from the initial days of Asian labor migration. According to activists of the Hawaiian Sovereignty Movement, part of Asian American political power in the islands has become suppressive of the rights and claims of indigenous Hawaiians.[21] That many Asian American writers from Hawai'i, including Eric Chock, were surprised at the criticism of Bamboo Ridge as neocolonial shows that this new political power is not evenly shared among Asian Americans in Hawai'i. The incongruity between Bamboo Ridge's own identification as an independent publishing house for people of color from Hawai'i and the criticism against it as neocolonial may well be a legacy of imperialism in the Pacific.

To live in this legacy requires the hard work of simultaneously acknowledging the grievances and claims of indigenous Hawaiians and continuing to undo the stigmas Pidgin speakers experience. In one of his short stories, Tonouchi says, "[w]e like standardize ehryting cuz it makes tings mo' easy fo' process, but wot would happen if we did'em da hod way."[22] The legacy of imperialism in Hawai'i means that there is no quick solution to the dilemma literature in Pidgin faces. But the ability of Pidgin to embrace doing things the hard way, as Tonouchi casts it, does offer a future for working out the relationship between Pidgin and Hawaiian.

The affection for Pidgin shown by writers such as Kanae and Tonouchi touches on several important concerns for understanding language difference and linguistic justice for a democratic culture. Her relationship with Pidgin has allowed Kanae to see that no language is intrinsically superior or inferior and that all languages should be given the space to develop and be valued. Yet the question of the indigenous language's particular vulnerability remains. Can the kind of Pidgin culture that Kanae and Tonouchi promote and support also contribute to the preservation and flourishing of the Hawaiian language? In the next section, I attempt to address this question by exploring the guerrilla philosophy Tonouchi attributes to Pidgin. The outsider perspective in this philosophy, in tandem with its staunch investment in linguistic justice, allows for new and nonprescriptive ways to envision interethnic and interracial relations where an affection for Pidgin does not come at the expense of Hawaiian.

Pidgin Philosophy

Tonouchi expresses a hopeful view of Pidgin and Hawaiian as "partners in resistance," although he does not elaborate on what this partnership will look like or how it will be achieved.[23] Here, I take Tonouchi's idea of himself as a Pidgin guerrilla and attempt to delineate Pidgin as method in envisioning linguistic justice. Prompted by language conflicts and the need for communication for supranational organizations, political philosophers have recently turned to exploring prescriptive theories of linguistic justice. For example, Philippe Van Parijs argues for a *lingua franca* – in his case, English – on the basis that increasing access to one language is more conducive to fostering distributive justice worldwide than trying to support multiple languages.[24] While he acknowledges "colonial attitude" as a problem between different language groups, his interest in the communicative efficiency of a lingua franca in the service of a "transnational-*demos*" precludes substantial engagement with the legacies of colonialism in his discussion of linguistic justice.[25] For Van Parijs, "transnational-demos" is a precondition to egalitarian justice on a global scale, and accordingly his conception of linguistic justice privileges language's function to facilitate understanding and to create common ground. As he puts it, "[b]elonging to a common *demos* is essential [for distributive justice]. Belonging to a common *ethnos* is not."[26] Once defined in this way, linguistic justice becomes mostly an issue of equal access to the language that is already the most powerful and influential. In contrast to this notion of linguistic justice, Tonouchi's guerrilla philosophy imagines linguistic justice not so much as an end but as a continued process of striving. Justice is viewed not simply as a matter of access to the dominant language but as questioning the inequalities along linguistic lines.

Tonouchi's conception of linguistic justice is tied to his understanding of Pidgin as inherently resistant to stable and fixed borders. Creole languages, Tonouchi intimates, share an awareness of the cultural politics of language standardization. Both examples of creole languages he mentions as spiritually kin to Hawaiian Pidgin – Singlish and "Jamaican patwa" – originate from colonial experiences and index the marginalization of groups relegated to the lower rungs of a social hierarchy.[27] Pointing to the countercultural uses speakers of creole have put the language to – "Most people in Singapore can talk British english, but dey raddah talk to each oddas in Singlish" – Tonouchi locates a critical consciousness in living in and with a language that breaks rules and crosses boundaries set up to keep some people in and some out. Calling the speakers of creole

"Pidgin peoples," he sees the countercultural agency of this critical consciousness as a global phenomenon: "All ova da globe get similar Pidgin kine movements going on."[28] Tonouchi's guerrilla philosophy exists in tandem with this countercultural agency to recognize and to challenge inequalities and injustices around language difference.

While well attuned to the dynamics of inclusion and exclusion around languages, the guerrilla philosophy of Pidgin is not focused on arguing for inclusion. It rejects the idea of linguistic justice as moving linearly from exclusion to inclusion and instead emphasizes the pursuit of linguistic justice through wit and strategy. Illustrations of this guerrilla philosophy can be found in several works by Tonouchi, but his collection of stories, *da word*, is particularly interesting for the way it engages with the metaphor of games. Two short stories that present games of words employing Pidgin bookend the collection. The opening story, "da word," is narrated by a boy who faces the prospect of transitioning from a vernacular culture of Pidgin at a local public school to a Standard English culture of college-prep private school. The narrator has a "love/hate" relationship with Laurie, a new student from Portland who, like the narrator, is academically strong but who, unlike the narrator, has an untroubled aspiration to test into a private school and has a learned disregard of Pidgin.[29] While they participate in a running game where they use big words on each other, making the other person look up the word, the game hits an unexpected obstacle when Laurie hears the narrator use the word "bumbye." After being cornered into a wager by Laurie, who dismisses the word as made-up, the narrator is baffled and upset when, against his initial conviction, he fails to find the word in several dictionaries. The last story of the collection, "pijin wawrz," departs from the rest of the stories in genre and language. The speculative fiction – written in Odo orthography, a system of phonemically transcribing spoken to written Pidgin invented by the linguist Carol Odo in the 1970s – is set in a world ruled by a supercomputer, Big Ben.[30] In this world, Pidgin is outlawed and Standard English is the only language permitted. A group of Pidgin rebels, inspired by the legend of the Pidgin Guerilla, attempt to access "the lost Pidgin Archives" with the hope of stealthily bringing back Pidgin.[31] The Archives turn out to be a trap set up by Ben to capture Pidgin rebels. But just as they are about to be apprehended, one of the rebels, Jimmy, successfully derails Big Ben by challenging his knowledge on the Pidgin word "da kine." As Big Ben enters a sequence of reviewing an endless list of sources to no avail, the rebels marvel at what their vernacular knowledge is able to achieve.

A glimpse of how Tonouchi views the fates of Pidgin and Hawaiian as linked can be seen in "pijin wawrz." In this dystopic world where Standard English rules, not only Pidgin but also Hawaiian is on the brink of extermination. Native Hawaiians are all rounded up and sent to Moloka'i, and their attempt to protect themselves by copyrighting Hawaiian and trying to make the state government and private industries pay for the use of Hawaiian words proves futile when Hawaiian words are simply stricken out of the local geography. Standardization is indisputably the enemy of both the Pidgin speakers and indigenous Hawaiians. A state-sponsored camp, Moloka'i is where the Pidgin Guerilla is said to have been imprisoned, and the Pidgin rebels discuss starting an immersion program in Pidgin modeled after what indigenous Hawaiians have used.[32] Pidgin speakers and Native Hawaiians are allied in the common struggle against Big Ben's regime.

By having these two stories bookend the collection, Tonouchi presents the idea of living in Pidgin as a ceaseless engagement in language games that reveal the production, distribution, and circulation of power through control over languages and their speakers. Although the games in "da word" and "pijin wawrz" have rules, the focus of the stories is not so much winning or losing as being placed in a position where one inevitably has to play these games. By painfully losing in his wager with Laurie, the narrator learns that the authority of dictionaries is established not just by including words he enjoys learning but also by excluding words like "bumbye" used frequently by his family and friends. By challenging Big Ben to figure out the meaning of "da kine," Jimmy emphasizes that linguistic knowledge is not just acquired through standardized protocols and codes but also through informal use in everyday settings. The games in "da word" and "pijin wawrz" bring attention to rules only to show the arbitrariness of these rules and the necessity on the part of the Pidgin speaker to subvert these rules or maneuver them to their advantage. They both concretize Tonouchi's guerrilla philosophy and show his interest in revealing the agonistic process that is necessary for the future horizon of linguistic justice or equality.

How does this guerrilla philosophy account for the affective registers of language difference? Affective manifestations of language difference, such as language pride, are an important dimension of ethnolinguistic nationalism. How the guerrilla philosophy handles the affective side of language difference may well offer insights into Tonouchi's view of language as *ethnos*. While his affection for Pidgin is palpable in his writings, Tonouchi is able to avoid the pitfalls of exclusionary ethnolinguistic nationalism by virtue of his attunement to Pidgin's origin as a creole language. A case in point is his own reflections on his fourth-generation Japanese Okinawan identity in *Oriental Faddah and Son* (2012), a collection of semi-autobiographical poems.[33] Micheline Soong notes in her introduction to *Oriental Faddah and Son* that "the trajectory of Okinawan immigrants is less widely known [to the American reading audience] because their stories are folded into the more widely known Japanese American experience of war and internment and reintegration into American society."[34] In Tonouchi's collection of poems, Okinawan is a distinct identity that cannot be entirely explained through or as Japanese identity. By setting up the relationship between Okinawan and mainland Japanese as parallel to that between Hawaiian and mainland American, Tonouchi brings into high relief the feelings and sentiments that can resonate across geographical distance and historical particularities. In "Palms Face Up," one of the several poems on hajichi tattoos – tattoos traditionally done most often on the back of women's hands in Okinawa – Tonouchi tries to understand the shame his grandmother felt over her hajichi tattoos. He fails to understand her explanation of Okinawan shame until she mentions the Japanese education in Okinawa that taught "you gotta be like da mainland."[35] "[Y]ou know da kine," Tonouchi says at the end of the poem as he understands his grandmother's shame through the shame he knows by being taught that Hawaiian ways are inferior to those of the mainland.[36] The antidote to language shame here is not language pride but the capacity to see connections between different conditions that similarly create shame in one's language. By focusing on the resonances and commonalities between his own experiences of growing up in Hawaii and Okinawan experiences he hears from his relatives and family friends, Tonouchi is able to avoid exclusionary tendencies of nationalism in his exploration of what that heritage means to him and how it translates into the practices of his everyday life.

In the scholarship on language rights, "ethnolinguistic democracy" and "ethnolinguistic equality" are often incompatible terms.[37] Defined as the idea that a language group should be able to represent itself using its own language, ethnolinguistic democracy supports all ethnic groups' languages. When this idea is put into practice, however, it often clashes with ethnolinguistic equality, or the idea that all language groups should be represented equally. Yet "democracy" and "equality" are both potent terms in Tonouchi's writings. Approaching these terms, as they relate to ethnolinguistic identity, through his guerrilla philosophy offers a decidedly different view of their compatibility than that offered by a mechanical, or strictly formal, approach to these terms. Regarding equality, in particular, guerrilla philosophy desists from thinking about it solely in terms of sameness and attempts to address the conditions under which an individual or a group experiences inequality. For example, in the poem "All Mix Up" in *Oriental Faddah and Son*, Tonouchi finds himself in a Japanese-language class in college, a suggestion made by others who are aware of the economic and social benefits of knowing Japanese. When he does poorly in class despite enlisting his grandmother to help him, Tonouchi wonders why, especially as the Japanese-language instructor tells him that his grandmother may not speak "proper Japanese."[38] In a chance conversation with his grandfather's friend, Tonouchi finds out that what his grandmother speaks is Chanpurū Uchināguchi, which is "Okinawan, Japanese, Hawaiian, English, Pidgin, all mix up togeddah in one."[39] Unlike his language instructor, who views this as a deviation from "proper Japanese," Tonouchi takes pride in his grandmother's language, which reflects the Hawaiian Okinawan experience. The poem ends with a subversion of what being smart means: "I guess I know little bit of something not too many people know, brah. Gotta be proud for be CHIBURU!"[40]

This seemingly simple poem actually holds several insights that can be helpful for discussions of linguistic justice. Chanpurū Uchināguchi indexes the unavailability of linguistic justice to Tonouchi's grandmother, who did not have access to either standard Japanese or English and whose language is viewed as improper. Nowhere in the poem, however, is there any suggestion that righting the linguistic wrong here should be done by including Chanpurū Uchināguchi in the school curriculum (a suggestion that has been repeatedly and understandably made for other languages in similar contexts). Tonouchi's poem disregards the educational institution as the standard of assessing what is proper language and turns away from viewing linguistic justice – at least in his grandmother's case – through institutional measures. Instead, the reader is left to reflect on the multiple experiences of social marginalization and discrimination that resulted in the grandmother's language. Implicitly, ethnolinguistic democracy or equality are not terms to be hastily viewed as incompatible within the existing institutional settings without a thorough examination of how these settings relate to the making of inequality in the first place. This reflective step, I suggest, precedes any prescriptive view of ideals such as democracy or equality when it comes to language and ethnicity in Tonouchi's guerrilla philosophy.

Literature, as a medium, is central to guerrilla philosophy because it allows Tonouchi to discard prescriptive views on language and instead to focus on creatively capturing the expressions of linguistic inequality. In theoretical discussions of why language diversity matters, aesthetic value – the idea that "[t]here are many different languages and, as a result, many different ways of expressing views or emotions, or even of producing art" and that this is beneficial for humanity – is only ambivalently upheld as a reason to support language diversity, curtailed by qualifiers such as the lack of uniform standards for aesthetic appreciation.[41] Tonouchi's writings resist the isolation of aesthetics as a discreet realm in human life and suggest that aesthetic experience should be embedded in social action and ethical deliberations, activities that are seminal to public conversations on what constitutes public good.

By way of conclusion, I would like to turn to a short story by Kanae, "Born-Again Hawaiian," to elaborate on the possibilities of literature in Pidgin's support for indigenous Hawaiian causes. In this short story, Kanae portrays a husband and wife, Sheldon and Manu, who suspend their marital conflict over the shared news of Manu's pregnancy and an imagined future for their unborn child rooted in Hawaiian heritage. Initially in the story, Sheldon, who disavows politics, cannot understand Manu, who in his eyes has become increasingly politically conscious since their dating days. She was Melissa then, not Manu. Much to his consternation, after attending classes at the University of Hawai'i, Manu now questions his lack of interest in indigenous Hawaiian history and culture and calls him "apathetic."[42] The couple is at a crossroads in their marriage until the end, when their conflict dissolves into shared excitement over their unborn baby. Sheldon realizes he wants to name the baby Kekoa, the Hawaiian word for warrior, revealing his own investment in indigenous Hawaiian culture, and the bond between the couple is renewed.

While it is never explicitly mentioned, the contours of this story point to the efforts of Hawaiian-language revitalization led by educators and activists like Larry Kimura, Pila Wilson, and Kauanoe Kamanā. Guided by the philosophy of linguistic self-determination and the commitment to the idea that a living people should have a living language, these educators and activists spearheaded a movement to start Hawaiian immersion programs and schools, overturning in 1986 the legal prohibition of using Hawaiian as a medium of education in schools, effective since 1896.[43] According to Kimura, by 2009 Hawaiian-language revitalization has grown to include more than 2,000 students receiving their entire education in Hawaiian, plus about 3,800 and 2,000 students taking Hawaiian language as a subject in K–12 and in college, respectively.[44] In light of the number of native speakers of Hawaiian in 1988 – fewer than 2,000 – Hawaiian immersion programs have successfully created a basis for preserving the Hawaiian language.[45] "Born-Again Hawaiian" suggests that a renewed interest in the language and the way of life associated with it came to exist even outside the immediate educational circles that use Hawaiian. Sheldon shows that the discovery of meaning in life and a rediscovery of Hawaiian language and culture can be intimately linked for ordinary people.

For advocates and supporters of Pidgin, borrowing from the lexicon of language preservation has been a way of both legitimizing Pidgin as a language and of creating collective concern for it. For example, hearing a longtime advocate of Pidgin, Eric Chock, observe that Pidgin's future may be uncertain given the decreasing number of younger speakers prompts Tonouchi to reflect on Pidgin's prospects similarly: "Is Pidgin really in danger of dying? Is Pidgin on da brink of death?"[46] This lexicon of language preservation unduly introduces the possibility of competition between Pidgin and Hawaiian because language preservation is an area where the question of limited resources and their fair distribution comes up acutely.[47] Kanae's short story offers a different relationship between Pidgin and Hawaiian in which Pidgin is the literary language that imagines a vibrant future for Hawaiian. In this relationship, Pidgin does not exist at the expense of Hawaiian. Rather, it sees its own survival as interlinked with the revitalization of Hawaiian.

Notes

1. I use the term "Pidgin" to refer to Hawaiian Creole English (or Hawaiian Pidgin English) because the writers I discuss here use this term for their language of writing. See Candace Fujikane and Jonathan Y. Okamura, eds., *Asian Settler Colonialism: From Local Governance to the Habits of Everyday Life in Hawai'i* (Honolulu: University of Hawai'i Press, 2008) for writings on Asian settler colonialism by Asian American and indigenous Hawaiian scholars and activists. See Iyko Day, *Alien Capital: Asian Racialization and the Logic of Settler Colonial Capitalism* (Durham, NC: Duke University Press, 2016) for a theory of Asian racialization in relation to settler colonialism.
2. Stephen H. Sumida, *And the View from the Shore* (Seattle: University of Washington Press, 1999); Gail Y. Okawa, "Resistance and Reclamation: Hawaii 'Pidgin English' and Autoethnography in the Short Stories of Darrel H. Y. Lum," in *Ethnicity and the American Short Story*, ed. Julie Brown (New York: Garland, 1997), 177–96; Rob Wilson, *Reimagining the American Pacific:*

From South Pacific to Bamboo Ridge and Beyond (Durham, NC: Duke University Press, 2000); Susannah Young-ah Gottlieb, "Homing Pidgins: Another Version of Pastoral in Hawai'i," in *American Babel: Literatures of the United States from Abnaki to Zuni*, ed. Marc Shell (Cambridge, MA: Harvard University Press, 2002), 163–87; Susan Y. Najita, "Pleasure and Colonial Resistance: Translating the Politics of Pidgin in Milton Murayama's *All I Asking for Is My Body*," in *Imagining Our Americas: Toward a Transnational Frame*, eds. Sandhya Shukla and Heidi Tinsman (Durham, NC: Duke University Press, 2007), 111–37.

3. Eric Chock, "The Neocolonialization of Bamboo Ridge: Repositioning Bamboo Ridge and Local Literature in the 1990s," *Bamboo Ridge: A Hawai'i Writers' Quarterly* 69 (1996), 11–25.

4. My discussion of allyship here does not assume any commensurability between indigenous Hawaiians and Asian Americans in Hawai'i. The two groups have different histories and experiences in Hawai'i, which affects their relationships to the state and each group's political strategies at various points in time.

5. Quoted in Lee A. Tonouchi, *Living Pidgin: Contemplations on Pidgin Culture* (Kāneo'he: Tinfish Press, 2002), 3.

6. Tonouchi, *Living Pidgin*, 30, 44.

7. Werner Sollors, *Beyond Ethnicity: Consent and Descent in American Culture* (New York: Oxford University Press, 1986).

8. Lisa Linn Kanae, *Sista Tongue* (Kāneo'he: Tinfish Press, 2001).

9. Kanae, *Sista Tongue*, 39 (my page number for the unpaginated chapbook).

10. Kanae, *Sista Tongue*, 28 (my page number).

11. Kanae, *Sista Tongue*, 28 (my page number).

12. Kanae, *Sista Tongue*, 52, 56 (my page numbers).

13. Pierre Bourdieu, *The Field of Cultural Production: Essays on Art and Literature* (New York: Columbia University Press, 1993).

14. Kanae, *Sista Tongue*, 52 (my page number).

15. Tove Skutnabb-Kangas, "Multilingualism and the Education of Minority Children," *Estudios Fronterizos* 8.18–19 (1989), 36–67. For a critical engagement with the term "linguicism" using Hawai'i as a case study, see Rubén Fernández Asensio, "Language Policies in the Kingdom of Hawai'i: Reassessing Linguicism," *Language Problem and Language Planning* 38.2 (2014), 128–48.

16. Tove Skutnabb-Kangas, "Indigenous or Immigrant Minorities? Who Is at Greater Risk?" *NORRAG News* 34 (2004), 16.

17. Skutnabb-Kangas, "Indigenous or Immigrant Minorities?", 15.

18. See John E. Reinecke's still-relevant 1935 study, *Language and Dialect in Hawai'i: A Sociolinguistic Study to 1935* (Honolulu: University of Hawai'i Press, 1969), for a discussion of Pidgin as a creole language in comparison to other creole languages in the Caribbean where plantations resulted in the creation of new languages.

19. Kanae, *Sista Tongue*, 17 (my page number).
20. Kanae, *Sista Tongue*, 56 (my page number).
21. Haunani-Kay Trask, "Settlers of Color and 'Immigrant' Hegemony: 'Locals' in Hawai'i," in *Asian Settler Colonialism: From Local Governance to the Habits of Everyday Life in Hawai'i*, eds. Candace Fujikane and Jonathan Y. Okamura (Honolulu: University of Hawai'i Press), 51–54.
22. Lee A. Tonouchi, "pijin wawrz" in *da word* (Honolulu: Bamboo Ridge Press, 2001), 135.
23. Tonouchi, *Living Pidgin*, 44.
24. Philippe Van Parijs, *Linguistic Justice for Europe and for the World* (Oxford: Oxford University Press, 2011).
25. Parijs, *Linguistic Justice*, 139, 28.
26. Parijs, *Linguistic Justice*, 196.
27. Tonouchi, *Living Pidgin*, 20.
28. Tonouchi, *Living Pidgin*, 20.
29. Lee A. Tonouchi, "da word," in *da word* (Honolulu: Bamboo Ridge Press, 2001), 12.
30. Kent Sakoda and Jeff Siegel, *Pidgin Grammar: An Introduction to the Creole Language of Hawai'i* (Honolulu: Bess Press, 2003), 24.
31. Lee A. Tonouchi, "pijin wawrz," in *da word*, 137.
32. Tonouchi, "pijin wawrz," 133, 135.
33. Lee A. Tonouchi, *Significant Moments in da Life of Oriental Faddah and Son: One Hawai'i Okinawan Journal* (Honolulu: Bess Press, 2012).
34. Micheline M. Soong, "Introduction: Lee A. Tonouchi—Guerilla Poet," in *Oriental Faddah and Son*, xix.
35. Tonouchi, *Oriental Faddah and Son*, 70–71.
36. Tonouchi, *Oriental Faddah and Son*, 71.
37. Joshua A. Fishman, "On the Limits of Ethnolinguistic Democracy," in *Linguistic Human Rights: Overcoming Linguistic Discrimination* (Berlin/Boston: De Gruyter, 1995), 49–61.
38. Tonouchi, *Oriental Faddah and Son*, 74.
39. Tonouchi, *Oriental Faddah and Son*, 76–77.
40. Tonouchi, *Oriental Faddah and Son*, 77.
41. Idil Boran, "Global Linguistic Diversity, Public Goods, and the Principle of Fairness," in *Language Rights and Political Theory*, eds. Will Kymlicka and Alan Patten (Oxford: Oxford University Press, 2007), 195.
42. Lisa Linn Kanae, "Born-Again Hawaiian," in *Islands Linked by Ocean* (Honolulu: Bamboo Ridge Press, 2009), 48.
43. Larry Kimura, "Aia Iā Kākou Nā Hā'ina – The Answers Are within Us: Language Rights in Tandem with Language Survival," in *American Indian Language Development Institute: Thirty Year Tradition of Speaking from Our Heart*, eds. Candace K. Galla, Stacey Oberly, G. L. Romero, Maine Sam, and Ofelia Zepeda (Tucson: American Indian Language Development Institute, 2010), 41–51.

44. Larry Kimura and Isiik April G. L. Counceller, "Indigenous New Words Creation Perspectives from Alaska and Hawai'i," in *Indigenous Language Revitalization: Encouragement, Guidance & Lessons Learned,* eds. John Reyhner and Louise Lockard (Flagstaff: Northern Arizona University, 2009), 127–28.

45. Kimura and Counceller, "Indigenous New Words," 122.

46. Tonouchi, *Living Pidgin,* 26.

47. Michael Blake, "Language Death and Liberal Politics," in *Language Rights and Political Theory,* 222–24.

CHAPTER 23

Celeste Ng's Little Fires Everywhere *and the Burning House of American Literature*

Anna Brickhouse

"Everyone in Shaker Heights was talking about it that summer: how Isabelle, the last of the Richardson children, had finally gone around the bend and burned the house down. All spring the gossip had been about little Mirabelle McCullough—or, depending on which side you were on, May Ling Chow—and now, at last, there was something new and sensational to discuss."[1] So begins Celeste Ng's *Little Fires Everywhere* (2017), a deceptively accessible novel that thinks about race and American literature across the sweep of time, from Nathaniel Hawthorne's *The Scarlet Letter* (1850) through our own moment and beyond. From its opening sentences, the novel's multiracial but predominantly white setting is clear: the wealthy suburban landscape of Shaker Heights in the late 1990s. Addressing its readers ever so casually, Ng's omniscient narrator luxuriates in the familiar pleasures of neighborhood gossip; we along with everyone in Shaker Heights can watch as the new and sensational scene unfolds. But the narrator's "you" is deceptive, and it comes with a requirement to take a side in a conflict that has not yet been specified. All we know is that this narrator has chosen to privilege, if only in the grammatical sense, a dominant cultural or European (American) name over a Chinese (American) one. The commitments of this narrative voice, the "side" it is on, are not yet clear.

These formal qualities of narration reflect the story's main subject: the evolution of two very different white families – and in particular two white mothers – who meet on the unequal playing field of landlord and tenant. The main storyline and the multiple prior histories in which it culminates are all framed by the burning down of the landowner's house; and the novel's epigraphs, taken from a real estate advertisement and a 1963 magazine article about social life in Shaker Heights, make clear that the history of property relations will constitute a significant part of the deep structure on which the story of the two white families rests. This history – like both the narrative voice and the "gossip" that inaugurates the novel – has an indelible racial background and produces its own complex and often ambiguous racial effects.

Shaker Heights is where "We're friendly people and we have a wonderful time!" – as per the second of the two epigraphs, which cites a woman of unspecified race from the "Shaker Heights Country Club," interviewed in the early 1960s. Like many suburbs, this planned community was conceived and developed to stand apart from what the narrator terms the "grimy city of Cleveland" – and it also brought this belief in the curative powers of planning to bear on the great color line problem of the twentieth century.[2] As the narrator explains, "a neighborhood association sprang up to encourage integration in a particularly Shaker Heights manner: loans to encourage white families to move into black neighborhoods, loans to encourage black families to move into white neighborhoods."[3] Only the prepositional phrase devoted to the "Shaker Heights manner" betrays a delicate irony regarding progressive racial policy.

James Baldwin famously phrased the irony this way in his 1963 meditation on race in America, *The Fire Next Time*: "Do I really want to be integrated into a burning house?"[4] Indeed, one thinks immediately of Baldwin when ninth grader Izzy Richardson – the "black sheep" of a very white family – decides to burn down the great family house at the end of Ng's novel.[5] Baldwin adapted the question – and the title of the book in which it appears – from an old song of the enslaved: "God gave Noah the rainbow sign. No more water, the fire next time."[6] Ng's novel does not cite Baldwin specifically, but it broadly evokes a continuous history of racial conflagration throughout American literature: from the fire that produces the racial "Monster" in Stephen Crane's 1898 novella of the same name to the flame-lit lynching scenes in James Weldon Johnson's *Autobiography of an Ex-Colored Man* (1912) and Jean Toomer's *Cane* (1923), and to the Crown Heights riot that Anna Deveare Smith titled *Fires in the Mirror* (1992) in her verbatim theater play of the early 1990s, just a few years before *Little Fires* itself is set. And Ng's novel recalls even more specifically the burning of Sutpen's plantation home in William Faulkner's *Absalom, Absalom!* (1936) and the burning of the master's great house in Toni Morrison's *A Mercy*, her 2008 novel exploring the seventeenth-century origins of race in America.

This essay reads *Little Fires Everywhere* as a metaliterary investigation into the relationship between literary and cultural form and the series of racial entanglements – black and white and Asian – played out in its neoliberal 1990s setting. The novel invites us to see that decade – from its discussions of presidential race to its often black/white and nationally delimited, Anglophone-based landscape of American literary criticism – from the vantage point of its moment of production during the waning Obama years and the rise of Trump. The novel explores the features of realist, postracial form in a suburban, domestic narrative that slowly reveals itself to be, instead, a racial tragedy: a tragedy about, among other issues, the global supply of reproductive material and labor that meets the demand for children among wealthy Americans. Finally, in its engagement with *The Scarlet Letter*, the novel asks what the role of race in Hawthorne can show us about racial discourse in the 1990s and about color-blindness as the mask of racial violence, reproductive and otherwise. In this way, Ng's novel testifies to the enduring power of American literature to imaginatively – spectacularly, as Morrison herself might say – unspeak and respeak the story of race in American history and culture.

***

As we learn in the opening pages, the racial conflagration framing Ng's novel has more than one source: "... little fires everywhere. Multiple points of origin. Possible use of accelerant. Not an accident."[7] True to its title, the book explores the burning house of America through the complex, polyvalent, and sometimes competing elements that define a flexible and enduring structure of white supremacy. The house that Izzy burns stands neither for slaveholding nor for the disinherited and repressed black familial line but for the very essence of Shaker Heights racial sensibility in a particular historical moment: the heyday of color-blindness, which gives rise to the future era of ideological postracialism during which Ng's novel was produced. Indeed, at the formal level, the book's opening frame exemplifies the postracialism it also scrutinizes. We quickly meet a small supporting cast of largely affluent nonwhite characters – Brian Avery, who is black and the son of a doctor and lawyer, is the boyfriend of Izzy's sister, Lexie; Serena Wong, who is Asian American and the daughter of one or more doctors, is Lexie's best friend – who do not discuss race with their white peers except in the most peripheral and superficial ways. But when May Ling Chow and her mother Bebe enter the novel a third of the way through, its self-consciously postracial mode implodes into a meditation on the potential violence of color-blind ideology and its legacy. The novel thus brings two distinct historical moments into sly dialectical relation: the late 1990s in which its action is set in richly textured detail and the last years of the age of Obama, in which the story itself came into being.

When Izzy's sister, Lexie Richardson, for example, announces that her "boyfriend Brian is going to be the first black president," the novel references both its historical frames simultaneously: both the waning of the Obama years in which Ng is writing and the moment in which Toni Morrison would call Bill Clinton "white skin notwithstanding . . . our first black president."[8] "After all," Morrison famously wrote in *The New Yorker* in September 1998, "Clinton displays almost every trope of blackness," starting with the single-parent household into which he was born – racialized tropes that she notices African American men in particular recognizing with a sense of trauma for the way they left "the President's body, his privacy, his unpoliced sexuality . . . the focus of persecution."[9] The narrator of *Little Fires Everywhere*, set during precisely this moment, describes the crisis from a quite different Shaker Heights point of view: "True, the country was now titillated by the president's tawdry indiscretions, but scandalous as it was, the whole affair felt faintly comic. Across the city, opinions ranged from *It has nothing to do with how he runs the country* to *All presidents have affairs* to the more succinct *Who cares?*"[10] In 1990s Shaker Heights, a critical analysis like Morrison's, framed by the long history of race in America, cannot emerge from within the framework of colorblindness: "I mean, we're lucky," says Lexie, "No one sees race here."[11]

The larger novel, of course, knows differently – and it presents a scenario much like the one Morrison offers, in which the second white family – the tenant family – presents certain tropes of blackness that set them apart in Shaker Heights: Mia Warren and her daughter, Pearl, are poor and subject to the whim of their landlord's mood, whether one of condescending kindness or cruelty. Mia cleans and cooks for the Richardson family, who owns the apartment she rents. There is, moreover, a traumatic mystery at the heart of Pearl's unknown paternity – one that has left Mia fugitive and vulnerable for reasons that the novel withholds at the start. This shadowy background – as landlord Mrs. Richards sees it, "this unwillingness to be forthcoming, to state your origins plainly" – has left the Warrens, her single-parent tenant family, in a state of precariousness that becomes especially clear when viewed through the lens provided by Morrison in the 1990s.[12]

As it happens, Morrison was also during that decade teaching a new generation of Americanists how to read race in American literature. "It only seems that the canon of American literature is 'naturally' or 'inevitably' 'white.' In fact it is studiously so": an argument that Ng's novel explores through a landscape of literary allusions that is overwhelmingly white, which is part of its meta-literary point, part of the racial ideology it both portrays and formally encodes.[13] *Little Fires Everywhere* teems with white readers. Izzy reads "The Love-Song of J. Alfred Prufrock" and Philip

Larkin's "This Be the Verse."[14] Moody Richardson, brother of Izzy and Lexie, can reference *Robinson Crusoe* – but as "a romantic at heart," he prefers Jack Kerouac, Frank O'Hara, Ranier Maria Rilke, Pablo Neruda, even Ernest Hemingway.[15] Under the tutelage of a mentor, Mia has read "books by the stack: Elizabeth Bishop, Anne Sexton, Adrienne Rich."[16] And Pearl, though she hasn't read as much "because (she has) moved so often," keeps a commonplace book and writes her own poetry.[17] She also knows fairy tales and how to retell them for alternative meaning, including "Rumplestiltskin" – a story with a reproductive plot that foreshadows the novel's explicit racial problem, the one named in its first sentence: the case of Bebe Chow, a Chinese immigrant and new mother experiencing food scarcity and postpartum depression, who leaves her baby, May Ling, at a fire station and then, after she has recovered, wants her back; meanwhile, a wealthy white Shaker Heights family, the McCulloughs, have adopted her.[18] Even the titles of children's books – *Goodnight Moon, Pat the Bunny, Madeline, Eloise, Blueberries for Sal* – become racial evidence of unrelenting whiteness under questioning by Bebe's lawyer, Ed Lim. As he points out, one need only contrast these books to the single American classic of children's literature featuring an Asian character, the white-authored *Five Chinese Brothers*, to understand the problem.[19]

***

But if the novel's canon of allusions is white and Western, it exists in part to be denaturalized and reframed by Ng's commentary on the centuries-long history of race in American literature. At the center of this commentary towers Hawthorne, perhaps because he was famous for avoiding the sort of racial "actualities ... so terribly insisted upon as they are, and must needs be, in America," as he put it in his preface to *The Marble Faun*.[20] Likewise, Ng's novel avoids insisting on – or even peripherally addressing – such actualities in Hawthorne. Instead, *Little Fires Everywhere* begins simply by flagging the utopian setting and the broadly philosophical questions about communities built on idealism that it shares with *The Blithedale Romance*, the dark romantic novel that critics have often associated with Hawthorne's experience at the experimental utopian community of Brook Farm in the 1840s. Shaker Heights in the 1990s no longer has Shakers as residents, but the goal of perfection still defines its late-century ethos: "perhaps the Shakers had lived it so strongly it had seeped into the soil itself."[21] Just as Hawthorne's ancestral Puritans have "mingled their earthy substance with the soil" of New England, leaving a legacy that "nearly two centuries and a quarter" have not fully eroded, Shaker Heights too – like transcendentalist Brook Farm refracted in *Blithedale* – has been founded "with the same idea of creating a utopia."[22] Like Hawthorne, Ng navigates the gap between a society's self-perception and its reality, exploring its "deep intolerance for flaws" and love of "regulation, the father of order."[23] And like Hawthorne, Ng plumbs the emotional depths of this utopia as it falls apart under the weight of its contradictions.

But her novel's deepest relationship is to *The Scarlet Letter*, which has offered Mia not only a name for her fatherless daughter, Pearl, but also an imaginative framework for raising her independently – since Hawthorne's Pearl, as the narrator puts it, was "of course born into complicated circumstances."[24] From the moment that Lexie asks Pearl – "Do you ever think about trying to find your father?" – the novel treads on the soil of its nineteenth-century American predecessor.[25] Mia offers an obvious analogue for Hester on several levels: She is an artist and approaches the world mainly to see its aesthetic possibilities; growing up, she suffers isolation surrounded by puritanical parents who believe art is a waste and therefore vaguely immoral; holding a camera, she has "a sudden image of herself as a sorceress, waving her hand over the field and transforming the boys below into pea-sized plastic dolls."[26] Like her literary ancestor who narrowly escapes being burned as a witch, she finds power and acuity of perception in the very art that separates her from society.

There is a kind of built-in triumph, in other words, in the name that Mia selects for her daughter – and in the flattering maternal parallel it sets up. Hester survives shunning and solitude to be "looked upon," eventually, "with awe, yet with reverence, too."[27] Because she lives without pursuit of "profit and enjoyment," following only the dual calls of art and motherhood, "people brought all their sorrows and perplexities, and besought her counsel, as one who had herself gone through a mighty trouble": "Women, more especially—in the continual recurring trials of wounded, wasted, wronged, misplaced, or erring and sinful passion—or with the dreary burden of a heart unyielded, because unvalued and unsought—came to Hester's cottage, demanding why they were so wretched, and what the remedy!"[28] Similarly, Mia too – with her austerity and her fatherless child – invites curiosity, and often reverence. She too opens the doors of her rental apartment to a series of young women suffering such "recurring trials" of their sex and asking her counsel: Izzy, rejected by her mother; Lexie, pregnant and ashamed; and, most important, Bebe Chow, who has abandoned her daughter, May Ling, and now wants to reclaim her.

But Ng's most striking engagement with *The Scarlet Letter* – and with the complex racial ideologies it helped to bequeath the United States across centuries – unfolds when the secret of her Hester-like heroine finally emerges. For when it does, it helps to clarify the twin stories of May Ling's adoption by a wealthy white family and Bebe's tragic derangement after the birth of a child she cannot support. Mia's secret is that she conceived her daughter, Pearl, under contract with a wealthy white family not unlike the one who adopts May Ling – though the event occurred years ago in New York City rather than Shaker Heights. The novel takes care to exempt Mia from willing participation in the reproductive economy in which she then found herself. She does not seek out surrogacy work, but rather is subsequently approached – accosted, virtually, and at the very moment when she has lost her tuition money under Reagan-era federal cuts to student aid – by a man with "a strange mix of recognition and hunger" in his eyes.[29] He asks for her egg, her womb, and her labor so that he and his wife can procure a child of their own straight from the moment of conception. In a tangle of beneficence ("She could help them. She would help them.") and clear-cut financial desperation, she agrees to what her parents soon call "sell[ing] your own child."[30]

Ng's novel thereby places Mia at the center of several interlocking strands of US economic history, playing out their consequences for a white and financially insecure young student in detail. Unrestricted free market activity has accelerated the wealth gap during the early 1980s between people like the Ryans and people like her parents, who cannot afford Mia's tuition after the decimating of student grants. During these same years, the reproductive body became legally available for sale for the first time in US history since Hawthorne's moment: during the era of slavery. The Ryans, who want to buy genetic material and reproductive labor, are thus in a prime economic position to choose exactly the surrogate they want: in this case, Mia, because she resembles Mrs. Ryan. Ng's novel is just as silent as Hawthorne's novel on the matter of her heroine's whiteness. But as *Little Fires Everywhere* slowly unfolds the close parallels between Hester and Mia, that silence becomes a form of articulation.

Like Hester, Mia makes a life-changing mistake as a result of her passion – though in her case, the passion is art, which draws her into the surrogacy contract in order to continue her studies. Like Hester, she then essentially pays for what she has done. She returns the maternity clothes the Ryans have bought her and leaves them nine hundred dollars, all the money she has to her name, to pay for medical expenses they have incurred. She runs with her unborn child, changes her identity, and lives at the edge of poverty with no permanent home. But she continues to practice and sell her art (like Hester, whose needlepoint supplies "food for her thriving infant and herself"), and she becomes a freer person intellectually and artistically as a result of her ordeal – precisely as did her nineteenth-century predecessor.[31] And ultimately, in refashioning Hawthorne's meditation on Hester's freedom from the constraints of society, Ng's novel lays bare the racial politics shaping her classic American predecessor in a subtle and innovative way.

Critics since at least the 1990s have recognized that Hester's faint racialization as one of Hawthorne's emblematic dark ladies marks the novel's anxieties regarding Native peoples, as well as its (dis)engagement with slavery, its unwilling but abiding attachment to what Morrison called "Africanist presence."[32] Moreover, Luther S. Luedtke recognized in 1989 that Hester's "rich, voluptuous, Oriental characteristic" registered Hawthorne's larger interest in East and South Asia and his corresponding use of Asian "themes, symbols, settings, character types, and storytelling techniques" – the residue of extraction, both literary and material, for the China trade route was central to the creation of the American bourgeoisie in the Northeast, including Hawthorne's seafaring family, whose wealth was built according to the Salem city motto: *Divitis Indiae usque ad ultimum sinum* ("To the farthest port of the rich East").[33] Ng's novel draws on both these strands of racialization, detailing the tropes of blackness surrounding Mia's family as well as the Orientalism of the white characters' investment in May Ling's Chinese heritage.

But its most devastating response to Hawthorne lies in the way that Mia's achievement of liberation and her fugitive independence from society asks us to reread Hester's as explained by Hawthorne:

> Her intellect and heart had their home, as it were, in desert places, where she roamed as freely as the wild Indian in his woods. For years, she had looked from this estranged point of view at human institutions, and whatever priests or legislators had established; criticizing all with hardly more reverence than the Indian would feel for the clerical band, the judicial robe, the pillory, the gallows, the fireside, or the church. The tendency of her fate and fortunes had been to set her free.[34]

Read through the lens that Ng's novel provides, the Hawthorne passage registers not merely the novel's racialization of its dark lady, but the far deeper and more pernicious racial structure of its conception of her freedom. When Hawthorne establishes the unboundedness of Hester's autonomy by aligning her with "the wild Indian," he is not merely harnessing racial otherness as a classic Romantic symbol for the conflict between individualism and society. He is also disclosing the racial under-pinnings of modern American freedom itself. "Indian" thus stands out in this passage as a "mark of colonial difference," as Lisa Lowe puts it, "an enduring remainder of the processes through which the human is univer-salized and freed by liberal forms, while the peoples who created the conditions of possibility for that freedom are assimilated or forgotten."[35] Hester's autonomous "intellect and heart" are not *like* that of the wild Indian; rather, her putative condition is made structurally and imagina-tively possible by the dispossession of the Indian from "his woods" in the first place – and by the broader histories of settler colonialism, slavery, and global capitalism that have shaped what it means to be human and to be free. But these broader histories are brought to the foreground by Ng's novel, which dramatically undoes its nineteenth-century predecessor pre-cisely by modeling its heroine's freedom on Hester's – but then back-lighting Mia's achievement of liberation with the juxtaposed story of Bebe Chow and the late twentieth-century racial entanglements revealed by her adoption case.

***

Hawthorne's novel, of course, never permits readers to glimpse whose stories must be occluded – nonwhite women's reproductive stories in particular – in order to stage Hester's trajectory as a triumph. *Little Fires Everywhere*, working against the grain of *The Scarlet Letter*, permits us to consider Mia's story only *after* we have witnessed the predicament of Bebe Chow. Aligning Mia and Bebe, the novel offers us a version of Hester refracted through a nineteenth-century racialized woman we will never know because Hawthorne (and arguably many of his critics) could not imagine the significance of her point of view. Ng's novel thus insists that we view its story of Mia's flight from contractual surrogacy "not in the abstract realm of reproductive choice," as legal theorist Dorothy E. Roberts puts it, "but in the real world that devalues certain human lives with the law's approval."[36]

As it happens, *Killing the Black Body*, Roberts's groundbreaking critique of the racial politics underlying *all* aspects of reproduction – from child-birth to birth control to abortion to surrogacy to assisted reproductive technology to adoption (all of which feature in subplots in *Little Fires*) – was first published in the same year in which Ng's novel is set, and it is hard not to read the two texts engaged in a sympathetic and productive conversation across the decades. Mia's story of (non)surrogacy, both texts insist, must not be read simply as the story of her own reproductive choice in conflict with that of the couple that hires her; it must be read with attention to the centuries-long history of slavery throughout the African diaspora that underlies it. For it is this history, as Roberts notes, that "enables us to imagine the commodification of human beings," and that allowed the "vision of fungible breeder women in the first place."[37] Moreover, when Mia first considers the reproductive proposal made by the Ryans and arrives at the familiar conclusion that "her womb was not an apartment for rent," she follows a logic that Roberts painstakingly denaturalizes in her study: "Feminist opponents of surrogacy miss an important aspect of the practice when they criticize it for treating women as *fungible* commodities. A Black surrogate is not exchangeable for a white one" – and particularly not in a historical moment when black female reproductive labor was being devalued ubiquitously throughout US media for its creation of what Roberts called a "new bio-underclass" emblematized in the 1980s and 1990s by the trope of the "crack baby."[38]

It is thus no accident that landlord Mrs. Richardson – in her nearly crazed support for May Ling Chow's adoption by her friends, the McCulloughs – invokes the racial panic surrounding so-called "crack babies" in the 1980s and 1990s:

> "It's just *providential*, as my mother used to say," Mrs. Richardson had told her husband on hearing the news. "There's simply no other word for it. You know what Linda and Mark have been through, all that waiting. I mean, I bet they'd have taken a crack baby, for goodness sakes. And then out of the blue the social worker calls them at ten-thirty in the morning, saying there's been a little Asian baby left at a fire station, and by four o'clock in the afternoon there she is in their house."[39]

The passage registers the age-old American tradition of racial disavowal, one that runs across centuries from the "inscrutable decree of Providence" that lifts the infant Pearl out of the "rank luxuriance" of her unknown origins in *The Scarlet Letter* through the single word "Asian," describing an abandoned baby in the 1990s.[40] An entire history of racial logic underpins Mrs. Richardson's breathless account as she speaks for a community precisely where "no one sees race."[41]

What the McCulloughs "have been through," carefully detailed in the novel, is a heartbreaking story of miscarriage and infertility – and one that conforms closely to Roberts's contemporaneous analysis of the racial underpinnings of US adoption policy: "a regime," in her acute formulation, that "always prefers a white family and accommodates white families' preferences."[42] As Roberts points out, for most white couples, adoption is "a second-best alternative only after they fail to conceive a genetically related child"; as if to emphasize this point, in Ng's novel the McCulloughs choose to adopt only after no fewer than seven wrenching, late-stage miscarriages and a diagnosis informing them that "even IVF would likely fail": then and only then, "after one last doctor's appointment full of heartrending phrases – *low-motility sperm; inhospitable womb; conception likely impossible* – they'd decided to adopt."[43] The grammatical interruption of these italicized phrases in the idiom of new reproductive technology suggests the extent to which it intersects with adoption policy. "New reproductive technologies are so popular in American culture not simply because of the value placed on the genetic tie," writes Roberts, "but because of the value placed on the *white* genetic tie."[44]

Ng's novel subtly conveys the extent to which this value, never quite articulated as such in progressive Shaker Heights, nevertheless shapes the actions of the McCulloughs once they realize that adoption presents "their best chance for a baby":

> They'd put their names on every waiting list they could find, and from time to time an adoption agent would call with a possible match. But something always fell through .... A year passed, then two, then three. Everyone, it seemed, wanted a baby, and demand far exceeded supply.[45]

Race goes unmentioned in this description of the neoliberal system of private adoption, with its procuring "agent" and its rhetoric of the familial "match." But the economy in which the McCulloughs are fully enmeshed was explicitly designed with a primary purpose: "to provide childless white couples with babies and with the type of babies they prefer."[46] As historian of reproductive politics Laura Briggs explains, the private system provided "a more efficient route to a healthy white baby" than did the public one, which was being targeted by politicians and in the press as immoral and ineffective throughout the 1970s and 1980s for trying to keep birth families intact when possible.[47] By the late 1990s, though, as the McCulloughs soon learn, the "consumer market for [white] parents" had increasingly withered, setting the stage for a dramatic increase in international adoption.[48] At the precise moment when black infants were being vilified in the press as frightening latent criminals – a generation of "crack babies" who would come to adulthood all too soon – the United States saw the greatest rise in the adoption of Asian children since the aftermath of the Korean War. Thus, the market "miracle" of the "little Asian baby" is found at the local firehouse: global "supply" without the expense and difficulty of going overseas to meet increasing national demand.

Ng's novel thus positions Mrs. McCullough's dream of a child and her loving openness to interracial adoption – along with Mrs. Richardson's fervent support for it – within a larger racialized economic and political context embodied in Bebe's precarious status as an impoverished Chinese immigrant restaurant worker without access to healthcare. When Bebe suffers the severe postpartum depression that leaves her initially unable to care for her baby, the novel is signaling a broader simultaneity, one that Roberts pointed out in the 1990s: the 1996 stripping of the welfare safety net and the 1997 Adoption and Safe Families Act, which made domestic adoption dramatically easier by favoring the so-called best interests of children over those of birth parents and families – or, as Roberts observes, by favoring the best interests of white families who wish to adopt.[49] *Little Fires Everywhere* details the convergence of these interests and racial ideology in painful detail as various characters move from observing the economic advantages that will accrue to May Ling Chow -- or Mirabelle McCullough, as her adoptive parents choose to name her – to denigrating her biological mother for "keep(ing) the cycle of poverty going."[50]

The latter comment is made, ironically, by a black character we know mainly as Cliff, according to the "Huxtable" nicknames that Lexie's boyfriend Brian gives his parents – the novel's reminder that color-blind politics went along with Cosby-era, "pull-up-your-pants" respectability politics and could have dire consequences for black families. "And what about all those black babies going to white homes?" asks Brian's mother. "You think that breaks the cycle of poverty?"[51] Brian himself may be headed to become the "first black president," but even at seventeen he already recognizes that this spectacular outcome, so often hailed as the preeminent sign of postracialism, serves to cloak – rather than end – racial injustice. When an already pregnant Lexie daydreams aloud about having his baby, he recoils in alarm when she cannot see through her avowedly color-blind lens that the stakes of such an event are not equal for them – and not only because she as a woman bears the biological consequences of pregnancy, but because he as a black man bears different consequences that are just as physical: "Everybody would say, oh look, another black kid, knocked a girl up before he even graduated from high school."[52] An unwed pregnancy would spell Brian's end on both figurative and literal levels: "I'd be dead. Instant. Instant death."[53]

In a sense, Ng's novel fictionally stages Roberts's groundbreaking argument from the 1990s that "the quest to secure Black women's reproductive autonomy can transform the meaning of liberty for everyone."[54] There are no substantive black female characters in the novel and yet – from May

Ling's adoption case to Mia's terminated surrogacy arrangement to Lexie's secret abortion to Brian's fear of being murdered for conceiving a pregnancy – *Little Fires Everywhere* bears out the ways in which all the story's reproductive contexts are silently enmeshed in what Saidiya Hartman has called the "afterlife of slavery."[55] It is this afterlife of racialized reproductive politics that shapes all outcomes indirectly. Even the novel's greatest beneficiaries of this afterlife – Mrs. Richardson and Mrs. McCullough – lose children as a result. Bebe Chow achieves reproductive liberty and reunites with her child, but only by fleeing the United States. Lexie aborts a child she wanted to keep, and Brian never knows his almost paternity. Mia and Pearl return to the fugitivity that surrogacy politics first set into motion. And Izzy, who sets the large Richardson house afire, runs away forever. No one finds the freedom imagined by Hawthorne for his "Oriental" Hester – but readers are closer to understanding the ongoing racial histories that gave his image of Hester its ambiguous meaning.

***

Three years after the publication of *Little Fires Everywhere* in 2017, Ng's novel was adapted as a widely viewed HBO television miniseries that began streaming in March 2020 – and in the midst of a global pandemic during which COVID-19 brought dramatic racial health disparities to the national foreground. And two months after the show began streaming, nationwide protests against police brutality erupted in response to the murder of George Floyd; *Little Fires* was still on the screen in many American homes as fires of outrage and despair burned throughout major American cities. How might Ng's novel speak indirectly to this later moment, the moment of its streaming adaptation? *Little Fires Everywhere* is dedicated, non-ironically, to "those out on their own paths, setting little fires."[56] By the end, we learn that Mia has encouraged Izzy to burn down her family's house, figuratively we assume, for the purposes of regeneration: "Like after a prairie fire," Mia explains. "The earth is all scorched and black and everything green is gone. But after the burning the soil is richer and new things can grow."[57] Setting her home aflame, Izzy responds in the only way she knows how to the problem posed in the novel by her mother and indeed by her known American world, a world that "would never quite be able to bring those two ideas into balance": "justice and order."[58] Indeed, the novel goes further than the television adaptation precisely by suggesting that true justice may often come at the expense of order.

At the same time, though, the show also pushes the original further than it could go on its own. The adaptation follows the novel faithfully save one major change – or rather, perhaps, it speaks a truth that was there all along: In this version of Ng's story, Mia and her daughter, Pearl, are black. The television series in this sense visually articulates what the novel tells us through its metaliterary work: that its reproductive politics are inseparable not only from the racial contexts of global immigration but also from the afterlife of US slavery. But a television adaptation cannot gesture to prior literary texts in quite the same way – and reviews of the HBO series were generally mixed. "Melodrama" was the repeating descriptor that critics used to denigrate the adaptation for what they saw as its failures to achieve complexity and subtlety.[59] Yet melodrama, as Susan Gillman has suggested, may be among the most appropriate modes, in both literature and visual culture, for capturing the excess, the contradiction, and the violence of American racial history – for suggesting "the irreducible historical identity of race itself as a melodrama in the United States."[60] For if the melodramatic imagination has at its core a search for "expressivity," a will to "utter the unspeakable," as Peter Brooks has argued, then the American melodramatic mode may be especially suited to the racial unspoken that Morrison so brilliantly charts in her work on literary whiteness.[61] But of course melodrama is only one of the genres of American literary racial thought – as Ng's metafictional novel powerfully shows. To unspeak and respeak the story of race in US history and culture: Toni Morrison would remind us that the task of American literature is ongoing, and so too is the work of its readers and interpreters.

Notes

1. Celeste Ng, *Little Fires Everywhere* (New York: Penguin, 2017), 1.
2. Ng, *Little Fires*, 23.
3. Ng, *Little Fires*, 159.
4. James Baldwin, *The Fire Next Time* (New York: Dial Press, 1963), 108.
5. Ng, *Little Fires*, 5.
6. Baldwin, *The Fire*, 120.
7. Ng, *Little Fires*, 7.
8. Ng, *Little Fires*, 38. Toni Morrison, "Comment," *The New Yorker* (October 5, 1998), 31–32.
9. Morrison, 31–32.
10. Ng, *Little Fires*, 151.
11. Ng, *Little Fires*, 42.
12. Ng, *Little Fires*, 149.
13. Morrison, "Unspeakable Things Unspoken: The Afro-American Presence in American Literature," *Michigan Quarterly Review* 28.1 (1989), 14.

14. Ng, *Little Fires*, 79.
15. Ng, *Little Fires*, 29–31, 51.
16. Ng, *Little Fires*, 206.
17. Ng, *Little Fires*, 31.
18. Ng, *Little Fires*, 55.
19. Ng, *Little Fires*, 263.
20. Nathaniel Hawthorne, *The Marble Faun* (Oxford: Oxford University Press, 2002), x.
21. Ng, *Little Fires*, 23.
22. Hawthorne, *The Scarlet Letter* (Cambridge, MA: Harvard University Press, 2009), 9; Ng, *Little Fires*, 22.
23. Ng, *Little Fires*, 22–23.
24. Ng, *Little Fires*, 231.
25. Ng, *Little Fires*, 43.
26. Ng, *Little Fires*, 194.
27. Hawthorne, *Scarlet Letter*, 263.
28. Hawthorne, *Scarlet Letter*, 263.
29. Ng, *Little Fires*, 209.
30. Ng, *Little Fires*, 220, 185.
31. Hawthorne, *Scarlet Letter*, 79.
32. Morrison's phrase is central to both "Unspeakable Things Unspoken" and *Playing in the Dark: Whiteness and the Literary Imagination* (Cambridge, MA: Harvard University Press, 1992).
33. Hawthorne, *Scarlet Letter*, 81. Luther S. Luedtke, *Hawthorne and the Romance of the Orient* (Bloomington: Indiana University Press, 1989), xxii, 24.
34. Hawthorne, *Scarlet Letter*, 199.
35. Lisa Lowe, *The Intimacies of Four Continents* (Durham, NC: Duke University Press, 2015), 7.
36. Dorothy E. Roberts, *Killing the Black Body: Race, Reproduction, and the Meaning of Liberty* (New York: Vintage Books, 1997), 279.
37. Roberts, *Killing the Black Body*, 278.
38. Ng, *Little Fires*, 215; Roberts, *Killing the Black Body*, 279, 19–21.
39. Ng, *Little Fires*, 113.
40. Hawthorne, *Scarlet Letter*, 87.
41. Ng, *Little Fires*, 42.
42. Roberts, *Killing the Black Body*, 275.
43. Roberts, *Killing the Black Body*, 272; Ng, *Little Fires*, 133.
44. Roberts, *Killing the Black Body*, 269.
45. Ng, *Little Fires*, 133.
46. Roberts, *Killing the Black Body*, 275.
47. Laura Briggs, *Somebody's Children: The Politics of Transracial and Transnational Adoption* (Durham, NC: Duke University Press, 2012), 112.
48. Briggs, *Somebody's Children*, 112.
49. Roberts, *Killing the Black Body*, xvii.
50. Ng, *Little Fires*, 154.

51. Ng, *Little Fires*, 154.
52. Ng, *Little Fires*, 175.
53. Ng, *Little Fires*, 175.
54. Roberts, *Killing the Black Body*, 7.
55. Saidiya Hartman, *Lose Your Mother: A Journey along the Atlantic Slave Route* (New York: Farrar, Straus and Giroux, 2008), 6.
56. Ng, *Little Fires*, frontmatter dedication.
57. Ng, *Little Fires*, 295.
58. Ng, *Little Fires*, 159.
59. See, for instance, Mike Hale's *New York Times* review lamenting that the show had "no way to get around the melodramatic core of the material" (March 17, 2020, www.nytimes.com/2020/03/17/arts/television/little-fires-everywhere-review.html); Constance Grady's review for *Vox* labeling the show "a ham-handed melodrama about race and motherhood" (March 19, 2020, www.vox.com/culture/2020/3/19/21185789/little-fires-everywhere-review-hulu-reese-witherspoon-kerry-washington-celeste-ng); and Megan Reynolds's review for *Jezebel* criticizing the adaptation for "Stifl[ing] Itself with Melodrama" (March 20, 2020, https://themuse.jezebel.com/little-fires-everywhere-stifles-itself-with-melodrama-1842378788).
60. Susan Gillman, *Blood Talk: American Race Melodrama and the Culture of the Occult* (Chicago: University of Chicago Press, 2003), 4.
61. Peter Brooks, *The Melodramatic Imagination: Balzac, Henry James, Melodrama, and the Mode of Excess* (New Haven, CT: Yale University Press, 1975), 4.

PART VII

Reflections and Prospects

For this closing section, I've asked four prominent scholars to comment on their field and to offer a sense of direction. These essays were written prior to the national and global protests of 2020, but the pressures that led to that response, and the brutal inhumanity of systemic white supremacy, have always been clear to anyone who pays any attention to the history of race in the United States. These closing meditations, then, speak to the realities that the broader world finally began to acknowledge through the 2020 protests – and they speak as well to the need for attention to the humanities in this time when literature might not seem like the most pressing concern. For many, though, it is clear that we are suffering for the lack of attention to the humanities; we are suffering for our inability to take in the stories of our past and imagine stories that offer a promising future.

The authors address a range of concerns and guide us toward a broader range still. P. Gabrielle Foreman sets the stage by considering "the response of Black creatives, particularly poets, to the re:memory project in slavery's many refracted afterlives and echoes. Can a resurrectionary poetics," she asks, "stitch the ephemerality and partiality of the Black past-present into a quilt of recovery?" In a consideration of archives and the urgency of a representational mode capable of attending to both presence and absence, Foreman presses us to look to a literature capable of doing justice to African American history beyond and in spite of the archival omissions that have produced motivated misrepresentations. Siobhan Senier extends this call for representational literature by relocating the centers of Native American literary history. Native Americans, she reminds us, "are *political* entities, with their own governance systems and their own claims to traditional territories, enshrined in treaty and international law." Accordingly, she argues, "Indigenous literature ... cannot be neatly absorbed into a unitary canon, even a 'diverse' or 'expanding' one. Indigenous writers and Indigenous texts need to be understood as emanating from tribal, collective centers." For Senier, the project of literary history requires us to "understand how communities take ownership of their own literary traditions." Min Hyoung Song draws us to communities as well, meditating on "the stories we tell, the stories we allow, and the stories that go untold," and thereby engaging "the work we must insist upon from literature, both lauding it for what it enables and being critical of what it might foreclose." As this volume has demonstrated, a focus on race in American literature leads one to the many lives lost and saved through the written word, and Song calls for a literature capable of attending to the possibilities for "the actual flesh-and-blood children standing there before us." Finally, Stephanie Li closes this section and the volume itself by bringing us to the present moment, to the contrast between Barack Hussein Obama and Donald J. Trump, the first one of the most literary of presidents and the second a leader who communicates primarily through often inflammatory tweets. "Literature," Li observes, "moves in tandem with the consciousness of a nation and the political struggles and debates that define historical moments. And just as whiteness has emerged as a salient and necessary category of identity in mainstream political and critical discourses, we are now witnessing a new recognition of the complex representative dynamics of whiteness in American letters."

It is unsurprising and perhaps even inevitable that a volume on race in American literature and culture would conclude with a meditation on the insistent structural realities of whiteness, but the volume also presses us to find other stories to tell and other narrative priorities to observe. The messiness of American history is a chaos of our own making, and the essays that have addressed this chaotic past together press for a collective understanding to which many Americans have been resistant. There is not a single story here, nor the hope that out of the many stories, one comprehensive story will emerge. There is no resolution available – but literary history is the story of ongoing negotiations with the threatening structures of race. Through literature, we can learn to manage those negotiations to greater purpose. We are the stories we tell, and our history can teach us how to hold to the many narrative possibilities passed down to us by those who have been fighting the most American of battles from the time of our nation's founding.

CHAPTER 24

What Is Missing?
Black History, Black Loss, and Black Resurrectionary Poetics

P. Gabrielle Foreman

Having to wade through – or wave off – the thick and heavy incredulity that there are Black pasts to recover or creative genius to appreciate is nothing new. It spills from the mouths and pens of generations of Western philosophers and statesmen, through centuries of intellectual gatekeepers who have not only questioned, but have erased and buried, the thinking and writing that Black people in the Americas have produced despite those who bet against us for pleasure or profit. It reaches back to the United States' founders and foundations, to Thomas Jefferson's dismissive commentary on Phillis Wheatley and his epistolary exchanges with Black astrologer and mathematician Benjamin Banneker. Yet faith in our own human creativity, even as others deny Black connections to either humanity or creativity, sent Alice Walker, for instance, to seek and find Zora Neale Hurston, to place a headstone on her unmarked grave and to republish what we now treasure as a once lost masterpiece, *Their Eyes Were Watching God.*[1] Likewise, June Jordan's assumption that Black literary soil has loam enough to sprout generations of genius spurred her to commemorate Phillis Wheatley and the difficult miracle of Black poetry in America.[2] *What does it mean to create, to master creativity, in the glint of the steeliest historical negation?* The miraculousness of Black persistence itself, as poet Tiana Clark reminds us, "is a tenacious ontological resolve, built and bred from struggle and resistance and transcendence."[3] Jordan's and Walker's responses to that question are examples of a go-back-and-get-it commitment that has also made way for collective resurrectionary poetics and practices and innovative archival approaches that counter the violence of historical erasure, especially in the eighteenth-century North America that this essay takes as its focus.

This piece looks to the response of Black creatives, particularly poets, to the re:memory project in slavery's many refracted afterlives and echoes. Can a resurrectionary poetics stitch the ephemerality and partiality of the Black past-present into a quilt of recovery? In my recent work, I'm particularly interested in poetry because its very form evokes the power of empty space or ground; I'm intrigued by the evocative potential of the ways in which words and lines give meaning to what is often called "white space." The poetic line as an organizing structure recalls the historical shard as opposed to the world-building that can happen in prose. If, in prose, words both build worlds and crowd pages, the use of empty space in meaning-making invites a meditation that offers a productive tension between historical plenitude and the unnameable (lack and absence) that is its inverse. That tension, of course, is critical in and to African American (literary) history.

Black poets who are deeply committed to exploring the past's afterlives in their own work also bring a Sankofa imperative to the methods and models they employ in the face of the ephemerality and refraction of Black historical lives in the Diaspora. If "a legible and linear narrative cannot sufficiently account for" shattered Black histories violently disregarded and disremembered, to build on Marisa Fuentes, Black poets join historians in employing "new methodologies that disrupt" and enlarge "conventional historical processes and methods."[4] Each group turns to the archive seeking to illuminate "marginalized and fugitive knowledge," as Fuentes puts it.[5] Poet-historians are likewise "stretching archival fragments" to give color to "extinguished, invisible," and etiolated "but no less historically important lives."[6]

In my larger work, I build on Herman Beavers's 2003 "The Archival Impulse in African American Poetry" and on his observation about "the recent turn in African American poetry ... toward a rumination on historiography, and by implication then, on history,"[7] and on Evie Shockley's examination of "the tradition of African American poetic engagements with slavery's history" and what she calls poets' head-on confrontation with "the evidence of the ongoing injuries and losses, the gaps and absences."[8] I'm particularly drawn to the material and metaphorical qualities of Black poetry's workings, as opposed, let's say, to the continuous procession of paragraphs on the page that create the world-making of the historical novel. In poetry, lines' ever-differing lengths, metrical units, and spatial registers act as building and organizing structures that recall the historical shard; the dynamic and variable relation between what is often called empty or "white space" and the poet's words are resonant with the continuous tension between what is historically "empty" and emptied, surviving and erased – what Shockley, via poet and critic M. NourbeSe Philip, calls w/holeness.

My focus is on the increasing number of poetry cycles, book sections, or entire volumes dedicated to Black pasts, as these are more likely to be informed by the author's deep engagement with historical records and methods. Poetry cycles use the space not only within but also between poems to bring attention to (and speak to the meta-condition of) forgotten, partial, or disremembered Black histories. Such writers as Elizabeth Alexander, Rita Dove, Tiana Clark, Honorée Jeffers, Tyehimba Jess, M. NourbeSe Philip, Natasha Trethewey, Frank X Walker, Carolyn Beard Whitlow, and Kevin Young represent a fraction of the poet-historians whose work sits at the shores of Black history and its losses.[9] As Beavers notes, in its dedicated return to the archive, this poetry demonstrates "the ways that history can burst past its boundaries, influencing, if not altering, the ways we navigate the present."[10] Indeed, in the ongoing turn to the Black past, these poets resurrect once disremembered histories piece by piece, demonstrating how poetry can also burst past history's (archival and methodological) boundaries to offer new work and new methods that influence both public history and public memory.

Tiana Clark joins this turn to the archive in her debut collection, *I Can't Talk about the Trees without the Blood* (2018), and it is her work on Wheatley that I'll take up here.[11] Clark's four Wheatley poems are as much a short cycle as a quatrain of poems that recalls perhaps the most famous of poems about the loss and lynchings that her book title references.[12] "Conversation with Phillis Wheatley#1," "Conversation with Phillis Wheatley #2," followed by poems by the same name numbered #7 and #14 are found in the first section, titled "I Can't Talk." Clark opens her first poetry volume – which necessarily stakes a claim to authorial presence and voice – with a denial that richly complicates the reality of the book in readers' hands. Poems entitled "Cross/Bite" and "Cottonmouth" launch the volume, followed by "Bear Witness" and "Soil Horizon," which starts with an epigraph by former US Poet Laureate and Pulitzer Prize winner Natasha Trethewey.[13] Clark's work highlights and contributes to ongoing poetic and historical groundings and genealogies and their (meta) critical tensions. The shared thematic of articulation that snakes through the pieces that precede the four Wheatley "conversation" poems (in a section, again, called "I Can't Talk") also signal the biting, dry, and toxic Black literary and historical ironies of not only bearing, but speaking, witness.

The four "Conversations with Phillis Wheatley" poems start in promising numeric sequence, with subsequent jumps (from #2 to #7 and from #7 to #14) that point to what is missing and lost. Only four of at least fourteen "conversations" appear, which highlights not only what hasn't survived in and over time but also that Clark's poetic conversations (and some of Wheatley's historical letters by citation and proxy) still exist. As fellow poet M. NourbeSe Philip puts it, "the fragment is both/and: containing the w/hole while being at the same time a part of the w/hole —it compels us to see both the w/hole and the hole: impulse to memory and impulse to amnesia."[14] The meta-conversations about Black literary genesis and genealogy in this section called "I Can't Talk" likewise recall the (not) talking book made iconic by Henry Louis Gates's reading of Wheatley's contemporary Olaudah Equiano. The now-famous scene in his 1789 narrative when, seeing others reading a book, he "put my ears to it, when alone, in hopes it would answer me; and I have been very much concerned when it remained silent" echoes Clark's own experience with putting her ear to Black cultural history itself.[15] Equiano wants not only to read but to animate the book, to talk with it. Likewise, conversations, as Clark calls her poems, are active; they require both talking and listening, speaking and hearing. Herman Beavers's discussion of the Black vernacular use of the term "hear" is instructive here. In Black communities, "hear" is also a command, as in "you be back in this house by dark, hear?" In this use, as Beavers puts it, its "aim is to target that place where aurality and obedience become synonymous."[16] To be in conversation, then, is to hear history, to grapple with the command to turn toward forgotten, scattered, disappeared voices, lives, and histories, to hear and bear witnesses to a Black past that has been disremembered.

Clark is not only in conversation with Wheatley but also with critics who engage (conceptual, spiritual, and theoretical) space that holds simultaneously missing and existing historical remnants. Significant critics and creatives have looked to epistolary exchanges, in particular, that record the inner lives of those who have become Black public touchstones. Clark explicitly positions herself as part of a "writing community" that emerges from "an 'unfolding' of early African-American women's literary production."[17] Likewise in community with scholars of that tradition, Clark cites and says she was inspired by Katherine Clay Bassard's essay "The Earliest Black Women's Writing Community."[18] Bassard builds on Hortense Spillers when she suggests that a Black women's writing community is "a corrective to the term 'tradition' with all of its patriarchal and elitist overtones"; the term "invokes the sense of a boundary or border (community) which remains actively and dynamically in the process of its own renegotiation."[19] Clark's content choices and citational practices display an active affiliation with a writing community that, as theorized by Spillers and Bassard, is meant "to revision the emergence of African-American women's authorship as a collective 'event.'"[20]

The Phillis Wheatley and Obour Tanner letters that Bassard centers make up one of the earliest Black community writing exchanges in the United States; yet that "community" was mediated by whites in various positions of power, oversight, and surveillance through whom the letters passed, as Clark and Bassard remind us.[21] The missives between the two women enslaved in different states in eighteenth-century New England are the only known letters between Wheatley and a Black comrade, friend, or colleague, enslaved or free.[22] Ever attentive to form as well as context, Clark chooses to write in couplets, like the two friends they were, with a single line at the bottom of every page, separated and alone. Clark notes that before she composed the Wheatley poems, she "researched her correspondence with Obour Tanner" and shares that "Wheatley's letters are all that survived their seven-year correspondence (approximately 1771/ 72–1778) [and that] most of the letters can be viewed at the Massachusetts Historical Society online archive."[23] Letters, written as they are in first person and in a genre that allows – even invites – intimacy and a glimpse of inner lives, prove as attractive to poets as they are to other researchers looking for clues in the archive. As critic Tara Bynum suggests, "Wheatley's letters remind us that she not only leaves us with the poems scholars know and teach often. She also leaves us with correspondence that demands a reconsideration of the archive, what we expect to find inside it, and what terms we use to bear witness to the realities of black women—in particular, those who look for each other in the Word of God and on the words of the page."[24] The page, more specifically, these poems, become what Bassard calls "a rhetorical meeting place" not only for Wheatley and Tanner but for Clark as well as for other poets who preceeded her.[25]

Through this short cycle, Clark is enacting several sorts of world-building; the writing community she draws (from) seeks to recover and also enliven connections between Black women's creative and critical genealogies and poets who turn to the muse of history, to borrow from Natasha Thethewey.[26] Clark's "Recovered Letter from Obour Tanner," as conversation #14 was titled when it was first published in *Obsidian*, resonates in concert with recent epistolary poems about the most famous of enslaved writers: Evie Shockley's "The Lost Letters of Frederick Douglass" to his daughter Rosetta in her fifties and Tim Siebles's "Douglass, a Last Letter."[27] By highlighting what's last (as a verb) and also what's lost in the corpus of the most well documented of nineteenth-century Black writers and activists, these poems point to the gaps and holes pockmarking the historical landscape.[28] As Clark's poems reach back to (and reach back for) Wheatley's correspondences, her "conversations" also echo Robert Hayden's "A Letter from Phillis Wheatley," which is likewise addressed to Wheatley's enslaved friend.[29] The almost forty-year gap in this call-and-response exchange between Hayden's "letter" *from* Wheatley and Clark's response *to* Wheatley from Tanner adds additional nodal points to a reverberating Black timeline as readers contemplate Clark's references to the varied lapses that passed between the women's surviving correspondence.[30] Though Clark/Wheatley's "final" letter only occupies that space because we don't know whether it was answered, Wheatley's plaintive words in the 1779 letter addressed to "Dear Obour" – "pray write me soon, for I long to hear from you" – is a cry and call that Clark answers. In doing so, not only Wheatley – but also Hayden – gets an answer.[31]

As Clark's poems speak to (and from) Wheatley and also add to the poetic conversation Hayden began, Clark's work comments on meta-dimensions across and over time.[32] Clark closes her essay about her historical poems and processes, "Pray Write Me Soon: On 'Conversation with Phillis Wheatley #2'" by citing Hayden and Wheatley.[33] Her poetry cycle also begins in writing community with both of these poetic ancestors. "Conversation #1" opens with what many might call a nod to Hayden's deeply influential poem "Middle Passage," which itself begins with and pivots around the italicized names of slave ships: *Jesus, Estrella, Esperanza, Mercy*. Clark's first Wheatley poem seems to fold Hayden's opening into her own; its italics and question likewise name the ships that for so many hundreds of thousands of girls who shared Wheatley's circumstances, were a death sentence or a fetid, airless tomb, closed before almost any could pass on stories about their own lives told in their own printed words.[34] When Clark opens with: *"Don't you hate your name?"* she reminds those of us who are and aren't aware of the heavy fact that Wheatley had to bear the name/memory of the slave ship, the *Phillis*, that vesseled her away from her family and homeland while she was still losing her baby teeth. Clark's Phillis answers the question via the middle passage:

> I was named as all things are named:
> after the things that carry them. Blacked
> out belly of my slave ship, the pitching
> womb of the ocean slapped against splint-
> ered and swollen wood. . .

The poem gives voice to Phillis's own experience as Clark's work also offers an answer to the question theorists and historians of slavery pose in the face of the archive's violent engulfings: "How can narrative embody life in words and at the same time respect what we cannot know?"[35] Clark's engagement with loss and gaps, with lapses and deferrals, with ongoing longing for community from Phillis forward, suggests that what narrative cannot hold, perhaps poetry can.

I want to return to Clark's section titles, or her book as a triptych as she puts it, and to the first of the three. "I Can't Talk" is both creation and commentary about Black history and historiography against such muting odds, and also a response to the violence Black communities, as well as archives, face as a matter of course and existence.[36] For, of course, "I Can't Talk" also recalls one of the most resonant literal and symbolic utterances of the era in which Clark's book was written: "I Can't Breathe."[37] Set against the other sections in the triptych, "About the Trees" and "Without the Blood" that together make up the book's title, the echo of "I Can't Breathe" nuances a poetic genealogy that starts with Wheatley and leads to Clark. Clark's through lines move in multiple directions/dimensions, both forward and backward as they also reach out and around; she embraces what she calls the "idea of 'stringing together impossibilities'" that unspool "like a vibrating timeline when I began to trace my literary origins."[38] As her triptych title brings Eric Garner into first view as the violent frame that holds the space in which she can't talk (but does nonetheless) and can't write (but does nonetheless), readers encounter these poems thru a doubly difficult set of questions about Black poetry's relation to voice, breath, and history.

Death and loss and resurrection hover over these poems as Clark explains them:

> The Conversation with Phillis Wheatley poems were born out of desperate need for belonging and survival, this wish to write to Wheatley inside the container of a poem, an epistolary ache. I wanted to pretend that she didn't die alone and cold and sick with her second manuscript unpublished and lost forever. I wanted to pretend that that still won't be a possibility for me or for other black women writers like me on the brink of burnout, free but struggling to survive.

Literary pretending and production are twinned here, a Black temporal coupling of erased pasts and implausible futures that brings a poetic matriarch and cultural descendants into conversation in Clark's vibrating timeline. Clark aspires to imbue the act of re/membering with the act of recovery (from Black burnout, Black loss, from the strangling power of effacement and erasure). Here is another example of how cultural daughters write Black history, and of how Clark claims multigenerational poetics and cultural genealogies as she also claims a broader community both for Wheatley and for herself in their own times and places.[39]

When Black poets return to the source – to lost letters, to loss letters, to delayed missives, and to what is missing – it is also a commentary on American letters, on belles lettres, on Black American letters lost in a tradition that for so much of its history did not recognize Black creative mastery.[40] *What, again, does it mean to create, to master creativity, in the glint of the steeliest historical negation?* What's missing in the archives of Black history is an endless series of lost and unpreserved papers and missing objects. But for Black communities, "missing" is not only items that weren't preserved in repositories; what's *missing* is also archival ache and historical longing over time. "Facing devastation again and again, Black folks need in and for each other becomes both time-traveling desire and reservoir knowledge," as Jessica Marie Johnson and Mark Anthony Neal write.[41] Their "oracle work" is a first cousin to what I call resurrectionary poetics.

In Wheatley's last known letter to Obour Tanner, she writes, "I hope our correspondence will revive—and revive in better times—pray write me soon, for I long to hear from you." Over many more years than those separating Wheatley's letters from Tanner's, Tiana Clark responds "to that urgent plea in my poems. I am trying to answer that longing by suspending time. A poem can attempt to answer a series of unanswerable griefs in verse."[42] In her essay, Clark uses the term "adynaton" as a refrain she uses to reframe American traditions of literary exclusion. The term names a figure of speech that magnifies its hyperbole to the point of impossibility in order to point to an inherent absurdity of whatever proposition – Black creative genius, let's say – is on the table. It is, as she puts it, "the formal principle of stringing together of impossibilities as a way of inverting the order of things, drawing attention to categories, turning the world upside down."[43] What is the difficult miracle of Black poetry, she asks, what is the difficult miracle of Black history and its archives, I ask, across unfree, interrupted, rarely-your-own terms, I-can't-breathe times and spaces, but adynaton?

This piece examines innovative archival approaches by Black poets that give ear to impossible mutings and space to historical hauntings.[44] How does Black poetry fueled by Sankofa imperatives use adynaton (again, an "inverting of the order of things, a drawing attention to categories" and classifications and turning them inside out) not only as a temporal but also as a methodological intervention? This piece takes up a shared longing for community and kin in action; it listens to the imperative for genealogical connections with cultural ancestors like Phillis Wheatley, who rejected impossibilities and in doing so brought the difficult miracle of Black writing in North America into being. Finally, this piece is painted on a canvas of more personal loss, a need to return to writing about poetry as a way to continue to be in conversation with my father, a poet of the Black Arts era, after he passed. Black poetry reaches back to the past structures and neighborhoods of meaning that bring these lost records, these loss records, home to those who recognize them. In doing so, it traces how cultural descendants go back to lost sources, using innovative methods and resurrectionary poetics to sit in conversation with Black historical hauntings and to make space for, make peace for, our living dead.

Notes

1. Alice Walker, "Looking for Zora," in *In Search of Our Mothers' Gardens: Womanist Prose* (San Diego: Harcourt Brace Jovanovich, 1983), 93–116; and also "From Their Eyes Were Watching God," in *I Love Myself When I Am Laughing: A Zora Neale Hurston Reader*, ed. Alice Walker (New York: Feminist Press at CUNY, 1979), 246–95.

2. June Jordan, "The Difficult Miracle of Black Poetry in America," Poetry Foundation (2006), www.poetryfoundation.org/articles/68628/the-difficult-miracle-of-black-poetry-in-america. Jordan was one of the many emerging, now famous, writers brought together by Margaret Walker Alexander at the 1973 Phillis Wheatley Poetry Festival at Jackson State University for the bicentennial publication of *Poems on Various Subjects, Religious and Moral*. The multiday gathering, held at the Institute for the Study of Life and Culture of Black People, which Dr. Margaret Walker Alexander directed, also included writers such as Alice Walker, Mari Evans, Nikki Giovanni, Lucille Clifton, Paula Giddings, Audre Lorde, Naomi Long Madgett, Carolyn Rodgers, Margaret Danner, and Margaret G. Burroughs.

3. Tiana Clark, "Pray Write Me Soon: On 'Conversation with Phillis Wheatley #2," Poetry Society of America, November 27, 2018, https://poetrysociety.org/features/in-their-own-words/tiana-clark-on-conversation-with-phillis-wheatley-2.

4. Marisa J. Fuentes, *Dispossessed Lives: Enslaved Women, Violence and the Archive* (Philadelphia: University of Pennsylvania Press, 2016), 6.

5. Fuentes, *Dispossessed Lives*, 6.

6. Fuentes, *Dispossessed Lives*, 7.

7. Herman Beavers, "The Archival Impulse in African American Poetry: Playing the Past," in *Rainbow Darkness: An Anthology of African American Poetry*, ed. Keith Tuma (Oxford, OH: Miami University Press, 2005), 173.

8. Evie Shockley, "Going Overboard: African American Poetic Innovation and the Middle Passage," *Contemporary Literature* 52.4 (2011), 795, www.jstor.org/stable/41472494.

9. Shockley, "Going Overboard," 792. The breadth of recent poets writing historical poems about eighteenth- and nineteenth-century Black experience is expansive. Evie Shockley includes this list of poets who have published volumes dedicated in their entirety to antebellum slavery and the Civil War: "Fred D'Aguiar (*Bloodlines*), Thylias Moss (*Slave Moth*), Vievee Francis (*Blue-Tail Fly*), Quraysh Ali Lansana (*They Shall Run: Harriet Tubman Poems*), and Camille Dungy (*Suck on the Marrow*), to name a few." Howard Ramsby II also has a "partial list of poems by various poets featuring ex-slaves, rebellious slaves, and other topics concerning slavery and struggles for liberation" on his blog about Black poetry, *Cultural Front*, www.culturalfront.org/2015/12/a-checklist-of-poems-featuring-ex-slaves.html.

10. Beavers, "The Archival Impulse in African American Poetry," 175.

11. Clark once had aspirations to be a historian but realized after a college internship at the Schomburg Center that what she had to say "wanted to come out figuratively." Virtual visit to Penn State University's graduate class, "Recovering the Black Past: Writers, Artists and the Archive," October 6, 2020.

12. Gwendolyn Brooks's "The Last Quatrain of the Ballad of Emmett Till" famously stands alone without any previous quatrains. Brooks's other Till poem is "A Bronzeville Mother Loiters In Mississippi. Meanwhile, A Mississippi Mother Burns Bacon."

13. Clark references more recent ancestor artists continuously. This section opens with an excerpt from Claudia Rankine; the third poem, "Bear Witness," is dedicated to and in conversation with Carrie Mae Weems's Roaming series in addition to Trethewey.

14. Shockley, "Going Overboard," 806. Quoted from Philip's discussion of the poetics of fragmentation in M. NourbeSe Philip, *Zong!* (Middletown, CT: Wesleyan Press, 2008), 202, paragraph 24.

15. This oft-cited passage is from Equiano's narrative; the concept of the "talking book" was developed from it and first introduced by Henry Louis Gates: "I had often seen my master and Dick employed in reading; and I had a great curiosity to talk to the books, as I thought they did; and so to learn how all things had a beginning: for that purpose I have often taken up a book, and have talked to it, and then put my ears to it, when alone, in hopes it would answer me; and I have been very much concerned when it remained silent" (Equiano, Interesting Narrative, 106–7, TEI pagination)[1]. http://dighist.fas.harvard.edu/courses/2015/HIST1993/exhibits/show/modeling-equiano/equiano-historical-context.

16. Beavers, "The Archival Impulse in African American Poetry," 178.

17. Katherine Clay Bassard, "The Daughters' Arrival: The Earliest Black Women's Writing Community," *Callaloo* 19.2 (1996), 515, https://doi.org/10.1353/cal.1996.0043. Bassard is citing Hortense Spillers, "Cross-Currents, Discontinuities: Black Women's Fiction," in *Conjuring Black Women, Fiction, and Literary Tradition*, eds. Marjorie Pryse and Hortense J. Spillers (Bloomington: Indiana University Press, 1985) and is also building on

Frances Smith Foster's *Written by Herself: Literary Production by African American Women, 1746–1892* (Bloomington: Indiana University Press, 1993), again creating writing community in citational practice and content.

18. Clark, "Pray Write Me Soon," https://poetrysociety.org/features/in-their-own-words/tiana-clark-on-conversation-with-phillis-wheatley-2.

19. Bassard, "The Daughters' Arrival," 515.

20. Bassard, "The Daughters' Arrival," 515.

21. Clark cites Bassard to note that because these missives were "hand delivered by a third party (usually male), they are prone to violation and interception. Perhaps more importantly, each letter is sent 'favd by' someone, and 'in care of' which marks the problematics of ownership for black women slaves, a qualification which framed even their most intimate attempts to communicate with each other." https://poetrysociety.org/features/in-their-own-words/tiana-clark-on-conversation-with-phillis-wheatley-2. Bassard, "The Daughters' Arrival," 516.

22. Of course, she has a poem dedicated to Scipio Moorhead. Phillis Wheatley, "To S. M. A Young African Painter, on Seeing His Works," in *Poems on Various Subjects, Religious and Moral* (London: A. Bell, 1773).

23. Clark, "Pray Write Me Soon," https://poetrysociety.org/features/in-their-own-words/tiana-clark-on-conversation-with-phillis-wheatley-2.

24. Tara Bynum, "Phillis Wheatley on Friendship," *Legacy: A Journal of American Women Writers* 31.1 (2014), 43, www.jstor.org/stable/10.5250/legacy.31.1.0042.

25. Bynum, "Phillis Wheatley on Friendship," 45. She cites Bassard's *Spiritual Interrogations*, 23.

26. Natasha Thethewey, "The Muse of History: On Poetry and Social Justice," convocation series, Lawrence University, November 1, 2016, Appleton, WI, https://lux.lawrence.edu/convocations/3.

27. Both poets' epistolary Douglass poems appear in *Rainbow Darkness: An Anthology of African American Poetry*. Also see Howard Rambsy II's blog on Black Poetry, *Cultural Front*, www.culturalfront.org/2011/04/evie-shockley-and-this-douglass-poetry.html. Honorée Jeffers also includes a series of "Lost Letters" in her *The Age of Phillis* (Middletown, CT: Wesleyan University Press, 2020), which was published after this essay was drafted.

28. Here, I'm channeling Alexis Pauline Gumbs, who in *M Archive*'s "From the Lab Notebooks of the Last* Experiments" notes that "*Last is a verb" (Durham, NC: Duke University Press, 2018), between preface and page 5, unpaginated.

29. Hayden's poem originally appeared in his (limited edition) 1978 collection *American Journal*, a short book of thirteen poems (including "American Journal," written for the bicentennial), which was bookended by his letter from Phillis Wheatley and his poem to Paul Laurence Dunbar. He calls his letter a psychogram because it adopts the poet's diction, style, and voice. The poem appears online here: https://interminablerambling.wordpress.com/2017/07/18/6623/.

30. Richard D. Daily also points out that though Clark's "recovered letter from Obour Tanner" is composed decades after Hayden's "A Letter from Phillis Wheatley, London 1873" (to Obour Tanner), the dated poetic letters situate Clark's as the prequel, as it's dated "New Port, February 6th, 1772." This adds another node to Clark's notion of reverberating timelines. Rick Daily during Tiana Clark Penn State University class visit, October 6, 2020.

31. May 10, 1779, to Obour Tanner. Wheatley's letters on the Massachusetts Historical Society's online collection are first shown in manuscript form. Though the transcriptions are available, they invite interacting with digital copies of letters written in Wheatley's own hand. See www.masshist.org/ database/viewer.php?old=1&ft=End+of+Slavery&from=%2Fendofslavery% 2Findex.php%3Fid%3D57&item_id=818. She signs this with her married name Phillis Peters. For more on Phillis Wheatley Peters, see Jeffers, *The Age of Phillis*, especially "Looking for Miss Phillis," 167–87. This prize-winning book, which was published after this essay was finished, is based on fifteen years of archival research, including long-term research at the American Antiquarian Society.

32. Though Hayden is a touchstone in her essay, "Pray Write Me Soon: Tiana Clark on 'Conversation with Phillis Wheatley 2,'" Clark notes that she found out about Hayden's Wheatley/Tanner poem after she composed her own "conversations." Discussion with the author during Penn State University author virtual visit, October 10, 2020. https://poetrysociety.org/features/in-their-own-words/tiana-clark-on-conversation-with-phillis-wheatley-2.

33. Clark follows what Michael Harper first called the "psychogram" style of Hayden's poem, adding that she researched Wheatley's diction by consulting her historical letters, most of which can be found at the Massachusetts Historical Society website. She underscores the use of elegant and carefully wrought eighteenth-century diction to simultaneously enhance "believabil-ity" and an informal intimacy. See Fred Fetrow, "Portraits and Personae: Characterization in the Poetry of Robert Hayden," in *Black American Poets between Worlds, 1940–1960*, ed. R. Baxter Miller (Knoxville: University of Tennessee Press, 1988), 54.

34. See Saidiya Hartman, "Venus in Two Acts," *Small Axe* 12.2 (2008), 2, www .muse.jhu.edu/article/241115. Her reference about the enslaved girl she calls Venus and mine about Phillis are merged in this sentence, in language that is largely hers.

35. Hartman, "Venus in Two Acts," 3.

36. Tiana Clark and Kevin Young, "Tiana Clark Reads Natasha Trethewey," June 20, 2018, podcast, 23:49, www.newyorker.com/podcast/poetry/tiana-clark-reads-natasha-trethewey. Clark uses this language in a *New Yorker* poetry podcast where she appears with poetry editor Kevin Young.

37. In case this reference fades, it refers to Eric Garner's last words as he was choked to death by an NYPD officer, Daniel Pantaleo, on July 17, 2014, while he was selling "loosies," or single cigarettes, which is considered a minor infraction under New York law. "I Can't Breathe" became a resonant

rallying cry to describe Black experience in the United States as second-class citizens whose rights and bodies and breath itself are under constant and continued assault.

38. Clark, "Pray Write Me Soon," https://poetrysociety.org/features/in-their-own-words/tiana-clark-on-conversation-with-phillis-wheatley-2.

39. We might note that Anna Murray Douglass's daughter Rosetta Douglass Sprague is the person who preserved her mother's reputation and highlighted her role as the conductor of the underground railroad stop at her home while Frederick Douglass traveled. Sprague and then her own daughter Fredericka Douglass Sprague Perry wrote and then reprinted *My Mother as I Recall Her* (1900). Sprague Perry delivered it before the Anna Murray Douglass Union chapter of the Women's Christian Temperance Union and dedicated it to the National Association of Colored Women. It was printed on the anniversary of Frederick Douglass's birthday, February 14, 1923, and then celebrated in such organizations as "Douglass Day." Sprague Perry inserted Anna Murray into that tradition well after her mother and grandmother had passed. This tradition is one contemporary Black women often still carry on when it comes to Wheatley's importance and situated literary activism. Frederick Douglass Papers at the Library of Congress: Family Papers (19). Manuscript Division (160,997); www.loc.gov/resource/mfd.02007/?sp=3. Rosetta Douglass Sprague, *Anna Murray Douglass, My Mother as I Recall Her, by Rosetta Douglass Sprague*, 1900, Manuscript/Mixed Material. www.loc.gov/item/mfd.02007/.

40. Sankofa is understood as a mandate, reminder, and affirmation to "go back and get it" or "return to the source." More literally, it is translated as "it is not taboo to go back and fetch what you forgot."

41. Jessica Marie Johnson and Mark Anthony Neal, "Introduction: Wild Seed in the Machine," *The Black Scholar* 43.3 (2017), 1–2, https://doi.org/10.1080/00064246.2017.1329608.

42. Clark, "Pray Write Me Soon," https://poetrysociety.org/features/in-their-own-words/tiana-clark-on-conversation-with-phillis-wheatley-2.

43. Clark, "Pray Write Me Soon," https://poetrysociety.org/features/in-their-own-words/tiana-clark-on-conversation-with-phillis-wheatley-2.

44. For more on historical hauntings that are both foreign and familiar, see Marisa Parham, *Haunting and Displacement in African American Literature and Culture* (New York: Routledge, 2008).

CHAPTER 25

Traditions, Communities, Literature

Siobhan Senier

This book is being compiled and sent to press during the inexorable runup to the 2020 US presidential election, the many mêlées of which included one over Elizabeth Warren's claims to Cherokee identity. Like most such media events, this one was co-opted and misrepresented for a variety of political purposes. What bubbles to the surface, however, are the cogent critiques of Indigenous intellectuals. Kim TallBear (Sisseton Wahpeton Oyate), Krystal Tsosie (Navajo), Rebecca Nagle (Cherokee), and many, many others continued to wrest the conversation back to a fundamental truth: Tribal identity and tribal citizenship are for tribal people to determine – not the media, not settler politicians, and not even individuals who may have Indigenous ancestry, but no lived connections to tribal communities. TallBear, who studies the history of genetic testing, has been especially sought out for commentary:

> Today, the Democrats peddle a story to Americans of multicultural progress, inclusion and absorption into the imperial state . . .. But that story, like the one sold by Republicans, is based in a worldview that holds private property as sacred and America as morally exceptional. For Indigenous people, private property has been, and is, devastating to our lives and cultures. It devastates the planet by enabling natural resource extraction, including Indigenous DNA, for the profit of settler societies. Meanwhile, the idea of moral exceptionalism in North America is informed by, and affirms, the genocide of Indigenous people: physically, symbolically, politically and scientifically. The stories that settlers insist on telling about the world, their world, have life-and-death repercussions for the planet, humans included.[1]

These words serve as an instructive reminder, too, for scholars and teachers of multicultural American literature. Simply put, Native Americans are not like other racialized groups in the United States. They are not one among many, or parallel to, other hyphenated ethnic minorities; they are *political* entities, with their own governance systems and their own claims to traditional territories, enshrined in treaty and international law. Indigenous literature, consequently, cannot be neatly absorbed into a unitary canon, even a "diverse" or "expanding" one. Indigenous writers and Indigenous texts need to be understood as emanating from tribal, collective centers.

In the volume at hand, the essays by Cari Carpenter, Kiara M. Vigil, and Melanie B. Taylor exemplify this growing assertion of Indigenous sovereignty, kinship, and resurgence in the field of Native American and Indigenous Studies. Decades ago, many of us in the field read Indigenous literature as "resistance," as always having to speak back to white literary nationalism. But as the foregoing essays show, Indigenous writing also emerges from distinctly Indigenous places, Indigenous intellectual histories, and Indigenous *communities*. Previously, we may have worried overmuch about the status of Native American literature vis-à-vis the US canon, with its seemingly endless push-pull of margin and center. But today, Native American and Indigenous Studies offers us ways to understand how communities take ownership of their own literary traditions – for example, in decolonial education (Carpenter); through Indigenous intellectual *networks* (Vigil); or through regional persistence (Taylor).

These writers have all done a superb job at showing how literary sovereignty operates at the textual level, so as I have been tasked with "concluding and reflecting," I would like to describe how certain tribal communities have maintained and circulated their own literary canons. It has been my privilege to witness how they do this, as I have participated in the making of some regional Indigenous anthologies. *Dawnland Voices: An Anthology of Indigenous Writing from New England* (University of Nebraska Press, 2014) gathered and gave new visibility to the voluminous literary traditions of a geographic area (in)famous for its "vanishing Indians." I invited eleven tribal community editors, representing ten distinct tribal nations, to choose texts they felt best represented their written traditions. Where New England has long figured in the settler imagination as the site of "the first Thanksgiving" and countless "massacres," migrations, and extinctions, *Dawnland Voices* has pushed back with almost 700 pages of mostly English-language texts spanning five centuries. It "resisted," perhaps, but also self-confidently expressed something tribal people have known all along: that they have generated ample amounts of writing from seventeenth-century political petitions to nineteenth-century language primers to twenty-first-century fiction and hip-hop poetry. Today, *Dawnland Voices* has migrated online, to dawnlandvoices.org. We publish a twice-yearly literary magazine of new work from both established and emergent writers, as well as electronic exhibits of archival materials selected by tribal historians.

What can we learn from the ways that tribal communities have cherished and preserved their own literary histories, more or less independent of what we might cheekily call the canon industrial complex? When I say "we," I mean people like those of us contributing to this volume: progressive academics devoted to notions of canon expansion. We feel increasingly under siege by a conservative retrenchment that is defunding and undermining our efforts. We labor on literary recovery, only to see recovered texts go out of print almost immediately. We watch the university and small presses that have long supported this literature have to curtail their operations or shut down entirely; and they surely watch in dismay as shrinking liberal arts curricula offer fewer and fewer courses in multicultural literature, with fewer and fewer assigned texts. Even the scholarship that supports the production of new knowledge about Indigenous literature seems to be losing steam to the disastrous elimination of tenure-track positions; there are just fewer *of us* researching and writing. It all feels like mutually assured destruction.

Intriguingly, however, as I have worked on *Dawnland Voices*, this sense of impending destruction has actually not been front and center for tribal editors and writers. Indigenous people are obviously more than acquainted with loss and apocalypse, and the tribal editors and writers have expressed all kinds of urgency – about the continuing pollution and extraction of their lands and waterways, about continued assaults on their governance, about virulent racism, about their own or their families' underemployment and precarity. But the "loss" of "Literature" has not been terribly high on their lists, even though their writings, by and large, are not on college syllabi. They are usually not in formal publication with major houses or small presses; they are not presented at professional conferences or studied in professional journals. They are often not even archived in university libraries or anywhere outside of tribal communities; you can't find them, generally, in WorldCat. And yet: if you talk to almost any Penobscot person, they know about Joseph Nicolar's 1893 *Life and Traditions of the Red Man* (or even have had a copy of it, long before Annette Kolodny and Duke University "recovered" it). If you talk to almost any Narragansett person, they know that Princess Red Wing published the magazine *The Narragansett Dawn* in the 1930s. They know, because they are sharing their own well-thumbed or even bootlegged copies of these texts. They are clipping them and saving them, in tribal offices and in their own living rooms. They are reading passages at public events, and they are reciting poems from memory.

Indigenous canonicity, then, is not a privatized or extractive industry; it is a profoundly collective, contributive endeavor. As we brought *Dawnland Voices* to press, the tribal editors all consulted extensively with their communities; no one, to my knowledge, unilaterally selected texts they thought were "the best." A notable example is Donald Soctomah, the Passamaquoddy tribal editor. Descended from generations of Passamaquoddy knowledge keepers, he is now the tribal historic preservation officer, in which capacity he maintains the tribal museum and archives.[2] He has contributed a great deal to those archives himself; when he served as tribal representative to the Maine state legislature (1999–2002), he told me, he used to walk across the street on his lunch breaks to the state archives and photograph as many documents as he could related to the state tribes. Soctomah started sharing some of those documents starting in 2002, when he began self-publishing books about Passamaquoddy history and distributing them out of the tribal museum. So he had a sense not only of what texts existed, but also of what texts were meaningful to other Passamaquoddy people. He therefore chose an early reading of wampum by his own great-grandfather, Sopiel Selmore, and the text of a speech by Lewis Mitchell, one of his predecessors in the state legislature. He had unique access to treasures like poetry by Sylvia Gabriel (quite well known for her basket artistry but not, I believe, for her writing) and Peter Mitchell, a World War II veteran who wrote often for tribal newsletters. Thanks to Soctomah's own extensive kinship networks, moreover, he was also able to recruit contemporary writings from family members and neighbors, including fantastic poetry by Natalie Dana, who is now working on a Passamaquoddy-language children's book.

What emerges in this kind of collective canonicity is a fluid group of texts not so much preoccupied with racialization or identity, with margins or centers – though those may certainly be concerns of individual texts. It is not a static tradition from which texts can be either "lost," "added," or made (forced?) to "stand the test of time." Rather, it is an ongoing, constantly negotiated engagement with this literature, and with its personal and collective uses. The Abenaki editor, Lisa Brooks, alludes to these processes in her introduction to the Abenaki section of *Dawnland Voices*. What is being "recovered," in Brooks's account, is not just a group of texts or even a literary history; it is nothing less than the Abenaki nation itself:

Writing has been an important tool in this process of recovery. Piles of documents and boxes of family photos fill so many living room corners, and they have been brought out time and again at kitchen tables, weaving images and written words into oral histories. The pages of those writings are stained with coffee, maple syrup, and macaroni stew, the lasting evidence of our interactions. Mothers, fathers, and grandparents now tell ancient stories at those tables to their children, nearly forgetting they first learned them from reading the books of stories gathered and relayed with great care by Joseph Bruchac. The language work of Henry Masta and Joseph Laurent, for years passed around as worn photocopies, now weaves its way through the poetry of Carol Bachnofer and Cheryl Savageau, even as it is used in the teaching and revitalization of language by Jesse Bruchac and Elie Joubert. Writing has been instrumental to this work.[3]

What is striking to me about this community model is that it does not seem to draw any hard lines between editing, archiving, writing, reading, interpreting, or even publishing. As the tribal editor, Brooks is selecting texts for inclusion in *Dawnland Voices*, but she is also consulting with other Abenaki people, and learning from them. As writers and publishers, the Bruchacs have found low-cost, sustainable ways of recirculating some of these older texts and newer ones for the benefit of other Abenaki people.[4] As readers, Brooks's family and neighbors are also insurgent archivists, willing to store and curate precious materials by whatever means necessary. Those kitchen-table, coffee-stained methods might be a meta-data librarian's nightmare, but they have obviously worked. Perhaps when you have never been given access to privileges like mainstream publishing, NEH grants, and repositories in major collecting institutions in the first place, you learn to work *with* partiality, ephemerality, and loss. You learn, maybe, to fill the gaps with oral tradition and collective memory.

You also learn, in many cases, exactly who has your materials, and where. This was the case with the Penobscot tribal nation, next to which the University of Maine in Orono is closely located. Penobscot knowledge keepers are intimately acquainted with the university's library and special collections. They have a formal process whereby they ask any scholar working on Penobscot culture or history to meet with their Cultural and Historic Preservation Committee.[5] The Penobscot editor, Carol Dana, took me to meet with this committee, and sitting with them was a tremendous privilege. We brought them a proposal, listing some writers and texts we already knew about. They filled this in and reshaped it with rapid-fire suggestions of historic and contemporary writers they valued, some of whom had not formally published: Go up there to the university library, they told me, and ask to see the *Wabanaki Alliance* newspaper, which contains some of these writers. I got to hear their concerns about the inclusion of particular texts and writers, though they were careful to say that at no point did they want to tell Carol Dana or me what to cut. (If they had, I believe we would gladly have complied.) This was a fascinating exercise in literary nationalism. On the one hand, the Penobscots understood what literary anthologists have always done, which is to place a heavy burden of representation on a group of texts, once those texts have been selected and formally rolled out under the heading of a national literature. On the other hand, they seemed to intuit what literary critics historically seemed a little slower to figure out: that canons are almost always multivocal, partial, and even internally contradictory.

When I initially recruited tribal editors to help compile *Dawnland Voices*, I knew nothing about the kinds of grievously unfunded yet extremely rigorous and multivalent methods that tribes were using to maintain their own literary histories. I knew (I thought) how to look through university and historical society finding aids for "forgotten" texts. I knew how to parse old newspapers for Northeastern writers. I even knew how to read between the lines of colonial histories, for hints about what kinds of writing Indigenous people were producing in a given moment.[6] But while gathering and publishing texts through such methods might have helped me *create* a canon of sorts, it would have presumed that the people themselves did not have access to these texts or memory. It could never have represented the texts that have been the most meaningful and enduring within specific tribal communities. Indeed, it would have entirely left out those myriad essays, poems, recipes, and histories that never attracted the attention of settler teachers, publishers, or collecting institutions – perhaps because they were not written *for* settlers – but that have been most cherished by communities because they document who the people are, where they come from, and where they are going.

In a sense, all of these functions – editing, archiving, publishing, curating, anthologizing, debating, citing, and reciting – are bundled together in what Lisa Brooks calls the gathering place. "The gathering place" is invoked often by Indigenous authors to describe any collective exercise of cultural authority and exchange. In Brooks's articulation, the gathering place could be the banks of a river where Native folks have historically come together for seasonal exchange and ceremony. It could be a kitchen table where families share traditional stories and gossip about tribal politics – indeed, where tribal politics gets done. Wherever the gathering place is, however, it implies collective meaning making, collective deliberation, and collective stewardship of knowledge. More profoundly, Brooks insists, it is processural:

> Gathering is . . . an activity that sustains us and our families. Yet, like the gathering of plants, intellectual and artistic gathering relies on carefully considered knowledge of the landscape and our impacts on it. Gathering without knowledge could get you and yours sick, could purge you. Gathering without foresight can destroy the roots of the very plants on which we rely for nurturance and healing. Gathering also requires distribution. One does not gather merely for oneself . . . does not view knowledge as something to be gathered within a vessel and preserved, or as a process of steady accumulation, of ever-growing accuracy or progress. Rather, this gathering relies on a process of exchange, which will constantly shape and change the state of the field.[7]

I don't want to romanticize these processes. The work of a small-scale community in maintaining its cultural heritage, literary or otherwise, can be extraordinarily powerful and sustaining; unquestionably, the kinds of work I have described here have not only kept these literary traditions alive – they have kept these people alive. At the same time, those processes can include considerable conflict. Like any small community, tribal communities can have long-standing disputes among particular individuals and families; and as in any community under stress of meager resources, tensions can become inflamed when a new publication, event, or institution arrives on the scene. The "cultural work" of a racist canonical text like *The Last of the Mohicans* can seem somewhat remote and abstract, compared to that of the damage done by a new book if some community members feel excluded, or if they question the authenticity or legitimacy of that publication. Painful disagreements happened a few times, to my knowledge, after *Dawnland Voices* was published, and I suspect that many more happened without my knowledge.

Some of these conflicts helped drive the decision to move *Dawnland Voices* to the web. On the Internet, an anthology can be a living document. We can edit and change texts, recursively, to authors' satisfaction; we can take them down if they cause too much controversy, or if we have unwittingly overstepped some cultural protocol.[8] In its online incarnation, dawnlandvoices.org tries to remain respectful of the gathering place, dispersing editorship and curation across multiple modes and sites. We have an editorial board including three tribal museums/offices, and we consult regularly with a much broader network that includes the original tribal editors of the book as well as many of the authors represented in that volume. The actual work of uploading digital items to the web is time-consuming and not necessarily a good use of tribal editors' time; indeed, it's not something that they necessarily want to do. Therefore, we enlist university students, for credit and/or pay, to help with this work. Undergraduate students have helped the Native editor of the *Dawnland* online magazine format and upload text and images for every issue but the first two. In some cases, they help proofread, under instruction to use a very light hand, and to consult with the tribal editor and authors. Students have also helped curate digital exhibits: for instance, researching and providing introductory text and metadata for the *Wabanaki Legislative News*, a mailing created by Donald Soctomah and his Penobscot counterpart in the Maine state legislature, Donna Loring, to update tribal members about their work.

At the heart of this work is *relationships*. Editing and web management are obviously technical skills, but they are also very much about relationships. This is true in any cultural context, but especially true with respect to Native American literature, which has a long and often unsavory history of being edited by non-Natives. If we keep in mind Lisa Brooks's cautions, that "[o]ne does not gather merely for oneself," that literature is not "something to be gathered within a vessel and preserved ... as a process of steady of accumulation, of ever-growing accuracy or progress," then we understand her assertion that "gathering relies on a process of exchange." Students who work on *Dawnland Voices* are only those who have taken courses in Native American and Indigenous literature, who have been present at Indigenous events where possible, and who are willing to *listen* to Indigenous authors and respect their desires, even if they as student editors do not necessarily understand or agree with these desires. They learn, in short, to treat these texts as gifts, not as objects.[9]

Perhaps what has enabled Indigenous people to see their literary traditions as vibrant and enduring, rather than endangered or "vanishing," is precisely that they see them as such collective enterprises, in which everyone has a stake. I have come to think of Indigenous canonicity as literary stewardship, in which texts are both objects and agents of fiduciary care – to the people and indeed to the lands and other-than-humans that have produced them, and that in turn care for those lands and kin. This is not a separatist matter, as both Brooks and TallBear would probably agree: Privatization and extractivism are affecting everyone, ecologically and culturally. But societies probably cannot continue handing off the business of literary stewardship to only a select group of scholars, teachers, or librarians. In cultural as in ecological crisis, we need all hands on deck.

Notes

1. Kim TallBear, "Elizabeth Warren's Claim to Cherokee Ancestry Is a Form of Violence," *High Country News*, January 17, 2019, www.hcn.org/issues/51.2/ tribal-affairs-elizabeth-warrens-claim-to-cherokee-ancestry-is-a-form-of-violence. For essays by Nagle, Tsosie, and others, see "Syllabus: Elizabeth Warren, Cherokee Citizenship, and DNA Testing," *Critical Ethnic Studies*, www .criticalethnicstudiesjournal.org/blog/2018/12/19/syllabus-elizabeth-warren-cherokee-citizenship-and-dna-testing.
2. The tribal historic preservation officer (THPO) is an official position within federally recognized tribes. Many THPOs deal primarily with issues like the repatriation of human remains and the management of tribal historic properties.
3. In Siobhan Senier, ed., *Dawnland Voices: An Anthology of Indigenous Writing from New England* (Lincoln: University of Nebraska Press, 2014), 276.
4. Siobhan Senier, "Bowman Books: A Gathering Place for Indigenous New England," *Studies in American Indian Literatures* 27.1 (2015), 96–111.
5. Since that time, the Penobscot Nation has created its own institutional review board and been a genuine leader in the field of cultural protocols. See Penobscot Nation Intellectual Property Working Group, "Developing Policies and Protocols for the Culturally Sensitive Intellectual Properties of the Penobscot Nation of Maine" (2014), www.sfu.ca/ipinch/project-components/community-based-initiatives/developing-policies-and-protocols-culturally-sensitiv/.
6. This is the fruitful approach taken by many historians of early American literature, including Drew Lopenzina, *Red Ink: Native Americans Picking up the Pen in the Colonial Period* (Albany: State University of New York Press, 2012), and Hilary E. Wyss, *Writing Indians: Literacy, Christianity, and Native Community in Early America* (Amherst: University of Massachusetts Press, 2003).
7. Lisa Brooks, "At the Gathering Place (Afterword)," in *American Indian Literary Nationalism*, eds. Jace Weaver, Craig Womack, and Robert Warrior (Albuquerque: University of New Mexico Press, 2005), 244–45.
8. Literary historians tend to consider publication as an absolute good, but there is a robust conversation now, precipitated by the rise of electronic publishing, around so-called open access. See, for instance, Kimberly Christen, "Does Information Really Want to Be Free? Indigenous Knowledge Systems and the Question of Openness," *International Journal of Communication* 6 (2012), 2870–93; Jane Anderson and Kimberly Christen, "'Chuck a Copyright on It': Dilemmas of Digital Return and the Possibilities for Traditional Knowledge Licenses and Labels," *Museum Anthropology Review* 7.1–2 (2013), 105–26.
9. On the emerging conversation around indigenized editing, see Anne Louise Mahoney, "Listening with the Heart: Editing Indigenous Manuscripts," *The Editors' Weekly* (blog; September 12, 2017), http://blog.editors.ca/?p=4510.

CHAPTER 26

Children of the Future

Min Hyoung Song

Talking about children unavoidably involves attention to storytelling, and to literature. This is so because children are never just children, but symbols of a whole social order pinned to prevailing ideas of what is to come. "We don't need Whitney Houston to tell us," Rebekeh Sheldon observes, "we already believe the children are our future."[1] And because children are so closely associated with the future, and the future so hard to imagine without thinking about children, there is a way in which people who are thought to be nonreproductive are pitting against both childhood and futurity. "The sacralization of the Child," Lee Edelman writes, "thus necessitates the sacrifice of the queer."[2] This comment, in turn, builds on an argument Lauren Berlant makes about how the very young and the unborn are representative of a pure potential that has become more important than the needs of those who are older and as a result less full of the promise of the future. She observes, "A nation made for adult citizens has been replaced by one imagined for fetuses and children."[3]

What follows might thus, at first, not seem like an essay about race in American literature, or about American literature at all. But it is. It is a meditation on the stories we tell, the stories we allow, and the stories that go untold. It therefore engages the work we must insist upon from literature, both lauding it for what it enables and being critical of what it might foreclose. We can never, it seems, just see the actual flesh-and-blood children standing there before us. What we see is mediated through our beliefs, which are themselves passed down to us by a complex history of societal conflicts and cultural attempts to resolve these conflicts. As Robin Bernstein explains, nineteenth-century America transformed colonial ideas of children into its opposite. Before, children were understood to be the bearers of original sin, and hence "inherently sinful and sexual." They needed a lot of discipline to set them onto the path of the righteous. Sometime around mid-century – under the pressure of a fast-expanding national territory and economy, in the throes of a spiteful debate about slavery, adjusting to burgeoning literacy rates and the gendered forms of storytelling that emerged in literacy's wake – children became something else. They "were not sinful but innocent, not depraved souls risking hellfire but holy angels leading adults to heaven . . . . Childhood was then understood not as innocent but as innocence itself; not as a symbol of innocence but as its embodiment. The doctrine of original sin receded, replaced by a doctrine of original innocence. This innocence was raced white."[4]

It's this kind of mediation, occurring over many decades and even centuries, that compels us to think of children as a category of personhood defined primarily by age and hence by a relationship to time. Their supposed innocence is also a function of time. Since they haven't been alive for very long (and born, presumably, with blank slates for minds), they haven't had the opportunity that time affords to gain experiences, to grow selfish and cynical and closed to the world, to grow dull and hard and insensitive to the wonders all around us. Time itself has yet to become quick. Days are long, weeks expanses, and months nearly unimaginable. Their whole lives stretch on, seemingly endlessly, before them. An infant born when the Twin Towers fell could live to see the ringing of the New Year's bell on the start of a new century. What will a child born in 2050 see if she were to live out the years hypothetically available to her, which would make her stooped and ancient when the next mid-century comes around? Time measured by children thus not only demonstrates the relativity of the speed of its passage but also figures the future, what lies ahead in the life of a child.

Just as importantly, the kind of time associated with the child takes the shape of a loop. A child is born, grows up, gives birth to his or her own child, and that child too grows up – a ceaseless cycle that, through heterosexual reproduction and binary gendered identities and ideas of racial filiation and class reproduction if not upward mobility, assures social continuity. It's these qualities we apparently cherish in the imaginary children we see whenever we see children. This makes children somehow frozen in time, always racing to an adulthood they can never reach. Perhaps individual children do grow up and grow out of childhood, but the figure of the Child cannot. As Edelman observes, the Child is like the popular comic strip and stage character orphan Annie, who must "stick out [her] chin / And grin / And say, 'Tomorrow! / Tomorrow! / I love ya / Tomorrow / You're always / A day /away.'"[5] Just as mind-twisting, however, since we imagine the Child as figuring the future she will likely have, or might have, we also always imagine her as old and stooped, living in ghostly form the life that is ahead of her. What disappears from view is the life that she is currently living now. The figure of the Child can never grow old and is also nearing the end of her life.

I provide these ideas in condensed form because they are already so familiar. I don't need to elaborate, even if we might argue over the details. We think of children as our future. They embody innocence. They carry the germs of the past and the present, promising to carry forward in time the social structures that we have known. Because of all of these beliefs, we feel a heavy moral obligation to take care of the children in our lives. There's almost a sacred duty to feed and clothe them, to make sure they get enough sleep, to advise them on how to form good habits, to make sure they know how to make good choices, to educate them, and in these ways do what we can to ensure they develop sturdy in body and mind so that they can be as prepared as possible for whatever might be coming their way.

All of this sounds so familiar and ready-made. Maybe we will argue about the constraints such beliefs entail on the lives of the children who are being made into symbols (we might ask, don't we want to let our children live free from the expectations that fill their days with lessons and sporting events and play dates?) or of the many who are left out of this story – the queer, the nonwhite, the disabled, the non-gender conforming, or simply the impoverished. Some of the braver among us might struggle to found a different vision of childhood, as more wild and free and, yes, queer.[6] Such arguments remain, nonetheless, predicated on the assumption that the current dominant beliefs are held deeply in place in our culture. What could be more rock-like or more ideologically durable than the view of children as the future? As I think about this question, I have come to realize that it is not a rhetorical one. There are intimations everywhere that our society might not care about children quite as much as it claims to.

Consider education. Over the past several decades, the rising cost of attending colleges and universities has exceeded the rate of inflation. When my first child was born, I sat in the hospital worrying about how I was going to pay for his college education. How much money would I need to save? How could I start to save right away, so that interest could help leverage the little contributions I could make? Did it make sense to open an account specifically designed to pay for college expenses, or would it be more flexible to start a general account that could be used for a wide range of purposes? If I saved too much, would it affect the kind of financial aid or scholarship he could receive? I suspect I am not the only parent who has had these thoughts at a time when we might expect a parent to be preoccupied with something more immediate. By the birth of my second child, I was able to push aside such concerns to focus on what was happening at that moment. Several years had passed by then, and I knew I wasn't going to save all that much for either of my children's college education. The satirical online publication *The Onion* succinctly captured my predicament, and the predicament of many parents, with this headline: "New Parents Wisely Start College Fund That Will Pay for 12 Weeks of Education."[7] My desire to plan for the future ran up against the hard exigencies of bills and expenses in the present. We would just have to manage somehow when the time comes round.

And what will happen when my kids finally end up in college? Even as the expense of college is going up, quality is going down – if measured by the number of poorly paid adjuncts teaching very expensive credit hours to undergraduates. The precarity and piece-meal nature of their jobs means they will be teaching a lot of students in many classes, they won't always have the time necessary to prepare, and there will be no guarantees they will be around when students need advising or letters of recommendation or simple conversation. The humanities have been hit the hardest, but the social sciences and the natural sciences aren't far behind in the challenges they face in placing their graduate students into the kind of positions that would allow them to do what they've been trained to do: teach, produce high-quality research, and do the service work that's both essential and easy to overlook. Every time I attend an academic conference, I meet one highly qualified young scholar after another who is almost finished or has recently finished their doctoral degree. They present brilliant work and are accomplished in ways I could not have imagined being when I was their age, and most are struggling to find full-time teaching posts. The same attitude that has frustrated their desire for tenure-track jobs (or even full-time nontenure-track jobs) also affects the lower schools, as K–12 education is marked by rigid standardization, low teacher pay, and unequal access. The education that someone from a wealthy neighborhood gets is entirely different from the kinds of educational opportunities available to those who are poor. Conditions for public grade school teachers across the board have also deteriorated so much that many students are refusing to get degrees in education, which means many schools, especially again in poorer neighborhoods, are finding it difficult to find qualified teachers to teach their students.

Consider the lives of the nonwhite and poor. As I write, the news is full of stories about the federal government's crackdown on asylum seekers on the southwest border. Children, some of whom are infants, were separated from their families and put into cages. Their days are marked by the buzz of always-on fluorescent bulbs and the noise of other children buzzing in the background; the buildings where they are housed are deliberately kept cold, so much so that they are referred to as the *hielera* or icebox. Lest we think such attitudes toward nonwhite children are a partisan matter, it's worth remembering that it was under the administration of another president belonging to another party that kept up, and even accelerated, rates of deportation of undocumented immigrants, many of whom were children. There was also no stoppage during this former administration of the deportation of young men who failed to get their citizenship and committed a crime. No matter how much they may have mended their bad habits and acceded to the confines of heterosexual reproductive and laboring life, the government seized many and returned them to the countries they left when they were mere boys or even toddlers. Some of the first and hardest hit by such policies were Cambodian refugees, whose families had fled the killing fields only to be left stranded with few resources in some of America's poorest neighborhoods.[8] Many of their neighbors were African Americans, who have for so long struggled in this country. The youth in this latter group have been disproportionately imprisoned at very young ages, and those who haven't have been surveilled, harassed, and even killed by the police. Tamir Rice was only twelve when he was murdered by a Cleveland officer. His crime was playing with a toy gun.

Maybe you think children as future and as innocent have, as Bernstein argues, always been white. Surely, then, white children enjoy the status such associations bestow? It was mostly white children attending elementary school who were murdered by a young man, himself barely an adult, carrying a high-powered rifle in Newton, Connecticut. It was mostly white teenagers who were murdered (by another white teenager) at Stoneman Douglas High School in Parkland, Florida. Neither has led to any meaningful change in national gun laws. The same is true for the hundreds of children, many of whom are white, killed every year because of gun violence. When we look more closely at the phenomenon of school shootings, Malcolm Harris reports that one major study discovered "other students expressed sympathy and understanding for shooters." Why? Because they "understood the target of these attacks to be the immiserating school itself, rather than a particular bully or clique of classmates."[9] As one way to substantiate how schools immiserate the lives of children, Harris offers this statistic: "Between 1981 and 1997, elementary schoolers between the ages of six and eight recorded a whopping 146 percent gain in time spent studying, and another 32 percent between 1997 and 2003, making it a threefold increase over the time surveyed, in addition to a 19 percent increase in time at school."[10] Being white does not spare a child from the conditions these figures represent.

If our society cared about children as much as is claimed, our society would do things a lot differently. We would offer free health care to young people and make sure they were informed about all of their reproductive choices – including abortion. We would make sure anyone who chooses to get pregnant has access to doctors, shelter, food, and anything else she might need. We would heavily subsidize day care so parents could work, and make sure all young people were enrolled in high-quality preschool programs. We would pay our teachers better, and teaching would be a prized profession that many young people would be eager to join. What if the average salary for a preschool, elementary, and high school teacher was $150,000 a year? We'd probably have as many students in schools of education than in schools of business and management; there'd be as many education majors as finance and economic majors. When students vote with their majors, they reflect macro-forces at work and reproduce societal valuation.

If our society cared about children as much as is claimed, we'd also make public college tuition free and subsidize higher education in numerous other ways – such as making sure professors and staff were all equally well paid – so that students could benefit from an advanced education. We'd imagine school as an enriching experience, and not training for a future job or as needing to maximize a return on investment. We wouldn't put police officers into schools, further increasing the likelihood that students will be criminalized. We wouldn't put young people in prison. Guns would be more thoughtfully and deliberately regulated. We'd be eager to welcome refugees and immigrants, many of whom want to come to the United States as families with young children, and offer lots of resources and services to make sure they were adjusting to life in a strange country. We'd find ways to promote the well-being of gay, lesbian, and transgender youth, affirming their right to exist.

Maybe we disagree about the particulars of what we might do differently if our society actually cared about children. I'm willing to have this debate. But I would be surprised if anyone believed the lives of children in the United States are already uniformly good and about to get better. And here's another thing, an important thing, we would do differently if our society cared about children as much as it claims. We would aggressively acknowledge the existential threat of climate change and channel as many resources as we could toward mitigation and adaptation. Nothing remarks on the negligence children suffer in our society more than the inattention that surrounds our environmental troubles.

Of course, there are many, many individuals who love and care for children, their own and others. They work tirelessly on their behalf and advocate for their many needs. As large as their numbers are, however, they remain individuals trying to hold back a flood. They are members of a civil society that is by its very nature ad hoc and loosely organized. There is, also, the formal sacralization of children. It's not permissible to speak dismissively of their needs or to threaten them in any way. It's political suicide for any politician to say he or she does not care about the welfare of children. Much of this official language of care for the child is, however, thin discursive tissue. Words and policies are at odds with each other.

As I think about this discrepancy, an incongruous poem comes to mind. It's Ezra Pound's "In the Station of the Metro." Margaret Ronda describes it beautifully when she observes, "Pound's modernist poem renders human life as spectral presence, evanescent as fallen petals, amidst the disorienting speed of urbanized existence."[11] It's so short it's difficult not to memorize: "In the apparition of these faces in the crowd; / Petals on a wet, black bough." It is thus easy to repeat, and to hold in mind as an image (hence, this kind of poetry was called by Pound imagism) that, like the apparition it explicitly conjures, haunts. We are here for only a brief time, mostly anonymous in the throngs of other people with whom we must share our existence, and then we are gone, but something ghostly remains against the backdrop of a great industrial rushing back and forth. I adore this poem for what it conveys so effectively. It captures something about my own experience of life at a moment of a great rushing forward, of accelerating changes that seem to be pushing us toward a destination we desperately do not want to reach. It also speaks, in an implicit way, to how childhood itself is even more "evanescent," a brief blip in the course of our lives regardless of what it might have felt like when we were experiencing it.

These are not the only reasons why I allude to this poem, however. I allude to it because for Asian American poets and literary scholars Pound endures as a complex cultural touchstone. His work translating classical Chinese poetry, if what he did could be called translation, and his interweaving of Chinese tropes into his own poetry challenge Asian American writers, and especially poets, to think about how they view the work they're doing. American ideas of China, and of the Orient, owe a great debt to Pound, who could not leave either alone. As Josephine Park puts it, "Pound burned into the American consciousness an Orient for the twentieth century; in casting about for a model that could renew poetry worn out by conventions of the nineteenth century, Pound discovered an image of reform in China that engaged him for the entirety of his career."[12] Asian Americans like me are the heirs of a dubious aesthetic inheritance.

I wonder, then, what Pound would say if he were to find himself in the present moment, looking into the multiracial faces of the crowds that comprise the major urban centers of this country, and in many other Western countries. I can't imagine it would be anything good. What I can imagine, all too easily, is how he might throw himself, again, into the arms of whatever brute fascist happened to be around. Adore the poem, not the poet. So let's flip things around a bit, and take on a more oppositional stance. The "we" used in this essay belongs to the faces who are gazing back at the poem's speaker. *We* are the faces of the crowd, of civil society. Our brown and yellow and black and white faces are looking past our hooded, slanted, epicanthic eyelids, seeing with our multihued pupils, or seeing nothing because some of us are blind. Each of us is as complex as entire universes, desiring and longing and striving for better worlds than what we have, caring for our children or the children of others and wanting for them a chance to bloom before their petals fall. When this "we" speaks, it speaks to demand a future for us all, and not just for a select few.

Notes

1. Rebekeh Sheldon, *The Child to Come: Life after the Human Catastrophe* (Minneapolis: University of Minnesota Press, 2016), 7.
2. Lee Edelman, *No Future: Queer Theory and the Death Drive* (Durham, NC: Duke University Press, 2004), 28.
3. Lauren Berlant, *The Queen of America Goes to Washington City* (Durham, NC: Duke University Press, 1997), 1. Quoted in Edelman, *No Future*, 21.
4. Robin Bernstein, *Racial Innocence: Performing American Childhood from Slavery to Civil Rights* (New York: New York University Press, 2011), 4.
5. Edelman, *No Future*, 18.
6. See, for example, Kathryn Bond Stockton, *The Queer Child, or Growing Sideways in the Twentieth Century* (Durham, NC: Duke University Press, 2009).
7. https://local.theonion.com/new-parents-wisely-start-college-fund-that-will-pay-for-1819576174.
8. For a vivid dramatization of how such policies affected Cambodian Americans, see the documentary *Sentenced Home*, directed by Nicole Newnham (2006).

9. Malcolm Harris, *Kids These Days: Human Capital and the Making of Millennials* (New York: Little, Brown, 2017), 39.

10. Harris, *Kids These Days*, 20.

11. Margaret Ronda, *Remainders: American Poetry at Nature's End* (Stanford, CA: Stanford University Press, 2018), 6.

12. Josephine Nock-Hee Park, *Apparitions of Asia: Modernist Form and Asian American Poetics* (New York: Oxford University Press, 2008), 24.

CHAPTER 27

Presidential Race

Stephanie Li

Barack Hussein Obama and Donald J. Trump could not be more oppo-site, and yet they were both elected to serve as president of the United States of America. Obama grew up in Indonesia and Hawaii, the son of a Kenyan economics student and an anthropologist born in Kansas. After college, he devoted himself to community organizing on Chicago's South Side and then became the first black editor of the *Harvard Law Review*. His best-selling memoir *Dreams from My Father: A Story of Race and Inheritance* (1995) is arguably the most literary of all books written by a president. He fashions scenes like a novelist and quotes William Faulkner and James Baldwin with ease. There has been no president in recent memory more devoted to American arts and letters; in 2009, he invited a largely unknown lyricist named Lin-Manuel Miranda to present a rap song that would evolve into the award-winning *Hamilton: A Musical* (2015), and before leaving office, he arranged to interview Marilynne Robinson about her writing process.

By contrast, Trump only promotes books and writers that support his narrow and often inaccurate version of reality. He has used his Twitter account to extol Christopher Bedford's *The Art of the Donald: Lessons from America's Philosopher in Chief* (2017), Jeanine Pirro's *Liars, Leakers, and Liberals: The Case Against the Anti-Trump Conspiracy* (2018), and Greg Jarrett's *The Russia Hoax: The Illicit Scheme to Clear Hillary Clinton and Frame Donald Trump* (2018), among many other overtly political texts. Just as these books indulge his administration's world of "alternative facts," Trump routinely lies about the most basic aspects of his upbringing and privilege.[1] He recently claimed that his father was born in Germany when in fact Fred Trump was born in New York.[2] A millionaire by the age of eight, Trump went on to receive hundreds of millions of dollars from his father, who also named his son president of the Trump Organization when he was only twenty-five years old. Trump subsequently pursued various business ventures involving real estate and reality television programming even as he has been trailed by accusations of sexual misconduct and racial discrimination for years. He names the Bible as his favorite book but frequently misquotes scripture, and he hardly lives a life of piety, charity, and service to others. Instead, since his election, Trump has strived to overturn Obama's signature achievements from the Affordable Care Act to our former president's cooperative and well-respected presence on the world stage as if to specifically refute the man who preceded him in the Oval Office.

These two men represent the extremes of our fraught political moment in nearly every way, from their modes of speech to their food preferences. Obama, who infamously favored arugula and Dijon mustard, was replaced by a man who gleefully serves a fast-food buffet of cheeseburgers and french fries to guests in the State Dining Room beneath a portrait of Abraham Lincoln. Obama speaks not just in full sentences but in thoughtful paragraphs. He cites the achievements of others and extols the work of allies. Trump meanwhile belittles longtime international partners and the work of governmental organizations like the FBI and CIA in his seemingly obsessive need to draw more and more attention to himself. The differences between these two men are so stark as to require that we consider how they are both inextricably linked to the racial realities of our nation. Trump represents a nativist backlash against the progressivism and inclusive vision of our first black president; his vision of "American carnage" sadly derives from the unity between red states and blue states that Obama called for, a unity that much of white America viewed as profoundly threatening to their own livelihood and sense of identity.[3] The two men are inverses of one another, and history will make clear that one could not even exist without the other. Obama's legacy will be inextricable from Trump while Trump has fostered a politics defined by dismantling the vision of Obama.

The stark racialized differences between Obama and Trump have led to analysis that more deliberately confronts the meaning of race in the United States. While it was certainly easy to racialize Barack Obama and extol him as the country's first black president, Trump's overt sympathies with white nationalists and such undeniably racist statements that Mexican immigrants are rapists and his reference to Haiti and African nations as "shithole countries" demand an inquiry into the workings of Trump's own racial identity.[4] Mainstream news sources from CNN to MSNBC to FOX News now more overtly speak about racial tensions, though often in ways that ignite conflict rather than think through differences and commonalities. However, even while politicians like Representative Steve King of

Iowa have been emboldened to ask, "White nationalist, white supremacist, Western civilization—how did that language become offensive?" there is at least an awareness even among mainstream Republicans that such comments are destructive.[5] Where Obama once spoke in coded ways to audiences with multiple racial backgrounds, politicians and pundits alike are now far more direct in describing the racial conflict at the forefront of our current political landscape.

In an October 2017 article published in *The Atlantic*, Ta-Nehisi Coates identified Trump as "our first white president." He explains that while all of the inhabitants of the Oval Office except one "made their way to high office through the passive power of whiteness," Trump is unique in deliberately and self-consciously mobilizing white power to his advantage.[6] Coates argues that Trump's core "ideology is white supremacy in all of its truculent and sanctimonious power"; only racism unites the wide-ranging positions he has advocated, from his call to build the wall on our southern border to his rejection of the Paris Climate Agreement.[7] His power tolerates no difference or recognition of authorities greater than the United States. For Trump, whiteness is the assumed foundation of his dominance, and he is unafraid to explicitly identify the menace of other racialized groups, from immigrants at our southern border to Muslims already living in our country. There is no way to comprehend the significance and shock of Trump's election without a recognition of the widespread threat to whiteness ignited by Obama's presidency and nurtured by population trends that will make the United States a majority minority nation in fewer than three decades.

Coates' powerful analysis reflects both the racialized dynamics at the core of Trump's political success as well as a significant change in literary and critical discourses about whiteness. Scholars like Robin DiAngelo, Eduardo Bonilla-Silva, Carol Anderson, and Michelle Alexander have provided new language, historical frames, and methodologies to understand how whiteness operates through institutionalized forms of power and privilege. Their work has revealed the prejudice at work in calls for "color-blindness," the racism that undergirds mass incarceration, and the dangers of white liberalism's defensive posturing. Such pioneering insights have at least allowed for a more open conversation about the social construction that is whiteness.

These new areas of inquiry and concern are reflected in texts by authors of contemporary American fiction. Literature moves in tandem with the consciousness of a nation and the political struggles and debates that define historical moments. And just as whiteness has emerged as a salient and necessary category of identity in mainstream political and critical discourses, we are now witnessing a new recognition of the complex representative dynamics of whiteness in American letters. For decades, whiteness operated as a silent, assumed category of identity. This was especially true in literary texts. Over twenty years ago, Toni Morrison wrote that "the readers of virtually all of American fiction have been positioned as white."[8] From Hawthorne to Hemingway, the American canon has been built upon the presumptions of whiteness or more specifically from the assumption that the characters of most value, power, and possibility are those who are white.

While Morrison's work as well as fiction by a wide range of writers of color defiantly resist this formulation, the past few decades suggest that her assumption about the racial positioning of American readers no longer holds among many white-authored novels. Contemporary white American writers no longer solely rely on racelessness to equal whiteness. Or as Sarah Brink, a white character in Lorrie Moore's novel *A Gate at the Stairs* (2009), comments, "racial blindness—now there's a very white idea."[9] Increasingly, white American writers are joining writers of color in their exploration of the lived realities of our racialized nation. However, rather than focus on the lives of racial minorities, these authors are demonstrating a refreshing awareness of how whiteness operates as its own social construction freighted with material and cultural advantages. Texts as diverse as Dave Eggers' *Heroes of the Frontier* (2016), Michael Chabon's *Telegraph Avenue* (2012), Clare Messud's *The Woman Upstairs* (2013), and George Saunders' *The Tenth of December* (2013) reflect a new awareness of the limitations and privileges associated with white subjectivity. While at times these works may be understood as reinscribing some of the presumptions of whiteness Morrison and other writers of color seek to make visible, they collectively herald a new stage in literature by white American authors: a commitment to what might be described as a postwhiteness sensibility. These authors no longer assume their whiteness to be a shared category of identity but instead question its construction and the limitations it imposes on a broader understanding of our national future.

George Saunders has spent decades writing about the white underclass, men and women who struggle to identify themselves with mainstream portraits of material success. His latest collection of stories, *The Tenth of December*, is especially concerned with how whiteness operates as a set of social expectations that breed anxiety, rivalry, and the casual exploitation of others. In "The Semplica Girl Diaries," the narrator, a white middle-class father, longs for the greatest status symbol in his dystopian society:

girls from impoverished nations whose brains are threaded with a microline so they can be hung in the air as lawn ornaments. The story speaks deeply to white concerns about social decline and the fierce competition required to maintain the entitlements associated with white privilege. Saunders' exploration of the intractable divide between the white elite and the struggling white poor, or, as the narrator describes, the white "middle," demonstrates how racialized fears are central to class anxieties.[10] The father in "The Semplica Girl Diaries" frequently reminds himself of guiding platitudes – "Have to do better! Be kinder. Start now" – that emphasize a can-do optimism with deep roots in American mythology.[11] He is certain that he has the power to change his circumstances and if only he can be a better person, he will be justly rewarded. This focus on personal initiative combines with a belief in his own special destiny: "have a feeling and have always had a feeling that this and other good things will happen for us!"[12] The merger of the narrator's personal sense of manifest destiny with his strong work ethic reflects the paradox of Calvinism. The early American settlers believed in predestination, the unconditional election of the appointed even as they strived to lead a righteous and pious life. The narrator's modern version of an antiquated belief underscores how deeply he is influenced by Protestant theology and a racialized view of his own individual exceptionalism. He is yet another incarnation of Morrison's "new white man" confident in his "vision of a limitless future."[13] However, whereas Morrison draws attention to early American writers who unproblematically assert the value, integrity, and independence of this figure, Saunders' story exposes the vulnerable underbelly of such an ideal. The narrator of "The Semplica Girl Diaries" senses and deeply desires his own special destiny, but it is less a reality than a promise he cannot fulfill.[14]

The work of George Saunders exemplifies how in these early decades of the twenty-first century, many white American writers are producing texts that evince a keen awareness of the privileges, entitlements, and material advantages of whiteness. By exposing whiteness as a manufactured but fundamentally exclusionary social identity, they join American writers of color who have explored for centuries the pernicious consequences of race on both black and white subjects. This new awareness of both the performative and material aspects of whiteness is not a direct consequence of our forty-fifth president. However, Trump has certainly activated new concern about both the threats of whiteness and the threats posed to whiteness. White nationalists and various white literary writers are similarly more inclined to name whiteness as a constitutive part of their identity. As these very different groups suggest, the recognition of whiteness does not necessarily lead to enlightened views on the creation of a more egalitarian society. Rather, white writers must contend with how to place their own experience of racialization against the history of other ethnic groups in the United States.

J.D. Vance's celebrated *Hillbilly Elegy: A Memoir of a Family and Culture in Crisis* (2016) demonstrates the challenges and pitfalls of equating the experience of whiteness to that of other racial minorities. A self-declared "hillbilly" who grew up amid his mother's history of drug addiction and troubled relationships, Vance found refuge and stability in the Appalachian values of his beloved Mamaw and Papaw. Published the summer before Trump was elected, *Hillbilly Elegy* was quickly identified by political pundits and social critics as key to understanding the rage of the white underclass that seemed to fuel the surprising election results of November 2016. Writing in *New York Magazine*, Frank Rich called Vance "his people's explainer-in-chief, the Ta-Nehisi Coates, if you will, of White Lives Matter."[15] *Hillbilly Elegy* seeks to chronicle a population in decline, victim not only of deindustrialization and shifts in globalized economies, but of a pervasive and most often self-induced isolation. The book is, as its title suggests, an elegy to a displaced and desperate people, though there is very little to lament in Vance's exemplary life; he attends college, graduates from Yale Law School, and becomes a successful attorney and, not to mention, a best-selling author. *Hillbilly Elegy* adopts a trajectory from culturally distinct self to American identity that reflects the basic journey of many immigrant narratives. In uniting his hillbilly heritage with his upwardly mobile, Ivy League–educated self, however, Vance recenters his roots as distinctly American. This is no elegy of antiquated hillbilly ways but a reassertion of values that reflect racialized privileges and the dominance of American whiteness.

Vance directly identifies himself as white and, in this way, suggests that he is racially conscious. Though hardly a progressive, presumably he is no purveyor of color-blind approaches to social life, and he even appears to recognize the dangerous effects of prejudice. He corrects the myth of the "welfare queen" as a "lazy black mom living on the dole," and observes, "I have known many welfare queens; some were my neighbors, and all were white."[16] However, there is a troubling slippage in Vance's approach to race. He refers to it only to dismiss its relevance to his life. He may be white, but as he emphasizes throughout the text, he grows up impoverished in various ways, and this impoverishment is the defining quality of hillbilly life. Notably, for much of his childhood, Vance is raised in a household with a combined income of over $100,000, but he continually bemoans the absence of stable father figures and his mother's general emotional and psychological instability, which in turn leads to debilitating substance abuse. Class and culture are repeatedly put forward as more salient categories of social impact than race. In this way, Vance ignores how his whiteness has contributed to his success. He is not blind to race, but he proves to be woefully blind to the powerful consequences of white privilege.

Vance begins his book by undermining its very existence. He explains, "My name is J.D. Vance, and I think I should start with a confession: I find the existence of the book you hold in your hands somewhat absurd." He admits that, at thirty-one, he has done "nothing great in my life, certainly nothing that would justify a complete stranger paying money to read about it." And yet his book has sold millions and is frequently cited as a text by which to understand Trump's shocking electoral victory.[17] Vance openly admits that he is no global visionary or entrepreneurial prodigy ("I haven't started a billion-dollar company or a world-changing nonprofit"). By affirming that he has done no more than achieve "something quite ordinary," Vance presents himself as disarmed by his own modest achievements.[18] The implication is obvious: He should not have to write this book. His graduation from Yale Law School and his comfortable life with his wife and two dogs should not be unusual or notable. But perhaps most importantly, readers should not need the explanation that his memoir seeks to provide. Vance's success should be a given, rather than a surprise.

Despite Vance's purported modesty and his gratitude to the people who have supported him throughout his life, most importantly his beloved grandparents, this rhetorical move operates from an unsettling set of assumptions. It takes for granted white male power in elite professional settings. Vance should not have to write this book. However, the social order is so disturbed that he must resort to penning his life story in order to elucidate the crisis in our midst, a crisis that leaves men like him in warehouse jobs rather than in corporate boardrooms. Vance may be a hillbilly with a traumatic family history, but he remains a member of America's most elite social group: heterosexual white men. Without explicitly mentioning race in this opening, Vance nonetheless animates important racialized assumptions.

Soon enough, though, Vance directly acknowledges his racial identity. He does so not only to frame the crisis of his book's title, but also to forcefully distinguish himself from white people he identifies as privileged. Whiteness for Vance does not equate the whiteness his readers may expect. He explains, "I may be white, but I do not identify with the WASPs of the Northeast. Instead, I identify with the millions of working-class white Americans of Scot-Irish descent who have no college degree. To these folks, poverty is a family tradition."[19] This self-description establishes a number of paradoxes for Vance. He identifies with working-class people, yet he makes a corporate salary working "as a principal for a leading Silicon Valley investment firm."[20] He graduated summa cum laude from The Ohio State University yet calls his people those "who have no college degree."[21] And as his memoir demonstrates, poverty is not really his family's tradition. His grandparents enjoyed a middle-class life in Ohio, and he was raised without the deprivations of penury.

As these descriptions demonstrate, Vance is both a member and an outlier of many social groups. However, he overtly embraces his hillbilly roots because for him they are the foundation of authentic Americanness and a seemingly rags to riches narrative that belies the white privilege that opens numerous doors for him. Throughout his memoir, Vance wants both to be part of an ethnic subgroup subject to various forms of prejudice and privation, and to be understood as the foundation of American identity. He claims groupings that are at once minority and mainstream. This troubling conception of the all-American hillbilly transforms whiteness into an overly expansive identity that assumes both dominant and imperiled qualities. Here, whiteness is not a category to question but one that overtakes all subject formations as he becomes both victim and victor. The work of Saunders and Vance suggests two paths forward for white American writers in the twenty-first century. While both acknowledge whiteness as foundational to the organization of contemporary society, Vance ignores the privileges that Saunders seeks to interrogate. The election of both Obama and Trump has profoundly shifted how we talk about race in the United States, and their presidencies have made clear that whiteness can no longer operate as an invisible, presumed position of authority. Amid our often frightening moment of political unrest, we have an opportunity to speak of whiteness as the historical force of domination and exclusion that led to centuries of injustice and that continues to define so much of contemporary American life. Though white writers have not led the way on progressive representations of race in US fiction, they may at last complete the important task of making whiteness visible.

Notes

1. US Counselor to the President Kellyanne Conway used the phrase "alternative facts" in an interview on *Meet the Press* on January 22, 2017, to defend then White House Press Secretary Sean Spicer's false claim about the number of people who attended Trump's inauguration as president of the United States.

2. www.theguardian.com/us-news/video/2019/apr/03/donald-trump-wrongly-states-his-father-was-born-in-germany-video.

3. In his inauguration speech, Trump described an impoverished and desperate country, declaring, "This American carnage stops right here and stops right now."

4. www.washingtonpost.com/politics/trump-attacks-protections-for-immigrants-from-shithole-countries-in-oval-office-meeting/2018/01/11/bfc0725c-f711-11e7-91af-31ac729add94_story.html?utm_term=.623c118ae70e.

5. King was removed from committee assignments in January 2019 by members of the Republican Steering Committee. www.nytimes.com/2019/01/15/us/politics/steve-king-offensive-quotes.html.

6. Ta-Nehisi Coates, "Epilogue: The First White President," in *We Were Eight Years in Power: An American Tragedy* (New York: One World, 2017), 341. See www.theatlantic.com/magazine/archive/2017/10/the-first-white-president-ta-nehisi-coates/537909/.

7. Coates, "Epilogue," 342.

8. Toni Morrison, *Playing in the Dark: Whiteness and the Literary Imagination* (New York: Vintage, 1993), xii.

9. Lorrie Moore, *A Gate at the Stairs* (New York: Random House, 2009), 86.

10. George Saunders, "The Semplica Girl Diaries," in *The Tenth of December* (New York: Random House, 2013), 118.

11. Saunders, "The Semplica Girl Diaries," 112.

12. Saunders, "The Semplica Girl Diaries," 113.

13. Morrison, *Playing in the Dark*, 34.

14. I offer a more detailed analysis of "The Semplica Girls" and its representation of whiteness in the conclusion to my book *Playing in the White: Black Writers, White Subjects* (New York: Oxford University Press, 2015).

15. Frank Rich, "No Sympathy for the Hillbilly," *New York Magazine*, March 20, 2017, http://nymag.com/intelligencer/2017/03/frank-rich-no-sympathy-for-the-hillbilly.html.

16. J.D. Vance, *Hillbilly Elegy: A Memoir of a Family and Culture in Crisis* (New York: HarperCollins, 2016), 8.

17. See "Six Books to Help Understand Trump's Win," *New York Times*, November 9, 2016, www.nytimes.com/2016/11/10/books/6-books-to-help-understand-trumps-win.html?searchResultPosition=1 and Rich, "No Sympathy for the Hillbilly."

18. Vance, *Hillbilly Elegy*, 1.

19. Vance, *Hillbilly Elegy*, 3.

20. jdvance.com (2018).

21. Vance, *Hillbilly Elegy*, 3.

Index

437